Be Merry and Wise

Be Merry and Wise

Origins of Children's Book Publishing
in England, 1650–1850

BRIAN ALDERSON AND FELIX DE MAREZ OYENS

THE PIERPONT MORGAN LIBRARY

THE BIBLIOGRAPHICAL SOCIETY OF AMERICA

THE BRITISH LIBRARY, LONDON · OAK KNOLL PRESS, NEW CASTLE

Dedicated by the authors
to
RAY AND PETER AND THE FAMOUS FIVE
and to
CONRAD OYENS

First published 2006 by
The British Library
96 Euston Road
London NW1 2DB
England
and
Oak Knoll Press
310 Delaware Street
New Castle
Delaware 19720
USA

In association with

The Pierpont Morgan Library
29 East 36th Street
New York NY 10016-3403

and

The Bibliographical Society of America
P.O. Box 1537
Lenox Hill Station
New York NY 10021

ISBN 0-7123-0668-4 (BL)
ISBN 1-58456-180-7 (OKP)

Designed by Bob Elliott
Typeset by Norman Tilley Graphics
Printed and bound in Hong Kong by
South Sea International Press

CONTENTS

PREFACE

ARLY in 1989 Paul Needham, at that time Astor Curator of
Printed Books and Bindings at the Morgan Library, and Felix
de Marez Oyens, at that time president of the antiquarian bookselling firm Lathrop C. Harper, put forward to me the idea of a
large-scale exhibition of children's books that would emphasize
the depth of the Library's holdings. As they well knew, and as is
outlined in the following Introduction, this would be by no means
the first such exhibition, but in this instance the intention would
be not to "show-case" the treasures of the collection, but to show
them in context, noting social, cultural and commercial factors
that can explain how they were created and how they became
works of great consequence.

As it happens, thanks to the generosity of many donors, and
especially the magnificent gifts from the late Elisabeth Ball, the
Library has notable holdings of children's books from the eighteenth and early nineteenth centuries that provide just such a
background. Many of them have never been fully described
before, and I was therefore very happy to see the project go ahead
and very curious to see what would materialize.

The exhibition was planned to take place around the holiday
period at the end of 1990 and work on it began at the start of that
year. Felix Oyens and I had asked Brian Alderson to join the team,
a person who had been involved in work with both historic books,
as founder of the Children's Books History Society, and modern
ones, as Children's Books Editor of the London *Times*. He and
Felix commenced an assessment of the Morgan holdings in
January 1990, but they were not able to carry out the plans of
collaborating with Paul Needham, who left the Library in that
year to become Director of the Books and Manuscripts Department at Sotheby's, New York.

The assembly of material for the exhibition, and the shaping of
it into a coherent history of the development of children's book
publishing in Britain down to the 1850s, proved an extensive
task. The two curators read and annotated much of the relevant
material in the Library, preparing both their exhibition notes and
the copy for a substantial catalogue as they went along. In the
event, however, the catalogue proved to be a work of such detail
that time forbade its production within the exhibition deadlines.
We did, however, recognize its manifest value as an unusually
subtle analysis of the role of the British book trade in creating and
exploiting the market for children's books. It is thus with great
pleasure that I welcome its appearance in print in a new guise as
a study of its subject, independent of, but clearly mirroring the
exhibition that was its *raison d'être*.

In the period between the exhibition and this publication, the
Library's holdings of children's books have grown dramatically
through the efforts of its curators and the generosity of its friends
and patrons. During her long career as a Fellow and Trustee of the
Library, Julia P. Wightman took a special interest in this collection
and greatly enlarged it with gifts in 1991 and a bequest in 1994.
Also a Fellow and Trustee, Elizabeth M. Riley bequeathed in 2003
a handsome sum for acquisitions in this field. Other donors have
helped with financial support and gifts in kind. As a result, the
Library is much stronger in games, harlequinades, and peepshows than one might think on the basis of Chapter 10. It now
has the first English version of "Beauty and the Beast" published
in 1759 (see item 51) and one of the first miniature libraries,
The Bookcase of Instruction and Delight (London, 1802), no less
ingeniously designed and elegantly furnished than the two
examples we borrowed for this occasion (items 163 and 165). But
we have resisted the temptation to make any substitutions or
additions: this catalogue reflects the Library's holdings at the
time of the exhibition although the authors have revised and
elaborated some of their findings in the light of recent scholar-
ship, including some of their own latest discoveries.

This catalogue is a collaborative effort in more ways than one.
The authors have worked closely with the Library's curators,
photographers, reading room staff, and publications department to complete the text and organize the illustrations. The
Bibliographical Society of America expressed interest in this
project at the very beginning and provided invaluable assistance
at the end. With the Society's support we have been able to present
a bibliographical analysis of children's books of unprecedented
sophistication and perspicuity. We have entrusted the design
and production of this volume to The British Library, which has
already published a number of fine books on related themes, also
touching on the origins and development of children's literature
in England. By joining forces in this way, we hope to produce more
than just a record of an exhibition but rather a copiously illustrated documentary history of these innovative publications, like
them combining entertainment and instruction so as to be fully
worthy of the title *Be Merry and Wise*.

CHARLES E. PIERCE, JR.
Director, The Pierpont Morgan Library

INTRODUCTION

THE first major exhibition of children's books at The Pierpont Morgan Library took place during the Christmas season of 1954–5 and is commemorated in a catalogue compiled by Herbert Cahoon: *Children's Literature: Books and Manuscripts*. The expressed aim of the exhibition was to put on display a goodly number of "important works for children" in their earliest form, and there can be little doubt that the enterprise was planned to give a splendid setting to one of the Library's many splendid treasures, the "dedication manuscript" of Perrault's *Contes de ma mere l'Oye* which had been acquired a year before as a gift of the Fellows.

At this time the Library did not have particularly strong holdings of children's books and much of the exhibition was composed of books borrowed from elsewhere. "The substantial framework" of the show, said Mr. Cahoon, consisted of "well over a hundred books, manuscripts and original drawings." However, a series of important acquisitions enlarged the scope and depth of the collection to such an extent that the Library could recruit its first Curator of Early Children's Books, Gerald Gottlieb, who displayed its more noteworthy holdings in a much more ambitious exhibition in 1975.

This exhibition, *Early Children's Books and Their Illustration*, was a further exercise in splendor: "not a history," wrote Charles Ryskamp in his preface to the sumptuous catalogue, but rather "a selection of masterpieces or milestones from the past two thousand years . . ." Manuscripts from the Morgan's peerless collection were set alongside printed books of comparable rarity—many of which had come to the Library as the gift of Elisabeth Ball. Gerald Gottlieb's exhibition and catalogue (now a collectors' item in its own right) made it clear to the public at large that The Pierpont Morgan Library had entered the ranks of American institutions with important collections of historical children's books.

Children's literature has continued to figure prominently in the Library's exhibition program. It offered expansive hospitality to *Beatrix Potter: The Artist and Her World* (1988), which had originated at the Tate Gallery in London. It has also held a number of small in-house displays, the most notable of which was "Forms of Combat," a richly entertaining diversion prepared by Gerald Gottlieb at the time of his retirement in 1983. But these smaller exhibitions were of a fairly informal nature, celebrating individual aspects of the collection, or displaying newly-acquired material. *Be Merry and Wise* returns to the tradition of a large-scale, fully catalogued exhibition, but on this occasion adopts a changed angle of view, an angle which may offer a glimpse of less obvious treasures than those usually so reckoned.

When the proposal for the exhibition was formulated, early in 1989, a consciousness of this changed viewpoint was already quite apparent. Felix de Marez Oyens then wrote of the making of children's books as being intimately related to their publishers' "perception of the current market." The masterpieces and

milestones of children's literature, he suggested, do not exist in splendid isolation, but share a literary, social and commercial inheritance with hundreds of "more obscure, less glamorous, but often exceptionally interesting contemporaries." Would not an exhibition featuring these works, unknown to fame, help to enhance our appreciation of the classics, highspots and celebrities?

In the event, the Morgan collection proved highly amenable to a strategy of this kind. The exhibition proposal was accepted, we were enlisted as guest curators, and the two of us began to explore the Library's holdings. As we worked our way through the collection we began to find that our exhibition was taking shape almost of its own accord. The original proposal had already envisaged restricting geographical coverage to the British Isles, but upon examining several thousand British books in the Library's vaults we realized that there might be profit in restricting the chronological coverage as well. A large proportion of the Morgan's British children's books derive, via Elisabeth Ball, from the library of the English collector Charles Todd Owen (d. 1941) and from the books catalogued and sold by the French bookseller Kirkor A. Gumuchian in 1930 (Elisabeth Ball's father bought almost the whole offering). These two giant accessions, shared out between the Morgan and the Lilly Library of Indiana University at Bloomington, are very rich in books from the eighteenth century and from the early decades of the nineteenth—the period when English children's literature was growing towards maturity. By comparison with such a wealth of examples, the Victorian and later periods were thinly represented (treasures enough, perhaps, but not the same depth or diversity of material). In consequence we found ourselves categorizing our selection so that it would, we hoped, give a clear "perception of the market," even though the perceived market was going to be one in its early stages of growth from being a very limited preserve to being a busy and complex industry.

The natural form for such a thematic approach was a chronological one and, since tradesmen were at the heart of the establishment of English children's literature, the chronological approach could not help being in essence a history of children's book publishing. With its large holdings of often little-known books from obscure entrepreneurs, the Morgan Library gave us an unparalleled opportunity to trace patterns of influence and development that would help to substantiate the crucial role which "the trade" played in the creation of this genre.

Nevertheless, even in primitive forms, the publishing of children's books is not an easy subject to summarize. The publisher may indeed be a prime mover, to a degree that does not prevail so obviously with adult books, but, on the one hand he must be shown to have some awareness of public expectation, and, on the other, he must be shown as not only responding to such expectation but also anticipating or even leading the way towards new concepts. Throughout the first part of this volume, therefore, the publishers of children's books can be seen creating norms for their business, which presumably adhere fairly closely to the known demands of the market, and then pressing beyond those norms, experimenting, and, where successful, carrying the market with them into areas of new and different possibility.

The challenge-and-response of this kind of development continues down to the present time—constantly complicated by the additional factor that (unlike publishing for adults) the writers, illustrators, printers, publishers and sellers of the goods are at one remove from their hoped-for readers. The final product, the children's book, is, through all its history, at the mercy of extraneous influences—philosophical, educational, ethical—which may play a part alongside simple economics in determining the reading experiences that are available to successive generations. Events in the historical section of this volume can be paralleled in the book trade of the present day.

We cannot claim that we have many revelations to offer in retracing this early history as seen largely through the Morgan collection. The "text" of Harvey Darton's *Children's Books in England*—that "children's books were always the scene of a battle between instruction and amusement"—remains unassailable, even though we have perhaps been able to point to the presence of a good deal more "amusement" than many people suspect. By good fortune, too, we have been able to carry the tale of the achievement of authorial freedom escaping from restraint through to its most dramatic climax: the publishing at Christmas 1854 of Thackeray's *The Rose and the Ring*, the "family manuscript" of which has been among the Morgan Library's foremost treasures since its acquisition in 1947.

Whereas previous exhibitions have tended to treat this wonderful document simply as a treasure, we have been able to give it its natural—and salient—place within the history of the genre. For *The Rose and the Ring* is the culmination of many events that we have portrayed here in earlier manifestations. First and foremost, of course, it marks the arrival of the author as a free, untrammeled agent writing solely for the delight of himself and his children; but, in addition, as we try to show, it also draws into itself a host of hints and references that relate to the children's literature that preceded it: the literature (and the illustration) of fairy tale, *Kunstmärchen*, and burlesque. Scattered throughout its text—and emergent too in Thackeray's life as a writer—there are features that can be related back to anything from John Newbery's fairings to the humor of both Punch and *Punch*.

* * * *

In working through and annotating material for the exhibition and this text we also bore in mind that the history of publishing is not the only history that can be written for children's literature. In his original proposal Felix Oyens had foreseen that there are also generic developments (whether of literary forms, like poetry, or of physical presentations like picture books and movable books) and there are diverse subdivisions within the market (books for the poor, books for very young readers, books used to promote other books). These features, which often shed light on publisher/reader relationships, also needed to be considered, and the shorter second part of the volume seeks to bring together a number of indicative examples which came to prominence in the Morgan stock. Some other intriguing sidelights (e.g., Shakespeare, and Punch and Judy) have also been incorporated into the chronological section in the form of "digressions."

The predominating difficulty in making our selection for the exhibition and in writing this bibliographical study has been the *embarras de richesses* which the Library has placed before us. In the initial stages of our work we were fairly clear about the historical steps that would be presented through our choice of examples. What we should also have bargained for, however, is, first, that—time and again—one example did not duplicate a companion example, but rather extended the point that we wished to make, and, second, that we found books that led us—time and again—towards unsuspected new aspects for discussion. (There were moments when we thought that the Morgan holdings of a single obscure publisher, such as the absurd and delectable George Martin of Great St. Thomas Apostle, would make him a fit subject for an exhibition all on his own; or when we thought we could digress forever on, say, the single image of a boy chasing butterflies with his hat.)

The discoveries we made for ourselves and the oddity (as opposed to the conventional sameness) of so many of our examples has placed a considerable strain on our self-discipline and on the limits we set both for the exhibition and this study. Books that seemed innocent of any complexity on their own began to acquire unexpected ramifications when placed in context with their fellows, pressing themselves forward as either additional examples of a trend or evidence to modify received wisdom. Not only did the number of books selected for consideration grow beyond our original limits but also the amount of space needed for their description and discussion. In view of the fact, however, that many of these items were being held up for consideration for the very first time we decided to err towards inclusiveness. More than one example of a phenomenon may often be given, in order to indicate that it veers towards the common rather than the unique; several variants of a market practice may be set out, in order to show that "common" does not necessarily mean uniform. As a result, this work takes on something of the character of an evidential handbook, containing details of a number of books that contribute towards the case that we are making but that did not appear in the exhibition itself. We should also note that—for all the scale of its possessions—the Morgan Library does not contain examples of every aspect of the early development of children's literature. We have therefore made judicious calls upon the holdings of several private and institutional collections to fill out obtrusive *lacunae*, and we would like to acknowledge here as well as in the formal acknowledgements list our gratitude to the librarians and collectors who have so generously allowed access to their resources.

In writing this study we have attempted to do justice to the material that we have chosen by placing it in what we hope will be a helpful context and by giving it as full a technical description as space allows. Neither of these procedures has been altogether straightforward.

At the heart of our difficulty has been the frequently lamented disregard in which children's books were—and are—held, very often by children and adults alike. During the period with which we are dealing, much of the production of "juveniles" was in the hands of obscure or anonymous writers, illustrators and publishers. Among the documents of the trade that have come down to us there is no detailed account of publishing houses or systematic list of their publications. (The Stationers Company Archives become very uneven for the period after 1740 when children's books began to appear in quantity—and *because* they were children's books nobody troubled too much to keep records of them anyway.)

In addition to this dearth of information there is also the dearth of comparative examples. By now the fragility and destructibility of children's books has acquired the status of a *cliché*, but this does not detract from the concomitant point, that so much evidence in the way of primary sources has been lost that all generalizations about trends or about individual books or publishers are extremely hazardous (see, for instance, our annotation to Hawkins's *The Seven Ages of Man* in entry no. 209).

Despite the many gaps in our knowledge—and, as will be evident in our acknowledgements, the widely dispersed resources that we have called on to try to fill these gaps—we have none-theless attempted to supply basic information both about the evolving structure of the children's book publishing industry and about the nature of each of our examples. In the first section of the catalogue much of the material has been arranged according to publisher, and for most of these individuals or companies we have given some preliminary, thumbnail details. For the individual books that make up our numbered sequence, we have sought to supply our reason for including that particular example and to draw attention to its relationship with other texts and/or their illustrations. The frequent indifference shown by children's book publishers to dating their products is a perpetual nuisance, and we have tried to justify dates that we have assigned on our own account.

Acknowledgement must be registered at this point to the continuing work in England and America of the librarians responsible for compiling the English Short-Title Catalogue. Access to publisher files and to records of individual books in ESTC has provided us with valuable guidance for estimating anything from the date of a book to the character of its publisher. At the same time though, the project confirms our awareness of the immense quantities of books that have gone out of existence. (For instance, in another edition of *The Seven Ages of Man* published by Homan Turpin [Cotsen copy] an advertisement is to be found for fifty-six children's books only fourteen of which are located in ESTC and then only in one or two copies.) No such aid has helped us through the busy decades at the start of the nine-teenth century and—from the point of view of all who are researching in the field of popular literature—we cannot urge strongly enough the need for publisher representation in the files of the projected Nineteenth-Century Short-Title Catalogue.

Our work on the physical description of books has also proved unusually tricky, with few models in the field to guide us. (The admirable bibliographies by such pioneers as Sydney Roscoe and Marjorie Moon have stopped short of full-dress collational formulae, and only in isolated instances, such as David Foxon's account of Godwin's Shakespeare chapbooks, has standard bibliographical analysis been applied to the ephemera of children's literature.) Certainly it is true that, bibliographically speaking, "children's books" cannot subsist as an individual category—to the bibliographer all books are just books. Never-theless, by virtue of their cheap production, their often distinctive illustrations and bindings, and their tendency to be in worn or defective condition, children's books do present notorious problems of technical description.

Here, therefore, is a summary of our procedures in organizing our descriptive entries for each book—which will, of course be modified for material not in codex form:

1. Title-page and imprint

a) author: where named or known, with dates; authors not named in the work, and putative authors, are cited in square brackets; invented authors, such as "Tommy Trapwit" or "Christopher Conundrum" appear only in the title statement and in the name index. (It may be deemed significant that about 250 of the total entries are of anonymous or "traditional" works.)

b) title: transcribed from the title-page with all subtitles and the statement of authorship but with no attempt at a quasi-facsimile transcription; ellipses indicate the omission of less significant information; in cases where the full title and imprint appear only on the cover this text will be used and will be noted as such; drop-head titles and the like have also been transcribed. Supplied information appears here, and in other parts of the entry, in square brackets.

c) place of publication: transcribed as given, with appropriate modifications in the case of absent or spurious addresses.

d) publication statement: transcribed in full, with addresses.

e) price: included if it appears on the title-page.

f) date: as given, followed by parenthetical comments, corrections and explanations in square brackets; undated works are assigned a probable period for their publication (ca.) or a probable year (with a query).

g) format: specified whenever possible in the standard nomen-clature of the hand-press period, noting paper size and the way the paper was folded (the designations of some of the smaller formats lacking the evidence of watermarks or deckles must be considered mostly conjectural); items printed on one side only are designated as broadsides, on both sides as broadsheets; the size of the leaf is expressed in millimeters, in the order of height first and then width.

2. Physical description

a) collation: the standard formulary for describing the sequence of gatherings, but with interpolated notes on significant features of the imprint and contents (e.g. dedications, incipits, adver-tisements, etc.); the presence and position of inserted leaves are recorded in the form (8+1), i.e., an inserted leaf follows the eighth leaf of the gathering; an entire gathering inserted in the center of another gathering is indicated with an angle bracket.

b) pagination: unnumbered pages (Pp.) are given in brackets; in unpaginated works, the number of leaves (Ff.) is also expressed in brackets. Errors and gaps in pagination are not indicated.

c) special features: according to the make-up of individual books, technical details may be given on such elements as typography, printing processes, paper (manufacture and watermarks), the number and nature of illustrations, etc. We have endeavored to distinguish woodcut illustrations from metalcuts, but are not entirely confident that we have succeeded in every case, especially when poor presswork has obscured the evidence for the repro-duction method.

d) binding: binders' tickets are noted if present.

e) bibliographical citations: keyed to full citations in the Refer-ences section at the end of this volume.

3. Provenance

We have been especially careful to include child ownership and presentation inscriptions along with more formal evidence of provenance. Morgan Library books are identified by accession numbers, followed by acquisitions information.

4. Commentary

After the bibliographical description of each item are remarks signaling its special characteristics, noting its historical significance, or developing themes introduced at the beginning of that chapter or section.

5. Illustrations

Most examples are illustrated and occasionally an illustration for an entry may be situated overleaf or on the next available color page in order to display it in color. The captions refer to the item number and the placement of the illustration in that work. Given the vagaries of pagination in early printed books, we indicate the placement of illustrations by signatures rather than page numbers. Some illustrations have been enlarged (to some advantage), but the actual size is recorded in every entry.

We hope that this fairly comprehensive account of our material, much of which has attracted little attention in the past, will serve to illuminate the day-to-day business of making books for children in the formative years of publishing. We hope too that it will encourage collectors, librarians, and those who trade in early children's books more fully to appreciate the minutiae of these elusive and often ephemeral objects.

Brian Alderson and
Felix de Marez Oyens

ACKNOWLEDGEMENTS

DURING our work on compiling and annotating this study we have received much willing support from friends, colleagues, and the curators of several collections within and beyond the confines of the Morgan Library. We offer the following, gathered alphabetically, our deepest gratitude, but, alas we can no longer directly thank Valerie Alderson (d. 2005) and such valued friends as John Kelly (d. 1992), Marjorie Moon (d. 1996), James Davis (d. 2000), and George Speaight (d. 2005):

Karen Banks	Richard Landon
Dr. L. G. E. Bell	Katherine Kyes Leab
Iain Bain	Margaret C. Maloney
Dennis Butts	Ian Maxted
Peter Courmont	Hope Mayo
Lawrence Darton	Paul Needham
Sue Dipple	Iona Opie
Inge Dupont	Conrad Oyens
Patricia Emerson	Marilyn Palmeri
Pat Garrett	Robert Rainwater
Mimi Hollanda	Patricia Reyes
Clive Hurst	Justin G. Schiller
Andrea L. Immel	Nigel Tattersfield
Elizabeth L. Johnson	Raymond M. Wapner
Dee Jones	

We are also grateful to the following libraries that loaned material for the exhibition and granted permission for reproductions in this catalogue:

> Department of Special Collections, Charles E. Young Research Library, UCLA; Osborne Collection of Early Children's Books, Toronto Public Library; Spencer Collection, The New York Public Library, Astor, Lenox and Tilden Foundations

The exhibition was supported by a grant from James M. Vaughn, Jr., Vaughn Foundation Fund.

Separate and particular thanks must be extended to two members of the staff of the Morgan Library: Anna Lou Ashby, Andrew W. Mellon Curator, and John Bidwell, Astor Curator of Printed Books and Bindings. After the departure of Paul Needham at the start of our project, it fell to Anna Lou to supervise our work in the Library and to smooth a path for what proved to be a complex exercise in book display. And when the exhibition closed she ensured that the text for this catalogue (already prepared, laboriously and accurately, by Kathleen Luhrs) would be preserved along with the photographs we ordered for the illustrations. The eventual arrangements to facilitate publication owe almost everything to the patient persistence of John Bidwell who obtained funding from several sources, helped to update the text, and tended the transatlantic connection with The British Library. Without the dedicated help of John and Anna Lou the following pages would never have seen the light of day.

I

VESTIBULUM: THEORY AND PRACTICE

CHILDREN did not figure very prominently in the early markets for printed books. Insofar as they were provided for at all, it was as creatures in need of instruction—which certainly made for profitable trade in the printing of primers, catechisms, and Latin grammars, but such schematic works were hardly the stuff of literature. When the child had learned to read he would have to find his enjoyment in works that were written and printed with his seniors chiefly in mind.

For this state of affairs to change there had to be a shift in the general perception of childhood itself. Some recognition was needed that education might be more subtly conducted than through the narrow channels of alphabets and syllabaries and predigested question-and-answer formulae. Some account had to be taken of the fact that children's minds go through stages of development, and also of the interesting notion that there might be a general benefit if learning were to become an experience that is pleasant rather than painful.

Such a change in attitude towards education could not help but bring with it new thoughts about the making of children's books—new thoughts that were perhaps most dramatically evident, and in a full European context too, in the publication of Comenius's *Orbis Pictus* (entry 1). Famed as a many-layered encyclopaedia with a revolutionary application of visual teaching methods, it is of signal importance as a children's book stemming from creative ideas about the nature of education.

Where Comenius led, others were to follow, and the purpose of this first chapter is to show how close the relationship was between educational theory and the production of children's books during the formative years of English children's literature. Ideas advanced by Locke, Rousseau and the Edgeworths not only influenced the growth of a literature designed for young readers but also directly fostered a number of books which achieved near-classic status.

1

JOHANNES AMOS COMENIUS (*vulgo* Jan Komensky, 1592–1670). *Orbis Sensualium Pictus . . . Die sichtbare Welt, das ist, aller vornemsten Welt-Dinge und Lebens-Verrichtungen Vorbildung und Benahmung.* [German translation by Siegmund von Birken (1626–81)]. Noribergae, Typis & Sumptibus Michaelis Endteri, Anno Salutis MDCLVIII [Nuremberg: printed and published by Michael Endter, 1658]. 8° (142 × 83 mm.).

)(^{8} (preliminaries including title with emblematic woodcut); A–V^8 (Latin and German text in parallel columns and illustrations). Pp. [16], 309, [11]. A single paper stock (watermark: small four-petalled flower, countermarked with initials MGK). Roman and italic type for Latin, gothic for German. 154 woodcuts by the Nuremberg artist Paulus Creutzberger (various sizes, but many about 70 × 50 mm.). The two woodcut volvelles of heavenly bodies on A5^v not included in the Morgan copy. Early nineteenth-century green quarter roan gilt, marbled paper covers, vellum corners (probably an Italian binding). References: Sadler p. 436 [facsimile]; Pilz pp. 76–86; Rammensee no. 312; Jarník p. LXXIV; Rosenfeld (facsimile).

Provenance: Lathrop C. Harper, Inc. 1978. PML 83013. Purchase: Julia P. Wightman.

Few books can more happily demonstrate the merging of a liberating theory and a liberating practice than this revolutionary little volume. "Proper understanding, proper action, proper speech," these are the necessary things says the Magister to his pupil at the start of the book, but his *alter ego*—Comenius himself—had already laid down in his preface that these desirable objects were to be gained: "Primum, *ad alliciendum huc Ingenia*, ne sibi crucem in Schola imaginentur, sed delicias." ["First of all by rejoicing the child's spirit, so that he sees his schooling not as a torture, but a delight"]. The central principle of Comenius's method lay in what the twentieth century called "visual education"—building up a picture of the world in a series of scenes and then using these not only to teach about objects and their relationships but also doing this bilingually so that the reader learned Latin terminology alongside German. Over and above this, however, there ran a broadly humane aim to develop the whole personality through knowledge. Nor was good humor lacking, as can be seen in an alphabet where the letters stand for noises made by appropriate animals (A2^v–A3^r).

Comenius developed his educational ideas in a number of theoretical works, collected in *Didactica Opera Omnia* (Amsterdam, 1657), but by then he had already formulated his ideas for a Latin picture book for unlettered children. A single proof sheet survives from an experimental *Orbis Pictus* (1653), printed at Sáros-Patak in Transylvania, where Comenius had established a school to work out his ideas. (Two copies of the proof are known: at Sheffield University and, in a different state, at Sáros-Patak College.) Lack of a skilled artist prevented progress, however, and the book needed the resources of a large publishing house for its proper completion. Within a year of publication of this first edition, an English translation by Charles Hoole, with "superior" copper-engravings, was published (Wing 2nd ed. C-5523); from that time on the *Orbis Pictus* became a "European book," its use and increasingly complex re-editing being especially prominent in Germany. In England a sequence of editions down to 1777 was supplemented by several rather muscle-bound reworkings of the Comenian idea, three of which follow here.

CXXXVI.

Ludi pueriles.

Kinderspiele.

Pueri

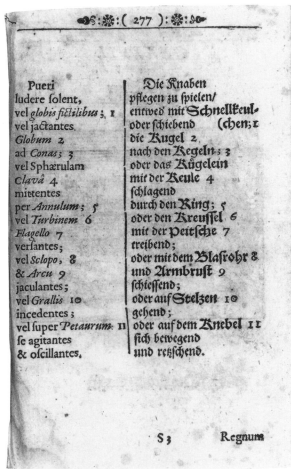

Pueri	Die Knaben
ludere solent,	pflegen zu spielen/
vel *globis fictilibus*; 1	entwed mit Schnellkeul-
vel jactantes,	oder schiebend (chen; 1
Globum 2	die Kugel 2
ad *Conas*; 3	nach den Kegeln; 3
vel Sphærulam	oder das Kügelein
Clavâ 4	mit der Keule 4
mittentes	schlagend
per *Annulum*; 5	durch den Ring; 5
vel *Turbinem* 6	oder den Kreussel 6
Flagello 7	mit der Peitsche 7
versantes;	treibend;
vel *Sclopo*, 8	oder mit dem Blasrohr 8
& *Arcu* 9	und Armbrust 9
jaculantes,	schiessend;
vel *Grallis* 10	oder auf Stelzen 10
incedentes;	gehend;
vel super *Petaurum* 11	oder auf dem Knebel 11
se agitantes	sich bewegend
& oscillantes.	und retzschend.

S3   Regnum

*Far left
and right*:
1. S2ᵛ–3ʳ,
reduced

Below left:
1. M7 verso,
reduced

XCIII.

Typographia.   Die Buchdruckerey.

Typographus	Der Buchdrucker
habet	hat
æneos *Typos*,	ehrne Buchstabe (schrifft)
magno numero,	in grosser Mänge/
distributos	so ausgetheilet sind
per *Loculamenta*. 5	in die Schrifftkasten. 5
Typotheta 1	Der Schrifftsetzer 1
eximit illos	nimt dieselben
singulatim,	einen nach dem andern/
& componit	und setzt
(secundùm *Exemplar*,	(nach der Vorschrifft/
quod	welche
Retinaculo 2	auf dem Tenakel[Halter]
sibi-præfixum habet)	vor ihm stecket) (2

Verba,

◄§ 2 §►

ELISHA COLES, the younger (1640?–80). *Nolens Volens: or, you shall make Latin whether you will or no . . . Together with the youths visible Bible: being an alphabetical collection (from the whole Bible) of such general heads as were judg'd most capable of hieroglyphicks. Illustrated (with great variety) in four and twenty copper plates.* London: Printed by Andrew Clark for T. Basset, at the George in Fleetstreet, and H. Brome, at the Gun at the West End of S. Pauls, 1675. 8° (165 × 108 mm.).

A⁸ (a)–(c)⁸ (preliminaries including frontispiece, grammar); B–L⁸ (biblical vocabulary including 23 full-page illustrations, lacking L7–8). Pp. [8] liv, [2], 156, [4]. Roman and black letter for English, italic for Latin. The engraved frontispiece shows a teacher and pupil, whose books are shelved, in medieval fashion, with the edges outwards; 21 copper engravings illustrate twelve words each, one contains ten illustrations and one only five. Contemporary sheep, lettering-piece and gilt rules on spine added later. References: Wing (2nd ed.) C-5079; Muir NBL 228; Gottlieb 95.

Provenance: Isaac James, Bristol 1798 (inscr.); Elizabeth Tyler (inscr.). PML 85507. Gift: Elisabeth Ball.

"From a Child thou hast knowne yᵉ Scripture," says the Magister to the pupil in the frontispiece here, echoing with his gesture

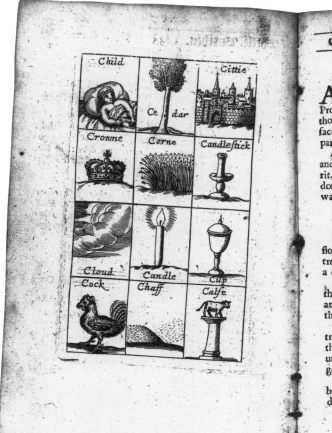

Right:
2. B7ᵛ–8ʳ,
reduced

Below right:
3. E1 recto,
reduced

the teacher in the *Orbis Pictus*. In the same way but without any acknowledgment, Elisha Coles echoes the Comenian method of displaying a "variety of Pleasant Emblems" in order to make the learning of Latin "more delightful to the younger Sort." (There is also a use of the word "visible" in the title which matches that in the English translation of *Orbis Pictus* as *Visible World* in 1659.) There, however, the equivalence stops. The rather admonitory tone of "whether you will or no" precedes a heavily technical (and unillustrated) account of Latin grammar, while the pictures are simply used to give a bit of spice to the quotations from the Bible set out in parallel columns of English and Latin. The organization of these excerpts alphabetically by key words must surely have led young readers more towards confusion than Comenian clarity. This is the first of three extant seventeenth-century editions.

❧ 3 ❧

JAMES GREENWOOD (d. 1737). *The London Vocabulary, English and Latin: put into a new method, proper to acquaint the learner with things as well as pure Latin words ... For the use of schools. The seventeenth edition corrected. By James Greenwood, author of the English Grammar, and late Sur-Master of St. Paul's School.* London: Printed for J. F. and C. Rivington, T. Caslon, S. Crowder, T. Longman, B. Law, E. Johnston, J. Wallis, and S. Bladon, 1777. Long 12° (145 × 85 mm.).

A⁶ (–A3·4; preliminaries); B–F¹² G² (text in parallel columns with illustrations, G2ᵛ Longman ads, G1·2 = A3·4). Pp. viii, 123, [1]. A single stock of unwatermarked laid paper. Italic type for the English words, roman for Latin. 26 cuts (about 47 × 66 mm. each). Original school binding of rough canvas over thin pasteboard. Reference: ESTC T169890; Johnson 47 (1767 ed.); Hockliffe 558 (1807 edition).

Provenance: John De Horne (signs. and initials); H. M. Gilbert (sign.); Gumuchian and Cⁱᵉ (1930 cat., no. 5214). PML 85639. Gift: Elisabeth Ball.

No acknowledgement to Comenius occurs here either, although *The London Vocabulary* is a fairly blatant adaptation and abridgment of the English *Orbis Pictus*. Everything has been simplified and cheapened in order to make the book attractive to purchasers in schools, and its popularity there is attested by its long life, from the first edition of 1711 to the twenty-sixth of 1817 and after. For another example of canvas used as a school binding, see entry 354.

Below left: 4. N2 recto   *Below right*: 4. Q6 recto

JOHN TRUSLER (1735–1820). *The Progress of Man and Society. Illustrated by upwards of one hundred and twenty cuts. Opening the eyes, and unfolding the minds of youth gradually. By the Rev. Dr. Trusler, author of Hogarth Moralized, Proverbs Exemplified, &c. &c.* London: Printed for the Author, John Trusler, at the Literary-Press, No. 62, Wardour-street Soho. Entered at Stationers Hall July, 1791. M,DCC,XCI. Price 6s Bound. Half-sheet 12° (155 × 90 mm.).

A⁶ (preliminaries including half-title with emblematic vignette captioned in the block *See with your own Eyes*, frontispiece of author's coat of arms, preface with tailpiece); B–Z⁶ (text and illustrations). Pp. [4], iii, v, 264. A single stock of wove paper. Roman type. 121 wood engravings by John Bewick repeated to 132 impressions (about 64 × 50 mm. each), the numerous tailpieces include at least three by the same artist, who also cut the half-title vignette and armorial frontispiece. Contemporary (perhaps original) sprinkled sheep. References: ESTC T013211; Muir NBL 482; Hugo 59; Morgan 293; Tattersfield JB51.

PML 83203. Purchase: Ball Fund.

[135]

The man who fishes for amusement, is called an Angler. His weapon is a long, slender fishing-rod; which he fastens a long hair line; at the end of which is a steel hook, that carries a bait; such as a worm, a small fish, or a piece of paste, as food for the fish he wishes to catch. This hook, with the bait, is let down into the water, to a certain depth; and if the fish sees it, and bites at it, the angler, who keeps his eye on the line, jerks, and hooks the fish; that is, catches the fish on the hook, and draws him out.

ANGLING.

BUT the most ingenious kind of angling, is what is called fly-fishing. At certain times of the year, particular sorts of flies swim about on the top of the water, and become food for the fish beneath. The angler knowing this, and what kind of fly certain fishes like best, makes such flies to imitate real ones,

N 2

[179]

THE PRINTER.

HAVING made paper, men next invented the art of Printing, or a more expeditious way of multiplying copies, than by writing them. Before the invention of printing, all books were written with the pen, and the time this took up, made them very expensive. The consequence of which was, that, not having books to read, few men learned to read, and people were very ignorant and uninformed: but, since this useful invention took place, books have been written and printed on all subjects; they are sold at a price, which most people can afford to pay; every one learns to read, to enjoy the advantage of books; and knowledge, thus generally communicated, has opened the minds of men, instructed them in the several sciences, made them more sensible, more rational, and more civilized.

Now, to give my reader some idea of the nature of printing, I must first tell him, that every letter is cast in a mould, so as to be all uniformly of the same

Trusler at least owns up to his source. "The idea of this work," he says in his preface, "is taken from the *Orbis Pictus* of Comenius, published in the year 1657, in folio, at Amsterdam." The facts there may be a little rough and ready, and Trusler was also rather dismissive of the *Orbis Pictus* as "merely a vocabulary, or, nomenclature;" nevertheless, he liked the idea of teaching children through pictures, "to cheat them into thought by amusement," and he thus turns the Comenian instrument into a simple encyclopaedia of manners, with dogged English explanations and no Latin at all. As he further says, though, the pictures (wood-engraved for cheapness) "are admirably executed" in a manner that "would not disgrace Hogarth." He thus draws attention to the closely observed and consistently lively images which John Bewick, younger brother to the more famous Thomas, designed and engraved for the book and which lift it above its pedestrian text. Bewick's children are especially attractive, portrayed with wit and affection.

Trusler clearly had problems financing this book as well as his *Proverbs Exemplified* (1790), which was also illustrated by John Bewick. "I could have wished to have reduced the price of this volume," he notes, but the production "has . . . been so expensive, that it will require the sale of many thousands to re-imburse me." The price of 6s. for *Progress* has been filled in by hand on the title-page, but the copy located by Hugo was one shilling cheaper at 5s.

⋅⋇ 5 ⋇⋅

[JOHN LOCKE (1632–1704)]. *Some Thoughts concerning Education.* London: Printed for A. and J. Churchill, at the Black Swann in Pater-noster-row, 1693. 8° (171 × 105 mm.).

A⁴ (2ʳ author's dedication *To Edward Clarke of Chipley, Esq*, 3ᵛ line 19 *Patronnge*); B–R⁸ S⁴ (S4 index). Pp. [8], 262, [2]. A single paper stock (post-horn watermark). Roman type. Contemporary sprinkled sheep over pasteboard. References: Wing (2nd ed.) L-2762A; Alston X, 111; Jean S. Yolton, "The First Editions of John Locke's *Some Thoughts concerning Education*," *PBSA* 75 (1981), pp. 315–21.

Provenance: John Debnam 1823 (inscr.). PML 75099. Purchase: Harper Fund.

Two editions of this date were printed for Churchill, and much ink has been spilled on which might be the original. Yolton's arguments are somewhat more persuasive than those published by others, and the exhibited edition is probably the first.

Locke would have known about Comenian principles through his association with the group of scholars—Boyle, Hartlib, et al.—who were responsible for founding the Royal Society and who were themselves sympathetic to the Moravian educationist. Nevertheless, Locke's *Thoughts* flowed typically from practical experience rather than from a preconceived theoretic framework. "The well Educating of Children" was important for familial reasons and also for social ones, "the Welfare and Prosperity of the Nation," and Locke applied his own observations of the mental and physical development of children to the construction of this almost epistolary guide to their upbringing.

The very pragmatism of the book was to be deeply influential (resting as it did on Locke's rationalist philosophy), and this is nowhere more obvious than in his paragraphs (§141–§151) on

reading. Like the best of twentieth-century specialists he fancied that *"Learning* might be made a Play and Recreation to Children" and that they might be "cozen'd into a Knowledge of the Letters" by games. When eventually they can read, "some easy pleasant Book" like *Aesop's Fables* or *Raynard the Fox* should be put into their hands. (But Locke, who apparently spent part of his university career reading romances, rather primly warns against works which will fill the young reader's head with "perfectly useless trumpery, or lay the principles of Vice and Folly.")

⋅⋇ 6 ⋇⋅

AESOP (early sixth century BC). *Aesop's Fables, in English & Latin, interlineary, for the benefit of those who not having a master, would learn either of these tongues. With sculptures.* London: Printed for A. and J. Churchil at the Black Swan in Pater-noster-row, 1703. 8° (183 × 111 mm.).

a⁴ (preliminaries, originally a full sheet with quire Y, –a4); A–V⁸ X⁸(8+1) (text, X8+1=a4); Y⁴ (table, the other half of sheet a, Y4ᵛ catchword *Aesop's*); 5 plates (facing A1ʳ, B5ʳ, C8ʳ, E3ᵛ, F5ᵛ). Pp. [6], 337, [9]. The copper-engraved illustrations printed on a sheet of a different paper stock from the letterpress. Roman and italic type for alternate words, black letter for "words in the English, to make up the Sense, where there are none to answer them in the Latin." The plates represent a total of 77 illustrations of animals keyed to the fable numbers (see overleaf). Contemporary English calf over pasteboard. References: ESTC T084704; Gottlieb 10.

Provenance: Alexander, David and John Horseburgh (signs., armorial bookplate); Justin Schiller, 1974. PML 65064. Purchase: Ball Fund.

When Locke in his *Thoughts* (entry 5) recommended Aesop as a first book for children, he added that "if his *Aesop* has *Pictures* in it, it will entertain him much the better"—a sentiment which clearly inspired the editing of this volume. "The Pictures of the several Beasts," runs the preface, will "make it still more taking to children," who will not merely be using it in Lockean fashion as a story book but will also, in Comenian fashion, be using it to learn Latin (or if they be "Strangers," to learn English). The attribution of the book to Locke occurred only after his death with the reissue in 1723 of the original sheets as a "second edition" with a cancel title-page giving A. Bettesworth as the publisher and naming Locke as author. Doubts were long harbored over the truth of this statement, but in *The Locke Newsletter* no. 6 (Summer, 1975) Robert H. Horwitz and Judith B. Finn published detailed evidence to show that the 1703 edition was initiated and supervised through all its stages by the philosopher. He refers to his plans for it as early as 1691 but work progressed only slowly, with William Grigg, at that time a Fellow of Jesus College, Cambridge, and a protégé of Locke, making the translation (from the Latin text used by Charles Hoole in his Aesop's *Fables* of 1657). Through his correspondence with Awnsham Churchill Locke can be seen as the active editor (albeit in slow motion), organizing Griggs's work to meet the needs of the interlinear form and, presumably, arranging for the inclusion of the "sculptures."

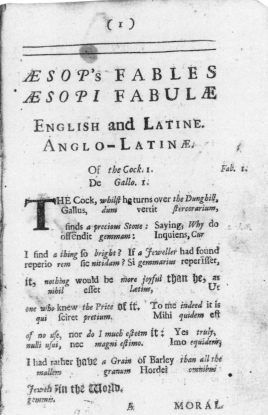

Left:
6. plate [1] and
A1 recto,
reduced

Below left:
7. engraving
opposite B2ʳ,
reduced

A RHINOCEROT

AN UNICORN .

 7

[THOMAS BOREMAN (fl. 1715–43), editor]. *A Description of Three Hundred Animals . . . With a particular account of the whale-fishery. Extracted out of the best authors, and adapted to the use of all capacities; especially to allure children to read.* London: Printed by J. T. [John Tilly] for Rich. Ware at the Bible and Sun in Amen-Corner, Tho. Boreman the Corner of St. Clement's Lane without Temple-Bar, and Tho. Game at the Bible in Prince's-street, against Stanhope-street End, 1730. 12° (162 × 90 mm.).

A⁴ (preliminaries, this quire forms a half-sheet with bifolium L); B–K⁶ L² (text); 57 leaves of engraved illustrations including frontispiece (this copy lacking the leaf paginated 116/7 with figs. 60–63, between F5 and F6, and also half the folding plate of a whaling scene between H2 and H3). Pp. [11], 212, [2] (the folding plate and blank reverse of 5 plates omitted from pagination), the figs. numbered 1–87 (bk. I), 1–113 (bk. II), 1–54 (bk. III) and 1–14 (bk. IV). Plates on different paper from text. Roman type. Title in red and black. The illustrations printed from 9 large copperplates on 5 sheets (one on one side, four on both sides), which were then divided into bifolia (including the unnumbered folding plate) and singletons for insertion. Contemporary English blind-panelled sheep. References: ESTC T135789; Lisney 126.

Provenance: Justin G. Schiller (bookplate). PML 84836. Purchase: Julia P. Wightman.

Locke expressed an understandable ignorance about "what other

Books" there were in 1693 "fit *to engage* the liking of Children," and his often reprinted words may well have been a prompt to forward-looking publishers to do something about the lack. Thomas Boreman, as will be shown later, was one of the first to make an attempt, and this early example of his work holds Lockean echoes: "most of the Books, which have been made use of to introduce Children into an Habit of Reading," says the preface, "tend rather to Cloy than Entertain them," and the author justly believes that his account of animals, complemented by pictures, will be sure to "engage their Attention." The pictures themselves in this first edition, and some of the animals, are a strange assemblage, with much taken from early and not very reliable sources: Dürer's rhinoceros, the leopard from Barlow's *Aesop*, and many creatures from Topsell's *History of Four-Footed Beasts*; the popularity of Boreman's compilation, which remained in print to the end of the century (see Roscoe J141), ensured that his images were copied in turn. Thomas Bewick refers to the *Three Hundred Animals* as a "wretched composition," and his dissatisfaction with it may have been one of the promptings that led him to work on his own *History of Quadrupeds* (entry 133).

A Little Pretty Pocket-Book, intended for the instruction and amusement of little Master Tommy, and pretty Miss Polly. With two letters from Jack the Giant-Killer; as also a ball and pincushion; the use of which will infallibly make Tommy a good boy, and Polly a good girl. To which is added, a little song-book, being a new attempt to teach children the use of the English alphabet, by way of diversion. [Probably edited by John Newbery]. London: Printed for Newbery and Carnan, No. 65, the North Side of St. Paul's Church-Yard, 1770. [Price Six-pence bound]. 24° (94 × 63 mm.).

A–F⁸ (A1ʳ title, A1ᵛ blank, A2ʳ dedication, A2ᵛ blank, A3ʳ introduction, A7ʳ *A letter from Jack the Giant-Killer*, B1·8 lacking, B3ʳ *The great A Play*, D8 *Fable I* lacking, E5ʳ *A little Boy and Girl at Prayers*, E7ʳ *A poetical description of the four seasons*, F3ʳ *Time's Address to Plutus and Cupid*, F4ʳ *Select proverbs*, F6ʳ⁻⁸ᵛ ads); engraved frontispiece (lacking). Pp. 90, [6]. One laid-paper stock. Roman and italic types. 54 (of 58) cuts of various sizes. Old gilt-blocked orange boards (*remboîtage*). References: ESTC T133644; Welsh p. 294; Roscoe J225(9); Johnson 48 (1767 ed.); Thwaite (1966) [facsimile of 1767 ed.].

Provenance: d'Alté Aldridge Welch (bookplate). Department of Special Collections, Charles E. Young Research Library, UCLA.

If Boreman took hints from Locke, then John Newbery took wholesale advice. *A Little Pretty Pocket-Book* (the lost original edition: ca. 1744) was probably one of his first publications, and its preface, addressed to "parents, guardians and nurses," is almost an epitome of Locke's pragmatic approach to child rearing, with "the great Mr. *Locke*" being mentioned on page 6. The book itself, with its illustrations of children's games and its jocular treatment of the alphabet, was obviously an attempt to "cozen" children into reading and also contains reference to an almost vanished teaching game that Newbery marketed: "Who will play at my Squares?" The "Seventh Edition" and now uniquely surviving copy of any edition of that game recently turned up in an attic in Maine and

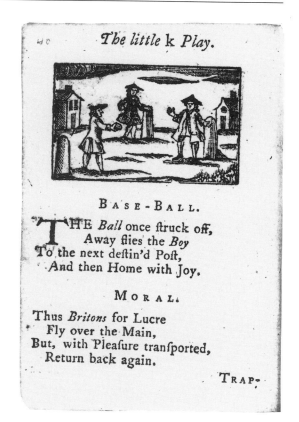

8. C4 verso, *enlarged*

was acquired by the Cotsen Children's Library at Princeton University. It appears that Benjamin Collins (1715–85) conceived the game and published it jointly with Newbery: *A Set of Squares, Newly invented for the Use of Children* (London: printed for J. Newbery and B. Collins, [between June 1743 and March 1744]. *Directions* booklet [A–B⁸] and 24 [of 56] *Squares*: 50 × 60 mm each [Christie's, London, 23 June 1993, lot 138]). The Newbery family's activities as children's book publishers are more fully dealt with in chapter V.

JOHN NEWBERY (1713–67), editor. *The Newtonian System of Philosophy. Adapted to the capacities of young gentlemen and ladies . . . Being the substance of six lectures read to the Lilliputian Society, by Tom Telescope, A.M. And collected and methodized for the benefit of the youth of these kingdoms, by their old friend Mr. Newbery . . . who has also added variety of copper-plate cuts, to illustrate and confirm the doctrines advanced.* London: printed for J. Newbery, at the Bible and Sun, in St. Paul's Church Yard, 1761. 18° (113 × 74 mm.).

A² (preliminaries, this bifolium belongs to the same third of a sheet as quire N); B–M⁶ N⁴ (text and 5 cuts, M3ᵛ–N4ᵛ ads); 9 etchings (lacking three including frontispiece). Pp. [4], 140. Laid, unwatermarked paper (plates on a different stock from text). Roman type. Contemporary marbled boards. References: ESTC T120522; Roscoe J348(1); Gottlieb 181; Morgan 222 (1794 rev. ed.); Johnson 22 (1776 ed.).

Provenance: *Elinor Rendel 11th March/90* (inscr.). PML 85536. Gift: Elisabeth Ball.

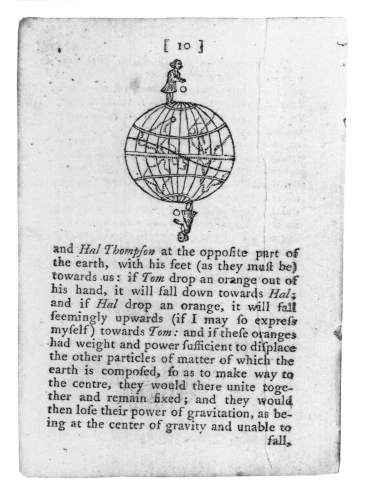

9. B5 verso, *enlarged*

9. plate between K2–3, *enlarged*

"The philosophic attitude is purely Lockeian, as the science is entirely Newtonian" says J.H. Plumb in his introductory essay to Gottlieb (p. xx), where he also notes the frequent neglect of "the influence of children's literature in changing the climate of ideas." Locke might well have been interested therefore to see how his advocacy of pleasant reading for children has here been instrumental in spreading his own philosophy. (Plumb gives "a conservative estimate" that 25,000 to 30,000 copies of *The Newtonian System* were sold between 1760 and 1800.) Certainly the book used many of Newbery's ploys to sustain the reader's interest, from the use of such phrases as "The Philosophy of Tops and Balls," which appears in the dedication, to the narrative setting for Tom Telescope's lectures. Tom himself appears more than a trifle unctuous, especially when lecturing the gentry on their social shortcomings, but Newbery ensures that he is amusingly needled into life by regular interjections from such youthful skeptics as Master Tom Wilson. In this first edition Newbery also takes the opportunity to advertise his *Pocket Dictionary* as an aid to understanding Tom Telescope's terminology.

❦ 10 ❧

[ANNA LAETITIA BARBAULD, née AIKIN (1743–1825)]. *Lessons for Children. Part I for children from two to three years old*. [Parts II–III for children of three, part IV for children from three to four years old]. London: printed for

J. Johnson, no. 72, St Paul's Church-Yard; by T. Bensley, Bolt Court, Fleet Street, 1800 [pts. II–IV: 1797–98]. Price Six Pence. 4 volumes. 24° (about 100 × 85 mm.).

Pt. I: [1–4¹² 5⁶]; pt. II: [1–3¹² 4⁶]; pt. III: A–D¹²; pt. IV: A–D¹² E⁶. Ff. 56 (*recte* 54); pp. 83 [1], 95 [1], 108. Pt. 1 wove paper (watermarked "B 1798"), other pts. laid paper (watermarked 1795 and 1796). Leaded type. Original marbled stiff wrappers, printed labels on front covers. References: ESTC N034061, N034059, N034052, N034054; Osborne I, 108 (other eds.); Morgan 14 (other eds.); Hockliffe 482 (1801 edition).

Provenance: Gumuchian & Cⁱᵉ (1930 cat., no. 460). PML 82211–4. Gift: Elisabeth Ball.

The theory that lies behind the writing of this famous series of "first readers," first published in 1778, may not derive directly from John Locke, but it is wholly consonant with his practical humanism. "This little publication was made for a particular child" says Mrs. Barbauld in her "Advertisement" to Part I, and her understanding of and affection for "Little Charles" illuminates the simple, everyday texts from which he is to learn to read.

> See here is Betty come from the fair.
> What has she brought?
> She has brought Charles a gun, and a
> sword, and a hammer, and some gingerbread.

Along with this unaccustomed comeliness, *Lessons for Children* were also printed in large type, well-leaded, and with few lines to the page—an intentionally functional setting aimed at further helping untutored readers. The universal success of the *Lessons* can be judged not only from its early translation into other European languages but also from the praise that it won equally from the Edgeworths and from Mrs. Trimmer (see entry 23).

◀§ **11** §▶

JEAN-JACQUES ROUSSEAU (1712–78). *Émile, ou de l'Éducation. Par J. J. Rousseau, Citoyen de Genève.* A La Haye, Chez Jean Néaulme, Libraire. MDCCLXII. Avec privilége de Nosseign. les Etats de Hollande & de Westfrise. [Paris: two printers for Nicolas-Bonaventure Duchesne, 22nd May 1762]. 4 volumes. 8° (193 × 119 mm.).

Vol. 1: π²<a⁴ (preliminaries including errata to vols. 1–2); A–Z Aa–Ff⁸ Gg⁴ (books 1–2, ± A5, ± B4, Gg2–3 Dutch privilege, Gg4ʳ errata to vols. 3–4); 2 engraved plates by Joseph de Longueil and Louis le Grand respectively after Charles Eisen (frontispiece and facing Aa7ᵛ). Pp. [2], viii, [2], 466, [6]. Vol. 2: π2 (π1 half-title); A–Y⁸ Z⁴ (books 3–4.1, ± H3, ± N6); Aa–Cc⁸ (index to vols. 1–2); engraved frontispiece by Le Grand after Eisen. Pp. [4], 407, [1]. Vol. 3: π²; A–Y⁸ Z⁴ (book 4.2, –Z4 blank); Aa⁸ Bb⁴ (index to vols. 3–4); engraved frontispiece by De Longueil after Eisen. Pp. [4], 384. Vol. 4: π2; A–Z Aa–Ee⁸ Ff⁴ (book 5); engraved frontispiece by J. J. Pasquier after Eisen. Pp. [4], 455, [1]. Different paper stocks for preliminaries, text, and plates. Two founts of roman type (vols. 1 and 4 from one press, 2 and 3 from another). Titles in red and black. Woodcut head- and tailpieces, the floral one at the beginning of the text signed [Nicolas] Caron. New quarter morocco, gilt edges. References: Gagnebin 1; McEachern 1A.

PML 17372–5. Purchase: Pierpont Morgan from J. Pearson & Co. 1911.

In contrast to the cool, widely acceptable practicality of Locke's *Thoughts*, Rousseau introduced in *Émile* a proto-Romantic, highly personalized view of education which was to be both influential and divisive. In these pages he completes the eighteenth century's invention of the child: "Les sages cherchent toujours l'homme dans l'enfant, sans penser à ce qu'il est avant que d'être homme"; and in semifictional form he sets out a passionate (but most unpractical) assertion of an educational program that would center itself on the developing capacities of the individual. His opposition to received opinion is often carried to extremes—Locke would have been surprised at his attack on fables, with its hilarious and absurd analysis of La Fontaine's "Le Corbeau et le Renard"—and with that famous phrase "je hais les livres" he commences his assault on what he sees as the irrelevant business of getting children to read. "Learning by experience" is essential, and when eventually a library is admitted it consists of one work—that manual for the independent spirit, *Robinson Crusoe*. The audacity and commitment with which such ideas are put forward ensured for *Émile* an influence into the next century, in England no less than on the Continent. The engravings illustrate Rousseau's classical allusions; thus, Thetis dipping Achilles in the Styx to render him invulnerable shows up the coddling by modern mothers of their children.

The publishing history of *Émile* during the year 1762 is a complicated one involving printers and publishers in Paris

Tom. I.   *Page 37*

Thetis, Liv. I.

11. vol. 1, frontispiece, *reduced*

(Duchesne), Amsterdam (Néaulme), and—without the author's knowledge—Lyons (Bruyset). The true first edition, published by Duchesne, was imposed and printed in two different formats. Jo-Ann E. McEachern has shown that the 12° formes were worked first but that the more expensive 8° issue was published first.

◀§ **12** §▶

[JOACHIM HEINRICH CAMPE (1746–1818)]. *The New Robinson Crusoe; an instructive and entertaining history, for the use of children of both sexes. Translated from the French. Embellished with thirty-two beautiful cuts* [by John Bewick]. London: Printed for John Stockdale, opposite Burlington House, Piccadilly, 1788. [Price 6s. sewed in four volumes, or 7s. bound in two.]. 4 volumes in 2. 12° (164 × 96 mm.).

Vol. 1: A–G¹² H¹⁰ (–H10). Pp. 173 [1] including frontispiece, and 6 full-page wood engravings. Vol. 2: A–G¹² H1 (lacking A12 text, H1=H10 vol. 1). Pp. 156, and 7 wood engravings. Vol. 3: A–F¹² G⁶. Pp. 137 [1], and 9 wood engravings. Vol. 4: A–H¹² I⁶ (I2ʳ ads, –I6

12. vol. 2, D4 verso, *reduced*

them, and, after lofing feveral of their company by famine and hardfhips, the reft with difficulty crawled back to the place where they had left Alonzo, carrying with them that pernicious gold for which they had expofed themfelves to the dangers of death in fo many miferable fhapes.

" In the mean time, Alonzo was employing himfelf in a far more ufeful manner. His knowledge in hufbandry pointed out to him a fpot of confiderable extent and fruitful foil, which he ploughed up by the affiftance of his fervants and the oxen he had brought with him. A plentiful harveft rewarded his toils. At intervals Alonzo and his fervants employed themfelves in fifhing ;

(25)

5   C

13. C1 recto, *enlarged*

blank). Pp. 177 [9], and 9 wood engravings. Contemporary, possibly original, half calf. References: ESTC T144879; Hugo 33; Carpenter 1; Gottlieb 139; Tattersfield JB44.

Provenance: *Mary Anne Thomlinson, Oct. 29 1813* (inscr.); Gumuchian & Cie (1930 cat., no. 4876); PML 83106–7. Gift: Elisabeth Ball.

Joachim Heinrich Campe was one of the most energetic of the educationists who tried to adapt and systematize Rousseau's ideas. Today he is probably best known for this bold attempt to rewrite Émile's single story-book, *Robinson Crusoe*, according to the Rousseauist philosophy—and indeed so widespread was the dissemination of his version that he was in some parts of Europe deemed to be the author of *Robinson Crusoe* itself. Campe did much to promote his *Robinson der Jüngere*. It was first published in Hamburg in 1779 (PML 86440–1, purchased from the bequest of Elizabeth M. Riley), and the author made translations into both French and English (the latter also published in Hamburg, dated 1781). Only with the four-volume London edition, however, anonymously translated from the French, did the book gain currency in England. Furnished with John Bewick's full-page desert-island views ("largely pirated from an earlier edition in French," according to Tattersfield), it stood out as an attractive

version of *Robinson Crusoe* for children but, understandably, it failed to oust Defoe's original and as a Robinsonnade it was soon to be overtaken by its famous competitor from Switzerland (see entry 15).

⊷ 13 ⊷

[THOMAS DAY (1748–89)]. *The History of Sandford and Merton. Altered from the original. For the amusement and instruction of juvenile minds.* York: printed by T. Wilson and R. Spence, High-Ousegate, 1802. Price sixpence. Half-sheet 12° (110 × 75 mm.).

A–G^6. Pp. 84. Laid paper watermarked 1802. Roman type. 21 wood-engraved illustrations including frontispiece. Contemporary boards.

PML 81751. Gift: Elisabeth Ball.

Thomas Day was one of England's leading Rousseauists. (He even attempted to educate a wife for himself according to Émilian principles—with predictably disastrous results.) Perhaps the most lasting product of his enthusiasm was the writing of the three volumes of *The History of Sandford and Merton* (1783–89) [PML 85516; Gottlieb 121], where he incorporated Rousseauist ideas into a book for children. In it Harry Sandford, child of nature, helps to reform spoiled Tommy Merton under the watchful eye and through the interminable lecturings of the Reverend Mr. Barlow.

Despite its unprepossessing subject matter the book became an enormous success, remaining in print down to the twentieth century and attracting appropriate satirical comments on the way. As might be expected, it was also very speedily abridged to make it approachable for younger or easily daunted readers. Richard Johnson, the hack who worked for Elizabeth Newbery and others, recorded in his daybook the completion of an abridgment in April 1790, and this 173-page reduction (Roscoe J92) has formed the base text for many more heavily abridged productions. Another edition, PML 83701 was printed for J. Wallis, with plates dated May 22nd, 1790. The York abridgment of Johnson's abridgment testifies to the selling power of the title. The edition was first published ca. 1795 under the spurious London imprint of A. Millar, W. Law and R. Cater (PML 81755), which the York firm adopted to de-provincialize themselves. The book carried wood engravings that also appear in the run-of-the-mill reprint shown here.

14. plate facing fo. 17ʳ, *enlarged*

◄§ 14 §►

[THOMAS DAY (1748–89)]. *The History of Sandford and Merton, abridged for children.* London: printed by Darton and Harvey, 1804. Price 4 pence. 24° (92 × 77 mm.).

[1²⁴] signed A–C⁸; engraved title and 6 plates (colored by a child) printed from one copperplate. Pp. 48. Printed from stereotype plates. Laid paper watermarked 1804 (same stock for letterpress and plates). Roman type. Original beige limp boards, relief illustration of a bird on either cover, series title *A New Toy Book for Children* on front cover. References: Gumuchian 2072; Darton *Check-list* G235.

Provenance: A. Brown (inscr.); Emma (inscr.). PML 84603. Purchase: Mrs. James M. Vaughn, Jr.

Once again, Johnson's abridgment has been used as the foundation for this popular, fourpenny edition. Indeed, the plan of the book tallies with that of the previous item, but the text is briefer and the Reverend Barlow's story of Alonzo and Pizarro has been replaced by his better known retelling of Androcles and the Lion. The edition also has a "new look" about it, with its simple engraved title-page, its specially engraved pictures and its use of a modern typeface. The phrase "Toy Book" on the cover is notable as a very early use of this term to designate a picture book or simple reading book for children (see entry 381).

be varied (see Ullrich chapters IV–V). Nevertheless, it was Campe's *Robinson* of 1779 (entry 12) that started the fashion for publishing imitation desert-island stories, or Robinsonnades, and these came to form a notable and continuing element in European children's fiction. Few such stories looked back to Rousseau, who is nonetheless patron of the genre, but crosscurrents of influence and imitation have flowed strongly from Campe down to such works as William Golding's latter-day morality, *Lord of the Flies* (1954).

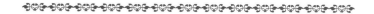

◄§ 15 §►

[JOHANN DAVID WYSS (1743–1818) &] JOHANN RUDOLF WYSS (1781–1830). *Der Schweizersche Robinson, oder der schiffbrüchige Schweizer-Prediger und seine Familie. Ein lehrreiches Buch für Kinder und Kinderfreunde zu Stadt und Land. Herausgegeben von Joh. Rudolf Wyss.* Zürich: Bey Orell, Füssli und Compagnie, 1812–13. 2 volumes bound in 1. 8° (176 × 103 mm.).

Vol. 1: π⁸ (1v engraved frontispiece signed J.H. Lips); 1–21⁸. Pp. [2] xii [2], 333 [3]. Vol. 2: π⁴ (–4 blank); 1–25⁸ 26⁴; folding engraved map (intended as frontispiece, here inserted at the end). Pp. v [1], 406 [2]. Laid paper (grapes watermark). Gothic type. Contemporary German or Swiss half calf and speckled boards. References: Ullrich pp. 182–3; Gumuchian 4906.

Provenance: H. Bradley Martin (1990 sale, part VI, lot 2504). PML 85998. Purchase: Gordon N. Ray Fund.

Inspired more by Defoe than Rousseau or Campe, "The Swiss

Robinsonnades · A DIGRESSION
(see entries 15–19)

From the time of its first publication in 1719, Daniel Defoe's *The Life and Strange Surprizing Adventures of Robinson Crusoe* found a large popular readership. Pirated editions and abridgments appeared almost at once, whereas abridgments specially intended for children began with John Newbery's *Wonderful Life* of ca. 1768 ("printed for the inhabitants of his island"—see Dahl no. 30); fantastic adventures, like Robert Paltock's *Peter Wilkins* (1751), showed how the theme could

Family Robinson" had its origins as a "Swiss Family Story." The pastor Johann David Wyss invented the tale for his own wife and children and turned it into a homemade book, which can still be seen in Zürich. Twenty years later his son Johann Rudolf prepared this edition for publication and thus launched one of the most popular of all Robinsonnades. Hardship and learning by experience are now discounted in favor of exotic adventures and a suitably prayerful family harmony (accompanied by such culinary delicacies as game hens and caviar!) The seemingly endless sequence of episodes strung out by Wyss (he added two more volumes drawn from the manuscript in 1826–7) came to exercise a hypnotic attraction—and were indeed extended by the Baronne de Montolieu in her widely circulated French translation of the work (Paris, 1814)—so that Johann Rudolf Wyss's hope that his book would be read by children "with a degree of mature understanding" has been amply fulfilled. (He was a bit worried about girls, who did not figure large in the story, simply because the Wyss children were all boys. With well-founded confidence, however, he assures his readers that his portrayal of the pastor's wife—bright, unflappable, resourceful—will go far towards establishing a proper balance between the sexes.)

The frontispiece by Goethe's friend Johann Heinrich Lips (1758–1817) is finely engraved, and there is really nothing in the physical production of the book to distinguish it in appearance from Germanic adult literature of this period.

⤙ 16 ⤚

[JOHANN DAVID WYSS (1743–1818) &] JOHANN RUDOLF WYSS (1781–1830). *The Family Robinson Crusoe: or, journal of a father shipwrecked, with his wife and children, on an uninhabited island. Translated from the German of M. Wiss.* London: printed for M. J. Godwin and Co., At the Juvenile Library, 41, Skinner-Street, 1814. 12° (175 × 95 mm.).

A¹² (1ᵛ imprint *Printed by Richard and Arthur Taylor, Shoe-Lane, London*); B–P¹² Q⁶ (Q6ʳ editor's note promising a continuation); ²B⁶ (ads); 4 illustrations after H. Corbould (including frontispiece), printed from two copperplates engraved by Springsguth and J. Dadley, and divided for insertion. Pp. xxiv, 346 [2], 12. Original or contemporary marbled calf gilt. References: Gottlieb 140; H.W. Liebert, "The Swiss Family Robinson, a bibliographical note," *Yale University Library Gazette* 22 (July 1947), pp. 10–13; Carpenter 6.

Provenance: *Robert Coverly's Book, Court Head, Sep. 20ᵗʰ 1857* (inscr.); Gumuchian & Cⁱᵉ (1930 cat., no. 4907). PML 83101. Gift: Elisabeth Ball.

Der Schweizersche Robinson found its way quickly into the English market, but not quite as directly as its publisher would have us believe. Far from being "translated from the German" as stated on the title-page, with the prospect of a second volume "as soon as the German copy of the Continuation can be procured," both this volume and its successor of 1813 are translated from the French of Baronesse Montolieu (see previous item). A comparison of the three texts finds the English one following all the many idiosyncrasies which the French lady introduced, from the initial spelling of the author as "Wiss" to dividing up his chapters differ-

ently and introducing episodes of her own invention. Use of the Montolieu version is the more likely given that the English translation was probably undertaken by the Godwins and that Mary Jane (William's wife) had already published several translations from the French.[1]

The early publishing history of *The Family Robinson Crusoe* is complicated. The first edition of the translation was published in 1814 in two issues, one in two volumes, the other in a single volume. They were printed from substantially the same setting of type pages with some adjustments such as pagination. The two-volume issue was apparently marketed first. In 1816 the translation of Wyss's "Continuation" was completed and this was published as volume two of what is in effect the first complete English edition. Volume one was simply a reissue of the 1814 one-volume issue with a cancel title. Only with the next edition of 1818 did the book finally acquire its definitive title *The Swiss Family Robinson.*

That is the end of the Godwins' involvement in Wyss's work, but we should also bear in mind that in the 1820s the Baronne de Montolieu, the French translator, gained permission from the Wyss family to continue their book, and *The Swiss Family Robinson* that found its way into Victorian nurseries was the hugely expanded Wyss/Montolieu joint text. (The Morgan Library has a long run of early French translations including a two-volume edition of 1814 with Maria Edgeworth's signature in both volumes: PML 85550).

[1] We are grateful to Dr. David Blamires for giving us access to his research on *The Swiss Family Robinson* as part of his, as yet unpublished, monograph on the relationship between German and English children's literature.

⤙ 17 ⤚

[DANIEL DEFOE (1661?–1731)]. *The Adventures of Robinson Crusoe. A new and improved edition. With engravings.* London: John Harris [the younger], St. Paul's Church-Yard, [ca. 1824–31]. 12° (138 × 84 mm.).

A⁴ (2ᵛ imprint *printed by Cox and Baylis, Great Queen Street*); B–P⁶ Q² (Q2 ads, quires A and Q same half-sheet); 12 hand-colored engraved illustrations dated Novʳ 1, 1818 (including frontispiece), perhaps printed from one copperplate on a single sheet, divided for insertion. Pp. viii, 170, [2]. Wood-engraved title-vignette. Calf gilt, by Root & Son. References: Moon *Harris* 199 (1); Gumuchian 4835; Dahl 144.

PML 84989. Gift: Mrs. Catherine G. Curran.

A handsome example of Defoe's own text, now adapted for the children of families who may well have been conscious of Mrs. Trimmer's strictures on *Robinson Crusoe* (see entry 23); "The most leading circumstances likely to amuse the fancy have been retained," says the publisher who now hopes that he has more fully emphasized the importance of "the aid of religion, and the exercise of patience and industry." This appears to be a third edition of the "new and improved" text. The hand-coloring was almost certainly carried out before publication, and Root's have copied the rosettes on the spine by which Harris was accustomed to denote a hand-colored edition.

❧ 18 ❧

Captain FREDERICK MARRYAT (1792–1848).
*Masterman Ready; or, the wreck of the Pacific. Written for
young people.* London: Longman, Orme, Brown, Green &
Longmans, Paternoster-Row, 1841–2. 3 volumes. 8° (170 ×
100 mm.).

Vol. 1: *A*⁴ (1v frontispiece, 2v imprint *London: Printed by
A. Spottiswoode. New-Street-Square*); B–T⁸. Pp. viii, 287, [1]. 42
wood engravings. Vol. 2: *A*² (1ᵛ frontispiece, 2ᵛ imprint *Printed by
J. L. Cox and Sons, 75, Great Queen Street, Lincoln's-Inn Fields*);
B–S⁸. Pp. [4], 269 [3]. 27 wood engravings. Vol. 3: *A*² (1ᵛ frontispiece, 2ᵛ Cox imprint); B–P⁸ Q² (Q2ᵛ author's note). Pp. [4], 225
[3]. 24 wood engravings. Original dark blue-gray fine-diaper
blind-blocked cloth, spines gilt-lettered (Westleys & Clark
binder's ticket in vols. 1 and 2); 6 leaves of publisher's ads dated
1st February 1841 bound in vol. 1 (*Wilson & Ogilvy, Printers,
Skinner Street*), 16 leaves of ads dated April 1842 in vol. 2
(*London: Manning and Mason, Ivy-Lane, St. Paul's*), 16 leaves of
ads dated October 1842 in vol. 3 (Manning and Mason imprint).
References: Sadleir 1583; Gottlieb 141; Carpenter 17.

Provenance: J. T. Lawrence (sign.); Gumuchian & Cⁱᵉ (1930 cat.,
no. 3970). PML 85529. Gift: Elisabeth Ball.

First edition, first issue. Much taken with *The Swiss Family
Robinson*, Frederick Marryat's children asked their papa to write
a (further) continuation for them. On consulting the work,
however, he found "difficulties which were to me insurmount-
able"—not so much the author's want of a knowledge of seaman-
ship (which Marryat saw as an almost universal failing) but rather
the "ignorance, or carelessness . . . displayed in describing the
vegetable and animal productions of the island." The criticism
would have been well taken by Johann Rudolf Wyss, who had
confessed in the original preface that his knowledge of natural
history and *Technologie* was, alas, limited and that he did not have
the time or the resources fully to investigate the accuracy of his
story. Even so, *pace* Marryat, the liberal exoticism of Swiss desert-
island life has a color to it that never quite found its way into the
verisimilitudes so faithfully served up by Masterman Ready.
Marryat's later attempt at a more complex, landlocked Robinsonnade, *The Children of the New Forest* (1846), was an altogether
more successful story and has claims to be the longest-lived work
of English fiction for children to have remained in print down to
the present.

❧ 19 ❧

ROBERT MICHAEL BALLANTYNE (1825–94). *The
Coral Island: a tale of the Pacific Ocean. With illustrations
by the author.* London, Edinburgh, New York: T. Nelson and
Sons, 1858 [Nov. 1857]. 8° (173 × 116 mm.).

*A*⁸ (1ʳ letterpress title) B–Z 2A–2D⁸ 2E⁴ (2E4 blank); 8 plates
(including frontispiece and pictorial title) apparently printed in
color lithography over a key-metalcut. Pp. 438, [2]. Original blue
diagonal wavy-grain blind-blocked pictorial cloth with gilt lettering. References: Quayle 12a; Sadleir 103; Carpenter 39.

19. color-printed title, *reduced*

Provenance: *Robert S. Morison from Mrs. Grew. Milson Nov. 13.
1858.* (inscr.). PML 57739. Purchase: Ball Fund.

First edition, published at six shillings; issue with "View from the
Hill-Top" replaced as frontispiece by the more exciting "Terrible
Encounter with a Shark."

Ballantyne was in some degree motivated by a design for
truthful yarn-spinning, rather like Marryat. But by making his
Robinsonnade a boyish adventure story rather than a celebration
of family life he gained for himself a good deal more room for free
maneuverings, and along with such writers as W. H. G. Kingston
(who, among many things, edited *The Swiss Family Robinson*),
he set the Victorian sea story on the path that would lead to the
masterpieces of *Treasure Island* and *Moonfleet*. Indirectly, too, he
may have found his way into *Peter Pan*, for it was in an introduction to the 1913 edition of Ballantyne's book that J. M. Barrie
wrote the famous sentence: "To be born is to be wrecked on an
island."

⊷ 20 ⊷

MARIA EDGEWORTH (1767–1849) & RICHARD LOVELL EDGEWORTH (1744–1817). *Practical Education.* London: printed for J. Johnson, 1798. 2 volumes bound in 1. 4° (262 × 200 mm.).

Vol. 1: π^2 (1 half-title lacking, 2^r title), A^4 (other preliminaries); B–F^4 G^4 (–3 blank) H–Z Aa–Zz 3A–$3C^4$ 3D1; engraved plate ("Alphabet") between G2 and G4. Vol. 2: c^4 (1 half-title lacking, 2 title); 3D2–4, 3E–3Z 4A–4Z 5A–$5F^4$; 5G–$5H^4$ (index), $5I^2$ (corrections, additions to index); 2 engraved plates ("Drawing Machine") between 5A1 and 5A2. Pp. x [2], 385 [1]; [4], 387–775 [1], [20]. Text paper watermarked 1797–98, plate paper 1794. Contemporary tree calf, gold-tooled spine. References: ESTC T137068; Slade 3A; Alston X, 331.

Provenance: George Gunning, March 1800 (inscr., bookplate). PML 82925. Purchase: Ball Fund.

First edition. "We have no peculiar system to support," say the authors at the start of their book, ". . . we rely entirely upon practice and experience." In doing so they united in a remarkable way the best of Locke and the best of Rousseau and produced a treatise which still rings true today. So far as children's reading is concerned, "practice and experience" led them to steer a judicious course between "teaching children in play, and making learning a task"—a procedure which was linked to their continuous advocacy of educating children through their own natural curiosity. Mrs. Barbauld's *Lessons* (entry 10) won special praise, but it was a sense of the lack of a suitable body of material for readers who had mastered her books that was to lead Maria Edgeworth to build upon her own first works as a children's author (see the following two entries). Richard Lovell Edgeworth's persistently inquiring mind had, in fact, produced a very early, privately issued simple reading book, itself called *Practical Education* and containing a first draft of the story of "Harry and Lucy" (1780). At the time when the present *Practical Education* came out, Maria's father also devised a little book developing (abortively) his ideas on the phonetic marking of texts: *A Rational Primer* (1799). In it he praised the newly published spelling book by "Mrs. Teachwell" (Ellenor Fenn). Towards the end of his life, he prepared a little primer in two volumes to be used by his son Lovell at his school in Ireland: *School Lessons* (Dublin: printed for the author by John Jones, 1817). The Morgan Library has a copy of this very rare work, given to Frances Maria Edgeworth by Lovell (PML 84925). The plain writing on everyday life and the retellings of simple fables "for the education of the poor" provide evidence of Edgeworth's unremitting concern for the practicalities of teaching.

⊷ 21 ⊷

[MARIA EDGEWORTH (1767–1849)]. *The Parent's Assistant; or, stories for children. Part I. Containing, The Little Dog Trusty; or, the liar and boy of truth. The Orange Man; or, the honest boy and the thief. Tarlton. Lazy Lawrence. The False Key, and Barring-Out. To which is prefixed, Address to Parents.* London: printed for J. Johnson, St. Paul's Church-Yard, 1796. 18° (134 × 84 mm.).

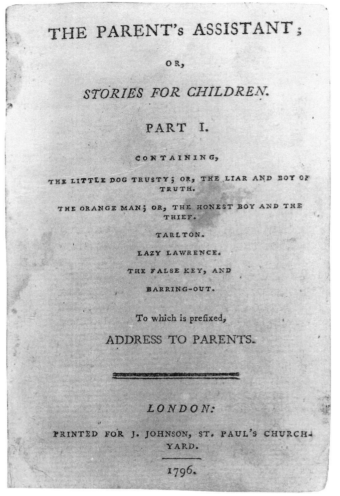

21. a1 recto

a^6 (title and preface); B–S^6 T^9 (T5 singleton) U^2. Pp. xii, 226. Original green quarter vellum. References: ESTC N038093; Slade 2B (i) (second issue); Osborne II, 880.

Provenance: *Wm and Reco Price's Book given them by Grandmama* (inscr.); Sotheby's, 3rd June 1975, lot 466. The Osborne Collection of Early Children's Books, Toronto Public Library.

Although appearing before *Practical Education*, the stories that make up the three parts of *The Parent's Assistant* nonetheless demonstrate the Edgeworth philosophy in action. Children, from lazy Lawrence to the schoolboy revolutionaries of "Barring-Out," are portrayed with unaccustomed vitality, learning right behavior through experience. The book rapidly assumed the status of a classic both in England and America and survived well into the twentieth century, as much as anything because of Maria Edgeworth's perceptive accounts of how children behave. (The original intention of dividing the tales into two parts "for different classes of children" seems to have been quickly abandoned. The utilitarian argument against fairy tales, given in the preface, was preserved for much longer but, as we shall see, to no great effect.)

This copy of *The Parent's Assistant* is apparently the only one extant of the first issue of the second edition. The second issue has a cancel title with the designation "second edition." The first edition had been published earlier in the same year and was first described by Justin Schiller (*The Book Collector* 23 [1974],

FRANK.
FOUR PARTS.
PART II.
———
SEVENTH OF THE SERIES OF
EARLY LESSONS,
BY MARIA EDGEWORTH.

22. enlarged

pp. 258–9); several copies are now recorded (including UCLA; and Baldwin Collection, University of Florida, Gainesville). The story "Barring-Out" was not included in the first edition. The first edition of Part II, volume one is also known in a single copy (Collection of M. Pollard, see *The Book Collector* 20 [1971] pp. 347–51); and that of Part II, volume two has not survived. The Osborne Collection owns the second edition of all three volumes. Only with the fourth edition of 1804 did *The Parent's Assistant* reach its definitive form and was the canon of seventeen stories finally established. Three stories for younger readers were transferred to Maria Edgeworth's series of *Early Lessons* (see next entry).

❧ 22 ❧

MARIA EDGEWORTH (1767–1849). *Frank, part I [–IV]: being the sixth [-ninth] part of Early Lessons. By the author of the Parent's Assistant, six volumes.* London: printed for J. Johnson, no. 72, St. Paul's Churchyard, by H. Bryer, Bridewell-Hospital, 1801. Price six-pence. 4 volumes. 16° (108 × 75 mm.).

Pt. I: A–G⁸. Pp. 111, [1]. Pt. II: A–G⁸ (G8 blank). Pp. 110, [2]. Pt. III: A–E⁸ F⁴ G². Pp. 91, [1]. Pt. IV: A² (probably making up the half-sheet with quires F and G of pt. III), B–G⁸. Pp. [4], 95, [1]. Apparently a single stock of unwatermarked laid paper. Original marbled wrappers, printed labels on front covers. References: Slade 6A (iii); Sadleir 766.

Provenance: *Thomas Browne Parker's book given him by his Mother Jan.ʸ 6ᵗʰ 1804* (inscr. pt. III); Gumuchian & Cie (1930 cat., no. 2341). PML 85276. Gift: Elisabeth Ball.

The ten parts of *Early Lessons* were got up by Joseph Johnson to resemble Mrs. Barbauld's *Lessons for Children* (entry 10), and they were probably devised by Maria Edgeworth and her father to form a sequence through which the Barbauld-trained reader could progress. The first two volumes of the series, "Harry and Lucy," originated in R. L. Edgeworth's experimental *Practical Education* of 1780—see entry 20—and later volumes included "The Purple Jar," "The Orange Man," and "Little Dog Trusty," lifted from *The Parent's Assistant* (see previous entry).

The four volumes of *Frank* show the Edgeworth method at its most mundane. Clarity and fluency are as always present in the writing, but the invariably tractable and prudent hero—to say nothing of his lovingly didactic parents—lacks all the natural energy of Rosamond, the heroine of previous volumes and one of the first real children to find herself in a children's book.

❧ 23 ❧

SARAH TRIMMER, née KIRBY (1741–1810), editor. *The Guardian of Education, a periodical work; consisting of a practical essay on Christian education . . . and a copious examination of modern systems of education, children's books, and books for young persons; conducted by Mrs. Trimmer.* London: published by J. Hatchard, bookseller to Her Majesty, opposite Albany House, Piccadilly [and F. C. and J. Rivington, no. 62, St. Paul's Church-Yard (vols. 3–5)]. J. Brettell, printer, Great Windmill Street, Haymarket [Marshall-Street, Golden Square (vols. 3–5); Bye and Law, printers, St. John's Square, Clerkenwell (vol. 2)], May 1802 – September 1806. 28 issues in 5 volumes. 8° (206 × 122 mm.).

Vol. I: A^2 (1 half-title lacking); B–Z AA–ZZ 3A–3X⁴. Pp. [4], 526 [2]. Vol. II: A^2; B–Z AA–ZZ 3A–3U⁴. Pp. [4], 517 [3]. Vol. III: A^2; B–Z AA– CC⁸. Pp. [4], 400. Vol. IV: A^2; B–U⁸ X⁴; Y–Z AA–EE⁸ FF⁶. Pp. [4], 436. Vol. V: A^2; B–Z AA–DD⁸ EE⁶. Pp. [4], 428. Wove paper, watermark-dates 1801–6. Contemporary sprinkled calf.

Provenance: Sir John Ogilvy Barᵗ of Inverquharity (armorial bookplate). PML 84831–5. Purchase: Julia P. Wightman.

Original edition, all published. Indefatigable as a writer for and about children, Sarah Trimmer was primarily concerned with the preservation of traditional, "establishment" values. *The Guardian of Education*, a magazine which she largely wrote herself, is remarkable for the vigor with which it prosecutes a campaign against infidel philosophers (Voltaire, Hume) and all who might want to modify religion as revealed to adherents of the Anglican communion. As an element in that campaign, Mrs. Trimmer determined to bring the whole of current children's literature under review, and *The Guardian of Education* thus assumes an importance not for any theoretical advances but as the first sustained critical account of the children's books of a given period. Mrs. Trimmer scrutinizes over two hundred books "for children" and over a hundred and fifty books "for young persons," and although many of her strictures now appear limited or ludicrous, they possess an earnest consistency and a capacity for literate argument which compare well with much modern reviewing of children's books.

Many of the books described in this and later chapters appear in these notices. There is a lengthy discussion of *Practical Education* and Maria Edgeworth's books; ("The want of religious instruction is strikingly apparent," she says of *Frank*.) There is a fascinated account of *Émile* ("*visionary, fallacious* and *dangerous*"), and although she is not keen on recommending *Robinson Crusoe*, which may lead to "an early taste for a rambling life," she can see its virtues when compared to the *Deism* of Campe's retelling.

The School Story · A DIGRESSION

(see entries 24–26)

As the nineteenth century progressed beyond the plans and restrictions of the guardians of education, so children's books came to be written and published from an increasingly complicated mixture of philosophies and motives. Certainly the educationists have never ceased to be an influence (they are with us still), but they have taken a place beside a changing array of different forces.

In one instance, however, a small educational revolution brought about a large new movement in the publishing of English children's fiction. The seriousness and sense of purpose which Thomas Arnold (1795–1842) introduced into English public school education when he became headmaster of Rugby School was celebrated in the boys' story *Tom Brown's School Days*, and from that one book flowed the strange and very English literary genre, "the school story." Probably no type of story was more popular, both with boys and girls, down to the 1930s, and despite a multitude of social and educational changes since then the genre is still capable (in, say, the "Choir School Books" of William Mayne, or in Antonia Forest's family saga) of inspiring work of great distinction. More surprisingly, the pranks, rivalries and sporting events that occur at the Hogwarts School of Witchcraft and Wizardry have proved a major element in the popularity of the "Harry Potter" books and have, according to some reports, stimulated a renewed enthusiasm for boarding-school education.

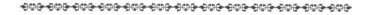

◄§ 24 §►

THOMAS HUGHES (1822–96). *Tom Brown's School Days. By an old boy. New edition. With illustrations by Arthur Hughes and Sydney Prior Hall.* London: Macmillan and Co., 1869. 8° (192 × 140 mm.).

a^2 (1^r half-title, –2) b^8 (1^r dedication to Mrs. Arnold, 2^r *Preface to the sixth edition*, 7^r *Contents*, 8^r list of illustrations pt. I) c1=a2 (list of illustrations pt. II); B–Z AA^8 BB^4 (BB4^v imprint *London: R. Clay, Sons, and Taylor, Printers*); steel-engraved frontispiece portrait of the author by C. H. Jeens after G. F. Watts, steel-

24. B1 recto, *reduced*

engraved pictorial title, 23 wood-engraved plates by J. D. Cooper after A. Hughes and S. P. Hall. Pp. xxii, 376. 35 wood-engraved in-text illustrations and initials by the same artists.

Original presentation binding, red morocco gilt, J.H.C.E. in gothic lettering on front cover, signed by the publisher, gilt edges. References: Osborne II, 998; Ray *English* 176.

Provenance: *John Harcourt Chichester Evelyn. from his father's old schoolfellow. with all good wishes August 11th; 1877.* (inscribed by the author); Blackwell's, Oxford (Centenary catalogue, no. 153). PML 83210. Purchase: Ball Fund.

First published anonymously in 1857 (see Sadleir 1235), *Tom Brown's School Days* rapidly established itself among the classic children's books of the Victorian period. As such it was probably among the books most frequently chosen as gifts or prizes, and this copy of the first illustrated edition is an example of the author using his publisher's "prize-binding" facilities to make a present to the son of an "old schoolfellow."

◄§ 25a §►

FREDERIC WILLIAM FARRAR (1831–1903). *Eric or Little by Little. A tale of Roslyn school.* Edinburgh: Adam and Charles Black, North Bridge, 1858. (The right of Translation is reserved). 12° (190 × 125 mm.).

A^6 (1^r half-title, 2^r title, 2^v imprint *Printed by R. and R. Clark, Edinburgh*, 3^r dedication to the Bishop of Calcutta, –6);

B,B2–R,R2⁸·⁴ S⁶ (S5ᵛ end of text, S6 ads); *T*1=*A*6 (ads); [1–3⁸] (ads). Pp. x, 394, [4]; [2], 46. Wood-engraved floral initials. Original blind-blocked purple bead-grain cloth, spine gilt-lettered. Reference: Sadleir 873.

Provenance: *R.C. Cann Lippincott with thanks for help in correcting proofsheets &c. From the Author. Harrow Nov. 8* (inscr.); Michael Sadleir (bookplate). Department of Special Collections, Charles E. Young Research Library, UCLA.

❧ 25b ❧

FREDERIC WILLIAM FARRAR (1831–1903). Autograph Letter, signed, to [Thomas Hughes], Harrow: Nov. 17 [1858]. (182 × 113 mm.).

Single leaf (2 pp.). Laid paper, blind impressed "Super satin."

MA 3548. Purchase: William Jovanovich.

The arrival of *Eric* within a year of the publication of *Tom* suggests that at least boarding-school life had become a theme worth pursuing, even if no more direct influence can be inferred. Farrar's presentation of the book to Hughes "as a tribute of admiration to the author of a noble and useful book" can be read either as praise from one who regarded himself as an independent equal or as a guarded attempt to recognize an influence; his earlier claim that *Eric*'s "faults lie thick as dust—but it is certainly a true picture for it is daguerreotyped from life" may be taken as a disguised criticism of the latent idealism in *Tom Brown's School Days*.

Farrar was indeed insistent on his special brand of socio-realism. "In all humility," he wrote in his preface, "I claim for the story a higher merit than that of style,—the merit of truthfulness." In this case the modern reader must add that the truthfulness has been laced with such religious zeal that what was essentially a story in *Tom* has become a tract in *Eric:* "Good spirits," pleads the author, "in pity, in pity shew him the canker which he is introducing into the sap of the tree of life." Alas, they don't, and from condoning foul language in Dormitory 7, Eric is little by little brought to his doom. He was also brought to sales figures that for a while must have matched those of *Tom*, but then to a degree of ridicule which has never affected his predecessor. ("Didn't I 'Eric' 'em splendidly?" asks Beetle at the end of Kipling's *Stalky & Co.*, having gleefully spoofed his seniors with a homily in the manner of Frederic Farrar.)

❧ 26 ❧

TALBOT BAINES REED (1852–93). *The Fifth Form at St. Dominic's by Talbot Baines Reed Author of "The Adventures of a Three Guinea Watch," "My Friend Smith," "The Cock-House at Fellsgarth," etc., etc.* London: The Office of "The Boy's Own Paper" 4 Bouverie Street and 65 St. Paul's Churchyard, [ca. 1918]. 8° (187 × 120 mm.).

*A*⁸ (1 blank, 2ʳ half-title, 3ʳ title) B–U⁸ (U5ᵛ imprint *Printed by William Clowes and Sons, Limited, London and Beccles*, U6ʳ–8ᵛ Religious Tract Society ads); halftone frontispiece signed J. F[innemore] *A notable battle was fought on the threshold of Greenfield senior's study.* Pp. 315 [1], [6]. Printed from stereotype plates. Original "series binding": green cloth, Art Nouveau floral design blocked in black on front cover and spine; yellow lettering. Reference: Alderson & Garrett 111–114 (other eds.).

Provenance: Douglas G. Parsonage (inscribed on title *To Douglas from Auntie Florrie Septʳ 1919*). Conrad de Marez Oyens, Paris.

Unlike Thomas Hughes or Frederic Farrar, Talbot Baines Reed was not concerned to use the boarding school story for statements about educational progress or moral degeneracy. For him (who had been a day-boy at the City of London School) the boarding school was a setting for storytelling only, and his many tales—mostly serialized in the *Boy's Own Paper*—did more than anything to arouse authors to the possibilities of the *genre roman*. *The Fifth Form at St. Dominic's* was first published in 1887 and is his best-known and probably his best book, unless one is allowed to include his pioneering *History of the Old English Letter Foundries* of the same year (for Reed was a typefounder, a typographical historian, and first secretary of the Bibliographical Society as well as a writer of school stories). Like *Tom Brown* (entry 24), Reed's books achieved huge sales through being published in series which were primarily intended as "rewards." The present volume is a more cheaply produced issue of a stereotyped edition, which originally had seven halftone plates and a Religious Tract Society imprint. At some point (ca. 1918?) the stock of plates came to be used only for frontispieces and down to the 1930s copies may be found with one or other of the seven subjects.

II

THE SALVATION OF SOULS

THE earliest reading matter intended for English children had little to do with liberal theories of education. It mostly took the form of simple instructional works like hornbooks or primers (see chapter XIX) or didactic texts like fable books (entry 6), or books on how to behave in society (courtesy books). If children wanted more entertaining fare, they could draw on the common stock of ballads, romances, and so on, which were made for a wide general audience (chapter III).

In the middle of the seventeenth century a new attitude developed towards the child as reader. For the first time authors set out to write books that they hoped would speak directly to the child's emotions. We may find it strange or even ludicrous today that the emotions they addressed were those of the religious enthusiasts: awe and contrition. These first writers for children were mostly adherents of the more proselytizing of the nonconformist sects. They desired nothing more than that the child should be stirred to a sense of its own wickedness and should be seized with an urge to repentance. In consequence, they devised books which were not didactic in the old way but sought through story, anecdote and admonition to engender an altogether deeper response in their readers than ever did a syllabary or Aesop's *Fables*.

Many of these books carried amongst their prefaces and introductions "an address to parents," which indicates that the author hoped that other adults would collude with him in this mission. But the substance of the books—earnest, stilted, abstract though it be—clearly indicates its ultimate reader to be a child rather than a grown-up. Furthermore, as James Janeway remarks (see entry 27), these "precious jewels," these children, were "not too little to go to hell." His book and those of his fellow writers were designed to save them from that fate.

⊸ 27 ⊱

JAMES JANEWAY (1636?–74). *A Token for Children: being an exact account of the conversion, holy and exemplary lives, and joyful deaths of several young children. To which is now added, prayers and graces, fitted for the use of little children.* London: printed for T. Norris, at the Looking-glass on London-bridge; and A. Bettesworth, at the Red Lion in Pater-noster-row, [ca. 1715]. 12° (141 × 82 mm.).

A¹² (A1 blank? lacking, A3ʳ author's dedication *To all Parents, School-Masters and School-Mistresses*); B–G¹² (D4ʳ title to pt. II, G11 Norris ads *Where all Country Chapmen may be furnish'd with all Sorts of Bibles, Common-prayers and History-books at reasonable Rates*, G12 Bettesworth ads). Pp. [24] 54, [8] 78 [4]. 4 cuts (20 × 42 mm. and smaller), repeated to 13 impressions, each placed at the beginning of an "example." Original or contemporary

sheep over pasteboard. References: ESTC N013474; Osborne I, 152; Sloane 102 (other eds.).

Provenance: *Nancy Oaten is My Name Engleland is my Nation pirtonister [?] is my Dwelling place and christ is My Salvation* (eighteenth-century inscr.); *Mary Oaten Her Book* (inscr.); John Oaten (sign.). PML 83134. Gift: Elisabeth Ball.

Registered in 1617 (Osborne 2 Ptt. 1672), Janeway's *Token* was among the earliest books aimed at the salvation of the child's soul. "Do but go to work in good earnest," he adjured the parents of his readers, "and who knows but that rough stone may prove a pillar in the temple of God;" and to that end he laid out with a sober grace his entreaties to children to live holy lives. The earliest editions were unillustrated, but in the eighteenth century simple

27. D8 recto

cuts were added, and from the evidence of this copy, with its several childish inscriptions, the book was appreciated. Not the least curious feature of this edition lies in the contents of the advertisements. Such works as *The Gentleman's Jockey* and *Coffee-house Jests* are hardly likely to have figured high among Janeway's recommendations for further reading.

❧ 28 ❧

JAMES JANEWAY (1636?–74). *A Token for Children.* Nottingham: Printed and sold by J. Dunn, Market-place; sold also by W. Baynes, Paternoster Row; Crosby & Co. and Williams & Smith, Stationer's-court, London, 1806. 12° (120 × 68 mm.).

A–B¹² C⁸ (pt. I); D⁴ E–F¹² G⁶ (pt. II). Pp. 64, 68. Wood engraving signed LEK. Original or contemporary blind-tooled sheep.

Provenance: Harriet Vincent (inscr. dated from Werrington,

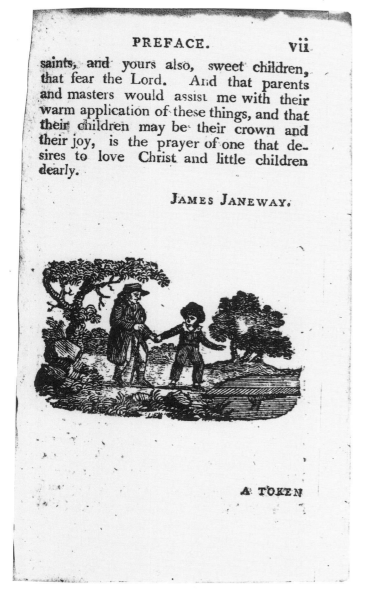

28. D4 recto, *enlarged*

Cambs, 1866); Gumuchian & Cⁱᵉ (1930 cat., no. 3168). PML 83133. Gift: Elisabeth Ball.

The *Token* continued in print for about two hundred years and must have had market appeal simply through its immediately recognizable title. Provincial printers like Dunn included it in their stock-in-trade, sometimes attempting to improve its appearance with new cuts. The Bewick-style wood engraving that Dunn has used as a space filler here lacks all relevance to Janeway's text, as well as any congruity with the book's seventeenth-century flavor. The Morgan Library has further evidence of the book's popularity in copies of a London edition for the Irish market in 1702 (PML 83131), a 1757 London edition (PML 81073), and a version re-edited for the children of Evangelical families in 1828 (see entry 300).

❧ 29 ❧

[H. PUNCHARD?, editor]. *A Looking-Glass for Children. Being a narrative of God's gracious dealings with some little children; recollected by Henry Jessey in his life-time. Together with sundry seasonable lessons and instructions to youth . . . by Abr. Chear, late of Plymouth. The third edition, corrected and amended. To which is added many other poems . . . by the said Abraham Chear. All now faithfully gathered together, for the benefit of young and old: by H. P.* London: Printed for Robert Boulter, at the Turks-Head in Cornhil, 1673. 8° (146 × 87 mm.).

A–F⁸ (B3ʳ Chear's poetry). Pp. 96. Original or contemporary blind-ruled sheep over pasteboard. References: Wing 2nd ed. P-30; Sloane 106; Morgan 187.

Provenance (see overleaf): *Josephus Gifford Liber ejus Hic Nomen pono quia Librum perdere nolo* (another inscr. of his dated April 1717); Thomas Bird (sign.). PML 84564. Purchase: Mrs. Hugh Bullock and Mr. and Mrs. August H. Schilling.

Jessey's *Narrative* and Chear's poetry were first published in 1672 (Wing 2nd ed. P-28). This third edition, only a year later, testifies to an immediate demand. Chear, a Baptist, wrote the devotional verses while imprisoned for his faith; those "written to a young Virgin, Anno 1663" include the ever memorable lines:

> 'Tis pitty, such a pretty Maid,
> as I should go to Hell.

Chear's poetry is written with some skill and must count among the earliest of the genre to be written directly for children. As such it is a clear harbinger of Isaac Watts's classic *Divine Songs* (entry 34).

❧ 30 ❧

The Mothers Blessing. Being several Godly admonitions given by a mother unto her children upon her death-bed, a little before her departure. [London:] Printed F. Coles, T. Vere, J. Wright, and J. Clarke, [ca. 1675]. 8° (132 × 84 mm.).

A⁸ B⁴ (A1 and B4 lacking, A2ʳ title, A5ʳ divisional title). Ff. [12].

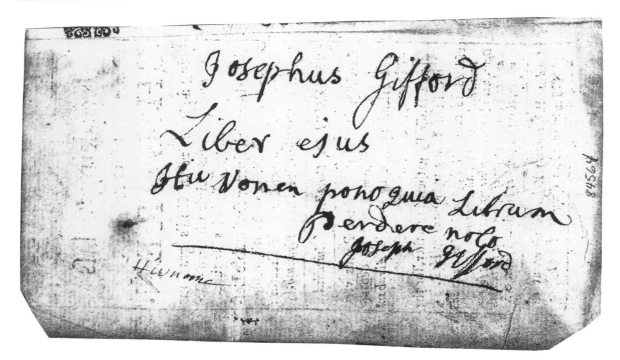

29. A1 verso

30. A2 recto

Black letter. 3 woodcuts (including Hodnett 762) repeated to 4 impressions. Modern leather. References: Sloane 57. Cf. Wing (2nd ed.) L-980–82 (Dorothy Leigh) and M-2937.

PML 68151. Purchase: Harper Fund.

The same publishers issued this text as a broadside. Unlike the heartfelt godliness of such as James Janeway, religion here seems to have been adopted as a veneer for the brute norms of adult control: "Give him no liberty in his youth, and wink not at his folly . . . Chastise thy Child, and be diligent therein, lest his shame grieve thee." For all that, the preface expressly states a wish to make these "hundred godly lessons" appeal to their intended audience: ". . . because Songs and rhimes may make a better impression, and stick faster in your memories, hear them in verse."

    The title cut (repeated on the divisional title) was printed from a much damaged block, which had survived at least 170 years, being first employed by Wynkyn de Worde in *The crafte to lyve well and to dye well* 1505 (STC 2nd ed. 792). It is ironic that in *The Mothers Blessing* it should represent a mother admonishing her children, for Wynkyn had also used it to show the Antichrist enthroned (*The byrthe and lyfe of Antechryst* [ca. 1525], STC 2nd ed. 670). The block of the next cut (A5ᵛ), showing a king holding a scepter, was very wormed and no doubt dated from the sixteenth century also (not in Hodnett). The third woodcut (B2ʳ) shows a puritan figure and its block had only a minor break.

❧ 31 ❧

[STEPHEN CRISP (1628–92)]. *A New Book for Children to Learn in. With many wholsome meditations for them to consider. With directions for true spelling . . . By S.C.* [London:] Printed and Sold by Luke Hinde, [ca. 1747]. 24° (92 × 68 mm.).

A–D¹² (D12ᵛ colophon *London: Printed and Sold by T. Sowle Raylton and Luke Hinde, at the Bible in George-Yard, Lombard-*

street). Pp. 96. Unwatermarked paper. Upwards of half a dozen type fonts represented on the title page, including large black letter. Modern buckram, original sheep covers preserved. Reference: Sloane 146 (earlier edition).

Provenance: Hannah Plumsted (inscr.). PML 81355. Gift: Elisabeth Ball.

While many of the puritan children's books were written without reference to the doctrines of particular sects, Stephen Crisp's *New Book* was an anthology which (apart from the alphabet and syllabary at the beginning) went in for some fairly abstract exhortations of distinctly Quaker coloring: "God that made the World...he is not a Man sitting as a man above the Stars . . . as many of the World and the Teachers thereof imagine. *But the true God . . . is an Eternal Spirit.*" Heavy cargo, which overweights the neat format and typography of its Quaker printers.

❦ 32 ❦

[BENJAMIN HARRIS sen. (fl. 1673–1705). *The Holy Bible, in verse*]. London: Benj. Harris Senior, at the upper-end of Grace-Church-Street, next Cornhill, 1698 (imprint of N.T. title). 32° (71 × 48 mm.).

A–D⁸ (A1–3, C6–8 and D⁸ lacking, C3ʳ divisional title *The New Testament, in verse. For the benefit of weak memories*). Ff. [32]. 9 of 16(?) woodcuts (49 × 40 mm. and smaller). Original panel-stamped sheep over thin beech boards, front cover: Indian hunter

shooting arrows at birds; back cover: vase of flowers (see overleaf). Reference: *Fellows Report* 1981–83, p. 371.

Provenance: unidentified early inscription inside front cover. PML 84565. Gift: Justin G. Schiller.

The shattered condition of this versified abridgment of the Bible is entirely made up for by the plain fact of its survival (the remaining stubs of the missing leaves fortunately render a complete collation possible). It is the earliest extant edition of the text, which was one of Benjamin Harris's energetic attempts to blend commerce and religious zeal and to suit the Scriptures to "weak memories" by putting them into doggerel. Harris was a virulent puritan whose anti-Catholicism is pungently expressed in his *Protestant Tutor* of 1679 and who was closely involved with the production of America's most famous early children's book, *The New England Primer*. He worked as author, printer, publisher, and bookseller in both London and Boston, and his publications mostly survive in fragmentary state because of the fatal combination of cheap production and widespread popularity. The Morgan Library also possesses a fragment of a 1724 American edition of *The Holy Bible in Verse* (Gottlieb 74, PML 85494), but the iconography of its primitive illustrations is quite different from the London edition.

In England the blocking in blind of pictorial panels on bookbindings goes back to the late fifteenth century but has to be considered a very archaic practice by the seventeenth century. In view of Harris's New England past and the American Indian scene on the front cover, it is possible that this copy belonged to an issue reserved by the publisher for the American market.

32. B7ᵛ–8ʳ, *enlarged*

32. rear cover binding panel, rubbing, *enlarged*

◆§ 33 §◆

[*The Beginning, Progress and End of Man*, incipit:] *Adam first comes on the stage / and Eve out of his side / was given to him in maridge / lift up and see the Bride.* Manuscript on paper. [England: ca. 1698]. Foolscap broadsheet (325 × 410 mm.), cut and folded to form a turn-up (165 × 105 mm.).

Single sheet of 4 metamorphoses with 8 flaps for turning up and down to reveal and conceal 13 quatrains and 8 pen-and-ink drawings. The paper is from a type of stock much imported into England during the last quarter of the seventeenth century (watermark: arms of Amsterdam, similar to Heawood 390). The reverse of the sheet shows 6 studies for the turn-up by the same hand, including a finished sketch of the second metamorphosis (a crowned lion carrying a scepter transforms into an eagle carrying an infant). References: Muir p. 210 and fig. 91; *Fellows Report 1984–86*, p. 278.

Provenance: ? Percy Muir; Sotheby's London, 5th Dec. 1986, lot 395. MA 4432. Purchase: Julia P. Wightman.

The idea of telling a pictorial story by getting the reader to turn up, or turn down, flaps on a sheet of paper dates from the middle of the seventeenth century. A turn-up printed by B. Alsop for T. Dunster in 1650 (Wing 2nd ed. B-1701) appears to be the model for a number of homemade versions and also, incidentally, for a glut of similar printed editions in North America at the end of the eighteenth century, known as Metamorphoses. The home-made manuscript exhibited here can be roughly dated from an

inscription on the reverse: "in the year 1698 there was a great snowfal on the third day of May." In text and illustration it follows the Alsop edition quite closely and thus is a *memento mori* rather than a puritan exhortation. Some phrasing is different and one extra stanza has been added on the upper flap of the last transformation:

> Ose Ose thou arte but dust
> thy gold and silver is but rust
> thy time is past thy glass is spent
> no golden bribes can death prevent

Secularized turn-ups, or harlequinades, became popular in the 1760s (see chapter X).

◆§ 34 §◆

ISAAC WATTS (1674–1748). *Divine Songs. Attempted in easy language for the use of children* . . . London: Printed for M. Lawrence at the Angel in the Poultry, 1715. 12° (150 × 83 mm.).

A^{12} (–A6·7 = D1·2, A10^v *Preface. To all that are concerned in the education of children*); B–C^{12} D^2. Pp. [20], 49, [3]. The frontispiece, an engraved portrait of the author by George Vertue after W. Hood, is a later insertion (as shown by the offsetting of the title onto a preceding flyleaf). Original gold-tooled red turkey over pasteboard, panelled sides with fillets, rolls and small tools; Augsburg gilt-blocked floral endpapers by Jakob Enderlin. References: Pafford B1; Stone *Watts* p. 45; Foxon p. 873; Alderson *Uncle Tom* pp. 44–5 (Osborne copy). On the manufacturer of the endpapers, see Haemmerle & Hirsch pp. 71–3, 120.

Provenance: *To M^{rs}. Elizabeth Abney / JW.* (inscribed by the author), one of Sir Thomas Abney's three daughters—the others being Sarah and Mary—to whom the book is dedicated; James Ward of Nottingham (Sotheby's, 28th July 1902, lot 24, sold to J. Pearson & Co. for Pierpont Morgan). PML 5522.

Divine Songs can justly claim to be the first classic text written for children in England. Its popularity lasted almost two centuries although, as this first edition confirms, its origins are firmly rooted in the puritan tradition of English children's literature. Of the three putative dedication copies, Elizabeth Abney's is apparently the only one extant. The publisher marketed the book in plain sheep (at least one surviving copy, Bonham's, 23rd June 1976, lot 150) and, less puritanically, in gilt turkey leather bindings (the three survivors have varying colors, but share the same design and tool-kit: PML, red; Dr. Williams's Library, London, red; W. A. White – Arthur Houghton copy, black).

◆§ 35 §◆

[Dr. Watts's Funeral Invitation. London: 1748]. Oblong broadside (demy half-sheet, deckle edge on three sides, 255 × 390 mm.).

Letterpress: You are desired to Attend the / Funeral of the late Reverend / ISAAC WATTS. D. D. from *Lo-/rimer's-Hall*, *London-Wall*, to the Burial-Ground in *Bunn-Hill-Fields*, on *Monday*, the

34. inserted portrait and A1r

5th Day of *December*, 1748, at One o'Clock in the / Afternoon. / The Corps will move between 2 / and 3 o'Clock, that it may be inter'd / an Hour before it is dark. Etching: border (225 × 265 mm.) showing a tomb, emblematic figures of Time and Death in a landscape, and a funeral procession in the foreground. Reference: *Realms of Childhood* 58.

PML 84438. Purchase: Ball Fund.

The invitation with its helpful note about the movement of the corpse are let in typographically to what was presumably a standard engraved sheet. Nevertheless, the writer of *Divine Songs* would surely have appreciated the *putti* on his mausoleum with their torches and Death nearby stroking an infant head:

> There is an Hour when I must die,
> Nor do I know how soon 'twill come;
> A thousand children young as I
> Are call'd by Death to hear their Doom.
> [Song X]

⌘ 36 ⌘

JOHN WRIGHT (fl. 1720–44). *Spiritual Songs for Children: or, poems on several subjects and occasions.* London: Printed for J. Murgatroyd, Chiswell Street, Moorfields, 1793. Six-Pence, bound and gilt. Half-sheet 24° (99 × 80 mm.).

[1–4¹²] signed A–H⁶ (1/1 frontispiece and 4/12 blank mounted as pastedowns, 4/10ʳ *Supplement*). Pp. 94 [2]. 23 wood engravings (82 × 57 mm. and slightly smaller). Original dab-colored floral boards. Reference: ESTC T160358.

Provenance: W. Brackett (sign.); Eliza Brackett (sign.). PML 82310. Gift: Elisabeth Ball.

First published by Joseph Marshall in 1727 (Foxon p. 907), *Spiritual Songs* suggests an influence from Isaac Watts. Where Watts was lyrical, however, Wright is argumentative, and his "songs," written mostly in jog-trot decasyllables, are not very singable. Among his earnest attempts to promote a Christian society there is an interesting plea to abolish Christmas:

A Journey from this World to the World
behind the Curtain.

*A Journey from this World to the World
behind the Curtain.*

'TIS known to all, this world is full of grief,
   I almost think 'tis but a civil thief;
It offers much, but little doth it give;
How can I chuse in such a world to live?
'Tis froward, peevish, changing, full of turns,
Sometimes it freezes, by and by it burns:
It shews be dainty things, but whilst that I
Upon them gaze, they slightly pass me by:
Much like a flea that skips upon my hand,
But yet it will not be at my command.
When I upon this world did meditate,
I quickly found it always came too late,
To help me in a strait, or else too soon;
For when I wanted, it was always gone.
So much distracted I went on;
To seek another world when this was done:
I went a little way, and there I found
A piece of blessed consecrated ground,
Where ev'ry dweller doth in safety lie,
And yet no man can claim a property:
'Tis common unto all without a ſtain,
'Tis watered too without one drop of rain.

No   36. 1/4ᵛ–5ʳ

You join the sacred name of God
   With mass, that idol vain;
And so in serving Christ, you nod
   To bring the Pope again.
As for the time when Christ was born,
   It is an hidden thing;
Some say it was in Capricorn
And some say in the Spring.

This late edition, with its curiously dense illustrations, is a testimony to the enduring influence of the puritan movement. Murgatroyd was a specialist in radical theology, and apart from a 1792 edition of Janeway's *Token* he does not appear to have been involved with other children's books. ESTC records nearly eighty productions with which he was associated as publisher or bookseller between 1787 and 1799.

Conscious that children were "very much delighted with little Poems, Histories, Emblems, and Fables," Foxton set out to lure them toward right conduct by incorporating emblematic incidents from real life into his moral songs. He was also conscious—as others have been since—that he may have been demeaning his art by adapting it to "the Capacities of Children," for he confesses that he has been "oblig'd to deface several Poetical Ornaments" in the course of composition. The first edition of Foxton's book owes much to Isaac Watts, not least its title, its publisher—by 1728 Ford was also the publisher of *Divine Songs*—and its blurb by the great man himself. Watts has some doubt about the high level of Foxton's "Language and Moral Instructions" but he does not seem to mind that the book is entirely secular in its leanings, with no direct "godly" purpose.

⋄§ 37 §⋄

THOMAS FOXTON (1697–1769). *Moral Songs. Composed for the use of children.* London: Printed for Richard Ford, at the Angel in the Poultry, near Stocks-Market, 1728. 12° (140 × 80 mm.).

A⁶ (2ʳ dedication *To William Archer, Esq.*; 6ʳ commendatory letter from Watts to Ford dated 26th Dec. 1727; 6ᵛ ad for three Watts titles); B–C¹² D⁶. Pp. x [2], 58 [2]. Publisher's device. Nineteenth-century sprinkled calf gilt, edges gilt. References: ESTC T140208; Opie *Three Centuries* (1977), 716; Pafford B196; Foxon p. 283.

Provenance: W. C. Hazlitt (sign.); Cornelius Paine (bookplate, sign.); George Bates (Jan. 1934 inscr.). PML 85615. Purchase: Harper Fund.

⋄§ 38 §⋄

A Guide from the Cradel to the Grave. Being a companion for young and old: wherein we may see the various stages of this life, from the tears of tender infancy, to the misery of old age, reduc'd to childhood. To which is added, the three great stepts to eternal salvation . . . With an instruction for children to be obedient to their parents. Printed in the Year DMCCXXXII [London: Edward Midwinter, 1732]. 12° (132 × 78 mm.).

[1⁸] (7ʳ–8ᵛ publisher's ads). Pp. 12, [4]. 10 cuts (77 × 60 mm. and slightly smaller). Old colored floral boards (*remboîtage*). References: ESTC T087902; Foxon G309.

Provenance: *Pillis Pentreath* (inscr.); Justin G. Schiller (Sendak bookplate). PML 84691. Purchase: Fellows Fund.

(2)
The First STAGE.

LORD, what is Man! a Sigh a Cry,
Looks up, and then begins to die!
Death steals upon us, while we're green ;
Behind us digs a Grave unseen.
'Tis true, the Babe does no Offence,
Grac'd, lik'd the Lamb, with Innocence ;
And when his Feet can take their Course,
He vainly rides the Hobby-Horse.
But surely this seems to presage
The Vanity of riper AGE ;
When knowing more, we practise less,
Unless it be in Wickedness.

38. 1ᵛ–2ʳ

(3)
The Second STAGE.

NOW see the Youth like Peacock fair,
Who seems to fly into the Air ;
He views far distant Shores and Strands,
And Princes Courts in foreign Lands.
If Nature can delight his Sense,
Or Learning give him Eloquence ;
Nothing is wanting to inspire,
Or make the Lookers-on admire !
Thus blest by Birth, by Riches more,
His Parts and Person all adore ;
And thus he spends his pleasing Time,
And glories in his Youthful Prime.

Essentially a moralized version of Shakespeare's "Seven Ages of Man" (see entry 209), this *Guide*, which has apparently survived in no other edition, introduces religion as a conventional reflex rather than out of any spiritual commitment. Because of this and the author's advice to children on their behavior toward parents and at home, the book may be seen as marking a transitional phase between the earnestness of the godly writers and the rationalism that became prevalent later in the century. The large relief illustrations confirm this sense of transition. The peacock youth of "The Second Stage" is much of his time, but the boy on his hobbyhorse conforms to an earlier iconography of children as nothing but small adults.

The pamphlet was apparently issued separately as well as with Midwinter's 1732 reprint of H. Parsons, *The History of the Five Wise Philosophers* (a version of the Barlaam and Josaphat legend), ed. Nicholas Herrick (London: J. Tracy, ca. 1725).

✧ 39 ✧

JOHN BUNYAN (1628–88). *Divine Emblems: or temporal things spiritualized. Calculated for the use of young people. Adorned with fifty copper plate cuts.* London:

Engraved, Printed and Sold by T. Bennett, Nᵒ. 7, Plough Court, Fetter Lane Holborn, Likewise Sold by T. Massey, Nᵒ. 18, Snow Hill, M. Trapp, Nᵒ. 1, Pater-noster-Row M. Gurney, Nᵒ. 128, and Wilkins, Nᵒ. 60, Holborn Hill, [ca. 1793]. Price Bound 1ˢ 6ᵈ. 16° (116 × 90 mm.).

A² (1ᵛ frontispiece portrait, 2ʳ title); B–F⁸ G² (text and 49 illustrations). Ff. [44]. Engraved throughout: frontispiece and title printed from a single small copperplate (100 × 157 mm.), the final quire (one-eighth of a sheet) from two somewhat larger plates, the remaining quires (all half-sheets) from two large copperplates each (about 320 × 220 mm.). The outer formes went through the intaglio press before the inner formes. Laid paper, watermarked with fleur-de-lys and initials IV. Contemporary (probably original) sheep. References: ESTC T059005; Praz p. 291; Sloane 182 (other eds.); Freeman pp. 206–28, 230, (other eds.); Johnson 21.

Provenance: Frances Ann Pattison (inscr. *given by her Grandmama Oct 9 1813 A Langston*); J. A. Fuller Maitland (armorial bookplate). PML 66116. Purchase: Harper Fund.

First published in 1686 as *A Book for Boys and Girls: or, country rhimes for children* (Wing 2nd ed. B-5489), Bunyan's verses depict homely scenes from which a suitable "comparison,"

39. E6 recto

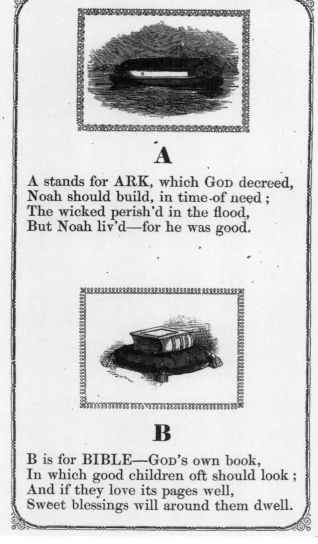

40. 5ᵛ–6ʳ, *reduced*

religious or moral lesson, may be derived. First supplied with cuts in 1707, the book gained wide popularity during the eighteenth century in abridged form (the 74 emblems reduced by 25); in 1724 it first acquired its current title. Bennett's edition is one of the most attractive; the framed oval pictures and the text were engraved together and project a certain formal dignity.

⤙ 40 ⤚

C. B. *The Little Christian's Sunday Alphabet. By a lady. Ninth thousand.* London: Seeleys, Fleet Street and Hanover Street, 1854. 18° (168 × 99 mm.).

[1¹⁸] (1ᵛ frontispiece by R. Langton after T.S. or S.T.; 3ᵛ *Preface to the second edition* dated 1850; 18 lacking). Ff. [18]. Printed on one side of the sheet only. 29 wood engravings, all illustrations hand-colored. Morocco gilt, edges gilt.

Provenance: Charles Todd Owen (binding). PML 85377. Gift: Elisabeth Ball.

The ardor of the puritans was renewed in the evangelizing movement of the nineteenth century, whose influence on children's books is explored later in this catalogue (chapter XIV). The relationship between the two movements can be clearly seen in this simple Victorian alphabet-book, with its fleeting resemblances to Bunyan's emblems and Watts's verses. "I publish it," says C.B. in her preface for parents, "in the sincere, unvarnished hope that it may call some infant minds to a love of holy things"—a hope with which James Janeway would surely have concurred.

III

ENTER TOM THUMB

Testimony abounds for the attractiveness of what Charles Lamb called "that beautiful Interest in wild tales which made the child a man." Some of the testimony, especially from the Savers of Souls, was negative: "As for play-books and romances and idle tales, I have already shewed in my *Book of Self-Denial* how pernicious they are," wrote Richard Baxter in the first part of his *Christian Directory* (1672); or, more pertinently: "And yet alas! how often do we see parents prefer a Tom Thumb, Guy of Warwick, Valentine and Orson, or some such foolish book, before the Book of Life!" (an expostulation in the editor's preface to *The History of Genesis*, 2nd edition [London: Printed by J.D. for W. Fisher and R. Mount, 1691; not in ESTC, copy in the Cotsen Children's Library]).

Much else was positive: From Philip Sidney to William Wordsworth and beyond, writer after writer remembered with affection the stories of fantasy and adventure that held their young imaginations—and we only have to look at the old advertisements of long-vanished booksellers with their lists of hacked-down romances or Mother Shipton folklore (or even to look at our own pulp fiction) to confirm that where reading enjoyment lay, there, too, lay a source of much trade.

"Popular literature," however, presented itself in many forms, whose chief common factor is a fugitive existence. We cannot easily gain a complete view of the themes or the selling patterns that prevailed from one generation to the next, because so much of the evidence has disappeared into the gutters or the jakes of their own time ("Boghouse Miscellanies," one commentator quaintly called them). Judging from what has survived, however, we can say that the printed forms in which popular literature reached the public were probably more diverse and more intricately priced than the common notion of "chapbooks" and "penny merriments" allows. In the following chapter a few notable examples of stories from "the pedlar's pack" are given, in the hope of demonstrating a little of this diversity and of the crude (but still easily comprehensible) sales-pitching that went with it. Perhaps we should also generalize from a remark quoted from Iona and Peter Opie in our first entry below, that much of this loved or vilified literature is decidedly more attractive in its intentions than in its execution. The imaginative potential of many a "wild tale" was seriously debilitated by the laborious prose or the abrupt surgical procedures of the hacks who made the texts. The objectors to "foolish books" may not have been as priggish as they sound.

∙⧽ **41** ⧼∙

R.I. [presumably RICHARD JOHNSON (1573–1659?)]. *The History of Tom Thumbe, the little, for his small stature surnamed, King Arthurs dwarfe: Whose life and adventures containe many strange and wonderfull accidents, published for the delight of merry time-spenders.* London: [A. Mathewes?] for Tho: Langley, 1621. 8° (137 × 85 mm.).

A–B⁸ C⁴ (A1ʳ title, lacking C4 presumably blank). Ff. [20]. Mostly black letter (82 mm.). 28 lines. Woodcut (81 mm. square) on title. Until the mid-nineteenth century bound second in the first of two tract-volumes of 25 seventeenth-century chapbooks, now in olive morocco gilt, edges gilt. References: STC (2nd ed.) 14056; Esdaile p. 85; *Fellows Report* 1954, pp. 38–40; R.I., *The History of Tom Thumbe*, ed. Curt F. Bühler (Northwestern Univ. Press for The Renaissance English Text Society, 1965); Opie *Fairy Tales* (1974), pp. 30–46.

41. A1 recto

Provenance: Narcissus Luttrell (1657–1732); Edward Wynne of Chelsea (Leigh and Sotheby's, 6th March 1786, lot 23, sold for £3 8s. to); John Baynes (d. 1787), bequeathed to; Joseph Ritson (Leigh and Sotheby's, 5th December 1803, sold to); Richard Heber (Evans, 8th December 1834, lot 1743 (II), £24 10s, to); Edward Vernon Utterson, who broke up the tract-volumes (Sotheby and Wilkinson, 19th April 1852, lot 1504); George Daniel (15th July 1852 inscr., Sotheby, Wilkinson and Hodge 20th July 1864, lot 1684, 12 gns. to); Henry Huth (1815–78), bequeathed to; Alfred H. Huth (Sotheby's, 8th July 1919, lot 7474, £41 to Quaritch for); John L. Clawson (Anderson Galleries, 20th May 1926, lot 425, $1,050 to Dr. A. S. W. Rosenbach). PML 45444. Purchase: Robert H. Taylor.

Writing of this text, the earliest complete version of an English folk tale to appear in print, Iona and Peter Opie remarked that it is "a glorious idea rather than a glorious story;" and if one considers what novelists have done with the idea, from Swift's Brobdingnag to Mary Norton's Borrowers, one can see what Mr. and Mrs. Opie meant. The adventures of "this little wonderous Gentleman" are pointlessly episodic, the storyteller doing little with his theme beyond having Tom trapped in puddings or eaten by various creatures or else (as happens too in "Jack the Giant Killer") provided with sufficient magical powers to make him invulnerable. Nor can it be assumed that the second part, promised by R.I., was any improvement. From the more extensive metrical version printed for John Wright in 1630 (STC 24115) and later reprinted for F. Coles, T. Vere, and J. Wright, ca. 1670 (Wing 2nd ed. T-1790), and from later chapbook editions, the continuations of the story appear to be only "more of the same" indited with less control.

   Despite its feeble text, however, this unique copy of *Tom Thumbe* offers an unusual glimpse of editorial attitudes towards popular themes early in the seventeenth century. For not only does "R.I." make a famous claim for the attractiveness of Tom Thumb's adventures ("the onely revivers of drouzy age at midnight; old and young have with his Tales chim'd Mattens till the Cocks crow in the morning"), he also places Tom within a veritable catalogue of contemporary storybook heroes: Guy of Warwick and "bould Sir Beuis of Hampton," Robin Hood and Adam Bell, Tom o'Lincoln and a couple of other notable Toms. So far from being a mere booklet to hawk about the streets, this *Tom Thumbe* is a celebration of the traditions that "compassed the Christmas fire-block" and implies a more sophisticated readership than its unsophisticated contents suggest.

   This appeal to a "literate" readership is perhaps confirmed in the book's carefully organized typography and design, which are far superior to the casual makeup and production of the seventeenth-century metrical versions. An examination of a photocopy of the ca. 1670 edition does, however, reveal a worm-eaten and possibly recut version of the 1621 titleblock, as well as yet another impression of the "court scene" block which we have already noted in F. Coles' edition of *The Mother's Blessing* (entry 30).

❧ 42 ☙

Tom Thumb's Folio; or, a new penny play-thing for little giants. To which is prefixed, an abstract of the life of Mr. Thumb, and an historical account of the wonderful deeds he performed. Together with some anecdotes respecting Grumbo the great giant. London: Printed for the People of all Nations;

42. fo. 10 verso, *enlarged*

and sold by T. Carnan, Successor to Mr. J. Newbery, in St. Paul's Church-Yard, 1786. [Price One Penny.]. Half-sheet 32° (95 × 61 mm.), imposed for work-and-turn.

[1¹⁶] signed A–B⁸ (1·16 mounted as pastedowns, 1ᵛ frontispiece and *Tom Thumb's Maxim in Trade and Politics*, 15ᵛ ads). Pp. 29, [3]. 9 cuts (including two illustrating fables). Original gilt-blocked and dab-colored floral wrappers. Reference: Roscoe J356(3).

Provenance: Simmons and Waters?, booksellers of Leamington (offered in their catalogue of ca. 1903). PML 81486. Gift: Elisabeth Ball.

Many of the early editions of the tales of Tom Thumb appear to be for a broad, popular market, which would have included children. Among the publishers who sought to adapt the story specifically for a child readership was (unsurprisingly) John Newbery, the range of whose activities are outlined in chapter V below. His *Tom Thumb's Folio* was originally listed in 1767 (about the time of his death), and the book was to remain in print with one of the Newbery firms for most of the rest of the century. As a revision of the prose original it has more order and character, being told in Newbery's hearty tones with contemporary comments and moral nudges incorporated on the way (but there is also a last hint of the old scatology when Tom makes use of the Giant Grumbo's pocket "for another Purpose, which was not altogether fair, but he could not help it"). In keeping with the story's always casual treatment, the main tale here ends on page 17 and the rest of the book is rather random supplementary matter including grammatical and moral lessons and a couple of fables.

◦§ 43 ξ◦

The Life and Death of Tom Thumb, the little giant. Together with some curious anecdotes respecting Grumbo the great giant, king of the country of eagles. Embellished with cuts. Gainsbrough: Printed at Mozley's Lilliputian Book-Manufactory, [ca. 1795]. (Price One Penny.). Half-sheet 32° (96 × 63 mm.), imposed for work-and-turn.

A^{16} (1·16 mounted as pastedowns, 1^v relief-cut frontispiece, 2^r title, 2^v blank). Pp. 31, [1] Laid paper (fleur-de-lys watermark). 6 cuts and one tailpiece. Original typographical and relief-cut yellow wrappers, from a series of street cries, "Buy a Mat" on front cover, "A Pig and Plumb Sauce" on back cover. Reference: ESTC N033571.

PML 81836. Gift: Elisabeth Ball.

As will be seen in chapter IX below, the Mozley family of Gainsborough made regular use of the Newbery lists to furnish themselves with saleable stock. In this adaptation of *Tom Thumb's Folio*, most of Newbery's text has been taken over verbatim, although "cuckaws" have now been upgraded to "eagles," the final fables have been cut, and there are fewer and much more worka-day illustrations. "Mr. Mozley's little Books," but not the delightfully named "Lilliputian Book-Manufactory," get an appropriate mention when Tom is gaining his education. The Morgan Library also owns two abridged penny editions of *Tom Thumb's Folio*, with only three illustrations, published at Brentford by P. Norbury (PML 81483 and 85577.1).

◦§ 44 ξ◦

The Life and Death of Tom Thumb, the little giant. And Grumbo the great giant, king of the country of eagles. Edinburgh: Printed at the Foot of the Horsewynd, [ca. 1780]. (Price One Penny). Half-sheet 12° (150 × 80 mm.), imposed for work-and-turn.

[1⁶]. Pp. 12. One half-sheet of laid, watermarked and counter-marked paper. 3 cuts. Folded, unopened, uncut (see overleaf). Reference: ESTC T169161.

PML 83119. Gift: Elisabeth Ball.

Newbery's *Tom Thumb's Folio* rapidly became a text that was adopted and adapted by publishers up and down the land. Usually (as with the previous item) the imitations followed Newbery's style fairly closely, but in this instance we find the *Folio* returned to the chapbook market with characteristic abandon. The text is cut, the Newbery chapter divisions and illustrations are done away with, and the half-sheet production, unsewn, converts the book entirely to a street vendor's stock-in-trade. An attempt to identify copy text for this chapbook edition serves chiefly to accentuate the problematic role of the Mozleys as purveyors of children's litera-

43. A9 recto, *enlarged*

ture (see chapters VIII and IX). From the reference to "eagles" rather than "cuckaws" we are almost certainly dealing with an abridgment of an earlier Gainsborough edition (entry 43). The Edinburgh printer has not edited his copy very carefully however, as at the point where Newbery and Mozley inserted a puff for their publications we now find reference to "Mr. Osborne's little books." This can be none other than the Osborne who appears as a London publisher on Mozley title-pages, an invention serving to de-provincialize the imprint in the same way that "Millar, Law, and Cater" did for Wilson & Spence of York (see entry 13).

◦§ 45 ξ◦

JOHN SHIRLEY (fl. 1680–1702). *The Renowned History (or the Life and Death) of Guy Earl of Warwick, containing his noble exploits and victories.* London: Printed by A. M. for C. Bates, at the Sun and Bible in Guilt-spur-street, and by John Foster, at the Golden Ball in Pye-Corner, [ca. 1705]. 4° (181 × 135 mm.).

A–K⁴ ($A1^r$ title, $A1^v$ blank, $A2^r$ *The Epistle to the Reader* signed John Shurly, $A2^v$ *The Argument*, K4 publishers' ads *Where any Country Chapmen or Others may be furnished with all sorts of Historys, small Books, and Ballads, at Reasonable Rates*). Pp. 79,

44. outer forme, *reduced*

45. E4 recto, *reduced*

[1]. Unwatermarked paper. Roman type. 12 woodcuts (134 × 132 mm. and somewhat smaller) repeated to 16 impressions. Nineteenth-century calf. References: ESTC T125807; Esdaile p. 233.

PML 85598. Purchase: Julia P. Wightman.

Guy of Warwick was the first of the merry tales named by R.I. in his introduction to *Tom Thumbe* (entry 41)—a farrago of furious adventures boiled down from a Middle English romance (based in turn on an even older French epic) by various seventeenth-century suppliers to the chap-trade. At least four editions of Shirley's version preceded this one, including an edition by the same printer for an earlier publisher, Philip Brooksby. These versions were no doubt read by children, as were the even more heavily abridged copies that were a staple of the eighteenth-century publishing industry (see the Aldermary Church Yard edition given in facsimile in Victor E. Neuburg's *The Penny Histories* [London, 1968]). The version shown here presumably counted as a "History" in the publisher's list of his wares on page 79, and was sold "stitchd" for 6d. or 1s. The long lines of print (and the prose) make for heavy going, but the large pictures would have proved amusing. Two quite different versions of *Guy* from around this date are also in the Morgan Library (Gottlieb 43 and 44; PML 3469.25 and 85493), the first being a metrical version published as a broadside. The earliest English *Guy of Warwick* in verse was printed at Westminster by Wynkyn de Worde ca. 1498 (GW 12586: one-leaf fragment, Bodleian Library) and in London by Richard Pynson ca. 1500 (GW 12587: three-leaf fragment, British Library).

Argalus and Parthenia. 97

did answer his Arguments for going Home, he still found out another: *Kalander* thus at last being overcome with Words, which Importunity had taught inexorable *Argalus*, was forced at last to yield to what he so long gainsaid.

'Tis now concluded *Argalus* must go; but yet *Kalander* must not leave them thus: There is no parting till her aged Uncle has warm'd his Fingers by *Parthenia*'s Fire. *Parthenia* sues, nor shall *Kalander* rest till he has promised to be *Parthenia*'s Guest.

To-morrow, next, when *Titan*'s early Ray had of a fairer Day an Earnest given, and with his trembling Beams had newly rouzed their poor Eyes from Rest, they left *Kalander*'s Castle, and that Night they at the *Palace of Delight* arrived, (for so that noble Place was

E

46. E1 recto

The most Illustrious

HISTORY

Of the Seven

CHAMPIONS of CHRISTENDOM.

THE FIRST PART

CHAP. I.

The Parentage and Birth of St George, and how he was stolen away by an inchantress.

NOT long after the destruction of Troy, sprung up the seven wonders of the world, the seven champions of Christendom, St George, for England, &c.

A 3

47. A3 recto, *reduced*

46

[Sir PHILIP SIDNEY (1554–86)]. *The Unfortunate Lovers: the history of Argalus and Parthenia. In four books. Adorn'd with cuts.* London: printed for Henry Woodgate, and Samuel Brooks, at the Golden-Ball, in Pater-noster-row, [ca. 1760]. Long 12° (141 × 81 mm.).

A–E¹² (A1ʳ *A catalogue of chapmens books*, A1ᵛ frontispiece and verse, A2ʳ title, A2ᵛ ads continued from A1ʳ *Where all country-booksellers, shop-keepers, school-masters and others, may be supplied at the most reasonable rates. N.B. Shop-Books, Pocket-Books, &c. and Paste-Boards of all sorts*, A3ʳ text, E12ᵛ blank). Lacking A6·7, D5·8, D6·7, E3·10, E4·9, E5·8, E6·7. Pp. 119, [1]. 3 cuts and one tailpiece. Stabbed and laced into original sheep binding over pasteboard. References: ESTC T128764; Esdaile p. 129; Tannenbaum 174.

PML 85654. Gift: Elisabeth Ball.

Originally published as a story in Sidney's *Arcadia*, *Argalus* must have appealed to seventeenth-century editors in quest of copy for the popular market. Many versions were published (listed in Wing under five different rubrics), one of which was the long poem by Francis Quarles. In the eighteenth century the story continued to find a place in the catalogues of the suppliers of "country booksellers . . . school-masters, and others," and in Woodgate and Brooks's list published here it lies alongside all the expected favorites: *Guy of Warwick* and the *Gesta Romanorum*, *Reynard the Fox* and *Robinson Crusoe*, *Robin Hood* and *Valentine and Orson*.

47

[RICHARD JOHNSON (1573–1659?)]. *The Illustrious and Renowned History of the Seven Famous Champions of Christendom. In three parts. Containing their honourable birth, victories, and noble atchievements . . . their combats*

*with giants and monsters . . . their relieving distressed ladies,
with their faithful love to them . . . Also, the heroic adventures
of St. Grorge's three sons. Adorned with cuts.* Glasgow:
Printed by Robert Duncan, 1788. Half-sheet 12° (170 ×
100 mm.).

A–I⁶ (A1ʳ title, A1ᵛ blank, A2ʳ preface, A3ʳ text). Pp. 108. 9 cuts
repeated to 13 impressions. Nineteenth-century half calf,
marbled boards, edges uncut. Reference: ESTC N028543.

PML 81414. Gift: Elisabeth Ball.

Richard Johnson, the putative editor of *Tom Thumbe*, was
certainly the purveyor of this medley of preposterous incidents
from the lives of St. George, St. Denis et al. His romance was first
published in 1596–97 (STC 14677–8) and, as with *Argalus*, popular renderings soon became common. The first edition of this
version may be that published by Norris and Bettesworth in 1719
(Esdaile p. 83), but once publishing for children got under way,
the still-substantial text was quickly reduced to proportions
manageable by inexperienced readers (see entry 382 for the
"chapbook" edition published in Tabart's series of popular tales).
In later times Richard Johnson was drawn upon for more
substantial renderings of the *Seven Champions* for children, most
notably by W. H. G. Kingston (1861) and by the great historian of
children's literature, F. J. Harvey Darton (1913).

❧ 48 ☙

*The History of the Noble Marquis of Salus and Patient
Grissel.* London: Printed and Sold in Aldermary Church-
Yard, [Cluer Dicey and perhaps his father, William Dicey, or
Richard Marshall, ca. 1750]. Long 12° (152 × 84 mm.).

[1¹²]. Pp. 24. 11 cuts, including a few not relating to the text.
Modern half calf and marbled boards. References: ESTC
T036507; Victor E. Neuburg, "The Diceys and the Chapbook
Trade" in: *The Library* 5th ser. vol. XXIV (1969), pp. 219–31.

PML 85562. Gift: Elisabeth Ball.

"Prosperity must be seasoned with some crosses, or else it would
corrupt us too much," says the anonymous adapter of this text,
hoping perhaps to temper the outrage of eighteenth-century
feminists with a moral sentiment. For this chapbook sustained in
print the medieval romance of Griselda (which had been used by
Boccaccio and Petrarch and had come into English literature
through Chaucer and Dekker), a tale that sought to urge on all
wives a degree of compliance much at odds with reality. Nevertheless, the publishing trade liked it. Adaptations for chapbooks
and ballads appeared in English no later than the start of the
seventeenth century (STC 12383–6), and editions for children
were popular until well into the nineteenth century (see entry
314). The example here comes from a prolific center of chapbook
publishing at the linked churchyards of Bow and Aldermary
where William and Cluer Dicey had their presses, alongside
Richard Marshall, the father of John who is soon to be seen here as
a significant publisher of children's books (chapters VI and XI).

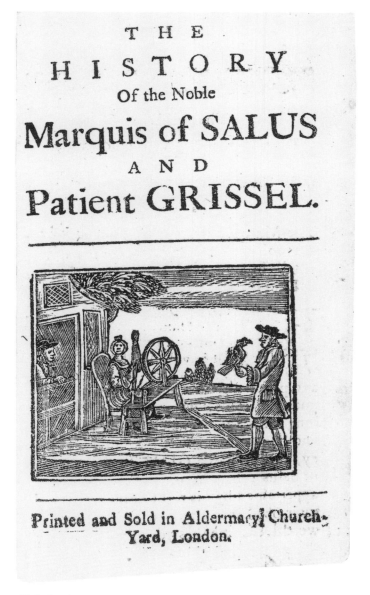

48. fo. 1 recto

❧ 49 ☙

*The Pleasant and Delightful History of Jack and the Giants.
Part the first* [second]. Nottingham: Printed for the Running
Stationers, [ca. 1775]. 2 volumes. 12° (163 × 90 mm.).

Pt. 1: A⁶. Pt. 2: A⁶. Pp. 12 each part. Unwatermarked, laid paper of
poor quality. 5 cuts to each part, not all relating to the text, the two
parts sharing one block. The two parts once bound together, now
separated. References: ESTC T068132 and T130590; Osborne II,
603.

Provenance: Gumuchian & Cⁱᵉ (1930 cat., no. 3152). PML 81400.
Gift: Elisabeth Ball.

Despite an agelessness that appears equivalent to that of Tom
Thumb, Jack the Giant Killer does not seem to have got into print
before the beginning of the eighteenth century. The earliest
recorded version of his adventures is a chapbook edition of Part II
only, published by J. White of Newcastle in 1711 (British Library
copy, now missing, see Esdaile p. 251; Opie (1974) pp. 47–50).

(7)

length, giving him a swinging stroke with both hands, he cut off both his legs, just below the garter, so that the trunk of his body made not only the trees to shake, but the earth tremble with the force of his fall; by which the Knight and his fair Lady escaped his rage.

Then had Jack time to talk with him: so setting his foot upon his neck, he said, thou savage and barbarous wretch, I am come to execute upon thee a just reward of your villainy. And with that he ran him through and through, when the monster sent forth a hideous groan, and so yielded up his life and breath into

49. pt. 2, A4 recto

12

was very sorrowful, because she loved Orson, and was resolved to marry none but him who had so nobly conquered the Green Knight.

CHAP. IV.

Valentine and Orson going in search of Lady Clerimond, who had the Brazen Head in her Possession.

VALENTINE and Orson having taken leave of the Duke of Acquitain, and his daughter Fazon, proceeded on their journey in search of the Lady Clerimond, and at last came

50. A6 verso, *reduced*

Once published, however, the *History* became a favorite with "the running stationers" (chapmen), and once the market for children's books was established his name was taken up as having a particular appeal. John Newbery especially exploited this with letters from him appearing in *A Little Pretty Pocket-Book* (entry 8) and regular mentions in titles and texts. Despite the value of his name as a byword there was an understandable reluctance to admit his violent and increasingly poorly devised adventures into the canon of children's literature. (Part the First of this Nottingham edition has a nice traditional flavor to its storytelling including such splendidly gruesome moments as the Welsh Giant's hara-kiri: "So taking the sharp knife, he ript open his belly from the top to the bottom, and out drops his tripes and trollybubs, so that hur fell down dead." Part the Second descends into mayhem for mayhem's sake.)

Judging by the ca. 1763 chapbook text from Shrewsbury, reprinted in Opie (1974), the two-part edition of *Jack* shown

here is an abbreviated version of the standard chapbook text. Abridgment has to some extent improved the pacing of the stories, but by cutting out a final section the Nottingham editors have lost the most renowned words of the *History*:

> Fee fau fum
> I smell the blood of an English man,
> Be he alive, or be he dead
> I'll grind his bones to make my bread.

❦ 50 ❦

The Famous History of Valentine & Orson, the two sons of the Emperor of Greece.

> *Reader, you'll find this book contains*
> *Enough to answer thy expence and pains.*

London: printed for, and sold by C. Sheppard, No. 8, Aylesbury Street, Clerkenwell. [Price One Penny.] 1804. Mary Rhynd, Printer, 21, Ray Street, Clerkenwell. Long 12° (155 × 95 mm.).

A^{12} (1^r title and cut, 1^v blank, 2^r text). Pp. 24. Laid, unwatermarked paper. 4 cuts. The illustrations were apparently not designed for this text. Boards. Reference: Osborne II, 614.

Provenance: *Beatrice Beddoe Oct. 23–1905* (inscr.). PML 85729. Gift: Elisabeth Ball.

This medieval French romance was popular throughout Europe, and a copy of the first edition, published by Jacques Maillet at Lyons, May 30, 1489, is in the Morgan Library (Goff V-11; PML 609). An English translation by Henry Watson was first printed by Wynkyn de Worde ca. 1510 (STC 2nd ed. 24571.3) and this has formed the source for countless abridgments and retellings, many in chapbook form. (A forerunner of the edition shown here—Gottlieb 46; PML 81637—was printed for the Company of Walking Stationers, and expands the title-page stanza with the two verses:

> And if with caution you will read it through
> 'Twill both instruct and delight thee too,

a sentiment which is arguable to say the least.) At the start of the nineteenth century the ramifying story was seen as a suitable case for reduction to picture-book proportions, and many adaptations for young children appeared. The Morgan Library has, for instance, a clutch of contrasting editions, ranging from the version which Benjamin Tabart included in his "popular tales" series in 1804 (see below, entry 382) to the engraved versions published by John Harris in 1807 (PML 81310) and Didier & Tebbett in 1808 (PML 80672). Nor was that the end. The Victorians published several large-format picture-book editions, and their example has recently been followed by one of the United States's leading picture-book artists: in 1989 Nancy Ekholm Burkert produced the story (complete with poster) as a "re-created folk play in verse," accompanied by a set of reproductions of highly ingenious paintings.

51. pl. [3], facing fo. 11ʳ, *enlarged*

51

[JEANNE-MARIE LE PRINCE DE BEAUMONT (1711–80)]. *Beauty and the Beast. A tale. A new and correct edition.* London: printed for the booksellers, 1816. 16° (123 × 80 mm.).

[1¹⁶]; 4 plates (copper engraving by W. H. Lizars). Pp. [3], 6–34. Wove paper (different stocks for letterpress and engraving, the first watermarked "C 17"). Original printed blue wrappers, *Price Sixpence* on front cover, *New Juvenile Library* ad on back cover. Calf gilt, by Riviere.

Provenance: Gumuchian & Cⁱᵉ (1930 cat., no. 502). PML 84079. Gift: Elisabeth Ball.

The traditions of popular publishing are here seen in a state of transition towards respectability. Not unlike the chapbooks of the eighteenth century, *Beauty and the Beast* is here abridged (from Mme Le Prince de Beaumont's original as translated in the *Magasin des Enfans: or, the Young Misses Magazine*, 1759); it is issued in paper covers in a single gathering; and it is "printed for the booksellers." On the other hand, few such little books would be sold by chapmen for as much as sixpence, and none would ever be found with such elegant, separately printed illustrations engraved

by a named artist. According to the final ad at least, twenty-four titles were in the series, all illustrated by Lizars and available bound together in four volumes at 14 shillings.

52

Rhymes for the Nursery. A pretty book for a good child. London: Printed and sold by J. & C. Evans, Long-lane, [ca. 1820]. 24° (95 × 51 mm.).

[1⁸]. Pp. 15, [1]. Laid paper. Small title vignette. 14 cuts (27 × 42 mm.) illustrating the rhymes, full-page cut of a mussel woman. Original engraved pictorial wrappers in red, advertising on front cover a hobbyhorse and whip for a halfpenny, on back cover a mask and book at the same price. Modern blue morocco gilt.

Provenance: Charles Todd Owen (binding). PML 85000. Gift: Elisabeth Ball.

As the eighteenth century drew to a close, the trade in 12° chapbooks and broadside ballads began to give way to a more diverse array of cheap books and song sheets, while new developments in printing technology (stereotyping, the iron press, the steam press,

The Lion ranges
Round the wood,
And makes the lesser
Beasts his food.

The Whale's the monarch
Of the main,
As is the Lion
Of the plain.

*Right and
far right:
52. fos.
2ᵛ–3ʳ,
enlarged*

etc.) were to offer wider opportunities to the purveyors of mass-market publications. Simple texts for children were obvious candidates for exploitation, not least because models existed in many of the small-format booklets in the lists of such publishers as the Newbery firms and John Marshall (see below, chapters V and VI).

J. Evans, who seems to have begun publishing at Long Lane in the 1790s, was possibly one of the first to try and develop a sustained output of these successors to the old Penny Merriments. He is known to have had business associations with the Marshalls at Aldermary Church Yard (a John Evans witnessed Richard Marshall's will in 1799), although, as with so many publishers of ephemera, the extent of the firm's activity is difficult to trace. This particular example, with an imprint combining John and Charles Evans, probably dates from the early 1820s and may have been printed from stereotype plates. Nevertheless, it has an antiquated air. The covers, in sanguine, could easily date back in their design to the beginning of the century, while the "rhymes for the nursery" and their accompanying pictures are drawn entirely from *The Royal Primer*, which Newbery and others had put together in the early 1750s (see entry 68).

❧ 53a ☙

Jacky Dandy's Delight. [cut] *This is Mr. Harliquin, who shews what is to be seen within.* London: Printed and Sold by J. Pitts, 6, Great St Andrew Street, 7 Dial, [ca. 1825]. 32° (91 × 50 mm.).

[1⁸] (8ᵛ imprint *Pitts Toy Warehouse*). Pp. 16. Wove paper. 16 cuts including title vignette (22 × 35 mm. each). Original pictorial yellow wrappers, cut of Harlequin on front cover (see overleaf), Man-in-the-Moon on back cover. Modern blue morocco gilt. Reference: Opie *Three Centuries* (1977), 448.

Provenance: Charles Todd Owen (binding). PML 83142. Gift: Elisabeth Ball.

❧ 53b ☙

The Easter Gift; being a useful toy for little Miss and Master to learn their ABC. London: Printed and sold by J. Pitts, No. 6, Great St. Andrew Street, Seven Dials, [ca. 1825]. One Halfpenny. 32° (95 × 55 mm.).

[1⁸] (2ᵛ *A was an Archer*). Pp. 16. Wove paper. Title vignette and 26 cuts (22 × 35 mm. each) illustrating a couplet for each letter of the alphabet. Original pictorial yellow wrappers, cut of a school-room scene on front cover, *Old Mother Cabbage* on back cover. Modern green morocco gilt.

Provenance: Charles Todd Owen (binding). PML 80761. Gift: Elisabeth Ball.

Just as Evans was associated with Marshall, so John Pitts of "the wholesale toy and marble warehouse" worked for Evans (and was possibly employed by Marshall when he first arrived in London from his home county of Norfolk). Pitts's biographer, Leslie Shepard (*John Pitts, Ballad Printer*. London: Private Libraries Association, 1969), while largely ignoring his output for children, states that he has found cuts in common use by these three printers, and there can be no doubt that the halfpenny and penny books put out by Pitts share all the rough-and-ready character of Evans's little productions. These two examples (now incongruously bound in gilt morocco) show Pitts working close to the tradition of children's rhymes. *Jacky Dandy* goes back to verses in *Tommy Thumb's Pretty Song Book* 1744 (Opie *ODNR* 259) and appears to have only slightly different contents from James Kendrew's chapbook of the same title and about the same date (Davis 37). *The Easter Gift* is based on "A was an Archer," but gives two verses for each letter, which diverts the rhyme into a new channel; this version apparently goes back no further than the beginning of the nineteenth century, and Pitts's greatest competitor and near-neighbor, James Catnach, did a chapbook edition of the same text at around the same time (Opie *Three Centuries*, 613). Both little books may have been printed from stereotype.

53a.
front
cover,
enlarged

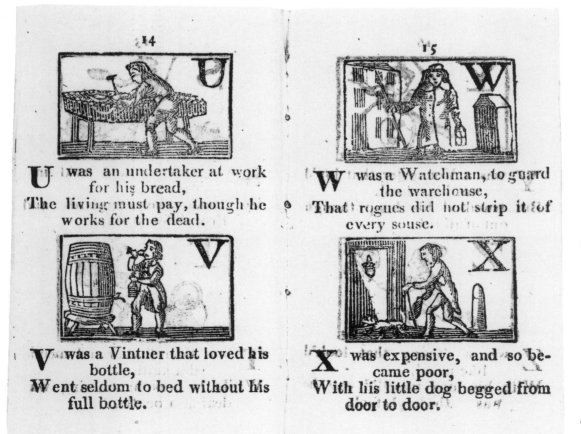

14

U was an undertaker at work
for his bread,
The living must pay, though he
works for the dead.

V was a Vintner that loved his
bottle,
Went seldom to bed without his
full bottle.

15

W was a Watchman, to guard
the warehouse,
That rogues did not strip it of
every souse.

X was expensive, and so became poor,
With his little dog begged from
door to door.

53b. fos. 7ᵛ–8ʳ, *enlarged*

O'd Woman of Stepney.

One Halfpenny.

54a. front
cover,
enlarged

54b. section [1], *reduced*

54a

The Old Woman of Stepney . . . [London:] Pitts Printer Wholesale Toy and marble Warehouse 6, Great st Audrew street 7 dials, [ca. 1825]. One Halfpenny. 32° (95 × 57 mm.).

[1⁸] (8ᵛ imprint *J. Pitts, Printer, Seven Dials*). Pp. 16. Wove paper. 15 cuts. Original pictorial yellow wrappers, cuts of the old woman on front cover, *Cat's meat Lass* on back cover. Reference: Hockliffe 822 (W. S. Johnson edition).

PML 80125. Gift: Elisabeth Ball.

54b

Old Woman of Stepney and Dame Trot (cover title). London: printed and published at the Nassau Press, 60, St. Martin's Lane, Charing Cross, W.C., [ca. 1850]. Panorama (110 × 2200 mm.), folded to 24° (110 × 100mm.).

Large single sheet (440 × 550 mm.) cut, after printing on one side, into 4 sections (110 × 550 mm. each) and joined to form a long continuous strip. The first two sections: *The Adventures of the Old Woman of Stepney*; the last two sections (here joined in reversed order): *Old Dame Trot and her Comical Cat*, slightly abridged. Each section comprises two pages of letterpress verse within type-ornament border and 4 full-page wood engravings colored by hand (first illustration to Dame Trot signed, but unidentified). Wove, unwatermarked paper. Original printed buff wrappers with wood-engraved vignette and typographical border.

PML 81550. Gift: Elisabeth Ball.

THE ADVENTURES
OF THE
OLD WOMAN OF STEPNEY.

There was an old woman who lived at Stepney,
And out of her nose there grew a plum tree.

All the children who knew her,
The plums they would steal,
But while fast asleep,
For fear them she should feel.

This old woman went
One fine day to the lawn
Of my Lord Cockagee,
And there shot a young fawn.

She tied up the hind legs
To the branch of her tree,
And so quitted the lawn
Of my Lord Cockagee.

OLD DAME TROT,
AND HER
COMICAL CAT.

Old Dame Trot,
    She went to the Fair,
With the Cat on her shoulder,
    To see the folks there.

Dame **Trot** and her cat,
    Sat down to chat;
The dame sat on this side
    And she sat on that.

"Puss," says the Dame,
    "Can you catch a rat
Or a mouse in the dark?"
    "Purr," says the Cat.

54b. section [3], *reduced*

The WISE-MEN of GOTHAM.   234

nted for & Sold by Bowles & Carver.   N°69 S.ᵗPauls Church Yard, London.

TAKE CARE. WE SHALL SOON
GET FAST HOLD OF THE MOON.

55. *reduced*

One of Pitts's wilder ventures was the publication of what must have been a local Seven Dials rhyme about the duel between the Old Woman of Stepney (out of whose nostrils "there grew a plumb tree") and a neighboring peer, Lord Cockagee. This rhyme bears all the marks of being composed for the street markets, but it survived beyond Pitts's halfpenny list to become part of the Nassau Press panorama shown here. W. S. Johnson operated his Nassau Press just south of the street in Seven Dials where Pitts had had his warehouse, and this amazing but tawdry survival, with its defective makeup and its random coloring, is typical of chapbook publishing in its final stages before being superseded by mass-market penny dreadfuls and cheap periodicals.

55

The Wise-Men of Gotham. London: Printed for & Sold by Bowles and Carver. Published as the Act directs. N° 69 St Paul's Church Yard, [copperplate ca. 1787–95, impression not before 1801 (watermark date)]. Oblong broadside (pot-size half-sheet, 182 × 271 mm.).

Etching (170 × 250 mm.): Bowles & Carver picture sheet 234 (for a description of the series, see entry 159), with title as transcribed above, and captioned *Take Care. We shall soon / get fast hold of the moon.* Laid paper. Reference: Bowles & Carver, pp. vii, 150.

Provenance: Walter Schatzki; B.M. Israel; C. F. van Veen (Sotheby's Amsterdam, 28th Nov. 1984, lot 37). PML 84760.185. Purchase: Mrs. Robert Horne Charles and Mrs. Donald M. Oenslager.

Anecdotes about the "Wise Men of Gotham" are among the earliest English folk satires to survive in print. A collection of tales, probably put together by the physician-extraordinary, Andrew Borde, is known from ca. 1565 (STC 2nd ed. 1020.5), and, as in the rest of Europe, these rustic mockings were natural source material for the compilers of chapbooks. However, as W. C. Hazlitt noted in 1876, "the printed editions evidently do not contain all the stories of this kind once extant" and the sunken-moon joke is absent from Borde's canon and from the chapbook editions that followed him, including the popular Bow Churchyard printing of the mid-eighteenth century. Nevertheless, the tale and its variants (Aarne-Thompson tale types 34 and 1335) are entirely in keeping with Gothamite wisdom. In some instances a traveler thinks that the moon has fallen into the water; then, when a cloud passes while his horse is drinking, he thinks the animal has swallowed it and cuts him open to let the moon out. Alternatively, attempts are made to rake up the moon, either to prevent it from drowning or in the belief that it is a cheese. Our Bowles & Carver print belongs among the latter interpretations and appears to be one of the earliest attributions of the tale to Gotham.

IV

SERIOUS BUSINESS

To the child of, say, the 1730s the words "children's books" (if they had any meaning at all) would have summoned up a very fuzzy image. Excluding the raw manuals of the school-room, he might have thought of a few fable books, whose function of entertainment would be inversely proportional to the length of their "Moral Applications." He might have thought of a scatter of pious works, aimed primarily at his salvation—even if they did include two best-sellers: the *Divine Songs* of Isaac Watts and *The Pilgrim's Progress* of John Bunyan (the latter not really a children's book anyway). For the rest, there was merely uncoordinated miscellanea—trials and errors—and a circumambient collection of forbidden Penny Histories and Shilling Shockers.

What was needed to change this state of affairs, to bring a degree of coordination, was a recognition on the part of the book trade that children constituted a public whom it might be profitable to serve. Changes in the concept of childhood at a psychological or even a spiritual level were already taking place—witness Comenius and John Locke, or those whom Darton called "the good godly" authors—but such changes could not be given an enduring life without the economic base and the continuing momentum of a specialist publishing industry.

That realization came to the English book trade with great rapidity in the few years surrounding 1740, rather earlier than in other countries. From a time of randomness and uncertainty a transition was made over barely five years to a time of experimentation, carried out with a much clearer sense of purpose than ever before. In this section we try to delineate the arrival of this new professionalism in children's book publishing, showing, to begin with, some unusual or remarkable books which appeared in no clear context, and going on to show the emergence of policy. Here we have not always adhered strictly to a chronology of title-page dates, as some books that illustrate points we wish to make had to be included in later editions.

⊸ 56 ⊱

HENRY WINSTANLEY (1644–1703). *All the Principal Nations of the World presented in their habits (or fashion of dressing) with a prospect of their capital citys and a geographycal description of the provinces . . . and as much of history of all, as could be contained in so small a space, all of which is most humbly . . . dedicated to the Honble James Herbert Esq. not for his improvement, but that it was part of his studjs and from whom I must own to have received most of my instructions in the composing of these cards . . . The use of these cards may be the same as with the common sort . . . And to make them profitable to a youth that shall desire them, I* woold give the one by one to him as he shall have learnt them by heart. Littlebury [Essex]: H. Winstanley fecit, [ca. 1675]. Foolscap half-sheets (7) and demy quarter-sheet (1): oblong broadsides (about 190 × 250 mm. each).

8 engravings: title and explanation within a border incorporating emblems of the four continents; 6 plates of 8 pictorial playing cards each showing cities, inhabitants, and text (13 hearts *Europe*, 13 diamonds *Asia*, 13 spades *Africa*, 9 clubs *America*), one plate comprising 4 playing cards (4 remaining clubs *America* and *Australes*) in upper half and world map in lower half. Two paper stocks (watermarks: foolscap countermarked with initials, type of Heawood 1944; fleur-de-lys, type of Heawood 1782–1801). The sheets were intended to be cut up for a full pack of 52 playing cards—the form in which they survive at the Guildhall Library, London—but this set in unused condition has remained undivided. Reference: *The Winstanley Geographical Cards* [a facsimile of the Guildhall set], Pasadena: H. & V. Wayland, n.d. On Winstanley, see Campbell Dodgson, "An English Engraver of the Restoration," *The Connoisseur* I (1901), pp. 72–6.

PML 81946. Purchase: Mrs. Gerard B. Lambert.

"I have always had a Fancy that *Learning* might be made a Play and Recreation to Children," said John Locke in 1693 (see entry 5). Here, nearly twenty years earlier, his precept is anticipated. These playing cards, perhaps the earliest produced specifically for children, are designed to introduce ideas about geography by way of recreation, and when Winstanley writes of their being "not for [the] improvement" of his pupil but as "part of his studjs," the implication is that master and pupil worked on the set together and that the Hon. James Herbert learned direct from that experience. The cards themselves are a testimony to contemporary attitudes in a world still lacking Oceania. (European priorities are especially nice, with England as King of Hearts and Romish Italy the knave.) The inventor and engraver, Henry Winstanley, was a remarkable entrepreneur, engineer as well as artist, and he may well have produced these sheets to be marketed by himself rather than through regular book trade channels.

⊸ 57 ⊱

AESOP (early sixth century B.C.). *Fables of Aesop and others, translated into English. With instructive applications; and a print before each fable. By Samuel Croxall, D. D. The seventh edition, carefully revised, and improved.* London: Printed for J. and R. Tonson in the Strand, 1760. 12° (166 × 96 mm.).

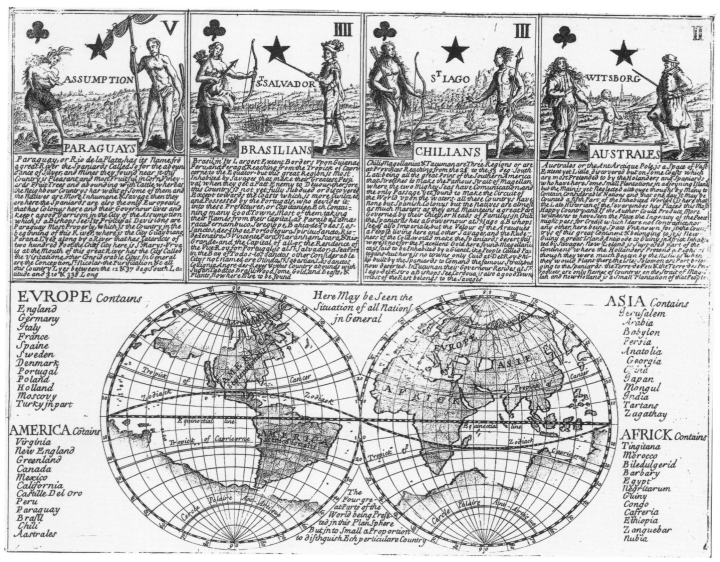

56. pl. [8], *reduced*

A[12] (1[r] blank, 1[v] frontispiece, 2[r] title, 2[v] blank, 3[r] editor's dedication *To the Right Honourable George, Lord Viscount Sunbury, Baron Halifax*, 6[r] Preface); a[6] (*Contents*); B–P[12] (B1[r] *Fab. I. The Cock and the Jewel*, P9[v] *Index*). Pp. [36], 329, [7]. A single paper stock, watermarked with large fleur-de-lys and countermarked with initials. One copper-engraving (frontispiece showing Aesop and a scribe surrounded by animals in a landscape); 196 metalcuts (70 × 52 mm.; one oval illustration within a rectangular frame to each fable, see overleaf) by Elisha Kirkall (ca. 1682–1742). Modern calf. References: ESTC T127929; Hobbs pp. 84–5 (20th ed., 1818); E. Hodnett, "Elisha Kirkall," *The Book Collector* 25, no. 2 (Summer 1976), pp. 195–209.

Brian Alderson, Richmond.

First published in 1722 (PML 150179), "Croxall's Aesop" was one of the best-selling smart children's books of the century. Success probably came to it less through the contribution of Croxall himself—his retelling of the fables and his applications are leaden—than through the illustrations. These are now known to be metalcuts (i.e. relief-engravings in soft metal and mounted type high to print like woodcuts). They were executed by Elisha

Kirkall, who took as a source-book the splendid Aesop that had been etched by Francis Barlow in 1666 (Wing 2nd ed. A-696). The modeling and the chiaroscuro in cuts like "The Stag looking into the Water" were to be a great influence on Thomas Bewick (entry 132).

58

PRIDEAUX ERRINGTON (fl. 1723-34). *New Copies in Verse, for the use of writing-schools: consisting of fifty-three alphabets. An essay on the virtues . . . all design'd to promote virtue and piety, especially in youth . . .* Newcastle upon Tyne: Printed by Isaac Lane, and Company, for the Author and Sold by the Booksellers in Town, 1734. 8° (153 × 99 mm.), turned chain lines.

A–K[8] L[2] (A2[r] author's dedication *To the Rt. Worshipful . . . William Ellison, Esq; Mayor . . . Aldermen . . . and Worthy Trustees of the Charity-Schools in Newcastle upon Tyne*, L2[r] errata, L2[v] blank). Pp. 162, [2]. Relief-cut bust of Homer (H4[r] tailpiece).

12 *ÆSOP's FABLES.*

FAB. VII. *The* Wolf *and the* Crane.

A WOLF, after devouring his Prey, happen'd to have a Bone ſtick in his Throat; which gave him ſo much pain, that he went howling up and down, and importuning every Creature he met, to lend him a kind Hand in order to his Relief; nay, he promiſed a reaſonable Reward to any one that ſhould undertake the Operation with Succeſs. At laſt the Crane, tempted with the Lucre of the Reward, and having firſt procur'd him to confirm his Promiſe with an Oath, undertook the Buſineſs; and ventur'd his long Neck into the rapacious Felon's Throat. In ſhort, he pluck'd out the Bone, and expected the promis'd Gratuity. When the Wolf, turning his Eyes diſdainfully towards him, ſaid, I did not think you had been ſo unconſcionable; I had your Head in my Mouth, and could have bit it off whenever I pleas'd, but ſuffer'd you to take it away without any Damage, and yet you are not contented.

The

57. B6ᵛ, *reduced*

Æ S O P's F A B L E S. 13

The APPLICATION.

There is a ſort of People in the World, to whom a Man may be in the wrong for doing Services, upon a double Score; firſt, becauſe they never deſerv'd to have a good Office done them; and ſecondly, becauſe, when once engag'd, 'tis ſo hard a matter to get well rid of their Acquaintance. This Fable is not an Example of Ingratitude, as at firſt Sight it ſeems to be, and as ſome of the Mythologiſts have underſtood it; to make it a Parallel in that Caſe, the Crane ought to have been under ſome Difficulties in his Turn, and the Wolf have refus'd to aſſiſt him when it was in his Power. The whole Streſs of it lies in this, That we ought to conſider what kind of People they are to whom we are deſired to do good Offices, before we do them; for he that grants a Favour, or even confides in a Perſon of no Honour, inſtead of finding his Account in it, comes off well if he is no Sufferer.

FAB. VIII. *The* Stag *looking into the* Water.

A STAG that had been drinking at a clear Spring, ſaw himſelf in the Water; and, pleas'd with the Proſpect, ſtood afterwards for ſome time con-

57. B7ʳ, *reduced*

Contemporary blind-paneled calf. References: ESTC T132174; Foxon p. 248; Hunt p. 58.

Provenance: Elizabeth Winship (eighteenth-century sign.). PML 68271. Purchase: Acquisitions Fund.

"Improvement" was certainly well to the fore in Prideaux Errington's mind in constructing this curious book, especially improvement "in all Christian Graces and Virtues." Where he differs from contemporary soul savers, however, is that here and in his preceding *Copies in Verse* (1723) he ingeniously wrenches his piety into a form that will permit him to string out stanzas, mostly in couplet form, whose initial letter comes in proper alphabetic sequence. (Predictably, he has problems with "X," and many obscure characters achieve brief poetic fame on account of their names: Xaca, Xenophanes, and Xequepeer, for instance. Xenophon and Xenocrates are most popular, apart from the dozen or so times when Errington retreats, lamentably, to the abbreviation "Xtians"). Both *New Copies* and its predecessor were privately published efforts and "offer'd to the easie Purchase of all Writing-Masters, for the use of their Schools." The printer,

Isaac Lane, worked only briefly in Newcastle (1734–36) before transferring his business to Durham.

✥ 59 ✥

CHARLES PERRAULT (1628–1703) and/or PIERRE PERRAULT DARMANCOUR (1678–1700). *Histories, or Tales of Passed Times. With morals. Written in French by M. Perrault, and Englished by R. S. Gent. The fourth edition, corrected. With cuts to every tale.* London: Printed for James Hodges, at the Looking-Glass, facing St. Magnus Church, London-Bridge, 1750. [Price bound 1s. 6d.]. Long 12° (136 × 80 mm.).

A–H¹² (A1ᵛ ad for a bilingual 2s. 6d. edition of the same fairy tales *very proper to be read by young Children at Boarding Schools, that are to learn the French Tongue, as well as in private Families*, A2ʳ dedication *To the Right Honourable the Countess of Granville* by the translator Robert Samber, F4ᵛ frontispiece to *The Discreet*

BLUE BEARD.

TALE III.

THERE was a man who had fine houfes, both in town and country, a deal of filver and gold plate, embroidered furniture, and coaches gilded all over with gold. But this man had the misfortune to have a *Blue Beard*, which made him fo frightfully ugly, that all the women and girls ran away from him.

One

59. A11 verso, *enlarged*

chapbook trade made much of "Cinderella" or "The Sleeping Beauty" until the second half of the century. Samber in his dedicatory essay makes a rather specious claim that the stories "tended to the Encouragement of Virtue, and the Depressing of Vice," while being well aware that some people thought them "very low and childish." For the publishers, however, the main reason for publication may have been to attract the lucrative educational market. J. Pote, the book's first publisher, moved his bookselling business to Eton at about the time of its publication, and we can see from Hodges' advertisement in this "fourth edition" that the book was already being sold with the French text alongside the English, a form which continued to be popular (see entry 374). The final tale, *The Discreet Princess; or, the adventures of Finetta. A novel,* is not Perrault's but by Marie-Jeanne L'Héritier de Villandon (1664–1734).

As owner of the 1695 dedication manuscript of *Contes de ma mere L'Oye* (Gottlieb 103), the Morgan Library has collected important holdings of early English and French editions of the text, and our inclusion of some of these later in the catalogue (entries 76, 111, 143, 374) shows the book becoming absorbed into the mainstream of publishing. Our annotation to the first of these dwells briefly on Benjamin Collins's involvement in an apparent piracy of Samber's translation under the initials of "G. M. Gent."

⊷ 60 ⊶

PHAEDRUS (fl. first century A.D.). *Select Tales and Fables with Prudential Maxims and other little lessons of morality in prose and verse equally instructive & entertaining for the use of both sexes . . . The whole embellish'd with threescore original designs, expressive of each subject, neatly engrav'd on copperplates . . . By B. Cole, engraver.* London: Printed for T. Osborn Grays-Inn, and J. Nourse at the Lamb, over against Catherine-Street, in the Strand. (vol. II: Printed for the Proprietor, 1746). 2 volumes bound in 1. 12° (142 × 83 mm.).

Vol. I: A² B–D¹² E⁴ (A and E the same half-sheet); engraved dedication to Prince Edward and title printed on two conjugate leaves from a single copper-plate, 30 engraved illustrations on 15 leaves printed from four copperplates by Benjamin Cole after J. Wale (see overleaf). Pp. [4], 80. Vol. II: A² B–D¹² E⁴ (A and E the same half-sheet); engraved title and frontispiece printed on two conjugate leaves from a single copperplate, 30 engraved illustrations on 15 leaves printed from four copperplates by the same artists. Pp. iv, 80. Same paper stock for plates and letterpress. Contemporary sheep.

Provenance: William Calvert 1797 (inscr.); Chris Calvert (sign.); Gumuchian & Cⁱᵉ (1930 cat., no. 1785). PML 84171. Gift: Elisabeth Ball.

In the dedication to his translation of Perrault (above) Robert Samber did not merely try to make a case for the "virtue" in the stories, he tried to do so at the expense of contemporary fabulists who "content themselves with Vending some poor insipid trifling Tale in a little tinkling Jingle." We cannot be sure whom he had in mind (hardly Dryden or Gay, surely?), but he does signal the popularity of the fable as a universal theme and the frequency with which it figures among the books given to children at this early period. Certainly the present text does not rise above the

Princess, F5ʳ divisional title *The Discreet Princess*, F6ʳ dedication to the Lady Mary Montagu); engraved frontispiece *Mother Goose's Tales* (a copy after Clouzier's engraving in the first French edition of 1697). Pp. 191 [1]. A single paper stock. Roman and italic type. 9 cuts from 8 blocks (*Sleeping Beauty* and *Riquet with the Tuft* share a block), each about 41 × 63 mm., including the full-page frontispiece (104 × 63 mm.) to the last tale. Nineteenth-century sprinkled calf gilt. References: ESTC N033009; Cahoon 102; Johnson 7 (1741 edition).

Provenance: Sam Hobhouse (early sign.); J. Dawson Brodie (bookplate); Alexander Gardyne 1883 (stamp); Charles Todd Owen. PML 83655. Gift: Elisabeth Ball.

The arrival of Mother Goose in Paris at the end of the seventeenth century was, in retrospect, one of the most momentous events in the history of children's reading. At the time though, it was not seen as such, being perhaps viewed as frivolity for adults rather than the first near-authentic documentation of folk tale tradition. Certainly, so far as England was concerned, the collection of "Tales of Passed Times" (which included seven perennial favorites) was not seen as particularly momentous. The book took over thirty years to arrive in English translation, and when it did so in 1729, it seems to have been slow to achieve any popularity—not even the

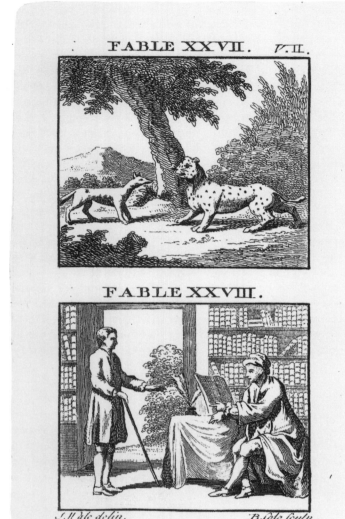

FABLE XXVII. *V. II.*

FABLE XXVIII.

J.Wale delin.   *B.Cole sculp.*

60. vol. II, plate facing C2^r, *enlarged*

insipid, even if it doesn't tinkle, but its presence shows how publishers were coming to use fables as the core of general compendia. By way of entertainment all of the "select fables" here are illustrated; by way of instruction the "other little lessons of morality" include some "counsels of wisdom," some proverbs, and some "Alphabets of Prudential Maxims" somewhat on the lines of Errington's *New Copies* (entry 58). The editor, though, cheats with "x" by making it begin words like "'xcuse' and "'xample."

As illustrators, both Wale the artist and Cole the engraver were involved in other fable books, the former making the designs for Dodsley's *Select Fables*, which was printed by Baskerville (Birmingham, 1761), and the latter cutting plates for *Gay's Fables Epitomized* by Daniel Bellamy the Elder, published "for the use of schools" by B. Creak (1733) [PML 60482 and 81998 respectively].

❧ 61a ❧

THOMAS BOREMAN (fl. 1715–43). *The History and Description of the Famous Cathedral of St. Paul's, London.* London: Printed for Tho. Boreman, Bookseller, near the two giants in Guildhall, 1741. [Price 4d]. 2 volumes. 64° (59 × 44 mm.).

Vol. 1: A–H^8 (A1 mounted as pastedown, A1^v frontispiece view of St. Paul's, A3^r poem to Master Tommy Boreman by Jack Heatherly, A5^v–C3^r list of subscribers, H6^v ads). Pp. 125, [3]. 9 full-page cuts. Vol. 2: A–H^8 (A1^v frontispiece-portrait of Christopher Wren, A3^r–8^v subscribers, G7^r *An Explanation of some of the hard Words*, H5^v remaining subscribers, H7^r ads). Pp. 121, [7]. 10 full-page cuts. Each volume consists of a single sheet of fleur-de-lys watermarked paper. Roman and italic type. Original floral boards (not uniform). References: ESTC T117671 and N033233; Stone V and VI; Gottlieb 174 (vol. 1); Johnson 5; Morgan 171.

Provenance: Elisabeth Ball. PML 83645, Gift: Elisabeth Ball; PML 84679, Gift: Lilly Library.

[54]
Four INDIAN KINGS.

[55]

CHAP. IV.

Of the strange conceptions four Indian Kings had of this great building ; and how they imagin'd it at first to be one great rock that grew in that place.

S A Ga Yean Qua Rash Tow, one of the four Indian Kings who were in this country about thirty-two years ago, amongst
D 4   other

61a. vol. 1, D3^v–4^r, *enlarged*

[52]
VULTURE.

61b. D2 verso

⊷ 61b ⊷

THOMAS BOREMAN (fl. 1715–43). *Curiosities in the Tower of London. Vol. I. The second edition.* London: Printed for Tho. Boreman, Bookseller, near the two giants in Guildhall, 1741. [Price Four pence]. 64° (56 × 42 mm.).

A–H⁸ (A1ᵛ frontispiece *White Tower*, A3ʳ poem addressed to the author by A.Z., A6ʳ–B4ᵛ subscribers, H7ʳ ads). Pp. 124, [4]. Apparently a single sheet of unwatermarked, laid paper. Roman and italic type. 13 full-page cuts. Modern green morocco gilt. References: ESTC T118393; Stone III note; Osborne II, 799; Johnson 5 (both vols.); Morgan 134 (both vols.).

Provenance: Elisabeth Ball. PML 84678. Gift: Lilly Library.

⊷ 61c ⊷

THOMAS BOREMAN (fl. 1715–43). *Westminster Abbey. Vol. II. By the author of the Gigantick Histories.* London: Printed for Tho. Boreman, Bookseller, near the two giants in Guildhall, 1742. [Price Four pence]. 64° (56 × 43 mm.).

A–H⁸ (A1 mounted as pastedown, A1ᵛ frontispiece *John Conduitt . . . monument*, A3ʳ–B4ʳ subscribers, H6ᵛ ads for all vols. in the 'Gigantick History' series except the tenth, *Cajanus the Swedish Giant*, the last in the series to be published). Pp. 123, [5]. A single sheet of watermarked paper. Roman and italic type. 5 full-page cuts. Original boards. References: ESTC N025905; Stone VIII; Osborne II, 800; Johnson 5 (vols. II and III); Morgan 309 (vols. II and III).

Provenance: Elisabeth Ball. PML 84680. Gift: Lilly Library.

Thomas Boreman was apprenticed to Mary Spicer, bookbinder, in 1715 and freed in 1723. He then sought to establish himself as bookbinder and bookseller, and has already been encountered (entry 7) as the author of some freshly devised if not very reliable natural histories for children. In that capacity he is one among various authors, translators and editors who were dabbling in children's books during the 1720s and 1730s. In 1740, however, with what now appears to be a stroke of genius, he decisively altered the concept of "children's books" for both producers and consumers. The stroke of genius was *The Gigantick History of the*

Two Famous Giants . . . in Guildhall, London, which he published in two volumes from his own stationer's stand in that building, and the significance was manifold. In essence, what Boreman did here was to combine a physically intriguing book—a tiny, dumpy volume bound in decorated paper and illustrated with cuts—with a new authorial voice (nicely summed up by the very word "gigantick," which not only puns on the subject of the book, but contains a happy piece of self-mockery in it). The author of *Three Hundred Animals* for older children had hit upon a way to talk to younger children without either patronizing them or sending them to sleep.

The *Gigantick History* could hardly not have been a success, and Boreman followed it up (as publishers have always done) with a series, of which we here give representative examples. *Curiosities in the Tower of London*, with its description of the animals in the Tower menagerie and the weapons in the armory, was rich in popular appeal, and although *St. Paul's* and *Westminster Abbey* rather lose momentum among epitaphs and architectural descriptions, you never lose the sense that Boreman was shaping and illustrating his material as best he could. Furthermore, in a gesture which mimicked the practice of publishers of adult books and which also gave him scope for generating sales, Boreman included lists of the children who subscribed to his "Histories," sometimes with their places of residence ("Master *Dicky Boys*, of Colchester, 7 sets"), sometimes with joky overtones ("Master Tommy Boreman;" "Giant Gogmagog 100 books").

It may seem uncharacteristic for Thomas Boreman to include in the *Curiosities* a dedicatory poem which contains the sentiment:

> *Tom Thumb* shall now be thrown away,
> And *Jack* who did the *Giants* slay;
> Such ill concerted, artless lyes,
> Our British Youths shall now despise.

But Tom Thumb and Jack the Giant Killer (who had not been in print for very long anyway) could afford to be benevolent. The "Gigantick Histories" were the first step towards making their place in the nursery secure for good.

⊷ 62 ⊷

The Child's New Play-Thing: being a spelling-book intended to make the learning to read, a diversion instead of a task . . . With entertaining pictures to each story and fable . . . The whole adapted to the capacities of children . . . Also a new-invented alphabet for children to play with, and a preface shewing the use of it. The eighth edition. To which are added, forty-eight new cuts, with moral and instructive verses to each. Designed for the use of schools, or for children before they go to school. London: Printed for Messrs. Ware, Hawes, Clark, Collins, Corbett, Dodsley, Hinxman, and C. Rivington, 1763. Long 12° (153 × 84 mm.).

A¹² (A3 + folded quarter-sheet: recto *A Apple-pye* and *A Was an Archer*, verso *This Alphabet is to be cut into single Squares for Children to play with*) (A1 portrait lacking, A2ʳ title, A2ᵛ *Preface*, A8ʳ *Alphabetical Pictures*); B–G¹² (F11ᵛ *Stories Proper to raise the Attention, and excite the Curiosity of Children*, G10ʳ *Songs*, G12ᵛ

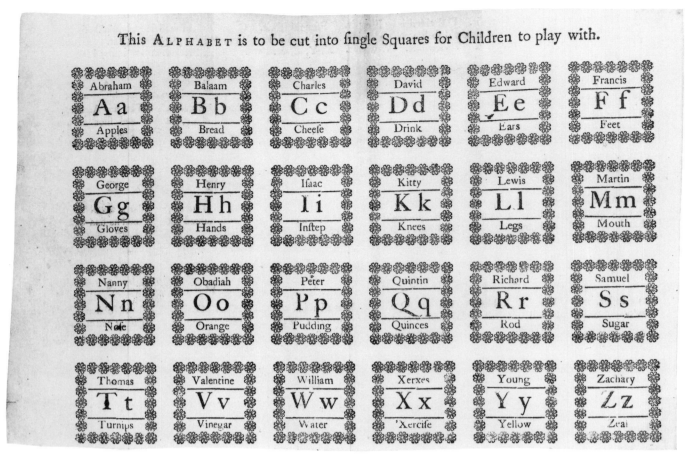

This ALPHABET is to be cut into single Squares for Children to play with.

62.

R. and J. Dodsley ad). Pp. 167 [1]. Folded quarter-sheet a different paper stock from the other sheets. Roman and italic types of various sizes. Typographical flowers around the alphabet squares, 61 cuts of various sizes. Contemporary sheep. References: ESTC N029767; Muir *NBL* 48; M. Treadwell, "London Trade Publishers 1675 – 1750," *The Library*, 6th ser., 4 (1982), pp. 99–134.

Department of Special Collections, Charles E. Young Research Library, UCLA.

First published by Thomas Cooper in 1742, shortly before he died, *The Child's New Play-Thing* continued its existence as the property of his wife Mary who may well have been responsible for its original conception and editing, rather than acting simply as a trade publisher. For, as we indicate in the next five entries, she showed herself aware of the potential which children's books held for an enterprising publisher, and she stands alongside Thomas Boreman and Benjamin Collins of Salisbury as one of the creators of the "new" children's literature. Although "designed for the use of schools," the book was edited rather for children to have at home "before they go to school," and the preface clearly sees home use to be the ideal. (The book was demonstrably an influence on Jane Johnson whose elaborate home-made "nursery library"* shows how one alert parent was adopting for her own family the new "play-way" methods.) The novelty of the pull-out alphabet, to be used for playing games, figures largely in the book's reputation for opening up new ideas. Equally though, attention should be drawn to the pleasant, miscellany style with rhymes juxtaposing lessons and with illustrated popular tales, "St. George," "Fortunatus," "Reynard," adjoining illustrated fables. Mary Cooper continued

to publish the *Play-Thing* up to the edition preceding this (the seventh), by which time shares in the book had also gone to Ware, Hitch, Corbett and Dodsley. In 1761 she sold her business to John Hinxman, formerly of York, who thus joins the 1763 conger.

* Further information on the nursery library and its relationship to contemporary publishing can be found in: (1) Johnson, *For Your Amusement*, item 1; (2) *Hand-made Readings; an Eighteenth Century Mother's Nursery Library* [exhib. leaflet]. Cambridge: Fitzwilliam Museum, 1995; (3) Mary Hilton, et. al. *Opening the Nursery Door; Reading, Writing, and Childhood 1600–1900*. London and New York: Routledge, 1997; (4) "Playing with Knowledge; Text, Toys and Teaching Children in Georgian England," Cotsen conference papers, *Princeton University Library Chronicle* LX:2, Winter 1999, passim; (5) Jane Johnson. *A Very Pretty Story; facsimile of the manuscript held in the Bodleian Library*. Introduction: Gillian Avery. Oxford: Bodleian Library, 2001.

of ENGLAND. 135

XVIII. *RICHARD* III. *Crook-back.*

From 1483 to 1485.

Richard, with deep Hypocrisy endu'd,
Ambitious, cruel, destitute of Good,

Yet courted publick Love by wholesome Laws,
And bravely fell, had Virtue been the Cause.

COTEMPORARIES,

Emperor of *Germany,* Frederick IV. 1440.

King of *France, Charles* VIII. —— 1483.

King of *Scotland, James* III. —— —— 1459.

64. F8 recto

⁓§ 63 ᠈⁓

The Travels of Tom Thumb over England and Wales; contain-
ing descriptions of whatever is most remarkable in the several
counties. Interspersed with many pleasant adventures . . .
Written by himself; and adorned with a suitable map.
London: Printed for R. Amey at Charing-Cross; and Sold by
M. Cooper in Pater-noster Row, 1746. Price 1s. 6d. Bound. 12°
(148 × 87 mm.).

*A*⁶ (A1 half-title lacking, A3ʳ dedication *To Prince William-*
Henry, The least Son of His Royal Highness Frederick, Prince of
Wales; B–G¹²; folding hand-colored engraved frontispiece map
(223 × 243 mm.). Pp. xii, 144. Original sheep. References: ESTC
T107830; Osborne I, 192.

PML 67307. Purchase: Acquisitions Fund.

Despite its larger size and its more severe aspect, *The Travels*
of Tom Thumb surely owes its conception to the "Gigantick
Histories" of Thomas Boreman. By choosing the folktale hero as a

guide to the counties, and by preserving throughout the text small
jokes about his littleness, the anonymous author has converted a
simple introduction to local topography into a pleasing and read-
able narrative. Small graphic touches give spice to his descriptions
of each county: "Upon attentively considering [Cheshire's] Form,
I could not liken it to any Thing so properly as an Urinal, such as
sick People take with them to Bed;" he is careful to keep his young
readers' attention by regular reference to figures of Romance (Guy
of Warwick, Fair Rosamond) and by nicely chosen quotations
such as the boast of Hugh Bigod, Earl of Norfolk (p. 115):

> *Were I in my Castle of* Bungey
> *Upon the River* Waveney,
> *I would not value the King of* Cockney

One would like to know more about Mary Cooper's involvement
in the making of the book, since it seems closer to her style than to
that of Robert Amey, who was a pamphlet seller.

⁓§ 64 ᠈⁓

The History of England. By Thomas Thumb, Esq. London:
Printed for M. Cooper, at the Globe in Paternoster-Row, 1749.
Long 12° (150 × 87 mm.).

A¹² (1+a²) (1ʳ title, 1+a² preface, 12 portrait of William the
Conqueror lacking), B–M¹² N⁸ (Nᵛ errata). Pp. 2, iv, 3–301 [3].
Paper stock watermarked RW. 30 relief-cut full-length portraits
of the Kings of England. Contemporary calf. Reference: ESTC
T098789.

PML 82492. Purchase: The Viscount Astor.

"I think it necessary here to advertise the Public, that I have now
by me in great Forwardness for the Press another . . . Work, which
will be a proper Companion to this." So wrote Tom Thumb in the
preface to his *Travels* (see previous entry), but without giving the
title for fear that "some one . . . among the laudable Society of
Booksellers, might employ some *great Author* to anticipate me in
my Subject." Presumably he was referring to this *History*, which
sustains, under more difficult circumstances, the easy manner of
his *Travels*. This time though, the book is fully the property of
Mary Cooper, and she has seen to it that the journey through
history is made easier by the relief-cut portraits of royalty with
their accompanying descriptive quatrains set vertically up the
sides of the portraits.

⁓§ 65 ᠈⁓

A Christmass-Box for Masters and Misses Publish'd accord-
ing to Act of Parliament. London: Printed for the Author
and Sold by M. Cooper in Paternoster Row and M. Boreman
in Guild-hall [Vol. II: Printed for M. Cooper . . . and
M. Boreman], 1746. 2 volumes. 32° (94 × 60 mm., vol. II:
95 × 56 mm.).

Vol. I: B–C⁸ (B1ʳ–2ʳ dedication by 'Mary Homebred' *To the tender*
parents of my Little Benefactors, B2ᵛ–C8ᵛ *Story I* [-X]); 12 engravings including title with vignette signed *T. Jefferys sculp.* (lacking
the second, originally inserted between B2 and B3). Pp. 56. Vol. II:

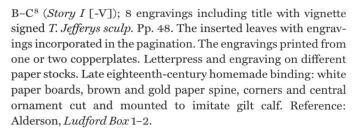

65. vol. 1, plate opposite C4ʳ, *enlarged*

65. vol. 2, *enlarged*

B–C⁸ (*Story I* [-V]); 8 engravings including title with vignette signed *T. Jefferys sculp*. Pp. 48. The inserted leaves with engravings incorporated in the pagination. The engravings printed from one or two copperplates. Letterpress and engraving on different paper stocks. Late eighteenth-century homemade binding: white paper boards, brown and gold paper spine, corners and central ornament cut and mounted to imitate gilt calf. Reference: Alderson, *Ludford Box* 1–2.

Provenance: *Elizᵗʰ Juliana Ludford* (1779–1859; adult inscrs.); Tone Price (Los Angeles Bookseller); Elvah Karshner. Department of Special Collections, Charles E. Young Research Library, UCLA.

First noticed by Wilbur Smith in his brief description of the children's books at UCLA, the title of *A Christmass-Box* is highly suggestive for its joining together the names of M. Boreman (presumably Thomas's widow) and Mary Cooper, the pre-Newbery progenitors of "diversion" in children's reading. The two volumes do not do much to extend this reputation since they contain contrived little tales about children whose names betray their humors (Sammy Trueman, Kitty Pert). Even in this, however, they have a chronological importance for, as far as we know,

A Christmass-Box is the first example of a collection of moral tales of an entirely secular character. (d'Alté Welch claims that the American edition, published at Boston as *A New Gift for Children* in 1762, is the volume that brought the Moral Tale to America, too.) This unique set of *A Christmass-Box* is part of a collection of children's books that belonged to the Ludford family of Warwickshire in the second half of the eighteenth century. Another example of a family collection is given below in chapter VII.

ᦸ 66 ᦷ

The Pretty-Book, being a new and pleasant method to teach children. [London:] Sold by Geo: Bickham in May's Buildings Covent Garden where is great variety, [ca. 1745]. 32° (77 × 49 mm.).

1² 2⁴ 3² 4⁸ (-1·2)5² 6⁴ 7⁶ (-1·6, -4, -5) 8⁴ (-1, -2)?. Pp. 64 (lacking pp. 33–6, 45–6, 51–60). Printed from two engraved copperplates on either side of a single sheet (outer forme including the title inked in red, inner forme in black). Text and 65 (of ?) illustrations, including frontispiece (in black).

66. frontispiece, *enlarged*

Original (?) floral boards. Reference: Alderson, *Ludford Box* p. 37, no. B.

Provenance: *John Ludford, March 17 1764* (inscr.) = John Newdigate Ludford (1756–1825), father of Elizabeth Juliana Ludford (see entry 65). The Osborne Collection of Early Children's Books, Toronto Public Library.

George Bickham (senior and junior) were primarily engravers and specialized in fine work such as writing-sheets. They also had a quiet line in plagiarism and several children's books from their shop are known which unabashedly copy texts and pictures previously published elsewhere. *The Pretty-Book* is a case in point but one which is of great interest in this formative period, for the frontispiece ("Delectando monemus . . .") and some other pages are taken from John Newbery's *Little Pretty Pocket-Book* (ca. 1744, see entry 8). The title has echoes of Mary Cooper's *Child's New Play-Thing* (1742), and the nursery rhymes come from her *Tommy Thumb's Pretty Song-Book* (ca. 1744), as does the scheme of printing one half of the book in red and the other in black. Thus the piratical Bickhams supply us not only with a glimpse of texts from early editions in a different guise but they also bear witness to the salability of the "new" literature.

✺ 67 ✺

The Famous Tommy Thumb's Little Story-Book: containing his life and surprising adventures. To which are added, Tommy Thumb's fables, with morals: and at the end, pretty

66. 4/4ᵛ–5ʳ, *enlarged*

stories, that may be either sung or told. Adorned with many curious pictures. London: Printed for S. Crowder, in Pater-Noster-Row; and sold by B. Collins, at the Printing-Office, in Salisbury, and by most eminent Booksellers, [ca. 1765]. 24° (82 × 52 mm.).

[1–2⁸] signed A–D⁴ (1/1ᵛ *Life*, 1/6ᵛ *Fables*, 2/6ᵛ *Stories*). Pp. 32. Relief-cut title vignette, 8 cuts (35 × 47 mm. and slightly smaller) illustrating the fables. Later wrappers. References: ESTC N008639; Opie *ODNR* p.132; Opie *Three Centuries*, 18; Osborne II, 597; Cahoon 147; Johnson 30.

PML 84794. Purchase: Julia P. Wightman.

Until recently, Mary Cooper's most noble children's book (and perhaps the most noble one of all time) reposed uniquely at the British Library in London: a lone, lorn "Voll. II" of *Tommy Thumb's Pretty Song Book*, "Sold by M. Cooper According to Act of Parliament," and probably published in 1744. (A second copy of vol. II only was sold at auction in London in 2001 and is now in the Cotsen Children's Library at Princeton.) This is the first known collection of English nursery rhymes, and not only does it yet again bring Tom Thumb into play as a conductor through a field of literature for children, it also, in its illustrations and in its small, parti-colored presentation continues Boreman's mood of near-frivolity. Although following much later, *The Famous Tommy Thumb's Little Story-Book* probably owes a debt to its predecessor, for as a tiny compendium of stories and fables it also contains nine nursery rhymes, two of which here make their first appearance in print ("This Pig went to Market" and "Little Boy Blue").

(24)

The NURSE and CROSS CHILD.

A Child in the cradle once cried and took on moſt violently, and would not be pacified by all that the nurſe could do. " Thou art the moſt troubleſome little raſcal that ever was born into the world, ſaid ſhe. An eternal bawler, with whom there is no living in the houſe. If you do not give over this noiſe preſently, I'll take and throw thee to

67. 2/4 verso

V

THE HOUSE THAT NEWBERY BUILT

As will have already been apparent, in any study of the emergence of English children's literature the name of John Newbery is inescapable. One of his earliest books, *A Little Pretty Pocket-Book*, appears in our first chapter to show the influence of Locke, along with the later *Newtonian System* (entries 8 and 9); and, as adumbrated in chapter III with *Tom Thumb's Folio* (entry 42), his firm had a pivotal role in the exploitation of popular children's wares by publishers. Furthermore, the publishing momentum developed by him and by his heirs and assigns was to carry his influence across the divide of the eighteenth and the nineteenth centuries.

In focusing on the Newberys in this chapter, we have thought it best to make a broad representation of the kinds of children's books they published and of their distinctive styles (which, as will be shown in chapter VI and IX, were imitated and pirated outright by the firm's competitors). As Sydney Roscoe has pointed out in his Newbery bibliography, without which our understanding of the progressive stages of the company would be much less clear, John Newbery's reputation as a bringer of sweetness and light to children's literature is not entirely justified, but what he did bring was great commercial agility, which served as a model both for those around him and for those who came after.

Without doubt, John Newbery himself must take center stage in any consideration of the importance of his house, even after his death in 1767 when the company broke up into two intermittently warring factions. What he did was, first, to perceive the value of the new imaginative appeal that Thomas Boreman and Mary Cooper had introduced into children's books and, second, to apply publishing energy to exploit it, perhaps following the example of a publishing colleague, Benjamin Collins of Salisbury. The bluff, rather avuncular manner in which so many Newbery texts are presented, vouches clearly for the personality of the man himself; his restless questing after new ideas, or new ways of recycling old ideas, has all the hallmarks of a true-born publisher (of any generation).

The list that Newbery built up between 1744 and 1767 provides good evidence of his diverse experimentation. No other eighteenth-century publisher could match it, and those, such as John Marshall (see chapter VI), who developed a large output were at this time very much in Newbery's shadow as far as innovation was concerned. Indeed, that held too for the activity of his successors: his son Francis and manager Thomas Carnan at the St. Paul's Church Yard address, and his nephew, also Francis, and his nephew's widow, Elizabeth, in the shop on the corner of Ludgate Hill. Both of these firms necessarily introduced new titles, but their thinking was dominated by that of the founder and they kept many of his books in print until the last decade of the century.

The first eight books in this chapter represent aspects of John Newbery's style as editor and publisher, even though we needs must exhibit editions reissued by the Carnan/Newbery partnership or others after his death. These are followed by three books that were first published by that partnership and by five from the competing firm set up by Newbery's nephew Francis and continued by his widow Elizabeth. We have sought examples demonstrating John Newbery's approach to educational, religious, and popular publishing, together with his experiment at producing a children's magazine. His successors are shown publishing traditional tales, moral and didactic verse, as well as abridged versions of literary classics. The Newbery firms figure also as publishers in eight of the books owned by Frances Laetitia Earle described below in chapter VII.

ᴥ 68 ᴥ

The Royal Primer: or, an easy and pleasant guide to the art of reading. Authoriz'd by His Majesty King George II. To be used throughout His Majesty's Dominions. Adorned with cuts. "London: Printed for J. Newbery, at the Bible and Sun, in St. Paul's Church-Yard. (Price bound 3d.)" [American forgery, not before 1799 (date of watermarked paper)]. 16° (97 × 80 mm.), turned chain lines.

A–E⁸ (A1ᵛ frontispiece *A good Boy and Girl at their Books*, A2ʳ title with Royal arms and border, E8 blank). Pp. 78, [2]. A single paper stock. Two sizes of roman type, italic type. 26 cuts (approximately 30 × 45 mm. each) and two full-page alphabet blocks (62 mm. square) of 12 illustrations each. Original colored floral boards. References: Gottlieb 65; Heartman 157.

Provenance: James William Ellsworth (bookplate designed by E. D. French 1895); Dr. A. S. W. Rosenbach (inscr.). PML 68291. Purchase: Ball Fund.

Although John Newbery started his children's book publishing enterprise with the varied delights of *A Little Pretty Pocket-Book*, much of his output during the 1740s was taken up with the more serious fare of his broadly educational "Circle of the Sciences" series. His editing of *The Royal Primer* ca. 1746 (published in association with Benjamin Collins, with whom he also shared *The Royal Battledore*, ca. 1753, Roscoe J21) may be seen as a typical attempt to liven up old introductory material for children, who might later turn to the "Circle." The core of the primer—alphabets, alphabet pictures, syllabaries, catechisms—had long been established, and indeed the American version, the *New England Primer*, was the most frequently printed early American children's book. Newbery's editing of the basic contents remained

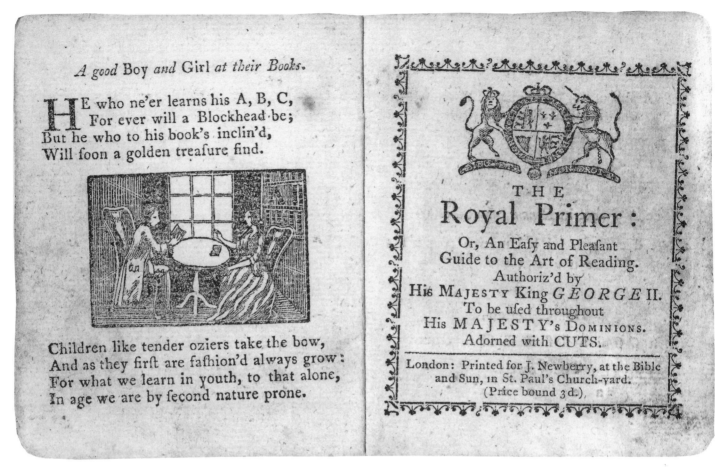

68. A1ᵛ–2ʳ, *enlarged*

fairly conventional except that he introduced rhymes, remarks, and pictures about animals and little biblical scenes.

The bibliography of *The Royal Primer*, in whose publication other booksellers were involved, is difficult since so much evidence has disappeared. This previously unrecognized forgery, however, (which appears oddly to have been made for a post-Colonial American market) follows Newbery's plan very closely, but substitutes a different set of subjects for the pictorial alphabet grid, and provides re-cut and mostly simplified versions of the illustrations, nearly all of which are reversed. The typographical ornament forming the title border is apparently identical to that used by the Boston publisher, John Boyles, for his 1770 edition of the same text (Heartman 163). The Morgan Library has no copy of the *Primer* with a genuine Newbery imprint, but its copy of the P. Norbury edition, published in Brentford ca. 1805, may represent a late use of the Newbery blocks (PML 85577.13).

◦ᶘ 69 ᶖ◦

The Fairing; or, a golden toy for children. Of all sizes and denominations, In which they may see all the fun of the fair, and at home be as happy as if they were there. Adorned with variety of cuts from original drawings. London: Printed for T. Carnan, Successor to Mr. J. Newbery, in St. Paul's Church-Yard, 1784. (Price Six-pence.). 24° (95 × 62 mm.).

A–I⁸ (A2ʳ dedication *To the true and genuine lovers of noise, this*

Or, GOLDEN TOY.   65
We were hurried from hence to another Booth, and placed before a Juggler with his Cups and Balls. See here he is. *Quick, Presto be gone.*

This conjuring Cur shewed us three empty Cups and three Balls. The Cups he turned down upon the Table, and then taking the Balls and throwing them away, as he pretended, he commanded the Balls and the Cups,
E   and

69. E1 recto, *enlarged*

Two Country Attornies overtaking a Waggoner on the Road, and thinking to crack a Joke on him, aſked why his Fore-Horſe was ſo fat, and the reſt ſo lean ? The Waggoner knowing them to be Limbs of the Law, anſwered, *That his Fore-Horſe was a Lawyer, and the reſt were his Clients.*

A Perſon of a College put his Horſe into a Field belonging to *Merton* in *Oxford,*

70.

70. C8 recto

book, which was calculated for their amusement, and written for their use, is most humbly inscribed by you know who, A2ᵛ *The preface. To the Critics of the Eighteenth Century,* I7ᵛ ads); etched frontispiece *Tom Trip with old Ringwood and Jouler and Tray Is riding to Town for a Fairing.... Huzza!* Pp. 141, [3]. 42 cuts, one of which is repeated (pp. 11 and 75). Original dab-colored floral boards. References: ESTC N028544; Roscoe J110(5); Johnson 31 (1768 edition).

Provenance: W. E. 1799 (inscr.), who was presumably responsible for the childish coloring of some of the cuts; Andrew White Tuer. PML 84001. Gift: Elisabeth Ball.

The Fairing, first advertised to be published at the beginning of 1765, stands at the further end of John Newbery's publishing career and shows him at his most swashbuckling and confident. From its opening exclamations: "Ha! ha! ha! ha! ha!," aimed at Mr. Critic, and "Hallo Boys, hallo Boys.—*Huzza*!," aimed at the reader, John Newbery, or his compiler, bundles one along through a vigorous fairground muddle of anecdotes, quips, and moral finger-wagging; they also manage to include the stories of "Dick Whittington" and "Puss in Boots" and a version of the song "There was a little man," which Benjamin Tabart was later to adapt for a picture book. No copies of *The Fairing* with John Newbery's imprint are recorded in Roscoe's bibliography and not many have survived from the near-twenty years preceding this edition, published by Newbery's son-in-law Thomas Carnan (who, with Newbery's son, continued the business in St. Paul's Church Yard).

70

[JOHN NEWBERY (1713–67)]. *Be Merry and Wise; or, the cream of the jests, and the marrow of maxims, for the conduct of life. Published for the use of all good little boys and girls. By Tommy Trapwit, Esq; adorned with cuts.* London: Printed for the Author, and sold by Carnan and Newbery at No. 65, in St. Paul's Church-yard, 1770. (Price Six-pence). 32° (95 × 60 mm.).

A–H⁸; (engraved frontispiece *he! he! he!*). Pp. 127 [1]. 12 cuts (36 × 47 mm. each), designed for this text. Brown morocco gilt. References: ESTC N027160; Roscoe J358(7); Welsh 319 (earlier eds.); Johnson 25 (1774 ed.).

Provenance: Charles Todd Owen (binding). PML 85565. Gift: Elisabeth Ball.

"Tommy Trapwit" has here produced one of John Newbery's most salable titles, the words perfectly summing up his humanitarian philosophy. In print for well over thirty years (so that the engraved frontispiece had to be replaced by one in relief), the book, in its first part at least, may well have appealed to good little gentlemen and ladies as well as boys and girls:

> Three gentlemen being at a Tavern, whose Names
> were *More, Strange* and *Wright*; says the last, there
> is but one Cuckold in Company, and that's *Strange*;
> Yes, answered *Strange*, here is one *More*; Ay!
> said *More*, that's *Wright*.

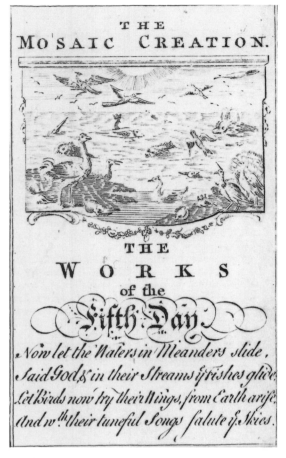

71. plate facing B5^v, *enlarged*

72. G6 verso, *enlarged*

⋟ 71 ⋞

[JOHN NEWBERY?, editor]. *The Mosaic Creation: or, divine wisdom displayed in the works of the first six days. Attempted to enlarge children's ideas . . . In prose and verse, with occasional remarks. Embellished with variety of copperplates, neatly engraved . . .* London: Printed for J. Newbery at the Bible and Sun in St. Paul's Church-Yard, [not after 1766]. Price 6d. 24° (98 × 63 mm.).

A–F^8 (A2^r preface, A3^r *A pastoral dialogue* by Elizabeth Rowe, D4^r *A poetical comment* by Addison, E1^r *Mr. Pope's Universal Prayer*, E7^r *Extract from the Works of Dr. Beveridge, Late Bishop of St. Asaph*, F3^v ads *Books . . . for . . . Children*, F5^r *For . . . Young Gentlemen and Ladies*, F7–8 blank, F8 mounted as pastedown); 7 engraved illustrations (including frontispiece), apparently printed on one sheet, which was then divided for insertion. Pp. 85, [11]. Different paper stocks for letterpress and engraving. Original dab-colored floral boards. References: ESTC N035290; Roscoe J248(3B).

Provenance: *Mary Eliz: Haynes's Book 1769* (and a similar inscription 1772); Andrew White Tuer. PML 81581. Gift: Elisabeth Ball.

John Newbery's happy-go-lucky willingness to go fishing in other men's ditches is well exemplified in this project, which probably originated in 1749, early in his career. As first published, *The Mosaic Creation* did not simply anthologize and dilate upon the first chapter of Genesis; it also went on to include extracts from Charles Rollin's *Belles Lettres* "embellished with a great variety of copperplates" under the title *Philosophy of Children* (Roscoe J321, subsequently published separately as such). According to Roscoe, this latter work shows Newbery plundering Boreman's *Three Hundred Animals* (entry 7), and in fact Boreman's frontispiece has been used as model for that of *The Mosaic Creation*. The other plates, with their combination of image and versified text, and the liberal use of printer's fleurons, give this production a more dignified air than is usual with Newbery's children's books.

⋟ 72 ⋞

The Holy Bible abridged: or, the history of the Old and New Testament. Illustrated with notes, and adorned with cuts. For the use of children. London: Printed for J. Newbery, at the Bible and Sun in St. Paul's Church-yard, 1757. [Price sixpence bound] (erased from this copy). 24° (98 × 64 mm.).

A⁸ (2ʳ *To the Parents, Guardians and Governesses of Great Britain and Ireland*); B–M⁸ (lacking B1·8, C1·8, D1·8, D4·5). Pp. [16], 176. 55 cuts. Original dab-colored floral boards. Reference: Roscoe J27(1).

PML 84788. Purchase: Julia P. Wightman.

Having incorporated some of Boreman into *The Mosaic Creation*, Newbery now incorporates some of *The Mosaic Creation* into this abbreviated Bible by recutting on wood the engravings for the Genesis chapter. (His journeyman even copied the crescent decoration at the bottom of the frames, so that they contrast noticeably with the very workaday cutting of the other blocks, two of which appear to be copied from *The Royal Primer*.) Such economies were typical of Newbery's pragmatic methods, but they do not detract too much from this abridgment, which may have its quaint moments—the naive pictures, the sudden slithers into genteel eighteenth-century diction—but more fairly represents its source text than most subsequent editions for children.

❧ 73 ❧

The History of Little Goody Two-Shoes; otherwise called, Mrs. Margery Two-Shoes. With the means by which she acquired her learning and wisdom . . . See the original manuscript in the Vatican at Rome, and the cuts by Michael Angelo . . . The fourth edition. London: Printed for J. Newbery, at the Bible and Sun in St. Paul's Church-yard, 1767. [Price Six-pence.]. 32° (95 × 61 mm.).

A–D⁸ (title, dedication, pt. I: *Goody Two-Shoes*); E–K⁸ (pt. II: *Mrs. Margery Two-Shoes*, I7ʳ *Appendix*, K6ʳ *Letter from the Printer* signed W.B., K7ᵛ book-ads, K8ᵛ ads for powders and pills); engraved frontispiece. Pp. 156, [4]. 17 cuts to pt. I, 18 to pt. II. Original floral boards. References: ESTC N018302; Roscoe J167(4); Osborne II, 889; Gumuchian 2753; Johnson 40 (1770 ed.).

Provenance: *Stephen Steele his Book, Novʳ 26. 1767* (inscr.); Elizabeth Hayden (sign.); *Thommas Hayden his Book was given to him on the Augest 25ᵗʰ1812* (inscr.). The Osborne Collection of Early Children's Books, Toronto Public Library (lacking C1·8, D–E⁸, F1·8, F2·7, F3·6; the Collection owns another imperfect copy, but containing those leaves missing from the copy here described).

Published towards the end of John Newbery's life, *Little Goody Two-Shoes* probably brought him more fame than all the rest of his books put together. This curious fact is perhaps only to be explained by the story's captivating title for, from its first page onwards, it proves to be nothing more than a Newbery contrivance, jamming a number of narrative ideas into a formless lump. (The strongest argument against Goldsmith's being the author is surely the tale's hopelessly inelegant construction.) Nevertheless, *Goody Two-Shoes*, with its recurring little tricks—the "trotting tutoress" teaching the alphabet, the "ghost story," the rhymes, and the cuts by Michael Angelo—hit the jackpot and was not only reprinted by the Newbery firms and their successors but also pirated and adapted and even put on the stage for well over a century, with several popular adaptations and pantomime versions lasting into the 1940s.

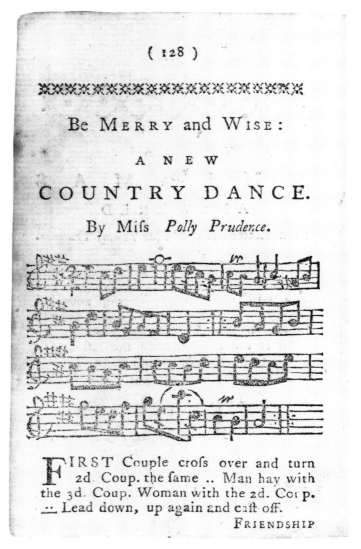

74. G5 verso, *enlarged*

❧ 74 ❧

The Lilliputian Magazine: or, the young gentleman and lady's golden library. Being an attempt to mend the world . . . London: Printed [by William Strahan?] for Newbery and Carnan, at the Bible and Sun, No. 65, in St. Paul's Church-Yard, 1768. [Price One Shilling.]. 12° (114 × 73 mm.), turned chain lines.

A1 (title=G1); B–G¹² (E7ᵛ musical notation to *That's My Honey*, –G1, G2–5 signed G1–4, G5ᵛ musical notation to *Be Merry and Wise: a new country dance. By Miss Polly Prudence*, G7ᵛ list of members of the Lilliputian Society, G11ᵛ *list of Subscribers, from Maryland*); 12 etched and engraved illustrations (including frontispiece *Leo the Great Lion*), printed from four copperplates and divided for insertion. Pp. [2], 142. 4 cuts including one signed by J. Bell (D8ᵛ). Original dab-colored floral boards. References: ESTC N033708; Roscoe J219(5).

Provenance: Richard Rasone (early sign.); Eliz.—(pencil sign. erased). PML 81224. Gift: Elisabeth Ball.

At the start of this work a dialogue takes place between A Gentleman and the Author. The Gentleman protests that at threepence a month the *Lilliputian Magazine* will have a hard job to pay "the necessary expences of paper, print and advertisements." "Very true," replies the Author, but virtuously adds that "my principal view is to promote learning" and that he hopes that after six months have passed, he will have obtained an enthusiastic readership.

Alas, his hopes did not materialize, and not a shred remains of the original parts in which the *Magazine* first appeared in 1751. (Jill E. Grey, in an article in the *Journal of Librarianship* vol. 2, no. 2 [April 1970], has pointed to evidence in the ledgers of William Strahan that he printed three monthly numbers.) Newbery's failure in this daring new ploy is not surprising since the formula for editing a successful children's magazine is hard to arrive at and many equally worthy ventures have failed since. Certainly he tried to leaven the lump of his rather heavy "Histories" in the magazine with jests, riddles, poems, and songs. ("Be Merry and Wise" appears as "A New Country Dance," and the "Morning Hymn" on pp. 101–2 is now known to be by Christopher Smart.) In the final analysis, the Newbery firms probably did well enough out of the *Magazine* since, in its present form as a compendium, it went through a number of editions from 1752 to ca. 1785.

⤙ 75 ⤚

Fables in Verse; with the life of Aesop, and the conversation of birds and beasts; with a variety of cuts for children. By their old friend, John Newberry. London: Printed for the Booksellers of all Nations, and Sold at the Corner of St. Paul's Church-yard [Elizabeth Newbery or John Harris], and at No. 55, Gracechurch-Street [Darton and Harvey], [not before 1801]. [Price Six-pence]. 18° (125 × 78 mm.).

A–B[6] (Life); C–G[6] (Fables). Pp. 84. Wove paper for the first quire, laid paper with fleur-de-lys watermark and date 1801 for quires B–G. 26 cuts (about 50 × 57 mm. each). Original or contemporary marbled boards. Reference: Roscoe J108; Darton *Check-list* G312.

PML 81622. Gift: Elisabeth Ball.

Fables in Verse for the Improvement of the Young and the Old. By Abraham Aesop, Esq. was first published in 1757 and must have been one of Newbery's best-selling titles (see entry 118). Roscoe lists reprints at regular intervals, and here we find what is essentially the same book surviving into the nineteenth century, with publication shared by either Elizabeth Newbery or her successor John Harris and William Darton the elder. He may be assumed the prime mover in this abridged edition of the original work (among other things, "Abraham Aesop" has disappeared) for in 1792 Darton & Harvey had bought the blocks for this and a quantity of other Newbery titles from the St. Paul's Church-Yard business. Twelve of the 38 blocks purchased for *Fables in Verse*, many of which derive from the influential series etched by Francis Barlow for his *Aesop* of 1666, were not used in this edition.

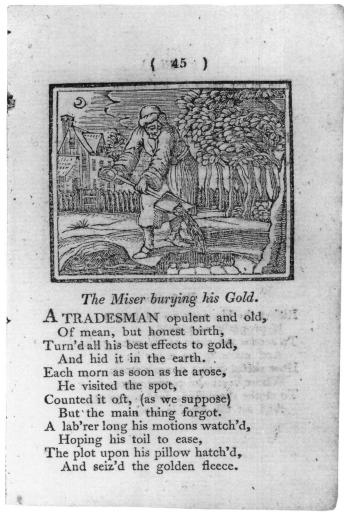

The Miser burying his Gold.

A TRADESMAN opulent and old,
Of mean, but honest birth,
Turn'd all his best effects to gold,
And hid it in the earth.
Each morn as soon as he arose,
He visited the spot,
Counted it oft, (as we suppose)
But the main thing forgot.
A lab'rer long his motions watch'd,
Hoping his toil to ease,
The plot upon his pillow hatch'd,
And seiz'd the golden fleece.

75. D5 recto, *enlarged*

⤙ 76 ⤚

CHARLES PERRAULT (1628–1702) and/or PIERRE PERRAULT DARMANCOUR (1678–1700). *Histories or Tales of Past Times, told by Mother Goose. With morals. Written in French by M. Perrault, and Englished by G.M. Gent. The sixth edition, corrected.* Salisbury: Printed and sold by B. Collins; also by Carnan and Newbery, in St. Paul's Church-Yard; and S. Crowder, in Pater-noster-Row, 1772. (Price 9d. neatly bound.). 12° (111 × 75 mm.).

A–N[6] (A1[v] frontispiece, A3[r] *Little Red Riding-Hood*, K1[r] *The Discreet Princess*, N6[v] ad for *The Polite Academy*). Pp. 156. 9 cuts (frontispiece full-page, others 41 × 62 mm.). Original dab-colored floral boards. References: ESTC N028549; Roscoe J279(2).

Provenance: Henry B. Wheatley (sign.); Elisabeth Ball. PML 84676. Gift: Lilly Library.

Although it would be agreeable to display an example that shows John Newbery himself publishing Mother Goose, arguably one of the two or three most important trade children's books of the eighteenth century, no such edition has come to light. Indeed, "light" is still lacking for a full account of what happened to Perrault in England.

76. frontispiece, *enlarged*

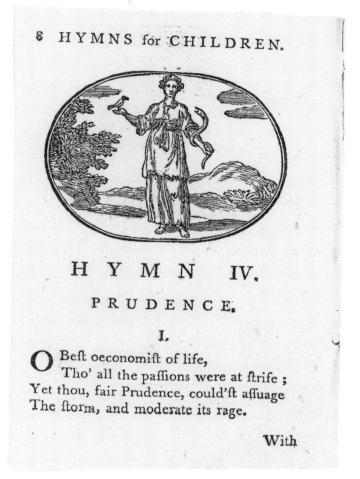

77a. B4 verso, *enlarged*

As we have seen above (entry 59), four editions of Robert Samber's translation are traceable down to 1750. After that the sequence divides. An uncertain "Samber" line continues by way of a so-called "6th edition" from Melvil (entry 374) and about the same time a so-called translation by "G.M. Gent." emerges from Benjamin Collins's shop at Salisbury. "G.M." is commonly identified with Guy Miège (ambassador and grammarian, 1644–ca.1718), but this obvious error is immaterial since the "G.M." version is exactly the same as Robert Samber's and the change of name may have been introduced to disguise a piracy (even though Collins and Hodges often collaborated). In any case, no "G.M." edition is known before a third of 1763 (Lilly Library), which Collins published in association with the London bookseller W. Bristow. The latter is not much in evidence as a publisher of children's books, although he traded from St. Paul's Churchyard "next the Great Toyshop." Was he a front-man for Newbery? This seems possible since in 1769 a fifth edition of "G.M.'s" text was published by Collins in Salisbury and Newbery and Carnan in London (Schiller Collection, now Cotsen Children's Library, Princeton University).

❧ 77a ❧

[CHRISTOPHER SMART (1722–71)]. *Hymns, for the Amusement of Children. Embellished with Cuts.* London: Printed for T. Carnan, in St Paul's Church Yard, 1771. Price Six-pence. 12° (106 × 74 mm.).

π^2 (engraving by W. Walker: 1^v dedicatee's portrait, 2^r title), A^2 (1^r dedication *To His Highness Prince Frederick, Bishop of Osnabrug,* 1^v blank, 2$^{r–v}$ *The Contents*); B–H^6 (H6^v ads). Pp. [6] ii, 83, [1]. 36 oval cuts (about 39 × 52 mm. each), some emblematic. Original gilt-blocked and dab-colored floral boards. References: ESTC N033384; Roscoe J338(2); Mahony & Rizzo 162; Johnson 36.

Provenance: *Eliza Cooper The gift of S. A. Willby, Boxted* (date of inscription deleted); Edgar S. Oppenheimer (1885–1959). PML 82512. Purchase: Julia P. Wightman.

❧ 77b ❧

A Poetical Description of Beasts, with moral reflections for the amusement of children . . . London: Printed for T. Carnan, at Number 65 in St Paul's Church Yard, 1773. 12° (115 × 75 mm.).

π^2 (engraving by Wm. Walker: 1^v dedicatee's portrait, 2^r title), 2π^2 (1^r dedication *To His Royal Highness Prince William Henry,*

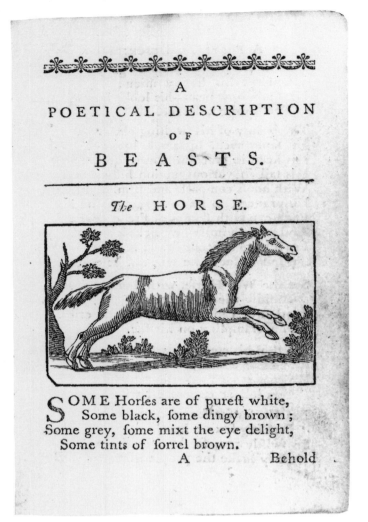

77b. A1 recto, *enlarged*

J. Lodge delin.et sculp.

78. plate facing F6ᵛ, *enlarged*

Knight of the Thistle, 1ᵛ blank, 2ʳ⁻ᵛ *The Contents*); A–F⁶. Pp. [6] ii, 72. 32 cuts (37 × 59 mm. each). Gilt and colored floral boards (perhaps not original). References: ESTC N040254; Roscoe J298(1); Johnson 29 (1777 ed.).

Provenance: *Miss Bent* (inscr.). PML 81602. Purchase: Julia P. Wightman.

After John Newbery's death many of his most successful publications continued to be sold by his son, Francis, and his son's partner, Thomas Carnan, from the address in St. Paul's Church Yard. They also introduced or commissioned new titles, among which *Hymns for the Amusement of Children* was one of the most distinguished. The author was the poet Christopher Smart, who was married to Carnan's sister and who had already written the "Morning Hymn" for the *Lilliputian Magazine* (entry 74). He did his work with a careful seriousness, finer but less approachable than his forerunner, Isaac Watts, and his brother-in-law responded by producing as comely a little book as the Newbery style would allow.

A couple of years later a rather similar style was adopted for the *Poetical Description of Beasts*, a work which sought to attach moral precepts to a versified fauna. This time the writer was casual to a degree and the result predictably puerile:

What awkward clumsy thing is that,
Clad with such furzy hair?
Oh, now I've got its name quite pat,
It is a sulky bear.

❧ 78 ❧

HENRY FIELDING (1707–54). *The History of Tom Jones, a foundling. Abridged from the works of Henry Fielding, Esq.* London: Printed for F. Newbery, at the Corner of St. Paul's Church-Yard, 1771. 12° (113 × 75 mm.).

A⁴ (1 blank mounted as pastedown, 2ʳ title, 3ʳ *Contents*); B–R⁶ S⁸ (S2ʳ ads, S8ᵛ blank, quires A and S forming a sheet); 6 etched illustrations (including frontispiece) printed from a single copperplate on a sheet divided for insertion. Pp. [8], 194, [14]. Different paper for letterpress and etching. Original gilt-blocked and dab-colored floral boards. References: ESTC N017172; Roscoe J132 (other eds.).

Provenance: *Sarah Burrows Janʳʸ· 18 1783* (inscr.), perhaps the unskilled colorist of the illustrations. PML 81793. Purchase: Ball Fund.

John Newbery's nephew, Francis, was already in business as a bookseller at the time of his uncle's death and had opened his shop on that famous site "the Corner of St. Paul's Church Yard" (i.e. the top of Ludgate Hill) around 1767. Most of Newbery's copyrights, however, went to his son and Carnan, and the nephew and his wife, Elizabeth, were left to develop their own line in children's books. Among their early schemes was one that seems to have met with ready response: the abridging of near-contemporary adult novels. Richardson's *Clarissa* and *Sir Charles Grandison* were early and successful efforts and their author might well have been pleased to know that they ran to more editions than equivalent abridgments of his rival Henry Fielding. *Tom Jones* does not seem to have fared very well, but several editions may have been read to pieces—Roscoe records what may have been the first edition advertised in December 1768 and did not know of either this edition or of one dated 1778, now in the Cotsen Children's Library.

ᦰ 79 ᦲ

[MARIE-CATHÉRINE DE LA MOTHE, Countess d'AULNOY (1650/51–1705)]. *Mother Bunch's Fairy Tales. Published for the amusement of all those little masters and misses who, by duty to their parents, and obedience to their superiors, aim at becoming great lords and ladies. Adorned with copper-plate cuts.* London: Printed for E. Newbery, at the Corner of St. Paul's Church-Yard, 1799. [Price Nine-Pence]. 24° (101 × 61 mm.).

A–M⁸; 12 engraved and etched illustrations (lacking 2: *Yellow Dwarf* and *Zalmandor and Amandina*) printed from three copperplates, divided for insertion. Pp. 192. Original dab-colored floral boards. References: ESTC N026265; Roscoe J17(5); Johnson 10 (ed. for F. Newbery, 1773).

Provenance: *Pollocks Collection* (inscr.). PML 85150. Gift: Elisabeth Ball.

The *féeries* of the Countess d'Aulnoy have a longer history in print in England than those of Perrault. A first collection appeared in London soon after its publication in France (1698), and both the collection and individual stories like "The White Cat" were well known by the middle of the eighteenth century. Francis Newbery, whose first edition of this neatly abridged text appeared in 1773, seems to have been the first person to apply to the Countess a name taken from popular literature, "Mother Bunch," probably in the hope of creating a rival to "Mother Goose." ("Mother Bunch" was renowned originally as an alehouse keeper. She arrived in literature in the seventeenth century with her name attached to jest and recipe books.) For a time Francis Newbery's strategy succeeded, and Mother Bunch stayed in print until the end of the 1820s; but the ornate and overly contrived nature of her stories could never compete with the direct and more intimate address of Mother Goose, who is still alive today.

ᦰ 80 ᦲ

The History of Sindbad the Sailor; containing an account of his several surprising voyages and miraculous escapes. London: Printed for E. Newbery, the Corner of St. Paul's Church Yard, 1794. 16° (107 × 75 mm.).

The Elephant rooting up the Tree whereon SINDBAD is placed.

80. H1 verso, *enlarged*

A–H⁸. Pp. 128. 6 wood-engraved illustrations (about 75 × 54 mm. each). Original gilt-blocked and dab-colored floral boards. Reference: Roscoe J171(1).

PML 82330. Gift: Elisabeth Ball.

"The Arabian Nights" was not published in an edition for children until Elizabeth Newbery got Richard Johnson to do a 263-page abridgment as (typically) *The Oriental Moralist* in 1791 (PML 75095). This had not precluded publishers from issuing individual stories, however, and several might be grouped together in children's compendia (entry 92) or quasi-chapbook editions (entry 130) at the end of the eighteenth century. This edition of *Sindbad* has been cunningly cobbled up from the last three chapters of *The Oriental Moralist*. These cover three voyages only of Sindbad, and are reproduced more or less verbatim as Voyages One, Three, and Seven in the present book. The other four voyages have been spliced in to make up a complete series.

ᦰ 81 ᦲ

MIGUEL DE CERVANTES SAAVEDRA (1547–1616). *The Life and Exploits of the Ingenious Gentleman Don Quixote, de la Mancha. With the humorous conceits of his facetious squire Sancho Panca. Abridged.* [Translated by Charles Jarvis]. London: Printed for F. Newbery, the Corner of St. Paul's Church-Yard, 1778. Long 12° (166 × 95 mm.).

81. frontispiece, *reduced*

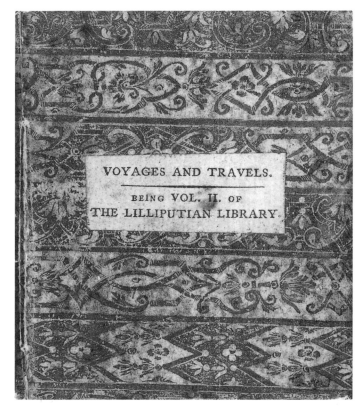

82. binding, *enlarged*

A⁶ (2ʳ *Life of the Author*, 3ᵛ *Contents*, 6ᵛ blank); A–L¹² (L12ᵛ blank); 6 etched illustrations (including frontispiece), apparently printed from a single copperplate signed Royce on a half sheet, divided for insertion. Pp. xi [1], 263 [1]. Different paper for letterpress and etching. Modern leather binding. References: ESTC T059476; Roscoe J50(1B); Osborne II, 870; Río y Rico 464.

PML 85603. Purchase: Ball Fund.

Although *Don Quixote* may have formed part of the Ludgate Hill Newberys' program for abridging the classics, its style of production is entirely different from their Fielding and Richardson editions with their child-size format and paper covers. At the very least, this substantial abridgment, with its worked-over etchings, should be seen as falling into the indeterminate category of books that may be intended for both children and adults. Charles Jarvis's translation was first published by the Tonsons and Dodsley in London in 1742 (Río y Rico 449).

✥ 82 ✥

[RICHARD JOHNSON (1733/4–93), editor]. *The Lilliputian Library; or, Gulliver's museum. Containing, lectures on morality. Historical pieces. Interesting fables. Diverting tales. Miraculous voyages. Surprising adventures. Remarkable lives. Political pieces. Comical jokes, Useful letters. The whole forming a complete system of juvenile knowledge, for the amusement and improvement of all little masters and misses, whether in summer or winter, morning, noon, or evening. By Lilliputius Gulliver, citizen of Utopia, and Knight of the most noble Order of Human Prudence. In ten volumes, price five shillings.* London: Printed [by Henry Baldwin] for W. Domville, under the Royal Exchange; and Byfield and Hawkesworth, at Charing-Cross, [not before 1779]. 10 volumes. 24° (99 × 78 mm.).

Vol. I: *Gulliver's Lectures.* Vol. II: *Voyages and Travels.* Vol. III: *[Aesop's Fables].* Vol. IV: *Gulliver's Tales.* Vol. V: *Lilliputian Letter-Writer.* Vol. VI: *Poetical Flower-Basket.* Vol. VII: *Merry Companion.* Vol. VIII: *Lilliputian Biographer.* Vol. IX: *Entertaining Medley.* Vol.X: *Lilliputian Fragments.* Each volume: A–E¹² (A2ᵛ *Advertisement*, vol. X E11ᵛ partial list of buyers). Pp. 120. Two paper stocks. 13 relief-cut illustrations including frontispiece. Relief-cut tailpieces. Original gilt-blocked paper boards, typographical label on front covers (label of vol. III lost). References: ESTC N002780; Roscoe J218.

PML 85685–85694. Gift: Elisabeth Ball.

The instigator of this remarkable venture was the printer Henry Baldwin, for whom Richard Johnson records making the compilation in 1779. (He was paid £20.) The ten volumes make up a large-scale miscellany of stories, poems, jokes, and general didactica, which Johnson pulled together from a variety of sources; indeed, he notes in his daybook that he laid out 20s. "for Books." Henry Baldwin does not feature as publisher on the title page, but Robert Baldwin of Paternoster Row joins with Domville and the others in at least one advertisement.

Unfortunately, no one thought out how to market these ten "Lilliputian Quartos," and from the "Advertisement" it is obvious that the publishers were trying hard to combine the selling of sets with subscriptions for individual volumes. Needless to say, they were not very successful, although an edition was published in Berlin (!) in 1782; Domville sheets for all volumes were apparently bought up as a remainder by Elizabeth Newbery and reissued for separate sale during the 1790s. The Morgan Library possesses a

copy of Volume IX, *The Entertaining Medley*, with a cancel title and A3 canceled, and although the book concludes with the original note "End of the Ninth Volume," it no longer appears to be part of the series (PML 83073). It is possible to see in Baldwin's plan a premonition of the miniature libraries that were to be so popular in the early years of the nineteenth century (entries 163–165), and the Domville set may well have made an impact on some members of the contemporary publishing fraternity. At the end of the final volume (pp. 118–120) is a list of "little pupils" who have honored the project with their "approbation and encouragement." Aside from Master and Miss Domville, three Master Baldwins, and two Miss Baldwins, it includes some twenty-two children who bear the names of prominent printing and bookselling families—among whom are numbered "Miss and Master Newbery."

THE
LILLIPUTIAN LIBRARY;
OR,
GULLIVER's MUSEUM.

CONTAINING,

Lectures on Morality.	Surprising Adventures.
Historical Pieces.	Remarkable Lives.
Interesting Fables.	Poetical Pieces.
Diverting Tales.	Comical Jokes.
Miraculous Voyages.	Useful Letters.

The Whole forming a complete System of
JUVENILE KNOWLEDGE,
For the Amusement and Improvement of
All little MASTERS and MISSES,
Whether in Summer or Winter, Morning, Noon, or
Evening.

By LILLIPUTIUS GULLIVER,
Citizen of Utopia, and Knight of the most noble Order of
Human Prudence.

In Ten Volumes, Price Five Shillings.

VOL. II.

LONDON:
Printed for *W. Domville*, under the *Royal Exchange*; and *Byfield*
and *Hawkesworth*, at *Charing-Cross*.

82. A1ᵛ–2ʳ, *enlarged*

VI
RIVALS AND IMITATORS, LONDON

CONFIRMATION of John Newbery's energy as a children's book publisher is apparent in the dearth of any sustained attempt to compete with him during his lifetime. Few children's books of any character appeared before 1767 that did not carry his imprint or follow his model, but from that time on production began to expand and diversify rapidly.

In this chapter and chapter VIII we seek to provide a simple chart to some of the chief features of this expansion. London, as always, was the center of activity and the source of most of the innovations that occurred, or at least of the creative variations on Newbery's themes. In the following brief survey of London trends we have tried to reconfirm how "children's literature" was a genre mostly created by publishers, and to give notes on some of the older or more prolific eighteenth-century firms. Our entries are grouped by publisher, with a brief general note on his activity whenever information could be gathered. The publishers themselves are arranged in roughly chronological sequence, i.e. according to the date of a firm's emergence or of its activity in the field of children's books.

JOHN MARSHALL (ca. 1755–ca. 1825)

John Marshall was the son of Richard Marshall, the printer of chapbooks (entry 48). Most of his apprenticeship was served with his father and he was freed on October 6, 1778. Soon after this, he introduced children's books as a new line in the family business. He was to become not only the chief competitor of the Newbery descendants but also (like William Darton, see entries 98–102) a publisher who was to carry forward new ideas into the changed light of the nineteenth century. There we shall meet him again in several guises, but with the six items that follow we merely note the early manifestations of his publishing style.

⁓ 83 ⁓

The Careful Parent's Gift. Being a collection of short stories to improve the mind and mend the heart. It is not only necessary to know what is good, but to put that Knowledge into Practice. Ticklepitcher. London: Printed and Sold by John Marshall and Co. at No. 4, Aldermary Church Yard, Bow Lane, [before Christmas 1787]. [Price Three-Pence Bound and Gilt.]. 24° (100 × 65 mm.).

A–E⁸ (A1 blank, A2ᵛ frontispiece, E8ʳ ads). Pp. 78 [2]. 25 full-page cuts (78 × 47 mm.). Original gilt-blocked red floral boards. References: ESTC N028594; cf. Alderson, *Ludford Box* 1–2c.

Provenance: *Mary Dendy Decʳ 24: 1787* (inscr.). PML 80644. Gift: Elisabeth Ball.

"Improving the mind and mending the heart" were Newbery sentiments, and putting a solemn epigraph by "Ticklepitcher" on the title page also has a Newbery flavor, but *The Careful Parent's Gift* takes us back to an earlier time, for it is essentially a re-edited version of *A Christmass-Box* (entry 65). What Marshall has done is to reprint "Mary Homebred's" stories, with the characters renamed; reproduce her engraved plates as cuts (usually reversed); and add some earnest, but illustrated, lucubrations on such subjects as Fame, Art, Religion and Rambling—an easy way to make a threepenny book. (In a note in the occasional newsletter *Juvenile Miscellany*, put out by the de Grummond Collection at the University of Southern Mississippi, Brian Alderson describes the fairly elaborate way in which Marshall carried out another piece of "borrowing" by putting Sarah Fielding's "fairy story" about the Giant Barbarico [from *The Governess*] into his story-book *The History of Good Lady Kindheart.*)

83. B5 recto, *enlarged*

20 *The* MASQUERADE.

The CHEROKEE CHIEF.

THIS figure reprefents a warrior come from beyond fea, as far off as from *North America*, where the people live by fighting and hunting, and their riches confift in their furs, bows and arrows

◄§ **84** §►

The Masquerade: containing a variety of merry characters of all sorts, properly dressed for the occasion. Calculated to amuse and instruct all the good boys and girls in the Kingdom . . . [London:] Printed and Sold by J. Marshall and Co. at No. 4, Aldermary Church-Yard, Bow-Lane, [ca. 1785]. [Price Three Pence, bound and gilt.]. 24° (98 × 63 mm.).

A–E[8] (A1 and E8 mounted as pastedowns, A1 blank, A2[v] *Frontispiece*, A4[r] *Advertisement*, E7[r] ads). Pp. 79 [1]. 19 oval cuts (56 × 43 mm.). Original gilt-blocked and dab-colored floral boards. References: ESTC N034926; cf. Osborne II, 911 ("illustrations engraved on copper").

PML 81730. Gift: Elisabeth Ball.

Another little book so steeped in Newberyisms that one wonders if it is not a direct copy of a (lost?) Newbery title. Quite apart from quoting *"Be merry and be wise"* at us from the title page, the book also introduces a miscellany of characters different from but presumably inspired by those in the *Lilliputian Masquerade* (entry 148c); they are presented with the rough bonhomie that we find in books like *The Fairing* (entry 69). In a new ploy, however, the editor claims that the illustrations for the book are based upon drawings by "a little gentleman of my acquaintance," who made them when he visited the masquerade.

20 *The* HISTORY *of*

Excufe me, Pufs, fays he, you'll find,
Many much abler friends behind :
To many more poor pufs apply'd,
But all with complaifance deny'd.

Friendfhip, like love, we feldom find
Sincere, unlefs to one confin'd.

Our little gentry, you may be fure, did nothing but read the ftory and fable dame *Wifhwell* left them till night came on, and then after fupper went to-bed, that they might be ready in the morning againft fhe called, and they had hardly breakfafted ere a thundering rap at the door announced the arrival of his Grace's coach and fix, with Dame *Wifhwell* in it, and fix

footmen behind. See here they are.

Mafter and Mifs GOODCHILD. 21

Well, in they get, and away they drive till they arrive at his Grace's houfe.

After the cuftomary compliments were over, my Lord and Lady enquired if they liked the cakes Dame *Wifhwell* brought? upon which they returned thanks, and rehearfed by heart the rules, letter, &c. the old gentlewoman left them, and fo pleafed his Grace, that he gave Mafter *Goodchild* a curious library of Books, in fine morocco binding. And fee here they are

in a fine Book-cafe, made on purpofe to hold them. The Dutchefs prefented Mifs *Goodchild* with this gold Watch, and her

B 3 Picture

◄§ 85 ◊►

The Whitsuntide Present for Little Masters and Misses or, the history of Master George and Miss Charlotte Goodchild. To which are added rules for behaviour, and the reward of virtue, an instructive story. By your old friend Nurse Allgood. London: Printed and Sold by John Marshall and Co. No. 4, in Aldermary Church-Yard, Bow Lane, [not after 24th January 1787]. [Price One Penny, Bound and Gilt.]. Half-sheet 32° (97 × 61 mm.), imposed for work-and-turn.

[1¹⁶] signed A–B⁸ (1·16 mounted as pastedowns, 1ᵛ verse *Come hither Master, and tell me* and frontispiece, 16ʳ verse *My pretty Miss pray let me know* and illustration, 3ʳ introductory verse, 4ʳ *A. Stands for Apple and all*, 14ᵛ ads). Pp. 30 [2]. 16 cuts (30 × 47 mm. and slightly smaller). Original gilt-blocked and dab-colored floral wrappers. Reference: ESTC T155485.

Provenance: *Sarah Cooke her Book January 24 1787 Sarah* (inscr.); A.S. Huber (sign.); Gumuchian & Cⁱᵉ (1930 cat., no. 5831). PML 81758. Gift: Elisabeth Ball.

Here again Marshall is to be seen following but not directly copying Newbery. The title echoes Newbery's *Whitsuntide-Gift* of ca. 1764, and the miscellaneous contents are edited in the style that he invented, not least with puffs interspersed into the text:

> And furthermore, if you attend
> to Learning, they will for you send
> to Mr. *Marshall's* (who they tell
> Does this with many others sell

Nevertheless, Marshall did introduce touches of his own, like a specially composed alphabet rhyme and two rhymed pictorial pastedowns, the one at the front addressed to boy readers and the one at the back to girls. There is also a hint of his future invention of miniature libraries in the "curious library" that the Duke of Goodmanners gives to Master Goodchild (see illustration on previous page).

◄§ 86 ◊►

[ELLENOR, Lady FENN, née FRERE (1743–1813)]. *Fables, by Mrs. Teachwell: in which the morals are drawn incidentally in various ways* ... London: Printed and Sold by John Marshall and Co. at No. 4, Aldermary Church-Yard, in Bow-Lane, [not before 1783]. 8° (148 × 91 mm.).

A–E⁸ F⁴ (A1ᵛ *Frontispiece*, E6 *An address to mothers*, F1ᵛ *Postscript*, F4ʳ *Index*). Pp. 88. 18 oval wood engravings framed with wood-engraved floral ornament (full-page frontispiece and smaller illustrations, one to each fable). Old floral boards (*remboîtage*). Reference: ESTC T073094.

Provenance: Charles Todd Owen (pencil-number). PML 80113. Gift: Elisabeth Ball.

Alongside his reworking or even direct copying of Newbery books (see entry 144b), Marshall also introduced a significant new development into his publishing program: the harnessing of authorial talent. Authors of some distinction like Sarah Fielding or Mrs. Barbauld were not unknown in children's literature, nor

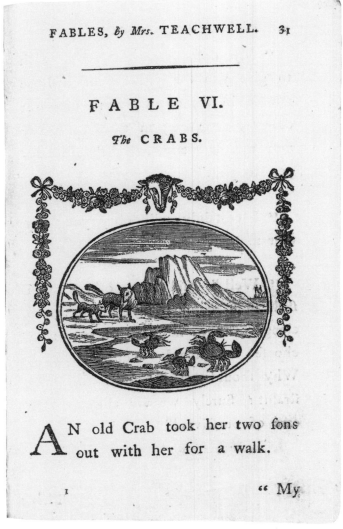

86. B8 recto, *reduced*

were editors and abridgers like Richard Johnson. What John Marshall did, however, was to find writers who were perhaps influenced by the growing interest in books for children and to encourage their activity. Foremost among the story writers whom he brought into his list were "the Kilners": Dorothy and her sister-in-law Mary Ann, whom he began to publish in 1780 (see entries 116 and 120). At the same time, though, he was attacking the market for what might be called "home education" by publishing a series of easy-reading books devised by "Mrs. Teachwell." This character (who clearly owes her name to Sarah Fielding's "Governess") was Ellenor Fenn of Dereham in Norfolk, the wife of Sir John Fenn the antiquary, whose books were drawn from her experience in teaching young children within the home. They thus have a pragmatic quality to them—how to catch "the volatile fancies of youth"—and develop a program (often based on dialogue) with more energy, but less grace, than is to be found in precursors like Mrs. Barbauld or successors like Maria Edgeworth.

Marshall's cavalier attitude toward dating his books makes for difficulty in determining the chronology of Lady Fenn's work, but she seems to have supplied him with a tranche of material at the beginning of the 1780s, which he published in a fairly closely linked series of volumes: *School Occurrences* (1782) which, "Mrs.

Teachwell" says here, was the first book she sent to "*Marshall* (the Children's Printer)," then *Fables* and, presumably, its companion *Fables in Monosyllables*, and then *Cobwebs to Catch Flies* (entry 87), which has claim to be her best-seller. These books were produced by John Marshall in more ceremonious fashion than his Newbery-style popular books. The octavo format was designed to give a spacious, legible page, and the ornamental pictures (never to be found in Barbauld or Edgeworth) followed the "new style" of wood engraving introduced by the Bewicks. In *Fables*, however, the cutting is too elementary to be by either master.

◦§ 87 §◦

[ELLENOR, Lady FENN, *née* FRERE (1743–1813)]. *Cobwebs to Catch Flies; or, dialogues in short sentences, adapted to children from the age of three to eight years. In two volumes* ... London: printed and sold by John Marshall, 140, Fleet Street, from Aldermary Church-Yard, [not before 1812]. 8° (148/150 × 96 mm.).

Vol. 1: engraved frontispiece; [1³²] signed *A*⁸ < B⁸ < D⁴ < E⁴ < F⁴ < G⁴ (2ʳ *dedication to Mrs. E**** D F*****, 32 blank). Pp. 64. 12 oval metalcuts (48 × 59 mm.), 8 wood-engraved tailpieces including one signed "Bewick" (hare). Vol. 2: engraved frontispiece; [1³⁶] signed A¹² < B¹² < C¹². Pp. 72. Watermarked laid paper. Frontispiece and half-sheet 17–20 (vol. 2) on blue paper. 13 oval metalcuts (same size), 5 wood-engraved tailpieces. Large roman type. Original pink paper boards, oval engraved labels on front covers. Reference: Hockliffe 545 (1817 edition).

Provenance: Charles Todd Owen (pencil-number). PML 80109–10. Gift: Elisabeth Ball.

Written in the shadow of Mrs. Barbauld's *Lessons* of 1778 (entry 10), the two volumes of *Cobwebs*, first published ca. 1783, provide progressive reading lessons, first with three-, four-, five- and six-letter words, then with one-, two-, three- and four-syllable words. The result makes it a forerunner of "Dick and Jane" and "Janet and John," but Lady Fenn is aware of the problems. In a note on her vocabulary control she says, "It is not very easy to introduce a number of such words, so that [some] Dialogues are particularly stiff and rambling." The popularity of *Cobwebs* is attested by this late Marshall edition, which retains Lady Fenn's various promotional addresses on the value of the book to mothers, and in her address to her "little readers," where she urges them to "remember the old proverb, '*Be merry and wise.*'" The old marbled covers have now been replaced by Marshall's later binding style, the engraved frontispieces have had to be reworked, and although some of the original oval cuts and the swagged surrounds have disappeared, a number of new vignettes have been added as space fillers. These are mostly wood engravings by John Bewick, originally cut for *The Beauties of Creation*, published in two volumes by George Riley in 1790, with an expanded edition in five volumes in 1793 (Tattersfield JB4–5). Mr. Tattersfield, whom we thank for drawing these details to our attention, notes in his catalogue that the Riley title, along with the blocks, was bought by Marshall in 1800 and that he is here found using John Bewick's work as stock-blocks.

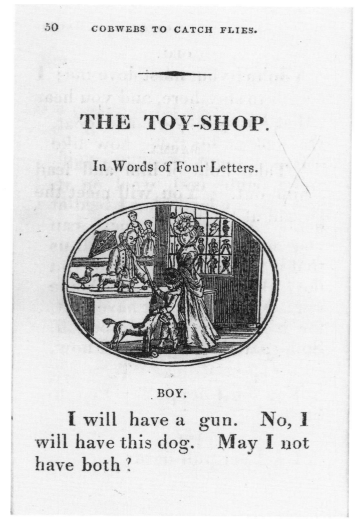

87. vol. 1, fo. 24ᵛ, *reduced*

◦§ 88 §◦

The Juvenile Magazine: or, an instructive and entertaining miscellany for youth of both sexes. For January [–June] *1788* ... London: Printed and Published by and for J. Marshall and Co. Aldermary Church-Yard, Bow-Lane, Cheapside, [1788]. To whom communications (Post paid) are requested to be addressed; and by whom any Hints for the Improvement of the Publication, will be thankfully received. 12° (154 × 95 mm.).

A² (forming a half-sheet with quire F, 1ᵛ *Answers and Acknowledgments to correspondents*, 2ʳ *The editor's address to her young readers*), B–E⁶ F⁴ (January), 2 colored engraved illustrations by Morris after Daniel Dodd on a bifolium < B2·5 and printed from one copperplate; G² H–L⁶ M⁴ (February), 2 engravings (one colored and signed by J. Taylor after Dodd) from one plate and divided for insertion, engraved music on a folding part-sheet inserted between quires L and M; N² O–R⁶ S⁴ (March), 2 engravings (one colored) from one plate; T² U–Z⁶ Aa⁴ (April), 2 colored engravings (*Little Hermit* misbound in June issue, the world map from the December issue inserted here); Bb² Cc–Ff⁶ Gg⁴ (May), 2 engravings (one colored, the map of Europe by

Sudlow on a folded quarter-sheet misbound in the April issue); Hh² Ii–Mm⁶ Nn⁴ (June), 2 engravings (one colored, the map of Asia lacking). Pp. 360. Double column. The coloring is in a child's hand throughout. Modern cloth, original tree calf covers preserved. References: Gumuchian 3473; Osborne I, 405; James, p. 18.

Provenance: *Charles Feilding. August 31ˢᵗ 1791* (inscr.); *Geraldine from Darling Mama. on her tenth Birthday: 1850: June. Clovelly* [Devon] (inscr.). PML 85197. Gift: Elisabeth Ball.

Marshall is here seen attempting a belated successor to the *Lilliputian Magazine* (entry 74) but with little more success than John Newbery. The *Juvenile Magazine* closed down in December 1788 after only twelve issues. Nevertheless, Marshall showed a much better sense than Newbery of the need for variety-within-unity, which is the hallmark of magazine publishing, and he gained this by appointing a regular editor, Lucy Peacock. She was one of the emergent band of ladies specializing in writing for children, and while one must admire her (or Marshall's) willingness to experiment with the content and production of the magazine, especially the folding maps and music ("composed for, and presented to the Juvenile Magazine by Mʳ Battishill"), the contents were too unrelievedly didactic to give it the common touch. (Lucy Peacock was later to diversify her interest in children's books by becoming a bookseller with a juvenile library in Oxford Street.)

JOSEPH JOHNSON (1738–1809)

Something of Johnson's distinctive character and importance has already been indicated in Chapter I, where he figures as the publisher of Mrs. Barbauld and the Edgeworths. As a bookseller and publisher closely associated with movements toward both political and religious nonconformity, he is a dominant figure (and indeed cannot really be seen as either a rival or an imitator of conventional Newberyism). A man of great integrity who went to prison in 1797 for selling a pamphlet by Gilbert Wakefield— "a seditious libel"—he won the respect of his authors, among whom were the redoubtable Mrs. Trimmer (entry 90) and Mary Wollstonecraft to whom he gave work and domicile for several years and whose children's book *Original Stories from Real Life* he published in 1788. He shunned unnecessary display and, although interestingly at one time involved with William Blake (who illustrated the second edition of *Original Stories* in 1791 [PML 84611] and Wollstonecraft's translation of Salzmann's *Elements of Morality* [PML 6007–9] in the same year), he had little use for adornments in publishing. Most of his children's books are notable for their rather somber appearance.

Johnson was born near Liverpool in 1738 and apprenticed to the London bookseller George Keith, being made free of the Musicians Company in 1761. He then set up his own business and eventually, in 1770, after several partnerships and a disastrous fire, moved to St. Paul's Churchyard where his shop became well known as a sort of informal club for the new talents whom he tried to foster. He died in 1809, and the business was continued by Rowland Hunter, his chief assistant, who, incidentally, had had his early education at Mrs. Barbauld's school at Palgrave.

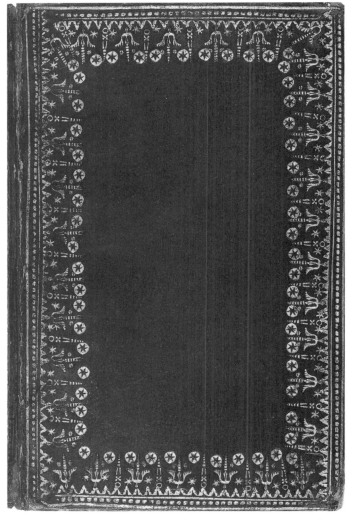

89.

◄§ 89 §►

ANNA LAETITIA BARBAULD, née AIKIN (1743– 1825). *Hymns in Prose for Children. By the author of Lessons for Children.* London: printed for J. Johnson, no. 72, St. Paul's Church-yard, 1781. 12° (142 × 85 mm.).

A⁶ (1ʳ title, 2ʳ *Preface*, –3·4); B–I⁶ K² (K1·2=A3·4, –K2 blank). Pp. vii [1], 98, [2]. Contemporary English gold-tooled red morocco, border on sides, small tools on flat spine, gilt edges, marbled endpapers. Reference: ESTC T053117.

Provenance: *Miss Monsons Gift to Charlotte Moore* (early inscr.). PML 82507. Purchase: Harper Fund.

First published three years after the first volume of *Lessons for Children* (cf. entry 10), *Hymns in Prose* can be seen as a simple continuous text for the child who has learned to read through the *Lessons*. Mrs. Barbauld wrote it because she doubted "whether poetry *ought* to be lowered to the capacities of children" and, in compensation, provided them with a series of vignetted scenes described in a language that Harvey Darton rightly believed "has been rivaled by few other writers for children." (Needless to say, prose was not deemed suitable by everyone and Harvey Darton's ancestor William Darton II published *Simple Truths in Verse* in

1816, in which Mary Belson Elliott converted Mrs. Barbauld's graceful prose into limping quatrains. The book was much reprinted and versions of it were popular in the United States.)

Johnson's production of the *Hymns* is typically restrained although the book was later to achieve decoration at the hands of Victorian wood engravers when John Murray put out a famous edition in 1864. There was also an early attempt by John Wallis to convert the hymns into a set of hand-colored, hieroglyphic reading cards (Opie Collection), and the book became one of the first texts for children in English to be widely translated into other languages.

◦§ 90 §◦

SARAH TRIMMER, née KIRBY (1741–1810). *Fabulous Histories. Designed for the instruction of children, respecting their treatment of animals.* London: printed for T. Longman, and G. G. J. and J. Robinson, Pater-Noster-Row; and J. Johnson, St. Paul's Church-Yard, 1786. 12° (165 × 97 mm.).

A[6] (title, dedication to Princess Sophia, *Advertisement*, introduction); B–K[12] L[6] (text, L6[v] ads). Pp. xi [1], 227, [1]. Previously contemporary sheep, now in modern cloth. References: ESTC T076171; Osborne I, 314.

Provenance: *From Mrs. Trimmer. Josepha Plymley 1798* (inscr.); W. Bateson (sign.); Herbert G. Norman (sign.); Edgar S. Oppenheimer (Sotheby's Hodgson's Rooms, 13th Oct. 1977, lot 2543). PML 82346. Purchase: Julia P. Wightman.

Johnson is here seen as partner in the publication of one of those eighteenth-century books that was to achieve its greatest circulation in the nineteenth century. One can faintly discern why this should be, since there is a modicum of child appeal in the allegory of family life displayed in "the history of the Robins" (a phrase which was later to be used as the main title for the book). Even so, the formality of Mrs. Trimmer's prose and her insistence upon moral applications are not very inviting, and the book may well owe its longevity to the opportunity that it offered to illustrators, none however being commissioned for this first edition.

HENRY ROBERTS (ca. 1710–ca. 1790)

Most of the published trade records are silent about Henry Roberts as bookseller, and he is only slightly more visible in his capacity of engraver. He was born at Haverfordwest in Wales, probably round about 1709–10, for he was apprenticed to the London engraver John Carwitham in 1724, and he remained in that city working at that trade for most of his life. Samuel Redgrave in his *Dictionary of Artists* (2nd ed., 1878) notes him as engraving landscapes and humorous prints, and says that he died "some time before 1790, aged about 80 years." He may well have been brother to James Roberts (1725–1799), who drew the pictures that Henry engraved for *The Sportsman's Pocket Companion* (ca. 1760) and *A View of the Wax Work Figures in . . . Westminster Abbey* (ca. 1770).

Redgrave also noted that Roberts was "careless in habit [and] engraved such works as would find a quick sale in his shop." This fits well with what we know of his involvement in children's books. He was, for instance, probably associated with Sayer in the production of harlequinades (his *Jobson and Nell* of December

22, 1770 being printed on paper with the same watermark as Sayer's and almost certainly from the same plate), and also produced harlequinades in association with L. Tomlinson, who more often partnered the Tringhams in such publications. The 1770s appear to be the time when Roberts was at his busiest publishing children's books. These were notable for their distinctively engraved, but not always dated, title pages. We should also draw attention to the advertisement for thirty-seven books and twenty-two turn-ups in *Sally Strawberry* 1779 (entry 342). From the titles listed there, a case can be made for Roberts's ceasing to trade early in the 1780s, when much of his stock and copyrights may have gone to Homan Turpin (see below).*

* We are grateful to Laurence Worms for biographical information in this note.

◦§ 91 §◦

The Tales of Orgar, the hermit of the mountains. Being moral and entertaining instructions for youth. Adorned with curious cuts. London: Printed for H. Roberts, Engraver, N° 56 almost opposite Great Turn Stile Holborn. Published according to Act of Parliam[t] Jan[y] 1772. Price Six Pence. 16° (95 × 75 mm.).

A[2] (frontispiece, title); B–F[8] (F3[r] *Ode on retirement*, F8 ads); engraved title and 8 illustrations printed from a single copperplate on one sheet, divided for insertion (frontispiece and title conjugate). Pp. 80. Different paper stocks for letterpress and engraving. Original dab-colored floral boards.

The Philosopher's Stone.

91. engraving opposite C8[r], *enlarged*

PML 84734. Purchase: Ball Fund.

A feeling for design, notable in the format, the engraved plates and the use of fleurons in the chapter titles, is the chief distinction of Roberts's work here. Orgar's tales are mainly typical moralities of little apparent relevance to child readers.

HOMAN TURPIN (ca. 1740–1791?)

Like Roberts, Turpin is one of a number of booksellers/publishers on the fringes of the children's book industry about whom one would like to know more. ESTC records and directories indicate that he was in business in the West Smithfield area from about 1764, and Plomer *1726* notes that he specialized in manuscript sermons. Certainly a fair proportion of his known output has a religious cast to it (including an edition of John Wright's *Spiritual Songs for Children*, see entry 36), and he may only have developed an interest in children's books through an association with Henry Roberts; they published jointly "Tommy Tell-Truth's" *Christmas Holidays; a poem, adorn'd with copper plates*, quite early in Turpin's career. In all probability (as we have noted immediately above), Turpin's list was greatly enhanced at Roberts's death or retirement, when he added Roberts titles to his list. About 1789 Turpin moved to premises at No. 18, near Gray's Inn Gate, Holborn, and he is likely to be the same Turpin whom Maxted records as dying there on March 6, 1791.

❧ 92 ☙

Oriental Stories; or, eastern tales, selected from the choicest among those nations which are remarkable for mirth and entertainment. Calculated to please and instruct youth of both sexes . . . London: Printed for H. Turpin, No. 104, St. John's Street, West Smithfield, [ca. 1785]. (Price one penny, bound and gilt). 32° (97 × 64 mm.).

A–B⁸ (A1 mounted as pastedown, A1ᵛ *Frontispiece* within type-ornament border: relief-cut portrait, perhaps representing or caricaturing Homan Turpin, with the bookseller's address underneath *where may be had great choice of Children's Books, wholesale and retail*, B8 ads). Pp. 30, [2]. 7 cuts. Original gilt-blocked and dab-colored floral wrappers.

Provenance: *AP* (initials in a contemporary child's hand). PML 84616. Purchase: Ball Fund.

One of thirteen penny-books that Turpin advertised in his catalogue at the end of *Harlequin* (entry 117), together with over fifty further items, including entertaining cards and harlequinades. This book is notable partly for giving four highly abbreviated stories from the *Arabian Nights* and partly for selecting these from unexpected sections of that rambling work. No Aladdin, no Ali Baba, but "Little Hunch-back" (pp. 17–23), which was later to be turned into a versified picture book by John Harris (PML 82202). Another Turpin imprint is *Young Aesop's Fables* (PML 81837; Gottlieb 13), whose engraved pages give rise to the thought that the copperplate may have originated in the shop of Henry Roberts.

92. *enlarged*

JOSEPH HAWKINS (ca. 1745–ca. 1795)

Hawkins is recorded as a printer in the Westminster Poll Books for 1774 (Maxted) but had died by 1796, when his son, also Joseph, was apprenticed to the engraver Charles John Downes (McKenzie 2549). He seems to have specialized in "little gilt books for the use of children," and in his *Strange Adventures . . . of the Nimble-footed Harlequin* (PML 85576.1) he advertises thirty-nine children's books sold wholesale from his Shire-Lane premises, with a Newberyish adage:

> These little Stories learn to read,
> And you'll be very good indeed.

After his death some of his cuts may have been sold to Robert Bassam (discussed below), in whose books they have been occasionally found.

❧ 93 ☙

The History of Felina, Princess of Purry-Mew Island, who was metamorphosed into a white cat. Including the history of the golden sparrow and Prince Squally-Wally; with their restoration and marriage . . . London: Printed and Sold by

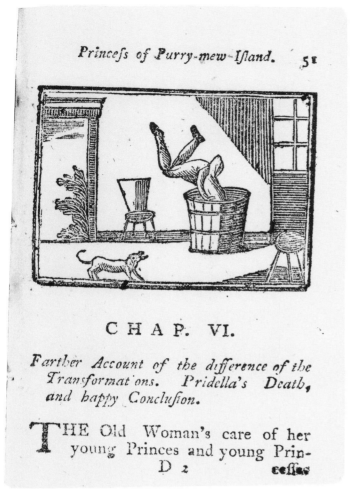

93. D2 recto, *enlarged*

94. fo. 16 verso, *enlarged*

Joseph Hawkins, Shire Lane, Temple-Bar, [ca. 1775]. [Price Three-Pence Bound and Gilt.]. 24° (94 × 64 mm.).

A–E⁸ (A1 and E8 mounted as pastedowns, A1ᵛ *frontispiece*). Pp. 79, [1]. 21 wood engravings (various sizes). Original dab-colored floral boards. Reference: ESTC N032790.

PML 83068. Gift: Elisabeth Ball.

Hawkins here publishes an absurd *Kunstmärchen*, very distantly related to Mme d'Aulnoy's "The White Cat" but handing over all control of the narrative to an Old Woman with fairy powers. The Morgan Library also has moral tales published by Hawkins: *The History of Master Tommy Cherry* (PML 82416) and *The History of Old Goody Careful* (entry 114). Another copy of *Felina* belonged to Frances Laetitia Earle, whose collection is described in the following chapter.

WILLIAM BARLING (fl. 1781–95)

Barling worked primarily as a bookbinder and stationer from about 1781, when he was freed of his apprenticeship. ESTC records only five books with his name in the imprint, but Howe notes that a son was involved in 1790 and that Mary Barling (?William's widow) was in business in 1817. She or other members of the family remain in the records up to 1836.

◄ 94 ►

The Merry Andrew: which contains a complete collection of riddles, calculated entirely for the amusement and improvement of youth. Adorned with cuts. London: Printed for, and sold Wholesale, by Barling & Co. No. 30, Warwick-Lane, [ca. 1789]. (Price Two Pence.). 32° (99 × 63 mm.).

[1³²] (1·32 mounted as pastedowns, 1ᵛ frontispiece, 32 blank). Pp. 62, [2]. 27 wood engravings, a wide variety of typographical ornament above and below the illustrated solution of each riddle. Original gilt-blocked green floral wrappers. Reference: ESTC N034857.

PML 80687. Gift: Elisabeth Ball.

This rough-and-ready production takes about half of its contents from the Newbery riddle book, *Food for the Mind*, a work that often seems to have been plundered (see entry 96). Barling may have published it in order to try and diversify his bookbinding business; the pretty flowered paper wrappers are presumably his own. The "Top" picture shows the riddling method, representing as it does an answer to the conundrum on the preceding page:

> You know I ne'er offend you
> Then why so cruel whip?...

ROBERT BASSAM (1754?–ca. 1815)

Son of a coffin maker, Robert Bassam was apprenticed to the printer Thomas Harrison in 1768, was freed in 1775, and became a liveryman of the Stationers Company in 1782. During the 1790s he must have run a fairly busy printing house since he took on several apprentices, but many of his books were cheaply done for a popular market: children's books and satires like *Lovers of Ale. An extempore sermon on malt. Preached at the request of two scholars, out of an hollow tree.* It appears that, after the death of the engraver and printer Thomas Hodgson, some of his stock and copyrights passed to Bassam who reissued some titles under his own imprint. The best-known of these is the *Curious Hieroglyphick Bible* first published in 1783 "with many woodcuts from the Beilby-Bewick workshop in Newcastle" (Tattersfield JB13). The Morgan Library has a good representation of Bassam's children's books, from which we have selected two contrasting titles.

95. frontispiece, *enlarged*

✂ 95 ✂

John, Julius and Henry, or the band of brothers; in which is introduced the story of Marac-Oublou, the faithful Indian. London: Printed & Sold by Robt Bassam N° 53, St John Street West Smithfield, [ca. 1790]. Price 4^d Bound. 32° (108 × 75 mm.).

A–D^8 (D8 mounted as pastedown, D8^r *Great variety of children's books from one penny to one shilling. Sold by J. Luffman, No. 5, Windmill-Street, Finsbury Square.*); engraved frontispiece and title (incorporating Bassam's calligraphic monogram) conjugate and printed from one copperplate. Pp. [4], 62, [2]. Original dab-colored floral boards.

Provenance: *William Jolliffe His Book Decr 7 1804* (inscr.); *James Jolliffe His Book No^v 22 1812* (inscr.). PML 80814. Gift: Elisabeth Ball.

A rather pointless tale, whose chief interest now lies in the brief account of Julius's soldiering against the colonists in the American War of Independence (whence he coolly writes home: "I had the misfortune to lose my right leg by a cannon ball"). The book is a handy example, however, of the complications that surround even the most humble publications, for in this edition, with its final Luffman advertisement, we see what is probably a hidden collaboration. Luffman was primarily an engraver and is probably responsible for the engraved title and frontispiece here (he did a very similar job for a book which he himself printed in association with Champante & Whitrow: *Travels and Adventures of Timothy Wildman*, PML 81590). Presumably, in return, he got copies to sell at his own shop. Bassam also published a different edition (PML 85576.2; Osborne II, 900) of *John, Julius and Henry*, again priced at fourpence. It has a typographic title, adds two short texts, *Advice to Youth* and *A Fable of a Drop of Water*, and is illustrated with stock cuts (Marac Oublou's coffin, for instance, appears in the book that follows this entry). As noted above, other books published by Bassam use blocks that had previously illustrated quite different texts published by Hawkins.

✂ 96 ✂

A Pretty Riddle Book, being a choice whetstone for the wit of young children. By Mr. Christopher Conundrum, riddle-maker in ordinary to the King and Queen of the Fairies. Adorned with cuts. London: Printed by R. Bassam, No. 53, St. John's Street, West Smithfield, [ca. 1795]. (Price Twopence.). 32° (97 × 61 mm.).

[1–2^{16}] (1^v frontispiece, 2/16^v blank). Pp. 63 [1]. 25 wood engravings (various sizes), several within typographical borders. Original gilt-blocked and dab-colored floral wrappers. Modern blue morocco gilt. Reference: ESTC T122887.

Provenance: Charles Todd Owen (binding). PML 85368. Gift: Elisabeth Ball.

Whatever Christopher Conundrum's relation to the fairies may be, he has magicked the contents of this riddle book mostly from Newbery's *Food for the Mind*, just as William Barling had done (entry 94). The choice of riddles and the style of the wood engravings differ from Barling's, but the principle of neighborly borrowing remains the same.

JOHN DREW (ca. 1744–ca. 1795)

Probably apprenticed to Richard Holt of Lincolns Inn Fields in 1758 (freed 1771!), John Drew worked as a journeyman printer before setting up as a bookseller and printer in about 1785, the

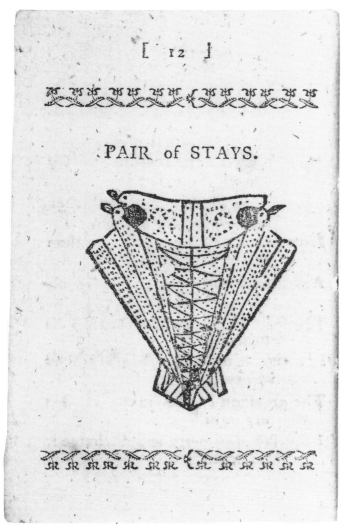

96. fo. 6 verso, *enlarged*

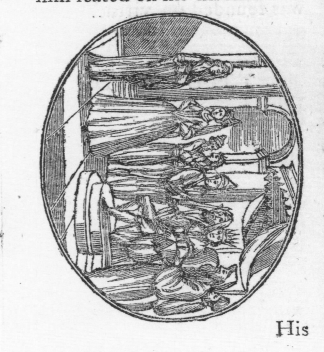

97. F4 recto, *enlarged*

year when, apparently, he went blind. Little is known of his activities as a publisher, which, judging from the advertisements in the following book, were probably undertaken as adjuncts to his printing business (and his selling of "Delarue's Incomparable Liquid").

❧ 97 ❧

[JEANNE-MARIE LE PRINCE DE BEAUMONT (1711–80)]. *Frederic and Matilda: or, Beauty and the Beast. An entertaining moral tale.* London: Printed by and for J. Drew, No. 31, Fetter-lane, 1791. [Price Three-pence.]. 24° (100 × 63 mm.).

B–F⁸ (B1 and F8 blank and mounted as pastedowns, B2ᵛ frontispiece *Matilda rides in royal state. Her sisters statues at her gate*, B4ʳ dedication, F5ʳ book-ads, F7ᵛ *Sold by J. Drew . . . in Bottles of 2s. and 1s. each*: *Delarue's Incomparable Liquid for Cleaning and Preserving all Kinds of House Paint; by which whatever is painted in Churches, Chapels, Houses, Rooms, &c. may be always kept clean, fresh and glossy*.). Pp. [2], 70, [8]. 10 wood engravings of various sizes in the text, including four oval illustrations too large for the width of the page and therefore landscaped. Original gilt-blocked and dab-colored floral boards. Reference: ESTC N028582.

Provenance: Justin G. Schiller (Sendak bookplate). PML 84688. Purchase: Julia P. Wightman.

Despite the false scent laid by the main title, Drew's little book is almost a verbatim reprint of Mme Le Prince de Beaumont's version of the old story as it appeared in the *Magasin des Enfans: or, the Young Misses Magazine* of 1759. (Matilda is almost always called Beauty and Frederic is only named when he turns into the Prince.) The rectangular wood engravings fit the story, with the Beast looking like an affable lion; the oval cuts were probably stock blocks.

WILLIAM DARTON I (1755–1819)

Like John Marshall, William Darton was a publisher whose activity and influence lasted well beyond the confines of the late eighteenth century. His firm and the separate bookselling enterprise set up by his son, William II, were both to continue under various members of the family right into the flood tide of Victorian publishing. (Nor was that to be the end—William's great-great-grandson, F. J. Harvey Darton, worked for an outgrowth of the original firms and came to write the standard history of English children's books, while other Dartons are associated with modern publishing and with the study of children's literature to this day. Indeed, information in this volume owes much to an elaborately detailed check-list of Darton's children's books by Lawrence Darton, a direct descendant of William.)

The original Darton firm was set up by William in 1787 after he had completed his apprenticeship and worked for some time as an engraver. Following a tentative start in White Lion Alley he moved his shop to Gracechurch Street and entered into partnership with Joseph Harvey. For many years thereafter, Harveys and Dartons alternated in the firm's imprint, but, regardless of who was at the helm, the company's philosophical roots in Quakerism, and its practical roots in bookish craftsmanship, ensured that throughout its development it held to an unwonted carefulness and sobriety in the choice and production of its stock. Of particular note was the regular experimentation with book design and illustrative techniques.

❧ 98 ❧

[WILLIAM DARTON (1755–1819), editor]. *Little Truths Better than Great Fables: in variety of instruction for children from four to eight years old.* London: Printed for, and Sold by, William Darton, White-Lion-Alley, Birchin-Lane, Cornhill, 1787. [Price Sixpence]. 18° (100 × 90 mm.).

A–G⁶ (±A2 *Introduction*); 4 engravings (perhaps by Darton) printed from two copperplates (frontispiece + pl. 3, plts. 2+4), divided for insertion. Pp. 84. Original marbled stiff wrappers, letterpress label on front cover. References: ESTC N033615; Gottlieb 182; Darton *Check-list* G224(1).

PML 85535. Gift: Elisabeth Ball.

This is one of the very few known institutional copies of what is assumed to be William Darton's first publication, and one of the very few editions issued from White Lion Alley before he moved to the familiar address in Gracechurch Street. According to Lawrence Darton, the work may have begun life as a "family book," recording incidents that actually happened and retaining family names, and that William Darton probably cut the charmingly naive engravings himself. The text of the book is in the Barbauld/Fenn tradition, using dialogue to promote interest in the subjects discussed and to encourage the child learning to read. For all its primness, there is an integrity about it that augured well for the fledgling publisher. A second volume followed in 1788.

❧ 99 ❧

[RICHARD JOHNSON (1734–93)]. *Juvenile Trials for Robbing Orchards, telling fibs, and other offences. With alterations and additions. Recommended by the author of Evenings at Home.* London: printed for Darton and Harvey, 1796. [Price Six-Pence]. 12° (113 × 77 mm.).

A–I⁶; engraved *Frontispiece.* Pp. 108. 15 cuts printed from the original Carnan blocks. Original dab-colored floral boards. Reference: Darton G531(1).

98. frontispiece

99.

PML 82170. Gift: Elisabeth Ball.

The Darton ledgers record that in 1792 (four years after Thomas Carnan's death) Darton & Harvey bought from the relicts of John Newbery the copyrights and blocks for a couple of dozen Newbery publications. *Juvenile Trials* was one of these (as was *Little Goody Two-Shoes*) and this edition shows the new publishers furbishing up their acquisition. An engraved frontispiece replaces the earlier cut, the introduction is abridged but, to make up for it, two more trials are added (without illustration). All of the original blocks are retained except for the first and the last (comparison with the Carnan ed. of 1786 = Roscoe J229(5); PML 82167).

❧ 100 ❧

[WILLIAM DARTON (1755–1819)]. *Trifles for Children; part 1* [2, III]. London: Printed [pt. III: Published] by W. Darton, and J. Harvey, Gracechurch Street, September 1st 1796 (pt. 1), Decr 30, 1796 (pt. 2, watermark-date 1797), June 20th 1798 (pt. III, engravings dated Jany 1. 1799). Price Sixpence. 18° and 24° (112 × 75 mm.).

Part 1: [1²⁰] signed A1·4 < ² A⁶ < A2·3 < B⁴ < C⁴ < D². Pp. [40]: 28 of engraved text and illustrations (including title-vignette) of animals and birds, perhaps all from only two copperplates; 12 of letterpress text (quire ²A). Engraving and letterpress on different paper stocks.

Part 2: [1²²] signed A² < B¹² < ²B²< C²< D² < E² (A2 misbound between B8 and B9). Pp. [44]: 20 of engraved text and illustrations (including title-vignette), perhaps all from two copperplates; 24 of letterpress text (quire B). Engraving and letterpress on different paper stocks.

Part III: [1²⁴] signed π² < A⁶ < B¹⁶. Pp. [48]: 4 of engraved illustrations including title (quire p), 12 of letterpress text (quire A), 32 of letterpress text (outer and inner formes) and engraved illustrations (outer forme, apparently from a single copperplate). Two paper stocks. Original marbled stiff wrappers. Pts. 1 and 2 modern blue morocco gilt. References: Osborne I, 142 (pts. 1–2); Darton G229(1); G230(1); G231(1); James p. 23 (pt. 2 only; this copy).

Provenance: pts. 1 and 2 *Mary Ann Herrick 1800* (inscr.); Charles Todd Owen (binding). PML 81525–6, 80914. Gift: Elisabeth Ball.

With almost perverse ingenuity Darton here contrives to combine letterpress and intaglio printing in a series of simple "first readers" ("with no regard to regularity of arrangement," as Mrs. Trimmer said of another, similar Darton title). The miscellaneous texts, which include homely descriptions and moral anecdotes, are sometimes typographic and sometimes engraved; the illustrations are all engraved, even when, as in part III, they accom-

Left and right: **100**. pt. 1, C1ᵛ–2ʳ, *enlarged*

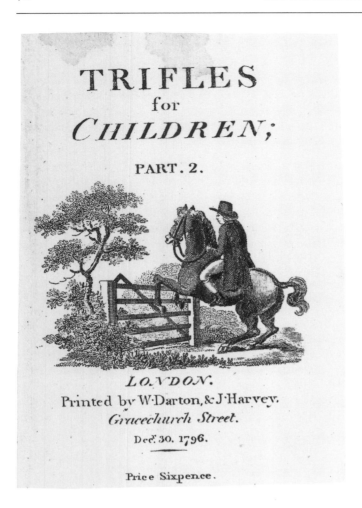

pany letterpress text. On several occasions Darton's engraver (probably himself) has copied, on copper, pictures that originated as wood engravings in the shop of Thomas Bewick at Newcastle upon Tyne. The printing method in part III was to produce an impression of all sixteen illustrations in quire B from one engraved copperplate, which was positioned in the intaglio press so as to leave the lower half of each page blank. The same side of the sheet was then run through the letterpress to print the outer forme of text.

❦ 101 ❦

[ANN TAYLOR (1782–1866) & JANE TAYLOR (1783–1824)]. *The New Cries of London, with characteristic engravings.* London: printed and sold by Darton and Harvey, Gracechurch-street, 1803. 12° (152 × 91 mm.).

A–B¹² (B12ᵛ imprint *Printed by Darton and Harvey, Grace-church-street.*). Pp. [48]. Engraved title including vignette (but imprint letterpress), 22 engraved illustrations probably by Isaac Taylor jun. (from two copperplates), the platemarks overlapping letterpress text on several pages. Original marbled wrappers. References: Muir *NBL* 683 (1804 ed.); Darton G917(1); Stewart A6a (no copy seen, misdated 1808); Andrea Immel, "Addenda to Stewart, *The Taylors of Ongar: The New Cries of London*" *PBSA* 82 (1988), pp. 595–604.

It is a pleasant thing for children to feed the poultry; but rather unsafe for a little child to go alone. In the west of England, a little boy went to feed some fowls, having the corn in his pin-cloth be-

fore him, the fowls ate it faster than he gave it to them; when a large cock pecked at the corn in the child's hand, and beat him down! The barley in his pin-cloth was scattered over him, and some

Above: 100. pt. 2, A1 recto, *enlarged*

100. pt. III, B10ᵛ–11ʳ, *enlarged*

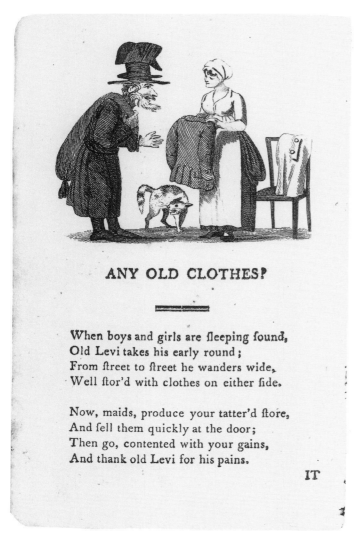

ANY OLD CLOTHES?

When boys and girls are sleeping sound,
Old Levi takes his early round;
From street to street he wanders wide,
Well stor'd with clothes on either side.

Now, maids, produce your tatter'd store,
And sell them quickly at the door;
Then go, contented with your gains,
And thank old Levi for his pains.

IT

101. A3 verso, *reduced*

102. frontispiece, *enlarged*

Provenance: *Mary Wilson to Thomas Burgess 1806* (inscr.); *to Mary Ann Burgess, 1820* (inscr.); *Phyllis Burgess 1886* (inscr.). PML 81284. Purchase: Ball Fund.

This time Darton combines letterpress text with superimposed engravings. Furthermore, he extends the usually fairly simple captioning of the cries by supplying a versified description of the trade and a prose lesson: "A good child will take more pleasure in relieving a poor beggar, or reading an instructive book, than in eating a Golden Pippin." With its tallish 12mo format, the book may also be seen as one of the steps towards the "new" style of picture book that is discussed in chapter XI. Some uncertainty prevails over the authorship of the *New Cries*. While it is generally accepted that Jane and Ann Taylor composed the verses for the second part, which was published in 1808, the text for the present first volume may be the work of William Darton, perhaps slightly polished by the Taylors.

❧ 102 ❧

[ANN TAYLOR (1782–1866) & JANE TAYLOR (1783–1824) and others]. *Original Poems, for infant minds. By several young persons* . . . London: printed and sold by

Darton and Harvey, Gracechurch-street, 1804. 12° (125 × 80 mm.).

A⁴ (A4ᵛ errata); B–E¹² F⁶ (F6ᵛ imprint); engraved frontispiece by Isaac Taylor jun. *A True Story.* Pp. [8], 107 [1]. Original red-roan-backed marbled boards. References: Stewart A1a; Darton *Check-list* G918(1).

Provenance: *R. Fowler to C H* (inscr.); C. Horton (sign.). PML 84825. Purchase: Julia P. Wightman.

A quotation from Isaac Watts on the title page now has the look of a premonition, for *Original Poems* was to vie with *Divine Songs* as one of the most popular children's books of the century. (Even Mrs. Trimmer sought to "recommend the work to an honourable place in *The Child's Library*" for all that she furnished objections to a number of poems, which she regarded as having "improprieties." See *Guardian of Education* vol. IV (1805), pp. 77–82.)

The inception of the book is now well known as an example of publisher's opportunism. Ann and Jane Taylor had been accustomed, from 1798 onwards, to send in readers' solutions or other contributions to Darton's annual *Minor's Pocket Book*. In 1803 the publisher realized that there was potential in their work and wrote to their father (a fellow engraver): "If they could give me some specimens of easy Poetry for young children, I would endeavour to make a suitable return in cash or books." "Books good, cash better," said the Taylors as they put together their submissions, for which they received a payment of £10. The only drawback was that, when the book was published, they discovered that it also contained poems by other hands, mostly by Adelaide O'Keeffe (1776–1855), with whom subdued wranglings went on over many years. This did not prevent Ann and Jane Taylor from preparing a continuation of *Original Poems*, which Darton published the following year. The Morgan Library possesses an integral set of the two volumes, with the third edition of vol. I alongside the first of vol. II, both dated by their original purchaser Ann Bruce, January 31st 1806 (PML 84826–7). By this time, the frontispiece to vol. I, by the Taylors' brother Isaac, had been re-engraved.

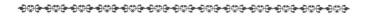

Grateful Tributes · A DIGRESSION

(see entries 103–110)

In her review of the Taylors' *Original Poems*, Mrs. Trimmer quoted in its entirety Ann's "My Mother." She described it as an "imitation of Cowper's delightful poem 'My Mary,'" and said that it would show children "how highly indebted they are to [their mothers] for the comforts and pleasures of infancy."

The sentiment caught on. In 1807 the engraver P. W. Tomkins, "by permission of Darton & Harvey," published an engraved picture book of the poem (see entry 103) and before long this single mawkish poem had become the foundation for a minor industry. "My Mother" itself was "borrowed," to be reprinted in magazines and anthologies, and an immense number of imitations were written celebrating every conceivable member of the family circle—and quantities of other entities too, such as "My Pony" and "My Bible."

William Darton II, of Holborn Hill (see chapter XI), was probably the most energetic publisher to exploit the craze. He made picture sheets of various versions of the poem, which he then converted, in cavalier fashion, into picture books (entry 104), and the Osborne Collection has his picture-sheet version of Ann Taylor's poem itself made into a dissected puzzle. Probably his most prolific collaborator on this enterprise was Mary Belson Elliott, who wrote many imitations and whose work may well have been the first to be collected under the generic heading "Grateful Tributes" (entry 109a). Other publishers too joined the fashion, beyond all hope of bibliographical clarification, but it is pleasant to discover that the satirizing of the poem—which became regular practice later in the nineteenth century—had an early beginning in standard picture-book form (entry 110).

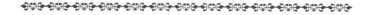

⤶ 103 ⤷

[ANN TAYLOR (1782–1866)]. *My Mother / A Poem Embellished with designs. / By a Lady—.* Manuscript on paper. [England, ca. 1807]. 4°? (275 × 185 mm.).

[1¹⁰] (all versos blank, 1ʳ title, 2ʳ incipit: *Who fed me at her gentle breast ...*, three-line stanza on fos. 2, 4–7 and 9, two stanzas on

103. fo. 4 recto, *reduced*

fos. 3, 8 and 10, original recension of the final stanza on 10ʳ *For God who lives above the skies ...*). Ff. [10]. Wove, unwatermarked paper, original tissue guards to protect the drawings. 9 half-page pencil drawings (2ʳ–10ʳ). Cursive script, brown ink. Stitched. References: Stewart II, p. 605; Muir *NBL* 457; Cahoon 161.

Provenance: F. R. Bussell (Sotheby's, 5–6th Feb. 1945, lot 240, nos. 23–416 in the auction catalogue sold as a single lot, £2,400 to Elkin Mathews Ltd.); Edgar S. Oppenheimer (1885–1959); Pierre Berès (Sotheby's, 2nd June 1982, lot 247); PML 84708. Purchase: Julia P. Wightman.

This manuscript has been called "the original holograph manuscript" (Muir, Cahoon, Stewart) for the first separate edition of Ann Taylor's *My Mother* (engraved and published by P. W. Tomkins, Nov. 1807, Stewart B2a), and the drawings have been attributed to Ann's brother, Isaac Taylor (Muir, Cahoon). Christina Duff Stewart reproduces one of Isaac Jr.'s original sketches for the poem (now in the Taylor Collection, The Osborne Collection, Toronto) side by side with Tomkins's engraving (Stewart pl. XXII), and the two are clearly quite unrelated. The handwriting in this elegant volume shows considerable similarity to Ann Taylor's hand as seen in autograph letters and poems of some years later, but there is no reason why the manuscript should not have been copied from Tomkins's engraved edition including the illustrations, rather than have served as his exemplar.

There is a tradition that Emma Hamilton was the model for these designs in *My Mother*, and several of Lady Hamilton's attitudes as engraved by Thomas Piroli after Frederic Rehberg (*Drawings faithfully copied from Nature at Naples* [London, 1794]) indeed bear a striking resemblance to the mother's poses in the Tomkins engravings and these drawings.

❧ 104 ❧

[ANN TAYLOR (1782–1866)]. *My Mother.* London: Published by William Darton Junr 58 Holborn Hill, 9th June 1815 [or later]. Engraved picture broadside ("No. 7.") cut up and stabbed to form a codex (112 × 90 mm.).

6 leaves: hand-colored illustration and verse on rectos, versos blank. Fo.1 drop-title, fo.3 sheet-number, fo.5 imprint. No wrappers. Modern blue morocco. References: Stewart B2b; Darton *Check-list* H620; James p. 60 (this copy).

Provenance: Charles Todd Owen (binding). PML 81514. Gift: Elisabeth Ball.

The engraved sheet from which William Darton's jigsaw is made (Hannas p. 124) is dated 1811, and pays scant attention to the orderly treatment of Ann Taylor's poem. The sheet contains two rows of three engraved pictures, each of which is topped and tailed by two stanzas of "My Mother" (see overleaf), but the order in which they are engraved, reading from left to right downwards, is: 4, 3, 1, 8, 11, 2, 7, 6, 5, 12, 9, 10. This absurd sequence was only slightly amended when the poem was reengraved in 1815, and with the conversion ff the sheet into a picture book, as here, confusion returned. The scrambling occurs because the title to the printed sheet stood over the center panel of verses, but in order to use it as title for the book that panel had to be placed before its left-hand fellow. At least, though, the publisher managed to get the apocalyptic final stanza at the end.

❧ 105 ❧

WILLIAM UPTON (fl. 1820). *The School Boy; a poem; by William Upton. With coloured engravings.* London: William Darton, 58, Holborn Hill, Sep. 1. 1820 [or later]. Price one shilling. Engraved picture broadside cut up and stabbed to form a codex (130 × 105 mm.).

6 leaves: hand-colored illustration and verse on rectos, versos blank. Fo. 1 drop-title *The School-Boy: by Mr Upton*, fo. 5 imprint. Original pink stiff wrappers, letterpress title label mounted on front cover. Modern brown morocco gilt. References: Osborne II, 668; Darton *Check-list* H1561.

Provenance: Charles Todd Owen (binding). PML 85862. Gift: Elisabeth Ball.

Upton's verses, modeled on Cowper/Taylor, are included here (see overleaf) as a token of the younger Darton's zest to commission sequels building on the success of *My Mother.* The Morgan Library also has in this particular group Mary Belson's *My Sister* (no. 24 in Darton's series: PML 83002) and William Jolly's *My Bible* (no. 22: PML 85104). Advertisements indicate that Darton also did a smaller version of *The School Boy*, no. 16 in his series of "coloured books," priced at sixpence.

❧ 106 ❧

My Father. London: Published by John Wallis, N° 42 Skinner St Snow Hill, April [1812?, year-date obscured in rebinding,

but not after 1818]. Etched picture broadside cut up and stabbed to form a codex—see overleaf (118 × 91 mm.).

6 numbered leaves: hand-colored illustration and verse on one side (1^v, 2^r, 3^r, 4^v, 5^r, 6^r). Fo. 2 title, fos. 4–6 imprint. No wrappers. Modern morocco gilt. Reference: Cf. Hannas p. 124 (Wallis's dissected puzzle of *My Sister*).

Provenance: *John / Leyland / augu xi 8181 / John / Leyland* (inscr.); Charles Todd Owen (binding). PML 83057. Gift: Elisabeth Ball.

All the evidence points to this being a homemade imitation of the kind of book noticed in the last two entries, where a broadside has been converted into a codex. The position and cropped state of the ownership inscription indicates that Wallis sold this impression as a picture sheet and that it was turned into a booklet by a later owner, subsequently to be girt in Mr. Charles Todd Owen's all-pervasive morocco. (James pp. 60–1 displays four Owen copies of grateful tributes: *My Mother* [see entry 104 above], *My Brother*, 1823; *My Sister*, 1812; and *My Aunt*, 1823.) The authorship of this version of "My Father" is uncertain, but the verses form part of a 12-stanza rendition found in *The Filial Remembrancer* (entry 109b).

❧ 107 ❧

The Mother's Present to her Little Darling, or the progress of life. London: Publish'd by G. Martin 6, Great St Thomas Apostle, [ca. 1820]. Price 6^d Col. 12° (105 × 90 mm.).

[1^12] (1·12 mounted as pastedowns, 1^v drop-title and imprint, lacking 5 and 6). Ff. [12]. Engraved throughout: printed from a single copperplate on one side of a sheet. 12 illustrations in

When first to walk you do me learn,
Thy tender help I often spurn,
Regardless of thy great concern,
My Mother.

107. fo. 4 recto

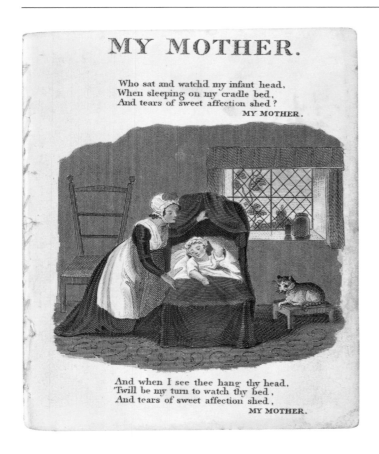

MY MOTHER.

Who sat and watch'd my infant head,
When sleeping on my cradle bed,
And tears of sweet affection shed?
MY MOTHER.

And when I see thee hang thy head,
'Twill be my turn to watch thy bed,
And tears of sweet affection shed,
MY MOTHER.

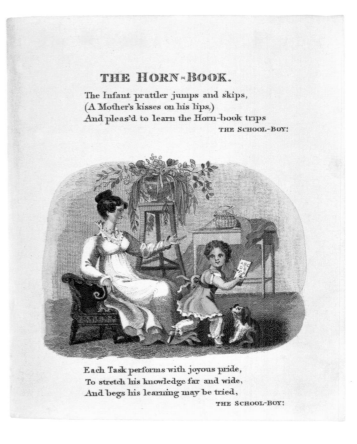

THE HORN-BOOK.

The Infant prattler jumps and skips,
(A Mother's kisses on his lips,)
And pleas'd to learn the Horn-book trips
THE SCHOOL-BOY!

Each Task performs with joyous pride,
To stretch his knowledge far and wide,
And begs his learning may be tried,
THE SCHOOL-BOY!

Top left: **104.** fo. 1 (stanzas 3 and 11)   *Top right*: **105.** fo. 1, *reduced*   *Below*: **106.** fos. 1ᵛ–2ʳ

MY FATHER.

Who took me from my Mothers arms
And smiling at her soft alarms
Show'd me the World, and nature's charms?
My Father.

Who made me feel and understand
The wonders of the sea and land,
And mark, thro' all the makers hand?
My Father.

publisher's coloring, each with rhyme. Original gray wrappers, no label. Modern morocco gilt. Reference: Osborne II, 653 (impression watermarked 1818).

Provenance: Charles Todd Owen (binding). PML 83049. Gift: Elisabeth Ball.

George Martin, as we shall see in chapter XII, was a publisher who forsook elegant production for speed and cheapness. This unidentified version of "My Mother" was planned from the start as a booklet and is typical of his rudimentary and rather charmingly opportunistic publishing practices.

◆§ 108 §◆

Kindness and Love between Brothers and Sisters, a pleasing domestic story, many pleasing plates. London: Edward Lacey, 76, St. Paul's Church-yard, sold by Henry Lacey, 64, Bold Street, Liverpool, [ca. 1840]. Price sixpence. 12° (169 × 101 mm.).

[1¹²] (1ʳ blank, 1ᵛ incipit: *Who, watchful ever to impart* . . ., 12ᵛ blank). Ff. 12. 12 half-page illustrations (hand-colored at the

Who, watchful ever to impart Sweet pleasure to his sister's heart, Became her horse, and lent his cart?

My Brother.

108. fo. 1 verso, *reduced*

publisher's) and text printed on one side of the sheet, perhaps from a stereotype plate. Original printed green wrappers, title, imprint and wood-engraved vignette (ship) on front cover, publisher's ads on back cover. Brown morocco, blind-tooled borders.

Provenance: Charles Todd Owen (binding). PML 82177. Gift: Elisabeth Ball.

An unidentified version of "My Brother," differing from those in tribute anthologies, but corresponding, albeit with a different order of stanzas, to a Hodgson edition of 1823 (PML 82801). Lacey published it as part of a series of "Superior Children's Books...divested of all the pernicious ribaldry, which, for many years, has disgraced much of the infantine reading." He also issued several other "tributes of affection," including *My Grandmother* (PML 82218).

◆§ 109a §◆

MARY ELLIOTT, née BELSON (ca. 1792–1860s?). *Grateful Tributes; or, recollections of infancy. By Mary Belson, author of "Industry and Idleness;"* . . . London: printed for W. Darton, Jun. 58, Holborn-Hill, opposite Ely-Place, 1817. Price Sixpence. 18° (134 × 86 mm.).

"And look with pity on the blind." *vide Page 32.* *My Grandmother.* *London Published by W. Darton Jun May 21.1818.*

109a. frontispiece

A[18] (1[v] *Preface*, 13[v] *My Bible by William Jolly*, 15[r] *My Grandfather by Mr. Upton*, 16[v] *My Grandmother by Mr. Upton*, 18[r] *My Childhood by Mr. Upton*, 18[v] imprint *S. Ashworth, Printer, Rochdale*); 6 engravings (*My Grandmother* frontispiece, *My Father* and *My Grandfather*, *My Mother* and *My Bible* conjugate, *Kind Brother* tipped onto A7[r]), presumably printed from a single copperplate. Pp. 36. Letterpress and engraving on different paper. Original printed buff stiff wrappers, front cover: imprint *printed by William Darton, Jun. 58. Holborn Hill. Price Sixpence, with Plates. 1818*, back cover: ads. References: Moon *Elliott* 99 (but with address error on cover); Darton *Check-list* H416(1).

Provenance: *Grandmothers Gift to F. Gibbons Nov[r] 15th 1820* (inscr.). PML 83063. Gift: Elisabeth Ball.

‑§ 109b §‑

Filial Remembrancer. Selection of the much-admired poems, My Father, My Mother, My Brother, and My Sister; with the father's address to his children; in imitation of Cowper. The third edition. Banbury: printed and sold by J. G. Rusher: Sold also by W. Rusher and Son, Banbury; J. Rusher, Reading; and by A. K. Newman & Co. Simkin & Marshall, Evans & Son, Walker & Co. and Law & Whitaker, London; and most other Booksellers, [ca. 1820]. 12° (130 × 78 mm.).

π[2] < A[12] (π1·2 mounted as pastedowns, π1[v] wood-engraved frontispiece *My Brother*, A2[r] *Preface*, A12[v] imprint *Printed and Sold by J. G. Rusher, Bridge-St. Banbury*, π2[r] wood-engraved device of the Prince of Wales). Pp. 26 [2]. Original printed blue-gray wrappers, title and price (fourpence) on front cover, Rusher ads on back cover. References: De Freitas p. 108; Opie *Three Centuries*, 734.

PML 84966. Gift: Elisabeth Ball.

One of the earliest attempts at anthologizing "grateful tributes" seems to have been a musical compilation, *The Nursery Concert*. The others are unidentified. As noted in the introduction to this digression, however, Mary Belson Elliott was the author who brought both a generic title and a popularity to the anthologies. Her book first appeared in 1811 and contained seven poems by M. Belson. In the edition described here four poems have been added. These were previously published in *The Nursery Concert* and then later by William Darton in "the Rev. David Blair's" *First, or Mother's Catechism*, 21st edition (1813; Darton *Check-list* H1221), and in the 38th edition of that book (1821) these four are credited to a Mr. Lynch. The confusions surrounding this gentleman, who may also be W. R. Johnson, are discussed in Moon *Tabart* under several heads.

The *Filial Remembrancer* from the publisher of Banbury chapbooks (see chapter XIII) and an impressive conger of London firms, shows the fashion spreading even wider and the editorial procedures getting more difficult to follow. Ann Taylor's (copyrighted) "My Mother" is present, unacknowledged; four poems come from the "grateful tributes" in *The Nursery Concert*. The others are unidentified.

110. *reduced*

‑§ 110 §‑

The Grandmother. "A Grandam's name is little less in love / Than is the doting title of a Mother." Shakespeare. London: printed by E. Hemsted, 19, Great New Street, for the proprietor, 1808. 16° (121 × 115 mm.).

[1[2]] (1[r] letterpress title, 1[v]–2[v] blank); 6 numbered leaves of hand-colored etchings (each an illustration with 3-line rhyme), perhaps printed from a single plate, then divided for insertion between the conjugate title leaf and blank leaf. Stabbed, original printed buff wrappers (watermarked *Cobb's Patent*).

Provenance: J. Prueci? (sign.); Gumuchian & C[ie] (1930 cat., no. 2795). PML 81876. Gift: Elisabeth Ball.

The wittily chosen quotation from Shakespeare prefaces a grateful tribute to end all Grateful Tributes, except that this parody was published very near the beginning of the sequence and should have been taken as an awful warning of what would happen to the genre. The anonymous author also, as the illustration shows, had a dig at the animal rights movement of his day.

JOSEPH MACKENZIE (ca. 1760–ca. 1820)

As a printer and bookbinder, Mackenzie first appears in the records in the *Universal British Directory* for 1790 (Maxted) but was in business well before then. He seems to have had no standing with the Stationers Company. Like his neighbor in Fetter Lane, J. Drew (discussed above), he turned out little children's books to be sold through his own shop. Going by the titles advertised in the following item, he clearly aped the programs of the Newberys and John Marshall. (One critic, had she known about it, would certainly have disapproved of his *Tommy Trimmer's Historical Account of Beasts.*) Howe traces Mackenzie through the commercial directories down to 1820 when he is listed as a pocket-book maker at 7 Dean Street, Fetter Lane.

❧ 111 ❧

[CHARLES PERRAULT (1628–1703) and/or PIERRE PERRAULT DARMANCOUR (1678–1700)]. *Fairy Tales from Mother Goose. 1 Little Red Riding Hood. 2 Blue Beard. 3 The Fairy. 4 Cinderella, or the Little Glass Slipper 5 Reward of Virtue and Learning.* London: Printed by J. Mackenzie, No. 17, Fetter-Lane, Fleet-street, [ca. 1795]. Pris Two Pence. 32° (102 × 61 mm.).

[1³²] (1·32 mounted as pastedowns, 1ᵛ frontispiece *Here Mother Goose in Winter Night / The old and young she both delights*., 14 lacking, 29ᵛ *The Reward of Learning and Virtue* [probably by Joseph Mackenzie], 31ᵛ–32ʳ ads). Pp. 61, [3]. 13 wood engravings. Original gilt-blocked and dab-colored wrappers.

Provenance: *Harriot Tyler October 2 1797* (inscr.). PML 84698. Gift: Justin G. Schiller.

The four Perrault tales are reprinted more or less verbatim from the standard Samber/G.M. version; the childishly simple cuts are from another source, apart from the well-known Mother Goose

frontispiece. The final "fairy tale" is a crude bit of puffery by Mackenzie for the books advertised at the end. These include the chapbook romance *Palidor and Fidele*, a copy of which is described in the next chapter (entry 121) and which itself contains a catalogue of twenty-eight 6d., 3d., 2d. and penny books printed and sold by Mackenzie.

GEORGE THOMPSON (ca. 1758–ca. 1810)

In all probability George Thompson is the apprentice bound to William Morgan, copperplate printer, in 1773 and freed in 1780. (One of his fellow apprentices was Thomas Ross, who may well have been the founding father of the long-lived business chronicled by Iain Bain in the *Journal of the Printing Historical Society* No. 2 (1966), pp. 3–22.)

Thompson was running his own printing shop by 1782 and is recorded as being a map- and bookseller at Long Lane by 1786; he later appears to have added children's book publishing to his varied activities. It is likely that he printed as well as published the *Tabby Cat* (described below), as the Morgan Library possesses a wonderfully devised *First Fairing for Children* which he both printed and sold. This is an alphabet book, with each letter fitted into a well designed but primitively cut woodblock, picturing a variant to the rhyme of "A was an Archer" (here an Angler). The book retains its decorative blue paper covers (PML 84103).

111. fo. 6 recto, *enlarged*

112. *enlarged*

⤐ 112 ⟜

The Life, Adventures, and Vicissitudes of a Tabby Cat. London: Published by G. Thompson, No. 43, Long-Lane, West-Smithfield, 1798. Price six-pence. 12° (108 × 71 mm.).

A–F⁶ G⁴ H² (A1ᵛ *Frontispiece*, H1ᵛ *Poetical extracts, From Tommy Tagg, Esq.*). Pp. 84. 14 wood engravings, all oval within rectangular frames (frontispiece 68 × 54 mm., others 37 × 52 mm. each). Original dab-colored floral boards. Modern red morocco gilt. Reference: ESTC N033474.

Provenance: *Mary Burchell April 21ˢᵗ 1803* (inscr.); Charles Todd Owen (binding). PML 82182. Gift: Elisabeth Ball.

By the end of the eighteenth century animal autobiography was a substantial genre in children's literature, Dorothy Kilner's *Life and Perambulation of a Mouse* (entry 120) being perhaps the most notable example. One motive behind such writing was to encourage kindness to animals, but few can have gone about the job in so drastic a manner as the anonymous author of this *Tabby Cat*. Rescued by little Harriet from being drowned, the cat proceeds to tell her (in a dream) the harrowing story of its early life, the bloodthirsty details of which set some kind of benchmark by which later tales of animal cruelty, such as Anna Sewell's *Black Beauty*, may be measured.

Thompson has obviously given care to the production of the book—see previous page— not least in the nicely framed, simple, but appropriate wood engravings (although the artist could not bring himself, like Master Henry, to crop the cat's ears with a pair of scissors). Tommy Tagg's concluding poetical makeweights include Prior's lines on the squirrel, which had first appeared in a children's book in *A Christmass-Box* (entry 65).

VII
FRANCES LAETITIA EARLE: HER BOOKS

DETERMINING provenance should figure high among the working priorities of all antiquarians and collectors (did Queen Elizabeth really sleep in that bed? Did Brahms own that piano?). Books, with their hospitality to the written word, may bring us into touch with former owners with peculiar directness and intimacy (see, for instance, William Beckford's caustic notes on the flyleaves of his books, or the marginalia of Samuel Taylor Coleridge), and children's books may do so with a certain poignancy as well. Endpapers that carry the signatures or bookplates of the great and the good do not convey quite the same determined sense of ownership as the up-and-down-and-round-about scrawls of children laying claim to one of what may be a very few treasured possessions.

Despite the efforts of the practitioners of "L'Histoire du livre," historical surveys of popular forms of literature to a large extent have had to be confined to producers rather than consumers. This is equally true of children's books. Although in the general run of things childish inscriptions are not uncommon—they occur throughout this study and a variety of them are more fully discussed in chapter XX—juvenile readers are hard to identify. They have tended and tend to treat their literary possessions roughly. Childhood lasts only a short time and afterwards the books connected with it will generally be neglected, if not thrown away. Substantial survivals of individual children's libraries, which allow us a deeper insight into the market for publishers' wares of a given period, are therefore of the utmost rarity. One such survival is the eighteenth-century Ludford family collection, discussed in Brian Alderson's *The Ludford Box* (1989). Another is this collection belonging to Frances Laetitia Earle from about the same time. A fortunate habit of Miss Earle's was not merely to put her name in the books she owned, but also to write the date and the place of acquisition or ownership, usually Reading in the County of Berkshire; from this clue it has been possible to trace her family background with some precision.*

Born on 3 March 1777 at Sonning in Berkshire, where her father was renting the Manor House, Frances Laetitia was the eldest (?) child of Timothy Hare Earle (1737–1816), gentleman, formerly of Moor Place, Hertfordshire. In 1788 (the year most prominent in the formation of Frances Laetitia's library) he bought Swallowfield Park, near Reading, and here the family stayed for nearly forty years, living, so it is said, "in very grand style." There were four other children, Timothy (b. 1780), William (b. 1782) and two more daughters, Mary Ann and Elizabeth Dorothy (shades of the the Kilners! see entries 116 and 120), but only Timothy's career is fully known, curving up from the time when he inherited Swallowfield in 1816 to his becoming high sheriff of Berkshire in 1821, then down as the family fortunes declined. He sold Swallowfield in 1824 and moved to Wokingham, where he died unmarried in 1836. Frances Laetitia also seems to have remained unmarried, dying only in 1865, the year of the first appearance of *Alice's Adventures in Wonderland.*

Twenty-four of Frances Laetitia's volumes have so far been recorded, the fourteen described here plus two in the Ball Collection at Bloomington and eight in the Opie Collection at the Bodleian Library (noted at the appropriate chronological points) The dates and places noted in her inscriptions conform to what we know of her life between 1788 and 1790, if we read "Moore" in entries 113 and 117 as referring to Moor Place, with which the family may have had a continued connection after moving to Reading. (Bath and London are doubtless part of the grand life.) We do not know how she acquired her books, whether from shops or as gifts or hand-me-downs, but there are some oddities in both the selection of titles (the Kilner *Peg-Top* and *Mouse* for an eleven/twelve-year old?) and in their dates (several books had been in print in later editions for a number of years before Frances acquired earlier ones). She may well have marked her ownership some years after acquisition. Miss Earle was certainly something of a bibliophile, for not only did she inscribe her books, she also looked after them carefully and seems to have taken delight in embellishing them. The regularity and the care with which the pictures are colored suggest a nice blend of eagerness and taste. (Given the clustering of the books in such a short period there is of course a possibility that she acquired them simply through a desire to exercise her artistic talents.) We also do not know how long "the Earle books" remained in the family, but there are strong indications that a descendant disposed of them at the start of the twentieth century to the booksellers Simmons and Waters of Leamington, Warwickshire, who offered a number of them for sale in an undated catalogue; Sydney Roscoe consulted the Simmons and Waters catalogue for his Newbery bibliography, but we have not been able to trace a copy. Frances Laetitia's books, all of which were produced by publishers featured in the two preceding chapters, are here entered according to the dates of her inscriptions.

The Morgan Library also possesses at least four eighteenth-century English children's books with the contemporary ownership inscription of "Mary Brookes." No other clue is given to where or when she lived, and she will be difficult to identify, but a striking feature of her books is the repair work done to their spines with strips of what appears to be soft deerskin (three are described in chapter IX). In the Ball Collection at the Lilly Library, Indiana University, is a copy of the Sayer harlequinade *The Little Pretty Huswife* (1771), touchingly inscribed "Mary Brookes given me by Papa when I had the small pox."

* We are indebted to Dennis Butts, former chairman of the Children's Books History Society, for some helpful and prompt assistance in this regard.

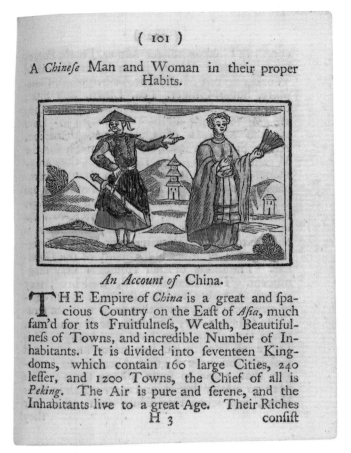

113. H3 recto, *enlarged*

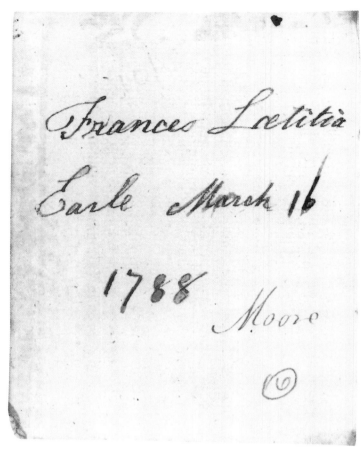

113. *enlarged*

◦§ 113 §◦

A Museum for Young Gentlemen and Ladies: or, a private tutor for little masters and misses. Containing a variety of useful subjects, and in particular, 1. Directions for reading with elegance and propriety . . . 2. Dying words and behaviour of great men . . . (Being a second volume to the Pretty Book for Children.). London: Printed for J. Hodges, on the Bridge; J. Newbery, in St. Paul's-Church Yard; and B. Collins, in Salisbury, [ca. 1750]. [Price One Shilling, neatly bound.]. 16° (108 × 82 mm.).

A⁴ (–4); B–O⁸ P⁸ (P8+1=A4). Pp. vi, 226. After quire C the paper stock changes (turned chainlines). 2 relief-cut diagrams, 25 relief-cut illustrations of various sizes (the first 16 colored by a child, presumably Frances Laetitia Earle). Original sheep-backed, gilt-blocked and dab-colored floral boards. References: ESTC N022004; Roscoe J253(1); Gottlieb 180.

Provenance: *Frances Laetitia / Earle March 16 / 1788 Moore* (colored inscr. on front pastedown). PML 83086. Gift: Elisabeth Ball.

This first edition of John Newbery's *Museum* is the most surprising of the Earle "survivals," coming to Frances some thirty-eight years after it was printed, and in fine condition too. Was it perhaps a book that her father had had as a child, and had he ever read it? The question is pertinent, because Newbery's "private tutor" includes the merry scatological ballad of "The Country Squire and

his Man John," which may have come as a shock to an eleven-year-old of genteel birth. For a censored copy of the third edition, see entry 378 in chapter XX.

N.B. The Opie Collection contains one book which should precede this entry: a copy of the Hawkins edition of *Felina* (probably the same printing as item 93 above). Frances Laetitia Earle has signed and dated this 1787 on its frontispiece. Two other acquisitions of hers are also dated March 16, 1788: the Ball-Lilly Library copy of *The Agreeable Storyteller* (printed for Joseph Hawkins, [1774?]), and the Opie copy of *Entertaining Memoirs of Little Personages, or moral amusements for young ladies* (printed for W. Tringham, [1785?]).

◦§ 114 §◦

The Pleasant and Instructive History of Old Goody Careful, and her two little scholars, Miss Charlotte Chearful and Miss Caroline Fearful. Now first printed from the original manuscript found in Goody Careful's cabinet of curiosities, after her death . . . London: Printed and Sold by Joseph Hawkins, Shire-Lane, Temple-Bar, [ca. 1775]. (Price only Two-Pence.). 32° (96 × 62 mm.).

A³² (1·32 mounted as pastedowns, 1ᵛ *Frontispiece. Goody Careful and her Scholars.*). Pp. 63, [1]. 23 cuts (including frontispiece) of varying size, all but three hand-colored by Frances Laetitia Earle. Original gilt-blocked and dab-colored floral wrappers. Reference: ESTC N038891.

Provenance: *Frances Laetitia Earle March / the 24 1788* (inscr. on frontispiece). PML 82307. Gift: Elisabeth Ball.

Joseph Hawkins should be grateful to Miss Earle for preserving one of his two-penny books in the near-pristine condition of this one. She may have done so because the story, once read, is unlikely to call for rereading. It was only devised as a framework into which the illustrations could be fitted. The reader's attention is drawn to almost each cut, with such directions as: "Here you may see him" and "Pray observe it.") The owner's coloring is the most attractive ingredient of the book.

114. *enlarged*

❧ 115 ❧

The Prettiest Book for Children; *being the history of the Enchanted Castle*; *situated in one of the Fortunate Isles, and governed by the giant Instruction. Written for the entertainment of little masters and misses, by Don Stephano Bunyano, under-secretary to the aforesaid giant.* London: Printed for E. Newbery, at the Corner of St. Paul's Church-Yard, [1784 ?]. 16° (103 × 69 mm.).

A⁸ (1ᵛ frontispiece portrait *Don Stephano Bunyano.*, 3ʳ *Preface*); B–H⁸ (H6ʳ ads). Pp. 122, [6]. 16 cuts (2 full-page including frontispiece, remainder slightly smaller than half-page), all but three hand-colored by Frances Laetitia Earle. Original gilt-blocked and dab-colored floral boards. References: ESTC N038939; Roscoe J48(2=3=5?).

115. frontispiece, *enlarged*

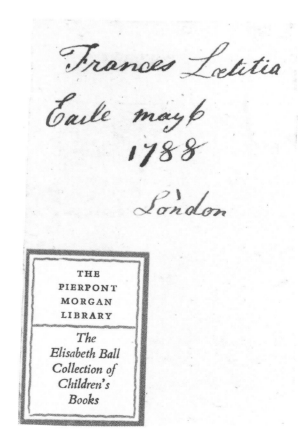

115.

Provenance: *Frances Laetitia / Earle May 6 / 1788 / London* (inscr. on front pastedown); Simmons and Waters, booksellers of Leamington (offered in their catalogue of ca. 1903). PML 81597. Gift: Elisabeth Ball.

Although this didactic compendium was put together after John Newbery's death, the first half—an instructional tour of the Giant's Castle—has many of the marks of his style of presentation (not least recommending Mr. Newbery's "pretty collection of little volumes, beautifully gilt" in preference to "idle stories" like *Tom Hickathrift* and *Jack the Giant-Killer*). The second half, however, deteriorates into a jumble of moral padding, with few illustrations, which Miss Earle clearly did not feel interested in coloring. Perhaps the most (unintentionally) entertaining part of the farrago is that moment in the retelling of the story of Theseus when Lady Charlotte remarks about the hero's escape with Ariadne: "but he soon despised her, my dears, (for that is the natural consequence of a young lady's going off with a man in such a manner)..."

❧ 116 ❧

[MARY ANN KILNER (1753–1831)]. *Memoirs of a Peg-Top. By the author of Adventures of a Pincushion* ... London: Printed and sold by John Marshall and Co. No. 4, Aldermary Church Yard, in Bow Lane, [ca. 1783]. 12° (117 × 78 mm.).

A–I[6] (A1 blank, A2[v] frontispiece). Pp. 108. 28 wood engravings (frontispiece 83 × 57 mm., remainder 46 × 60 mm. each), all but one hand-colored by Frances Laetitia Earle, frontispiece (see p. 88) and title within type-ornament border. Original gilt-blocked and dab-colored floral boards. Reference: ESTC N035178.

Provenance: *Frances Laetitia / Earle May 6 1788 / London* (inscription on front pastedown). PML 82819. Gift: Elisabeth Ball.

With the two volumes of *The Life and Perambulation of a Mouse* (entry 120) this book serves to give representation in our study of John Marshall's promoting the work of Dorothy Kilner and her sister-in-law, Mary Ann. (A third member of the family, Elizabeth, figures as "S.W." at entry 197.) Few copies of their books can have been so affectionately treated as Frances Laetitia's colored *Peg-Top*. Marshall published another 12° edition about the same time (A–I[6] K[2]: PML 82817–8), which probably preceded the edition owned by Miss Earle.

N.B. Two further books dated by Frances Laetitia Earle on May 8, 1788 are in the Opie Collection: a companion "for young gentlemen" to the Tringham *Entertaining Memoirs* noted above in entry 113, and *Mother Bunch's Fairy Tales*, published by Elizabeth Newbery in 1784.

❧ 117 ❧

The History of Harlequin and Columbine, shewing the wonderful tricks and metamorphoses performed by the fancyful hero in his motley jacket, to gain his fair mistress ... [London:] Printed for H. Turpin, Bookseller, No. 104, St.

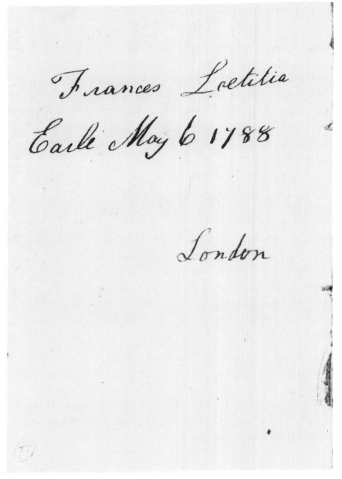

116. *enlarged*

John's-Street, West-Smithfield, [ca. 1785]. [Price Six-Pence, Bound and Gilt.]. 12° (109 × 73 mm.).

A–I[6] (A1[v] *Frontispiece*—see p. 88, I3[r] ads, I6[v] *Where may be had Money for any Library, or parcel of Books, &c.*). Pp. 99, [9]. 23 cuts (65 × 54 mm. and smaller), all but one hand-colored by Frances Laetitia Earle. Original gilt-blocked and dab-colored floral boards. Reference: ESTC N032835.

Provenance: *Frances Laetitia / Earle April* [deleted] *May 6 / 1788 / Moore* (inscr. on front pastedown—see overleaf). PML 81814. Gift: Elisabeth Ball.

From this point on, Frances Laetitia's engagement with her books lessens. Fewer pictures are colored, except in *The Easter Gift*, for which we have no date of acquisition, and some uncertainty prevails over her treatment of *The Life and Perambulation of a Mouse* (see note to entry 120). Nevertheless, most of these remaining books have been preserved in fine condition, with the decorated paper covers still sound and two nice examples of pictorial bindings printed in sanguine. Two volumes are of especial rarity: the above *History of Harlequin*, a fusty succession of anecdotes and ditties, and J. Mackenzie's *Palidor and Fidele*, a generously printed redaction of a quasi-romance whose wanton use of stock-blocks is mitigated by the printer's liking for setting them within borders of fleurons (see the illustration for entry 121).

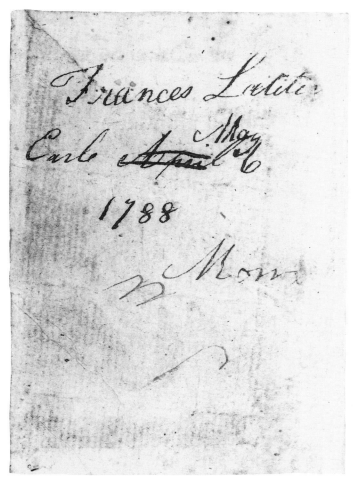

117. *enlarged*

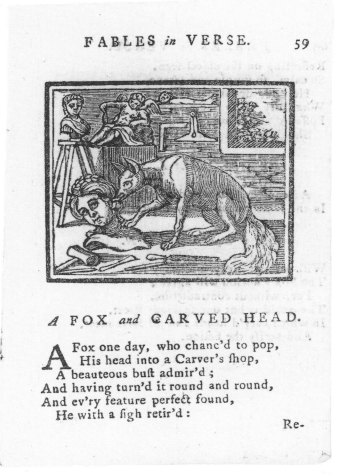

FABLES *in* VERSE. 59

A FOX *and* CARVED HEAD.

A Fox one day, who chanc'd to pop,
His head into a Carver's shop,
A beauteous buft admir'd ;
And having turn'd it round and round,
And ev'ry feature perfect found,
He with a figh retir'd :

Re-

Above: **118.** E6 recto, *enlarged*   *Below:* **118.** *enlarged*

❧ **118** ❧

*Fables in Verse, for the improvement of the young and the old;
by Abraham Aesop, Esq. To which are added, fables in verse
and prose; with the conversation of birds and beasts, at their
several meetings, routs, and assemblies; by Woglog the great
giant. Illustrated with a variety of curious cuts, by the best
masters. And with an account of the lives of the authors, by
their old friend Mr. Newbery . . .* London: Printed for the
Booksellers of all Nations, and sold at Number 65, in St.
Paul's Church-yard [i.e. Thomas Carnan], 1783. [Price 6d.
bound.]. 12° (113 × 76 mm.).

A–M⁶ (E2·5 lacking, M3ᵛ ads). Pp. 138, [6]. 36 half-page wood
engravings (49 × 57 mm.) including 16 hand-colored by Frances
Laetitia Earle. Original buff pictorial boards, four cuts illustrating
fables, printed in red: *The Stag looking into the Water* and *The
Eagle and the Crow* on back cover, *The Husbandman and the
Stork* and *The Lion and other Beasts in Council* on front cover (see
overleaf) (from a series of blocks cut and signed by J. Bell, apparently after Elisha Kirkall's illustrations for Croxall's Aesop of
1722). References: ESTC T084722; Roscoe J7A(10).

Provenance: *Francis l Earle 1788 / Reading* (inscription on verso
of front free endpaper). PML 83731. Gift: Elisabeth Ball.

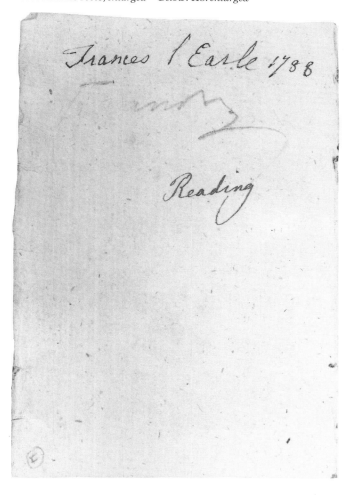

116. frontispiece, *enlarged*

FRONTISPIECE.

Accept this Gift, my Son, its Magic Power,
Shall still befriend you in each evil Hour;
Wave it around, and instantly you'll find,
You'll travel swifter than the fleeting Wind;
Thro' this with Speed, you'll every Wish
obtain,
And to the Summit of Ambition gain.

117. *enlarged*

118. front cover,
enlarged

ᵉᔤ **119** ᔤᵉ

Frontispiece

Lovelace forces Clarissa to leave her Fa- thers House

SAMUEL RICHARDSON (1689–1761). *Clarissa; or the history of a young lady. Comprehending the most important concerns of private life. Abridged from the works of Samuel Richardson, Esq. author of Pamela, and Sir Charles Grandison. A new edition.* London: Printed for E. Newbery, at the Corner of St. Paul's Church-Yard, [not after 1788]. 12° (111 × 71 mm.).

A–P⁶ (P5ʳ ads); six engraved illustrations printed from one copperplate on a single sheet divided for insertion, all but the last colored by Frances Laetitia Earle. Pp. 176, [4]. Original gilt-blocked and colored floral boards. References: ESTC N027171; Roscoe J315(4); Gottlieb 185.

Provenance: *Frances Leatitia / Earle 1788 / Reading* [erased] (inscr. on verso of front free endpaper). PML 85586. Gift: Elisabeth Ball.

N.B. The Opie Collection has two further books dated simply 1788 by Frances Laetitia Earle: *The Twelfth-Day-Gift* (printed by T. Carnan, 1788), and volume IX of W. Domville's "Lilliputian Library," *Lilliputius Gulliver* (n.d.). Here she gives Wargrave as the place of acquisition.

Above: **119.** engraving inserted opposite K1ᵛ, *enlarged   Below:* **119.** *enlarged*

74   PERAMBULATION *of a* MOUSE.
Frugal's ducks, for the sake of seeing them waddle; and then, when they got to the pond, he sent his dog in after them, to bark and frighten them out of their wits.

And as I came by, nothing would serve him but throwing a great dab of mud all over the sleeve of my coat. So I said, Why, Master *Sam*, you need not have done that, I did nothing to offend you, and however amusing you may think it to insult poor people, I assure you, it is very wicked, and what

120. vol. I G1 verso, *enlarged*

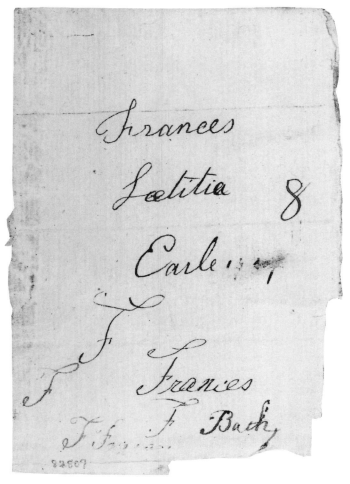

120. vol. I, *enlarged*

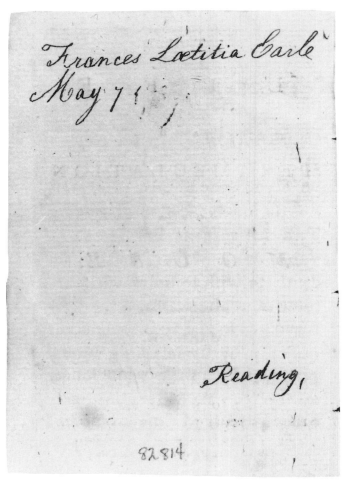

120. vol. II, *enlarged*

◦§ 120 ◊◦

[DOROTHY KILNER (1755–1836)]. *The Life and Perambulation of a Mouse* [*vol. II*]. London: Printed and sold by John Marshall and Co. No. 4, Aldermary Church-Yard, in Bow Lane, [not before 1783–4]. [Price Six Pence Bound and Gilt.]. Two volumes. 12° (112 × 74 mm.).

Vol. I: A⁶ (1 blank mounted as pastedown, 2ᵛ *Frontispiece*, 3·4 and 6 lacking) B–I⁶ K² (B1ᵛ end of the introduction, K2 blank mounted as pastedown). Pp. 110, [2]. 26 wood engravings (frontispiece full-page, remainder half-page), all but two hand-colored by Frances Laetitia Earle. Original gilt-blocked and dab-colored floral boards. Vol. II: A–H⁶ I⁴ (A1 and I4 mounted as pastedowns, A1ᵛ *Frontispiece*, A3ʳ *Dedication. To Master ****** signed M.P., I3ʳ ads). Pp. 99, [5]. 22 wood engravings (frontispiece full-page, remainder half-page), none colored. Original gilt-blocked and dab-colored floral boards.

Provenance: vol. I: *Frances / Laetitia / 8 / Earle 1789* [date erased] / *F / F Frances / F Bath / F Frances* (inscr. on pastedown); vol. II: *Frances Laetitia Earle / May 7 1789* [year-date erased] / *Reading.* (inscr. on verso of title). PML 82809 (vol. I), 82814 (vol. II). Gift: Elisabeth Ball.

These are the most problematic volumes in the Earle Collection. The inscriptions are indecisive, with dates erased: volume I (see

previous page) was acquired (or read) at Bath, and has lost its title page, while volume II has the Reading location. Furthermore, the hand-coloring is desultory in places in the first volume; the second has no coloring at all. This may be the second edition of volume I and the first edition of volume II; another edition by Marshall of volume I, with a separate quire for all of the preliminary matter, is probably the first (PML 85514, inscribed by Mary Brookes).

N.B. Between this entry and the next belongs the Ball-Lilly Library copy of "Solomon Sobersides," *Christmas Tales*, John Marshall n.d., inscribed *Miss Fanny Earle London June 7 1789*.

◦§ 121 ◊◦

The Entertaining History of Palidor and Fidele: written for the amusement and instruction of youth. Adorned with curious cuts. London: Printed and Sold by J. Mackenzie, No. 198, Upper Thames Street, [not after September 1789]. (Price Six Pence.). 12° (110 × 69 mm.).

A–E¹² (A1 and E12 blank mounted as pastedowns, A2ᵛ frontispiece *Palidor and Fidele taking their leave of each other when the king and queen enters the room.*, E9ʳ ads, E10ʳ *N.B. Good Allowance to those that Buy a Quantity to sell again.*, E11 blank). Pp. 112, [8]. 43 cuts (including frontispiece) of various sizes, type-

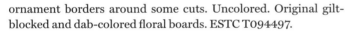

121. *enlarged*

121. frontispiece, *enlarged*

ornament borders around some cuts. Uncolored. Original gilt-blocked and dab-colored floral boards. ESTC T094497.

Provenance: Frances Laetitia Earle (inscr. on pastedown: *1789* [last numeral changed from 8] *September / London*). PML 85555. Gift: Elisabeth Ball.

N.B. The Opie Collection has one book dated simply "1789 Reading" by Frances Laetitia Earle: *Six Pennyworth of Wit; or, little stories for little folks of all denominations* (printed for T. Carnan, [1780?]).

❧ 122 ❧

[RICHARD JOHNSON (1733/4–93)]. *The Adventures of a Bee, who invites all his little friends to sip his honey, and avoid his sting. Embellished with cuts.* London: Printed for F. Power, (Grandson to the late Mr. J. Newbery) and Co. No. 65, near the Bar, St. Paul's Church-Yard, 1790. [Price Four Pence.]. 24° (96 × 61 mm.).

A⁸ (+ A1 title, A2ʳ *To the little masters and misses of Great Britain*) B–F⁸ (F7ᵛ ads). Pp. [4], 92. 12 wood engravings (34 × 49 mm.), all but four hand-colored by Frances Laetitia Earle. Original

gilt-blocked and dab-colored floral boards. References: ESTC N016199; Roscoe J2.

Provenance: *Frances. Laetitia. / Earle. / January 13 1790 / Reading* (inscr. on recto of front free endpaper). PML 81560. Gift: Elisabeth Ball.

First edition. See illustrations overleaf.

❧ 123 ❧

[RICHARD JOHNSON (1733/4–93)]. *The Youthful Jester; or, repository of wit and innocent amusement. Containing, moral and humourous tales, merry jests, laughable anecdotes, and smart repartees. The whole being as innocent as it is entertaining. Embellished with cuts.* London: Printed for E. Newbery, the Corner of St. Paul's Church-Yard, [late 1789 or early 1790]. [Price Six-Pence.]. 16° (111 × 75 mm.).

A–H⁸ (A1ᵛ frontispiece, A3ʳ dedication signed *Little Momus*, quires E and F reversed). Pp. [8], 120. 13 wood engravings (frontispiece full-page, remainder half-page), none colored. Original gilt-blocked and dab-colored floral boards. References: Roscoe J395(1); Muir NBL 922; Osborne I, 271.

(2)

city, will prove equally amuſing
and inſtructive to you. See how
hard he and all his friends and relations are at work for you.

A hive of Bees may be compared
to a large family of little folks, in
which ſome are idle and indolent,
others lively and active; ſome procure the honey with great labour,
while others feed upon it in eaſe
and

Above: 122. A3 verso, *enlarged*   *Below*: 123. D6 recto

Frances Laetitia
Earle
January 13 1790

Reading

Above: 122. *enlarged*   *Below*: 123.

THE YOUTHFUL JESTER.   51

banter him, and one of them told the
fellow he would prove him to be a horſe
or an aſs. " Well, (ſaid the hoſtler)
and I can prove your ſaddle to be a mule."
—" A mule ! (cried one of them) how
can that be ?"—" Becauſe (replied the
hoſtler) it is ſometimes between a horſe
and an aſs." The two ſcholars rode a-
way without ſaying a word more.
    A dignified clergyman, going down to
his living to ſpend the ſummer, met near
his houſe, as you here ſee, a comical old

                                    chimney

March 25. 1790
reading.

125. binding, *enlarged*

Provenance: Frances Laetitia Earle (inscr. on verso of front free endpaper: *March 25. 1790 / reading.*). PML 85660. Gift: Elisabeth Ball.

First edition.

❧ 124 ❧

[STEPHEN JONES (1763–1827)]. *The Life and Adventures of a Fly. Supposed to have been written by himself. Illustrated with cuts.* London: Printed for E. Newbery, At the Corner of St. Paul's Church-yard, [ca. 1788]. [Price 6d.]. 16° (108 × 71 mm.).

A–H⁸ (A1ᵛ frontispiece signed JBwk, A3ʳ *Contents*, A5ʳ dedication, A6ʳ–B1ᵛ *Preface* signed S.J., H5ᵛ–8ᵛ ads including dissected maps). Pp. 121, [7]. 12 wood engravings by John Bewick (frontispiece 95 × 58 mm., remainder circular within square frames 49 × 51 mm.). Uncolored. Original gilt-blocked and dab-colored floral boards. References: ESTC T117748; Roscoe J190(3); Hugo 4109; Tattersfield JB36.

Provenance: *Frances L. Earle / March 25. 1790 / Reading.* (inscr. on front pastedown); Simmons and Waters, booksellers of

Leamington (offered in their catalogue of ca. 1903). PML 82151. Gift: Elisabeth Ball

Perhaps the first edition. See illustrations overleaf.

❧ 125 ❧

The Easter-Gift; or, the way to be very good. A book very much wanted, and which ought to be read by the parents as well -as children . . . London: Printed for T. Carnan, Successor to Mr. J. Newbery, in St. Paul's Church-Yard, 1785. [Price Two-Pence bound.]. 32° (97 × 63 mm.).

[1³²] signed A–D⁸ (1·32 mounted as pastedowns, 1ᵛ frontispiece *The Lady of the Red Knot* and verse signed T. Tagg, 30ʳ *The books usually read by Master Billy and Miss Kitty are these . . .*, 32ʳ illustration *The Gentleman of the Red Ribband* and verse signed Woglog). Pp. 59, [5]. 19 cuts (about 32 × 40 mm. each), all colored by Frances Laetitia Earle. Original buff pictorial wrappers printed in red, different typographical border on each cover surrounding a pair of unidentified cuts (about 47 × 34 mm.). References: ESTC N028546; Roscoe J97(4).

Provenance: *Frances / Laetitia / Earle* (inscr. on title); Simmons

THE *Frances Laetitia Earle*

EASTER-GIFT

OR,

The WAY to be VERY GOOD.

A Book very much wanted, and which
ought to be read by the *Parents* as
well as *Children*:

For in it they may chance to find.
Something to mend the Heart and Mind.
                                    WOGLOG.

Adorned with CUTS.

LONDON:

Printed for T. CARNAN, Suc-
ceffor to Mr. J. Newbery, in St.
Paul's Church-Yard. 1785.
[Price TWO-PENCE bound.]

124. frontispiece, *enlarged*

124. *enlarged*

THE *Frances Laetitia Earle*

EASTER-GIFT

OR,

The WAY to be VERY GOOD.

A Book very much wanted, and which
ought to be read by the *Parents* as
well as *Children*:

For in it they may chance to find.
Something to mend the Heart and Mind.
                                    WOGLOG.

Adorned with CUTS.

LONDON:

Printed for T. CARNAN, Suc-
ceffor to Mr. J. Newbery, in St.
Paul's Church-Yard. 1785.
[Price TWO-PENCE bound.]

and Waters, booksellers of Leamington (offered in their catalogue of ca. 1903). PML 83060. Gift: Elisabeth Ball.

Although placed last in the sequence (because the inscription is undated), *The Easter Gift* has contents and coloring of a kind which suggests that it was an early rather than a later acquisition.

N.B. The Opie Collection has one other book inscribed by Frances Laetitia Earle with the location "Reading" but without a date: *The Polite Academy; or school of behaviour for young gentlemen and ladies* (printed for R. Baldwin, and B. C. Collins, Salisbury, 1786).

125. fo. 2 recto, *enlarged*

VIII

RIVALS AND IMITATORS,
THE PROVINCES

Many changes in the pattern of English life during the eighteenth century were to affect the making and distribution of books: the growth of population and the rise of the mercantile classes, improvements in communications, technological change and, more specifically, the gradual freeing of the book trade from the centralized control of government and, internally, of its regulatory body, the Stationers Company.

These factors particularly encouraged entrepreneurial activity by printers and booksellers in provincial centers, and as the eighteenth century progressed more and more towns began to show some activity in book production, often allied to the printing of local newspapers. Books which commanded a sure sale tended to have regional interest: guidebooks, topographies, local histories, directories, etc., but where catchment areas were large enough booksellers might also engage in more general publishing. An obvious field of development was popular literature: cheap editions of classic titles, chapbooks, and what Merridew of Coventry called "small Libraries for Youth." Such publications could be produced with limited capital resources and fitted into the established distribution channels of the street and market traders and the "running stationers."

The following selection of provincial books aims to show a cross section of the juvenile output of local printers and booksellers towards the end of the eighteenth century. It is arranged by town, chronologically according to the emergence of a children's book trade, even though the earliest publications of the booksellers included did not in each case relate to children's literature. The index of publishers and printers contains references to other places where English children's books were published, notably those covered in chapters XII, XIII, XIV, and XIX.

YORK: Spence, Wilson

The Spence and Wilson firms had between them an existence in York of more than sixty years as printers, publishers and booksellers, but their varying partnerships remain to be explored. A T. Spence and a T. Wilson were both trading in the city in the 1750s, and the families came together as Wilson & Spence in the late 1780s, soon to be joined by Joseph Mawman. (He left for London in 1801, where he took over the famous bookselling business in the Poultry owned by Charles Dilly.) T. Wilson and R. Spence continued in York, with the firm eventually evolving into Thomas Wilson & Sons before fading away in the late 1830s. R. Spence was also associated with Wilson's traveler, Richard Burdekin, when the latter set up his own business in 1813.

During this period these various partnerships were very active in the north of England, publishing on their own or in association with other provincial colleagues, especially Mozley of Gainsborough (see below). They also forged links with the London trade

(hence Mawman's departure?), although the joint imprint that they used "for A. Millar, W. Law, & R. Cater" looks like a more or less plausible invention equivalent to Mozley's "Osborne and Griffin" (see entry 145b). The "Wilson group" was responsible for putting out many children's books in the Newbery style, and its list was greatly enhanced towards the turn of the century when the Bewick blocks (discussed in chapter IX) were purchased from Hall and Elliot of Newcastle.

❧ 126 ❧

Fairy Tales, pleasing and profitable for all little gentlemen and ladies. York: Sold by R. Spence, Bookseller in High-Ousegate, [not after 1788]. (Price One Penny.). Half-sheet 32° (100 × 60 mm.), imposed for work-and-turn.

[1¹⁶] (1ʳ front cover: wood engraving of a maritime scene, 1ᵛ alphabet and vowels, 3ʳ *The Story of Princess Frutilla*, 7ʳ *The Story of Finetta*, 16ʳ ads, 16ᵛ back cover: another maritime scene). Pp. 30, [2]. 9 cuts (*The Giant's Wife*—see overleaf—and *The Giant* full-page, remainder smaller). First bifolium serves as covers, otherwise unbound as issued. Reference: ESTC N028584.

Provenance: *Sarah Cooke Swinton 1788* (inscr.); A.S. Faber (sign.); Gumuchian & Cie (1930 cat., no. 2464). PML 82418. Gift: Elisabeth Ball.

Whether this little half-sheet production should be regarded as a chapbook or not is a moot point, but it certainly employed the lackadaisical editorial methods of the chapbook industry. The stories have been taken from Mme d'Aulnoy—probably the Newbery "Mother Bunch" version—and have been edited down and furnished with stock blocks to make up a self-contained booklet. Carelessness is especially evident in the first story, which can have made little sense to contemporary readers since it is really part of "The White Cat" and is here included out of context.

The choice of these two stories by the publisher nonetheless points to ways in which certain fairy-tale themes, now associated with the Brothers Grimm, became popular long before *Kinder- und Hausmärchen* appeared. "Frutilla" bears a considerable likeness to "Rapunzel" and (as the Opies noted in *Classic Fairy Tales*) "Finetta" is, in essence, "Hansel and Gretel."

❧ 127 ❧

Picture Alphabet; designed for the instruction and amusement of all the little gentry in the kingdom. Adorned with

126. fo. 11 verso

forty-nine cuts. York: printed by Thomas Wilson and Son, High-Ousegate, 1812. (Price one penny.). 48° (86 × 56 mm.).

A¹⁶ (1ᵛ frontispiece *Do not, unthinking youth, too soon engage, In all the giddy vices of the ages!* . . . , 15ᵛ imprint *From the Office of Thomas Wilson and Son, High-Ousegate, York.*, 16ʳ ads, 16ᵛ blank). Pp. [29, 3]. Laid paper. Wood-engraved frontispiece (portrait of a youth), 24 wood-engraved capital letters (18 mm. square) and 24 wood engravings (20 × 29 mm.) illustrating the alphabet. Original printed gray wrappers, wood engraving of a book on front cover *In useful learning pray employ your time* . . . , wood engraving of a monkey on back cover *The Ape is full of mimickry and art* . . . , both blocks copied from cuts first seen in Newbery's *Food for the Mind*. Modern brown morocco gilt.

Provenance: Charles Todd Owen (binding). PML 81393. Gift: Elisabeth Ball.

The covers, the frontispiece, and the blocks for this unusual alphabet all bespeak an eighteenth-century origin. As one of the Wilson firm's later publications, it provides a good example of the way in which "old-fashioned" styles coexisted with the new and more colorful "modern" publishing discussed in chapter XII.

127. A8 verso, *enlarged*

COVENTRY: Luckman, Suffield, Merridew

Thomas Luckman was apprenticed to the printer James Jopson in Coventry in 1744 and presumably set up on his own in the early 1750s. He had a variegated career, now attempting to establish newspapers, now publishing religious works (including some for young people), and eventually giving up printing in 1771, only to resume again nine years later. He was elected mayor of Coventry in 1782 and died in 1784, when his widow Mary apparently took over the business. She developed quite a line in children's books, relying heavily on London models, which was maintained when she joined with the bookseller William Suffield about 1798.

The firm of Nathaniel Merridew (1763–1823) was a separate, competing enterprise, coming into being when Merridew completed his apprenticeship in 1784. He appears to have remained a working printer up to the time of his death, and, like Thomas Luckman, he was elected mayor of his city in 1822.

❧ 128 ❧

[WILLIAM COWPER (1731–1800)]. *The Diverting History of John Gilpin: as related by the late Mr. Henderson. Shewing how he went farther than he intended and came home safe at last.* Coventry: Printed and Sold by M. Luckman, and by all other Booksellers, [ca. 1790]. 24° (86 × 77 mm.).

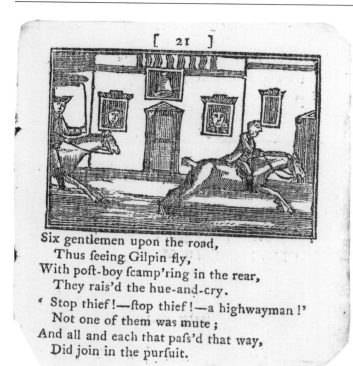

[21]

Six gentlemen upon the road,
 Thus feeing Gilpin fly,
With poft-boy fcamp'ring in the rear,
 They rais'd the hue-and-cry.
' Stop thief!—ftop thief!—a highwayman !'
 Not one of them was mute ;
And all and each that pafs'd that way,
 Did join in the purfuit.

[A¹²] (1·12 mounted as pastedowns, 1ᵛ frontispiece *Gilpin Draper*, 12ʳ ads). Pp. 22, [2]. 4 wood engravings (frontispiece 69 × 65 mm., others 44/48 × 63 mm.). Original gilt-blocked greenish wrappers.

PML 84628. Purchase: Ball Fund.

"John Gilpin" first appeared anonymously in the *Public Advertiser* on 14 November 1782. A few months later the actor John Henderson introduced it in a program of readings at Freemasons' Hall, and the ballad (still anonymous) took off like a skyrocket. Chapbook and broadside editions soon followed in great numbers. Many of these were published for a general readership, and at the moment it is possible to argue that Mary Luckman's production is not only among the earliest provincial editions of the poem but also the first that appeared as part of a "children's list." (The publishing date must be conjectural. Mary Luckman was in business by 1784 and Henderson died in 1785, but the list of twenty children's books on p.[23] "printed and sold by M. Luckman" indicates that she had been trading for some time, or was advertising as hers books published by her husband.) This printing of the ballad is not listed by Norma Russell in her *Bibliography of William Cowper* (1963) although she there notes a *Young Gentleman and Lady's Poetical Preceptor* published by Luckman ca. 1794 which includes other Cowper material. She also

Above: **128.** A11 recto, *enlarged*   *Below*: **129.** A11ᵛ–12ʳ, *enlarged*

(22)

O.

———

Mr. O'Cypher, I pray,

What have you to fay ?

You ftand for Nothing,

And may go away.

(23)

ON

Aerial Caftle-Building.

He dreams of riches, grandeur and a crown,
He wakes and finds himself a fimple clown.

ALNASCHAR was a very idle Fellow, that never would fet his Hand to any Bufinefs during his Father's

describes a popular edition of *John Gilpin* printed in London for W. Lane (1785–6) whose title is exactly replicated by Luckman. The earliest provincial edition recorded by Russell is a Bury printing "not before 1789."

❧ 129 ❧

A Visit to those Respectable Ladies and Gentlemen, called the Twenty-four Great Letters; who all reside at a large house, called Alphabet-Hall: Wherein the strictest attention to politeness and good-breeding is constantly paid. Also a short conversation between ten comical figures: To which are added, virtuous maxims of a good child. Coventry: printed and sold by Luckman and Suffield, [ca. 1799]. [Price One Penny.]. Half-sheet 32° (99 × 62 mm.).

A[16] (1·16 mounted as pastedowns, 1[v] frontispiece, 3[r] *Alphabet Hall*, 8[v] *To the Reader*, 9[v] comical figures, 12[r] *On Aerial Castle-Building*, 15[r] *Maxims*). Pp. 31, [1]. Laid paper. Type partly leaded. 18 wood engravings (frontispiece full-page, remainder half-page). Original gilt-blocked orange wrappers.

Provenance: Andrew W. Tuer (pencil note). PML 81475. Gift: Elisabeth Ball.

Although the "respectable ladies and gentlemen" and their rhyme have been imported from John Newbery's *Little Pretty Pocket-Book* (entry 8), most of the wood engravings for the rhyme—and the rest of the book—may well be local inventions. It would be nice to think that the whole compendium was the brainchild of Mary Luckman, who advertised the book in *John Gilpin* (entry 128). At some stage, presumably after the title was copied, a decision was made to increase the "Newbery alphabet" by adding the letter *J*, so Alphabet Hall here contains twenty-five, not twenty-four, residents. (See illustration on previous page.)

❧ 130 ❧

The History of Ali Baba, or the forty thieves destroyed by a slave. Coventry: Printed and Sold by N. Merridew, [not before 1801 (apparent watermark-date)]. [Price Six-pence.]. 18° (112 × 75 mm.).

A–F[12·6] (A1[v] frontispiece, F2[r]–6[r] *Friendship. A Tale*, F6[r] imprint *Merridew, Printer, Coventry*). Pp. 107, [1]. Laid paper. Wood-engraved frontispiece and pictorial title vignette; 10 other wood engravings (oval illustrations within rectangular frames) to *Ali Baba*, each surrounded by a type-ornament border; 1 wood engraving to *Friendship*. Original blue boards, wood engravings and type-ornament border on sides. Reference: ESTC N028577.

Provenance: *Sarah Comberbach. The Gift of Mrs. Bass.* (nineteenth-century inscr.); Gumuchian & C[ie] (1930 cat., no. 304). PML 85551. Gift: Elisabeth Ball.

This is one of the children's books advertised by Merridew as forming "a small Library for Youth" (advertisement in another of his "Arabian Nights" titles, *The Fisherman*, PML 83061). As a ploy to sell groups of books the idea was a good one, especially if the other titles provided as good a sixpenny worth as this. The tale is sensibly abridged and attractively bound and illustrated, and even

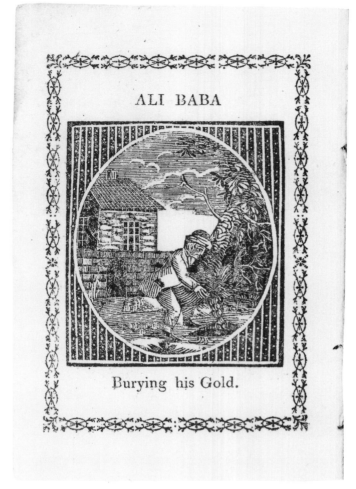

130. A8 verso, *enlarged*

the fable "Friendship" is not too weightily didactic. Other titles in the "Library" were Burder's *Early Piety*, Watts's *Songs*, *History of Joseph*, Quarll's *English Hermit*, *Robinson Crusoe*, *Prince Lee Boo*, and *Goody Two-Shoes*.

NEWCASTLE UPON TYNE:
Charnley, Saint, Slack, Hodgson, Beilby, Bewick

Like York, Newcastle was a city very prominent in the northern book trade during the eighteenth century and had its own Stationers' Company among the city guilds. It was a major center for the production of chapbooks, song sheets, and other popular printing, including children's books. Foremost among the publishers of these was the bookseller-printer Thomas Saint (1738–88), who was admitted to the Stationers' Company in 1761 and soon after became a partner of his employer John White, a notable printer of chapbooks and founder of the *Newcastle Courant*. After White's death in 1769 Saint continued the business, being the first to draw on the artistic skills of Thomas Bewick, who had been apprenticed to the engraver Ralph Beilby in 1767. Saint employed Bewick to cut blocks for a number of children's books in the early part of his career, many of which were pirated from London publishers, usually the Newbery firms, and now finding themselves more happily illustrated. An example is included in a late York printing in chapter IX (entry 146b). Later, by commissioning the larger fable books (see entry 132), he helped the prolific wood engraver on the road to fame.

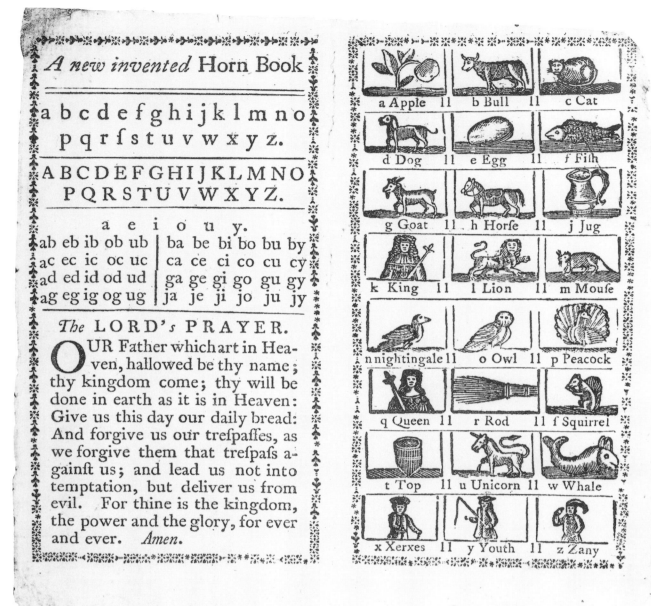

131.
enlarged

ᵈᵍ 131 ᵍᵉ

A new invented Horn Book. [Newcastle?, 1769]. Broadside, one-sixth (?) of a sheet (145 × 145 mm.).

The hornbook can be folded in half to form a two-leaf battledore, the left page containing the alphabet, vowels, and the Lord's Prayer, the right page an alphabet illustrated with twenty-four small wood engravings (about 11 × 18 mm. each) by Thomas Bewick. Type-ornament border around both pages. Roman and italic type. This copy was apparently never mounted for use. References: Hugo 2; Johnson 12.

PML 68164. Purchase: Ball Fund.

Our inclusion of this battledore in the catalogue was, on the strength of information in Hugo, to show some of Thomas Bewick's early work as a woodcutter. As is often the case in popular lore, however, wishful thinking supersedes hard evidence, and there is no conclusive reason to believe that the *New Invented*

Horn Book is his work or even that it was printed in Newcastle. What can be said is that the Beilby ledgers record the cutting of twenty-four alphabet pictures in 1769 but when they were used cannot be certainly ascertained.

The *New Invented Horn Book* is nonetheless a good example of the exploitation of the pictorial "grid" that had first appeared in the Collins/Newbery *Royal Battledore*, but the copying is so elementary that Thomas Bewick might well be happy not to be associated with it.

ᵈᵍ 132 ᵍᵉ

AESOP (early 6th century B.C.). *Select Fables, in three parts. Part I. Fables extracted from Dodsley's. Part II. Fables with reflections, in prose and verse. Part III. Fables in verse. To which are prefixed, the life of Aesop; and an essay upon Fable. A new edition, improved* . . . Newcastle: Printed by and for T. Saint, 1784. 12° (172 × 96 mm.).

(17)

no track behind them ; waſte the prime of their
days in deliberating what they ſhall do ; and
bring them to a period, without coming to any
determination.

An indolent young man, being aſked why he lay
in bed ſo long, jocoſely and careleſsly anſwered
———Every morning of my life I am hearing
cauſes. I have two fine girls, their names are
Induſtry and Sloth, cloſe at my bed-ſide, as
ſoon as ever I awake, preſſing their different
ſuits. One intreats me to get up, the other
perſuades me to lie ſtill : and then they alter-
nately give me various reaſons, why I ſhould riſe,
and why I ſhould not. This detains me ſo long,
as it is the duty of an impartial judge to hear
all that can be ſaid on either ſide, that before
the pleadings are over, it is time to go to
dinner.

B 3   F A-

132. B3 recto, *reduced*

(153)

F A B L E   XXXVII.

The Fox *and the* Ape.

ONCE upon a time, the beaſts were ſo void
of reaſon as to chooſe an Ape for their
King. He had danced, and diverted them with
playing antic tricks, and truly nothing would
ſerve, but they muſt anoint him their ſovereign.
Accordingly crowned he was, and affected to
look very wiſe and politic. But the Fox, vexed
at his heart to ſee his fellow brutes act ſo fooliſh-
ly, was reſolved the firſt opportunity, to convince
them of their ſorry choice, and puniſh their
jackanapes of a king for his preſumption. Soon
after, ſpying a trap in a ditch, which was baited
with a piece of fleſh, he went and informed the
Ape of it, as a treaſure, which, being found upon the waſte, belonged to his Majeſty only. The
Ape, dreaming nothing of the matter, went very
briſkly to take poſſeſſion, but had no ſooner laid
his paws upon the bait, than he was caught in
                                                          the

132. N5 recto, *reduced*

b⁶ (*Life* and *Essay*); A–Z Aa–Bb⁶ Cc⁴ (Cc4+1) (*Fables*, Cc4+1 *The index*), lacking an engraved frontispiece by Ralph Beilby (absent in most copies). Pp. xii, 308, ii. Laid paper from a single stock. Roman type, headings and morals in italic. 142 wood-engraved oval illustrations within rectangular frames (about 60 × 44 mm. each) by Thomas Bewick, title vignette and 37 tailpieces including repeats. Nineteenth-century English polished calf gilt, edges gilt. References: ESTC T078508; Roscoe, *Bewick* p. 149; Hugo 24; Tattersfield JB p. 67.

Provenance: Edward Jackson Barron, F.S.A. (armorial book-plate). PML 52926. Gift: Mrs. Samuel C. Chew.

Saint first employed Bewick to illustrate *Select Fables* in 1774–5, soon after his apprenticeship ended. This later edition shows a far more elaborate treatment of the illustrations, with Bewick clearly learning much from the metalcuts that Elisha Kirkall had done for the much-reprinted Aesop edited by Samuel Croxall, first published in 1722 (entry 57). Bewick's mature style is here evident, with the perspective and texture of his small-scale scenes achieved

through "white-line engraving"—the creation of pictures not as black outline drawings with crosshatched shading but as compositions that achieve form through the modulation of the black printing surface with "white-line" shading. According to Tattersfield JB p. 67, Thomas acknowledged a contribution from his brother John, but "few of the illustrations betray his hand and none do so clearly."

✃ 133 ✃

[Ralph Beilby (1744–1817) & Thomas Bewick (1753–1828)]. *A General History of Quadrupeds. The figures engraved on wood by T. Bewick.* Newcastle upon Tyne: printed by and for S. Hodgson, R. Beilby, & T. Bewick, Newcastle: sold by them, by G.G.J. & J. Robinson, and C. Dilly, London, 1790. Demy 8° (207 × 129 mm.).

π⁴ (1ʳ title and vignette, 1ᵛ blank, 2ʳ *Advertisement*, 2ᵛ *Index*); A–Z Aa–Ee⁸ Ff⁴ (A1ʳ *The Horse*, Ff3ʳ *Addenda*). Pp. viii, 456. Wove

133. U8 verso, enlarged detail

133. X1 recto, enlarged detail

paper, apparently unwatermarked. 201 wood-engraved illustrations by Thomas Bewick; title vignette and 101 tailpieces (pictorial and floral) including repeats, several signed in the block by Bewick. Contemporary polished calf. References: ESTC T061242; Roscoe (1953) 1b variant B.

Provenance: Hercules Scott of Brotherton (armorial bookplate); Sydney Roscoe (booklabel). The Osborne Collection of Early Children's Books, Toronto Public Library. Gift: Felix de Marez Oyens, 1991.

Bewick's work on Aesop was a mere prelude to the wood engravings that were to make him famous and bring a renewal to the techniques of book illustration in Europe and America. These engravings are to be found in the *Quadrupeds* and in his two-volume *History of British Birds*, all of which were compiled (largely by Beilby) as much for adolescent readers as for adults. Bewick's delineation of animals in these books was made with such accuracy (and self-assurance) that they were immediately copied, and versions of his cuts turn up over and over again in the children's books of the time. Of equivalent importance are Bewick's famous "tale pieces"—those tiny narrative illustrations which he engraved as comic or admonitory observations and placed promiscuously throughout all three books. These are marvels of observation, often containing a visual message or story, and they too were from time to time enlarged and used as part of the contents of children's picture books.

The joint publishers in Newcastle, of whom Hodgson was the only professional, fixed the price at 12s. for the royal-size paper issue (100 printed) and 8s. for the demy-size or "common paper" issue (1500 copies).

❧ 134 ☙

Mother Chit-Chat's Curious Tales and Puzzles: or, master and miss's entertaining companion. Containing a short history of the Creation . . . With select stories, tales, jests, riddles, great variety of amusing questions of sport and pastime . . . Addressed to all the little gentry in and about Newcastle . . . The fifth edition enlarged. Newcastle: Printed for T. Slack, 1777. [Price Six-pence]. 12° (117 × 72 mm.).

A² (1ᵛ ads, 2ʳ *Preface*); ²A B–K⁶ (lacking H2, half of H3 and all of quire I, K4ʳ *Riddles*) L⁴ (half-sheet with quire A). Pp. [4], 128.

Original gilt-blocked and dab-colored floral boards.

Provenance: Martha Cooke (inscr. dated 1784–86); H. Faber (sign.). PML 85099. Gift: Elisabeth Ball.

Thomas Slack (1719?–1784) was an entrepreneur of considerable ability, printer, bookseller, and publisher of the long-lived *Newcastle Chronicle*. He had a line in school books and children's books, *Mother Chit-Chat* being a remarkably informal collection of anecdotes, etc., for the local "little Gentry." It was obviously too informal for Martha Cooke or whoever attended her, for major excisions have been made after page 96 and a number of (improper?) words elsewhere have been inked out.

BRENTFORD: Norbury

Philip Norbury I was apprenticed to the printer John Moore of Southwood in 1754 and was freed in 1761. Soon after, he set up as printer at Brentford, just west of London, where he seems to have thrived in all respects. Three sons were apprenticed to him, Henry, Philip II, and William, and his business with its associated circulating library and other adjuncts continued until 1842. As a publisher of children's books, he specialized in chapbook-style publications (the Morgan Library has a bound collection which includes such titles as *The Cries of London, The Entertaining History of Tommy Gingerbread, The Babes in the Wood*, and the *Humours of a Fair*). As with Saint of Newcastle, many of these were based on Newbery publications, and elsewhere (entry 148d) we show Norbury to be a buyer of Newbery materials.

❧ 135 ☙

[TOBIAS GEORGE SMOLLETT (1721–71)]. *The Comical Adventures of Roderick Random, and his friend Strap, with their voyage to South America, &c. Adorned with cuts.* Brentford: Printed by P. Norbury, nearly opposite the Market-Place, and Sold by all Booksellers in Town and Country, [not before 1795 (watermark date)]. Price 6d. Bound. 24° (83 × 69 mm.).

A–E¹² (A1 and E12 mounted as pastedowns, A1ᵛ *Frontispiece*, E12 blank). Pp. 118, [2]. Laid paper. 6 wood engravings (frontispiece full-page, remainder half-page), hand-colored by a child. Gilt-blocked and dab-colored floral boards, perhaps original.

(31)

company of horfemen coming up, he rode
off, and left me ftanding motionlefs like a
ftatue.

This company confifted of three men
in livery, well armed, with an officer,
who was the perfon from whom *R-ft*
had taken the pocket piftol's the day before; and who making known his mif-
B 4   fortune

135. B4 recto, *enlarged*

PML 85592. Purchase: Julia P. Wightman.

Norbury was so given to using other publishers' texts that it is not surprising to find the same abridgment of *Roderick Random* for children published by H. Turpin in 1776 in an illustrated edition of the same size (ESTC N028244).

✑ 136 ✑

A Description of Westminster Abbey, its monuments and curiosities . . . Interspersed with cuts . . . Brentford: Printed by P. Norbury, nearly opposite the Market-Place: and Sold by all Booksellers in Town and Country, [ca. 1800]. (Price 6d bound.). 24° (90 × 68 mm.).

A–D¹² (A1ᵛ frontispiece-view of the Abbey, D12ᵛ imprint *Printed by P. Norbury, New-Brentford*). Pp. 96. Laid paper, unwatermarked. Roman and italic type. 12 cuts (frontispiece full-page, remainder smaller). Original colored floral wrappers. Modern brown morocco gilt. Reference: ESTC T165014.

Provenance: Charles Todd Owen (binding). PML 85370. Gift: Elisabeth Ball.

Norbury's publication was undoubtedly inspired by Boreman's of about sixty years earlier, but the texts of their children's guides are quite different, Norbury's being rather shorter than Boreman's three-volume set (see entry 61c).

WORCESTER: Gamidge

Worcester has long been noted among printing historians as having the longest surviving provincial newspaper, which was founded in 1709 as the *Worcester Post-Man*, and was re-christened *Berrow's Worcester Journal* when taken over by

(23)

Reprefentation of the Tomb of Sir Ifaac Newton.

On this monument the great Sir Ifaac is reprefented reclining upon four folios which are entitled Divinity, Chronology, Optics, and Phil. Prin Math. and pointing to a fcroll fupported by cherubs. On the back ground is a pyramid, from whence projects

136. A12 recto, *enlarged*

Harvey Berrow. As a bookseller he is found dealing in children's books and in 1752 advertised for sale a dozen Newbery titles and the Collins/Newbery "Sett of Fifty-Six Squares." His contemporary, Samuel Gamidge, was a bookseller who began publishing on his own account in the late 1750s. He seems to have liked turning out editions of popular texts, garlands, etc., including some children's books, and was associated for some publications with like-minded London booksellers such as S. Crowder and H. Roberts. The pattern of his publishing is not easy to trace since, like many of his contemporaries, he did not regularly date his productions. He died in 1777 when the business was saved from bankruptcy by his wife Ann (1734–1817) who continued to run it until 1798. A daughter, Elizabeth, had also been apprenticed to him but had died before completing her term. See Margaret Cooper, *The Worcester Book Trade in the Eighteenth Century* (Worcestershire Historical Society, 1997).

✑ 137 ✑

The History of Worcester: with an account of whatever is most remarkable for grandeur, elegance, curiosity, or use in the antient city. The whole embellished with thirty-two views of public buildings, &c. Worcester: Printed for S. Gamidge, 1774. [Price Six Pence.]. 24° (112 × 87 mm.).

A⁴ B–G⁸. Pp. 104. 31 wood engravings. Original or contemporary gilt-blocked and dab-colored boards. Reference: ESTC N008999.

PML 83065. Gift: Elisabeth Ball.

137. E6ᵛ–7ʳ

This competently produced *History of Worcester*, for all its cover decoration, looks more like a book for general sale than for children. At sixpence it was quite a bargain compared with some of the rough sixpenny books put out by other publishers of popular books at the time, although the title promises one more cut than the contents deliver.

GAINSBOROUGH: Mozley

John Mozley began his printing and publishing business in Gainsborough ca. 1775. One of his earliest productions was *The Pilgrim's Progress* "the 57th edition, adorned with cuts" (1776), and that set the tone for his subsequent activity. Reprints and reworkings of classic and popular texts flowed from his press, sometimes apparently in conjunction with London publishers, although this, as we note in the next chapter, may have been a diversionary tactic to deflect charges of plagiarism. He or his son Henry nonetheless developed commercial associations with other provincial publishers, especially Thomas Wilson of York, and by the time the enterprise moved to Derby in 1815, it is said to have been "in a fairly large way of business" (see J.S. English's note on "The Mozleys of Gainsborough," in *Factotum*, Occasional Paper 3, pp. 21–23).

The "way of business" continued into High Victorian times, and the firm's conversion to an altogether more respectable species of children's publishing is traced below through entries 274 and 293.

❧ 138 ❧

The Lilliputian Story Teller, or entertaining miscellany; embellished with curious cuts. London: Printed for W. Osborne and T. Griffin, in St. Paul's Church-yard, and J. Mozley, Gainsbro', 1785. 24° (100 × 60 mm.).

A–H⁸ (A1ᵛ *Frontispiece. Every pretty moral Tale, Shall o'er the Infant's mind prevail.*, A3ʳ *To all good little masters and misses who have a true relish for Lilliputian learning*, A3ᵛ *Contents*). Pp. [6], 121, [1]. 13 wood engravings (frontispiece 79 × 52 mm. (see overleaf), remainder oval illustrations 50 × 41 mm.), the first four in childish coloring. Gilt-blocked floral wrappers (probably original). Blue morocco gilt, by Bayntun of Bath. Reference: ESTC N033711.

Provenance: *Maria Partridge Francis 1791* (inscr. on dedication page); Charles Todd Owen (binding). PML 82183. Gift: Elisabeth Ball.

Use of the term "Lilliputian" in the title and prelims to this collection of stories provides an immediate clue to Mozley's source: Domville's *Lilliputian Library* (entry 82). As we note later (see entry 145), the cooperating London booksellers, Osborne and Griffin, are spurious.

138. *enlarged*

139. D7 verso, *enlarged*

⊰§ 139 §⊱

The Eventful History of King Arthur, or, the British Worthy: being a true account of the many diabolical machinations which were formed against that great deliverer of his country. Adorned with cuts. Gainsbrough: Printed by H. and G. Mozley, [not before 1797 (watermark date)]. Price Four Pence. 32° (96 × 63 mm.).

A–F⁸ (A1ᵛ frontispiece *King Arthur*, F8 blank). Pp. 93, [3]. Laid paper. 18 wood engravings of various sizes, including frontispiece. Original gilt-blocked and dab-colored floral boards.

Provenance: Justin G. Schiller (Sendak bookplate). PML 84687. Purchase.

This unusually smart-looking volume (with John Mozley's sons on the title page) is still a piece of hack publishing. The story does not come from Malory but from Dryden, and the illustrations are brought in from sundry quarters, none having had anything to do with King Arthur when originally cut. The cut here reproduced is one of at least five that were copied from etchings in Elizabeth Newbery's *Mother Bunch's Fairy Tales* (entry 79), where it was

used to illustrate the story of "Princess Zamea and the Prince Almanzon."

HUDDERSFIELD: Brook, Lancashire

According to Berry & Poole, Joseph Brook began printing at Huddersfield in 1778. He did not build up a very lively list, concentrating on official documents for the locality and on such works as *The Duties of a Christian Soldier* by the Vicar of Brotherton. In the 1790s he formed a partnership with Lancashire, but the firm does not seem to have survived long into the new century.

The two children's books here described, representing the two imprints, do not suggest that Brook had much ambition to publish children's books. Certainly they are home-produced and not copies of London works. They are competently printed and bound, but these virtues do not quite compensate for the books' dullness of tone and appearance. A similar monotony is found in the Morgan Library's other Brook & Lancashire imprints: *Tales of the Castle* 1799 (PML 81589) and *General History of the World* 1802 (PML 83088).

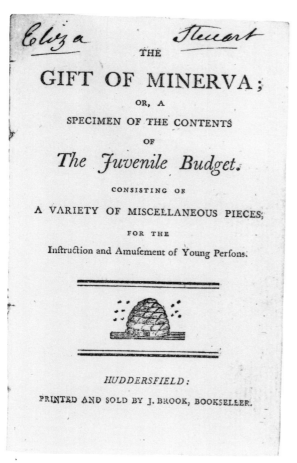

140. A1 recto

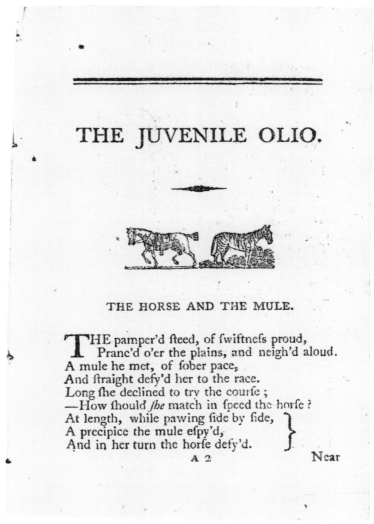

141. A2 recto

❧ 140 ❧

The Gift of Minerva; or, a specimen of the contents of The Juvenile Budget. Consisting of a variety of miscellaneous pieces, for the instruction and amusement of young persons. Huddersfield: printed and sold by J. Brook, Bookseller, [ca. 1790]. 12° (120 × 75 mm.).

A–I⁶. Pp. 108. 8 cuts of various sizes including title vignette, head- and tailpiece. Original colored floral boards.

Provenance: Eliza Steuart (sign.); Gumuchian & Cⁱᵉ (1930 cat., no. 2731). PML 83091. Gift: Elisabeth Ball.

❧ 141 ❧

The Juvenile Olio: containing fables, tales, anecdotes, &c. &c. for the use of young persons. Embellished with cuts. Huddersfield: printed and sold by Brook and Lancashire, Booksellers, 1799. 16° (138 × 92 mm.).

A–D⁸ (D8ᵛ imprint *Printed by Brook & Lancashire, Market-Place, Huddersfield.*). Pp. 64. Laid paper. 33 blocks impressed to form 29 illustrations. Original gilt-blocked and colored floral boards.

Provenance: Charles Todd Owen (pencil note). PML 82308. Gift: Elisabeth Ball.

Four cuts are shared with Brook's *Gift of Minerva* (entry 140). The text is entirely unrelated to William Fordyce Mavor's work of the same title, published by Elizabeth Newbery in 1796 (Roscoe J239).

BURSLEM: Tregortha

John Tregortha began printing and publishing about 1795, and the approximately one dozen eighteenth-century books of his that are known indicate a largely popular output for adults and children, whether *Mother Bunch's Closet Broke Open* (1800?) or an abridgment of *Sandford and Merton* (1799).

❧ 142 ❧

The Adventures of a Silver Three-pence containing much amusement and many characters with which young gentlemen and ladies ought to be acquainted. Adorned with cuts. Burslem: Printed and Sold by J. Tregortha, [ca. 1816 (watermark date)]. 32° (94 × 58 mm.).

142. D7 recto

143. frontispiece

A[16] B–F[8] (A1[v] frontispiece *Read and be wise . . .*). Pp. 112. Three paper stocks (quires A–C laid, quires D–F wove paper). 17 cuts repeated from 14 blocks of various sizes. Modern green morocco gilt, original or contemporary marbled wrappers bound in. Reference: ESTC N016200.

Provenance: Charles Todd Owen (binding). PML 82188. Gift: Elisabeth Ball.

Tregortha's edition of *The Adventures of a Silver Three-pence* is an abridgment of the text first published by Elizabeth Newbery, haphazardly illustrated with blocks that came to hand at the time of publication.

EDINBURGH: Paterson

D. Paterson worked as a publisher in Edinburgh during the last two decades of the eighteenth century and probably specialized in chapbooks. The following unusual edition of Perrault, which maintains the line of editions acknowledged to "R. Samber, Gent.," is very like a chapbook, with its cheap paper, its varied and unevenly printed cuts, and its use of the moral fairy tale of the "Widow and her Two Daughters" as a filler.

❧ 143 ❧

CHARLES PERRAULT (1628–1703) and/or PIERRE PERRAULT DARMANCOUR (1678–1700). *Mother Goose's Tales. Histories or tales of past times. With morals. Written in French, by Monsieur Perrault. Englished by R. Samber, Gent.* Edinburgh: printed by D. Paterson, 1780. (Price Sixpence bound.). 18° (119 × 73 mm.).

A–C[18] D[9] (A1[v] *Contents*, A2[r] translator's dedication to the Countess of Granville, C5[r] divisional title to *The Discreet Princess* by Mlle L'Héritier de Villandon, C6[r] dedication to Lady Montague, D1 lacking, D5 singleton, D6[v]–9[r] *The Widow, and her Two Daughters* by Mme Le Prince de Beaumont); engraved frontispiece *Mother Goose's Tales*. Pp. 125, [1]. 11 cuts of various sizes. Original sheep-backed marbled boards.

Provenance: Mary Hittone (sign.). PML 83653. Gift: Elisabeth Ball.

As we have already noted on several occasions, the demand for copy for juvenile books during the last part of the eighteenth century tended to exceed the supply. "Mary Homebred's" crude *moralités* in *A Christmass-Box* were re-edited by John Marshall (entry 83); *Tommy Thumb's Folio*, once edited by Newbery, became standard fare (entries 42–44); the translations of fairy tales by Perrault, Mme d'Aulnoy, and Mme Le Prince de Beaumont were apparently regarded as being "in the public domain."

These are not isolated examples, however. One of the values of the depth of the Morgan holdings is that it enables us to see a variety of "copycat" publications, which, if they were not outright infringements of "copyright," at least showed how urgently printers and booksellers sought material and how ready they were to reap where somebody else had done most of the sowing. We certainly know that some effort was made to protect ownership at this time. At the beginning of a collection of severely moral tales, *Old Heads on Young Shoulders* (London: Printed for J. Cooke, 1774; PML 85593), there stands a fierce notice:

> This WORK being entered in the HALL-BOOK
> of the Company of Stationers; whoever presumes
> to pirate the Whole or any Part thereof, shall
> be prosecuted as the Law directs.

There must be some doubt if anyone would want to pirate such histories as "Lorenzo; or, the fatal effects of reading books containing libertine principle" (several seductions, murders, and suicides occasioned by deism), but, as we try to show in the following entries, a number of lighter works for children tended to travel from one publisher to another in ways which may or may not have involved "piracy."

MARSHALL DERIVES FROM NEWBERY

144a

JOHN NEWBERY (1713–67), editor. *The Twelfth-Day-Gift: or, the Grand Exhibition. Containing a curious collection of pieces in prose and verse (many of them originals) which were delivered to a numerous and polite audience, on the important subjects of religion, morality, history, philosophy, polity, prudence, and oeconomy, at the most noble the Marquis of Setstar's, by a society of young gentlemen and ladies, and registered at their request, by their old friend Mr. Newbery . . . The fourth edition.* London: Printed for T. Carnan and F. Newbery, Jun. at Number 65, in St. Paul's Church-Yard, 1777. 24° (111 × 74 mm.).

A–S⁶ (A1ᵛ dedication *To his Grace the Duke of Galaxy, The most noble the Marquis of Setstar, The Right Honourable the Countess of Twilight, and the Young Gentlemen and Ladies of Great-Britain and Ireland, and the British Colonies . . .*); 9 illustrations (including frontispiece—see overleaf) in a worn impression from an engraved copperplate on one sheet, divided for insertion. Pp. [6], 209, [1]. Letterpress on different paper stocks from the engraving. Original pictorial boards, contemporary deerskin spine, 4 fable cuts by J. Bell in the same arrangement as on F. L. Earle's copy of the 1783 *Fables in Verse* (entry 118) but here printed in black. References: ESTC N034488; Roscoe J366(5); Morgan 297.

Provenance: Mary Brookes (rebacking; contemporary sign.). PML 81230. Gift: Elisabeth Ball.

144b

[JOHN NEWBERY (1713–67), editor]. *The Twelfth-Day-Gift; or, the Grand Exhibition. Containing an account of a society of young gentlemen and ladies, who meet every twelfth-day, to shew their improvement in learning, virtue, and happiness, and, by their example, endeavour to mend the world . . .* London: printed and sold by John Marshall, No. 17, Queen-Street, Cheapside, and no. 4, Aldermary Church-Yard, [ca. 1795]. 12° (158 × 94 mm.).

A1 (title); B–N⁶; engraved frontispiece by J. Piggot after Newbery's artist. Pp. [2], 143, [1]. 8 wood engravings (42 × 59 mm.). All illustrations in early hand-coloring. Contemporary marbled boards, new leather spine. References: ESTC T174793; Morgan 298 (later Marshall ed., 2 vols., 1820).

Provenance: J. H. Duffield (early sign.). PML 80114. Gift: Elisabeth Ball.

John Newbery's anthology *The Twelfth-Day Gift* was published just before his death in 1767 and continued in print through his son's and Carnan's business until at least 1788 (Roscoe J366[7]). The early editions, as the one shown here (overleaf), were illustrated with copper engravings. At first sight John Marshall appears to be copying these engravings onto wood for his later large-format edition. However, the Newbery engravings had not stood up well to reprinting, and by 1788 Carnan was reillustrating with cuts. It is these very blocks that Marshall is using, presumably having bought them and the copyright from the defunct business in St. Paul's Church-Yard. Marshall did, however, go so far as to commission a new copper engraving for the frontispiece, and this makes by far the best rendering of Newbery's famous maxim "Trade and Plumb-cake for ever, Huzza!"

144a. frontispiece, *enlarged*

Trade and Plumb-cake for ever, Huzza!

144b. *reduced*

GAINSBOROUGH PIRATES LONDON

❧ 145a ❧

The Valentine's Gift: or, a plan to enable children of all sizes and denominations to behave with honour, integrity and humanity. Very necessary in a trading nation. To which is added, some account of old Zigzag, and of the Horn which he used to understand the language of birds, beasts, fishes, and insects . . . London: Printed for T. Carnan and F. Newbery Junior, at No. 65, in St. Paul's Church-Yard, 1774. Price Sixpence bound. 32° (94 × 64 mm.).

A–H⁸ (A2ʳ dedication, H6ʳ–8ᵛ ads); etched frontispiece *The Valentines*. Pp. 122, [6]. 25 cuts (45 × 35 mm. and slightly smaller). Original pictorial boards, contemporary deerskin spine, wood engravings of children's games: "Blind Man's Buff" on front cover, "Battledore and Shuttlecock" on back cover. Reference: Roscoe J368(3).

Provenance: Mary Brookes (rebacking; contemporary sign.). PML 82173. Gift: Elisabeth Ball.

❧ 145b ❧

Tommy Trip's Valentine Gift: a plan to enable children . . . to behave with honour . . . Adorned with cuts. London: Printed for W. Osborne and T. Griffin, in St. Paul's Church-Yard; and J. Mozley, Gainsbrough, [ca. 1785]. 32° (102 × 64 mm.).

A–H⁸ (A1ᵛ frontispiece *The Valentines*, A3ʳ dedication, H7 blank, H8 blank and mounted as pastedown). Pp. 124, [4]. 26 cuts (frontispiece 82 × 49 mm., remainder 47 × 35 mm. and slightly smaller). Original gilt-blocked and stencil-colored floral boards.

PML 82171. Gift: Elisabeth Ball.

The slightly changed title does little to disguise a straight piracy of a Newbery volume that was in print until at least about 1790 (Roscoe J368[6]). The text is a line-for-line reprint with only minor variations. Newbery's cuts were obviously copied onto another set of blocks and thus converted into inferior, reversed images. Corroboration may reside in the form of the imprint; Osborne and Griffin appear to have been "front" names for Mozley's piratical operations. They turn up on a number of his

145a. A4 recto, *enlarged*

145b. A5 recto, *enlarged*

title pages, looking very plausible, but their initials keep changing and sometimes their address too. The Morgan Library has a Mozley edition of *Little Jack Horner's Tales and Stories* "printed for W. Osborn and J. Griffin in Holborn . . . 1786" (PML 83595).

BEWICK TAKES OVER FROM RUBENS

ᵍ§ 146a ᵍ⁰

[RICHARD JOHNSON (1733/4–93]. *The Picture Exhibition; containing the original drawings of eighteen disciples. To which are added, moral and historical explanations, published under the inspection of Master Peter Paul Rubens, professor of polite arts.* London: Printed for T. Carnan, in St. Paul's Church-Yard, 1783. [Price 6d.]. 24° (111 × 76 mm.).

A⁴ (2ʳ *Advertisement* signed P. P. Rubens, P.P.A., 3ʳ *Contents*); B–G⁶ H² (H2+3) (H2+1ʳ signed H3 end of text, H2+1ᵛ ads). Pp. [8], 77, [5]. 18 wood engravings (58 × 38 mm. and slightly smaller—see overleaf). Original gilt-blocked and dab-colored floral boards. References: ESTC T139050; Roscoe J280(2).

Provenance: *Mrs. Pollocks Collection* (pencil note); S. & W. (pencil note, presumably Simmons and Waters, booksellers at Leamington). PML 82169. Gift: Elisabeth Ball.

ᵍ§ 146b ᵍ⁰

[RICHARD JOHNSON (1733/4–93]. *The Picture-Room: containing the original drawings of eighteen little masters and misses. To which are added, moral and historical explanations. Published under the inspection of Master Peter Painter, professor of polite arts. The cuts by Bewick.* York: printed by T. Wilson and R. Spence High-Ousegate, 1804. (Price sixpence.). 24° (109 × 77 mm.).

A–G⁶ (A1ᵛ frontispiece, A2ʳ title, G5ᵛ–6ʳ ads, G6ʳ imprint *Printed at the Office of T. Wilson and R. Spence, High-Ousegate, York*). Pp. 81, [3]. Frontispiece (77 × 51 mm., originally commissioned by Wilson & Spence from the Bewick workshop for their edition of *The Sugar Plumb*, 1788); 18 wood engravings by Thomas Bewick, all rectangular (50 × 38 mm.) except the last oval (53 × 39 mm.), which was taken from the workshop blocks for Saint's *Choice Collection of Hymns*. Original gilt-blocked and dab-colored floral boards. References: Hugo 194; Morgan 231 (an edition of 1800).

146a. D2 verso, *enlarged*

146b. C4 verso, *enlarged*

PML 82168. Gift: Elisabeth Ball.

A double jump occurs in this instance of north-country piracy. Scarcity of evidence prevents a full explanation, but the probable sequence of events is as follows:

1. Thomas Carnan publishes *The Picture Exhibition* for Christmas 1773, Richard Johnson having completed work on the text on 6 January 1772 (Roscoe J280).

2. Some time after this the text is pirated in Newcastle upon Tyne by Thomas Saint, who in 1781 commissions wood engravings from the Beilby/Bewick workshop.

3. Saint issues the piracy under a slightly changed title, publishing it not under his own name but "for the booksellers in town and country," and the book continues on his list until his death, after which his successors, Hall and Elliot, sell the stock of blocks to Thomas Wilson of York.

4. Wilson and his partner(s) reprint a number of Saint titles such as the present one, making the legitimate claim "The cuts by Bewick" although they had no compunction about distributing the blocks differently among the titles.

The Morgan Library has several other examples of these York < Newcastle < London titles, such as *The Renowned History of Primrose Prettyface* (1798), following Marshall's original but with his illustrations reworked on a smaller scale within framed ovals

(PML 82161), and *A Collection of Pretty Poems . . . By Tommy Tagg Esq.* (1800), with wood engravings that add much detail to, but subtract the primitive force from, the original Newbery cuts (PML 81605).

GAINSBOROUGH REFURBISHES LONDON

◄§ 147a §►

Food for the Mind: or, a new riddle-book. Compiled for the use of the great and the little good boys and girls in England, Scotland, and Ireland. By John-the-Giant-Killer, Esq . . . London: Printed for the Booksellers of Europe, Asia, Africa, and America; and sold by T. Carnan and F. Newbery, Jun. at Number 65, St. Paul's Church Yard, 1778. [Price Six-pence.]. 32° (94 × 60 mm.).

A–H[8] (A1[v] warning against the "paltry Compilations" of F. Newbery, John Newbery's nephew, as opposed to the "useful Publications" to be had from F. Newbery *fils*, H5[r] ads). Pp. viii, 112, [8]. 68 cuts (37 × 47 mm.). Original pictorial boards, contemporary deerskin spine, wood engravings of children's games on covers (identical to Mary Brookes's copy of *Valentine's Gift*, entry 145a). References: ESTC N028548; Roscoe J190B(6).

90   FOOD *for the* MIND; *or,*

OF all the arts in which we shine,
    Or sciences acquir'd,
There's none so difficult as mine,
    Less practis'd, more admir'd :
Behold my whimsical attire,
    How aukward my address ;
The trade which I take up for hire,
    Millions unknown profess.

                    I fiddle,

147a. G1 verso, *enlarged*

Provenance: Mary Brookes (rebacking; contemporary sign.). PML 82300. Gift: Elisabeth Ball.

⊸§ 147b ℈⊷

A New Riddle Book. Compiled for the use of the great and little good boys and girls, of England, Scotland and Ireland. By John the Giant-Killer, Esq . . . Gainsbrough: Printed at Mozley's Lilliputian Book-Manufactory, 1791. [Price 6d.]. 32° (97 × 65 mm.).

A–G⁸ (A6 lacking); H⁸ (1ʳ *Conundrums. By Lancelot Loggerhead, Esq., 3ʳ Rebusses, 5ʳ Epitaph. By Mr. Gray, 5ᵛ Epitaph. By a Nobleman on his deceased Lady, 6ʳ On Stephen the Fiddler, 6ᵛ Inscription on an Urn at Lord Cork's, to the memory of the Dog Hector, 7ʳ An Epitaph on an honest Fellow. To the Memory of Signior Fido,* 8ᵛ blank and mounted as pastedown). Pp. 127, [1]. 51 cuts (37 × 47 mm.). Original gilt-blocked and dab-colored boards.

PML 80811. Gift: Elisabeth Ball.

108   Food for the Mind, or

MERRY ANDREW.

147b. G6 verso, *enlarged*

72   FOOD FOR THE MIND; OR,

OF all the arts in which we shine,
    Or sciences acquir'd,
There's none so difficult as mine,
    Less practis'd, more admir'd :
Behold my whimsical attire,
    How awkward my address ;
The trade which I take up for hire,
    Millions unknown profess.
I fiddle, sing, prate, laugh and cry,
    To draw the thoughtless in;
And num'rous other antics try,
    To bait the subtle gin:

147c. E4 verso, *enlarged*

ᕽᔞ 147c ᔞᕽ

Food for the Mind; or, a new riddle-book: compiled for the use of the great and the little boys and girls in England, Scotland, and Ireland. By John the Giant-Killer, Esq . . . York: printed by Wilson, Spence, and Mawman, Anno 1797. [Price six-pence.]. 24° (114 × 82 mm.).

A–F⁸ (A2ʳ *Preface*, A4ʳ *New Riddle Book*, F5ᵛ blank, F6ʳ–8ʳ *The Story of the Good and Naughty Boy*, F8ᵛ ads for twelvepenny down to twopenny books). Pp. 95, [1]. 68 cuts—see previous page (37 × 47 mm.). Original gilt-blocked and dab-colored floral boards. Reference: ESTC N028545.

Provenance: *Edm. Page Septʳ. 27ᵗʰ 1805* (inscrs.); *Edm. Page to his God son E. Page* (inscr.); Gumuchian & Cⁱᵉ (1930 cat., no. 2588). PML 83569. Gift: Elisabeth Ball.

John the Giant-Killer and his riddles are ubiquitous in eighteenth-century children's book publishing. We have already described a cheap abridgment put out by a part-time publisher (entry 94); now we find John Mozley using Newbery's original as the basis for a production from his Lilliputian Book Manufactory (i.e. without the "assistance" of Messrs. "Osborne and Griffin"). He retains Newbery's preface; he recuts Newbery's blocks (reversed throughout); but he makes a sensible change to the layout, so that the riddles do become riddles, and he also brings in Lancelot Loggerhead etc. at the end. The York piracy by Wilson, Spence, and Mawman is almost an enlarged replica of Newbery's edition, and this time not reillustrated by Bewick but extended with an arbitrary story to fill up the final sheet.

BRENTFORD MOVES IN ON LONDON

ᕽᔞ 148a ᔞᕽ

The Comical Adventures of a Little White Mouse; or, a bad boy happily changed into a good boy. A useful lesson to all young people . . . London: Printed for H. Turpin, No. 104. St. John's-Street, West-Smithfield; and sold by all Booksellers in Town and Country. Where may be had the greatest Choice of Children's Books, Wholesale and Retail, as cheap as any Shop in London, [ca. 1785]. 18° (110 × 77 mm.).

A–F⁶ (A1ᵛ *Frontispiece*); G⁹ (1ᵛ end of text, 2ʳ–9ʳ ads, 5 singleton, 7–8 signed H1–2). Pp. 89, [1]. 10 full-page wood engravings including frontispiece (about 89 × 55 mm. each). Original dab-colored floral boards. Reference: ESTC T085911.

Provenance: *Crunchback* (early inscr.); Charles Todd Owen (pencil note). PML 81599. Gift: Elisabeth Ball.

ᕽᔞ 148b ᔞᕽ

The Curious Adventures of a Little White Mouse; or, a bad boy changed, in a very comical manner, into a good boy . . . Brentford: Printed by P. Norbury and Sold by all Booksellers

in Town and Country, [not before 1794 (watermark date), not after 1803 (inscription date)]. Price Six-pence. Full-sheet 24° (110 × 76 mm.), three quires worked together.

A–F⁸ (A1 and F8 mounted as pastedowns, A1ᵛ *Frontispiece. Mary Muffin Courting Colin Clump*, F3ʳ *The mouse's petition*, F5ᵛ *Rules of life. In verse*, F7ᵛ *The pleasures of retirement*). Pp. 95, [1]. Laid paper. 10 wood engravings (full-page frontispiece 88 × 56 mm., half-page illustrations 41 × 55 mm.). Original gilt-blocked and dab-colored floral boards.

Provenance: . . . *Goslings 1803* (erased inscr.). PML 80652. Gift: Elisabeth Ball.

ᕽᔞ 148c ᔞᕽ

The Lilliputian Masquerade, occasioned by the conclusion of peace between those potent nations, the Lilliputians and Tommythumbians . . . London: Sold by T. Carnan, In St. Paul's Church-Yard, 1783. Price of a Subscription Ticket not Two Guineas, but Two-Pence. 32° (98 × 63 mm.), turned chainlines.

[1³²] signed A¹⁶<B⁸<C⁸ (1·32 mounted as pastedowns, 1ᵛ frontispiece, 2ᵛ introductory verse). Pp. 63, [1]. 20 wood engravings: full-page frontispiece, small mask on title, illustrations (31 × 43 mm.). Original gilt-blocked and dab-colored floral wrappers. References: ESTC T170000; Roscoe J220(2).

PML 82159. Gift: Elisabeth Ball.

ᕽᔞ 148d ᔞᕽ

The Lilliputian Masquerade, occasioned by the conclusion of peace between those potent nations, the Lilliputians and Tommythumbians . . . Brentford: Printed by P. Norbury, and Sold by all Booksellers in Town and Country, [ca. 1795]. Price Two-Pence. 32° (97 × 62 mm.).

[1³²] (1·32 mounted as pastedowns, 1ᵛ *Frontispiece*, 3ʳ introductory verse, 32ʳ imprint *Norbury, Printer, Brentford*). Pp. 63, [1]. 20 wood engravings (Carnan's blocks). Original gilt-blocked and dab-colored floral wrappers. Reference: ESTC T171753.

PML 82158. Gift: Elisabeth Ball.

ᕽᔞ 148e ᔞᕽ

The Lilliputian Masquerade, occasioned by the conclusion of peace between those potent nations, the Lilliputians and Tommythumbians . . . London: Printed for the Booksellers, [ca. 1800]. (Price Two Pence.). Full-sheet 32° (94 × 56 mm.), four quires worked together.

A–D⁸ (A1ᵛ frontispiece *The Characters in the Masquerade*, A2ᵛ introductory verse, D6ᵛ ads, D7ᵛ and D8 blank). Pp. 59, [5]. Laid paper. 20 wood engravings: full page frontispiece, mask on title,

A Little White Mouse. 13

B

148a. B1 recto

14 *The Curious Adventures of*

Way before them; and very mer-rily they passed the Day.

Colin could plough and sow, and reap and mow; *Mary* could brew, and bake, and make a cake; be-sides, she made the very best Plumb Pudding

148b. A7 verso

16 The LILLIPUTIAN

fufely; had he but been more fparing, he might have been happy at this Minute.--- However, in fpending what he had, if he met with no folid Satisfaction, he met with fome Amufement; but the Mifer who denies himfelf the common Neceffaries of Life, can neither meet with Sa-tisfaction nor Amufement.

Only behold how fufpicioufly he looks about him, as if fomebody wanted to run away with the Key of his Cheft. Now, Ladies and Gentlemen,

---" Say,

148d. fo. 8 verso

14 *The* LILLIPUTIAN

but been more fparing, he might have been happy at this Minute: ---However, in fpending what he had, if he met with no folid Satis-faction, he met with fome Amufe-ment.---But the Mifer who denies himfelf the common Neceffaries of Life, can neither meet with Satisfaction nor Amufement.

Only behold how fufpicioufly he looks about him, as if Somebody

wanted to run away with the Key of his Cheft.---Now, Ladies and Gentlemen. ---*Say,*

148e. A7 verso

illustrations (30 × 41 mm.). Original dab-colored floral wrappers. Modern green morocco gilt. Reference: ESTC N033710.

Provenance: Charles Todd Owen (binding). PML 82200. Gift: Elisabeth Ball.

Norbury's relationship to other members of the trade is in need of investigation. At first glance his edition of the *Little White Mouse* may appear to be a piracy of Turpin's original, with an interesting recutting of the illustrations—thematically the same, not reversed, but reduced in visual scope so that the main incident only is given in a framed oval. However, allowing for the discrepancy between the dates when Turpin was active (up to 1789) and Norbury (ca. 1794 onward), there is no reason why the latter should not simply have taken over rights (if any) to the older publisher's book.

Some such possibility gains credence when we find in the Morgan Library a copy of Turpin's *The Picture Alphabet* (PML 82302), reprinted by Norbury using Turpin's original blocks ("using" is too polite a word; some show up as little more than blotches of ink; PML 81392). Moreover, Norbury also seems to have acquired blocks from the St. Paul's Church-Yard Newberys, rather as Darton and Marshall had done in 1793: witness *The Lilliputian Masquerade*, sold by T. Carnan in 1783, and reproduced by Norbury employing the same blocks barely a dozen years later. Yet, another edition of *The Lilliputian Masquerade*, "printed for the booksellers," *is* a piracy. The cuts are not reversed but show up as inferior copies of the Newbery/Norbury pictures.

HARRIS IN PARIS (AND ELSEWHERE)

❧ 149a ☙

The Old Woman and her Pig. London: Griffith and Farran, successors to Newbery & Harris, corner of St. Paul's Church Yard, [ca. 1860]. Royal 16° (175 × 112 mm.).

[1¹⁶] (1·16 mounted as pastedowns, 1ᵛ drop-title *The Old Woman and her Pig. An Ancient Tale in a Modern Dress*, illustration *Finding the silver penny*, incipit: *A little old woman, who lived in a house*). Ff. 16. Printed on one side of a sheet of wove paper, then mounted on cloth to make an "indestructible" book for the youngest children (see chapter XIX). 14 half-page wood engravings in publisher's hand-coloring. Original printed yellow wrappers, title (as given above) and wood engraving of a pig on front cover, publisher's ads and imprint *Wertheimer and Co., Printers, Finsbury Circus* on back cover. Reference: Opie *Nursery Companion* pp. 96–100, 126. A different text from the earlier Lewis version at entry 198.

Provenance: The Osborne Collection of Early Children's Books, Toronto Public Library. Gift: Felix de Marez Oyens.

❧ 149b ☙

[*The Children's Comical and Picturesque Toy-Book, containing the most favourite stories in humorous style*. Paris: Truchy's Juvenile Library, 1838. Oblong 16°]. The two

3   THE OLD WOMAN AND HER PIG.

PIG WON'T GO OVER THE STILE.

But how shall I paint her vexation and toil,
When, in crossing a meadow, she came to a stile,
And found neither threats nor persuasions would
    do
To induce Mr. Piggy to climb or creep through?
She coax'd him, she strok'd him, she patted his
    hide,
She scolded him, threaten'd him, thump'd him
    beside;
But coaxing, and scolding, and thumping proved
    vain,
Whilst the evening grew dark, and 'twas likely
    to rain.

149a. fo. 3 verso, *reduced*

original etched copperplates for printing all 32 illustrations of these four stories, which were published collectively under the above title (Gumuchian 1710–11) and issued separately as follows: *Old Mother Hubbard and her Dog* and *The Comical Adventures of Old Dame Trot and her Comical Cat* (Gumuchian 4321), the two combined on a single copperplate, each with the illustrations numbered 1–8, and designated with the letters *H* and *T* respectively (masked before pulling impressions); *Further Adventures of Dame Trot and her Comical Cat* (Gumuchian 4321–22) and *The Remarkable Adventures of an Old Woman and her Pig* (Gumuchian 4334–35; Moon 708 note), the two combined on another copperplate, each with the illustrations numbered 1–8, and designated with the letters *F* and *P* respectively, scene 2 in *F* signed BP (also masked before printing). [Paris: J. H. Truchy, French and English Library, 1838]. 475 × 635 mm. each.

Provenance: *Aumont et Herh . . . Rue St. Jacques 2* (presumably the copperplate makers, inscription engraved on the back of both plates); Gumuchian & Cⁱᵉ (1930 cat., no. 1710). PML (with an impression commissioned in modern times). Gift: Elisabeth Ball.

149c. fo. 10 recto, *reduced*

149d. fo. 10 recto, *reduced*

⋙ 149c ⋘

The Paths of Learning Strewed with Flowers or, English grammar illustrated . . . London: John Harris, corner of St. Paul's Church-Yard, [not before 1825 (watermark date)]. Royal 16° (177 × 106 mm.).

[1¹⁶] (1ʳ blank, 1ᵛ title and imprint *Published September 25ᵗʰ 1820, by Harris and Son, Corner of Sᵗ Pauls Church Yard,* 2ʳ *The purpose of this little work...* [repeated in letterpress on cover-title], 2ᵛ–3ʳ blank, 3ᵛ alphabet, 16ʳ *Interjections,* 16ᵛ blank). Ff. 16. Etched throughout: apparently printed from a single copperplate on one side of the sheet (watermarked J. Whatman 1825). Title vignette, two wreaths, and 13 half-page illustrations, all in publisher's hand-coloring, with 4- or 5-line explanations. Original buff boards, letterpress title (as transcribed above) on front cover, Harris's wood-engraved circular Athena device on back cover, ad inside back cover for *Harris's Cabinet of Amusement and Instruction, Consisting of the most approved Novelties for the Nursery; Printed in a superior manner upon good paper, 1s. 6d.*

each . . . *neatly coloured* to which *Paths of Learning* belongs. References: Moon *Harris* 602(2); Osborne II, 728; Hockliffe 612; Opie *Nursery Companion* pp. 46–9, 124.

PML 84994. Purchase: Fellows Fund

⋙ 149d ⋘

The Paths of Learning Strewed with Flowers: or, English grammar illustrated . . . New York: published by S. King, 136 William-street, [not before 1825 (copperplate date)]. Royal 16° (178 × 110 mm.).

[1¹⁶] (1ʳ blank, 1ᵛ title and imprint *Publish'd by S. King, N. York, 1825,* 2ʳ *The purpose of this little work...* [repeated in letterpress on cover-title], 2ᵛ–3ʳ blank, 3ᵛ alphabet, 16ʳ *Interjections,* 16ᵛ blank). Ff. 16. Etched throughout: apparently printed from a single copperplate on one side of the sheet (unwatermarked). Title vignette, two wreaths, and 13 half-page illustrations, all in publisher's hand-coloring, with 3- to 5-line explanations. Original

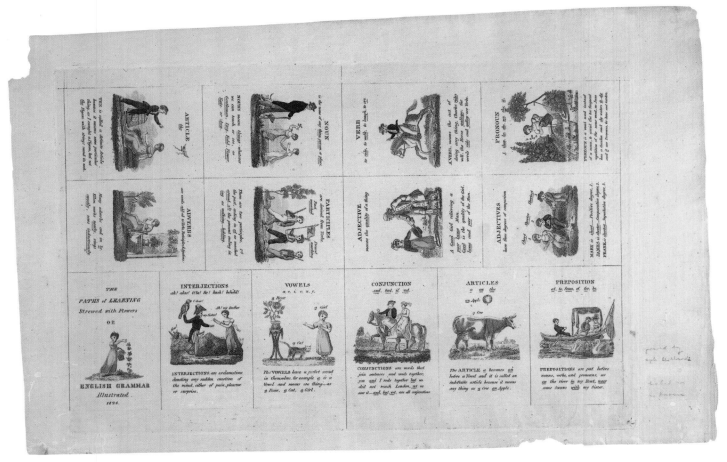

149e. *reduced*

buff boards, letterpress title (as transcribed above) and type-ornament border on front cover, ad on back cover *S. King's Cabinet of Amusement & Instruction, Consisting of the most approved novelties for the Nursery . . . neatly coloured* to which *Paths of Learning* belongs (at 37½ Cents).

Provenance: Gillett Griffin. PML 81047. Purchase: Ball Fund

⤐ 149e ⤏

The Paths of Learning Strewed with Flowers or English Grammar Illustrated. [Hartford, Connecticut: Asaph Willard], 1826 [copperplate date, impression possibly later]. Full sheet (345 × 525 mm.).

Etching (290 × 490 mm.) showing 14 pages of illustrations (all hand-colored) and text, including title page as transcribed above. The sheet of unwatermarked wove paper intended for division and quiring to form a codex, but here left intact. The sheet has survived as part of a small remainder. References: Shoemaker 27650; *Realms of Childhood* 119.

PML 84446. Purchase.

As one of the leading publishers of the children's-book revolution of the early nineteenth century, John Harris finds a place in chapter XI. His most famous books were widely copied in a variety of ways, and here we see two instances of how they made their way to foreign markets.

The two French copperplates—apart from being rare survivals of the surface from which intaglio printing of children's books was carried out—are interesting for showing a series of Harris re-interpretations, which were commissioned by the bookseller-printers Truchy in Paris. Truchy specialized in English reprints, if not on the scale of a Baron Tauchnitz, and here he is found reprinting four of Harris's most popular texts, with a selection of Harris's original illustrations now converted to fit a whole oblong page. It is not certain whether Truchy published his editions of these English picture books under license or under the skull-and-cross-bones.

The unfolded, uncut sheet to make up a copy of *The Paths of Learning* is more certainly a piratical piece of work, being one small element in the mass American exploitation of English children's books that had been going on since the 1760s. Asaph Willard has reduced both the length and the format of the book, presumably so that he could fit a complete printing onto a single plate, and the finished print has been hand-colored in advance of being cut and folded. We include with this rather pretty piece of borrowing Harris's original book on which it was based and a description of the Morgan copy of another, quite different, United States piracy, which follows Harris in every detail (not exhibited).

Giant Thundol, with Two Heads, dragged ashore.

150b. pl. [4], *reduced*

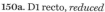

The Death of Thundol, the two-headed Giant.
D   page 66.

150a. D1 recto, *reduced*

INNES LETS DEAN DO MOST OF THE WORK

⋙ 150a ⋘

Jack, the Giant Killer, And Jack, and the Bean Stalk. Re-written by a lady. Illustrated with many coloured engravings. London: Dean and Co. Threadneedle-Street, [ca. 1845]. 18° (140 × 90 mm.).

C¹⁸(C1+1) (1ᵛ frontispiece *The mighty Cornish Giant, the first one whom Jack slew*, 1+1 title) D¹⁸ E¹⁸ (–7·12, 8·11, 9·10, and 13–18; these canceled leaves presumably formed part of another Dean six-penny popular tale, with which this edition of *Jack* was worked together). Pp. [3] 38–104 (plates excluded from pagination). Full-page frontispiece and 14 half-page illustrations (8 leaves), all wood-engraved and hand-colored. Original gilt-decorated cloth, lettered on both covers *Popular Tales. Jack the Giant Killer. And Jack, and the Bean Stalk.*

Provenance: Gumuchian & Cⁱᵉ (1930 cat., no. 3155). PML 80677. Gift: Elisabeth Ball.

⋙ 150b ⋘

Innes's Edition. The Surprising History of Jack the Giant-Killer. Embellished with Superior Colored Engravings. London: Printed and Published by J. Innes, 61, Wells Street, Oxford Street, and may be had of all booksellers, [ca. 1845]. Price Sixpence. 18°? (137 × 85 mm.).

A–C⁶ (A1 and C6 blanks mounted as pastedowns, C5ᵛ imprint *J. Innes, Printer, 61, Wells-street, Oxford-street, London*); 2 pairs of conjugate plates (1·2: full-page frontispiece and 2 half-page illustrations; 3·4: 4 half-page illustrations), all wood-engraved and hand-colored. Pp. 34, [2]. Original printed pink wrappers,

wood engraving on front cover (*Jack killing the Giant with his Pick-axe*, repeated from plate 4). Modern blind-stamped morocco, by Morrell of London.

Provenance: Charles Todd Owen (binding). PML 80733. Gift: Elisabeth Ball.

Borrowing other publishers' ideas and making free with authors' copyrights has never ceased (oriental piracy has been much in vogue of late). These two versions of *Jack the Giant Killer*, dating from just before the middle of the nineteenth century, show one publisher, Innes, not so much stealing from a competitor, Dean & Co., but rather heavily leaning upon Dean's priority in the field. He chooses a page size and illustrative layout similar to his model; he follows Dean's text, with a few modifications; and his artist, while not slavishly copying the earlier pictures, uses them as the pattern for his own designs, most of which give a reverse treatment of the same scenes. (Innes, however, balked at including the "three ladies, tied up by the hair of their heads, and almost starved to death.")

X

"THE DAWN OF LEVITY"

THE title for this chapter has been taken from F. J. Harvey Darton's *Children's Books in England*, where he felicitously applied it to the excited awakening of English children's literature at the start of the nineteenth century. What he had chiefly in mind was the arrival of a host of new nursery picture books, the subject of our next two chapters. We have borrowed his phrase at this point to describe some events that preceded the publishing of those books and that would form part of a greater trend within which the picture books themselves do have a prominent place.

Featured here is the use of the printing press for a variety of unexpected and essentially playful purposes. Precedents existed for almost every development that we describe, but from about 1770 onwards these developments came together and gathered momentum in an unprecedented way. The apparently sober, homogeneous world of children's books, where so much looked exactly like so much else, was brightened and variegated by entrepreneurs with new ideas to try. These ideas might be related to books (miniature libraries, doll books, etc.) or they might have to do more with games and broadsides (puzzles and such educational devices as writing sheets), but in most cases their realization depended on a wider and more imaginative use of intaglio printing (engraving and etching), with hand-coloring thrown in.

In order to give form to our discussion of these engines of levity we have divided the chapter into ten sections, each of which is devoted to explaining a particular device and giving some characteristic examples. Our approach is broadly chronological, setting out each new publishing ploy as it touched on, or came to be adopted by, the children's book market. Several children's book publishers were closely connected with these developments, but most of our comments on their individual activity and significance will be found in the chapters that follow.

HARLEQUINADES

"Harlequinades" or, more prosaically, "turn-ups" were a portent of good things to come rather than a perfected achievement. We have already noted the origins of the genre in the seventeenth century and described the mechanism of the cut-paper flaps (entry 33). At that date, however, the "turn-up" theme was a didactic one, and it was only with the arrival of a commercial movement in the 1770s that change took place. This movement was not really inspired by any wish to appeal to children. The turn-ups that were produced by the chief publisher of such goods, Robert Sayer, were primarily a means of cashing in on the public's enthusiasm for *commedia dell'arte* (hence the term "harlequinade"). Most of the versified narratives making up the texts that were illustrated by flap-pictures were vapid abridgments of already vapid entertainments and no creative use was made of the metamorphic principle.

What did matter about harlequinades, however, was first their "play" aspect: they are among the first mass-production "movables" in print. Secondly, they and related material were produced on a large scale from engraved plates and sold hand-colored as well as plain to an English popular market. Obviously, such newfangled devices appealed to children; they also laid the groundwork for more varied developments in the future. (Among these developments was the genus, popular today, which goes by the title "heads-bodies-and-legs," where horizontal flaps are moved to allow the making of a large variety of funny figures. This type of movable was, in 1853, the subject of a playful experiment by William Makepeace Thackeray. He cut four harlequinade-like flap changes in a manuscript set of *Metamorphoses*, which he made in Philadelphia for the children of his friend William Reed. The manuscript is reproduced in *A Book of Drawings*, with a note by Agnes Repplier, published in a limited edition by the Pennell Club in 1925.)

The harlequinades that are described here have been chosen to demonstrate the checkered history of the genre over a period of about fifty years. An understanding of its evolution is hampered, however, by the small number of examples surviving and by the fact that these sheets usually were printed from at most two copperplates, which may have led a peripatetic existence. Turn-ups with the same title and contents but with different imprints have sometimes survived in widely separated collections. Only a full census and close comparative study will determine the life span of the plates from which harlequinades were printed.

One step towards this has been made by the theater historian and authority on toy theaters, George Speaight. In an article in *Theatre Notebook* (vol. 45, 1999, pp. 70–84) he compares what is known of the text of two pantomimes to the structure of two turn-ups: *Harlequin's Invasion* (1770—the earliest harlequinade, based on a 1759 entertainment by David Garrick) and *Mother Shipton*, discussed below in entry 152. Speaight also provides a near-complete list of all known turn-ups with a note of the stage productions on which they were probably based.

◆§ 151 ◇

Harlequin Cherokee or the Indian Chiefs in London. London: Publish'd as the Act directs by Robᵗ Sayer, Map & Printseller, Nº 53, in Fleet Street, Febʸ 24ᵗʰ 1772. 6ᵈ Plain. 1ˢ Colour'd. Book 12. Turn-up: two half-sheets, one cut up to form flaps attached to the other (unfolded but turned down: 190 × 320 mm.).

Two engravings, colored by hand at the publisher's; each with four scenes, which are shown in various transformations by turning the flaps up or down and are accompanied by six-line verses. Folded three times to a narrow format in original gray paper

HARLEQUIN CHEROKEE
or the Indian Chiefs in London.
London Published as the Act directs Oct. 24, 1772 by
Rob.t Sayer, Map & Printseller N.o 53. in Fleet Street.
6.d Plain, 1.s Colour'd.
Book 12.

Here Harlequin that artful thief
You see is like an Indian Chief
What can his meaning be for this
Since Europe all is known for his
Must Savage Wilds become his prey
Turn up and then attend the lay.

Here's a Ship likewise a Cargo
By fancy brought without Embargo
For it is known to all the Nation
No Duty's paid for Frolickation
The Young & Old may laugh and play
But turn it up and then away.

See here in pleasures ample round
The strange Americans are found
Tho' they seem odd to stare & Grin
Yet we as Wildly stare at them
It is the Custom of each Nation
Which causes all the Consternation.

Here Harlequin you see again
No doubt he's something in his brain
For I have heard with Fun and Frolick
He never yet has had the cholick
And if still further you would know
Pray Turn it up and we will shew.

151. *reduced*

wrappers. References: ESTC N032889; Muir NBL 824; Osborne II, 1051; Speaight p. 80 (querying source in a 1762 production by J. Love of *The Witches; or Harlequin Cherokee*); McGrath 3.

The Osborne Collection of Early Children's Books, Toronto Public Library.

A late example in the Sayer series. His no. 1, *Adam and Eve*, was first published ca. 1767. The story is typically incongruous, not least because it unexpectedly introduces a North American theme into the conventions of the *commedia*. No doubt this was an attempt to capitalize on the celebrity of three Cherokee Indian chieftains who visited London in 1762 accompanied by two veterans of George Washington's campaigns (see Richard Altick, *The Shows of London* [Cambridge, Mass., and London: Harvard University Press, 1978], pp. 46–7).

ᕦ§ 152 §ᕤ

[E.?] TRINGHAM, jun. (fl. 1771–86). *Mother Shipton.* London: Printed & published by I. Strutt, Little Queen Street, Lincoln's Inn Fields; E. Burns, N° 54, Tottenham Court Road and E. Newbery, Corner of S.t Paul's Church Yard, Sept.r 10.th 1800. Price Six Pence Coloured 1 Shilling. Turn-up (unfolded but turned down: 180 × 305 mm.).

Four etched scenes, each with two movable flaps for transformation and three six-line verses. Apparently printed from two copperplates, publisher's coloring including gouache. Folded

three times to a narrow format, modern mounting and boards. References: ESTC N035369; Roscoe J250A; Osborne II, 1052; Speaight p. 79; McGrath 5.

The Osborne Collection of Early Children's Books, Toronto Public Library.

On February 13, 1771, William Tringham "under St. Dunstan's Church, Fleet Street" and three other booksellers published their turn-up of *Mother Shipton*, with the engraving being done by his son, who was presumably E. Tringham. They may have been inspired to the task by the staging of a "Mother Shipton" harlequinade, for within a couple of weeks Robert Sayer came forward with his *Mother Shipton, or Harlequin in despair*, Book 7 of his turn-up series, dated March 2nd, 1771 (a second part, sub-titled *Harlequin in the dumps*—Book 9—appeared on "Sep.r y.e 9.th 1771." PML 84950). The few iconographic similarities between the Tringham and Sayer versions could easily be accounted for by their relationship to a common theatrical source.

What fate befell William Tringham's turn-up we do not know, but with this *Mother Shipton* from I. Strutt and his partners we find a revival of Tringham junior's original plates. The former imprint has been burnished out and replaced by the new publishers, and since their addresses were not so long LONDON has been added in large caps. In all other respects the nineteenth-century customers were being offered a thirty-year-old production.

Speaight notes a 1770 pantomime by G. Colman, *Mother Shipton*, and ascribes the source of the turn-up to a later restaging of *Mother Shipton* as *Harlequin's Museum* (1792) without realizing that Strutt's plates were earlier than that date and must surely relate to the 1770 piece.

Mother Shipton herself is a figure who stands somewhere between folklore and the chapbook tradition. She was born in 1488, offspring of the devil and a lady named Sontibles, and she was celebrated by the makers of popular literature as a worker of wonders and a prophetess. Her cave at Knaresborough in Yorkshire can still be visited by the curious.

◦§ 153 §◦

The Magpie and the Maid. [London:] Pub^d by S. Poole N°. 126 Pall Mall, 1815. Turn-up: probably a single sheet, one of its halves cut, pasted, and folded to make up flaps for lifting (unfolded but turned down: 192 × 302 mm.).

Eight illustrations arranged in four sections, presumably printed from a single large aquatinted copperplate, which may be combined in various transformations by turning the flaps up or down, and three six-line verses to each section. Colored by a contemporary hand, perhaps at the publisher's. Folded three times to a narrow format, with original engraved pictorial (rebus) label, also dated 1815, mounted on buff paper wrappers. References: Osborne II, 1052; Speaight p. 81 (noting an 1815 pantomime of the same title by G. Dibdin); McGrath 6.

The Osborne Collection of Early Children's Books, Toronto Public Library.

A further example of a "late" harlequinade, emanating from an extremely obscure publisher at a high-class address. The Ball Collection at Bloomington, Indiana, has a George Martin version of the same theatrical interlude, *The Maid and the Magpie* [n.d.], but in this instance the two treatments are not closely related.

◦§ 154 §◦

The Riding Master, or, Harlequin on Horseback. London: Published by G. Martin, 6, G^t St Thomas Apostle, [ca. 1820]. Price 6d. Coloured. Turn-up: half-sheet, partly cut up and mounted to form flaps for lifting (unfolded but turned down: 99 × 302 mm.).

Eight illustrations arranged in four sections and hand-colored at the publisher's, probably printed from a single etched copperplate, which may be combined in various transformations by turning the flaps up or down, and three four-line verses to each section. Folded three times to a small square format in original orange wrappers, letterpress title-label mounted on front cover.

Department of Special Collections, Charles E. Young Research Library, UCLA.

I. Strutt and partners (see entry 152) were not the only ones to benefit from the dispersal of Tringham's copperplates for turn-ups. The harlequinade of *The Riding Master* was first published in this neat square format by E. Tringham on 31 May 1783, priced at 3d. plain and 6d. colored. In time *The Riding Master* plates, along with some others (e.g. *Harlequin's Imprisonment*), came into the hands of George Martin, who replaced Tringham's imprint with

153. cover-label, *reduced*

his own and reissued the little books at the uniform price of 6d. colored. The small format is very suitable for this harlequinade's typically unimpressive narrative. George Martin's slaphappy methods are noted below (chapter XII).

HIEROGLYPHICS

The idea of using printed pictures to symbolize ideas has among its roots the emblem-book tradition, whose earliest exponent is Andrea Alciati's *Emblematum Liber* (Augsburg, 1531). In emblem books, however, the picture was primarily intended to make a complex statement that needed a written interpretation, whereas in hieroglyphic books the picture may stand either as a substitute for a word or as its phonetic equivalent. The earliest such book for children was *Geistliche Herzenseinbildungen* by Melchior Mattsperger, with engravings by Hans Georg Bodenehr and published at Augsburg in 1685. That was a handsome piece of book production, a claim that cannot easily be made for the first English hieroglyphic Bible for children, which came from the shop of Thomas Hodgson, probably in 1784. He had commissioned forty-six of its many small illustrations from the Beilby/Bewick workshop, and John Bewick would later add improvements when he worked for Hodgson in London. The book was a great success with new editions being called for every year;

Harly is gone, the ſcene is chang'd,
A Drummer in his place is rang'd;
So merrily he beats the Drum,
That to the end you all may come.

Harly a Bag of Gold preſents,
The Old Man takes it, and Conſents;
Which ſerves to prove that ſaying true,
'Tis money makes the Mare to go.

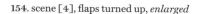
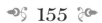

154. scene [4], flaps turned up, *enlarged*

eventually the rights passed to Robert Bassam and others, by which time *A New Hieroglyphical Bible* was also on the market. Needless to say, Mrs. Trimmer was upset by the godlessness of such levity, and we note her strictures on Thompson's edition in chapter XVIII (entry 356).

❧ 155 ❧

A Curious Hieroglyphick Bible; or, select passages in the Old and New Testaments, represented with emblematical figures, for the amusement of youth: designed chiefly to familiarize tender age, in a pleasing and diverting manner, with early ideas of the Holy Scriptures. To which are subjoined, a

155. front cover

short account of the lives of the Evangelists, and other pieces, illustrated with cuts. The thirteenth edition. London: Printed and Sold by Robert Bassam, No. 53, St. John's Street, West-Smithfield: (by Assignment, from the Executors of T. Hodgson,) H.D. Symonds, Pater-noster-Row, Scatcherd and Whitaker, Ave-Maria-Lane, and may be had of all the Booksellers, 1796 [but not before 1802]. [Price One Shilling bound.] Entered at Stationers-Hall agreeable to Act of Parliament. 18° (132 × 85 mm.).

A^6 (1 mounted as front pastedown, 1^v frontispiece, 2^r title, 2^v blank, –3·4, 5^r dedication, 5^v *Advertisement* for *Emblems of Mortality*, 6^r *Preface*); B–M^6 ($M4^r$ *On the Incomparable Treasure of the Holy Scriptures*, incipit: *Here is the Spring where Waters flow*, $M4^v$–6^r Lives of the Evangelists, $M6^v$ *Doomsday; or, A Call to Judgment*, incipit: *Come to Judgment, come away!*) N^2 (=A3·4; 1^r last three stanzas of "Doomsday," *A Prayer for the true Use of the Holy Scriptures*, 1^v *Questions and Answers out of the Holy Scriptures*, 2^v imprint *Printed by R. Bassam, No. 53, St. John's Street, West Smithfield*). Pp. [8], 136. Laid paper, fleur-de-lys watermark, countermarked with initials IV and date 1802. Wood-engraved frontispiece and 520 wood-engraved illustrations (including repeats) of various sizes, a variety of type-ornament borders (one on each page of the biblical part). Original pictorial yellow boards, wood-engraved foliate border, an angel subduing

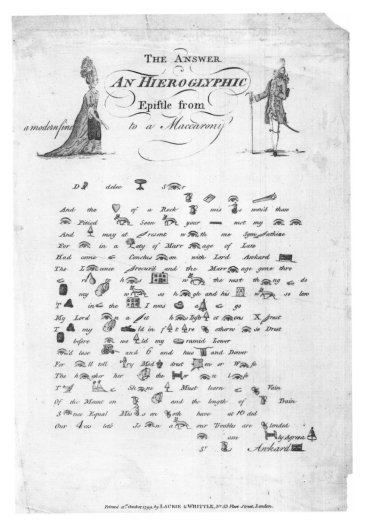

155. M3 recto

156. *reduced*

the devil by holding up the *Hieroglyphick Bible* on front cover, *Agnus Dei* and angel heads on back cover. References: ESTC T139135; Clouston, pp. 12–13; Johnson 33; Tattersfield JB13; Hockliffe 416.

Provenance: John Dyer (early inscr.). PML 86031. Gift: Felix de Marez Oyens, 1991.

Hodgson's hieroglyphs were primarily simple riddles—a picture of feet for the word "feet"—with answers at the bottom of the page. Occasionally, though, the pictures would have an emblematic quality, such as doves for "love," or a bosomy lady with a dagger for "jealousy." The book had a long and influential life. James illustrates an edition dated 1834 (p. 89), and Osborne II lists six variant editions. It may also have prompted an interest in the wider use of hieroglyphics, for we soon find John Wallis issuing hieroglyphic puzzle cards, and Linda Hannas records two hieroglyphic dissected puzzles of the Lord's Prayer and the Creed published by Richard Carpenter in 1790.

❧ 156 ❧

The Answer. An Hieroglyphic Epistle from a modern fine [Lady, *in rebus*] *to a Maccaroni* [Gentleman, *in rebus*]. London: Printed by Laurie & Whittle, N° 53 Fleet Street, 21st

October 1799 [this impression not before 1814 (watermark date)]. Broadside (post half-sheet, 372 × 240 mm.).

Engraving (335 × 235 mm.) of an epistolary satire in cursive script and hand-colored rebus, incipit: *Dear delectable Sir / Your letter I saw / And the heart of a Rock your misfortunes wou'd thaw . . .* Verso blank.

PML 84441. Gift: Elisabeth Ball.

Mrs. Trimmer's views on fine ladies and macaronis are guessable but, however disapproving, they would hardly run to objections about their using hieroglyphics in secular correspondence, especially when the epistles carry the satirical overtones of this one. The sheet is not really intended primarily for child readers, but the puzzle element in it and the likely enjoyment to be derived from construing the verses give it child appeal and show the way in which picture sheets brought new life to popular publishing in the 1790s. Furthermore, the method of incorporating the hieroglyphics (phonetic and ideogrammatic) was later to be copied by Catherine Sinclair and others in their letters for children published during the 1860s. Several such were published at Edinburgh (see Darton p. 221), and they may have revived the fashion, for the Morgan Library owns a manuscript rebus letter by Harry Palmer, written from Rudge, near Ross, and dated 12 February 1863 (MA 3963).

The term "maccaroni" (or, more usually, "macaroni") has nothing to do with foodstuffs. It means a dandified fellow and, according to *OED*, was first used thus ca. 1760.

WRITING SHEETS

Writing sheets and exercise books also have a long history, at least dating back to the woodcut and typographical copy books of the Italian writing masters in the sixteenth century. Sheets for young schoolchildren began to be popular in England from the early decades of the eighteenth century, and their decorative borders soon accommodated narrative or fable themes as well as ornamental motifs.

Naturally, printer/publishers of children's books saw writing sheets as easily claimable territory, and we meet many publishers already discussed (e.g. Bickham, Hawkins, Dicey & Marshall), either issuing sheets or advertising them among their stock-in-trade. Robert Sayer, the harlequinade man, also produced hand-colored sheets. The boom time for sheets, or the period from which most have survived, began in the 1790s and continued for about forty years. Laurie & Whittle, "successors to the late Mr. Robert Sayer," were the most prominent of the publishers in this period, and we show here two of their many sheets with religious themes and a much less usual secular sheet. A later example of the genre, published by the prolific William Belch (in partnership with J. Phelps), is discussed at entry 238 in chapter XII.

◄§ 157a ℈►

Christ Blessing Little Children. London: Published by Laurie & Whittle, 53 Fleet Street, 2ᵈ Novʳ 1795 [plate date, this impression not before 1854]. Broadside (post-size full sheet, 485 × 385 mm.).

Writing sheet (numbered 55), printed on the mould side from an etched copperplate (450 × 355 mm.) and hand-colored. Laid paper, post-horn watermark, countermarked GC & Co 1854. Illustration *Suffer little Children to come unto me and forbid them not* (top) and ten other biblical pictures (sides), empty cartouche (bottom); the central area left blank for calligraphic exercise (uncompleted).

Private Collection.

◄§ 157b ℈►

A New School Piece, Design'd and Extracted from the Revelation of Sᵗ John. London: Publish'd by Laurie & Whittle, 53, Fleet Street, Novʳ 9, 1803 [plate date, this impression not before 1811]. Broadside (post-size full sheet, 460 × 360 mm.).

Writing sheet (numbered 78), printed on the mould side from an etched plate (430 × 340 mm.) and hand-colored. Laid paper, post-horn watermark, countermarked J. Whatman 1811. Illustration *The twenty four Elders fall down before him that sat on the Throne, and worship him that liveth for ever and ever. –Rev.ⁿˢ Ch. IV, ve. 10* (top) and 8 other biblical pictures (sides), empty cartouche (bottom); the central area left blank for calligraphic exercise (uncompleted).

Private Collection.

157b. *reduced*

◄§ 158 ℈►

The Entertaining History of Robin Hood, & Little John, &c. London: Publish'd by Laurie & Whittle. 33 Fleet Street, June 24. 1809 [plate date, an early impression probably of the same year]. Broadside (post-size full sheet, 480 × 385 mm.).

Writing sheet (numbered 93), printed on the mould side from an etched copperplate (440 × 360 mm.), uncolored. Laid paper, post-horn watermark, and date 1808, countermarked King & Ford 1808. Large framed illustration *Merry making in Shirewood &c.* (top) and six smaller ones (sides), unframed illustration *Burning the Nunnery* (bottom); the central area left blank for calligraphic exercise (uncompleted—see overleaf).

Private Collection.

PRINTS

The oldest German xylographic broadsides date from the second decade of the fifteenth century. Woodcuts of saints and other religious subjects survive mounted inside the lids of wooden boxes or inserted in manuscript codices, and can be seen nailed to walls and doors in old-master paintings of the Netherlandish schools. Medical and astrological images were also not uncommon, while social and political satire found popular markets in the sixteenth and seventeenth centuries. The earliest known catchpenny prints specifically for children's entertainment were published in Holland (Amsterdam, Leyden, Haarlem, Schiedam) from the third quarter of the seventeenth century onwards. This Dutch

The Entertaining History of Robin Hood, & Little John, &c.

158. *reduced*

tradition is invariably described as unique until the late eighteenth century, but the recent discovery of a remarkable, large colored woodcut picture sheet preserved inside the lid of an English seventeenth-century children's desk (private collection) reveals how much may have been lost: *A Pleasant History of the World turned upside down* (London: Printed for George Minnkin and are to be so'd at is shopp at the Parrot in Shoo Lane [undated]; demy broadside [about 510 × 340 mm.]). No seventeenth-century publisher at this address appears to be known (his name does not appear in ESTC or in the publishers' index to Wing), but his neighbor at the Falcon in Shoe Lane, Francis Leach, was the first to license a woodcut of this popular subject in the Stationers' Register of 12 March 1656. No copy of Leach's print has survived; see Sheila O'Connell, *The popular print in England 1550–1850* (London: British Museum Press, 1999), p. 123. A George Minikin at the King's Head in St. Martin's Lane advertised a pack of cards of the counties of England in the "Term Catalogue" for 1676 (Edward Arber, *The Term Catalogues 1668–1709*, I, 237).

Some of the social and commercial forces that led to the establishment and growth of English publishing for children also led to the expansion of the popular print trade, with its very different emphasis on political commentary and satire. (In 1775 Sayer and Bennett's catalogue had well over fifteen hundred single prints and sets of prints listed, including portraits, landscapes, and decorative prints, as well as drolls.) Undoubtedly the popularity of print shops, with their enticing window displays, alerted booksellers to the potential of graphic art for children, and throughout this chapter we can perceive how interaction takes place between the engraved work done for single prints and its adaptation to more specialized wares such as harlequinades, dissected puzzles, and board games.

The Bowles & Carver sheets in the following description represent a typically ambitious eighteenth-century print publishing venture. With the upswing in specialist children's book publishing, firms like the Dartons also developed their own lines of prints exclusively aimed at the juvenile and educational market.

❧ 159 ❧

[Children's Prints]. London: Printed for & Sold by Bowles & Carver. N° 69 in St Paul's Church Yard, 1787–95 [no impressions before 1801 (watermark dates)]. Broadsides, the majority oblong (pott-size half-sheets, about 274 × 181 mm. each).

201 etchings (about 169 × 243 mm. each): Bowles & Carver picture sheets 10–24, 26–35, 37–71; 73, 77–81, 83, 85–9, 92–124, 131–9 (oblong); 140; 141–4 (oblong); 145; 146–8 (oblong); 149; 150, 152–68 (oblong); 169; 170 (oblong); 171; 172–7 (oblong); 178; 179–96, 199–202 (oblong); 203–4; 216, 219, 221–2, 226–7, 230 (oblong); 233; 234, 236–40, 243, 247–8 (oblong); 250–1; 252–6 (oblong); 257. All on the same laid-paper stock (watermark: royal arms, countermark: 1801). Reference: Bowles & Carver.

Provenance: Walter Schatzki; C. F. van Veen (Sotheby's Amsterdam, 28th Nov. 1984, lot 27). PML 84760. Purchase: Mrs. Robert Horne Charles and Mrs. Donald M. Oenslager.

One of the largest of the late-eighteenth-century printsellers was Carington Bowles (1724–1793), whose shop at 69 St. Paul's Churchyard was almost next door to the Newbery/Carnan establishment. Bowles published and sold a vast range of prints, and the Morgan Library possesses no fewer than 201 examples of his picture sheets in impressions published after his death by his son Carington II, under the imprint of Bowles and Carver. Many of these picture sheets would not only have been enjoyed by children but were produced with children chiefly in mind, and the following list has been selected to represent comic scenes, educational pictures, narratives, and puzzles:

B & C 10: *The Animal Performers* [a single large image of three dressed animals—a cat, dog, and monkey singing "A New Song"]. CP 1. PML 84760.1.

B & C 70: *Saucepan* [and 34 other objects, the last *Music Book*]. CP 57. PML 84760.59.

B & C 77: *Puzzle-Brain Mountain*. CP 60. PML 84760.62.

B & C 121: *Miss in her Chaise* [and three other children's games]. CP 79. PML 84760.102.

B & C 141: *A, B and C, I'll fight you all three* [and eight other alphabet scenes of fights and punishment]. CP 90. PML 84760.116.

B & C 158: *The Wonderful Pig of Knowledge* [a single image of the pig exhibiting her literary skill at a drawing-room levee]. CP 105. PML 84760.132.

B & C 160: [The World turned upside down, fourteen scenes]. CP 107. PML 84760.134.

B & C 173: *Flying a Kite*; *Cricket* [and seven other children's games]. CP 118. PML 84760.147.

159. B & C 70, *reduced*

159. B & C 77, *reduced*

159. B & C 121, *reduced*

159. B & C 160, *reduced*

159. B & C 240, *reduced*

B & C 174: *John Gilpin.* CP 119. PML 84760.148.

B & C 204: *Dear Doll do not roam, But prithee go home.* Not in CP. PML 84760.176.

B & C 221: *M[r] Patrick O'Brien—The Irish Giant* [a portrait]. CP 146. PML 84760.179.

B & C 238: *Noddle Island* [an island landscape composed in the manner of 240]. CP 153. PML 84760.188.

B & C 239: *The Isle of Man—the Rocks of Scilly at a distance* [an island landscape composed in the manner of 240]. CP 154. PML 84760.189.

B & C 240: *The Isle of Dogs.* CP 155. PML 84760.190.

DISSECTED PUZZLES

What was eventually to be known as the jigsaw puzzle had a hesitant beginning. Until recently it was assumed that the invention dated back to the early 1760s when John Spilsbury (1739–69) issued from his print shop at Russell Court, Covent Garden, the first of his dissected maps "to facilitate the teaching of geography." This was simply a print, pasted to a thin mahogany board and then cut into simple outline pieces that could be pushed together to make up the original picture. There is, however, reason to believe that an educational aid of this kind was first used during the 1750s through the agency of Mme Le Prince de Beaumont who was then running a school in London with a prospectus advertising among other things "les cartes de geographie en bois." The evidence is fully discussed by Jill Shefrin in her monograph on Charlotte Finch, the tutoring of the children of George III, and the use of dissected maps in their education: *Such Constant Affectionate Care* (Los Angeles: The Cotsen Occasional Press, 2003).*

The idea did not take immediately, perhaps because Spilsbury died before he could fully exploit his invention, but by the 1780s several publishers involved with the print trade (including Carington Bowles) were "diversifying" into dissections. Education remained a dominant motive, and several children's book publishers like John Wallis, John Harris, and the Dartons developed special lines in primarily educational puzzles; but the play element was especially encouraged through purely entertaining themes such as a quarrel scene from *Tristram Shandy* (1795) or the adaptation to puzzle form of hieroglyphic sheets and race games.

* Jill Shefrin has also compiled for the same publisher a valuable account of Spilsbury's activities, especially in relation to an eighteenth-century cabinet specially constructed to house his puzzles: *Neatly Dissected . . . John Spilsbury and Early Dissected Puzzles* (Los Angeles, 1999).

◆§ 160 §◆

Chronological Tables of Roman History from the foundation of the City to the Augustan age. London: Published by J. Wallis N° 16 Ludgate Street. and E. Newbery, Corner of S*t* Paul's Church Yard. October 20*th* 1789. Oblong broadside (royal full sheet, 405 × 585 mm.), dissected to form a jigsaw puzzle.

Engraving, mounted on soft wood and backed with a sheet of plain laid paper (against warping), cut apart into 42 interlocking pieces. 32 medallion portraits of Roman rulers, from the founder Romulus to the emperor Augustus, each with text in a copperplate hand. Reference: Hannas p. 93.

Department of Special Collections, Charles E. Young Research Library, UCLA.

An example of one of the simplest of the educational puzzles, each compartment forming an individual piece which needs only to be put into its appropriate chronological place. The idea of dissecting across the natural boundaries was a later refinement.

TABLE GAMES

The use of printed sheets to make "race games" dates back to the sixteenth century. One of the most famous, *The Game of the Goose*,

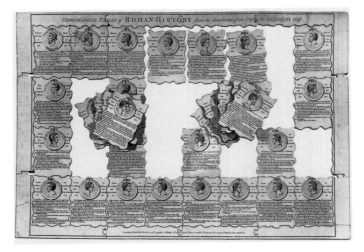

160. *reduced*

was registered at Stationers Hall in 1597, and one of the earliest surviving examples, *The Game of the Snake* (ca. 1680), was played in very similar fashion.

The association of such entertainments with gambling did not do much to encourage their adaptation for children however, and when, along with the growth of the print industry, table games for children began to be manufactured they tended to have a strongly moral or educational flavor. (As our examples show, they also shied from recommending dice, preferring the apparently more innocent "teetotum," a six-sided piece of wood or metal which could be spun like a top.)

Carington Bowles (see the section *Prints* above) is counted among the earliest dealers in children's games with his involvement in John Jeffreys's *Journey Through Europe; or the play of geography* (1759), which was advertised as "to be played in all respects the same as the game of Goose." As with other novelties, game sheets took time to catch on, and although Robert Sayer, the publisher of harlequinades, seems to have dabbled in the genre (his *Royal Geographical Amusement* came out in 1774), the upsurge of popularity came only with the increased activities of the 1790s. The Wallis/Newbery *Game of Human Life* (entry 161) was one of the first manifestations of a new spirit of inventiveness, and over the following twenty years both printsellers, like Laurie & Whittle, and publishers, like John and Edward Wallis, vied with each other in seeking thematic variants for the old "Game of Goose" formula.

◆§ 161 §◆

The New Game of Human Life. London: Published according to Act of Parliament, by John Wallis, N° 16, Ludgate Street, and E. Newbery, the Corner of S*t* Paul's Church Yard, July 14: 1790 [impression possibly later]. Broadside (super royal full sheet, 465 × 670 mm.).

Hand-colored engraved race game on paper, printed from a single copperplate (sheet virtually trimmed to the plate-mark), divided into 16 equal sections for mounting on linen and folding. Text within the oval track: *Rules of the Game*; in the outside corners: *The Utility and Moral Tendency of this Game* and *Directions for*

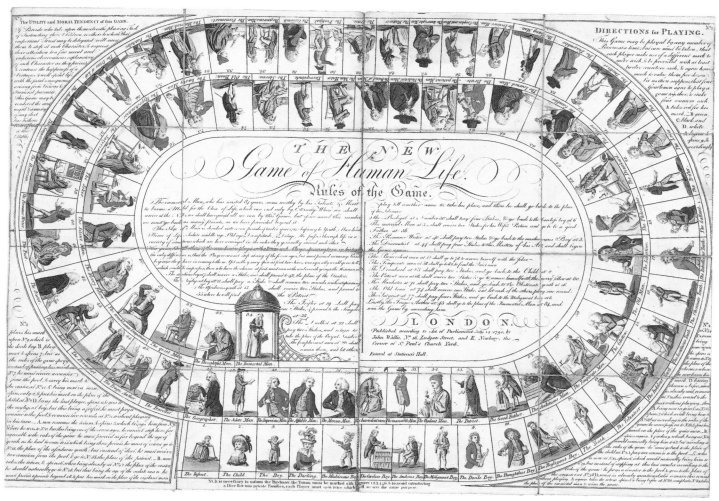

161. *reduced*

Playing. References: Hannas pp. 32, 115; Whitehouse pp. 46–7; Shefrin 35.

PML 85566. Gift: Elisabeth Ball.

Both F. R. B. Whitehouse and Hannas describe the importance of this game in *Table Games* and *The English Jigsaw Puzzle*. Not only did it daringly bring back into circulation for children a game design chiefly associated with gambling, the spiral *Royal Game of the Goose*, but it also required the use of a teetotum, which may have avoided "introducing a Dice Box into Private Families" but did indeed "answer the same purpose." (As a guard against possible depravity, however, the publishers suggest that parents might like to call a halt after each move in the game to request attention for "a few moral and judicious observations explanatory of each Character." The publishers also help, with implied judgments: if you land on The Romance Writer you must pay two stakes and go back to The Mischievous Boy at 5.) Hannas notes that this game closely follows a French model but with some of the characters "anglicised": The Ambitious Man is none other than the Prince Regent. Whatever the source, however, the game is a remarkable blending of the old use of moral figures with a new encouragement of play while, technically, it shows the scale on which engraving and hand-coloring could now be used for popular goods. The game was also sold dissected, as a jigsaw puzzle.

☙ 162 ❧

The Swan of Elegance. A new game designed for the instruction and amusement of youth. London: Published by John Harris, Corner of St Pauls Church Yard, Decr 20th 1814. Broadside (royal full sheet, 600 × 480 mm.).

Hand-colored engraved race game on paper, printed from a single copperplate, divided into twelve equal sections for mounting on linen and folding. Original green marbled paper board slipcase (205 × 125 mm.), colored engraved pictorial title-label. References: Moon *Harris* 1057 (not seen); Whitehouse pp. 49–50.

Published with: *Rules and Directions for Playing The Swan of Elegance, a new moral game . . .* London: printed for J. Harris, the corner of St. Paul's Church-Yard, 1815. 16° (161 × 100 mm.). [1^8] (1^v imprint *H. Bryer, Printer, Bridge-street, Blackfriars, London,* 7^v–8^v ads *New Games,* 8^v imprint). Pp. [16]. Paper watermarked "Howard & Lunno 1814." Original wrappers made up from a waste sheet of *Mrs. Carter's Celebrated Treatise on the Art of Cookery: in which economy and elegance are united. An improved edition. Printed for J. Harris and E. Crosby.*

PML 85346. Purchase: Ball Fund.

"Elegance" is the word, although it applies rather less to the swan

162. *reduced*

than to the tasseled bandana in which he is wrapped, with its engraved pictures of children in various states of virtue. The game itself is simple enough, the players moving counters and gaining advantages or paying forfeits according to the nature of the child on whom they land. The instructions are given in verse:

Passionate Jem

Oh! Jem what a shame 'tis to kick the poor cat
Now your passion I quickly will cool;
So go back to Harry, the game fresh begin,
Pray! amend, and no more play the fool.

Which is just like going down the last long snake in Snakes and Ladders.

Something went amiss in the planning of this game. Two places, Ann (no. 2) and Phoebe (no. 19), instruct the player to proceed to a character called Ned who helps a gentleman up from the ground; however, neither his place nor its accompanying rhyme can be found on the board.

MINIATURE LIBRARIES

During the 1790s Ellenor Fenn was a force to be reckoned with in the promotion of what might be called home-reading-without-tears (see entries 86 and 87). A number of her books from this period mention or advertise boxes of letters and other equipment which were designed to help children learn through play. These experiments culminated in a series of brilliantly conceived "miniature libraries" initiated by her publisher, John Marshall. They were sets of tiny books, planned around themes and housed in wooden boxes whose lids were made to resemble the front of a

bookcase. The first of these was actually the largest, *The Juvenile, or Child's Library* (1799–1800), but it was quickly followed by the smaller *Infant's Library* (1800–1)—sixteen little books in a box—which proved to be the most popular of a whole succession of imitations. The volumes were mostly little picture books on various subjects, all prettily bound in glazed paper with decorated paper labels. Marshall later varied his formula with a series of inventive sets of highly attractive boxed cards and other playthings.

⋘ 163 ⋙

Bibliothèque des Enfants. London: Printed and Sold by John Marshall. No. 4, Aldermary Church-Yard, Bow-Lane, Cheapside, [not before 1802 (watermark date vol. 8)]. 16 volumes. 64° (58/55 × 47/42 mm.).

Vocabulaire pour la Bibliothèque des Enfants. Tom. I [V, IX, XIII]: [1^{38}] (vol. 1: 1^r title, 1^v blank, 38^r imprint *Printed by John Marshall, No. 4, Aldermary Church Yard, of whom may be had a great variety of Publications for Children; Libraries, &c.*, 38^v blank); [1^{32}] (vols. 5 and 9: 1^r title, 1^v blank, 32^r imprint, 32^v blank; vol. 13: 1·32 blank, 2^r title, 2^v blank, 30^v imprint, 31 blank). Pp. 75, [1]; 62, [2]; 62, [2]; 59, [5]. Wove paper, vol. 1 watermarked 1801. Original mottled (vol. 13 marbled) boards, engraved title-label on front covers.

Tom. 2 (Outdoor scenes, incipit: *Votre maman donne la charité*), *Tom. 3* (Furniture and other objects, incipit: *Cette piramide se nomme un obélisque*), *Tom. 4* (Buildings and landscapes, incipit: *Pourquoi ne vous asseyez vous pas?*), *Tom. 6* (Rural and naval scenes, incipit: *Ceci se nomme un Moulin à eau*), *Tom. 7* (More outdoor scenes, incipit: *Allez dans le champ*), *Tom. 8* (Flowers, incipit: *Dites moi, je vous prie maman*), *Tom. 10* (Farming and related activities, incipit: *Voici un beau champ de bled*), *Tom. 11* (Birds, incipit: *L'Oie est un oiseau précieux*), *Tom. 12* (Girls' games, incipit: *Je ne peux pas fair tourner mon bendalore bien*), *Tom. 14* (Boys' games, incipit: *Voici de petits garçons qui jouent aux soldats*), *Tom. 15* (Quadrupeds, incipit: *Ce superbe animal se nomme un Zèbre*), *Tom. 16* (Insects, animals, etc., incipit: *Ce petit garçon court après un Papillon*). Each volume: [1^{16}], outer forme printed from an etched copperplate, inner forme letterpress (1^r title, 1^v–2^r blank, 2^v illustration, 3^r incipit, 15^r illustration, 15^v–16^r blank, 16^v colophon). Pp. 28, [4]. 13 full-page illustrations. Laid paper (vols. 10 and 12), wove paper (watermarked 1802 in vol. 8, 1801 in vol. 16). Original monochrome-glazed boards (pink, white, green, yellow or purple), engraved title-label on front covers.

Original wooden box, lined with pink paper, four compartments containing four volumes each, thus forming a portable library, sliding lid with engraved pictorial hand-colored and varnished label, showing the title and a glazed Georgian bookcase, scrollwork pediment forming a handle at the top of the lid.

Provenance: *Sold by Tabart & Co. at the Juvenile School Library, No. 157, New Bond Street; Where is constantly kept on Sale the largest Collection of Books of Amusement and Instruction in the World, from one penny to five guineas in price.* (letterpress label mounted on the bottom of the box). Peter Courmont, New York.

15

Ces enfants-ci
jouent à la croſſe.
L'un jete la balle,
et l'autre ſe tient
prêt à la frapper
de ſa croſſe.

163. vol. 15, fos. 7ᵛ–8ʳ, letterpress, intaglio

Minet, minet,
viens ici mon
joli petit minet.
Je vais demander
à Marie qu'elle
me donne du lait
pour toi.

163. vol. 15, fos. 8ᵛ–9ʳ

Although sets of *The Infant's Library* are not all that uncommon, some companion sets which Marshall enterprisingly issued in other languages are extremely rare. The Courmont set of the French version is apparently the only known complete example of its kind. To Marshall's credit, he did not merely translate his English version for this production. The sixteen volumes are all separately edited with the needs of the French-learner in mind, and the first volume in each group of four books is a French/English vocabulary for the picture books that follow. A further interesting feature of this set is the Tabart advertisement on the back of the box, which shows that his "Juvenile and School Library" stocked miniature libraries, and indeed such items can be observed on display in his shop in the illustrations of "Tabart's Juvenile Library" as reproduced in the frontispiece of Moon *Tabart*.

❦ 164 ❧

A History of Flowers. London: Printed and Sold by John Marshall, 140 Fleet Street, [April 21 1801 (date on the cards)]. 2 volumes. 64° (44 × 36 mm.), illustrations on separate cards (75 × 49 mm.).

Each volume: [1¹⁶]. Pp. 30 [2]. A total of 14 hand-colored illustrations mounted on card, presumably printed from one copperplate on a single sheet and then cut up.

Original gilt-decorated paper boards (red vol. 1, white vol. 2), engraved label on front covers. See overleaf. Volumes and cards preserved in original wooden box (90 × 63 × 37 mm.), floral engraving under varnish on the lid. Reference: Alderson *Miniature Libraries* 5.

The Osborne Collection of Early Children's Books, Toronto Public Library.

Once seized by the idea of putting books in boxes, John Marshall went on to produce a number of imaginative schemes which aimed to link learning and play. Among these was a series of "Infant's Cabinets" in which sets of illustrated cards were boxed up with two miniature books that gave brief explanations of the pictures. The general intention seems to have been educational: "find a card and read all about it." Children doubtless found ways of converting didacticism into play.

❦ 165 ❧

The Book Case of Instruction. London: Published by John Wallis, 42 Skinner Street, Snow Hill, Decʳ 11, 1812 [date of box-label, books dated 1813]. 10 volumes. 18° (vols. 1–4, 100 × 64 mm.), 32° (vols. 5–10, about the same measurements).

1: *The Good Childs Cabinet of Natural History. Embellished with 32 fine engravings. Vol. 2. Birds*; 2: *Vol. 1. Beasts*; 3: *Vol. 4. Insects*; 4: *Vol. 3. Fishes*. Each volume: [1¹⁸] (1ᵛ frontispiece, 2ʳ title, 18ᵛ blank). Pp. [36]. Laid paper (two stocks, Britannia watermark, one countermarked with date 1809, the other with name of the mill J. Rump). Etched frontispiece, title dated Janʸ 4ᵗʰ 1813 and 31 half-page illustrations, apparently printed from two copperplates about as large as the full sheet (uninked area overlapping letterpress text). Original marbled boards, colored paper spines, etched pictorial title-labels on front covers. Reference: Cf. Alderson *Miniature Libraries* 7 (Wallis's *Elegant Present of Natural History* 1801, another boxed miniature library, containing *Flowers* as well as an earlier edition of the above four titles).

5: *Rewards for Attentive Studies or, stories moral and entertaining*; 6: *The History of England from the Conquest to the Death of George II*, 31 wood-engraved portraits; 7–8: *Scripture History; or, a brief account of the Old and New Testament*, 64 wood-engraved portraits; 9: *Short and Easy Rules for Attaining a Knowledge of English Grammar. To which are added a few letters for the formation of juvenile correspondence*; 10: *Exercises for Ingenuity: consisting of queries, transpositions, charades, rebuses, and riddles*. Each volume: A–D⁸ (A1ʳ title, imprint *London: printed for John Wallis, 42, Skinner Street, Snow Hill; By F. Vigurs, 14, York Street, Covent Garden*). Pp. 64. Wove paper (watermark date 1809). Original marbled boards, colored paper spines, engraved title-labels. Reference: Cf. Alderson *Miniature Libraries* 4 (earlier edition of 5, 6 and 9 in another of Wallis's boxed miniature libraries, *The Book-Case of Knowledge*).

Original wooden box, lined with pink paper, two compartments containing the ten volumes, thus forming a portable library (see overleaf), an empty drawer underneath with engraved label listing *Contents. 1. Natural History of Birds, 32 Plates*, [etc.]; sliding lid with engraved pictorial hand-colored and varnished label, showing the title and a boy handing a book to a girl from a glazed

164. Boxed miniature set, *intaglio*

Georgian bookcase, carved pediment showing a globe and forming a handle at the top of the lid.

Provenance: Sydney Roscoe (pencil notes in his hand, Sotheby's London, 1st June 1989, lot 328). The Osborne Collection of Early Children's Books, Toronto Public Library. Gift: Felix de Marez Oyens, 1991.

Once John Marshall had shown the way, other publishers were quick to market alternatives to his *Juvenile* and *Infant's* libraries. As might be expected, John Wallis, with his involvement in maps, games, puzzles, and so on, was one of the foremost competitors. This *Book Case of Instruction* appears to be a fairly latecomer on the scene but incorporates a number of themes that were already present in some of Wallis's earlier boxed libraries.

DOLL BOOKS

Among the later inventions of this fertile period were the "paper doll books," which emanated chiefly from S. & J. Fuller's Temple of Fancy in Rathbone Place. A trial run can probably be seen in their *Lecture on Heads; a chimney ornament for all ages* (ca. 1808), in which a single bald-headed visage could be slotted into a variety of be-hatted torsos to illustrate a series of rather satirical verses; but the prompting idea may well have come from the earlier use of paper dolls by the fashion trade as a cheap means of displaying dress samples. (Sayer and Bennett in their catalogue of 1775 advertise what may have been a precursor, *The Children Metamorphosed* with "changing head-dresses, toys &c." The Child's Toy Warehouse in Lower Thames Street was also found to be selling a paper doll with dresses and hats ca. 1780.)

Nevertheless, it was only with Fuller's publication of *Little Fanny* (entry 166) that a consistent effort was made to market these "histories in a series of figures," and some eleven titles emerged from The Temple of Fancy, several of them running to two or more reprints. Competitors were less successful. J. Aldis of Moorfields (see chapter XII) produced a *History and Adventures of Little William* and of *Little Eliza* (both 1810) with eight complete cut-out figures each, and the Wallises attempted a variation (entry 167), but the result does not seem to have encouraged the production of additional titles.

◦§ 166 §◦

[AMELIA TROWARD? (m. Samuel Rainbow Girdlestone 1827)]. *The History of Little Fanny, exemplified in a series of figures.* London: Printed [by D. N. Shury, Berwick Street, Soho] for S. and J. Fuller, Temple of Fancy, Rathbone Place, Where are also sold books of instruction in every branch of drawing, colours, and every requisite used in drawing, 1810. 16° (127 × 97 mm.).

a⁸; 7 hand-colored aquatint cut-out figures (head-portrait of Fanny, costumes and hats for her various guises). Pp. 15 [1]. Original printed gray paper wrappers including ads front and back for books and "fancy articles," the letterpress titling, etc., replicated on a publisher's slipcase of printed gray paper over pasteboard with a slit at one edge for a carrying ribbon. References: Haining, pp. 14–15; Hockliffe 707.

165. *reduced*

165. *reduced*

Provenance: *Sold by A. Loriot Toyman. Stationer & Perfumer to the Prince & Princess of Wales N° 60 New Bond St London* (engraved label); *S. Caroline Palmer the gift of Lady Blandford* (1811 inscr. of her sister Elizabeth). The Osborne Collection of Early Children's Books, Toronto Public Library.

The first edition of *Fanny* was almost certainly the earliest of the Fuller series and typifies the genre: a crudely devised narrative making a heavy moral point, divided up into scenes, and calling upon the reader to dress and redress the hero/heroine in appropriate costumes. Fanny begins her story in a white frock and then a greatcoat with muff and bonnet. She runs away and is abducted, thus having to beg and run errands in various guises, only to be restored to civilization and another frock at the end (see overleaf). She is dressed by the simple procedure of poking the tab of her neck into slots in the costumes, with the hats then being added. Because of their small size the latter often got lost.

Notes by Frederick Alger in the Osborne Collection suggest Amelia Troward as a possible author of *Fanny*. A late reprint of the book (ca. 1830) attributes it to "Dr. Walcot," who may or may not be the poetaster "Peter Pindar." For a Fuller doll book adapted to Shakespearean themes, see entry 211.

⊷§ 167 §⊷

St. Julien, the Emigrant; or, Europe depicted: exhibiting the costumes, and describing the manners and customs of the various nations. London: printed for the author; and sold by I. and E. Wallis, 42, Skinner Street, Snow-Hill. Vigurs, printer, 5, Princes Street, Leicester Square, 1812. 16° (133 × 106 mm.).

[1^16]; hand-colored engraved frontispiece map of Europe, seven hand-colored engraved cut-out figures (head of St. Julien, fitting costumes, and hats for his various guises). Pp. 32. This copy lacks the German costume and has the Spanish one in duplicate. Original printed yellow wrappers with relief-cut vignette, blue ribbon through a slit in the inner margin, original printed slipcase with the same vignette, and advertising dissected maps. Reference: Osborne II, 1053.

The Osborne Collection of Early Children's Books, Toronto Public Library.

The Wallises' single attempt at competing with the Fullers shows

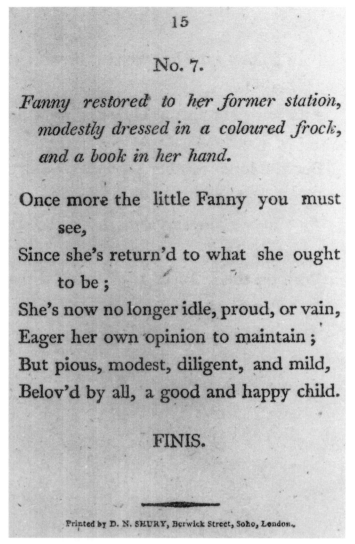

166. a8 recto

166. final cut-out figure

the firm adapting a doll book to their own cartographic interests. Our hero follows the course marked on the frontispiece map, dressing in different costumes as his journey (told in prose) progresses. In 1812 the Fullers also introduced an item which allowed for a display of costumes of the nations (a favorite theme in semi-educational children's books at this time), *Lucinda the Orphan*.

TOY THEATERS

The Toy Theater, or Juvenile Drama, emerged during the period that is under review and from time to time involved the publishers of children's books. This is not true for the founders of the fashion such as William West (see chapter XVI), but Hodgson & Co., whose publications are discussed in chapter XII, was deeply involved in publishing toy-theater sheets, which are described by George Speaight in his *History of the English Toy Theatre* (1969) as "excellent examples of the Juvenile Drama at its best." We therefore include an example of Hodgson & Co.'s work, recognizing its family relationship to the harlequinades, the prints, and the doll books that are also featured in this chapter. The influence of toy

theater on Thackeray and indirectly on his ideas for *The Rose and the Ring* are noted in chapter XVI.

⋅§ 168 ৡ⋅

Hodgson's Grand Procession in Edward the Black Prince, 19 Feb. 1823, 13 hand-colored engraved plates; *Hodgson's General Combat in Edward the Black Prince,* 18 Oct. 1822, plain engraved plate; *Scene[s] in Edward the Black Prince,* 28 Jan.–6 March 1823, 13 (?) hand-colored engraved plates (four (?) scenes each to three acts and one plate of "Side Wings"). London: Hodgson & C° 10. Newgate S^t, 1822-3. Each plate 1^d plain, except the double-size battle sheet 3^d All half-sheets (about 190 × 230 mm.); *General Combat*: two half-sheets joined (190 × 525 mm.).

Grand Procession plate 2 watermarked 1822, plate of scene 3, act 1, watermarked 1820. This set lacks nine plates illustrating *Grand Procession* (of the four present, one has been cut up for use and has therefore lost its numbering); also lacking are the plates for scene

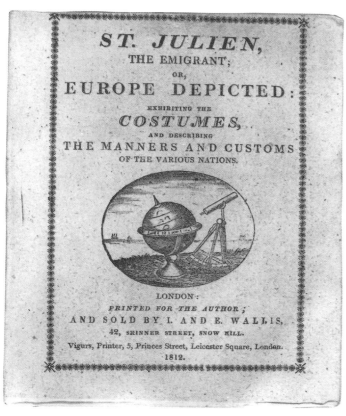

167. *reduced*

3, act 2, and scenes 2 and 3, act 3. A play-book for *Edward the Black Prince* was presumably also published. Reference: Speaight p. 187.

Thomas Fisher Rare Book Library, University of Toronto.

PEEPSHOWS

Peepshows originated in Germany as *Perspektivische Vorstellungen*. Their chief manufacturer and perhaps their inventor was Martin Engelbrecht, who around 1730 began to issue sets of scenes, engraved and hand-colored, which could be slotted into a wooden box so that a miniature three-dimensional world became visible through a viewing device. Engelbrecht's scenes were often very elaborate and do not seem to have caused a rash of imitations, but almost a hundred years later his ideas were adapted to newer production methods. The wooden box was done away with and the perspective scenes were built up in paper concertinas with peepholes at one end. The "Temple of Fancy" set a model here with their *Areaorama* of 1825, which Percy Muir has described as "among the most elegant and beautifully finished of any."

Very soon the making of peepshows became a European craze, with examples being imported into England from Germany and France. The manufacturers do not seem to have had children in mind as a special public for their wares; peepshows were often made to celebrate special occasions (e.g. the Great Exhibition, or

Below: **170**. *unfolded, reduced*

the opening of the Crystal Palace) and would be sold to visitors as souvenirs.

The "Tunnel under the Thames" proved to be much the most popular theme (a tunnel lending itself particularly well to peep-show perspectives). A few ambitious examples were produced in the 1820s, before part of the tunnel collapsed, but around the time of its completion in 1843 at least a dozen "perspective views" were in print.

169

The Areaorama. A View in the Regents Park. London: S. & I. Fuller, 34, Rathbone Place, Pub^d May 1, 1825. Peepshow (109 × 138 × ca. 750 mm., unfolded).

Eight hand-colored engraved illustrations cut out and joined by a folding strip of black paper, the first and last mounted on board. Original pink board slipcase, engraved green paper label. Reference: McGrath 20.

The Osborne Collection of Early Children's Books, Toronto Public Library.

170

A View of the Tunnel under the Thames, as it will appear when completed. London: M. Gouyn, 7 Fish St Hill, Augt 1 1829. Peepshow (110 × 140 × ca. 630 mm., unfolded).

Seven hand-colored engraved illustrations cut out and joined by a folding strip of blank paper (see previous page), the first and last mounted on board. Marbled board slipcase, colored engraved paper label (*Price 2^s Superior Edition 3^s Pub^d Decr 1828*), perhaps not originally belonging to this edition.

Provenance: *W. & A. Essex, Bazaar, No^s 333, 4, 5 & 6, Soho Square* (engraved label). The Osborne Collection of Early Children's Books, Toronto Public Library.

XI
THE INNOVATORS

WHILE not all of the experiments and innovations noted in the previous chapter occurred before the beginning of the nineteenth century, those that did are enough to indicate a stirring on the part of tradesmen, a growing awareness that the market was ready to support new ideas about what children might enjoy. This awareness was also reflected in the publishing of conventional children's books (as opposed, say, to harlequinades or miniature libraries), and from about 1800 onwards a group of publishers can be perceived as what today we might call "market leaders" in this different approach. Some, like John Marshall and John Wallis, were prime movers in the change itself, others like William Darton and John Harris, successor to Elizabeth Newbery's firm, took longer to accustom themselves to the revolution, and again others were new figures on the scene. This chapter attempts to distinguish the varying character of these firms and to provide several examples of their output which may typify their publishing style. We need to stress, however, that this period sees the Morgan Library's holdings of children's books at their strongest and that we could have included dozens of alternative examples to make the same demonstration, both in this chapter and in the following one, which will deal with some of the lesser (but not necessarily less prolific) publishers of the period.

JOHN MARSHALL; ELEANOR MARSHALL; THE CARVALHOS

As may be gathered, John Marshall is at this time ubiquitous. We have observed him as something of a Newbery look-alike; we have observed him as perhaps the foremost man of ideas; and we shall later see him among the promoters of evangelical religion. Here, though, we show various examples of his impressive performance as an innovative and sometimes imitative book publisher, noting at the same time the still insufficiently explained gap in his activities during several years on either side of 1810.

John Marshall died in 1824, and his business was carried on for a few years by his widow, Eleanor. Eventually she assigned some stock and copyrights to David Carvalho, who may well have found them to be his most profitable line of trade, judging from his continuance of "Marshall-style" publishing into the 1830s. The chronology is uncertain; for instance, the Morgan Library has an edition of *Johnny Gilpin's Journey to Vauxhall* "printed and sold by Marshall & Co." as late as 1833 (PML 85022), while D. Carvalho is found publishing *The Multiplication Table in Verse*—a Marshall title (see PML 81698)—in a different edition of his own in the early 1830s (entry 177b). Because of the interconnections, a note on and examples of Carvalho publishing are included in this sequence.

◆§ 171a §◆

[CECIL BOYLE? (d. 1865)]. *Little John; or, the picture-book. By Sabina Cecil, author of Little Eliza, Little Hariet, Little William, &c.* London: printed and sold by John Marshall, 140, Fleet Street, From Aldermary Church-Yard, 1818. Price One Shilling. 12°? (120 × 100 mm.).

[1⁶] (1ʳ title, 6ʳ imprint, 6ᵛ ads); 10 hand-colored engravings by J. Piggot, including frontispiece, printed from three copperplates (Aldermary Church Yard address, dated Febʸ 1. 1800, and July 1. 1800—see overleaf). Pp. 11, [1]; illustration numbering retained from previous use of the plates. Different paper stocks for letterpress (watermarked Ruse & Turner 1817) and engraving. Large, leaded roman type (two sizes for text, more for title). Original green stiff wrappers, shaped colored engraved label *Little John* mounted on front cover. Blue morocco gilt.

Provenance: Charles Todd Owen (binding). PML 85066. Gift: Elisabeth Ball.

◆§ 171b §◆

The Picturesque Instructor. London: printed and sold by John Marshall, 140, Fleet Street, From Aldermary Church-Yard, 1818. Price One Shilling. 12°? (120 × 100 mm.).

[1⁶] (1ʳ title 1ᵛ blank, 2ʳ alphabet, 2ᵛ–3ᵛ larger alphabet, 4ʳ *The Apply-Pye alphabet*, 6ᵛ imprint); 10 hand-colored engravings printed from two (?) copperplates (Aldermary Church-Yard address, dated Decʳ 22 1801), and inserted in the middle of the quire. Pp. 12; illustration numbering 2–11 retained from previous use of the plates. Different paper stocks for letterpress (watermarked Newton 1816) and engraving. Large sizes of roman type. Blue morocco gilt.

Provenance: Francis Stania Brentford? (inscr.); Charles Todd Owen (binding). PML 81396. Gift: Elisabeth Ball.

John Marshall's earliest ventures into picture-book publishing are hard to determine for want of evidence. What we do know, however, is that he was one of the first to try to exploit the use of hand-colored engraved plates in making books for young children. By good fortune these plates were re-used at later dates, thus providing evidence for editions that may have disappeared.

In "Sabina Cecil's" *Little John* we can see Marshall hiring someone to cobble up a simple reading book in 1818 based upon plates dated 1 February and 1 July, 1800, when they had been used for Marshall's abortive *Picture Magazine or Monthly Exhibition.* In *The Picturesque Instructor* of the same date we see the resurrection of a small alphabet book of 1801, now furnished with some letterpress additions. The Morgan Library also possesses a little

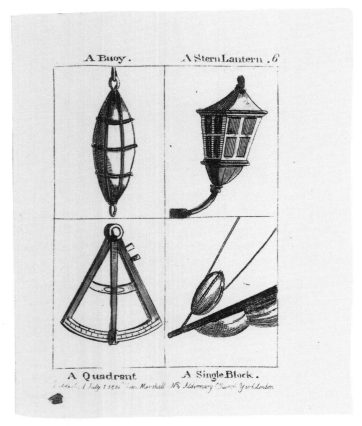

A Buoy.   A Stern Lantern. 6

A Quadrant   A Single Block.

Above and right: 171a. 4ᵛ and facing pl., *reduced*

book with the same main title, "printed and sold by E. Marshall" (watermark-date 1823), showing simple objects—"A neat doll. A new hive"—with plates dated 9 February, 1802 (PML 81553).

❧ 172 ❧

LUCY PEACOCK (fl. 1785–1816). *Emily; or, the test of sincerity. By Lucy Peacock, author of "The Visit for a Week,"* &c. &c. London: printed and sold by John Marshall, 140. Fleet Street, From Aldermary Church-Yard, 1817. 12° (168 × 101 mm.).

A² (1ʳ half-title, 2ʳ title); B–G¹² (G11ʳ imprint, G11ᵛ and G12 blank); 11 hand-colored etchings (including frontispiece, and 5 conjugate pairs in quires E–F), printed from at least two and no more than six copperplates. Pp. [4], 141, [3]. Letterpress on paper watermarked P & Cᵒ 1815, plates on a different stock (apparently watermarked Whatman 1811). Original or contemporary tree sheep.

Provenance: *Edith Howard From Margy 1859* (pencil-inscr.). PML 84643. Purchase: Ball Fund.

Having called upon Lucy Peacock to edit his *Juvenile Magazine* as long ago as 1788 (entry 88), John Marshall here resumes the connection and publishes what may well be the last of her novels for children. (Good little Emily and her destitute Mamma receive a fortune after being kind to Mr. Miles, who had pretended to be destitute himself. The *Juvenile Review* of 1817, a Trimmeresque publication, noticed the book, which had first come out in 1816, but complained about Mr. Miles's "use of artifice" to test his

friends' sincerity.) Marshall has given *Emily* a fittingly sumptuous appearance. Few children's novels of the time (Harris's *Felissa* is a notable exception), and certainly few of Lucy Peacock's previous effusions, were garnished with a dozen or so gaudily hand-colored prints.

❧ 173 ❧

Marshall's Edition of the Popular Story of Aladdin; or, the wonderful lamp. Embellished with coloured engravings. London: printed and sold by John Marshall, 140, Fleet Street, From Aldermary Church-Yard, [ca. 1824]. Price Sixpence. 16° (110 × 92 mm.).

A² (1+B⁸) (A1ʳ title, A1ᵛ text, A2ᵛ end of text and imprint *Printed and Sold by John Marshall, 140, Fleet Street, from Aldermary Church-Yard, London; Of whom may be had a Variety on the same Plan*); 6 hand-colored etchings (including frontispiece), printed from three copperplates and inserted as three pairs of conjugate leaves (around *A*1·2, B3·6, B4·5). Pp. 20. Letterpress on laid paper, etching on wove. Roan-backed marbled boards, original stiff wrappers lacking.

Provenance: *George Wilson the gift of his Aunt Leroux March 30ᵗʰ 1828* (inscr.); Gumuchian & Cⁱᵉ (1930 cat., no. 278). PML 85571. Gift: Elisabeth Ball.

Marshall had participated in the revival of nursery rhymes when in 1792 he acquired the rights to the Newbery-Power *Mother Goose's Melody* (whose illustrations Nigel Tattersfield has recently shown to be by Thomas Bewick). He retained the book in his list, later enlarging its format and adding hand-coloring. In the 1820s

8

When little John can spell the names of these things, his papa will tell him the use of them.

172. etching opposite C9ᵛ, *reduced*

173 (note). PML 85572, front cover

he began to publish his "editions of popular stories." These may have been inspired by Tabart's earlier series (see entry 382) but are designed to a different format and employ lurid hand-coloring as well as gaudy paper bindings (see entry 358c), both highly distinctive Marshall trademarks. This undated version of *Aladdin* is an abridgment of the usual Galland text. From the same series the Morgan Library also has copies of *Beauty and the Beast*, with the beast looking like a brown bear, dated 1821; and *Cinderilla* and *The Master Cat* in later undated editions, printed and sold by E. Marshall, the former with an 1826 watermark (PML 81466, 85572 & 85412).

❧ 174 ❧

Parlour Puzzles; or, the fireside enlivened: consisting of seventeen original enigmas, to which are added, some of the choicest conundrums. Illustrated by a variety of curious devices. London: printed and sold by John Marshall, 140, Fleet Street, From Aldermary Church-Yard, 1823. Price one shilling. 12°? (152 × 96 mm.).

[1²] (1ʳ blank, 1ᵛ title, 2ʳ *Conundrums*, 2ᵛ *Solutions of the enigmas* and imprint); 17 numbered hand-colored etched illustrations (see overleaf), printed from three copperplates apparently on one side of a single sheet of wove paper, divided into six pairs of conjugate leaves and inserted in the middle of the quire (the innermost conjugate pair watermarked Rump 1821). Pp. [4]. Original white-speckled green wrappers, oval colored engraved label *Parlour Puzzles* mounted on front cover.

Provenance: Charles Todd Owen (pencil note). PML 85020. Gift: Elisabeth Ball.

Along with nursery rhymes and fairy tales, John Marshall also developed a line in books of round-games or games of forfeits. Many of these were "games of questions and commands," variations of which were published by several houses. (The most famous, if only because of its title, was *Aldiborontiphosky-phorniostikos* from A. K. Newman; see Gottlieb 196, PML 85542, and Opie *Nursery Companion* pp. 108–12, 127.) E. Marshall's *Hopping, Prating, Chatt'ring Magpie* (1829) has for a frontispiece "the little Party sitting round the fire playing at the New Game." *Parlour Puzzles*, however, carries no forfeits with it, being simply a series of rebus riddles, somewhat in the tradition of the "hieroglyphic books" (see entry 155). Some of the conundrums may be of interest to bibliographers, including: "Why is an unbound book like a lady in bed? *Because it is in sheets.*"

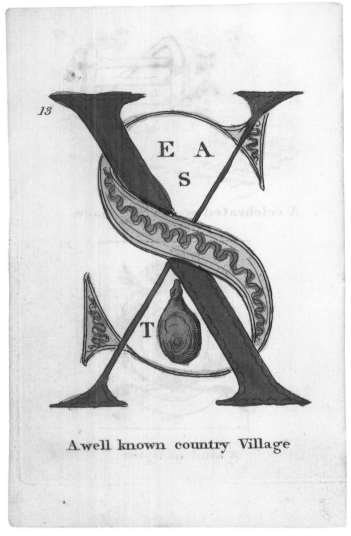

13

A well known country Village

174. East Ham in Essex, *reduced*

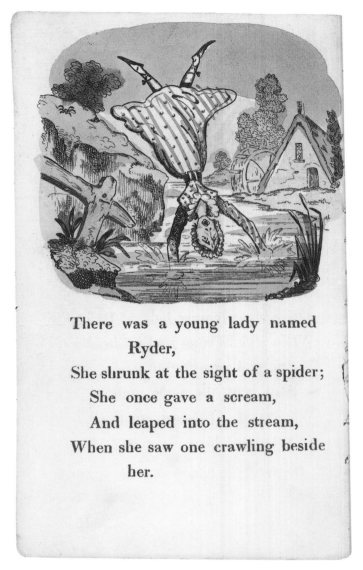

There was a young lady named
Ryder,
She shrunk at the sight of a spider;
She once gave a scream,
And leaped into the stream,
When she saw one crawling beside
her.

175. fo. 15 verso, *reduced*

❧ 175 ❧

Anecdotes and Adventures of Fifteen Young Ladies. Embellished with engravings. London: Printed and Sold by, E. Marshall, 140, Fleet Street. From Aldermary Church-Yard, [not before 1825, not after 1827]. 16° (180 × 110 mm.).

[1¹⁶] (1 frontispiece *There was a young lady of Greenwich* misbound between 15 and 16). Ff. [16]. Printed on one side of a single sheet: 16 hand-colored etched illustrations (upper half of the page) attributable to Robert Cruikshank and printed from one copperplate, letterpress on lower half of the page. Paper watermarked J. & T. Jellyman 1825. Original orange stiff wrappers, shaped colored engraved label *Anecdotes of Fifteen Ladies. Price One Shilling and Sixpence*. Reference: Hockliffe 722.

Provenance: *Louisa Jane Boodle from her affectionate Sister Susan October 8ᵗʰ 1827*. PML 81681. Gift: Elisabeth Ball.

Long famed in the annals of children's literature is *Anecdotes and Adventures of Fifteen Gentlemen*, which John Marshall published ca. 1821 and from which Edward Lear got the idea and the form of the limerick (see Darton pp. 204–5). The book was in fact directly inspired by *The History of Sixteen Wonderful Old Women*, which

John Harris had published in 1820, but while Harris did nothing further with the idea, Marshall (and/or his widow) pursued it, and this is one of several limerick, or near-limerick, books that they produced, sometimes matching Lear himself:

> There was a young lady of Greenwich,
> Who was fond of fried bacon and spinach,
> And she dined once a week
> Upon bubble-and-squeak;
> What a whimsical lady of Greenwich!

❧ 176 ❧

The Barn that Tom built. A new game of forfeits. Embellished with 16 coloured engravings. London: printed (by assignment of E. Marshall) by D. Carvalho, 74, Chiswell Street, Finsbury Square, [not before 1830, not after 1832]. 16° (180 × 110 mm.).

[1¹⁶] (1ᵛ frontispiece *Come, let us all merry merry be, And play at forfeits now with me*). Ff. [16]. Printed on one side of the sheet:

16 hand-colored etched illustrations (upper half of the page), perhaps by Robert Cruikshank and apparently printed from a single copperplate, letterpress (two sizes of roman type, at least partly leaded) on lower half of the page. Paper watermarked Ruse & Turner 1830. Later blue wrappers (original cover lacking).

PML 83211. Gift: Elisabeth Ball.

The Morgan Library possesses a number of picture books, mostly "games of questions and commands" (see entry 174), with the same imprint as this. They confirm evidence from elsewhere that E. Marshall titles were moving *en bloc* to D. Carvalho. *The Barn that Tom Built* is an example of the traditional "Jack" rhyme, rewritten and converted to use as a memorizing game. It was first published by John Marshall in 1817 (Opie *Three Centuries* 423). Another forfeit game, *The Pretty, Playful, Tortoise-Shell Cat*, published on assignment by Carvalho (PML 83214), gives a different view of the group of children seen round the fire in the *Magpie* (note to entry 174) and advertises also *The Frisking, Barking Lady's Lap-Dog* (PML 83213).

❧ 177a ❧

The Infant's Tutor; or, amusing alphabet. By a lady. Illustrated with numerous engravings. London: printed & published by S. Carvalho, 8, Craven Street, Charles Square, Hoxton, [not before 1825]. 16° (169 × 102 mm.).

[1⁸] (1ᵛ title, 2ʳ incipit: *A was an Angler and he caught a trout*). Ff. [8]. Printed on one side of the half-sheet: letterpress and 27 hand-colored wood engravings (mostly four to the page). Paper watermarked Catshall Mill 1825. Modern russet morocco, gilt edges.

Provenance: Charles Todd Owen (binding). PML 85039. Gift: Elisabeth Ball.

❧ 177b ❧

The Multiplication Table, in verse. By the author of the Pence Table in Verse. London: printed and published by D. Carvalho, 74, Chiswell Street, Finsbury Square, [ca. 1830–2]. 12° (174 × 105 mm.).

[1¹²] (1ᵛ title and incipit: *Twice one are two—good little boys*, 2ʳ imprint). Ff. [12]. Printed on one side of the sheet: letterpress (roman type, leaded) and 12 hand-colored wood engravings (slightly smaller than half-page). Unwatermarked. Modern brown morocco.

Provenance: Charles Todd Owen (binding). PML 81699. Gift: Elisabeth Ball.

The publishing activities of the Carvalhos (who sound more like a team of acrobats) are obscure. The Morgan Library has a mysterious undated chapbook *Cinderella*, printed in Bristol and published by a certain J. Carvalho of Hennage Lane, Leadenhall Street, and this may mark the family's earliest publishing endeavor (PML 80386). We have not yet found any other J. Carvalho offering, but the Library has several cheap books put out by S. Carvalho, the earliest of which may be two battered story

177a. fo. 1 verso, *reduced*

books illustrated with crudely engraved and colored plates: *The History of Jack the Broom-Boy* (Gumuchian 6126; PML 81704) and *The History of Anne and her Seven Sisters* (PML 81549). These booklets were published from an address at 18 West Place, Nelson Street, City Road, probably ca. 1820 (Gumuchian's suggested date). They therefore precede *The Infant's Tutor*, described above, just as all of S. Carvalho's output appears to precede David Carvalho's books. David (perhaps S. Carvalho's son) published a slightly altered and less colorful "fourth edition" of *The Infant's Tutor* from his Chiswell Street address, where he began his business and worked from 1830–32 and from where he also published the books assigned to him by E. Marshall. His own independent edition of *The Multiplication Table in Verse* is mentioned in the introduction to this chapter.

THE WALLIS FAMILY

In all probability, the founder of this busy company was the John Wallis from Yeovil in Somerset who was apprenticed to William Johnson, bookseller of Ludgate Street, in 1760 and freed in 1769. He apparently opened his own shop at Yorick's Head, 16 Ludgate Hill, in 1775, and although declared bankrupt in 1778 he continued to trade and gradually developed his specialization in maps, dissected puzzles and children's games (see entry 161). He was quick to appreciate the new mood in children's book publishing, which indeed he had helped to foster, and vied with John Marshall at the start of the new century in the production of picture books and miniature libraries (entry 165). A set of Twelfth Night cards published by John Wallis the elder is discussed in chapter XVI (entry 335).

In 1794 Wallis took as apprentice his son, John the younger (freed in 1806), and another son, Edward, later also joined the firm. The former managed a bookshop of his own at 188 Strand from 1808 but moved in 1814 to Sidmouth in Devon where he ran his Marine Library for about eight years. He remained associated with the London family enterprise, in which Edward began to play a dominant role, becoming a partner in 1813 and sole proprietor on his father's death in 1818. Much of the publishing endeavor seems to have been devoted to producing picture books (alongside the flourishing trade in maps and dissected puzzles). Several changes of address occurred which were summarized in Linda Hannas's *The English Jigsaw Puzzle*:

1778–1805	16 Ludgate Street
1805–1811	13 Warwick Square
1812–1847	42 Skinner Street
1823–1847	also, 14 High Street, Islington.

The Morgan Library possesses large quantities of Wallis picture books, which span the whole period from the days of the infant's libraries to the era of *Struwwelpeter*. In the following brief selection we give only a few examples to indicate this range.

❧ 178 ❧

JOHN OAKMAN (1748?–1793). *A Second Holiday for John Gilpin; or a voyage to Vauxhall; where, though he had better luck than before, he was far from being contented.* London: printed for J. Wallis, Jr., At his Universal Juvenile Library & original Dissected-Map Warehouse, Removed from Ludgate-street, to No. 188, Strand, (Next Door to the Crown-and-Anchor Tavern), 1808. Brettell and Co. Printers, Marshall-Street, Golden-Square. 24°? (108 × 95 mm.).

[1¹²] (12ᵛ printer's imprint); 3 engravings (inserted to face 3ᵛ, 6ᵛ, 11ᵛ). Pp. 24. Watermark-date 1807. Maroon morocco gilt. Reference: Russell *Cowper* 211–12 (earlier eds.).

Provenance: Charles Todd Owen (bookplate, binding). PML 85021. Gift: Elisabeth Ball.

John Wallis junior is here seen at the moment of his removal from his father's address to snug tavernside premises in the Strand. The Gilpin sequel by John Oakman that he chose to convert into a fashionable small square picture book was first published as a broadside in 1785 (when J. Wallis, Sr., published a dissected puzzle of the original).

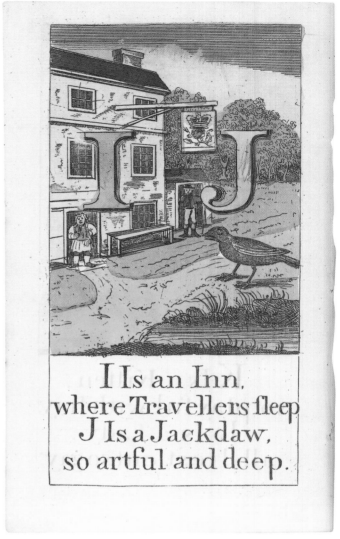

179. 1/7 verso, *reduced*

❧ 179 ❧

The Darling's Delight or Easy ABC being the first step, of the ladder to learning. London: Published by J. Wallis & Son Skinner Street, & J. Wallis Junʳ Marine Library Sidmouth, [not before 1816 (date and initials IP inscribed on the wall of the schoolroom in the YZ illustration)]. 8° or 16° (177 × 106 mm.).

[1–2⁸] (1ᵛ *Frontispiece*, 2ʳ title, 3ᵛ incipit: *A is an Archer, so bold and so free*, –2/8 blank). Ff. [16]. Etched throughout, printed on one side of the sheets: 14 hand-colored illustrations, each with four-line verse (except frontispiece). Original pink stiff wrappers, engraved floral title-label mounted on front cover. Maroon morocco gilt.

Provenance: Charles Todd Owen (bookplate; binding). PML 80657. Gift: Elisabeth Ball.

There is an almost Victorian feeling to these engraved pages, with the hand-colored letters superimposed on variably jumbled pictorial scenes. Investigators of character stereotyping in children's books will find double cause for thought in the caricatures for:

Q is a Quaker, who cocks up his chin,
R is a [Jewish] Rogue, wou'd fain take him in.

ᵉᵍ 180a ᵍᵉ

Blue Beard; or, female curiosity, a juvenile poem. Illustrated with elegant engravings on copper. London: printed for J. and E. Wallis, 42, Skinner-Street; and J. Wallis, Marine Library, Sidmouth, [ca. 1816]. Price 1s. coloured. - 6d. plain. 16° (124 × 101 mm.).

A–B⁴ (A1ᵛ imprint *J. Pittman, Printer, Warwick Square, London*, A2ʳ incipit *Beneath a castle's dreary pile*); 16 illustrations printed from one etched copperplate on a quarter sheet, divided into two bifolia and inserted (1·2 around quire A, 3·4 around B2·3), hand-colored as issued. Pp. 16. Brown morocco gilt.

Provenance: Charles Todd Owen (binding). PML 83580. Gift: Elisabeth Ball.

ᵉᵍ 180b ᵍᵉ

Nathaniel Numeral's Novel Notions of Acquiring a Knowledge of Numeration. Displayed in six elegant copper plates. London: printed for E. Wallis, 42, Skinner-Street; and J. Wallis, Marine Library, Sidmouth, Decʳ 8ᵗʰ 1817 (date on first plate and probably the date of impression) [this copy issued in 1818 or slightly later]. 16° (128 × 105 mm.).

[1–2⁸] (1ᵛ incipit: *1 One 2 Two Ma'am how d'ye do*, 2/8ʳ *31 Thirty-one 32 Thirty-two Pray Cobbler mend my shoe*). Ff. [16]. Stipple-engraved throughout, printed from two copperplates on one side of two half-sheets from different paper stocks (the first water-marked 1815, the second 1817). Original gray stiff wrappers, letter-press title and wood-engraved vignette on front cover.

Provenance: *Sold by A. Rutherfurd, Kelso* (nineteenth-century trade label). PML 67548. Purchase: Ball Fund.

Two examples of J. and E. Wallis's fairly late use of the squarish 16° format, which had become fashionable a dozen years earlier with Harris's *Old Mother Hubbard* (see entry 187). Both books enhance a sense of Wallis's eclecticism: the uncolored *Nathaniel Numeral* with its stippled caricatures and the typographic versification of *Blue Beard* with its almost emblematic scenes, arranged four to a page. The anonymous author of the poem has cravenly side-stepped the discovery behind the locked door:

And Irene fainted on the ground,
For through a vivid flame,
Her frantic eyes beheld a sight,
A sight we cannot name.

ᵉᵍ 181 ᵍᵉ

The Adventures of Ulysses, a tale for the nursery. London: published by E. Wallis, 42, Skinner-Street, 1820. 18° (125 × 81 mm.).

29 Twenty-nine   30 Thirty
Mifs don't be so flirty.

180b. 2/7 verso, *reduced*

A–D⁶ E² (E2+1ʳ end of text and imprint *Printed by T. Davis, 102, Minories, London*, verso blank); 16 hand-colored etchings (including frontispiece—see overleaf), printed from a single copperplate on a sheet of wove paper watermarked 1815, then divided for insertion. Pp. 53, [1]. Letterpress a different wove-paper stock. Original printed wrappers, wood engraving on front cover. Modern blue morocco gilt.

Provenance: Charles Todd Owen (binding). PML 83905. Gift: Elisabeth Ball.

This apparently unrecorded retelling of the *Odyssey* for children is unrelated to Charles Lamb's version of the same title first published in 1808 by Wallis's neighbor in Skinner Street, William Godwin. With a cover-title that reads *The Wonderful Adventures and Escapes of Ulysses, King of Ithaca*, the book sounds like a product of fairy tale rather than heroic epic, and Wallis confirms this judgment by having his adaptor and illustrator conduct us through events with speed and drama. The nursery is not spared the gruesome details of cannibalism and revenge, reinforced by a series of powerfully conceived and finely executed etchings. Altogether, this is one of the most surprising and outstanding children's books of the period.

ᵉᵍ 182 ᵍᵉ

WILLIAM COWPER (1731–1800). *The Diverting History of John Gilpin.* London: E. Wallis, 42, Skinner Street, [ca. 1840]. 12° (203 × 130 mm.).

[1–3⁴] (1ʳ title, 1ᵛ imprint *K. Chandler, Printer, 17, Bridgewater Square, London*, 3/4ᵛ blank). Pp. 23, [1]. 21 wood-engraved illus-

181. frontispiece

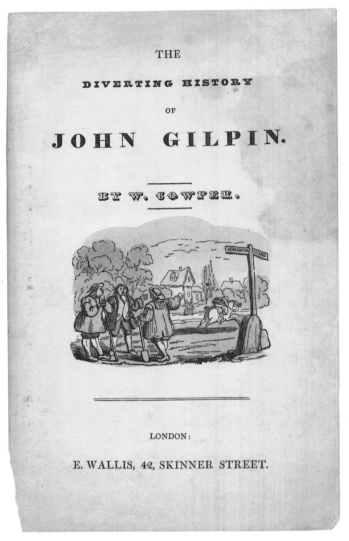

182. *reduced*

trations within rectangular frames (63 × 90 mm. each), colored by hand (probably as issued). The title-vignette is a repeat of the block on 2/4ᵛ, without frame. Maroon morocco, by Morrell.

Provenance: Charles Todd Owen (binding). PML 85030. Gift: Elisabeth Ball.

Edward Wallis is here seen towards the end of his career recalling one of his father's early successes. The hand-colored wood engravings appear to be a new series and resemble etchings in their energetic treatment of the familiar scenes.

The design of the book, with its larger page size, shows Wallis joining the movement that would lead to the "quarto" picture books of the Victorian heyday. Dating, however, is difficult. The Morgan Library possesses another book from the same series as this: *The Horse that Tom Bought*, in original covers (PML 83212). This was printed by Wood & Chandler from a Beech Street address, where they were working 1835–38 (Todd). This *Gilpin* is printed by Chandler alone and, since it is not advertised in the list on the back of *The Horse*, may be slightly later in date.

JOHN HARRIS (1756–1846)

John Harris was born in 1756 and was apprenticed to the bookseller Thomas Evans (Moon; not in McKenzie), for whom he continued to work after he was out of his time. Eventually, however, he became Elizabeth Newbery's manager in the famous

shop "at the Corner of St. Paul's Church Yard," whose fame he was to extend after he took over the business in 1801.

Harris's first years as a publisher were careful ones. He husbanded the resources that he had gained from Elizabeth Newbery, and most of his excursions into the new and unknown were in association with John Wallis (games and miniature libraries) or with T. Hughes and Champante and Whitrow (harlequinades). In 1805 he burst upon the market with *Old Mother Hubbard* (entry 187), the first of his engraved picture books, and his success at exploiting the formula enabled him to become *primus inter pares* of picture-book publishers. Thanks to his astuteness he managed to achieve an equivalent triumph a couple of years later when he converted William Roscoe's poem *The Butterfly's Ball* into a picture book (1807; Gottlieb 159), launching not just a best-selling book but a best-selling series, in which his competitors gleefully joined.

For the next twenty years or so the firm of Harris was among the most prominent of all children's book publishers, not merely in the production of picture books, which Harris systematized within his "Cabinet of Amusement and Instruction," but also in a continuing production of more conventional and more earnest story books and books on factual subjects. His career, and the comparative decline that set in when his son, John Harris II, took

TEMPERANCE.

WHAT is the reason that the cheeks of Charles glow like a cherry, while his sister always looks as pale as ashes? —I can explain this to you presently.

Charles is not so greedy as his sister, and does not eat so much trash. Not that he dislikes cakes, or fruit, or other nice things that come in his way; but he is not always thinking about them, nor will he strive to procure them at any rate. He has no objection to eat

GLUTTONY.

THE little girl who is so unfortunate as to have this character, is never so happy as when she is pampering her appetite, and devouring all before her: this is the chief substance of her thoughts from morning till night; and whilst those who are wise take food to satisfy their hunger, and support their bodies, she is constantly loading her stomach beyond what it can well bear. Little does she think how many want a meal, who would be glad of what she eats in waste.

184. A6ᵛ–7ʳ, *reduced*

over the business in ca. 1824, are charted by Marjorie Moon in her checklist, *John Harris's Books for Youth* (1976; revised ed., 1992), where extensive descriptions and notes are given. John Harris outlived his business, which passed to Messrs. Grant and Griffith in 1843. He died at the age of ninety in 1846, after which, under various designations and with varying success, the "successors to John Newbery" preserved the business at the Corner of St. Paul's Church Yard until almost the end of the century.

❧ 183 ☙

The Dog of Knowledge; or, memoirs of Bob, the spotted terrier. Supposed to be written by himself . . . By the author of Dick the Little Poney. London: Printed for J. Harris (Successor to E. Newbery), at the Juvenile Library, Corner of St. Paul's Churchyard, 1801. 18° (129 × 81 mm.).

A⁶ (1ʳ title, 1ᵛ imprint *S. Gosnell, Printer, Little Queen Street, Holborn*, 2ʳ dedication *To the lovely children of the most noble the Marquis of W—*, 3ʳ *Advertisement*, 5ʳ *Contents*); B–Q⁶ R³ (R2 singleton, R2ᵛ Harris's ad for *Dick, the little poney* [Roscoe J241(2)], R3ʳ *Juvenile pieces. New Publications, Libraries, &c. in French and English, for youth of both sexes*); engraved frontispiece *Bob supplicating the Cottage Matron*. Pp. xii, 183,

[3]. Laid paper watermarked 1799 (letterpress), wove paper (frontispiece). Wood-engraved title-vignette signed [John] Lee. Contemporary blue half roan gilt and gray boards (final quire R⁴ from vol. III of a Darton and Harvey edition of Priscilla Wakefield's *Mental Improvement* accidentally inserted between quires Q and R). Reference: Moon *Harris* 212(1).

PML 84010. Purchase: Ball Fund.

Said by Mrs. Moon to be "probably the first book published by John Harris alone," *The Dog of Knowledge* bears all the marks of the eighteenth century continuing into the nineteenth. Like *The Adventures of a Silver Three-Pence* ([1801]; PML 82510), which is simply a Newbery reprint with advertisements for a hundred or so ex-Newbery items "sold by J. Harris," *The Dog* has the severe appearance and the all-too-formal diction of Elizabeth Newbery's moral tales.

❧ 184 ☙

Take Your Choice: or the difference between virtue and vice, shown in opposite characters. London: printed for J. Harris, successor to E. Newbery, corner of St. Paul's Church-yard, By J. Swan, No. 6, Angel Street, 1802. 12° (157 × 97 mm.).

185 (note). design for frontispiece, *reduced*

185. frontispiece, *reduced*

A–B[12] C[6] (A1[r] half-title, A1[v] frontispiece *The balance of worth* and six-line verse, A3[r] *A word of advice*, C6[r] imprint *James Swan, Printer, Angel Street, Newgate Street*). Pp. [60]. Laid paper, watermark: fleur-de-lys, Neckinger 1801. Wood-engraved frontispiece, publisher's title-device signed Berryman, wood-engraved headpiece and 5 tailpieces, 16 larger wood engravings (almost half-page) including two signed Lee, one Berryman and one F.J. or F.T. Old pink boards, yellow spine. Reference: Moon *Harris* 847(1).

Provenance: *William Oates. The gift of George Paley Esq[re] October 25 1803 1803* (inscr.). PML 81816. Gift: Charles Ryskamp in memory of Mrs. Sherman Post Haight.

Locked still within eighteenth-century concepts, John Harris nonetheless seems to be questing here after new formulae—probably under the influence of books being put out by William Darton, who was publishing volumes in this larger format with prominent illustrations at the head of sections. In *Take Your Choice* he introduces the "opposite characters" in parallel, with "Industry" alongside "Idleness," say, rather as Hogarth had done. Furthermore he has singled out the virtuous half of each page opening by setting the text in a decorated border; then he has headed each section with an attractive sequence of wood engravings. Some of these, and some of the tailpieces, are after the Bewicks.

⋘ 185 ⋙

Gratitude: or, the juvenile writers. London: printed for J. Harris, successor to E. Newbery, at the Original Juvenile Library, corner of St. Paul's Church-yard, 1808. 18° (111 × 72 mm.).

A–C[6] (A1[v] imprint *H. Bryer, Printer, Bridge-Street, Blackfriars*); 3 hand-colored engravings including frontispiece dated 1806 (the second lacking). Pp. 36. Laid paper. Bound up with seven other tales in the series: later half calf gilt. Reference: Moon *Harris* 329.

PML 84453.8. Purchase: Mrs. Alexander O. Vietor in memory of her daughter, Barbara Foster Vietor (1956–1966).

Moral or instructive stories never disappeared from Harris's list and, even at the height of his "Butterfly's Ball" period, he organized

the publishing of the uniform series of tales to which *Gratitude* belongs. In this instance, however, he plays a pretty narrative game. The children in the story had already appeared in other volumes of this series, but now, on a trip to London, they visit "HARRIS'S Original Juvenile Library" to buy some books and "when they arrived at home, they found their own names, histories, and characters, exhibited with amazing exactness" in the publications they had bought. In gratitude to Mr. Harris they all write stories for him, and these are then printed in the rest of the book.

The Morgan Library owns the original wash drawings, perhaps by William Mulready, for three of the stories in the series (PML 84706.1–9). Comparison between the drawings and the reversed engravings reveal an accurate tracing of the originals onto the plate.

⋘ 186a ⋙

Dame Partlet's Farm; containing an account of the great riches she obtained by industry, the good life she led, and alas, good reader! her sudden death; to which is added, a hymn, written by Dame Partlet, just before her death. And an epitaph for her tomb-stone. London: printed for J. Harris, (successor to E. Newbery) St. Paul's Church-yard, 1806. 16° (125 × 101 mm.).

A–D[8] E[4] (A1[v] imprint *Printed by J. and E. Hodson, 15, Cross-Street, Hatton-Garden*, A2[r] rhyme (see note below), E3[r]–4[v] ads, E4[r] printer's imprint). Pp. 68, 3, [1]. Wove paper watermarked 1805. 13 half-page wood engravings including one signed Lee (C8[v]). Original printed yellow wrappers. Green morocco, by Morrell. References: Moon *Harris* 178(2); Hockliffe 89 (1804 edition).

Provenance: Charles Todd Owen (binding). PML 81361. Gift: Elisabeth Ball.

⋘ 186b ⋙

Dame Partlet's Farm; an account of the riches she obtained by industry, the good life she led, and alas! good reader, her death and epitaph. New edition. London: Grant and Griffith,

48   DAME PARTLET'S FARM.

Do see her standing at the door
    To all her servants talking,
Directing them to mind their work
    Whilst she abroad was walking.

See Peggy Partlet with the corn
    To feed the hen and chickens:
The geese too stretching out their necks
    To gather up some pickings!

186a. C8 verso, *reduced*

successors to John Harris, corner of St. Paul's Churchyard,
[ca. 1848]. 12° (175 × 105 mm.).

A–B¹² (A1ᵛ frontispiece, A2ᵛ imprint *London: Printed by S. & J.
Bentley, Wilson and Fley, Bangor House, Shoe Lane*, B12ᵛ same
imprint). Pp. 48. 13 hand-colored wood engravings (different
blocks from 186a; 75 × 85 mm.). Original printed buff stiff wrappers. Red morocco, by Morrell.

Provenance: Stassin et Xavier (mid-nineteenth-century Parisian
booksellers at 9 rue du Coq-S.-Honoré, who specialized in English
children's books; their label pasted above the ads on back cover);
Charles Todd Owen (binding). PML 80654. Gift: Elisabeth Ball.

First published in 1804, *Dame Partlet's Farm* is rightly described
by Mrs. Moon as "a charming production, but still in the 'old style'."
It has various Newbery touches: the "Goody Two-Shoes" setting;
the jumble of story, precept, and verses; and the description of
books "got from the corner of St. Paul's Church Yard" together
with the celebrated rhyme: "At HARRIS'S, St. Paul's Church-yard,
Good children meet a sure reward . . . "
   At the same time the book is produced in the "new" squarish
16mo format with stiff-paper printed covers and with more of the
"Bewick-style" wood engravings that gave distinction to *Take Your
Choice* (entry 184). Although *Dame Partlet* was not reprinted in
this form after 1806, the text was revived during the sober season
of the 1830s; an essentially eighteenth-century book finds itself
refurbished with hand-colored cuts and printed in the tall 12mo
format of Harris's Cabinet. Thus it continued into Grant and
Griffith's list in the 1840s.
   The penciled claim on A1ᵛ of PML 81361 that "this book was
written by Dʳ James Hodson" (a relative of the printer?) has not so
far been substantiated from any other source.

DAME PARTLET'S FARM.   33

Her cousin left her all his goods,
    A bull and fifteen cows;
A noble flock of sheep she had,
    A boar and fourteen sows.

Three carts, two waggons, and a plough,
    A roller and a harrow;
And whistling in a wicker cage,
    A blackbird and a sparrow.

B 5

186b. B5 recto, *reduced*

⤙ 187 ⤚

[SARAH CATHERINE MARTIN (1768–1826)]. *The
Comic Adventures of Old Mother Hubbard and Her Dog:
illustrated with fifteen elegant engravings on copper-plate.*
London: printed for J. Harris, successor to E. Newbery, at the
Original Juvenile Library, the corner of St. Paul's Church-
yard, 1805. 16° (116 × 95 mm.).

[1–4⁴] (1ʳ blank, 1ᵛ title *The Comic Adventures of Old Mother
Hubbard and Her Dog*, illustration, and imprint *Publish'd June
1–1805. by J. Harris, Succeser to E. Newbery, Corner of Sᵗ Pauls
Church Yard*, 2ʳ dedication *To J . . . B . . . Esqʳ. M.P. County of . . .
at whose suggestion and at whose House these Notable Sketches
were design'd . . . 1805 SMC*, 2ᵛ–3ʳ blank, 3ᵛ incipit: *Old Mother
Hubbard / Went to the Cupboard . . .*, 4/4ʳ end of rhyme . . . *The
Dame said your Servant / The Dog said Bow. Wow*, illustration,
4/4ᵛ blank). Ff.[16]. Engraved and etched throughout, printed on
one side of the sheet probably from a single large copperplate.
15 hand-colored illustrations (about 70 × 80 mm. each; the first
on title, the second beneath six lines of verse, remainder each
beneath four-line verse). Laid paper, watermark: armorial shield
and date 1794. Original yellow stiff wrappers, letterpress title (as

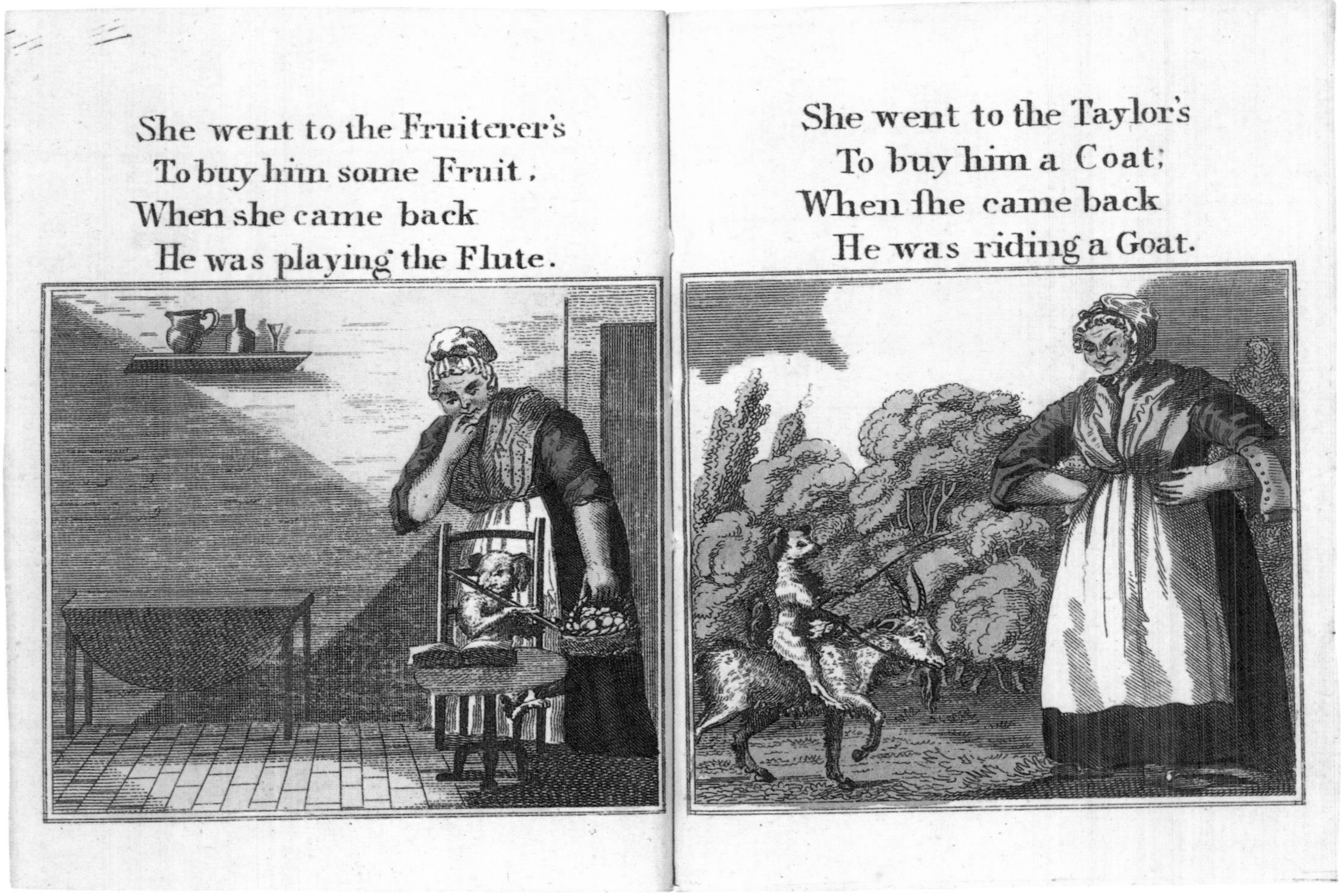

187. 3/3v–4r

transcribed above) on front cover, on lower cover Harris's ad for *Dame Partlet's Farm* (1804) at one shilling. Modern morocco gilt. Reference: Moon *Harris* 559(1).

Provenance: *1/6* (price inscribed on front cover); Charles Todd Owen (binding). PML 81009. Gift: Elisabeth Ball.

Not seen by Marjorie Moon when she compiled her checklist, this impression of the first state of the first edition of what she calls "probably the most significant book that JH ever published" is outstanding. Not only is it on fine eighteenth-century laid paper and in near perfect condition (albeit bound according to C. T. Owen's unfortunate specifications), it is also finely hand-colored and carries on its front cover what is probably the original bookseller's price of 1s. 6d.—points not recorded in Moon. The Morgan Library also has a copy of Sarah Catherine Martin's *Continuation* of 1806, probably colored by a former owner (PML 81008).

188a

[WILLIAM COWPER (1731–1800)]. *The Diverting History of John Gilpin. Shewing how he went farther than he intended, and came safe home again. Illustrated with humorous engravings.* London: printed for J. Harris, successor to E. Newbery, at the Original Juvenile Library, corner of St. Paul's Church-yard, 1808. 16° (123 × 94 mm.).

A8 (1v imprint *H. Bryer, Printer, Bridge-Street, Blackfriars*, 8r end of text and same imprint, 8v blank); 8 hand-colored etchings including frontispiece, probably printed from a single copperplate on a half-sheet, divided for insertion. Pp. 15, [1]. Different stocks of wove paper for text and illustration. Original printed gray stiff wrappers, series title *Harris's Cabinet of Amusement and Instruction* and wood engraving of his shop on front cover, bookseller's inscription *Gilpin* and price *1/6*; ad on lower cover . . . *the Proprietor can with confidence assert, that no Establishment of a similar description can produce an Assortment equal to that which is to be found at his House. A Catalogue will be delivered Gratis.* Modern red morocco gilt. References: Russell *Cowper* 195; Moon *Harris* 171.

Provenance: Charles Todd Owen (binding). PML 81861. Gift: Elisabeth Ball.

188b

Peter Prim's Pride, or proverbs, that will suit the young, or the old. London: Published by J. Harris, Corner St Paul's Church Yard, Dec. 26–1810 [this impression not before 1825 (watermark-date)]. 16° (123 × 91 mm.).

[1–44] (1r blank, 1v title, 2r illustration captioned *Never too old to learn*, 4/4r illustration captioned *The more the merrier but the less*

Every Crow thinks her own young the whitest.

189b. 4/1 verso, *reduced*

the better fare, 4/4ᵛ blank). Ff. [1], 15. Stipple-engraved throughout, printed on one side of the sheet probably from a single copperplate. 15 illustrations, hand-colored at the publisher's. Wove paper. Original pink stiff wrappers, original letterpress label mounted on front cover: *Harris's Cabinet. Prim's Pride* [in manuscript] *One Shilling Coloured*. Brown morocco gilt. References: Moon *Harris* 680 (recording a half-sheet of letterpress, presumably inserted with earlier impressions); Opie *Nursery Companion* pp. 94–5, 126.

Provenance: Charles Todd Owen (binding). PML 85073. Gift: Elisabeth Ball.

Harris's success with his engraved picture books was unprecedented. Harvey Darton reports a sale of 40,000 copies in the first year of Roscoe's *Butterfly's Ball* and of the even more popular *Peacock "At Home"* by Mrs. Dorset. Like most professional publishers before and since, Harris plowed back resources and turned his rather random few titles into a list. For ten years or so he edited into his "Cabinet of Amusement" a succession of square format picture books, whose style varied according to what he saw as the demands of the text. Thus, there were simply composed books like his elementary version of *Peter Prim's Pride*, with foregrounded pictures that plainly and elegantly illustrate a selection of proverbs; or he might combine engravings with letterpress as in the 1808 *John Gilpin*. (An edition of 1806 was entirely engraved, Moon *Harris* 170.)

189a

Peter Piper's Practical Principles of Plain and Perfect Pronunciation. Printed and published with pleasing pretty pictures, according to Act of Parliament. London: printed for J. Harris, corner of St. Paul's Church-yard, April 2, 1813. 16° (125 × 99 mm.).

A¹⁶ (1ʳ title, 1ᵛ imprint *H. Bryer, Printer, Bridge-Street, Blackfriars, London*, 2ʳ *Peter Piper's Polite Preface*, 3ʳ incipit: *Andrew Airpump ask'd his Aunt her Ailment*, 15ʳ *Note to V. p. 26*, 15ᵛ *Advertisement*, 16ʳ ad for *Paddy O'Murrough*, 16ᵛ same imprint). Pp. 29, [3]. Wove paper, watermarked 1812. 24 hand-colored wood engravings. Original typographical wrappers. Modern morocco. Reference: Moon *Harris* 629(1).

Provenance: *1/6* (price inscribed on front cover); contemporary signature (unidentified); Charles Todd Owen (binding). PML 81389. Gift: Elisabeth Ball.

189b

Peter Piper's Practical Principles of Plain and Perfect Pronunciation. To which is added, a collection of moral and entertaining conundrums. London: John Harris, St. Paul's Church-yard, [ca. 1835]. 12° (174 × 101 mm.).

1² 2–3⁶ 4⁴ ? (collation doubtful because of resewing; 1ʳ blank, 1ᵛ frontispiece, 2ʳ title, 2ᵛ imprint *London: printed by Samuel Bentley, Dorset Street, Fleet Street*, 2/1ʳ preface, 2/1ᵛ blank, 4/2ʳ conundrums, 4/3ᵛ same imprint, 4/4ʳ ads, 4/4ᵛ blank). Pp. 34, [2]. Wove paper, unwatermarked. Wood-engraved floral frontispiece, 24 wood engravings (same blocks as in the first edition above, but framed; two blocks replaced: *Billy Button* for *Bobby Blubber*, *Gaffer Gilpin* for *Gaffer Grumble*; *Vincent Veedon view'd his vacant Vehicle* has replaced *Villiam Veedon vip'd his Vig and Vaist-coat*, but the original illustration remains), all hand-colored. Original decorated fine-diaper brown cloth wrappers, yellow endpapers. Green morocco, by Morrell. References: Moon *Harris* 629(6); Opie *Nursery Companion* pp. 75–6, 125.

Provenance: Maria Blake (sign.); Charles Todd Owen (binding). PML 81388. Gift: Elisabeth Ball.

189c

Tom Tickle's Family History Versified by Himself. London: printed for J. Harris and Son, corner of St. Paul's Church-yard, [1822 copperplate-date, this impression not before 1832 (watermark-date)]. 8° (175 × 105 mm.).

[1¹⁶] (1ʳ blank, 1ᵛ drop-title *Tom Tickle's Family History*, illustration, incipit: *My Father he left me his Horses and Plough*, imprint *London Published June 20ᵗʰ 1822, by Harris & Son corner of Sᵗ Pauls*, 16ʳ explicit: *To Tom Tickle who now bids you kindly farewell*, same imprint, 16ᵛ blank). Ff. 16. Engraved throughout, printed from two copperplates on one side of two sheets of different wove paper stocks (dated 1825 and 1832) from the same mill (IIS & S). 16 half-page stipple illustrations,

189c. fo. 6 verso, *reduced*

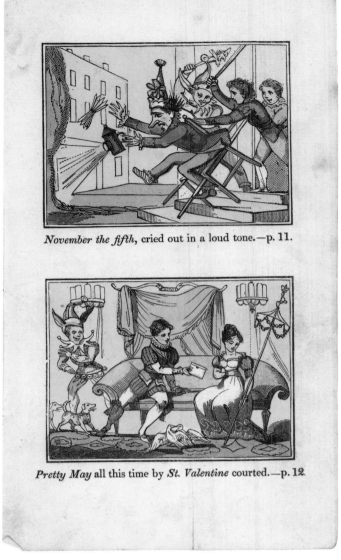

November the fifth, cried out in a loud tone.—p. 11.

Pretty May all this time by *St. Valentine* courted.—p. 12.

189d. plate facing A6[v], *reduced*

hand-colored as issued, each accompanied by four-line rhyme. Original blue flexible boards, letterpress title (as transcribed above) and wood-engraved vignette on front cover, wood-engraved device of *Harris's Cabinet of Amusement & Instruction* (showing his shop and St. Paul's Cathedral) on back cover, back pastedown *Harris's list of 1s. 6d. books coloured.* References: Moon *Harris* 888; Gumuchian 5602.

Provenance: *Chassereau's Fancy Warehouse, 21, North Street. Brighton* (nineteenth-century bookseller's label). PML 83040. Gift: Elisabeth Ball.

⤌ 189d ⤍

[CHARLES LAMB (1775–1834)]. *The New Year's Feast on his Coming of Age.* London: J. Harris and Son corner of St. Paul's Church-yard, 1824. 12° (177 × 105 mm.).

A¹²(12+1)(1[r] title, 1[v] imprint *London: printed by S & R. Bentley, Dorset Street, Fleet Street,* 2[r] signed A2 *Preface,* 2[v] blank, 3[r] incipit: *The Old Year being dead, the young Lord, New Year's Day,* 5[r] signed B5, 12[v] same imprint, 12+1[r] ads, 12+1[v] blank); 12 half-page

wood engravings with letterpress captions on one side of three inserted bifolia (between 3 and 4, around and between 6·7), hand-colored as issued. Pp. 24, [2]. Wove paper watermarked Balston & Co 1823. Original printed pink stiff wrappers. Reference: Moon *Harris* 576. Not in Lucas.

Provenance: *Sarah Margaret . . .* (erased inscription); Charles Todd Owen (pencil-note). PML 81633. Gift: Elisabeth Ball.

About 1817 the "Cabinet" underwent a transformation as Harris began to issue books of taller size, perhaps copying a model which Marshall and Wallis had introduced earlier in the century and which Marshall seems to have been reviving at this time with books like *Mother Goose's Melody* (1816). In some instances—see also *Dame Partlet's Farm* (entries 186a and 186b)—Harris would re-edit a square format book into a tall one. The *Peter Piper* of 1813 is smartened up no end for its reappearance in a larger size and with the cuts put into frames (first published in 1819). In other instances a new book was designed for the new format. *Tom Tickle* is an example of a fully-engraved book, with Harris calling upon one of his favorite (but still unidentified) artists for the lively stipple-engravings; *The New-Year's Feast* is primarily typographic, and even its six plates have been given letterpress legends.

With regard to the authorship of *The New Year's Feast*, Mrs. Moon notes that the text is a versification of an essay in the *London Magazine* signed "Elia's Ghost" and reprinted in *Last Essays of Elia*. The preface to the present book makes clear that the versifying has been done by the same hand as the original, so the assumption must be that Charles Lamb is the author.

⋙ 190 ⋘

[MARIE-CATHERINE DE LA MOTHE, Countess d'AULNOY (1650/51–1705)]. *The Celebrated Fairy Tales of Mother Bunch, now republished with appropriate engravings, for the amusement of those little masters and misses, who, by duty to their parents, and obedience to their superiors, are likely to become great lords and ladies.* London: printed for J. Harris, corner of St. Paul's Church Yard, 1817. 2 parts in 1 volume. 18° (136 × 85 mm.).

Pt. 1: *A²* (1ʳ half-title, 1ᵛ blank, 2ʳ title, 2ᵛ imprint *H. Bryer, Printer, Bridge-Street, Blackfriars, London*); B–G⁶ I² (I2ᵛ same imprint); 6 hand-colored stipple engravings. Pt. 2: A²; B–G⁶ I²; 6 hand-colored stipple engravings. Perhaps all 12 illustrations (including frontispieces) printed from a single copperplate, the sheet then divided for insertion. Pp. [4], 76, [4],76. Laid paper (letterpress), wove (engraving). Original marbled boards, red roan spine gilt. Reference: Moon *Harris* 470.

Provenance: *Farindon Lane 1818* (inscr.). PML 84696–7. Purchase: Ball Fund.

Harris's first use of the D'Aulnoy fairy tales was in the continuing line of editions from the Newbery "Mother Bunch" of 1773 (see entry 79). By nineteenth-century standards, however, that was a mean edition, and in this new reprint of the stories he makes them fit company for the refined drawing rooms of a more sophisticated clientele. He also removes the intrusive tale of "Little George at the Castle of Instruction" from the center of the collection to the end, where it forms a moral coda. Harris published in the same year a companion edition of Perrault's tales in two parts, with illustrations by the same hand.

WILLIAM DARTON II (1781–1854)

The emergence of William Darton I as an influential publisher has already been noticed (chapter VI). In 1804, the year of *Original Poems for Infant Minds* (entry 102), his son William set up an independent business after having served an apprenticeship with his father. He found premises at 40 Holborn Hill, moving to No. 58 in 1808. For five years of trading, from 1806–1811, he worked with his brother Thomas, and their joint initials are often found on their publications at this time.

From the start it seems clear that these younger Dartons were less inhibited in their publishing policy than their cautious, serious-minded Quaker father. Linda Hannas notes in *The English Jigsaw Puzzle* that, where William I's publishing of dissected puzzles, etc., held to a largely educational aim, William II widened the scope of his productions and included table-games with dice or teetotums, which were anathema to his parent.

190. part 2, frontispiece

W. & T. Darton also published many picture sheets, writing sheets, and other engraved material (some already noted in the digression on "Grateful Tributes"), and they were therefore in a good position to cash in on the boom in picture books after the arrival of *Old Mother Hubbard*. Unlike with Harris, however, there is both waywardness in William Darton's policy (not for him a nicely regimented and numbered "Cabinet") and a much greater variation in format, in subjects dealt with, and in quality of production—a feature that was to characterize the Holborn Hill enterprise beyond William II's retirement in 1836 and into the difficult years when the new forces in Victorian publishing began to compete with the old established firm. (In that connection there is a telling mistake in Thackeray's *Vanity Fair*. In chapter 46 Amelia Osborne goes to "Darton's Shop" to buy Christmas books for her beloved Georgy—Maria Edgeworth's *Parent's Assistant* and Thomas Day's *Sandford and Merton*—but Thackeray places the shop in Newbery's old quarters in St. Paul's Churchyard).

The books described here represent only a small portion of the Morgan Library's holdings of Darton material. Because of the heavy emphasis on picture books in this section, the point should be made that, like John Harris, William Darton II published a large quantity of often rather severely produced moral and didactic works during his long career.

191. 2/1 verso, *reduced*

192. fo. 16 recto

❧ 191 ❧

The Adventures of Old Dame Trot and her Comical Cat. Part I. London: William Darton and Son, Holborn Hill, [ca. 1830]. Sixpence coloured. 16° (129 × 102 mm.).

[1–2⁸] (1ʳ blank, 1ᵛ drop-title, incipit: *Old Dame Trot, Going to the Fair*). Ff. [16]. Etched throughout, printed perhaps from a single copperplate on one side of the sheet. 16 larger-than-half-page illustrations, dab-colored as issued, most with four-line rhyme, the second with eight-line, the third with seven-line rhyme. Original buff wrappers, letterpress title (as transcribed above) and wood engraving of a tiger's head on front cover, sheep's head on back cover. Brown morocco. References: Opie *Three Centuries* 366; Darton *Check-list* 320(8).

Provenance: Charles Todd Owen (binding). PML 85080. Gift: Elisabeth Ball.

In Lawrence Darton's *Check-list* an effort is made to trace the complex history of *Dame Trot*, whose text may be based on an 1803 edition by T. Evans (Opie *ODNR*, p. 320). William Darton II's first printing of the rhyme must have been one of his earliest publications and did not carry his imprint but was issued merely as "Sold at all Juvenile Book Shops," with one of the two known copies printed on paper with an 1803 watermark.

  These facts, taken with the rhyme's close similarity to *The Comic Adventures of Old Mother Hubbard* (item 187), raise unanswered questions about the relationship between Darton's cat and Harris's dog. Could the former have preceded the latter?

  The first dated edition of *Dame Trot* appeared under the

imprint of W. & T. Darton in 1807, with a spoof attribution "to the pen of the Dutchess of L****" and "with elegant engravings after Sir Joshua." The Morgan Library has a later printing of this version (PML 80888) watermarked 1814, but the later copy described here is the first to have descriptive legends ("Recreation," "Discourse" etc.) in a manner perhaps copied from Godwin's *Gaffer Gray* (item 202).

❧ 192 ❧

Death and Burial of Cock Robin. [London:] Published by W. Darton Junʳ 40 Holborn Hill, Janʸ 31ˢᵗ 1806 (copperplate-date, early impression presumably of the same year). 16° (118 × 91 mm.).

[1¹⁶?] (1ʳ blank, 1ᵛ drop-title, incipit: *Who killed Cock Robin?*, imprint). Ff.[16]. Etched throughout, probably printed from a single copperplate on one side of a sheet. Wove paper with 1806 watermark-date. 16 larger-than-half-page illustrations, each accompanied by a rhyme of five to eight lines. Uncolored. Original covers lacking. Modern morocco gilt. References: Osborne II, 675; Opie *Three Centuries* 312 (late impression); Darton *Check-list* H235(1); James p. 37 (this copy).

Provenance: Charles Todd Owen (binding). PML 81368. Gift: Elisabeth Ball.

Further evidence of Darton/Harris competition can be seen in William Darton's publication early in 1806 of the earliest picturebook version of the traditional Cock Robin rhyme (with the Hare seen carving on a gravestone the actual date of the hero's demise: O^ct 25, 1805). Harris was to respond to this a few months later with his *Happy Courtship . . . of Cock Robin, and Jenny Wren. To which is added, Alas! the doleful death of the bridegroom* (Moon *Harris* 144).

Around this time William and Thomas Darton began to invade the Hubbardonian Library too, by publishing their own *Sequel to the Comic Adventures* (cover-date 1807 but already advertised in 1806), in which Mother Hubbard's dog has "got him a wife," who creates a good deal of trouble (PML 85079). This is a different sequel from the one by "W.F," published by Harris in 1806 (Moon *Harris* 562).

❧ 193a ☙

[MARY ELLIOTT, née BELSON (ca. 1792–1860s?)]. *The Mice, and their Pic Nic. A good moral tale, &c. By a look-ing-glass maker.* London: Printed for the Author, by W. and T. Darton, 58, Holborn Hill, 1810. 16° (128 × 102 mm.).

A–B^8 (A1^r blank, A1^v wood-engraved *frontispiece*, A2^r title, A2^v *Entered at Stationers' hall*, A3^r incipit: *A mouse, of a free, open, generous nature*, B7^v end of text, imprint *Printed by W. and T. Darton, 58, Holborn Hill*, B8^r full-page wood engraving *The Scramble*, B8^v blank); two bifolia (around A3·6 and B4·5) with four full-page wood engravings: *Content, Harmony restored*; *A journey, A general muster*. Pp. 30, [2]. Wove paper water-marked E & S 1809. Original tan flexible boards, four wood-engraved illustrations on covers including the Darton printer's device, price "1/" inscribed on front cover. References: Moon *Elliott* 178; Darton *Check-list* H467(2).

PML 81615. Gift: Elisabeth Ball.

❧ 193b ☙

[MARY ELLIOTT, née BELSON (ca. 1792–1860s?)]. *The Baby's Holiday. To which is added, The White Lily. Illustrated by Coloured Engravings. By Mary Belson.* London: William Darton and Son, Holborn Hill, [ca. 1830]. Price Sixpence. 16° (131 × 101 mm.).

[1^16] (1^r title, 1^v blank, 2^r incipit: *As Marian at her nurse's knee*, 9^r *Preface to The White Lily*, 10^r incipit: *The sun declin'd, the evening breeze*, 16^v imprint *Printed by W. Darton, jun. 58, Holborn-Hill*); 8 hand-colored numbered etchings, dated 16th Sept. 1812, appar-ently printed from two copperplates on two quarter-sheets of different wove paper (one with 1809 watermark-date) and divided for insertion (no. 4 inserted as frontispiece). Pp. 32. Original yellow stiff wrappers, letterpress title on front cover, wood engraving of a duck's head on back cover. Modern morocco gilt. References: Moon *Elliott* 13 (the one-shilling first edition of 1812 by Wm. Darton jun.); Darton *Check-list* H399(2).

Provenance: Charles Todd Owen (binding). PML 85088. Gift: Elisabeth Ball.

193a. front cover, *reduced*

❧ 193c ☙

[MARY ELLIOTT, née BELSON (ca. 1792–1860s?)]. *The Children in the Wood: a tale for the nursery. With copper-plates. Revised and corrected, with additions, by Mary Elliott.* London: William Darton, 58, Holborn Hill, 1826. Price Sixpence. 18° (139 × 89 mm.).

A^18 (18^r imprint *William Darton, 58, Holborn Hill*, 18^v ads of *Sixpenny Books*); five etchings, printed perhaps from a single but no more than three copperplates: the first inserted as a folded frontispiece (139 × 182 mm.), the others on two bifolia (around A7·12 and between A9·10). Pp. 35, [1]. Original buff stiff wrappers, letterpress title on front cover, ads on back cover. References: Moon *Elliott* 40; Darton *Check-list* H409(2).

Provenance: *Jane Freestone from her Mamma 1829* (inscr.). PML 83098. Gift: Elisabeth Ball.

Mary Elliott (née Belson) has already been encountered as an author of "Grateful Tributes" (entry 109a) and a versifier of *Hymns in Prose* (entry 89). She was something of a sheet-anchor in William Darton II's publishing activities, turning out a large and varied body of work which found much favor in its day. A full insight into her contemporary importance can be gained from Marjorie Moon's *The Children's Books of Mary (Belson) Elliott; a bibliography* (Winchester, 1987). Neither Mrs. Moon in this work, however, nor Lawrence Darton in his *Check-list* of the Darton firms were able to pin down firm dates for Mary Belson Elliott's birth and death. Our speculative dates (ca. 1792–1860s) are based on our interpretation of their notes.

The three examples of her work catalogued here show her progress (if that is the right word) from her early poetic endeavors

Engraved for THE CHILDREN IN THE WOOD: a tale for the Nursery.

...and, after a great deal of trouble, the pretty babes were at last found stretched in each other's arms; with WILLIAM'S arm round the neck of JANE, his face turned close to hers, and his frock pulled over her body.

London, William Darton 58 Holborn Hill.   *see page 31.*

193c. frontispiece, enlarged

to the confident, not over-sentimental retelling of "The Babes in the Wood." *The Mice and their Pic Nic*, in its pictorial covers, is a well-turned rendering of the fable of the town mouse and the country mouse; *The Baby's Holiday* is a less successful attempt to refashion "The Butterfly's Ball" with babies and cupids at center stage; and *The Children in the Wood* gains a curious force from its densely etched, weirdly proportioned illustrations.

❧ 194 ❧

[RICHARD ROE? (fl. 1808–13)]. *The Good Boy's Soliloquy; containing his parents' instructions, relative to his disposition and manners. By the author of the Invited Alphabet, &c.* London: Printed by William Darton, Jun. 58, Holborn-Hill, 1813. (Price One Shilling.). 16° (125 × 99 mm.).

[1⁸] (1ʳ title, 1ᵛ blank, 2ʳ *To the reader*, 3ʳ incipit: *The things my parents bid me do*, 8ᵛ imprint *Printed by W. Darton, jun. 58, Holborn-Hill*); 16 leaves with oval engravings, dated 15 April 1811, printed on one side of the sheet. Pp. 16. Wove paper (different stocks for letterpress and intaglio). Original brown pictorial stiff wrappers, wood engraving of birds on front cover, a shepherd on back cover. Green morocco, by Morrell. References: Darton *Check-list* H1282(2); James p. 56 (this copy).

Provenance: Charles Todd Owen (binding). PML 81329. Gift: Elisabeth Ball.

Given the daunting title of these salutary verses, it is cheering to

report that *The Good Boy's Soliloquy* is nothing more nor less than a satire on its kind. (Indeed, there is something almost Carrollian in the author's anxious disclaimer to his reader that he does not want to "be accused of putting a number of naughty things into your head, which, it is *most* probable, you *never* think of yourself.")

To begin with, every appearance of moral adjuration is maintained: "I must abhor to steal or wrong; I must not have a railing tongue." But as the jog-trot rhythms move to "lighter themes," the author draws closer and closer to the kind of parody that was to culminate in the *Cautionary Verses* of Hilaire Belloc:

> I must not scamper in the mire,
> Or fry the snow upon the fire
> I must not blow the candle out,
> Or throw the smutty snuff about.

The comedy is heightened by the elegant and wittily detailed engravings. Samuel Wood, who published editions in New York from 1818 (Welch 460.1), may have taken the whole thing seriously, for he commissioned from Nancy Sproat (1766–1826) a properly moral *Good Girl's Soliloquy*, 1819 (Welch 1245.1)

For many years "the Author of the INVITED ALPHABET" [R. R.], and hence of this "courtesy book," has been assumed, on no clear evidence, to be one Richard Ransom(e). The announcement at the end of the soliloquy, however, supported by remarks in the preface, gives every reason for attributing this book and the *Invited Alphabet* and the *Assembled Alphabet* to a Richard Roe.

The Morgan Library owns a copy of the 1811 first edition as well, with the same provenance (PML 80883; Gottlieb 36). *The Assembled Alphabet* makes an appearance in chapter XIX.

194. plate [12], *reduced*

❧ 195 ❧

[JOHN BUNYAN (1628–88)]. *The Pilgrim's Progress, from this world, to that which is to come. Part I. With twelve coloured plates.* London: William Darton, 58, Holborn Hill, 1823. Price one shilling. Engraved and etched picture broadside, cut up and stabbed to form an oblong codex. (86 × 101 mm.).

12 leaves, printed on one side only: illustration and caption on facing versos and rectos, hand-colored at the publisher's. Fo. 1ᵛ incipit: *I looked, and saw him open the book and read therein,* 10ʳ and 11ᵛ plate-imprint *London: William Darton, Holborn Hill, 1822.* Original pink stiff wrappers, letterpress title-label (as transcribed above) on front cover. Modern morocco gilt. Reference: Darton *Check-list* H116.

Provenance: Charles Todd Owen (binding). PML 81536. Gift: Elisabeth Ball.

As we have already seen in "Grateful Tributes" (entries 104–105), Darton sold his picture sheets also as little books. As a result the original narrative becomes a series of disjunct scenes whose cheerful colors are presumably there to make up for the fact that the "story" has disappeared. As well as this first volume of a 2-volume *Pilgrim's Progress,* the Morgan Library owns two other made-up booklets in the same series, *The History of Prince Lee Boo* 1823 and *Robinson Crusoe* 1823 (PML 84609 and 81161). The missing second volume contrives to recount the pilgrimages of both Christiana and Tender-Conscience in its twelve leaves.

195. fo. 9 verso, *enlarged*

A FULL LENGTH PORTRAIT OF

OLD MOTHER HUBBARD AND HER DOG.

196. frontispiece

❧ 196 ❧

[SARAH CATHERINE MARTIN (1768–1826)]. *The Adventures of Old Mother Hubbard and her Wonderful Dog. With coloured engravings.* London: William Darton and Son, Holborn Hill, [ca. 1830]. 18° (137 × 87 mm.).

[1¹⁸] (1ᵛ frontispiece *A full length portrait of Old Mother Hubbard and her dog*, 2ʳ title, 15ᵛ–16ʳ nursery rhymes: *This little pig went to market*; *Let us go to the wood, says this pig*; *The man in the wilderness asked me*; *Pussy-cat, pussy-cat, where have you been?*; *Hiccory, diccory, dock*; *Little Miss Muffett*), Pp. [1], 34, [1]. The sheet printed on one side only. 15 wood engravings (frontispiece full-page, remainder half-page), hand-colored as issued. Original green stiff wrappers, letterpress title, *Price Sixpence* and wood-engraved vignette of a dog's head on front cover, stag's head on back cover. Reference: Darton *Check-list* H1107(1).

PML 85896. Gift: Elisabeth Ball.

From the imprint "William Darton and Son," this sixpenny picture book must have been published in the early 1830s, by which time Sarah Catherine Martin's verses had entered "the tradition" and become common property. The design of the covers and the pages suggests comparison with similar books being put out by Thomas Dean & Co, a firm discussed in the next chapter.

BENJAMIN TABART (1767 or 1768–1833)

"Lively and unconventional" said F. J. Harvey Darton of Benjamin Tabart in 1932, but also "an elusive person; probably attractive if one could catch him." And so he remained up to the point when, in 1989, Marjorie Moon was completing work on her bibliography of his "Juvenile Library" (Moon *Tabart*). At that point she was approached by a direct descendant of the bookseller, K. Jane Evans, who was working on a family history* and was able to give dates for his birth and death as well as new details of his checkered business career. Even so his early years remain obscure, except that he probably worked for the engraver and printseller Francis (*né* François) Vivares, whose daughter Susanna (1759–1839) he married in the 1780s.

Tabart appeared on the London bookselling scene in 1801 with a fully fledged Juvenile Library in premises at 157 New Bond Street (corner of Grafton Street). The Bodleian Library possesses a catalogue issued by Tabart soon after his shop opened, which shows him not merely stocking a large range of current educational and recreational books but also giving information about his stock in a systematic and intelligent way. Almost certainly he was running this enterprise in association with the City bookseller, Richard Phillips of Blackfriars (who enters many Tabart publications in the Stationers' Register), but the novelty and flair of several books published by Tabart have a liveliness which is very different from Richard Phillips's dowdy educational publications. Tabart was to develop his business for a dozen years or so before there was an inevitable slowing of momentum, and about 1812 there are telltale signs of instability (especially changes of address); eventually his name is preserved not on publications of his own but as the editor of *Fairy Tales, or the Liliputian library* (1817), an extensive anthology that was to remain in print as *Popular Fairy Tales* with one publisher or another to the end of the 1830s.

Only a skeletal representation of Tabart's publishing is given in this chapter, partly because a number of his books are to be found elsewhere in the catalogue (see especially his wide-ranging series of individually published "Popular Stories" in chapter XX).

---

* Published privately in 1991 as *Tabart of Fonthill; From England to Van Diemen's Land* and revealing not just Benjamin's complicated genealogy but also the emigration of his family to Tasmania—hence their elusiveness.

❧ 197 ❧

[ELIZABETH KILNER (fl. 1802–08)]. *A Puzzle for a Curious Girl . . . Second edition.* London: printed for B. Tabart, Juvenile Library, New-Bond-Street; and J. Harris, corner of St. Paul's Church-yard, 1803. 12° (130 × 83 mm.).

A² (1ʳ half-title, 1ᵛ imprint *Printed by T. Davison, White-friars*, 2ʳ title, 2ᵛ blank); B–M⁶ (M6ʳ same imprint, catchword *At*, M6ᵛ blank); N² (ads *At B. Tabart's Juvenile and School Library*). Pp. [4], 130, [2], [4]. 12 etched illustrations (at the beginning of chapters). Original red-roan-backed marbled boards. References: Moon *Harris* 961(2); Moon *Tabart* 91(2).

Provenance: *C.L. Powys and S.C. Powys 1807 Given us by Miss Lockwood* (ink- and pencil-inscrs.); *Miss Emily has read this book* (pencil-inscr. partly erased, facing title) *10 Oct. 1811* (below the end of text). PML 83506. Gift: Elisabeth Ball.

CHAP. XII.

THE MYSTERY DISCLOSED.

MRS. Belfast, on her daughter's entrance, laid aside her writing, and seating herself by her, thus began :

" Not

197. K4 verso

Since they were both setting up similar businesses, but in different parts of town, Tabart and Harris may well have found it prudent to cooperate over publishing ventures (or else Richard Phillips was acting as some kind of middleman). In any case, *A Puzzle* was an attractive enough book to start a list with, being for its time an amusing detective story and, thanks to its pictorial chapter heads, a neat piece of book production. Elizabeth Kilner, as "S.W.," is named as the author of *A Puzzle* in the title statements of three other books by her published by Tabart: *A Visit to a Farmhouse* (1804), *Scenes at Home* (1810) and *A Visit to London* (1805), whose preface reveals that the author is a woman, and one of whose chapters describes a visit to the Juvenile Library in Bond Street (Osborne, p. 194). S.W.'s identity was finally established through the sale of a quantity of annotated books from the Kilner family (Sotheby's London, 2 June 1988, lot 228).

❧ 198 ❧

[MATTHEW GREGORY ("MONK") LEWIS (1775–1818)]. *[A] True History of a Little Old Woman, who found a silver penny . . .* London: printed for Tabart and Co. The Juvenile and School Library, 157, New Bond-Street; and to be had of all booksellers. C. Squire, Printer, Furnival's-Inn-Court, Holborn, 1806. 16°? (127 × 105 mm.).

[1⁴ 2² 3⁴] (1ʳ title, its first word in this copy erased, 1ᵛ incipit: *Some six years ago, (or perhaps it was more)*, 2ᵛ–3ʳ, 2/1ᵛ–2ʳ and 3/2ᵛ–3ʳ blank, 3/4ᵛ *Moral*); [4²] (ads including for *Popular Stories*); 13 etched illustrations (including the last, a folded strip also comprising the final verses), apparently printed from four copperplates dated 27 May-1806, on both sides of a sheet divided into three bifolia for insertion (around 1/2·3, 2/1·2 and 3/2·3) and a 4-leaf panorama printed on one side only (inserted between 3/4 and 4/1). Pp. 20, [4]. Wove paper with watermark-date 1805. The plates colored by hand—see overleaf, presumably at the publisher's. Original yellow wrappers, letterpress title on front cover, ads on front and back covers. References: Moon *Tabart* 96A(1) and Appendix D; Osborne II, 607; Hockliffe 861.

Provenance: Early inscription on title erased. PML 85018. Gift: Elisabeth Ball.

Soon after the previously noted volume was published, Tabart launched his most famous venture, the "Popular Stories for the Nursery," a collection of fairy tales and the like published in individual booklets (entry 382). With this *True History*, however, he took the nursery story generally known as "The Old Woman and her Pig" and not only used "Monk" Lewis's versification but also arranged that its climactic ending should be represented in panorama form. The Ball copy presumably belongs to the first or an early edition and has the plates carefully colored. The Morgan Library also has a copy of an 1808 edition (printed for Tabart by W. Marchant), in which the paint has been laid on a little more thickly (PML 81547), but see the Moon Appendix for a discussion of various states.

Attribution of authorship to "Monk" Lewis is based on a passage in Margaret Baron-Wilson's *Life and Correspondence of M.G.L.* (London, 1839), pp. 202–15, noted by Marjorie Moon with acknowledgment to Iona Opie.

❧ 199 ❧

The History of Little Red Riding-Hood. In verse. Illustrated by engravings. Second edition. London: Published at the Juvenile Libraries of B. Tabart and Co. New Bond-Street, and J. Harris, St. Paul's Church-Yard. Printed by E. Hemsted, Great New-street, Fetter-lane, 1808 [this issue not before July 1816 (date of plates)]. 16°? (134 × 118 mm.).

[1–2² 3²(2+1)] (1ʳ title, 3/2+1ʳ *Moral* and printer's imprint, 3/2+1ᵛ blank); frontispiece and 11 numbered etched illustrations, perhaps from three copperplates, divided into six bifolia (frontispiece·III around quire 1, I·II inside quire 1; IV·VII around, V·VI inside quire 2, VIII·XI around, IX·X inside 3/1·2). Pp. [1], 1–11, [2]. Two wove paper stocks, that for the etchings watermarked 1814. Illustrations I–VII and X hand-colored by an early child owner. Original yellow wrappers, letterpress title *The Renowned History . . .* on front and back covers. References: cf. Moon *Harris* 621 and *Supplement* 621; cf. Moon *Tabart* 128(3).

PML 84977. Gift: Elisabeth Ball.

M. G. Lewis made a neat entertainment out of the versified "Old Woman and her Pig" and may possibly have been retained by Tabart to do the same for Perrault's *Little Red Riding-Hood*. The verses have the same meter and a similar liveliness, although we

7

At her wits' end was she, when a *Dog* came in sight,
" Honest Tray," she exclaimed, " take the trouble to bite
My pig who won't cross yonder stile to the right ;
Or else I shan't get to my cottage to-night !"—
" I bite him," quoth Tray, " sure you're running your rigs,
I'll not injure a hair of his tail, please the pigs ;
And I'd have you to know too," he added with smiles,
" They're only lame dogs that *I* help over stiles."

London, Pub. by Tabart & Cº May 17 1805, New Bond St.

198. 1/4ʳ and facing plate, *reduced*

11

" O Grandmamma dear! you have got such long arms !"
The Wolf said, " my love, they'll protect you from
              harms."
" But O ! what long ears you have got, Granny dear !"
" The better," he said, " your sweet accents to hear."
" And O ! Grandmamma, you have got such large eyes !"
" The better to see you, my love," he replies.
" And O ! what long teeth !" she exclaim'd in affright :
" The better to eat you"—he said with delight.
And so without further delay or advice,
Ate Little *Red Riding-hood* up in a trice.

199. 3/2ᵛ and pl. XI, *reduced*

insertion. Pp. 71, [1]. Wove paper, unwatermarked. Original marbled boards, blue roan spine gilt. References: Stewart A9a; Moon *Tabart* 171; Alderson *Moon* 100; Hockliffe 777.

Provenance: *Miss Walker April 3rd 1820 Branthill* (?) *near Wells Norfolk* (inscr.). PML 84452. Purchase: Mrs. Alexander O. Vietor in memory of her daughter, Barbara Foster Vietor (1956–1966).

Ann Taylor's *Autobiography* goes some way towards further narrowing our view of Tabart as a "commissioning editor," since she there records that the work of revising "The World Turned Upside Down" was sent to the Taylor family by Richard Phillips, "who paid us 24 guineas for the operation." As with the two previous books, the versifying is nicely turned; the illustrations, by Isaac Taylor, Jr., respond to the sometimes gruesome fantasies with notable graphic power. A comparison of *Signor Topsy Turvy* with the versified text in the Ryland edition of ca. 1770 (PML 84610) shows that although the books have similar dimensions, the Taylors in no way "revised" the material but rather invented entirely new texts and in many cases new examples.

WILLIAM GODWIN (1756–1836) AND M. J. GODWIN & CO.

Most publishers discussed in this catalogue were dyed-in-the-wool professionals. Whether through apprenticeships or family connections, they were bred to their calling. (A digression on private publishing can be found at the end of chapter XII.) With William Godwin, however, we meet a species whose presence is never to die out (though always endangered): the hopeful amateur.

Known to his contemporaries primarily as the radical-minded author of *An Enquiry Concerning Political Justice* (1793), Godwin entered the book trade in partnership with his second wife, Mary Jane, whom he had married after the heartbreaking death of his first, Mary Wollstonecraft. They opened their "Juvenile Library" at a shop in Hanway Street, just off Oxford Street, in 1805, and moved to new premises in Skinner Street, Snow Hill, in 1807. They had minimal capital, and their experience derived mostly from Mary Jane's work as editor and translator for the Phillips/Tabart combine. Neither was well fitted for a life of commerce; they were swindled by their manager, Thomas Hodgkins, in whose name the business was run until 1808 as the name Godwin was not one to inspire affection and confidence amongst a clientele of respectable parents. Furthermore, Mary Jane seems to have been rather an unsympathetic character—Lamb called her "the Bad Baby"—and in consequence of this and of their chronic cadging the partnership has always appeared somewhat ludicrous as well as ineffectual.

By comparison with most of the other companies represented in this chapter, however, M. J. Godwin & Co. is a firm that deserves recognition and praise. They were not content to follow a fashion so much as to work up their own ideas, as witness the attempts to bring originality to their series of colored books culminating in the elegant *Beauty and the* Beast of 1811 (including two folding plates of music), and their experimentation with publishing styles. Godwin's *Fables Ancient and Modern*, published under the pseudonym of Edward Baldwin, was, for instance, issued as a two-volume set with pictorial head-pieces to each fable and in a one-volume popular edition with the same illustrations reduced in size and placed within a series of composite grids. Furthermore,

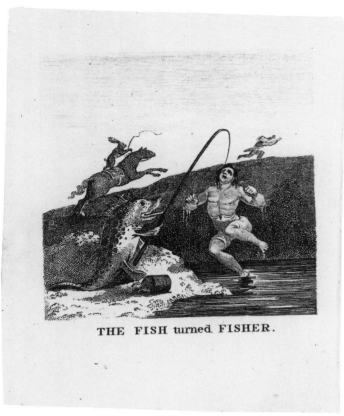

THE FISH turned FISHER.

200. etching opposite B7r, *reduced*

are spared a panoramic view of Little Red Riding Hood being devoured by the wolf. The book was another joint enterprise with John Harris and was first published with a title dated 1807 and a frontispiece dated 1 Jan. 1808. The British Library has a copy of the second edition with the plates dated 1808. The Ball copy of the second edition has the plates dated 1816 and with Tabart's Piccadilly address. (Also, plates IX, X, and XI, which were misnumbered in 1808, are now corrected.) Presumably a remainder of second-edition sheets was joined with impressions of the copperplates in a new state, well after Tabart had moved his shop from New Bond Street.

❧ 200 ❧

[ANN TAYLOR (1782–1866), JANE TAYLOR (1783–1824), & Rev. ISAAC TAYLOR (1759–1829)]. *Signor Topsy-Turvy's Wonderful Magic Lantern; or, the world turned upside down. By the author of "My Mother," and other poems. Illustrated with twenty-four engravings.* London: printed for Tabart & Co. at the Juvenile and School Library, no. 157, New Bond-Street; and to be had of all booksellers: By B. M'Millan, Bow Street, Covent Garden, 1810. [Price 3s.6d. Bound]. 16° (129 × 104 mm.).

B–C16 D4 (B1r title, B1v blank, B2r *Advertisement*, B2v blank, B3r *Introduction*, D4v ads *Elementary Books Lately published by R. Phillips, Bridge Street, Blackfriars; and to be had of Tabart and Co.*, and printer's imprint); 24 etchings (including *frontispiece*) by Isaac Taylor, Jr. (1787–1865), printed from fewer copperplates (six?) on one side of the sheets, divided into single leaves for

201a. 1/3 verso, *reduced*

201b. B3 verso, *reduced*

few other children's book publishers of the period could boast of having published two substantial works that have remained as classics until the present day, *The Swiss Family Robinson* (entry 16) and *Tales from Shakespear* (see entry 205).

As with Benjamin Tabart though, innovative ideas ahead of public taste did not sort well with under-capitalization. The Godwins' lack of financial means caused continuous woe (exacerbated by private calamity: Mary Jane's daughter Claire chased after Byron, by whom she had the unfortunate Allegra; William's daughter Mary [see entry 203] eloped with Shelley; and his stepdaughter Fanny committed suicide). The final years before bankruptcy in 1825 were largely spent in selling stock—eventually from an accommodation address in the Strand.

❦ 201a ❦

Tom and his Cat: the surprising history of a good boy; who for his diligence in his learning was rewarded with a fine cat; and through the clever tricks of his cat became heir to the throne. London: printed for Thomas Hodgkins, at the Juvenile Library, Hanway-Street, (opposite Soho-Square) Oxford-Street; and to be had of all Booksellers, 1806. Price 1s. Plain, or 1s.6d. Coloured. 16° (125 × 103 mm.).

[1–4⁴] (1ʳ blank, 1ᵛ illustration, plate-imprint *London, Published, July 17. 1806, by Thoˢ Hodgkins, Hanway Street*, incipit: *Little Tom was so good*, 4/4ʳ ending *And ow'd all his good luck / To his comical Cat*, 4/4ᵛ blank). Ff. [16]. Etched throughout: 16 illustrations (about 85 × 78 mm.), each accompanied by four-line rhyme, perhaps printed from a single large copperplate on one side of the sheet (divided for quiring); hand-colored as issued.

Wove paper, no watermark. Original blue wrappers, letterpress title (as transcribed above) on front cover, ad on back cover. References: Kinnell p. 95; Alderson *Gobwin* 4.

Provenance: Henry Bell (signs.); C. A. M. Bell (sign.), pencil inscription perhaps by one of the Bells: *For pleasour / For pleasaeir*. PML 81557. Gift: Elisabeth Ball.

❦ 201b ❦

Tom and his Cat [etc.]. London: printed for M.J. Godwin and Co. At the French and English Juvenile and School Library, 195, (St. Clement's), Strand, 1823. 8° (180 × 112 mm.).

[1¹⁸] signed A²<B⁸<c⁸ (1·18 mounted as pastedowns, 1ʳ *B.M'Millan, Printer, Bow-Street, Covent Garden*, 1ᵛ title, 2ʳ blank, 2ᵛ headline, illustration, incipit, 9ᵛ blank, 18 blank). Pp. 33, [3]. Title, headlines, and four-line rhymes printed letterpress (inner formes only). 16 etched illustrations, identical to those in the 1806 edition, but the original copperplate(s) cut up to omit the text portion; hand-colored as issued. Wove paper, no watermark. Original olive stiff wrappers, letterpress title and *Price 1s.6d.*

Coloured on front cover, the Godwin wood-engraved device *Esop instructing children* on back cover.

PML 83035. Gift: Elisabeth Ball.

Even while establishing the business at Hanway Street, the Godwins commenced a series of what they called their "copper plate" books in the Hubbardonian style, beginning with Charles Lamb's "Paraphrase on the King and Queen of Hearts" (1805). Indeed, the meter of *Tom and his Cat* shows the pervasive influence of the rhyme and, although the anonymous author (Mrs. Godwin?) has tried to inject a narrative into the usual trail of stanzas, it proceeds with no consistency. In the 1s. plain issue the illustrations appear rather amateurish, but when colored as here they take on a warmth that endorses their intended comicality.

Tom and his Cat, in one form or another, lasted the life of the Juvenile and School Library itself. Our second example not only shows how the firm tried to preserve a "modern look" for the series by reissuing it in the larger format that John Harris and others made popular, it also reveals through its date and its St. Clement's address that this was one of the last editions to come from the failing company, its publications eventually appearing with the spurious imprint of "William Jackson." The text is now entirely typographical, but the pictorial portion of the original plates remains.

◄§ 202 §►

[THOMAS HOLCROFT (1745–1809)]. *Gaffer Gray; or, the misfortunes of poverty: a Christmas ditty* . . . London: printed for M.J. Godwin & Co., at the Juvenile Library, 41; Skinner-street; And to be had of all Booksellers and Toymen throughout the United Kingdom, 1816. Price 1s. Plain or 1s. 6d. Coloured. 16° (108 × 90 mm.).

[1–4⁴] (1ʳ blank, 1ᵛ heading *Charity*, frontispiece, title *Gaffer Gray* and plate-imprint *Printed for Thoˢ Hodgkins, Hanway Street, May 26. 1806*, 2ʳ incipit: *Ho! why dost thou shiver and Shake, Gaffer-Gray!*, 4/4ʳ heading *The Welcome*, illustration, end of rhyme as given below, 4/4ᵛ blank). Ff. [16]. Etched throughout: text and 13 illustrations probably by William Mulready (see the next entry), perhaps printed from two copperplates on one side of the half-sheets (divided for quiring); uncolored as issued. Wove paper, watermark-dates 1810. Original pink wrappers, letterpress title (as transcribed above) on front cover, ads on back cover. Blue morocco gilt. References: James p. 43 (this copy); Alderson *Gobwin* 3 (1808 wrappers).

Provenance: A. W. Tuer (pencil-note); Charles Todd Owen (binding). PML 85672. Gift: Elisabeth Ball.

Originally preceding *Tom and his Cat* by a month or two, *Gaffer Gray* is anything but Hubbardonian, being rather a piece of Godwinesque social criticism. Parson Trulliber, Lawyer Doublefee, and Squire Guzzle show no charitable inclinations, even though the snow lies thick, and

> The poor man alone,
> When he hears the poor moan,
> Of his morsel a morsel will give, Well-a-day!

The ballad comes from the novel *The Adventures of Hugh Trevor*

202. 3/2 recto

(1794–7, 6 vols.) by Godwin's erstwhile friend Thomas Holcroft. Its transference to this picture book shows a concern to emphasize its radical sentiments, first by engraving the whole text on its own before it is "diluted" with pictures, and second by supplying summary legends of one or two words, whose use in picture books may have started here but was much exploited by William Darton II, who is found doing the same thing in his *Memoirs of Little Jack Horner* (plates dated June 19, 1806), and in other picture books.

Like *Tom and his Cat* and other titles in the series, *Gaffer Gray* was reissued later in the firm's life, in larger format with letterpress text, and the original copperplates cut up for imposing and printing the illustrations individually (PML 85673).

◄§ 203 §►

[MARY WOLLSTONECRAFT SHELLEY, née GODWIN (1797–1851)? and JOHN TAYLOR (1757–1832)?]. *Mounseer Nongtongpaw: a new version* . . . London: printed for the proprietors of the Juvenile Library, 41, Skinner Street, 1808. 16° (120 × 101 mm.).

[1⁸] (1ʳ title, 1ᵛ explanation of *"Je vous n'entends pas"* and imprint *Printed by Richard Taylor and Co., Shoe Lane*, 2ʳ incipit: *John Bull, from England's happy Isle*, 8ʳ *Conclusion*, 8ᵛ same imprint); 12 hand-colored etchings, apparently printed from two copperplates on one side of the sheets (divided for insertion). Pp. 16, illustrations numbered I–XII. Different paper stocks for letterpress (this half-sheet not watermarked) and plates (watermarked

V

203. *reduced*

Budgeon & Vilmotte 1808). Modern brown morocco. References: Opie *Nursery Companion*, pp. 118–22, 127–28; Kinnell p. 95; Alderson *Gobwin* 6.

Provenance: Francis Bishop (early inscr.); Charles Todd Owen (binding); Elisabeth Ball. PML 84986. Gift: Lilly Library.

This example of the Juvenile Library's copperplate series is the first edition of the reworking of Charles Dibdin's music hall song by Godwin's daughter Mary, who was "in her eleventh year" at the time. (Later, as Mary Shelley, she would write *Frankenstein*). The plates are by William Mulready, who probably assisted in the reworking of the text. His work as a children's-book illustrator needs to be more fully defined. By 1808 he was well known to the Godwins, for one of William Godwin's earliest efforts for his company had been the writing of "a true history of the early years of an artist" [i.e. Mulready], entitled *The Looking Glass*, "calculated to awaken the emulation of young persons of both sexes in the cultivation of the fine arts." (Geoffrey Summerfield in his essay *"The Making of the Home Treasury"* notes that Henry Cole consulted Mulready about illustrating his projected series [see entry 312] and reprinting *The Looking Glass*; he also looked at *Gaffer Gray* and *The Little Old Woman*. Later Cole recorded Mulready as saying that for these books "Godwin had never paid him anything though he was poor at the time.") The John Taylor, who, correspondence suggests, assisted in the new version of Dibdin, had had a companion ballad reprinted in the series: *Monsieur Tonson* (1807/8).

204

[CHARLES LAMB (1775–1834) & MARY ANN LAMB (1764–1847)]. *Poetry for Children, entirely original. By the author of "Mrs. Leicester's School." In two volumes . . .* London: printed for M.J. Godwin, at the Juvenile Library, no. 41, Skinner Street, 1809. 2 volumes. 12° (135 × 83 mm.).

Vol. I: A^2 (1^v imprint *Mercier and Shervet, Printers, No. 32, Little Bartholomew Close, London,* 2^r *Contents*); B^6 (B2·5 and B4 here in facsimile) C–I⁶ K⁴ ($K4^r$ same imprint, $K4^v$ ads; quires A and K presumably make up a half-sheet); etched frontispiece. Pp. iv, 103, [1]. Vol. II: A^2 (here in facsimile); B^2 C–K⁶ L^2 ($L2^v$ end of verse, same imprint; quires A, B and L originally made up a half-sheet); etched frontispiece. Pp. iv, 104. Wove paper. Modern green morocco gilt, top edges gilt, by Riviere & Son. References: Darton p. 193; Kinnell p. 96; Lucas pp. 351–429 and 490–7.

Provenance: Dr. A. S. W. Rosenbach. PML 61319. Gift: John F. Fleming.

William Godwin maintained a precarious friendship with Charles Lamb, who (as already noted) did not care at all for Mary Jane. Nevertheless, it was Godwin who encouraged Lamb to turn his hand to writing for children (thus gaining a prose *Ulysses* that was entirely creditable and, probably from Lamb, poetic renditions of *The King and Queen of Hearts*, 1805 [PML 19273], *Beauty and the Beast*, 1811 [PML 16547], and *Prince Dorus*, 1811). Lamb made use of his connection with Godwin to gain help in his efforts to occupy and sustain his unstable sister Mary. Among the results were the stories that made up *Mrs. Leicester's School* (1809) and the now exceedingly rare *Poetry for Children*. The verses seem to be modeled closely on the Taylors' *Original Poems* (entry 102), full as they are with everyday detail and a plain diction. Only occasionally, however, do they escape from the trite or the maudlin towards the Taylors' degree of naturalness.

205

CHARLES LAMB (1775–1834) [& MARY ANN LAMB (1764–1847)]. *Tales from Shakespear. Designed for the use of young persons. By Charles Lamb. Embellished with copperplates. In two volumes . . .* London: printed for Thomas Hodgkins, at the Juvenile Library, Hanway-street (opposite Soho-Square), Oxford-street; and to be had of all booksellers, 1807 [actually 1806]. Two volumes. 12° (169 × 101 mm.).

Vol. I: A^6 (preliminaries); B–K¹² L^{12} (–L6·7, $L12^v$ imprint *T. Davison, Printer, Whitefriars*; 10 etchings (including frontispiece), probably printed from a single copperplate on one side of a sheet (divided for insertion, one illustration to each tale). Pp. ix, [3], 235, [1]. Vol. II: π^2 (= vol. I, L6·7?); A^2 B–L¹² M^{12} (–M6·7=A1·2?, $M11^v$ ad for Baldwin's *Fables*, –M12 blank?); 10 etchings (distributed as in vol. I). Pp. [4], 261, [3]. Different wove paper stocks for letterpress and etching. Original sheep, bifolium of publisher's ads printed by T. Davison bound in at the end of vol. II. References: Darton pp. 191 and 358; Kinnell p. 95; Wells p. 150; Lucas pp. 1–206 and 204–8.

205. vol. II, etching opposite I3ʳ, *reduced*

Provenance: Erased inscription dated 1823. PML 17043–4. Purchase.

Although credited to Charles Lamb on the title page, this abridgment, bowdlerization, and proseification of Shakespeare was mostly the work of his sister (Lamb only did the tragedies). Condemned by a modern critic (Geoffrey Summerfield in *Reason and Imagination*) as the depredation of burglars "who stole nothing of value," the retellings nonetheless found and retained a large public for at least one hundred and fifty years. Such success may be partly explicable in the same terms as guides to the opera are explicable—they give the audience the plot so that they can think about the detail. Just as tenable is the theory, based upon overseas sales of the book, that it provided a crib for readers with uncertain command of English.

The posed illustrations for this first edition of *Tales* have a certain theatricality about them and may be after William Mulready. They are certainly not by Blake, as some optimists have hitherto suggested.

Shakespeare · A DIGRESSION

(see entries 206–211)

The prominence which the Lambs' retelling of the *Tales* won for itself has tended to obscure the fact that Shakespeare was too marketable a commodity to be neglected by other makers of children's books and school books (his fate now as then). Leaving aside their subversive influence on teachers' perception of English history, or the use of "King Lear and his Three Daughters" as a quasi-folk tale in story collections, the texts of the plays also furnished material that could be more directly edited or adapted for young readers. Most of the following examples show publishers doing just that, before Godwin and the Lambs made their large-scale assault.

⊸ 206 ⊱

JEAN-BAPTISTE PERRIN (fl. 1768–86). *Contes Moraux Amusans & instructifs, à l'usage de la jeunesse, tirés des tragédies de Shakespeare. Par M. Perrin, editeur de la nouvelle édition du Dictionnaire de Chambaud, &c. &c.* Londres: Chez Law, Robson, Cadell & Elmsly, 1783. 12° (168 × 97 mm.).

A¹² (2ʳ dedication *A Mylady Charlotte Finch*, 3ʳ *Préface*, –6·7, 10ʳ *Subscription*, 12ᵛ *Table*); B–P¹² Q²=A6·7 (Q2+1 *Les Livres suivans par le même Auteur*). Pp. xix, [1], 340, [2]. Laid paper. Contemporary sheep. Reference: ESTC T067403.

Provenance: *Griffith 1784*? (erased inscription); Edgar S. Oppenheimer; P. Berès (Sotheby's Hodgson's Rooms, 21st April 1977, lot 1988). PML 85602. Purchase: Julia P. Wightman.

Given the title of this collection of abstracts from "le poëte favori des *Anglois*," the reader may be forgiven for expecting travesty upon travesty. As it turns out though, M. Perrin, who "carefully instructs or perfects LADIES and GENTLEMEN in the FRENCH language," has made an honest attempt properly to reflect the substance of his chosen tragedies. (Some are omitted: "Titus Andronicus" is so "horrible & monstrueux, qu'elle n'est propre, qu'à être représentée devant des *Cannibals*.") M. Perrin's method is to give for each play a brief *Sommaire* and then to launch into a retelling of the substance of the thing including some more or less direct, but translated, quotations. The "conte" is indeed there, but there is no moralizing worth speaking of.

⊸ 207 ⊱

The History of King Lear, and his three daughters; shewing, the fate which will attend those who are undutiful, and the reward which providence will bestow on the virtuous and good. Written for the amusement and instruction of youth. (Adorned with cuts). London: printed for W. Moore, No. 8, Leadenhall-Street, 1794. [Price Sixpence.]. 18° (110 × 75 mm.).

and his Three Daughters.   35

" Heav'ns drop your patience down ;
You fee me here, ye gods, a poor old man,
As full of griefs as age, wretch'd in both ;
I'll bear no more ; no, ye unnatural
Hags, I will have fuch revenge on you
  both,
That all the world fhall————I will do
Such things, what they are yet I know
Not, but they fhall be the terror
Of the earth ; you think I'll weep,
This heart fhall break into a thoufand
Pieces firft.——Oh ! Gods, I fhall go mad."
                                    Ye

207. C6 recto, *enlarged*

FABLES CHOISIES.   103

FABLE XXVI.—L'HIRONDELLE et les PETITS
OISEAUX.

UNE Hirondelle qui avoit acquis beaucoup d'expérience
dans ses voyages, vit un fermier qui ensemençoit son
champ. " Voyez-vous," dit-elle, aux petits Oiseaux,
" ce que cet homme fait ? Il sème de la graine de chanvre
qui deviendra un jour votre ruine, si vous n'y prenez
garde, car les filets des oiseleurs sont tous faits de lin ou
de chanvre. Croyez-moi, dépêchez-vous de manger
cette graine."—" Manger du chenevis, quand nous avons
tant de mets délicats ! Non, non, belle voyageuse, man-
gez-le vous-même." Dès que la chenevière fut verte,
l'Hirondelle leur dit : " Arrachez cette maudite herbe
brin à brin ; si vous ne le faites, votre perte est infail-
lible."—" Prophète de malheur ! babillarde ! voyez le
bel emploi qu'elle nous donne. Tous les oiseaux du roy-
aume pourroient à peine éplucher ce canton. Amusons-
nous, mes amis, et laissons là cette vieille radoteuse."

                    F 4

208. F4 recto, *reduced*

A–F[6] (A1 and F6 mounted as pastedowns, A1[v] frontispiece, E6[v]
blank, F1[r] *A lamentable song of King Lear and his three daughters*,
F5[v] and F6 blank). Pp. 69, [3]. Laid paper. 14 cuts (frontispiece
full-page, remainder 46 × 58 mm. and slightly smaller). Contemporary marbled paper boards. Reference: ESTC N0177707.

PML 81606. Purchase: Julia P. Wightman.

As noted above, the essential "King Lear" story appears on
occasion in story anthologies of this period. Here, though, the
Shakespeare play is the base of the "History," with some sizeable
quotations and with a happy ending. Under these circumstances,
the Bard will probably be glad to find himself acknowledged only
in the middle of page 8. The "Lamentable Song" that closes the
book is after the version in Percy's *Reliques* and does not have a
happy ending.

✺ 208 ✺

J. OUISEAU (fl. 1784–1829). *The Manual of Youth.
Containing, I. Sixty fables, French and English, ornamented
with one hundred and twenty cuts . . . furnishing . . . a series
of elementary lessons, in the several styles of drawing.
II. Remarks on rhetoric . . . III. A large collection of extracts,*

in prose and verse. London: Printed for H. D. Symonds,
20, Paternoster Row, 1807. Large 12° (178 × 102 mm.).

A[6] (1[r] half-title, 1[v] imprint *S. Gosnell, Printer, Little Queen Street,*
6[v] ad for the same author's *A Practical Geography*); B–S[12]
(S11[r]–12[v] *General index*, S12[v] printer's imprint). Pp. xi, [1], 404,
[4]. Wove paper. 120 wood-engraved illustrations, some signed
Austin. Contemporary half roan.

Provenance: [Name scored through] *Surrey Place* (inscr.). PML
84546. Purchase: Fellows Endowment Fund.

Published apparently as a schoolbook, this English-French
compendium includes a number of substantial passages from
Shakespeare in the sections devoted to Rhetoric and Extracts.
M. Ouiseau, like M. Perrin before him, also had a taste for the
more bloodthirsty passages. As far as illustration goes for the
"Fables" in the first section of the book, an "entirely new Plan"
has been offered. Each fable in French has a typical fable scene,
sometimes copied from Barlow, but the English equivalent has a
different or an enlarged detail of the previous image, with the idea
that it can be used for lessons in drawing.

209. engraving opposite 1/8ʳ, *enlarged*

Shylock lends Antonio Money.

210. engraving opposite A2ᵛ, *reduced*

ᴄ§ 209 §ᴇ

The Seven Ages of Man, beautifully described by the immortal Shakespeare. The whole adorned with curious copper-plate cuts. The world's a stage, and men and women merely players. London: Printed and Sold by J. Hawkins, Shire-Lane, Temple-Bar, [ca. 1785]. [Price only Sixpence, bound and gilt.]. 36° (86 × 70 mm.).

π1 = 4/6 (recto title, verso blank); [1–4¹².⁶ (–4/6)] signed B–G⁶; [5⁴] (ads); 8 engravings, printed from a single copperplate on a part-sheet, then divided for insertion. Pp. [2], 70, [8]. Laid paper. Two sizes of roman type. Gilt and colored floral boards (*remboîtage*). Reference: ESTC N037098.

PML 85604. Purchase: Harper Fund.

This is an ingenious adaptation to moral purposes of Jaques's famous speech from *As You Like It*, each age being quoted and then commented upon. The artist adds a more than routine contribution, especially with the interior scenes where, after Hogarth, he includes emblematic pictures on the walls.

At least two other editions are known, both apparently with the same plates as the Hawkins edition. The earliest was published by H. Roberts and has an engraved title dated "Sepʳ 5ᵗʰ 1771" (Birmingham City Library); the other has a Homan Turpin imprint and is undated (private collection). All three publishers are discussed in chapter VI.

ᴄ§ 210 §ᴇ

[MARY ANN LAMB (1764–1847)]. *The Merchant of Venice. Embellished with three copper plates.* London:

printed for the proprietors The Juvenile Library, 41, Skinner-Street, 1808. Royal half-sheet 36° (117 × 80 mm.).

π1 (recto title, verso imprint [*Richard Taylor and Co. Shoe Lane.*]) = C6 (last leaf of *King Lear* from the same press); A–C⁶ (C6ᵛ end of text and printer's imprint); 3 engravings, presumably printed together with three others for *King Lear* from a single copper-plate, then divided for insertion. Pp. [2], 36. Laid paper (letterpress), wove (engraving). Modern morocco gilt. References: D. Foxon, "The Chapbook Editions of the Lambs' *Tales from Shakespeare*," *The Book Collector* 6 (1957), pp. 41–53; *Realms of Childhood* 107 (an 1811 edition of *Midsummer Night's Dream*).

PML 61321. Purchase: Harper Fund.

Returning to Lamb and Godwin, we find in the Morgan Library one of what David Foxon described as "the greatest rarities of more recent English literature." It is a little book deriving from Godwin's attempt to capitalize on the *Tales* by issuing them separately in "chapbook" style, with engraved plates and probably inspired by Tabart's series of "Popular Tales." The scheme may not have been a success. Eight tales were published by the proprietors of the Juvenile Library in this form. Godwin also issued them bound together in various combinations, in order to use up overstocks. The Morgan copy of *The Merchant of Venice*, without wrappers and with the plates uncolored, almost certainly once formed part of such a collective volume, which has subsequently been broken up.

ᴄ§ 211 §ᴇ

Young Albert, the Roscius, exhibited in a series of characters from Shakspeare and other Authors. Douglas. Barbarossa. King Richard III. Hamlet. Othello. As you like it. King Henry IV. London: published by S. and J. Fuller, at the Temple of Fancy, 1811. 12° (145 × 102 mm.).

A¹²; 7 hand-colored engraved cut-out figures (head-portrait of Albert, costumes and hats for his various guises). Pp. 22, [2]. Original printed gray boards, traces of a pink ribbon, original printed slipcase. Reference: Osborne I, 420.

Provenance: *Sold by, / A. Loriot, Toyman, &c / No. 65 New Bond Street, London.* (engraved label). The Osborne Collection of Early Children's Books, Toronto Public Library.

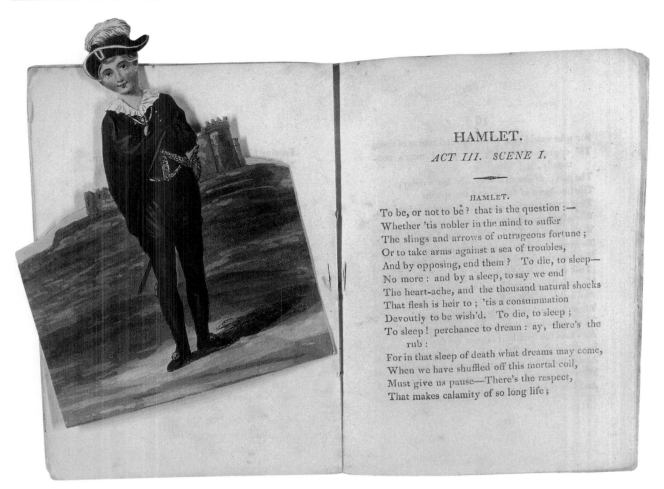

211. cut-out figure [4] and A8ʳ, *reduced*

Published at the Temple of Fancy, where also were to be found the doll books discussed in chapter X. *Young Albert* is a later and slightly larger and more elaborate addition to the series. He has dresses (and speeches) for five Shakespearean roles, but unfortunately in this instance he cannot play Othello, for his "blacked up" face is missing.

JAMES LUMSDEN

What little we know of this unusual publisher is to be found in Sydney Roscoe's *James Lumsden & Son of Glasgow*, completed by R. A. Brimmell (Pinner, 1981). The firm seems to have been founded ca. 1780 by James Lumsden I, an engraver and printer; he was succeeded by James II (1778–1856), who eventually rose beyond trade and became Lord Provost of Glasgow in 1843–45. For some thirty years, from 1790 onwards, the Lumsdens developed a children's book list which Mr. Roscoe singles out for its "distinctive quality . . . a certain trimness" in all aspects of production.

Apparently the Lumsdens had no designs on expanding their trade far beyond southern Scotland, which was perhaps just as well, since they made liberal use of "London" titles and texts in the editing of their list. They carried on an obscure selling arrangement with G. and J. Ross, the Edinburgh chapbook printers, and engaged in much chapbook selling on their own account as well (see chapter XIII); however, their chapbooks had little of the individual character of their more carefully designed children's-book series.

The five books noted here represent only a small part of the Morgan holdings of Lumsden titles, but others have necessarily been included in the chapters on book production (XVIII and XIX), as well as in that on chapbooks.

❧ 212 ❧

The New Testament of our Lord and Saviour Jesus Christ: translated out of the Greek. Appointed to be read by children. A new edition. Ornamented with Copperplate Cuts. Glasgow: Sold Wholesale by J. Lumsden & Son, at their Lilliputian Book Manufactory, 1799. [Price Twopence]. 32° (101 × 61 mm.).

A–B⁸ (A1 and B8 mounted as pastedowns, A1ᵛ title); 8 etchings (each showing two scenes), printed from a single copperplate on one side of a quarter-sheet (divided into four bifolia and inserted around A2·7, A4·5, B2·7 and B4·5). Pp. 47, [1] (pagination including the plates). Laid paper, no watermark. Original blind-blocked and dab-colored floral wrappers. Reference: Roscoe & Brimmell 31 (known to them only from an advertisement).

PML 81587. Gift: Elisabeth Ball.

Not seen by Roscoe, this early example of a Lumsden children's book is remarkable for its "Dutch-paper" wrappers and its use of the term so fashionable at Gainsborough: "at their Lilliputian Book Manufactory." The text draws upon Newbery's abridgment

212. etching opposite B8^r, *enlarged*

213a. pl. A1

(Roscoe J27), and Lumsden used it again with these engravings about fifteen years later (Roscoe & Brimmell 32; the Morgan Library has several copies, one on paper watermarked 1815: PML 80920).

❦ 213a ❧

[MARIE LE PRINCE DE BEAUMONT (1711–80)]. *Beauty and the Beast. A tale. For the entertainment of juvenile readers. Ornamented with elegant engravings.* Glasgow: Published and Sold by J. Lumsden & Son, [not before 1818 (watermark-date)]. 18° (131 × 85 mm.).

A¹⁸ (18ᵛ *James Lumsden and Son Have always on hand a great variety of Children's Books, Lotteries, &c. and the Completest Assortment of Sixpenny and Shilling Drawing Books in the Kingdom*); 6 etched illustrations (including frontispiece), printed from a single copperplate on one side of a part-sheet (divided into three bifolia, marked A–C, and inserted around A1·18, A5·14 and A8·11). Pp. 48 (plates included in pagination). Different wove paper stocks for letterpress (watermark-date 1812) and intaglio printing (1818). Small oval wood engraving of the Beast's palace on A18ᵛ. Original pink stiff wrappers, engraved title-label on front cover. References: Roscoe & Brimmell 53; Hugo 4270; Hockliffe 8.

PML 81282. Gift: Elisabeth Ball.

❦ 213b ❧

The History of Goody Two Shoes. With the adventures of her brother Tommy. Embellished with elegant engravings. Glasgow: Published by J. Lumsden & Son. & sold by Stoddart & Craggs, Hull, [not before 1815 (watermark-date)]. Price sixpence. 18° (132 × 83 mm.).

[1¹⁸] signed A⁶ <B⁶ <C⁶ (1ʳ drop-title *Improved edition. The renowned history of Goody Two-Shoes and her brother Tommy*); etched frontispiece (*Tommy Two Shoes Showing the Indians The Watch*) and title (as transcribed above, with vignette) printed from one copperplate and inserted not as a bifolium, but with stubs around 1·18; six etched illustrations (each consisting of two scenes), printed from a single copperplate on one side of a part-sheet (divided into three bifolia, marked A–C, and inserted around 2·17, 5·14 and 8·11). Pp. 52 (plates included in pagination). Two small wood engravings (18ʳ⁻ᵛ). Original pink stiff wrappers, engraved title-label on front cover. Reference: Roscoe & Brimmell 79.

Provenance: Gumuchian & Cⁱᵉ (1930 cat., no. 2759). PML 83560. Gift: Elisabeth Ball.

Two examples of Lumsden's Sixpenny Books, alike in their getup, but with different ornamental labels on their pink covers and with

THE PIGEON CARRYING THE LETTER

MARGERY SUSPECTED FOR A WITCH

213b. pl. A2

two styles of etching: single ovals with elaborate lettering, double framed ovals with captions. There is speculation, beginning with Hugo, that the wood engraving in *Beauty* may be by Bewick, but this seems unfounded since the Lumsdens had clearly found an artist in Glasgow who could produce admirable cuts in the Bewick manner. (Note, too, the highly comic letter from Lumsden to Bewick, reprinted in Roscoe and Brimmell pp. xix–xx.)

The link between Glasgow and Hull cannot be easily explained. According to C. W. Chilton's *Early Hull Printers and Booksellers* (Kingston-upon-Hull, 1982), Stoddart & Craggs had only a brief partnership for a year or two after 1808. Stoddart then disappears and Craggs continues at various addresses up to 1847. How Lumsden's *Goody Two Shoes* and one other title, *Christmas Tales* by "Solomon Sobersides" (Roscoe & Brimmell 57), both printed ca. 1814, came to carry the Hull imprint is a mystery. Did Stoddart remain in the business up to 1814? Were there earlier printings of the two books? Or did Lumsden—who seems to have been casual in his dealings with the Sassenachs—come to an agreement in 1808, perhaps while visiting Hull, and only get round to implementing it, without further inquiry, in 1814?

214

Vicissitude: or the life and adventures of Ned Frolic. An original comic song. For the entertainment of all good boys and girls in the British Empire. Glasgow: published and sold by J. Lumsden & Son, 1818. Niven, Printer. 16°? (138 × 87 mm.).

A⁸ (1ʳ title, 1ᵛ blank, 2ʳ incipit: *When I was a youngster, my Mother*); 4 hand-colored, etched illustrations (including frontispiece), presumably printed from a single copperplate on one side of a part-sheet (divided into two bifolia and inserted around A1·8 and A3·6). Pp. 16. Wove paper. Original plain blue-green stiff wrappers. Reference: Roscoe & Brimmell 22; Hockliffe 873.

Provenance: Gumuchian & Cⁱᵉ (1930 cat., no. 5748). PML 81319. Gift: Elisabeth Ball.

The Lumsden style here appears to be in transition, not merely in the choice of text (a drinking song), but also in the use of fine composite illustrations made up from groups of tiny pictures. The hand-coloring is probably the publisher's since the book was apparently issued only in color, but it has a rather clumsy amateur appearance.

215

The Marvellous History of Mynheer von Wodenblock. Embellished with beautiful coloured plates. Glasgow: published by J. Lumsden & Son, [ca. 1835]. 24° (117 × 74 mm.).

[1⁸]; six etched illustrations (each showing two scenes, except frontispiece), printed from a single copperplate on one side of a quarter-sheet (divided into three bifolia, marked A–C, for insertion: A<1·8, B<3·6, C in the middle of the quire), all hand-colored as issued. Pp. 26, [2] (plates included in pagination). Wove paper, no watermark. Original gray wrappers, relief-cut ads on front cover *Lumsden & Son's improved edition of coloured twopenny books*, and back cover *Lumsden & Son Publishers of the coloured prints price one halfpenny; Upwards of 500 kinds . . . Maps of every Country in the world elegantly coloured, price 3ᵈ only!* Brown morocco, by Morrell. Reference: Roscoe & Brimmell 98.

Provenance: Charles Todd Owen (binding). PML 84120. Gift: Elisabeth Ball.

Listed, but not seen (and therefore misdated "1815?") by Roscoe, this example of "late" Lumsden publishing comes from a period when the influence of such London publishers as Dean was probably making itself felt (see chapter XII). The story too (whence did it come?) has all the air of laborious farce, triggered by the permanent British belief that "foreigners are funny," which was to be a characteristic of Victorian popular literature. The etched illustrations in simple line—the National Library of Scotland in their communication to Roscoe and Brimmell described them as wood engravings—add much hilarity to the tale of this sad Mynheer, who is literally carried away by his newly invented false leg. The hand-coloring appears to have been applied by stencil.

VICISSITUDE. 5

IV.

I soon became tir'd of the calling,
   My place I resolv'd not to keep,
But as I was still fond of bawling,
   Apprentice I went to a *Sweep!*
But folks were so cursed uncivil,
   They mock'd at poor NED night and day,
So when they call'd out—" *there's the devil!*"
   From Master I scamper'd away.

CHORUS.*

So then to be cheerful and happy,
   And end the fatigues of the day,
A jorum I took of brown nappy,
   Which made me quite jocund and gay.

* This Chorus to be continued to the end.

A 3

214. A3r and
facing plate,
reduced

215. etched
bifolium C,
enlarged

XII

EPIGONES

THE publishers discussed in the previous chapter were aware of the need to develop a varied list of children's books. Most of the publishers discussed in the present chapter were less directly creative. Conscious of the growing demand for children's picture books and also of the ease with which these might be produced from engraved plates, they set about producing "a line" of books, perhaps as an adjunct to other printing or publishing activities. They effectively supplied the needs of young consumers who scarcely cared to discriminate between one illustrated version of a common text and another.

Several of these printer-publishers are obscure figures, and although the Morgan Library may have a fair representation of their output, we still know little of their background or the vicissitudes of their careers in the children's book trade. In consequence we have made no attempt to treat them chronologically but, so far as the London publishers are concerned, have arranged them in alphabetical order. This London list is followed by a brief section on provincial publishers, arranged alphabetically by place, which seeks to indicate to what extent the new style of picture book spread outside the metropolis. In a number of instances (e.g. the Hodgson firms, G. Martin, A. Park) the Morgan Library has considerable resources from which we have been able to select only a few examples. The extent of its holdings is therefore a testimony to the vigor with which the publishing of picture books for children was pursued once Wallis, Harris, Darton et al. had provided the models.

J. ALDIS

We have not so far been able to find out anything about J. Aldis who, with his name engraved on a sack of flour in *John Bull* and on the parents' tombstone in *The Children in the Wood*, may well have been chiefly an engraver and printer. The two books described below are typical productions at the lower end of the market: cheap paper, hasty engraving, and rough coloring. We should record, however, that in 1810 Aldis was responsible for producing at least two wallets of booklets and cut-out figures, *The History and Adventures of Little William* and *Little Eliza*. The latter appears in Gumuchian as "A Companion to Little Fanny," which seems to point to an attempt by Aldis to cash in quickly on the success of the Fuller series of doll books (see entry 166).

◆§ 216a ◆

The Children in the Wood and Robin Redbreast so Good. [London:] Published by J. Aldis, 9 Pavement, Moorfields, June 27, 1808 (plate-imprint as well as year of impression; watermark-date 1807). 12° (115 × 90 mm.).

[1¹²] (1ʳ blank, 1ᵛ drop-title as above, illustration, incipit: *In the*

County of Norfolk, 2ʳ imprint as above). Ff. [12]. Etched throughout: apparently printed from a single copperplate on one side of a sheet. Each leaf with larger-than-half-page hand-colored illustration and four-line rhyme. Lacking original wrappers. Brown morocco gilt.

Provenance: Charles Todd Owen (binding). PML 83540. Gift: Elisabeth Ball.

◆§ 216b ◆

John Bull's Staff of Life. London: Published by J. Aldis, 9 Pavement, Moorfields, April 6, 1809. Price 6ᵈ Plain, or 1ˢ coloured. 12° (115 × 90 mm.).

[1¹²] (1ʳ blank, 1ᵛ drop-title, illustration, incipit: *Says Charles to His Father*, 2ʳ imprint, 5·8 lacking). Ff. [12]. Etched throughout: apparently printed from a single copperplate on one side of a sheet. Each leaf with larger-than-half-page illustration in publisher's coloring and four-line rhyme. No watermark. Original engraved gray-blue pictorial wrappers, front cover: title and

216a. fo. 3 verso

The corn's took to the mill,
Which with stones has the power;
To grind it quite fine,
And then it's call'd flour.

216b. fo. 11 verso

imprint as above and illustration of *The corn's took to the mill*, back cover: illustration of *Then the Baker with water*. Blue morocco gilt.

Provenance: Anna Welchman (early sign.); Charles Todd Owen (binding). PML 85041. Gift: Elisabeth Ball.

Aldis's *Children in the Wood* must be one of the briskest recensions ever of the lengthy old ballad, its curt phrasing matched by the uncompromising engravings. The similar treatment of both verse and picture in *John Bull* suggests that the same creative talents were at work here, perhaps Aldis himself.

Other Aldis books in the Morgan Library are *The Life of Brushtail the Squirrel, that could play and not quarrel* (1806; PML 82197) and two copies of *Will Wander's Walk* (1806; PML 85579 and 84077 [Gottlieb 157]). These provide conclusive proof of how ready small publishers were to turn to "levity" (Darton's word), even before *The Butterfly's Ball* appeared.

W. BELCH—see LANGLEY

B. BLAKE

Like Aldis, B. Blake is an obscure figure, and there is little likelihood that he shares any relationship with his celebrated namesake over the river at Lambeth. William indeed would probably have been appalled at the jog-trot reduction of Bunyan's masterpiece with its rough pictures; but one hopes that he would have had a little sympathy for the faintly satirical prints of Dame Pastime's quizzical counting book.

JOHN BUNYAN (1628–88). *Scenes from Bunyan's Pilgrim's Progress, in easy verse, for the instruction of children. With twelve coloured engravings.* London: Published by B. Blake, 13, Bell Yard, Temple Bar, [impression not before 1825 (watermark-date)]. Price sixpence. 12° (105 × 93 mm.).

[1¹²] (1ʳ blank, 1ᵛ title, illustration with two-line quotation from Matthew 7.7, and imprint as above, 2ʳ illustration, incipit: *With sins on his back that resemble a load*). Ff. [1], 1–11. Etched throughout: probably printed from a single copperplate on one side of a sheet. Each leaf with almost-full-page illustration in publisher's coloring and four-line rhyme (except on title). Original yellow front wrapper (back wrapper removed), letterpress title-label (as transcribed above). Maroon morocco gilt.

Provenance: Charles Todd Owen (binding). PML 83775. Gift: Elisabeth Ball.

217b

Seventy-Eight Quizzical Characters, for the amusement of children. By Dame Pastime. London: Published by B. Blake, 13, Bell Yard, Temple Bar, [impression not before 1822 (watermark-date)]. Price sixpence, coloured. 12° (105 × 88 mm.).

[1–4²(?) 5–6²] (1/1ʳ blank, 1/1ᵛ incipit: *A Hunchback quizzical comical blade* and imprint as above). Ff. [12]. Etched throughout: probably printed from a single copperplate on one side of a sheet. Each leaf with almost-full-page illustration—see overleaf—in publisher's coloring and a couplet. Original gray front wrapper (back wrapper removed), letterpress title-label (as transcribed above). Maroon morocco gilt.

Provenance: Charles Todd Owen (bookplate, binding). PML 83518. Gift: Elisabeth Ball.

J. BUSHNELL

"Neatly executed coloured engravings" is rather an optimistic cover advertisement for a book that is anything but neat and was also available plain. This reinforces the impression that Bushnell had not yet got his act together as a publisher (and probably never did). The idea for the book is a nice one—games for every day of the week except the Sabbath—but is marred by the poor verses and by such slips as showing a bow and arrow where a popgun should be. The half-filled advertisement space on the back cover suggests uncertainty about the arrival of future titles.

218

A Fortnights Journal of Juvenile Sports by Charles, Thomas and Harry . . . London: Published as the Act directs by J. Bushnell, 6 Bear Street Leister Sq, [impression not before 1820 (watermark-date), not after 1825 (inscription-date)]. Price 6ᵈ Plain, 1ˢʰ Colour'd. 16° (116 × 89 mm.).

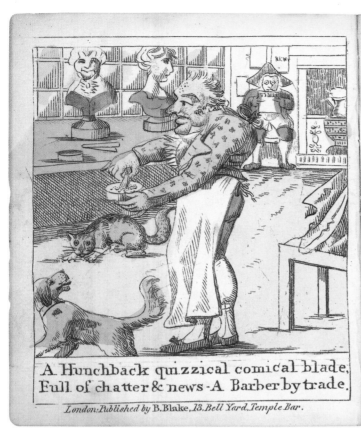

A Hunchback quizzical comical blade,
Full of chatter & news – A Barber by trade.

London: Published by B. Blake, 13, Bell Yard, Temple Bar.

Two queer Customers going to pop,
Into the well known gossiping shop

Above: **217b.** fos. 1ᵛ–2ʳ   *Below left:* **218.** fo. 2 recto   *Below right:* **218.** fo. 8 recto

A Fortnight's JOURNAL of Juvenile Sports
BY
CHARLES, THOMAS and HARRY

By perusal You'll learn how light easy & Gay
Charles Thomas & Harry are amus'd with their Play

LONDON.
Published as the Act directs by J. Bushnell, 6 Bear Street Leister Sq.
Price 6ᵈ. Plain, 1ˢʰ Colour'd.

SATURDAY

Harry now names the Game,
Which is Cricket to day,
Behold them united,
How cheerfull they play.

[1–2⁸] (1/1 and 2/8 mounted as pastedowns, 1/1ᵛ *Frontispiece*, 1/2ʳ title, 1/3ᵛ *Monday*, incipit: *Charles proposd they begin with / The whipping of Tops*, 2/8ʳ *Sunday*, ending: *Each prays to his Maker / With Christian-like Zeal*. Ff. [16]. Etched throughout: apparently printed from two copperplates on one side of two half-sheets. Each leaf with three-quarter-page illustration in publisher's coloring and four-line rhyme (couplet on title). Original engraved yellow wrappers, title on front cover, ad on back cover. Maroon morocco gilt.

Provenance: inscription dated July 26th 1825 (name erased); Charles Todd Owen (binding). PML 81691. Gift: Elisabeth Ball.

J. BYSH

Unlike Aldis, Blake, and Bushnell, J. Bysh has a definable career, and his output as a picture-book publisher was prolific. According to Brown, he began trading no later than 1818 from 52 Paternoster Row and moved to Cloth Fair after 1821. He published a large number of sixpenny and shilling colored books and, as we see below, sought to gain a place for himself in the market by advertising them as "Bysh's Editions," or even "Bysh's Cabinet" series (see PML 82997, for *The Feathered Tribe* [n.d.]).

⋙ 219a ⋘

The Adventures of Mother Goose. London: Published by J. Bysh, 52, Paternoster Row & Sold by C. Penny, Wood Sᵗ, [ca. 1820]. Price 6ᵈ Colour'd. 24° (94 × 85 mm.).

[1¹²] (1ʳ blank, 1ᵛ frontispiece, *Well may the folks with wonder stare . . .*, 2ʳ title, 2ᵛ–3ʳ blank, 3ᵛ incipit: *Accus'd of witchcraft Mother Goose*, 5 and 6 lacking). Ff. [12]. Wove paper. Etched throughout: probably printed from a single copperplate on one side of a sheet. Each leaf with three-quarter-page illustration (uncolored) and four-line rhyme (except title). Original gray wrappers, hand-colored etched pictorial title-label mounted on front cover *Mother Goose and her Golden Egg Price Sixpence*. Blue morocco gilt, edges gilt.

Provenance: Charles Todd Owen (binding). PML 85873. Gift: Elisabeth Ball.

⋙ 219b ⋘

Bysh's Edition of the History of the Children in the Wood. A tale in verse. Embellished with eight coloured engravings. London: Printed by T. Richardson, 98, High Holborn; for J. Bysh, 8, Cloth Fair, West Smithfield, [not before 1825 (watermark-date)]. Price Sixpence. 16° (140 × 92 mm.).

[1⁸] (1ʳ blank, 1ᵛ heading *Death of the parents*, illustration, incipit: *In Norfolk's fertile plains as histories tell*, 8ʳ *The uncle's remorse*, ending: *At length, a maniac in a cell he lies— / By all forsaken—he unpitied dies*, 8ᵛ blank). Ff. [8]. Printed on one side of a half-sheet (inner forme). Each leaf with a half-page wood engraving in publisher's coloring and four couplets (letterpress). Original brown-gray wrappers, letterpress title (as transcribed above) and wood engraving (repeated from 4ʳ) on front cover, ads on back cover. Red morocco gilt.

219a. fo.11 verso

Provenance: Charles Todd Owen (binding). PML 83776. Gift: Elisabeth Ball.

Two examples from the opposite ends of Bysh's career. *Mother Goose*, for all the pretty label on its cover, is an incompetent piece of work, a nonsensical sequence of verses adapted from an equally nonsensical harlequinade and issued plain when the title page says colored. (The C. Penny associate in the imprint is listed by Todd as in business at Wood Street from 1812–25).

The Children in the Wood, from Cloth Fair, is a much later production, completed before 1830, when Thomas Richardson the printer moved to 245 High Holborn. Compared with Aldis's earlier picture-book version of the story (entry 216a), this more formal treatment is sadly lacking in vigor both in the pictures and the verses.

W. COLE—see HODGSON

DEAN & MUNDAY ETC.

Of all the publishers noted in this survey the firm that began as Dean & Munday is the longest-lived and the most consistent in its trading policies. Like the two Darton companies, it evolved through generations of proprietors and through varieties of publishing fashions, but unlike them it lasted into modern times (and, indeed, still exists in the twenty-first century as an imprint within Egmont Books, Ltd., "supplying great value books . . . to the promotional market"). Unlike them too—then as now—its forte lay in the publishing of popular or mass-market wares. At no time did it put its name to a book of great consequence in the development of children's literature.

The beginnings of the firm are obscure. Hearsay recorded by Darton (p. 208) maintains a connection between Thomas Dean and the Bailey family, printers in the vicinity of Leadenhall Street from about 1745 onwards. McKenzie records a Thomas Dean apprenticed to Susan Bailey (widow of Thomas Bailey II?) of Bishopsgate Street Within in 1797; he was freed in 1804 and a year later had a press at Ball Alley, Moorfields, where Susan Bailey witnessed a document (Todd); 1805 seems to be the date when he commenced the printing business, and hearsay goes on to maintain that he took Munday as his apprentice at about the same time. What happened then we do not know, but by 1814 Todd records the firm trading as printers and booksellers at 35 Threadneedle Street under the direction of Mary Anne Dean and Anna Maria Munday, and from this date publishing activities began to get under way. The imprint Dean & Munday continues down to 1842, with premises at 40 Threadneedle Street being added to the address in 1837; then, from 1843–46, the usual imprint was Dean & Co., and from 1847–71, after George Alfred Dean had become a partner, the designation was Thomas Dean & Son. Within this period the address changed too, becoming variously 31, 11, and 65 Ludgate Hill during the years 1856–70. After that it became 160A Fleet Street.

In all this time the activities of the firm are strangely amorphous (not least in the peculiar publishing cooperative established with A. K. Newman of the Minerva Press between about 1815 and 1825, which seems, as we discuss in the following entry, to have been initiated by Dean & Munday as printers). In matters of style, no books can be singled out that have the wild simplicity of, say, George Martin's, or the up-market dignity of John Harris's, and as a result the company appears here with some run-of-the-mill examples, scattered between this section and later chapters (see index). For despite a considerable volume of books published during the first half of the nineteenth century, Dean & Son only came into their own with the picture books and movables of High Victorian times.

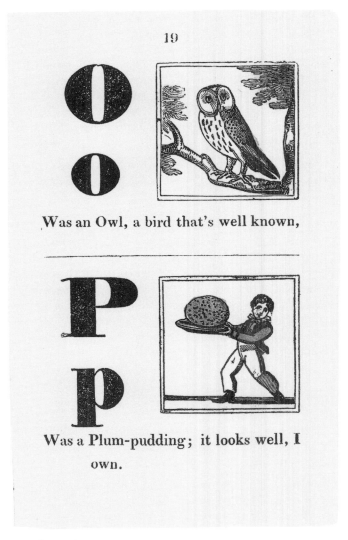

220. fo. 10 recto

❧ 220 ❧

The Infant's Alphabet. Embellished with twenty-seven neat coloured engravings. London: printed for A. K. Newman & Co. Leadenhall-street, [and Dean and Munday, ca. 1825]. Price Six-pence. 16° (138 × 85 mm.).

[1¹⁶] (1·16 blank and mounted as pastedowns, 2ʳ title, 2ᵛ–3ʳ blank, 3ᵛ incipit: *A a Was an Angler, and he a fish caught*). Pp. 30, [2]. Printed on one side of the sheet. Wood-engraved vignette on title, 26 wood engravings (35 mm. square) illustrating the alphabet, all in publisher's coloring. Original printed orange wrappers, title and wood engraving (repeated from *P p was a Plum-pudding*) on front cover with imprint *London: printed and sold by Dean and Munday, Threadneedle-street*, back cover with ads of *Children's Toy Books* including the present title.

Provenance: Gumuchian & Cⁱᵉ (1930 cat., no. 6123). PML 85075. Gift: Elisabeth Ball.

Anthony King Newman, son of Charles Newman, gentleman, of Penryn, Cornwall, was apprenticed to William Lane at the Minerva Press in Leadenhall Street from 1794–1801. Lane was famous for his publishing of romances and gothic thrillers, which he exploited by establishing a chain of circulating libraries in London and the provinces. Newman succeeded to the Minerva Press about 1804, some ten years before Lane's death.

The proximity of the Minerva Press to the printing houses of the Baileys and Dean & Munday may account for the cooperative venture between Newman and the more recently established firm. Dorothy Blakey, the Minerva Press bibliographer, claims without citing documentary evidence that Dean & Munday initiated such a venture, preparing and printing editions of which Newman would take a proportion with his own title-page. The arrangement may well have been more complex, however, for Newman was already publishing moral stories for children on his own account (e.g. W. F. Sullivan's *The Young Truants* [1817]) and, as we note below (entry 246), he had also gained a picture-book list from Didier & Tebbett. Possibly, therefore, he was more positively involved in the editorial policies of the new firm and helped to finance Dean & Munday's expansion into the field of picture books, taking part of their editions under his own imprint for his circulating libraries.

❧ 221 ❧

[JEANNE-MARIE LE PRINCE DE BEAUMONT (1711–80)]. *Beauty and the Beast; or, the magic rose. Embellished with a coloured engraving.* London: printed and

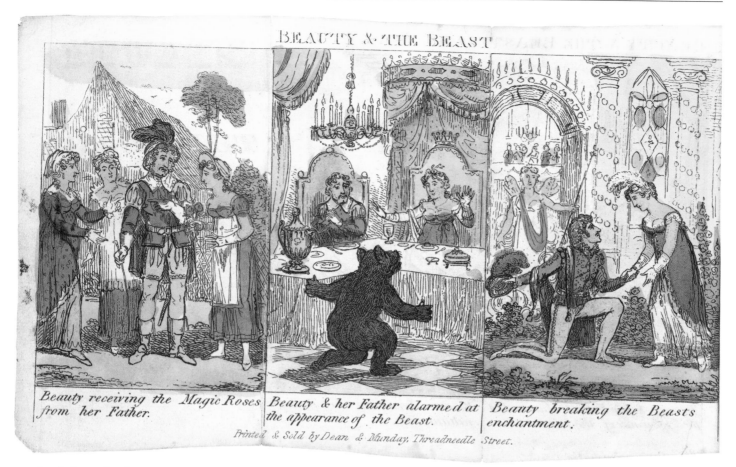

BEAUTY & THE BEAST

Beauty receiving the Magic Roses from her Father.

Beauty & her Father alarmed at the appearance of the Beast.

Beauty breaking the Beasts enchantment.

Printed & Sold by Dean & Munday, Threadneedle Street.

221. frontispiece, *reduced*

sold by Dean and Munday, Threadneedle-street, 1824. 16°
(136 × 78 mm.).

B[16] (1[r] title, 16[v] imprint *Dean and Munday, Printers, Threadneedle-street*); folding etched frontispiece by George Cruikshank (unsigned), hand-colored at the publisher's, showing three scenes: *Beauty receiving the Magic Roses from her Father, Beauty & her Father alarmed at the appearance of the Beast, Beauty breaking the Beasts enchantment.* Pp. 3–34. Original printed yellow wrappers, title and wood engraving on front cover, ads on back cover. Red-morocco-backed marbled boards. References: Hearne p. 208; cf. Cohn 63.

Provenance: Gumuchian & C[ie] (1930 cat., no. 503). PML 84047. Gift: Elisabeth Ball.

Dean & Munday's reluctance to date their children's books makes it difficult to determine when any publishing activity grew from their initial work as printers. They probably began by issuing chapbooks, such as those described in the next chapter, but they do not figure significantly in the annals until the 1820s, when they published several series of popular, hand-colored books for children. This dated edition of *Beauty and the Beast* belongs to one of the earliest of these series, "a fairy tale library," begun in 1819 and unillustrated apart from the composite frontispieces, which were apparently designed for the most part by either George or Robert Cruikshank (see Alderson *Picture Book*, p. 56).

222a

Deborah Dent and Her Donkey; and Madam Fig's gala: two humorous tales. Embellished with seventeen beautifully-coloured engravings. London: Dean and Munday, Thread-needle-street; and A. K. Newman & Co. Leadenhall-steet, [ca. 1825]. Price One-Shilling. 18° (168 × 96 mm.).

[1–3[6]] (1/1[r] blank, 1/1[v] *Frontispiece*, 1/2[r] title, 1/2[v]–3[r] blank, 1/3[v] incipit: *Deborah Dent had a Donkey so fine*, 2/5[v] *Madam Fig's Gala*, incipit: *Johnny Fig was a green and white grocer*). Pp. 35, [1]. Printed on one side of the sheet. Unwatermarked. 16 half-page wood engravings in publisher's coloring (those on 2/1[v] and 2/5[v] repeated to form the frontispiece). Wrappers lacking. Green morocco, by Morell.

Provenance: Charles Todd Owen (binding). PML 81862. Gift: Elisabeth Ball.

222b

Deborah Dent and Her Donkey; and Madam Fig's gala: two humorous tales. Embellished with seventeen neatly coloured comic engravings. London: printed and sold by Dean & Munday, Threadneedle-street, [not before 1826]. Price one-shilling. 18° (166 × 95 mm.).

222b. front cover, *reduced*

223. fo. 16 verso, *reduced*

[1¹⁸] (1ᵛ *Frontispiece*, 2ʳ title, 11ᵛ *Madam Fig's Gala*). Pp. 35, [1]. Printed on one side of the sheet. Paper watermarked T Barratt 1826. 16 half-page wood engravings in publisher's coloring (those on 7ᵛ and 11ᵛ repeated to form the frontispiece). Original printed pink stiff wrappers, title and wood engraving (Deborah and her donkey taking tea; this cut does not occur in the book) on front cover, Dean & Munday ads *Juvenile Publications* on back cover. Black morocco gilt.

Provenance: Charles Todd Owen (binding). PML 81292. Gift: Elisabeth Ball.

Along with *Dame Wiggins of Lee* (entry 310) *Deborah Dent* stands out as one of Dean & Munday's most original and fanciful productions. The rhyme has a jolly rhythm to it and, with its accompanying illustrations, emerges as one of the last successful inventions in the Hubbardonian tradition. C.T. Owens's dogged pursuit of early English picture books in all their variants shows that Dean & Munday issued the book first with Newman & Co. and later, with changing formats, under their sole imprint.

DIDIER & TEBBETT—see NEWMAN

R. DUTTON

From the imprint on the cover of the book described below, Dutton appears to be yet another printer selling his own wares. Brown lists him at 10 Birchin Lane between 1799 and 1802 and at 45 Gracechurch Street from 1803 to 1817, a combination of addresses and dates which suggests a neighborly relationship with William Darton I.

⤙ 223 ⤚

Aunty Ann's Drawing Book, or exhibition of pretty pictures, for the entertainment of her little nephews and nieces. London: printed and sold by R. Dutton, 45, Gracechurch Street, 1808. 16° (124 × 103 mm.).

[1¹⁶] (1ʳ incipit: *Here you see a cross child lying upon the ground*). Ff. [16]. Etched throughout: probably printed from a single copperplate on one side of the sheet. 16 half-page illustrations, the fifth and sixth signed Walkinshaw sc. Original gray wrappers, letterpress title (as transcribed above) on front cover. Maroon morocco gilt.

Provenance: *Elizabeth Walkers Book* (contemporary inscr.); Charles Todd Owen (binding). PML 85574. Gift: Elisabeth Ball.

Presenting those most popular of protagonists in books, naughty and silly children, "Aunty Ann" adopts a pleasantly conversational tone, which invites her young readers to be amused at the foolish goings-on in the pictures. These appear to be in the rather unusual medium of soft-ground etching; the artist who signed two of them, A. Walkinshaw, is recorded by Bénézit as an engraver of portraits between 1796 and 1810.

224. unfolded frontispiece

J. FAIRBURN

John Fairburn of 110 Minories was the son of another John, who was a printseller at 146 Minories between 1793 and 1810, later moving to Broadway, Blackfriars. John II specialized in prints and engraved books; he promoted his name (as did Bysh and others) by often placing it in front of his editions of otherwise well-known texts. He started in business some time before 1820 and continued at his Minories address until 1843, when the imprint changed to John Butler Fairburn and then Sarah Anne. Some grisly late writing sheets, apparently printed lithographically in the 1850s, bear an address at Featherstone Street, City Road. For John Fairburn the younger in his role as seller of A. Park's publications, see entry 247.

❧ 224 ❧

BENJAMIN FRANKLIN (1706–90). *Franklin's Morals, for the entertainment & instruction of youth.* London: Printed & Publish'd by J. Fairburn 110 Minories, [not before 1818]. Price Sixpence. 24° (97 × 82 mm.).

[1²] (folded frontispiece *Employ thy Time well if thou meanest to gain leisure* …, recto blank); [2²²] (1ʳ title, 1ᵛ–2ʳ blank, 2ᵛ incipit: *Sloth like Rust consumes faster than Labour wears*…). Ff. [24]. Etched throughout: apparently printed from a single copperplate on one side of a full sheet. 46 oval illustrations (two to a page, four on frontispiece) with Franklin's maxims as captions, author's portrait on title. Frontispiece in early coloring. Original yellow wrappers, letterpress title on front cover, ads on back cover.

Provenance: *Crewe Hall Library. Juvenile Books.* (bookplate of Richard Monckton Milnes, first Baron Houghton, with shelf-mark "Box 24f"). PML 84992. Purchase: Fellows Fund.

A handsome example of Fairburn's copperplate printing, but with only the folding frontispiece hand-colored. The 1818 watermark and the list of twelve 6ᵈ books on the back cover help to suggest a date for J. Fairburn II getting into his stride.

THE HODGSONS AND WILLIAM COLE

An attempt was made by Trevor Hall and Percy Muir in *Some Printers and Publishers of Conjuring Book* (Leeds, 1976) to sort out the many confusions about the dates and locations of the activities of this group of publishers. In summary, the position is roughly as follows:

A Thomas Hodgson, printer and stationer, was in business at 11 King Street, Cheapside, from 1799 to 1830 (Maxted). A printing and publishing business, associated with him, was set up at 43 King Street about 1820, and this firm, Hodgson & Co., moved to 10 Newgate Street in 1822 only to be taken over by William Cole in 1825. In the aftermath of the takeover, Orlando Hodgson, one of the partners in Hodgson & Co., started his own business at 21 Maiden Lane, whence he moved to Cloth Fair in 1828 and Fleet Street in 1836, where he remained until 1844 (but with a printing house at Isleworth in Middlesex). There may well have been printing undertaken by various Hodgsons at other addresses during this period.

The Morgan Library has large holdings of Hodgson children's books, still in need of analysis in terms of both their chronology

225. fo. 10 recto

226. front cover, *reduced*

and the sources for their texts and illustrations. The small selection here is designed to show different aspects of the Hodgson-Cole ventures, to which may be added the example drawn from Hodgson's busy involvement in toy-theater sheets seen at entry 168 above.

⪚ 225 ⪙

The History of the Seven Champions of Christendom. London: printed by and for William Cole, Juvenile Press, No. 10, Newgate-street, [not issued before 1825, impression not before 1822 (watermark-date)]. Sixpence. 24° (96 × 90 mm.).

[1¹²] (1ᵛ frontispiece *The Seven Champions parting at the Brazen Pillar*, 2ʳ title, imprint *London, Pub. by Hodgson & Cᵒ 10, Newgate Sᵗ.*, 2ᵛ–3ʳ blank, 3ᵛ incipit: *A Lady fair is here set free*, 12ʳ ending *The champions bold, do soon descry, | And they the whole did quick destroy*, 12ᵛ blank). Etched throughout: apparently printed from a single copperplate on one side of a half-sheet. Frontispiece, title-vignette, ten three-quarter-page illustrations (each captioned with a quatrain), all colored by a contemporary hand (probably at the publisher's). Original gray wrappers, letterpress title on front cover (as transcribed above), Cole's ads on back cover. Brown morocco gilt.

Provenance: Charles Todd Owen (bookplate, binding). PML 84978. Gift: Elisabeth Ball.

One complicating factor in the complicated Hodgson story is that some intermediate trading took place between Orlando Hodgson and the printer and publisher of popular books Thomas Hughes (see Hall & Muir, esp. pp. 30–1). Such a connection may well have begun before the breakup of the Hodgson company in 1825, and

the present picture book looks very like an earlier Hughes publication, with Hodgson & Co.'s name engraved over the burnished-out forerunner's imprint. The fact that the Hodgson sheets are then bought by Cole, who puts his own covers on, occasions surprise that a work of so little consequence should pass through the hands of three proprietors.

⪚ 226 ⪙

Hodgson & Cᵒ's Tom Thumb. London: Hodgson & Cᵒ, [ca. 1820]. Six pence. 8° (158 × 95 mm.).

[1⁸] (1ʳ blank, 1ᵛ drop-title *Hodgson's Tom Thumb*, illustration captioned *Tom punished for thieving*, incipit: *For stealing cherry stones pray mind!*). Ff. [8]. Etched throughout: printed from a single copperplate on one side of the sheet. Eight half-page hand-colored illustrations, each with one-line caption and four-line rhyme. Original gray wrappers, hand-colored etched pictorial label (including title and imprint as transcribed above) mounted on front cover. Brown morocco gilt.

Provenance: Charles Todd Owen (bookplate, binding). PML 83053. Gift: Elisabeth Ball.

In format, printing method, binding, and price, this versified *Tom Thumb* is strikingly similar to Belch's *British Sports* (entry 235) and *Capitals of Europe* (entry 236); the Hodgson series to which it belongs was therefore no doubt the inspiration for the "late Belch style." For another impression of the same copperplate and a note on the treatment of the text, see entry 359.

Fly Catcher.

227. fo. 8 verso, *reduced*

❧ 227 ❧

The Young Naturalist's Cabinet of Birds. Beautifully engraved and coloured. London: printed by and for William Cole, Juvenile Press, No. 10, Newgate-street, [not before 1825]. Oblong 24°? (81 × 101 mm.).

[1¹⁰ 2² (?)] (1/1ʳ *Chaffinch, Goose*, 2/2ᵛ *Black Headed Bunting, Jay*). Ff. [12]. Etched throughout: perhaps printed from a single copperplate on one half-sheet. 12 illustrations in publisher's coloring, with captions. Original gray wrappers, letterpress title on front cover (as above), *Picture Books* ads on back cover. Red morocco gilt.

Provenance: Charles Todd Owen (binding). PML 81429. Gift: Elisabeth Ball.

Advertised as a picture book, this *Cabinet* is entirely that, its twelve leaves being simply devoted to pictures of sixteen birds with their designations (and who now knows what a "rollar" may be?). The small oblong shape is unusual at this time.

❧ 228 ❧

The History of Beasts. Embellished with copper plates. [London:] Pub. by Hodgson & Cᵒ 10 Newgate Sᵗ 1824. (113 × 73 mm.).

Set of 12 unnumbered cards. Etched throughout: perhaps printed from a single copperplate, cut up and mounted. Each card with hand-colored illustration, five quatrains and imprint. Original wallet of buff cardboard, with flap, hand-colored etched pictorial title-label mounted on the front.

PML 83069. Gift: Elisabeth Ball.

The purpose of these cards in their decorated case is not entirely clear, although they may have been inspired by the beautifully engraved reward-cards that were a specialty of R. Miller of Old Fish Street (see entry 244). The animal pictures are mostly copied from Bewick's *Quadrupeds* (entry 133).

THE FOX.

Sly Renard, oftimes unawares,
  Your poultry catches by his snares;
But when the well known hounds he spies,
  To' scape how many ways he tries,

By night what prowling steps he takes,
  And mazy hole in bank forsakes;
He spares no victim in his way,
  Should any from the henhouse, stray;

Sometimes between the enclosed gap,
  His leg is caught in farmers trap;
But sooner than be ta'en alive,
  He'll many an artfull, Scheme, contrive;

All animals, he makes his foes,
  Is feard and hated, where he goes,
They wish the cruel felon, dead,
  That dares disturb the peacefull shed,

Beneath the grapry, bowr he stood,
  Trying, to get delicious, food,
But now alas, in evil hour;
  He cries behold, these grapes, are sour.

Pub. by Hodgson & Cᵒ 10, Newgate Sᵗ 1824.

228. *enlarged*

❧ 229a ❧

The Scripture History of Joshua, the Brave and Samson, the Strong . . . London: Pubᵈ by Hodgson & Cᵒ 10, Newgate Street, March 21, 1823 [date of inserted title and date of issue; impression not before 1821, (watermark-date)]. 12° (171 × 102 mm.).

[1/1ʳ title, 1/1ᵛ blank; 2¹²] (2/1 blank, 2/1ᵛ heading *Joshua destroying Jericho*, illustration, incipit: *Great Joshua, Jericho did burn*, 2/12ʳ *Samson pulling down the Philistines, House*, ending *To God, with all his might he cried, / Tore down the house, & bravely died!*, 2/12ᵛ blank). Ff. [13]. Etched throughout: apparently printed from a single copperplate on one side of a full sheet, title printed from a separate plate on different paper and at a later date. Hand-colored illustration and six-line rhyme on title; each of the other leaves with headline, hand-colored illustration (about 100 mm. square) and four-line rhyme. Original pink wrappers, large hand-colored etched pictorial title-label on front cover *Hodgson's The Scripture History of Joshua, and of Samson*. Dark blue morocco gilt, edges gilt.

Provenance: *H Robarts November 1839* (inscr.); Charles Todd Owen (binding). PML 80705. Gift: Elisabeth Ball.

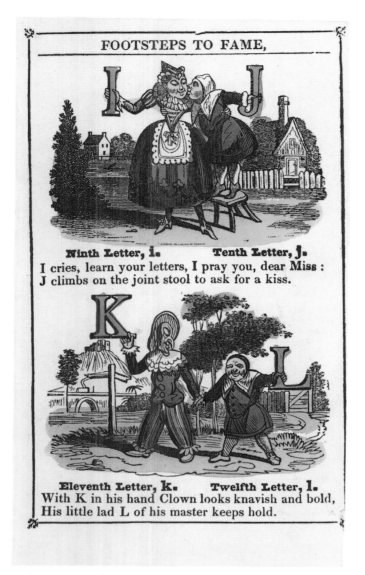

FOOTSTEPS TO FAME,

Ninth Letter, i.   Tenth Letter, j.
I cries, learn your letters, I pray you, dear Miss :
J climbs on the joint stool to ask for a kiss.

Eleventh Letter, k.   Twelfth Letter, l.
With K in his hand Clown looks knavish and bold,
His little lad L of his master keeps hold.

229b. fo. 4 recto, *reduced*

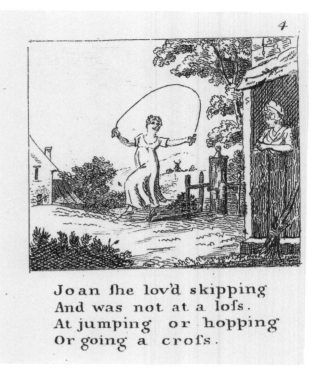

Joan she lov'd skipping
And was not at a lofs.
At jumping or hopping
Or going a crofs.

230. fo. 4 recto

(Orlando Hodgson was also busy with other engraved and printed goods such as writing sheets and toy-theater equipment, see chapter X.) In *Joshua the Brave* we see an example of one of the many all-engraved books which the firm published on Old Testament themes. The much later *Footsteps to Fame* is one of the large series of sixpenny books which Orlando Hodgson brought out in letterpress, with letterpress covers and brightly hand-colored wood engravings.

◄§ 229b ►

Footsteps to Fame, and a waggon load of gold. By Louisa Lovechild . . . London: O. Hodgson, Cloth Fair, West Smith-field, [ca. 1832]. Price sixpence. 8° (175 × 104 mm.).

[1⁸ (1.8 mounted as pastedowns, 1ᵛ title, 2ʳ incipit: *You booby, cries Granny, learn great A from me*). Ff. [8]. Printed on one side of the sheet only (inner forme). 14 wood engravings in publisher's coloring (one on title, 13 illustrating the alphabet). Original pink wrappers, letterpress title on front cover. Orange morocco gilt, edges gilt.

Provenance: *Stassin et Xavier / Libraires / Rue du Coq Sᵗ Honoré N. 9 / Assortiment nombreux et varie de / livres Anglais, Alle-mands, Italiens / Espagnols, Portugais, Langues du Nord. / Vente, Achat, Echanges* (contemporary engraved Parisian bookseller's label); Charles Todd Owen (binding). PML 81351. Gift: Elisabeth Ball.

Much of the Hodgsons' book production in later years was concerned with the tall 12mos of Harris's later "Cabinet" style.

T. & R. HUGHES

McKenzie records that a Thomas Hughes, third generation of a printing dynasty working around High Holborn, was freed from his apprenticeship by patrimony in 1780. Whether or not this is the same Thomas Hughes who worked as a bookseller in partner-ship with William West in 1801–2 is uncertain, but after the bankruptcy of the partnership this T. Hughes set up on his own and continued to trade as a bookseller until the early 1830s, first at Stationer's Court, then, soon after, at 35 Ludgate Street, and finally (ca. 1827) at 3, Broadway, Ludgate Hill. For a few years (approximately 1806–9) Thomas Hughes was joined by R. Hughes, who could have been the not-immediately-related Robert, who was apprenticed to the printer Charles Clarke of Northumberland Court, Strand, for seven years from 1787.

Judging from the surviving titles, Hughes was a middle-of-the-road bookseller and publisher, feeding a known market with what he hoped would be acceptable fare. At the end of his career his stock seems to have been made over to Orlando Hodgson (see entry 225), but it is possible that some copyrights (e.g. *Jack and his Brothers*, etc.) passed to David Carvalho (on whom see entries 176 and 177b).

231. frontispiece, *reduced*

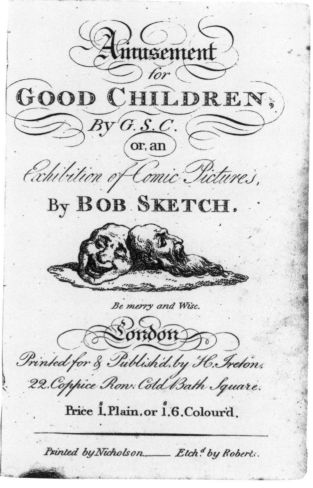

231. *reduced*

◦§ 230 §◦

The Comic Adventures of Jumping Joan. And her dog cat and parrot. Embellished with 15 engravings. London: Printed for T & R Hughes 35 Ludgate St, Published 1 August 1807 (plate-date, impression possibly somewhat later). 16° (101 × 90 mm.).

[1¹⁶] (1ʳ blank, 1ᵛ title, 2ʳ incipit: *Here am I little / Jumping Joan. / When nobodys with me / I'm always alone*, 16ᵛ blank). Ff. 16. Etched throughout: presumably printed from a single copper-plate on one side of a full sheet. Unwatermarked. 15 larger-than-half-page illustrations, each with four-line rhyme. Lacking wrappers.

PML 81501. Gift: Elisabeth Ball.

One of T. Hughes's earliest publications was a harlequinade, *Harlequin's Habeas* (1803), and he was clearly keen to exploit the new pictorial fashion in children's books. He does not seem to have done more than follow the lead of others, however, and this edition of *Jumping Joan* is a rather tame attempt at imitating *Old Mother Hubbard*.

H. IRETON (otherwise unrecorded)

◦§ 231 §◦

Amusement for Good Children, by G.S.C. or, an exhibition of comic pictures, by Bob Sketch. [vignette of two masks, captioned:] *Be merry and Wise.* London: Printed for & Publish'd by H. Ireton, 22, Copice Row, Cold Bath Square. Printed by Nicholson.—Etchᵈ by Roberts, [not before 1800 (watermark-date), not after 1804 (inscription-date)]. Price 1ˢ. Plain, or 1ˢ.6. Colour'd. 12°? (163 × 101 mm.).

A–C⁶ D² (A1ʳ text, D2ᵛ imprint *Nicholson, Printer, Warner Street*); plain etched title and 12 etched plates in publisher's coloring including frontispiece. Pp. 3–42. Wove paper. Contemporary marbled stiff wrappers. Maroon morocco, by Morrell.

Provenance: *James Davies's Book 1804* (inscr.); Charles Todd Owen (binding). PML 85558. Gift: Elisabeth Ball.

"Be merry and Wise" runs the rubric on the title-page—an eighteenth-century phrase in a book that straddles the divide of old and new. The random, moral/satirical text, the heavy jocularity, the uncertainty as to whether "good children" really are the audience, all bespeak the influence of John Newbery. On the other hand, the page size, the mixing of letterpress and intaglio printing, the caricatures, and the strong hand-coloring all belong to newer movements.

The book's slightly mysterious, slightly ambiguous presence is emphasized by the difficulty of accounting for its various progenitors. Who was G.S.C.? Which Roberts was involved with the etching? What else did H. Ireton publish at that poetical resort in Clerkenwell: Coppice Row, Cold Bath Square? Nothing is known of his activities, although his printer, Nicholson, arrives at a neighboring address for the years 1813–14. A further peculiarity is the book's adoption for the American market by Warner & Hanna in Baltimore in 1806–8 (Welch [1963] 140.1–2). More copies of these American editions are recorded than of their English source.

LANGLEY & BELCH

The first-named of these two publishers, who shared a partnership for some twelve years, is probably the Edward Langley who was apprenticed to the printer Thomas Pasler in 1785 and freed in 1792. Such dates certainly do not contradict the probable commencement of Langley's publishing activities at 173 High Street, Borough [i.e. Southwark], about 1803. At this time he seems to be casting around for a style, and the early examples of his work that we exhibit suggest an influence from the Dartons, both in their presentation of moral anecdotes through a combination of picture and text and in the actual style of illustration, as well as in the letterpress-outer forme, intaglio-inner forme method of production.

There is thus a possible early connection with William Belch, who was William Darton I's first apprentice, bound to him in 1788 and made free of the Clothworkers Company in 1795. Belch's activity at this time is obscure. Even before he was out of his apprenticeship, he was sharing with William Darton in the publishing of a work in parts, *A Cabinet of Quadrupeds*, and was also spending time in Wales. (He was registered as of Pontypool when he married at Neath in 1803, and he is described as "of Cardiff" in an 1805 imprint to *Quadrupeds*.) He nonetheless forged some kind of working relationship with Langley at this time, and in 1807 Langley & Belch were in business at the 173 High St. address.

The partnership lasted about a dozen years, during which they published many children's books and some engraved writing sheets. In 1819 the business failed and the partners went their separate ways, with Langley continuing at the old address until ca. 1825, and with Belch at Newington Butts and 258 High Street, Borough, whence he issued children's books, engraved sheets, and some dissected puzzles (the sheets often in conjunction with J. Phelps of Paternoster Row). Some time in the mid-1830s Belch moved to 6 Bridge Street, Union Street, Borough, but in 1843 failed once more, at which time he probably retired to Wales. He died at Neath, aged seventy-four, in 1847.

◂§ 232 §▸

Light Reading for Leisure Hours. By a writer. [London:] Printed & Sold by Edwd Langley Borough, [ca. 1805]. 18° (132 × 82 mm.).

[1^18] (1·18 mounted as pastedowns, 1^v frontispiece, 2^r title, 2^v *Preface*, 3^r text). Pp. [36]. Wove paper. Outer forme: text printed letterpress; inner forme: illustrations and title printed from a large etched plate. 35 illustrations (two to a page including frontispiece, one to the title), the first seven hand-colored by the original child owner. Contemporary marbled stiff papers. Brown morocco gilt. Reference: James p. 36 (this copy).

Provenance: *E. Doubleday his book* (contemporary inscr., and repeated initials); Charles Todd Owen (binding). PML 81301. Gift: Elisabeth Ball.

An early example of Edward Langley's publishing style before he was explicitly joined by Belch. The makeup and visual appearance of the book show a direct influence from William Darton I, especially in the wedding of moral anecdotes set in letterpress to densely engraved pictures. Langley's trade connections are not clear at this date, but the Morgan Library has a copy of his *Leaves of Recreation*, dated 1 November 1803, and published in association with the engravers Champante & Whitrow. Here, too, there is a Dartonesque set of plates, backed up with typographic texts (PML 82181).

◂§ 233 §▸

The Blossoms of Reason, for the entertainment of youth. London: Printed & Sold by Langley & Belch, 173, High Street Borough, [ca. 1810]. 18° (130 × 85 mm.).

[1^18] (1·18 mounted as pastedowns, 1^v frontispiece, 2^r title, 2^v *Preface*, 3^r text). Pp. [36]. Wove paper. Outer forme: text printed letterpress; inner forme: illustrations and title printed from a large etched plate. 35 illustrations uncolored (two to a page including frontispiece, one to the title). Original printed gray stiff wrappers, front cover with short title, imprint, *Price 6d. plain, and 1s. coloured*, wood engraving and type-ornament border, back cover with ads for 6d. and 2d. books.

Provenance: George Morris (early signs.). PML 81554. Gift: Elisabeth Ball.

A transitional work published early on in the Belch/Langley partnership (one of the storytelling scenes includes an advertisement for "Langley's books"). Despite the choice of issue – 6d. plain, 1s. colored—the work retains an eighteenth-century feel, not least through its alternation of letterpress and engraved pages and its trite moralizing.

◂§ 234 §▸

Langley's Sports of Europe, Asia, Africa, and America. Coloured. London: printed and published by E. Langley, 173, High Street, Borough, [not before 1825 (watermark-date)]. Price sixpence. 8° (183 × 112 mm.).

[1^8] (1·8 mounted as pastedowns, 1^v drop-title *Langley's Sports of the Four Quarters of the Globe Price 6 Pence*, illustration, incipit: *The Spaniards take a vast delight*). Ff. [8]. Etched throughout: printed from a single copperplate, on one side of the sheet. Eight half-page illustrations in publisher's coloring, each with caption

Right:
232. fos. 1ᵛ–2ʳ

Below:
233. front cover

and four-line rhyme (see overleaf). Original gray wrappers, front cover with letterpress title (as transcribed above), lower cover with Langley's ads for *Sixpenny Coloured Books*.

PML 81494. Gift: Elisabeth Ball.

A typical Langley production from the end of his career.

◆§ 235 §◆

British Sports for the Amusement of Children . . . London: Printed, Published & Sold by W. Belch, Newington Butts, [not before 1825 (watermark-date)]. 8° (152 × 90 mm.).

[1⁸] (1ʳ title, illustration *Pheasant Shooting* and rhyme, incipit: *See the Fowler takes his aim*, 1ᵛ–2ʳ blank, 2ᵛ *Rabbit Shooting*). Ff. [8]. Etched throughout: printed from a single copperplate on one side of the sheet. Eight half-page illustrations in publisher's coloring, each with caption and four-line rhyme (see overleaf). Original blue-gray stiff wrappers, hand-colored etched pictorial title-label *Price 6ᵈ Colᵈ* mounted on front cover. Black morocco gilt.

Provenance: Charles Todd Owen (binding). PML 81695. Gift: Elisabeth Ball.

This and the previous item show that after Langley and Belch split up, they continued to issue very similar picture books. As noted above (entry 226), these later productions by Belch appear to be influenced by the all-engraved books from the Hodgson firms.

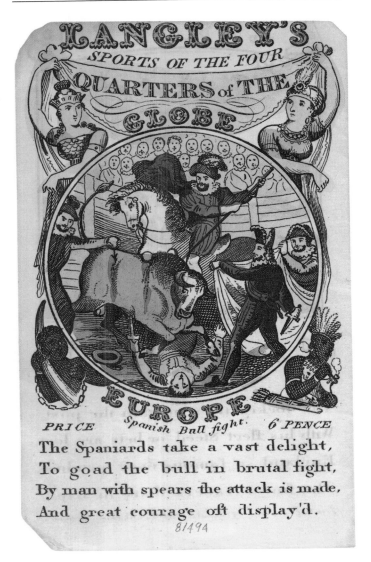

234. fo. 1 verso, *reduced*

ANGLING.

Angling will oft our patience try,
Ere we a dish of Fish supply;
Yet many love the rural sport,
And to the Brook or Lake resort.

235. fo. 8 verso

◈ 236 ◈

Capitals of Europe for the Instruction and Amusement of Children. London: Printed Published & Sold by W. Belch, Newington Butts, [not after 1830]. Price 6ᵈ Coloured. 8° (157 × 98 mm.).

[1⁸] (1ʳ blank, 1ᵛ title, illustration *Constantinople* and rhyme, incipit: *The stately buildings that arise,* 2ʳ *Madrid*). Ff. [8]. Etched throughout: printed from a single copperplate on one side of the sheet. Eight half-page illustrations in publisher's coloring, each with caption and four-line rhyme. Original gray stiff wrappers, hand-colored etched pictorial title-label mounted on front cover. Reference: Gumuchian 1053.

Provenance: *Thomas Eborel Cooke August 1ˢᵗ 1830* (inscr.). PML 84993. Purchase: Fellows Fund.

Belch's activities as an independent publisher were increasingly channeled into a program of engraved books. *Capitals of Europe* is one of many books in the series which rely upon a factual base for their copy.

◈ 237 ◈

W. Belch's, Good & Bad Apprentice. London: Printed & Sold by W. Belch, Newington Butts, [not after 1830–1]. 8° (155 × 96 mm.).

[1⁸] (1ʳ blank, 1ᵛ–2ʳ title, 1ᵛ illustration *The Industrious Apprentice at Church* and rhyme, incipit: *Steady to industry and truth,* 2ʳ *The Idle Apprentice Playing in the church yard*). Ff. [8]. Etched throughout: printed from a single copperplate on one side of the sheet. Eight half-page illustrations in publisher's coloring, each with caption and four-line rhyme. Original blue-gray stiff wrappers, letterpress ads for children's books, lotteries and drawing books inside front cover, for writing-sheets (see next entry) inside back cover *School Pieces (in very great variety) with three whole-sheet flourishing ditto, Plain and Coloured . . . slip copies, black lines, map files and flourishing school-piece books.*

Provenance: *Edward Taylor's Book Great Kelk* [East Riding of Yorkshire] *Decemer 11 1830 1831* (inscrs.). PML 82408. Gift: Elisabeth Ball.

The Good and Bad Apprentice is an excursion into traditional

AMSTERDAM.

Here commerce holds a potent reign,

And gives the Dutchman distant fame,

Boats and canals in every street,

You may in this vast City meet,

moralizing. The content and sequence of the illustrations are drawn from William Hogarth's set of prints "The Idle and Industrious Apprentice" (1747), but Belch has edited out the seamier incidents such as the idle apprentice's whoremongering. The Morgan Library also has an even later treatment of the same theme, published at Derby by Thomas Richardson ca. 1835 (PML 80236).

❧ 238 ❧

The Life of Jonathan. London: Printed & Sold by W. Belch, 258 High St Boro & J. Phelps 27, Paternoster Row, [impression not before 1825 (watermark-date)]. Broadside (post-size full sheet, 475 × 385 mm.).

Writing sheet, printed from an etched copperplate (450 × 360 mm.) and hand-colored. Wove paper. Large illustration *And Saul cast a javelin at him to smite him: whereby Jonathan knew that it was determined of his Father to slay David. 1st Sam: Chap. 20. Ver. 33* (top) and six smaller biblical ones (sides), empty cartouche (bottom); the central area left blank for calligraphic exercise (uncompleted—see overleaf).

Private Collection.

Belch sold biblical writing-sheets during most of his career. Impressions could be struck as needed, and the active life of a copperplate might span a decade or more.

J. L. MARKS

John Lewis Marks is one of the last booksellers/publishers to represent the style that emerged at the beginning of the century. He began trading ca. 1822 at 17 Artillery Street and concentrated

Above:
236. fo. 6 recto, *reduced*

Right:
237. fos. 1^v–2^r, *reduced*

W. BELCH'S,

THE INDUSTRIOUS APPRENTICE
AT CHURCH.

Steady to industry and truth,

At church behold the pious youth,

Conduct like this gives friends delight,

There's nothing like beginning right.

London, *Printed & Sold by* W. Belch, *Newington Butts.*

GOOD & BAD APPRENTICE

THE IDLE APPRENTICE PLAYING
IN THE CHURCH YARD.

Ah, sad reverse, this idle lad,

Gambles with companions bad,

The Beadle comes and with his whip,

Makes the wicked youngster's trip.

238. *reduced*

239. fo. 1 verso, *reduced*

on cheap series, reprints of popular titles, and fancy goods (ads include "one shilling books with beautiful plates," "Marks's Comic Nursery Tales" at sixpence, a variety of halfpenny, penny, and twopenny books, together with prints and valentine letters), as well as on toy theaters and jigsaw puzzles. He gives the impression of keeping a watchful eye on the publications of such competitors as Dean & Munday, and after his move to Long Lane, West Smithfield, in 1839 he begins to publish larger-format picture books such as "Aunt Jaunty's Tales" in foolscap quarto. Marks had a close working relationship with William Raine, printer and publisher of Baltimore, Maryland, judging by the near-identity of his toy-book lists and toy-book illustrations with those of his American colleague. His firm continued until quite late in the century with an S. Marks, still recycling the texts and cuts of earlier years.

Our example, *Little Dame Crump*, is typical of Marks's six-penny series; the text is a strangely contorted reworking of *The Old Woman and her Pig*.

❧ 239 ❧

Marks's History of Little Dame Crump and Her Little White Pig. London: Pub^d by J. L. Marks, 17, Artillery St^t Bishopsgate, [not before 1828 (watermark-date)]. Price, Six Pence, Coloured. 8° (178 × 108 mm.).

[1⁸] (1^r blank, 1^v title, illustration and rhyme, incipit: *Little Dame Crump with her little hair broom*). Ff. [8]. Etched throughout: printed from a single copperplate on one side of the sheet. Eight larger-than-half-page illustrations in publisher's coloring, each with four-line rhyme. Original buff wrappers, etched title and vignette on front cover. Red morocco, by Morrell.

Provenance: Charles Todd Owen (binding). PML 81422. Gift: Elisabeth Ball.

GEORGE MARTIN

We have already encountered George Martin as a producer of newly designed harlequinades (entry 154), but although he was very active as a publisher of engraved work, very little is known of his career. Born George Samuel Martin, the son of a glazier, he was apprenticed to George Mitchell, a bookseller, in 1795, turned over to Thomas Hurst, the Paternoster Row bookseller, in 1800, and presumably freed in 1802. Todd records him as a printer at Hand Court, Upper Thames Street in 1812, but it was after his move to nearby Great St. Thomas Apostle, between Queen Street and Bow Lane, a year or two later that his output of cheap engraved books for children began to proliferate. He remained at that location for over thirty years, removing to nearby Friday Street in 1845, after which date he disappears from the records.

These sparse details are worth noting in view of the Morgan

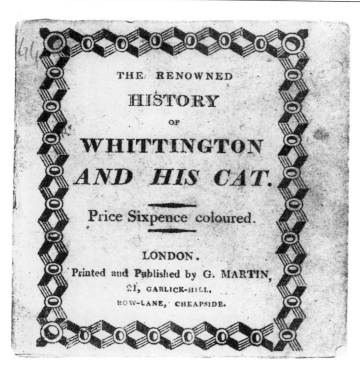

240. front cover, *reduced*

Thinks he to make my Crown Secure
More royal blood Ill spill
The Duke d'Enghien in the night
My Mameluckes shall kill

241. fo. 4 recto, *reduced*

Library's holdings of Martin's children's books, which show him to be a publisher of hypnotic awfulness. From an advertisement in *The Adventures of Dame Winnifred* of ca. 1823 (entry 243) Martin's energy may be gauged: 41 sixpenny colored books, 16 ditto at one shilling, three ditto at 1/6, six sixpenny "battle doors", 18 story books at one shilling, 42 turn-ups at sixpence and one shilling, and 52 engraved sheets of natural history. Judging from surviving examples, however (of which the Morgan holds well over a dozen), this large output was produced with a slapdash eccentricity of engraving, lettering, and coloring that is wondrous to behold. Indeed, such is Martin's determination to put "production" ahead of all questions of editorial control that he succeeds in creating for himself a quaintly amateurish distinctiveness. The following examples show some of the ways in which this manifested itself.

◀§ 240 ৡ▶

The Renowned History of Whittington and His Cat. London: Printed and Published by G. Martin, 21, Garlick-Hill, Bow-Lane, Cheapside, [ca. 1814]. Price Sixpence coloured. 12° (101 × 95 mm.).

[1¹²] (1·12 mounted as pastedowns, 1ᵛ drop-title, illustration, incipit: *Dick Whittington when very young*). Ff. [12]. Engraved throughout: printed from a single copperplate, on one side of the sheet. 12 three-quarter-page illustrations in publisher's coloring, each with four-line rhyme. Original gray wrappers, letterpress title (as transcribed above) within type-ornament border on front cover, single-column ads within the same border on back cover. References: Gumuchian 5832; Osborne II, 615 (copy watermarked 1814).

Provenance: John Callin (child signs.); Charles Todd Owen (pencil note). PML 84082. Gift: Elisabeth Ball.

An early Martin production, issued from his first address as publisher and with short ads.

◀§ 241 ৡ▶

The Life of Bonaparte. London: Printed and Published by G. Martin, 6, St. Thomas-Apostle, Bow-Lane, Cheapside, [ca. 1815]. Price Sixpence coloured. 12° (102 × 95 mm.).

[1¹²] (1·12 mounted as pastedowns, 1ᵛ drop-title *Buonaparte*, illustration, incipit: *From humble birth and lowly mein*). Ff. [12]. Engraved throughout: printed from a single copperplate on one side of a sheet. 12 three-quarter-page illustrations in publishers coloring, each with four-line rhyme. Bound in maroon morocco, preserving original gray wrappers, letterpress title (as transcribed above) within type-ornament border on front cover, single-column ads within a different border on lower cover.

Provenance: Charles Todd Owen (bookplate, binding). PML 82196. Gift: Elisabeth Ball.

An early and primitive-looking production from Martin's second address. The rhyme must have been composed during Napoleon's brief exile on Elba; it prophetically ends:

> Then he to Elba in a trice
> A prisoner was sent
> Now to Return to France again
> Is Bony's full intent

◀§ 242 ৡ▶

A Juvenile Calculator. [Part the First]. [London:] Publsh'd by G. Martin 6. Great Sᵗ Thomas Apostle, [ca. 1820]. Price 6ᵈ. Coloured. 12° (102 × 95 mm.).

242. fo. 1 verso

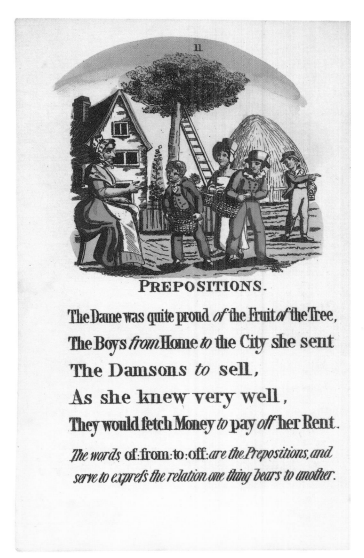

243. fo. 11 verso, *reduced*

[1¹²] (1·12 mounted as pastedowns, 1ᵛ drop-title, illustration, incipit: *1 and 1 make two, Pray give something new*). Ff. 12. Engraved and etched: printed from a single copperplate on one side of a sheet. 12 nearly full-page illustrations in publisher's coloring, each with two-line rhyme captions. Original gray wrappers, title-label removed from front cover, letterpress double-column ads on back cover.

PML 80680. Gift: Elisabeth Ball.

This first part of *A Juvenile Calculator* was soon followed by Martin's publication of the second and third parts in separate volumes.

❧ 243 ❧

The Adventures of Dame Winnifred and Her Numerous Family: or The Infants Grammar. London: Published by G. Martin, 6, Great Sᵗ Thomas Apostle, [not before 1822 (watermark-date), not after 1826 (inscription-date)]. Price 1ˢ 6ᵈ Coloured. 4° (198 × 121 mm.).

[1¹⁶] (1ʳ blank, 1ᵛ title, illustration, 2ʳ *Articles*, 2ᵛ–3ʳ blank, 3ᵛ *Nouns*, 16ʳ *Future tense*, 16ᵛ blank). Ff. 16. A single paper stock (watermarked Basted Mill 1822). Etched throughout: printed from four copperplates on one side of four sheets. 16 nearly half-page illustrations, in publisher's coloring all except title with caption, five-line rhyme and brief grammatical explanation. Original orange stiff wrappers, hand-colored etched title-label *Dame Winniefred or the Infants Grammar* on front cover, letterpress ads inside covers for books priced from 6d. to 1s.6d. including "turn up and down books" and "copper-plate engravings." Reference: James p. [49] (this copy).

Provenance: *Emma Barston Leicester Dec. 13ᵗʰ 1826* (inscr.); Charles Todd Owen. PML 85364. Gift: Elisabeth Ball.

Although there is little to be said for its wayward approach to the grammatical theme, *Dame Winnifred* belongs to the most expensive class of books published by George Martin; two other books in this category were *The Gay Old Lady's Disasters in Pursuit of Pleasure* and *A Visit to Fifteen Counties, or an over-notable Dame Marketting*.

R. MILLER

Richard Miller of 24 Old Fish Street, Doctor's Commons, is another specialist in engraved work for children who finds no place in standard trade reference books. Perhaps his most characteristic work is to be found in several series of elegantly engraved cards which were used as school or Sunday school rewards (e.g. a sequence of Dr. Watts's *Divine Songs*, or poetical effusions about birds and beasts). These were also bound up and published as books along with other works in "Miller's Juvenile Library." Later Miller moved across the river from the City, to 37 Harleyford Place, Kennington.

≈§ 244 §≈

[CHARLES PERRAULT (1628–1703) and/or PIERRE PERRAULT DARMANCOUR (1678–1700)]. *Blue Beard or the Fatal Effects of Curiosity. Embellished with Col^d Engravings.* [London:] Published by R. Miller, Old Fish Street, [not before 1820 (watermark-date)]. 12°? (131 × 85 mm.).

A^8 B^4 C^8 (A1 and C8 blank and mounted as pastedowns, A2^r text, C6^v imprint *Miller, Printer, 24, Old Fish Street, Doctor's Commons*, C7 ads); six etchings, hand-colored at the publisher's including frontispiece *Fatima and her sister going to visit Blue Beard* and conjugate title with vignette, apparently printed from a single copperplate. Pp. 36, [4]. Original printed leather-backed boards, title . . . *from Miller's Juvenile Library. One shilling* on front cover, back cover with ads for *Instructive Books, published by R. Miller* including *Costumes* advertised as available on two kinds of paper ("extra-super large Cards" and "fine drawing paper," each at 2s.).

PML 83912. Purchase: Ball Fund.

A standard reprint of this Perrault tale, with the colored engravings less carefully executed than Miller's sets of reward cards.

NEWMAN

Something has already been said of Newman's place as a publisher, specifically his relationship with Dean & Munday. With the two books described here, however, we see his earlier incursion into children's book publishing. *The Wonderful Adventures of Captain Gulliver* with its Didier title page and its Newman cover shows him taking over the children's-book list of Didier & Tebbett, small publishers, who lasted from ca. 1803 to ca. 1810. (The Morgan Library also has two copies of *The Jack-Daw "at home"* by a "Young Lady of Rank," the third edition of which is published by Didier in 1809, printed by G. Schulze, and the fourth edition of which is printed by Lane, Darling & Co. at the Minerva Press for A.K. Newman.)

Pomona's Frolic, however, seems to be a book instigated by Newman. It is a distant, ornately verbose relation of Roscoe's *Butterfly's Ball*, seeking to blend "Amusement and Instruction;" in its advertisement list are found many of the children's books that came to Newman from Didier's.

≈§ 245 §≈

Pomona's Frolic; or, the Grand Jubilee of the animated fruit. Part the first [second]. London: printed at the Minerva Press, for A. K. Newman and Co. Leadenhall-street, 1810. 2 volumes. 24° (99 × 79 mm.).

Pt. I: A–D^12 E^4 (A1^r half-title and imprint *Lane, Darling, and Co. Leadenhall-Street*, A1^v blank, A2^r title, A2^v blank, A3^r *Preface*, E4^v same imprint); five etchings including frontispiece *Prince Melon requesting of his Majesty to give a grand Entertainment.* Pp. 104. Pt. II: A–D^12 E^8 (A1^r title, A1^v blank, E8^v same imprint, quires E of both parts together forming a half-sheet); seven etchings includ-

245. pt. I, pl.[4] facing D1^r, *reduced*

ing frontispiece *Queen Peach carving for her illustrious Guests.* Pp. 112. Wove paper (the letterpress stock watermarked 1809). The 12 etchings of both parts perhaps printed from a single copperplate on a half-sheet, divided for insertion; all colored by a contemporary hand, presumably as published. Original gray wrappers, letterpress title and ads on covers. Brown morocco gilt.

Provenance: Charles Todd Owen (binding). PML 85332–3. Gift: Elisabeth Ball.

A very elaborate production with fine colored etchings, unpriced, but later advertised at 1s. each part.

246. *reduced*

◦§ 246 §◦

The Wonderful Adventures and Discoveries of Captain Lemuel Gulliver. London: printed at the Minerva Press, for A.K. Newman and Co. Leadenhall-street, 1811. Price 1s. plain and 1s.6d. coloured. 12° or 16° (123 × 108 mm.).

[1–2⁶ or 1–2⁸ (?)] (1/1ʳ *Frontispiece*, imprint *London, Published by Didier & Tebbett 75, Sᵗ Jamess Strᵗ 1ˢᵗ April, 1808*, 1/1ᵛ–2ʳ blank, 1/2ᵛ *Gulliver first discovered by the Lilliputians*, 2/6ʳ or 2/8ʳ *Gulliver leaving Lilliput*, 2/6ᵛ or 2/8ᵛ blank). Ff. 12 or 16?]. Engraved throughout: printed from one or two copperplates on one side of the sheet. 12 larger-than-half-page illustrations in publisher's coloring, each except frontispiece (see previous page) with headings and six-line rhyme. Original gray wrappers, letter-press title (as transcribed) with type-ornament border on front cover, ads surrounded by the same border on back cover. Red morocco gilt.

Provenance: Charles Todd Owen (binding). PML 82923. Gift: Elisabeth Ball.

An expensively priced but cheaply produced picture book. The confusing order in which Gulliver's adventures are presented and the unfortunate rebinding of the volume render an exact collation impossible.

A. PARK AND FAMILY

Arthur Park was an engraver and lithographer who worked in a number of areas of popular publishing: picture sheets, Twelfth-Night sheets, and toy-theater equipment. His early productions, done in association with J. Goulding, were probably freelance engravings (some for the Hodgson firms). He opened his shop at 47 Leonard Street ca. 1830, and from there were published a variety of printed goods, including cheap children's picture books with the Park imprint. Arthur Park left for the United States in 1842 (Hannas; Speaight says ca. 1835) and died there in 1863. The business was continued by Archibald Alexander Park (a brother?) and then by Sarah Park (his widow?) and Alexander Park (their son?). The latter moved premises several times after 1867 and the business closed in 1880.

'Twas Rouen saw the closing scene,
    Courageous died, the guiltless Fair;
Her look undaunted and serene,
    Made England blush that brought her there.
Thus fell the Heroine renown'd,
    Victim of Treason, foul and dark;
Her Memory, by Glory crown'd,
    Blazon'd — THE VALIANT MAID OF ARC."

247. fo. 8 recto

◄§ 247 §►

Park's History of Joan of Arc, called the Maid of Orleans.
London: Printed & Published by A. Park, Nº 47, Leonard Sᵗ
Tabernacle Walk. Sold by J. Fairburn, 110, Minories, [ca.
1838]. Price 6ᵈ Coloured. 8° (176 × 111 mm.).

[1⁸] (1·8 mounted as pastedowns, 1ᵛ drop-title and Park imprint,
illustration, incipit: *The Maiden Joan of Arc was poor*). Ff. [8].
Engraved throughout: presumably printed from a single copperplate on one side of the sheet. Eight larger-than-half-page illustrations, in publisher's coloring, the one on title with six-line
rhyme, the others with eight-line rhyme. Original yellow wrappers, engraved pictorial title (as transcribed above) on front
cover. Modern boards with gold-thread embroidery, gilt edges.
Reference: James p. 86 (this copy).

Provenance: Charles Todd Owen (pencil-note). PML 81756. Gift:
Elisabeth Ball.

For Fairburn's own publishing ventures, see entry 224.

◄§ 248 §►

*Park's Amusing History of Little Jack Horner. Embellished
with coloured engravings.* London: printed and published by
A. Park, 47, Leonard Street, Finsbury, [ca. 1838]. 8° (173 ×
106 mm.).

[1⁸] (1·8 mounted as pastedowns, 1ᵛ drop-title and imprint, illustration and first stanza). Ff. [8]. The sheet printed on one side
only (inner forme). Eight wood engravings (about 100 × 85 mm.
each), publisher's coloring, each leaf (except the first) with two
letterpress stanzas. Original buff wrappers, wood engraving
(same block as the final illustration) and title (as transcribed
above) on front cover.

Provenance: Katé. K. Woodhouse (sign.). PML 84004. Gift:
Elisabeth Ball.

Park printed many similar picture books using either copperplates or wood blocks and letterpress.

STEVENS & CO.

We have found no information at all about the firm of Stevens &
Co., perhaps a short-lived printing establishment turning out a
few children's books to help turnover. An undated children's book
published by G. Stevens alone is *The Reward of Merit* (PML
85057).

◄§ 249 §►

The Juvenile Numerator. London: Publish'd by Stevens & Cº
Nº 10 Borough Road Sᵗ Georges Fields, July 1ˢᵗ 1810. 24°?
(107 × 102 mm.).

[1¹²] (1·12 mounted as pastedowns, 1ᵛ *Frontispiece*, 2ʳ title and
pictorial border, 2ᵛ–3ʳ blank, 3ᵛ incipit: *One Two Buckle my Shoe,*
8ʳ *Eleven Twelve A Cat on the Shelf,* 12ʳ *Nineteen Twenty, My
belly's Empty: So pray Dame give me some pudding*). Ff. [12].

249. fo. 4 recto, *reduced*

Etched throughout: printed from a single copperplate on one side
of a half-sheet? Each leaf with full-page illustration. Contemporary or original plain blue-gray wrappers. Red morocco gilt.

Provenance: Charles Todd Owen (binding). PML 85054. Gift:
Elisabeth Ball.

Iona and Peter Opie (*ODNR*, 1951) record the first appearance in
print of "One, two, Buckle my shoe" as being in *Songs for the
Nursery* (1805). This is one of the earliest adaptations of the
rhyme to make a picture book and the first to give it an educational
flavor through a title. Other publishers including D. Carvalho
were to copy this later on.

THOMAS TEGG

Thomas Tegg had an upbringing of variable fortune. He was born
at Wimbledon in 1776, orphaned at the age of five, sent to Scotland
to be schooled on the cheap, and then apprenticed to a loutish
bookseller. He ran away, and after a gradual journey back to the
south (during which he briefly sold chapbooks in the streets of
Berwick), he took up bookselling again and in 1799 started his
own business. Although he became best known as an auctioneer
and as a master of the cheap reprint and remainder trade, he also
established a line in printselling and in 1808 he could advertise
"a large collection (the largest in England) of new popular
Humorous and Political Caricatures by Woodward, Rowlandson,
Cruikshanks . . ." This was the side of his business that led him to
produce a number of comic booklets, which would have included
children among their readers. Much later in his career he engaged
in a famous quarrel with the American purveyor of didactica
"Peter Parley" (see entry 303); a brief account is given by Harvey
Darton (pp. 224–45). Tegg died in 1845. His son William continued publishing under his own name until 1890.

250. fo. 2 recto, *reduced*

◦§ 250 ◦֍

The Loves of M͏ʳ Jenkins and Polly Pattens. [London:] Pub. by T. Tegg, 111 Cheapside, Jan. 1-1809. 12° (121 × 113 mm.).

[1¹²] (1ʳ blank, 1ᵛ title within border, 2ʳ incipit: *M͏ʳ Jenkins smok'd his pipe*). Ff. [12]. Etched throughout: perhaps printed from a single copperplate on one side of the sheet. Paper watermarked 1808. Each leaf, except title, with larger-than-half-page illustration (uncolored) and four-line rhyme. Original covers removed. Modern blue morocco gilt, by Bayntun.

Provenance: Charles Todd Owen (binding). PML 81446. Gift: Elisabeth Ball.

This is no. II in *Tegg's Entertaining Magazine for Youth, To be continued on the First Day of every Month*. The Morgan Library also owns a plain copy of no. III in the series, *Crackbrainiana or Trifles for Exercising the Mind by Peter Puzzle-Cap, Conjuror to the Lilliputian Society*, (illustrated in James p. 56).

OUTSIDE LONDON

The quest to exploit the formula of the "new" picture book was not confined to London and its environs. Printers and engravers in many provincial towns attempted versions and variations on their own account, much as, say, a generation earlier Luckman of Coventry or Mozley of Gainsborough had been inspired by the examples set by the Newberys. For the student of this movement, however, a knowledge of these provincial publishing firms is more difficult to acquire than of the myriad London entrepreneurs, and the following are presented with few notes on their publishers. They have been chosen to show the spread of activity in England only, and they are listed alphabetically according to the place of

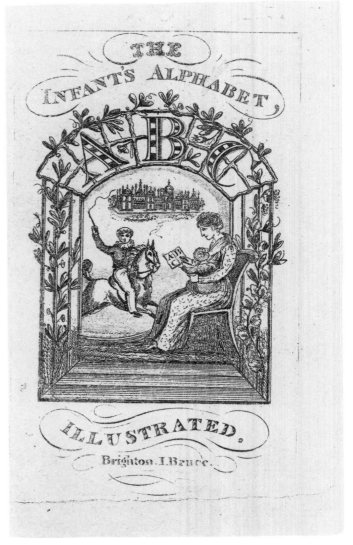

252. front cover, *reduced*

publication. For the record, we should note the presence in the Morgan Library of several engraved picture books and such from Scottish publishers, including Thornton & Brydone and W. Darling, both of Edinburgh.

BATH

◦§ 251 ◦֍

Scripture History; or leading facts of the Old Testament . . . Bath: Published by James Fryer, [ca. 1830]. Fourpence Plain – Sixpence Coloured. 8° (174 × 105 mm.).

[1⁸] (1ʳ heading *The Three Children in the fiery furnace*, illustration, incipit: *Unhurt, amidst the burning flame*). Ff. [8]. Etched throughout: apparently printed from a single copperplate on one side of the sheet. Each leaf with heading, larger-than-half-page illustration in publisher's coloring, and four-line rhyme. Original pale-blue stiff wrappers, etched pictorial titles on sides: an illustration of Paradise on front cover, the Expulsion on back cover. Black morocco gilt.

Provenance: Charles Todd Owen (binding). PML 80706. Gift: Elisabeth Ball.

"Scripture Histories" were a publishing line to which the Hodgsons lay claim, either in the form of booklets or writing sheets. Although the contents of this provincial picture are entirely different, its physical production book bears a strong resemblance to Hodgson's *Scripture History* (entry 229a.). It is possible that the copperplates used by Hodgson and Fryer have a common source.

BRIGHTON

⋙ 252 ⋘

The Infant's Alphabet. Embellished with copper plate engravings. Brighton: Printed & Published by I. Bruce, [not before 1831]. Six Pence. 8° (176 × 105 mm.).

[1⁸] (1·8 mounted as pastedowns, 1ᵛ title, 2ʳ incipit: *A An Archer. B A Bullock*). Ff. [8]. Etched throughout: apparently printed from two copperplates on one side of two half-sheets. Paper watermarked W. Joynson 1831. 27 small illustrations including title-vignette, colored by a contemporary hand. Original green stiff wrappers, etched pictorial title on front cover. Black morocco gilt.

Provenance: Charles Todd Owen (binding). PML 81424. Gift: Elisabeth Ball.

One of several picture books in the Morgan Library printed and published by I. Bruce, whose shop no doubt took advantage of Brighton's increasing popularity as a resort for the leisured classes.

BRISTOL

⋙ 253 ⋘

[JEANNE-MARIE LE PRINCE DE BEAUMONT (1711–80)]. *Beauty and the Beast. A tale. Ornamented with Cuts.* Bristol: Printed and Sold by Philip Rose, Broadmead, [not before 1800 (watermark-date)]. Price Six Pence. 12°? (132 × 80 mm.).

[1²⁰] (1·20 mounted as pastedowns, 1ᵛ *Frontispiece*, 20ʳ imprint *Printed by Philip Rose, 58, Broadmead, Bristol*). Pp. 39, [1]. Wove paper. Seven full-page oval wood engravings (including frontispiece), each within the same type-ornament border. Original blue-gray stiff wrappers, letterpress title on front cover. Reference: Hearne p. 208.

Provenance: *Elizabeth Napper 1838* (pencil inscr.); Gumuchian & Cⁱᵉ (1930 cat., no. 501). PML 84044. Gift: Elisabeth Ball.

Philip Rose appears to have been one of the leading printers in Bristol during the first thirty years of the nineteenth century. He printed some substantial works, sometimes in association with London publishers, but also developed a line in chapbooks and in slightly fancier books such as this standard reprint of Mme De Beaumont's fairy tale.

253. fo. 10 verso

GUILDFORD

⋙ 254 ⋘

[THOMAS RUSSELL (1748–1822)]. *The Adventures of the Guildford Jack-Daw. Interspersed with anecdotes of some little good and bad boys. For the use of children. Embellished with cuts.* Guildford: printed for J. Russell, and sold by J. Evans, Pater-noster-row; R. H. Westley, Strand; and W. and J. Stratford, Holborn-Hill, London, [not before 1794 (watermark-date)]. (Price One Shilling.) 18° (129 × 81 mm.).

A² (= E3·4; 1ʳ title, 2ʳ dedication); B–D⁶ E⁶ (–3·4) F–G⁶ (G2ʳ *End of the Guildford Jack-Daw*, G2ᵛ blank, G3ʳ divisional title *The Conceited Magpye. A tale, in verse*, G3ᵛ blank, G5ʳ incipit: *A Magpye, of her cage grown tir'd*); etched frontispiece *Little Jack Barrett and his Daw*. Pp. [4], 68. Laid paper (frontispiece on wove paper). 15 wood engravings (33 × 50 mm. each) by John Russell (1745–1806). Original gilt-blocked and dab-colored floral boards. Reference: ESTC T187802.

Provenance: *James Morton His Book 1808* (inscr.); *From Mʳˢ Evans at Ventnor ap. 1911* (inscr.); George Hubbard (bookplate dated 1916). PML 81592. Gift: Elisabeth Ball.

254. frontispiece

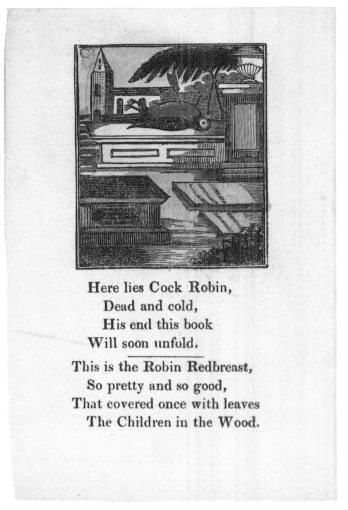

255. frontispiece, *reduced*

Probably a piece of opportunistic publishing, adapting a newly fashionable mode of book design to a local story for local sale. The patterned binding, in eighteenth-century floral paper, suggests a time lag in taste—or possibly the prudent use of overstocks. The author and the artist were brothers. Both their father and grand-father were book- and printsellers in their native town of Guildford.

STOCKPORT

✺ 255 ✺

The Death and Burial of Cock Robin. Embellished with neat engravings on wood. Stockport: S. Dodge, [not before 1829]. 18°? (140 × 90 mm.).

[1⁸(4+1)?] (1ᵛ frontispiece *Here lies Cock Robin, / Dead and cold, / His end this book / Will soon unfold . . .* misbound at the end, 2ʳ title, 2ᵛ *Little Robin Redbreast / Sat upon a tree; / He noddled with his head, / And warbled merrily*, 3ʳ incipit: *Who kill'd Cock Robin?*, 8ᵛ blank). Pp. 17, [1]. 15 half-page wood engravings (the frontispiece signed L), wood-engraved title-vignette of Cock Robin's tombstone dated 1829, all illustrations colored by a contemporary hand. Tan morocco, by Morrell.

Provenance: Charles Todd Owen (binding). PML 81315. Gift: Elisabeth Ball.

Bath and Brighton, Bristol and Guildford, with their genteel hinterland, seem natural places to find children's book-production going on; Stockport, though, on the threshold of the industrial revolution with Lancastrian cotton-spinning starting to boom, is perhaps a much less likely location.

TAUNTON

✺ 256 ✺

The Winter's Night; or, the admiral, the farmer, and the old marine, a tale, in rhyme. For children. With five etchings. Taunton: Printed and Published by J. W. Marriott, Taunton Courier and General Printing-Office, East-Street. [Entered at Stationers'-hall.], 1815. Price two shillings. 16° (131 × 99 mm.).

[1–2⁸] (1/1ʳ title, 1/1ᵛ blank, 1/2ʳ incipit: *His cattle sold, – his bargains made –*, 2/7ᵛ imprint *Marriott, Printer, Taunton*, 2/8 blank); 4 soft-ground etchings (lacking one), apparently printed from a single plate. Pp. 30, [2]. Paper watermarked O & P 1812.

*The Farmer at the Alehouse Door
Mounts his Mare to crofs the Moor*

256. pl. [1] facing 1/2ʳ, *reduced*

this sermon, I know that it will sell by the hundred thousand.")

Children's books are not excluded from enterprises of this sort, and we offer here a selection, from the sublime to the ridiculous, of privately funded efforts to get through to the market and, in our first example, a truly private piece of book-making.

ᨁ 257 ᨁ

SOPHIA ELIZABETH BURNEY (1777–1856). *Stories for Miss Cecilia-Charlotte-Esther Burney. Aged five years. Written by Sophia Burney. Printed by Frances Burney.* [England: 1793]. 16°? (113 × 91 mm.).

[1⁴ 2²(1+1) 3–6² 7²(1+1) 8² 9⁶(–6)?] (1/1ʳ title, 1/1ᵛ *List of the Contents,* 1/2ʳ *Story I,* 9/5ᵛ colophon: *So here ends the Story of little Martin, and here likewise ends this little Book, which we hope Cecilia will like, as we wrote it on purpose to give her pleasure; and Uncle Inny was so good as to draw three beautiful Pictures for it. The End*). Pp. [2], 48. MANUSCRIPT on wove paper (unwatermarked). Written in Frances's "printed" script, mostly upright but occasionally sloping, in brown ink (through p. 27 "The Story of Norbury," and colophon page) and black ink (contents page, and from p. 28 "The Story of Charles" onwards). Nine watercolor drawings (45 × 75 mm. and smaller), those on pp. 6 (Halsted), 11 (Amelia feeding her little brother, Master Frederic) and 26 (Norbury's chaise overturned) presumably by Edward Francesco Burney (1760–1848), the remainder by Frances (1776–1828) and/or Sophia. Marbled wrappers (original?), resewn (earlier stab-holes visible); an original flyleaf at the beginning, two lines of letterpress on verso: *Titchfield Street, / Wednesday, September 18th.* The volume is preserved in an embroidered silk moiré pouch, no doubt part of the original gift.

Provenance: Cecilia Charlotte Esther Burney (1788–1821); Henry Burney (1814–93), *Henry Burney from his affectionate Aunt Cecilia Burney. August 23rd 1818* (inscr.). MA 4160. Purchase: Ball Fund.

Original limp green roan, oval letterpress title-label on front cover.

PML 81736. Gift: Elisabeth Ball.

John William Marriott was a busy printer in Taunton during the first half of the nineteenth century and was publisher of the local newspaper, the *Taunton Courier.* He seems to have been proud of this venture into children's books for he issued it conventionally bound in yellow paper (PML 83596) and in this superior binding. The Morgan Library also has another picture book with a Taunton imprint, *The Juvenile Scrap-book,* printed and sold by J[ohn] Bishop ca. 1831 (PML 83278). It appears to have been made up from stock-blocks acquired from various sources.

Privately Published · A DIGRESSION
(see entries 257–264)

While decisions whether or not to publish a book are usually based upon commercial assessments of its likely success, certain books (including some of the highest merit) have found their way onto the market through the determination of their authors to get them there (e.g. Proust and Joyce). The reasons for this desire may vary, with vanity at one end of the scale and an urgent belief in the importance of what one has to say at the other—with a fair degree of commercial hopefulness thrown in. ("Even if the publisher is blind to the potential of

Making books at home for the family has long been a source of great private satisfaction (the Victorians were to excel at it, producing a great multitude of illustrated manuscript stories, family magazines, etc. etc.). In this little eighteenth-century booklet we see a particularly charming example, notable as much for the affection displayed in it as for its association with a distinguished family. Sophia, Frances, and Cecilia Burney were the granddaughters of the famous musicologist Charles Burney (1726–1814), and the nieces of the novelist Fanny Burney d'Arblay (1752–1840) and of the classicist Charles Burney (1757–1817). "Uncle Inny," who did three of the pictures, was Sir Joshua Reynolds's friend, the artist and engraver Edward Francesco Burney. (For a genealogical table by Althea Douglas of the large and complicated Burney family, see Joyce Hemlow, *A Catalogue of the Burney Family Correspondence 1749–1878* [New York Public Library, 1971].)

The two children, writing for their younger sister do not attempt any rounded storytelling, but rather give her short accounts of incidents in the places and among the people that she

257. embroidered pouch, *reduced*

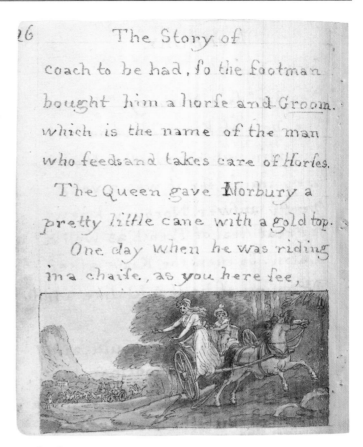

257. fo. 26

knows. Eighteenth-century children's literature with its liking for good boys and girls (and for *Sandford and Merton*) resonates in the text, but there is no horrid moralizing and many glimpses of true family pleasures, from sharing dolls to getting a present of a sheepfold or dabbling in the water like a duck.

❧ 258 ❧

[WILLIAM BLAKE (1757–1827)]. *For the Sexes | The Gates of Paradise | Mutual Forgiveness of each Vice | Such are the Gates of Paradise . . .* [London:] Publishd by W Blake Lambeth, 17 May 1793 (plate-imprints) [revised with re-engraving of illustrations and additional engraving of text from ca. 1818 onwards, impressions pulled by Blake himself between 1825 (watermark-date) and 1827]. "Blake 8°" (227 × 139 mm.).

21 engravings (90 × 70 mm., 100 × 65 mm. and smaller) printed on rectos only of 21 separate leaves, stabbed to form a codex: title (Bentley's 3rd state), *Frontispiece* (1st state), illustrations 1–16 (1st states) numbered in the copperplates, *The Keys of the Gates* (2nd state) numbered 17–18 in Blake's hand, *To the Accuser who is The God of This World* and pictorial tailpiece numbered 19 by Blake. Wove paper watermarked J Whatman 1825. Binding not after 1833: half calf and marbled boards, spine lettered in gilt *The Gates of Paradise by Blake 1793*, gray endpapers. References: Keynes *Blake* 53D ("Third state"); Keynes *Paradise* v. I, p. 49, copy D ("Third state;" with commentary accompanying the Trianon Press facsimiles); Bentley *Thorne* 11; Bentley *Blake Books* 45D.

Provenance: Blake's widow, Catherine Blake; Frederick Tatham, the Blakes' executor, who also owned the copperplates and presumably pulled the impressions for copies F–L; *Thomas Boddington 1833* (inscription and bookplate, sold at Sotheby's,

4 Nov. 1895, lot 94, £21 to Quaritch); *W. A. White 18 Nov. '95* (inscrs.); Dr. A.S.W. Rosenbach (acquired from White in 1929). PML 63936. Gift: Mrs. Landon K. Thorne.

Originally published as "For Children" in 1793, *The Gates of Paradise* was reissued towards the end of William Blake's life as "For the Sexes." The word "published" is here used advisedly since that is how Blake describes his plates in their imprints, and in the prospectus of his own books, dated 10 October 1793, in which he offered this "small book of engravings" at three shillings. One wonders what the children's book buying public of 1793 made of such a remarkable offering of simple emblems with complicated meanings. The earliest state of the title lists the artist's friend and associate, the established bookseller Joseph Johnson (see chapter VI), as co-publisher, but there is no evidence that Johnson ever advertised the book.

Commercially the book proved a complete failure and, as the late Geoffrey Keynes has pointed out, only one copy can be shown to have found its way into the hands of a child. Nevertheless, this sequence of emblematic engravings amounts to one of the most mysteriously evocative picture books ever published.

❧ 259a ❧

The Careless Child's Alphabet. Designed to fix the learner's attention to the shape of the letters. Containing, I. The roman small letters twelve times repeated, and placed promiscuously. II. A large collection of those pairs of letters that are

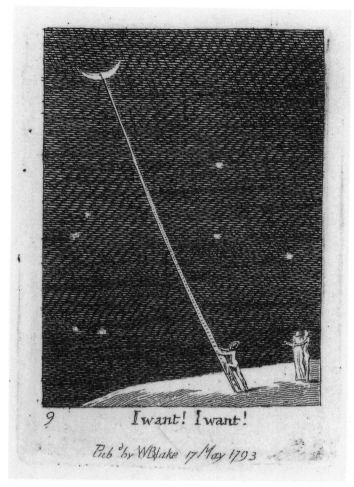

258. fo. 11 recto, *reduced*

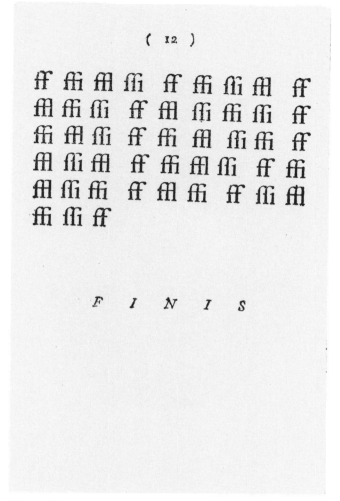

259a. fo. 6 verso

nearly alike in form. III. The roman capitals repeated twelve times, and placed promiscuously. IV. To which is added, the joined letters, repeated as often as the capitals, and placed promiscuously. Northampton: printed for William Adam, 1776. Half-sheet 12° (131 × 81 mm.), imposed for work-and-turn.

A⁶ (1ᵛ *Preface*, 2ʳ *The Manner of using the following Alphabets*, 6ʳ⁻ᵛ ligatures). Pp. 12. Original gilt-blocked and dab-colored stiff wrappers. Reference: ESTC T186690.

PML 81474. Gift: Elisabeth Ball.

◆§ 259b §◆

JAMES FISHER (fl. 1803–27). *Scripture Riddles, taken from some of the historical passages of the Old Testament; with appropriate keys, in form of a dialogue. Adorned with cuts for the entertainment and instruction of little boys and girls . . . Third edition.* Northampton: Printed for the Author, by W. Cooper, Parade. Sold by Hamilton and Adams, London; W. Cooper, Northampton; and may be had of all other booksellers, 1827. Price one shilling and sixpence. 12° (185 × 115 mm.).

A⁶ (1ᵛ *Frontispiece*, 2ʳ title, 2ᵛ *Entered at Stationer's Hall*, 3ʳ *Advertisement*, 4ʳ *Riddle I*, incipit: *If ancient things you wish to see*) B–G⁶ H⁴ (H4ᵛ imprint *Cooper, Printer, Bookbinder, &c. Northampton*). Pp. 92. 20 wood-engraved illustrations. Original gray boards.

Provenance: *Ann Bromley Warner, Evesham, May 13ᵗʰ 1828. The gift of her Mother* (another inscription in the same hand: *The Author of this book has been blind ever since he was two years of age*). PML 85180. Gift: Elisabeth Ball.

Placing these two authorial experiments next to the Burneys' manuscript and Blake's engravings demonstrates most completely how wide the span can be in private publishing (and suggests that Gotham lies nearer to Northampton than to Nottingham).

The Careless Child's Alphabet is possibly the maddest book ever produced in the interests of educational progress (and that takes some doing). The author is truly anxious to be helpful, believing that children will learn the alphabet more easily by having to spot individual letters in unfamiliar relationships. So weird and unrelated to reality are his groupings that the pamphlet looks more like a type specimen than a child's ABC.

In the much later *Scripture Riddles* Northampton seeks to redress the balance by delving so deeply into explanation that the

260. etching opposite c5ᵛ, *enlarged*

importance of the thing to be explained is lost behind the blind author's ingenuity.

> Riddle 10.   While I was acting like a saint
> One gave me that which did me pain;
> I kept it though he much did want
> to take it back with him again.

The answer (of course) is: Eglon, King of Moab.

❧ 260 ☙

The History of Little Sam the Soldier. Written by a friend . . . The fifth edition corrected and enlarged. Embellished and adorned by nine elegant copper-plates. London: printed for the author. Sold by T. Greenhill, Gracechurch Street, H.D. Symmonds, No. 20, Paternoster-Row, T. Vernor, No. 10, Birchin Lane, and all other Booksellers, [ca. 1790]. Price one shilling. 18° (128 × 75 mm.).

a–i⁶ (a1ʳ title, a2ʳ *Preface*, i5ᵛ ads for two illustrated books by the same author at sixpence each, i6 blank and mounted as paste-

down); frontispiece (mounted as pastedown) and 9 oval etchings, printed from one or two copperplates. Pp. 105. Laid (letterpress) and wove (intaglio) paper. Original gilt-blocked and dab-colored floral boards. Reference: ESTC N028578.

PML 83071. Gift: Elisabeth Ball.

"The same Author as *Sam*" was among the most persevering of private entrepreneurs, for he also published *The Travels . . . of a Kite* and *The History . . . of the Ashton Family*. Perhaps he was widely disseminated, since *Sam* is here claimed to be in a corrected and enlarged fifth edition, but it is hard to credit that even a public brought up on *Sandford and Merton* would relish this factitious attempt "to inculcate RELIGION, MORALITY, VIRTUE and BENEVOLENCE" (pp. 103–4).

❧ 261a ☙

The Dove Cot, or the raven's visit, a poetic tale, third edition. Embellished with engravings. London: printed for the author, 1812. Price 6d. Coloured 9d. 16° (123 × 95 mm.).

A⁸ (1 title or blank lacking, 2ʳ incipit: *A Dove secluded in her House*); 4 etchings in original hand-coloring, printed from a single copperplate on a quarter-sheet, divided into two pairs of conjugate leaves for insertion around a2·7 and a3·6. Pp. [16]. Original gray wrappers, front cover with letterpress title (as transcribed above) and inscribed "Colᵈ."

Provenance: Charles Todd Owen (binding). PML 81867. Gift: Elisabeth Ball.

❧ 261b ☙

[E. ROBSON (1791–1819) or JANE ROBSON]. *Hartlepool and Seaton: written for the amusement of the author's nephews.* Darlington: 1817. 16°? (115 × 103 mm.).

[1⁶ 2⁴(4+1)] (1/1ʳ title, 1/1ᵛ imprint *Printed by E. Robson*, 1/2ʳ incipit: *This is the town of Hartlepool*, 2/4+1ʳ footnote *Whilst this little work was in the press, Robin Hood was unfortunately killed by the accidental discharge of his gun*, 2/4+1ᵛ imprint *Darlington, Printed by E. Robson*); 11 etchings by E. Robson, printed from as many copperplates, signed and dated ER 1817. Pp. 21, [1]. Paper with 1815 watermark-date. Original gray stiff wrappers.

Provenance: *Jane G. Backhouse from her Aunt Jane Robson* (inscr.); Gumuchian & Cⁱᵉ (1930 cat., no. 2960). PML 85612. Gift: Elisabeth Ball.

Not even the square 16mo picture books were immune from the amateur (interestingly, the Burneys had already decided in 1793 that that was a nice way to fold and cut their paper for Cecilia's little book). *The Dove Cot* shows the amateur laboring to exploit what he hopes is a funny fable: Parson Raven has designs on Mrs. Dove and tries to persuade her that her husband is faithless, only to meet with general derision at the claws of the dove tribe when they find out. (That seems to be the plot, but the verse is so badly managed that it tends to obscure the author's intentions.)

Hartlepool & Seaton is a merrier piece, a willfully distorted version of "The House that Jack Built," done with an exclusively

261b. etching opposite 2/3ᵛ, *reduced*

263. fo. 2/6ᵛ, *detail*

local audience in mind. Indeed, the text may well have been merely a support to the publication of the extremely accomplished etchings. The Robsons and Backhouses were prominent Quaker families in Darlington—a notable Quaker town.

◄§ 262a §►

The History of the Celebrated Nanny Goose, from the original MS. Illustrated by coloured engravings. London: printed for S. Hood, no. 39, Tottenham-Court-Road, 1813. 12° (162 × 100 mm.).

A–B⁶ C⁶(6+1) (A1ʳ title, A1ᵛ imprint *Jones, Printer, 24, Wardour-Street, Soho, London*, A2ʳ editor's dedication *To the Right Honorable the Lady William Beauclerk* (Maria Janetta Nelthorpe), C6+1ᵛ same imprint); 4 etchings including frontispiece, printed from at least two copperplates, hand-colored as issued (see overleaf). Pp. 38. Letterpress on a paper stock watermarked 1811, etching on at least two paper stocks watermarked 1808 and 1811 respectively. Original blue boards, title on front cover mostly lost, on back cover Hood's ad for *The Adventures of a Hackney Coach*. Brown morocco gilt. References: Facsimile edition, Friends of The Osborne and Lillian H. Smith Collections of Early Children's Books, Toronto Public Library, 1973; Osborne II, 602; Alderson *Moon* 42.

Provenance: Charles Todd Owen (binding). PML 82851. Gift: Elisabeth Ball.

◄§ 262b §►

The History of the Prince Renardo and the Lady Goosiana. London: H. Fores, Spur Street, Leicester Square, 1833. 12° (174 × 103 mm.).

A–B¹² C⁶(6+1) (A1ʳ blank, A1ᵛ frontispiece, A2ʳ title, A2ᵛ list of illustrations). Pp. 62. 5 full-page hand-colored wood engravings signed I.E.A.D. (see overleaf). Original printed green stiff wrap-

pers, title on front cover. Red morocco, by Morrell. References: Facsimile edition, Friends of The Osborne and Lillian H. Smith Collections of Early Children's Books, Toronto Public Library, 1973; Osborne II, 602.

Provenance: Charles Todd Owen (binding). PML 83483. Gift: Elisabeth Ball.

The standard reference books give no clue to the character or extent of S. Hood's involvement in publishing, and it seems likely that he was a front man for "the editor" of *Nanny Goose*, whose story was destined for an aristocratic circle. (Judith St. John notes in her afterword to a facsimile of *Nanny Goose* that the dedicatee's husband was to become eighth Duke of St. Albans in 1816.) Nevertheless, the story has a touch of "the folk" about it, being not only the first known edition of the tale that eventually turned into the "The Three Little Pigs" but also a pleasantly unpretentious account with amateurish pictures to match.

The same cannot be said for the later, also aristocratic, reworking, published by the obscure firm of H. Fores. *Prince Renardo* uses much of the material in the earlier book but gives it an unnecessary fireside setting and overelaborates the plain storytelling of its source. (Judith St. John notes that a versified retelling of the story, "The Fox and the Geese," appeared in *The Treasury of Pleasure Books*, published by Grant & Griffith in 1850, while the first known appearance of "The Three Little Pigs" was in James Orchard Halliwell's *Nursery Rhymes of England* [fifth edition, 1853]).

◄§ 263 §►

Rev. WILLIAM LISLE BOWLES (1762–1850). *The Little Villager's Verse Book; consisting of short verses for children to learn by heart; in which the most familiar images of country life, are applied to excite the first feelings of humanity and piety. Seventh edition, ornamented with thirty engravings on wood.* London: Longman, Rees, Orme, Brown, and Green, [1829 or 1830]. 4° (170 × 110 mm.).

[1–2¹⁰ (1/5,6 and 2/5,6 disjunct; these innermost half-sheets of the two quires were originally worked together, but misimposed: 1/5,2/6 and 1/6,2/5 had to be separated before binding)] (1/1 and

Above: **262a**. plate [3], *enlarged*   *Below*: **262b**. A7 recto, *enlarged*

2/10 mounted as pastedowns, 1/1ᵛ frontispiece *The Villager's Cottage*, 1/2ʳ title, 1/3ʳ *Preface*, 1/4ʳ *Index*, 1/5r *Path of Life*, incipit: *Oh Lord—in sickness and in health*, 2/9ᵛ imprint *Allbut, Printer, Devizes*, 2/10 blank). Pp. 38, [2]. Paper with 1828 watermark-date. 33 wood engravings including frontispiece. Original gray boards, red spine, title, impression of frontispiece cut and *Price one shilling* on front cover, ad and review quotes dated Aug.–Sep. 1829 on back cover.

Provenance: Gumuchian & Cⁱᵉ (1930 cat., no. 894). PML 83534. Gift: Elisabeth Ball.

William Lisle Bowles, a brief but powerful influence on the young Coleridge, spent much of his long life as vicar of Bremhill in Wiltshire. These simple, not to say simpleminded, lyrics were written for "the Poor Children of my own Parish," whom Mrs. Bowles instructed, idyllically, "on the Garden Lawn before the Parsonage House." The verses were apparently first issued privately, and this seventh edition was printed by a local man (using stock blocks?), even though it had now gained a London publisher. F. C. Morgan's catalogue of his 1911 exhibition at Malvern records at no. 119 a later printing which sees the book returning to a "private" capacity: "London: The Proprietor, 14 Dalston Rise, 1837."

๏ 264 ๏

[Lady DELAMERE of Vale Royal]. *Life and Adventures of Mʳ Pig and Miss Crane. A nursery tale. Embellished with designs.* [Chester: privately printed for a town bazaar, by Thomas and William Crane, Newgate Street, not before 1832 (watermark-date)]. Oblong 4°? (157 × 200 mm.).

25 disjunct leaves printed on one side, stabbed to form a codex (1ʳ title, 2ᵛ incipit: *Young Master Pig you here may see*, 3ʳ illustration, 24ᵛ *Moral*, incipit: *Behold the crisis of our awful story*, 25ʳ illustration). Lithographed throughout: title and 12 full-page illustrations on rectos (the first signed with monogram VR), and 12 leaves with four-line rhymes on versos (ten lines on the last). Illustrations printed on a different paper stock from the text, and with tissue guards. Original buff wrappers, pink paper spine, lithographic title repeated on front cover. Reference: Crane, p. 3; Spencer, p. 11.

Provenance: M.G. Cotes (early sign.); unidentified leather bookplate. PML 84816. Purchase: Julia P. Wightman.

Walter Crane's father, Thomas, and uncles William, John, and Philip ran a private lithographic press in Chester from ca. 1829 to ca. 1839, mostly reproducing Thomas's portraits of the nobility (including the late duke of Westminster) and the famous (the violinist Paganini); their efforts included at least three productions in book form. Lady Delamere's verses with Thomas Crane's designs are an early example of the illustrated private fancies which the Victorians so much enjoyed. The book is not listed in the general catalogue in Michael Twyman's *Early Lithographed Books* (London, 1990).

264. fo. 25 recto, *reduced*

A DISTINCTION must be drawn between the earlier popular books that are treated in Chapter III and those displayed here. The former were mostly published to be sold wholesale among "the company of running stationers," who then hawked them direct to the public. The market was probably reckoned to be a fairly undifferentiated mass of readers who liked the unsophisticated fare that was the stock-in-trade of the chapmen.

By the early nineteenth century, however, the chap-trade was on the wane. With the growth of children's books as a specialist field of publishing, there was scope for printers and booksellers working in a large catchment area to develop their own line in cheap books without having to rely on the traditional centers of chapbook publishing. Traditional texts—alphabet rhymes, riddle books, nursery rhymes, fairy tales—were coming to the fore in abundance, so as long as there was a sufficiency of none-too-discriminating demand there would be no difficulty over supply. "Chapbook" is still useful as a generic term for these "penny histories," but the attention that publishers were now giving to their physical production—with neat and often bespoke wood engravings and with covers in colored sugar-paper or brushed with a colored wash—shows greater sophistication in technique and suggests, perhaps, growing sales through the established retail trade.

The Morgan Library possesses a large and varied stock of these nineteenth-century chapbooks as well as many examples of equivalent productions from the United States. In making our selection we have tried to include at least one typical example from every English publisher represented in the collection, thus demonstrating the number of provincial printers who were involved in this kind of small-time trade. (Other printers put in an appearance in the section devoted to battledores, chapter XIX.)

The entries are arranged in alphabetical order according to place of publication, but with London coming first. Almost all of these little books are undated but most belong within the first forty years of the nineteenth century. All were printed on unwatermarked wove paper, except some Scottish productions. From about 1834 onwards, the development of a national transport system and the growing power of London as a publishing center would put an end to many local enterprises of this kind.

LONDON: T. & J. ALLMAN

◄§ 265 §►

The Knife-Grinder's Budget of Pictures & Poetry, for boys and girls. London: printed for T. and J. Allman, 1829. 32°? (87 × 55 mm.).

[1¹⁴] (1·14 mounted as pastedowns, 1ᵛ *Frontispiece*, 2ʳ title, 3ʳ incipit: *"Come buy my fine Apples,"* 14ʳ imprint *W. Walker, Printer,*

Otley). Pp. 27, [1]. 24 wood engravings (frontispiece full-page, remainder half-page). Original printed yellow wrappers, wood engravings, rhymes and *Price one penny* on both covers. Reference: Osborne II, 646.

PML 80192. Gift: Elisabeth Ball.

Thomas and Joseph Allman began trading during the teens of the nineteenth century. As publishers they made a specialty of safe, insipid books, a prudent policy that kept them in business for almost a hundred fifty years. They were not significant as chapbook publishers, and *The Knife-Grinder's Budget* suggests, in its title if nowhere else, a degree of sharpness rarely equaled by their later productions. (Indeed, the book probably originated with Walker of Otley, since copies are known with his sole imprint.)

265. enlarged

L said conversation would
be quite the belle,
Provided the company
thought it as well.

In talking and joking he
seem'd in his glory,
And proposed to tell them
a comical story.

M prais'd the mutton, 'twas
done quite the thing,
So vastly well dress'd, 'twas
fit for a king,

The chickens how tender,
as he was a sinner,
He'd doubts if the King ever
had such a dinner.

266. A8ᵛ–9ʳ,
enlarged

LONDON: J. BAILEY

~§ 266 §~

The New Rhyming Alphabet, or the invitation of A to all the letters. London: Printed and Sold by J. Bailey, 116, Chancery Lane, [ca. 1815]. Price Two-pence. Half-sheet 32° (97 × 63 mm.).

A¹⁶ (1·16 mounted as pastedowns, 1ᵛ *Frontispiece*, 2ʳ title, 3ʳ incipit: *Great A, on a time, quite happy and free*, 16 blank). Pp. 30, [2]. Relief-cut frontispiece of two crossed keys, signed R, captioned *A Bishop's Armorial Bearings*, 26 half-page woodcut or metalcut capital letters of the alphabet, each with elaborate floral ornament. Original printed pink wrappers, title and cut within border on front cover, ads on back cover.

PML 80371. Gift: Elisabeth Ball.

We do not know if there is any connection between the Baileys who were printing in the Bishopsgate area (and who fostered the early efforts of Dean & Munday) and the Baileys farther west in Chancery Lane. They appear to have come from East Smithfield, where John Bailey had a press in 1799, moving eventually to 116 Chancery Lane in 1808. Here he continued until ca. 1824, when the business passed to Joseph Bailey (his son?), who continued it at various addresses until the 1840s. Bailey produced a quantity of chapbooks, of which this *New Rhyming Alphabet* is notable for putting to "educational" use a striking set of decorative initials.

LONDON: J. CARVALHO, S. CARVALHO

~§ 267a §~

[CHARLES PERRAULT (1628–1703) and/or PIERRE PERRAULT DARMANCOUR (1678–1700)]. *The Curious Adventures of the Beautiful Little Maid Cinderella, or the history of a glass slipper.* London: Printed for J. Carvalho, Hennage Lane, Leadenhall-Street, by J. Baker, Bristol, [ca. 1815]. Price One Penny. Quarter-sheet 32° (95 × 56/62 mm.).

[1⁸] (1ʳ blank, 1ᵛ frontispiece and rhyme, incipit: *Here Cinderella, you may see*, 2ʳ title, 8ʳ imprint *John Baker, Printer, Bristol*). Pp. [5–]19, [1]. Seven wood engravings (see overleaf). Original pictorial blue-gray wrappers, two biblical cuts on each cover.

PML 80386. Gift: Elisabeth Ball.

~§ 267b §~

[CHARLES PERRAULT (1628–1703) and/or PIERRE PERRAULT DARMANCOUR (1678–1700)]. *The Fairy Tale of Cinderella and her Glass Slippers.* London: Printed by S. Carvalho, 8, Corner of Craven Street, City Road, [ca. 1825]. Quarter-sheet 32° (97 × 60 mm.).

[1⁸] (1·8 mounted as pastedowns, 1ᵛ *Frontispiece*, 2ʳ title, 2ᵛ

267a. 7ᵛ, *enlarged*

267b. 3ᵛ, *detail*

blank). Pp. [16]. Eight wood engravings. Original printed buff wrappers, title and price *One Penny* on front cover, wood engravings on both covers.

PML 80387. Gift: Elisabeth Ball.

The reticent Carvalhos have already been discussed (see chapter XI), and only through these chapbooks can we gauge the possibility that J. Carvalho was the founder of the business (might he have come from Bristol?). No connecting link can be made to S. Carvalho through *Cinderella*, however, since the two chapbook editions described here are unrelated.

LONDON: DEAN & MUNDAY

⮜ 268a ⮞

[CHARLES PERRAULT (1628–1703) and/or PIERRE PERRAULT DARMANCOUR (1678–1700)]. *Puss in Boots: or, the miller's fortunate son.* London: printed and sold by Dean & Munday, Threadneedle-street, [ca. 1825]. Price One Penny. Quarter-sheet 32° (102 × 60 mm.).

[1⁸] (1·8 mounted as pastedowns, 1ᵛ *Frontispiece. The Marquis of Carabas and the Princess dancing,* 2ʳ title, 2ᵛ blank, 8ʳ imprint *Dean & Munday, Printers, Threadneedle-street*). Pp. 15, [1]. 7 wood engravings including frontispiece and title-vignette. Original printed gray wrappers, series *No.] [15.* and title on front cover, ads on back cover, wood engravings on both.

PML 81241. Gift: Elisabeth Ball.

⮜ 268b ⮞

[ARABIAN NIGHTS]. *The History of Abou Cassim, and his Unfortunate Slippers, or avarice punished.* London: Printed and sold by Dean and Munday, Threadneedle-street, [ca. 1830]. Price Twopence. Half-sheet 32° (101 × 62 mm.).

A¹⁶ (1·16 mounted as pastedowns, 1ᵛ *Frontispiece,* 2ʳ title, 2ᵛ *Explanation of the frontispiece,* 3ʳ *Abou Cassim's Pantoufles,* 13ʳ *The Jugglers.* Pp. 31, [1]. 10 full-page wood engravings (including frontispiece) to *Abou Cassim,* 5 smaller cuts illustrating *The Jugglers.* Original printed yellow wrappers.

PML 81231. Gift: Elisabeth Ball.

⮜ 268c ⮞

[CHARLES PERRAULT (1628–1703) and/or PIERRE PERRAULT DARMANCOUR (1678–1700)]. *The History of Blue Beard.* London: published by Dean and Munday, Threadneedle-street, [ca. 1835]. Half-sheet 16° (104 × 84 mm.).

[1⁸] (1·8 mounted as pastedowns, 1ᵛ frontispiece *Blue Beard,* 2ʳ title, 2ᵛ blank, 8ʳ imprint *Dean and Munday, Printers, Threadneedle-street*). Pp. 15, [1]. 8 wood engravings of various sizes, including frontispiece and title-vignette. Original printed gray wrappers, title, wood engraving, and series *No.] [24.* on front cover, ads on back cover.

PML 81233. Gift: Elisabeth Ball.

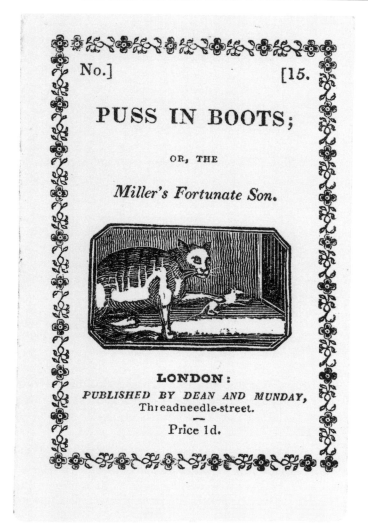

268a. enlarged

27

figure or letter throughout the alphabet, and usualy concluded with the figure of 7.

We would recommend to our little readers who are not so fond of their books as they ought to be, to study these figures with attention, and by endeavouring to form something like the letters, they may be inculcated on their memories, it would certainly help them, and if the dunce will not

Above: **268b.** A14ʳ, *enlarged*   *Below*: **268c.** frontispiece

Dean & Munday have also been noticed above (chapter XII), and these three undated chapbooks may well represent late editions of the firm's earliest efforts to generate turnover in their publishing business. From the series numbering it is clear that they are part of a concerted program of chapbook reprints of popular texts, but each example here shows a variation in style of production.

LONDON: JAMES WALLIS

⊸§ 269 §⊶

Wallis's Juvenile Tales. The Talisman of Truth; a tale. London: Printed and Published by James Wallis, 77, Berwick Street, Soho, [ca. 1812]. 36° (84 × 67 mm.).

C⁶ (1ʳ drop-title), worked together with five other separately issued and bound tales in the series, including *The Shepherdess* (quire B) and *The Good Shepherd* (quire F). Pp. 12. 4 wood engravings, one or more perhaps after George Cruikshank. Original rust wrappers, title (as above) on front cover, ad on back cover. Reference: cf. Cohn 826.

BLUE BEARD.

Provenance: Albert M. Cohn (armorial booklabel); Sherman Post Haight and Anne Lyon Haight (bookplates). PML 81088. Gift: Mrs. Sherman P. Haight.

There seems to be no connection between James Wallis and the other publishing Wallises, nor is it altogether clear if our James Wallis of Berwick Street is the same James as the one recorded by Maxted, who, working from Paternoster Row, was twice bankrupt (in 1801 and 1805). If so, he certainly seems to have done better in Berwick Street, where Brown records dates of 1812 and 1825 and where, according to Cohn, he got the young George Cruikshank to design illustrations for his chapbook series *Wallis's Juvenile Tales*. In his catalogue raisonné of Cruikshank (1924), Cohn listed fifteen titles in the Wallis series, omitting the three tales which he was to acquire later for his own collection and which are now in the Morgan Library.

ALNWICK: W. DAVISON

Born in Newcastle-upon-Tyne, William Davison (1780–1858) was apprenticed there to a chemist, probably in 1794. On completing his time, he set up shop in Alnwick in 1802 as "chemist and druggist," but also had an interest in printing. This led him to an association with John Catnach (1769–1813; father of the Seven Dials ballad-monger, Jemmy Catnach), and they produced several books together around 1807, a year before Catnach moved on to Newcastle. After 1808 Davison developed his own printing business alongside the pharmacy, and he published a number of substantial books as well as quantities of primers, alphabets and "children's books in great variety." He did a considerable business in stereotyping, and many of his children's chapbooks, which ranged from eight-page halfpenny books to thirty-six-page two-penny books, were printed from stereo plates. Davison's reputation as an energetic businessman has been enhanced through an assumed connection with Thomas Bewick who was thought to have produced many wood engravings for his use. The assumption is erroneous, however, and it is likely that most of Davison's chapbook cuts "by Bewick" were done by a local copyist. (See Peter Isaac's introduction to the facsimile of Davison's *New Specimen of Cast-Metal Ornaments* published by the Printing Historical Society in 1990.)

⊷ 270 ⊶

Tom Thumb's Play-Book; to teach children their letters, by a new and pleasant method. New and improved edition. Ornamented with pictures. Alnwick: stereotyped and printed by W. Davison, 22, Bondgate street, [ca. 1830]. Price twopence. 18° (141 × 87 mm.).

[1¹⁸] (1·18 mounted as pastedown, 1ᵛ Roman capitals, 2ʳ title, 2ᵛ Roman small letters, 4ᵛ Syllables of Two Letters. Lesson I, 16ʳ The cat and the dog, 18ʳ The Lord's Prayer, imprint Printed by W. Davison, Alnwick.) Pp. 35, [1]. 26 wood engravings (inner and outer formes sharing only one block), some after Thomas Bewick. Original printed pink wrappers, title, border and wood engraving of a dog on front cover, ads on back cover. Reference: Peter Isaac, *William Davison of Alnwick, pharmacist and printer* (Oxford, 1968), pp. 24 and 28–9.

PML 86948. Gift: Julia P. Wightman

One of Davison's primers, using a number of stereotyped pictorial blocks, after Bewick. The Morgan Library also has a good representation of Davison's extensive line in battledores.

BANBURY: J. G. RUSHER

⊷ 271a ⊶

Jack the Giant Killer, a hero celebrated by ancient historians. Banbury: printed by J. G. Rusher, [ca. 1820]. 32°? (86 × 58 mm.).

[1⁸] (1ʳ title, 1ᵛ incipit: *Kind Reader, Jack makes you a bow*, 8ᵛ full-page illustration). Pp. 15, [1]. Six half-page wood engravings (one in two impressions); one full-page wood engraving, perhaps by John Lee after William Marshall Craig. Stitched, as issued. References: De Freitas p. 111; Osborne I, 33; Johnson 90 & p. 49; Hockliffe 22.

PML 83811. Gift: Elisabeth Ball.

⊷ 271b ⊶

The History of a Banbury Cake; an entertaining book for children. Banbury: Printed and Sold by J. G. Rusher, Bridge-Street, [ca. 1830]. Price One Penny. Half-sheet 16° (115 × 69 mm.).

[1⁸] (1ʳ blank, 1ᵛ frontispiece *The Banbury Cake travelling to Bristol with miss Nancy, and master Tommy*, 2ʳ title, 2ᵛ Preface, 8ʳ imprint *Printed by J G Rusher, Banbury*, 8ᵛ blank). Pp. 15, [1]. 4 wood engravings. Original printed blue-gray wrappers, title and wood-engraved vignette on front cover, 2 oval wood engravings *The Tiger* and *The Greyhound* on back cover, ads inside both covers, unopened and edges uncut. Reference: De Freitas p. 109; Morgan 4.

PML 83823. Gift: Elisabeth Ball.

> At Rusher's fam'd Warehouse
> Books, Pictures and Toys
> Are selling to please
> The good girls and boys.

This early publicity jingle celebrates a firm of considerable note in the south midlands. Its founding father appears to be William Rusher, hatter, bookseller and stationer, with offices at Banbury, Oxford and Reading; all of these towns supply evidence of members of the Rusher family being active in civic or commercial affairs. Banbury, though, was where the famed warehouse was to be found and where printing, as opposed to bookselling, was carried out. (In 1802 Philip Rusher had even lodged a patent for a new form of printing type "to diminish the trouble and expence of printing, and to render it much more uniform and beautiful." The British Library has a copy of *Rasselas* so printed.)

The firm's exploitation of conventionally printed chapbooks was the work not of Philip but of John Golby Rusher. Probably during the late teens and the 1820s, he put out the two series that constitute the main body of Rusher chapbooks: the sixteen-page, self-covered series selling at 1d (often found folded but unopened), and the sixteen-page series in sugar-paper covers, also at 1d. The Morgan Library has nearly complete sets of these not

271a. fo. 8 verso, *enlarged*

272. front cover, *enlarged*

uncommon chapbooks, and we show here one specimen from each series. *The History of a Banbury Cake* also demonstrates Rusher's deft use of his town's name and traditional associations in marketing his popular wares. This even gave rise to Edwin Pearson's early and highly unreliable study of "nursery toy book literature" being given the title *Banbury Chap Books* (London: Arthur Reader, 1890).

BIRMINGHAM: T. BRANDARD

272

[CHARLES PERRAULT (1628–1703) and/or PIERRE PERRAULT DARMANCOUR (1678–1700)]. *Diamonds and Toads or Humility Rewarded, and pride punished. Adorned with cuts.* Birmingham: Printed by T. Brandard, [ca. 1815]. Price One Penny. Quarter-sheet 32° (99 × 57/58 mm.).

[1⁸] (1·8 mounted as pastedowns, 1ᵛ *Frontispiece*,5 2ʳ title, 7ᵛ imprint *T. Brandard, Printer*, 8 blank). Pp. 14, [2]. 5 wood engravings (the first 2 making up the frontispiece). Original gray wrappers, wood engraving on front cover *Rope Dancing*, 2 smaller cuts within type-ornament border on back cover *Queen and Horses*. References: Osborne II, 596; Morgan 21.

PML 80373. Gift: Elisabeth Ball.

The rise of Birmingham to become England's second largest town came with the development of the industrial revolution during the second half of the eighteenth century (a period that coincided with the printing activity there of the great John Baskerville). As a result, a large trade in popular books, chapbooks, and tracts was engendered, and T. Brandard was one of perhaps a dozen local printers who went in for such work. This penny edition of Perrault's *Diamonds and Toads* follows the customary chapbook text of the story and employs the gimmick, commonly used by chapbook publishers, of placing a stirring illustration on the upper cover regardless of any question of relevance to the contents.

CHELMSFORD: I. MARSDEN

273

The Good Child's Reward: in a scriptural alphabet of verses, for children; and a Christian anthem. Chelmsford: Printed and Sold by I. Marsden, [ca. 1815]. Price two-pence. Half-sheet 12°? (127 × 69 mm.).

273. frontispiece, *enlarged*

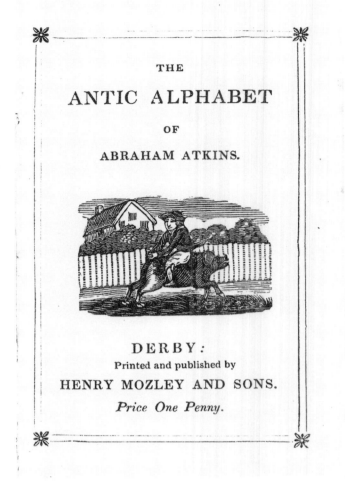

274b. fo. 2 recto, *enlarged*

[1¹²] (1·12 mounted as pastedowns, 1ᵛ frontispiece, 2ʳ title, 3ʳ *Alphabetical Verses*, incipit: *A, my dear, stands for angels*, 10ʳ *Christmas anthem*, incipit: *This is the day that Christ the Lord*, 12ʳ imprint *Marsden, Printer, Chelmsford*). Pp. 23, [1]. 24 small alphabet-cuts making up the frontispiece, 27 wood engravings (26 relating to the verse, the last a tailpiece). Original printed blue-green wrappers, title on front cover, wood engraving of a school scene on back cover. References: Osborne II, 680; Morgan 28.

PML 80822. Gift: Elisabeth Ball.

Like some other chapbook printers (see Rusher, Kendrew, Keys, et al.) Marsden devised a simple formula for the production of his wares and then fitted a series of chosen texts into the standard format: duodecimos in sugar-paper covers. At twopence a time, though, his little books may have faced competition from the more common halfpenny and penny series, and copies of some titles (e.g. *Abou Cassim*) are often found in unread condition. *The Good Child's Reward*, with its handsome alphabet, shows Marsden at his best.

DERBY: H. MOZLEY AND SONS

❧ 274a ☙

[JEANNE-MARIE LE PRINCE DE BEAUMONT (1711–80)]. *The History of Beauty and the Beast.* Derby: printed and published by Henry Mozley and Sons, [ca. 1825]. Price One Penny. Half-sheet 16° (131 × 81 mm.).

[1⁸] (1·8 mounted as pastedowns, 1ᵛ frontispiece, 2ʳ text, 8ʳ imprint *Henry Mozley and Sons, Printers, Derby*). Pp. 15, [1]. 5 wood engravings including frontispiece. Original printed yellow wrappers, numbered *14.*], title (as transcribed above) and a repeat of the cut from 5ᵛ on front cover, wood engraving illustrating 8-line verse *Morning Admonition* on back cover.

PML 84970. Gift: Elisabeth Ball.

❧ 274b ☙

The Antic Alphabet of Abraham Atkins. Derby: Printed and published by Henry Mozley and Sons, [ca. 1830]. Price One Penny. Half-sheet 24° (101 × 64 mm.).

"The master-cat, who went still
on before, met with some reapers,
and said to them, 'Good people,
you who are reaping, if you do not
tell the King, that all this corn belongs to the Marquis of Carabas,
you shall be chopped as small as
herbs for the pot."

See Page 18.

275a. frontispiece, *enlarged*

WAGON LOAD OF GOLD.

Here's a library of books,
In which you take pleasure,
'Tis far better than gold,
Or all other treasure.

275b. fo. 2 recto, *enlarged*

[1¹²] (1·12 mounted as pastedowns, 1ᵛ frontispiece, 2ʳ title, 3ʳ incipit: *Abraham Atkins wrote an Alphabet*, 12ʳ imprint *H. Mozley and Sons, Printers, Derby*). Pp. 23, [1]. 14 wood engravings. Original printed green wrappers, numbered 5.] and titled *Antic Alphabet* on both covers, wood engraving of a *Shipwreck* and four-line rhyme on front cover, *The Liar* on back cover.

PML 83943. Gift: Elisabeth Ball.

In 1815 the Mozleys of Gainsborough (see chapter VIII) moved to Derby, where there was clearly more scope for their not incon-siderable energies. Henry Mozley, son of the founder John, was head of the firm at this stage, and J.S. English estimates that he employed more than thirty-five people, a very large number for a provincial establishment (*Factotum* Occasional Paper 3, p. 21). Production of "nineteenth-century style" chapbooks was a natural field of activity for the firm and we show nos. 5 and 14 from two different penny-book series. In about 1845 the Mozleys also opened a London office, by which time High Church preoccu-pations had taken over and chapbook publishing turned to tract publishing (see chapter XIV).

DERBY: T. RICHARDSON

◄§ 275a ℈►

[CHARLES PERRAULT (1628–1703) and/or PIERRE PERRAULT DARMANCOUR] (1678–1700)]. *The History of Puss in Boots.* Derby: Printed by and for Thomas Richardson, Friar Gate, [ca. 1825]. 32°? (100 × 62 mm.).

[1¹⁴] (1·14 mounted as pastedowns, 1ᵛ frontispiece, 2ʳ title). Pp. 27, [1]. 10 wood engravings including title-vignette. Original printed yellow wrappers, title, wood-engraved vignette and *Price one penny* on front wrapper, ad for Richardson's one-penny children's book series and for *An excellent Assortment of halfpenny Books and Lotteries* on back cover. Reference: Osborne I, 41.

PML 80235. Gift: Elisabeth Ball.

Another version of the same fairy tale appeared in *Richardson's Library of Amusement.*

⋙ 275b ⋘

Wagon Load of Gold. Derby: printed by T. Richardson, [ca. 1830]. Price one halfpenny. 48°? (80/87 × 44/51 mm.).

[1⁶] (1ʳ title, 1ᵛ incipit: *Here's a fine golden watch*). Pp. 11, [1]. 12 wood engravings, each (except title-cut) with four-line rhyme (see previous page). Stitched, 1ʳ·6ᵛ dyed yellow, as issued, to resemble wrappers, edges unevenly trimmed.

PML 80257. Gift: Elisabeth Ball.

⋙ 275c ⋘

Butterfly's Ball. Derby: Printed by Thomas Richardson, [ca. 1830]. 48°? (87 × 51 mm.).

[1⁶] (1ʳ drop-title, incipit: *The trumpeter Gad-fly / Has summoned the crew*, 6ᵛ imprint [as above]). Pp. 11, [1]. 12 half-page wood engravings, each with four-line rhyme. Stitched, 1ʳ·6ᵛ dyed yellow, as issued, to resemble wrappers.

PML 80225. Gift: Elisabeth Ball.

This is not Roscoe's verse, and is also different from the Otley recension (see entry 283b.).

⋙ 275d ⋘

The Renowned History of the Seven Champions of Christendom. With a coloured engraving. Derby: Thomas Richardson, Robert Sears and Co., 53, Paternoster-Row, London, [ca. 1835]. Half-sheet 12° (138 × 88 mm.).

A⁶ (1ʳ title, 6ᵛ imprint *Printed by Thomas Richardson, Derby*); frontispiece of 2 wood engravings in publisher's coloring. Pp. 12. Original green wrappers, letterpress title and *Price Two-pence* on front wrapper, ad for *Richardson's Library of Amusement* on back cover. Reference: Osborne I, 14.

PML 80214. Gift: Elisabeth Ball.

Thomas Richardson was a prolific publisher of chapbooks and popular literature. Born in 1797, he was apprenticed to the Mozleys and moved with them to Derby in 1815. According to Appendix III of the catalogue of the Osborne Collection, he married a Miss Handford in 1818 and thereupon took over the printing and bookselling business of one Marriott, initially running it as Richardson & Handford and then trading simply under his own name. He published a great variety of cheap reading matter and children's books ("Library of Amusement"), often with well executed hand-colored illustrations. We display here a cross section of examples (he also specialized in battledores, cf. PML 83338–45).

Like his former employers, Richardson also became involved in religious publishing, but as a notable supporter of the Roman Catholic cause. About 1837 he opened an office in London at 21 Great Russell Street, as well as one in Dublin. His son succeeded him in business, and he died in 1875. The business closed in 1888.

276a. back cover, *enlarged*

DEVONPORT: S. & J. KEYS

⋙ 276a ⋘

The History of Tom Thumb. "My name is Tom Thumb, From the fairies I've come . . . Devonport: printed by S. & J. Keys, [ca. 1840]. Quarter-sheet 24°? (96 × 57 mm.).

[1⁶] (1·6 mounted as pastedowns, 1ᵛ incipit: *In good king Arthur's happy reign*). Pp. 11, [1]. 10 wood engravings. Original light gray wrappers, title and imprint divided over both covers with 2 wood engravings and typographical borders.

PML 83873. Gift: Elisabeth Ball.

⋙ 276b ⋘

Tom the Piper's Son, with all the fun that he has done. Devonport: printed by and for Samuel and John Keys, [ca. 1840]. Quarter-sheet 24°? (104 × 61 mm.).

[1⁶] (1·6 mounted as pastedowns, 1ᵛ incipit: *Tom, Tom, the Piper's Son*). Pp. 11, [1]. 10 wood engravings. Original yellow wrappers,

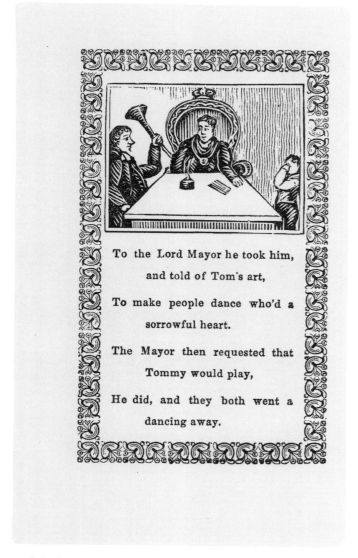

276b. back cover, *enlarged*

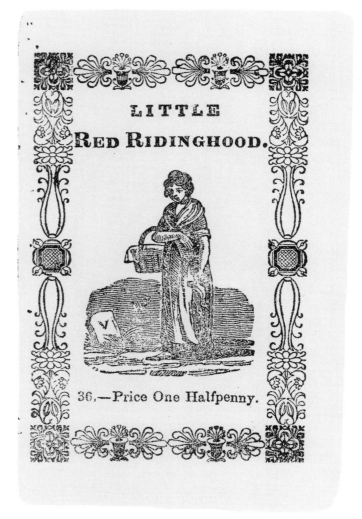

277. fo. 1 recto, *enlarged*

title and wood engraving within type-ornament border on front cover, wood engraving and the last four verses (within the same border) on back cover. Reference: Morgan 52.

PML 83861. Gift: Elisabeth Ball.

Samuel and John Keys were the sons of the Devonport printer and stationer Elias Keys, who emerges as a publisher only in 1829 and continued to run his business with his sons as partners until 1873. It appears that the Keys series of well over two dozen chapbooks may have formed a separate list within the family firm's output, as their imprints consistently omit mention of the father's name.

DUNFERMLINE: J. MILLER AND SON

⌐§ 277 §⌐

Little Red Ridinghood. Dunfermline: J. Miller and Son, Booksellers, [ca. 1825]. Price One Halfpenny. Quarter-sheet 24° (98 × 60 mm.).

[1⁶] (1ʳ title, number *36.* and price within floral border, 2ᵛ text, 6ᵛ

border, alphabet, and imprint as above). Pp. 11, [1]. Paper dyed yellow throughout. 12 wood engravings of various sizes, not all relating to the story. Stitched as issued.

PML 80938. Gift: Elisabeth Ball.

Scotland was a mighty producer of chapbooks, many of which ("printed for the booksellers") were for adults rather than for children. This single halfpenny example of a children's chapbook must stand, with the Lumsden items in chapter XII and with the Caw & Elder, Paterson, Ross, and Lumsden items that follow in this chapter (entries 278–82), as a small representation of a huge industry that deserves study on a far larger scale than can be accorded here.

EDINBURGH, see entry 280 and after Glasgow

GLASGOW: LUMSDEN AND SON

Lumsden has been discussed as a publisher of children's books (chapter XI), and one book (entry 212) has already been shown as an early example of the twopenny booklets that we include below as "chapbooks." (In fact, as Roscoe points out, Lumsden did a separate trade in "chapbooks proper," briefly summarized as "stupidity and dirt," which are not related to the children's book business at all.)

PETER PUZZLECAP, Esq.

278. fo. 7 verso, *enlarged*

279. engraving opposite 5ʳ, *enlarged*

We also note with the Lumsden items a *Gulliver* from G. Ross at Edinburgh, who is inextricably tangled with Lumsden. The little book corresponds to an edition "published by J. Lumsden & Son, 1815" (PML 80922; Roscoe 45) and is presumably one of those pieces initiated by Ross as printer and then issued in association with Lumsden.

◦§ 278 §◦

Gammer Gurton's Garland of Nursery Songs, and Toby Tickle's collection of riddles. Compiled by Peter Puzzlecap, Esq. Embellished with a variety of cuts. Glasgow: Published and Sold Wholesale, by Lumsden and Son, [ca. 1820]. [Price Twopence]. Half-sheet 32° (99 × 61 mm.).

[1¹⁶] signed A^8 < B^8 (1ʳ title, 1ᵛ *Gammer Gurton's advice to all good children*, 2ʳ incipit: *Cock-a-Doodle-Do*, 13ᵛ *Story of Little Scug the squirrel*). Pp. 32. 26 wood engravings. Original wrappers with wood-engraved caricatures, front cover: *I feel your pulse & take your fee / To die you'r then at liberty*, back cover: *This worthy Magistrate they say / Takes his three gall^{ns} every day*, bookseller's

inscribed identification on front cover *Gammer Gurton*. Reference: Roscoe & Brimmell 17.

PML 80931. Gift: Elisabeth Ball.

The Morgan Library has four copies with variant covers of this popular rhyme-and-riddle book. Many of the pretty little wood engravings in their oval frames are inspired by Bewick designs. The covers of this copy employ two satirical pictures that have nothing to do with the book's contents.

◦§ 279 §◦

ISAAC WATTS (1674–1748). *Watts' Divine Songs, in easy language, for the use of children.* Glasgow: published by Lumsden & Son, [ca. 1815]. Price Twopence. Half-sheet 32° (99 × 61 mm.).

A^{16} [1·16 mounted as pastedowns, 1ᵛ title and wood-engraved vignette, 2ʳ *A General Song of Praise to God*, incipit: *How glorious is our heavenly King*); 14 illustrations printed in red from a single engraved copperplate on one side of a quarter-sheet, divided into

280. back cover, *enlarged*

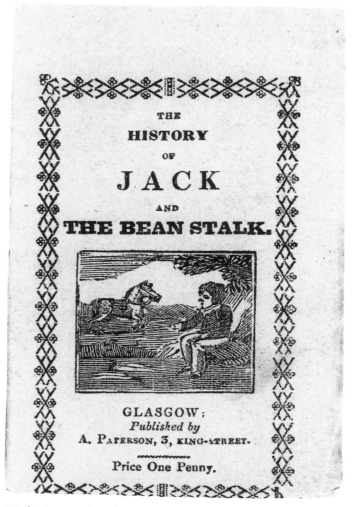

281. front cover, *enlarged*

four bifolia for insertion around A2·15, A4·13, A6·11 and A8·9. Pp. 47, [1]. Laid paper, fleur-de-lys watermark. Original plain gray wrappers. Reference: Roscoe & Brimmell 39.

PML 80934. Gift: Elisabeth Ball.

This chapbook fairly closely follows the style of the *New Testament* (entry 212). The simple engravings are given the appearance of woodcuts, but their framing and the red printing bring a touch of class to the production. In true chapbook style the oval wood engraving on the title page also does duty for "Rules for Daily Practice" in *Gammer Gurton* (entry 278).

❧ 280 ❧

Adventures of Captain Gulliver, in a voyage to Lilliput. Edinburgh: Printed and published by G. Ross, [1815]. Half-sheet and quarter-sheet 32° (96 × 58 mm.).

*A*⁸ B–C⁸ (A1 and C8 mounted as pastedowns, A1ᵛ frontispiece *Captain Gulliver*, A2ʳ title). Pp. 47, [1]. Laid paper (quires A–B) and wove (quire C). 13 wood engravings, including frontispiece (full-page) and 12 oval illustrations in rectangular frames (45 ×

34 mm.). Original printed blue-gray wrappers, front cover with *Price Twopence* and series title *From Ross's Juvenile Library* within wood-engraved cartouche, and bookseller's inscribed identification *Gullivers Travels*, back cover with wood-engraved left profile *Spaniard*, which turned upside down becomes a right profile *John Bull*. Reference: Roscoe & Brimmell 45 (Lumsden issue).

PML 80869. Gift: Elisabeth Ball.

This is a complete Ross production—imprint, covers, and all. However, sheets were supplied to Lumsden for distribution under his own imprint, with the title and both formes of the last quire reset.

GLASGOW: A. PATERSON

❧ 281 ❧

The History of Jack and the Bean Stalk. Glasgow: Published by A. Paterson, 3, King-street, [ca. 1820]. Price One Penny. Quarter-sheet 32° (100 × 64 mm.).

[1⁸] (1ʳ drop-title). Pp. 16. 7 wood engravings (36 × 46 mm. each).

Gum. 1660

Riddle me, riddle me,
Riddle me ree,
None are so blind
As they that won't see.

282. frontispiece, *enlarged*

13

Here's prinny with gun,
Sword, and gorget so smart,
He's going to France,
To fight Buonaparte.

283a. fo. 7 recto, *enlarged*

Original gray wrappers, title (as above), wood engraving and type-ornament border on front cover, same title but different wood engraving and border on back cover, the cover cuts unrelated to the story. Reference: Gumuchian 1624.

PML 80115. Gift: Elisabeth Ball.

Paterson had no apparent business relations with Lumsden, and his production of *Jack and the Bean Stalk* seems more typical of chapbooks put out by the English provincial trade than those of his Glasgow neighbor. His text for the story follows the original prose version published by Tabart in 1807 (see entry 382) but with modifications, chiefly the removal of references to the woman-helper being a fairy.

EDINBURGH: CAW AND ELDER

282

Toby Tickle's Puzzle-Cap; or a new riddle book. Edinburgh: Printed and Sold Wholesale, By Caw and Elder, High Street,

1819. Price Twopence. Half-sheet 32°? (100 × 59 mm.).

[1–2⁸] (1/1 and 2/8 mounted as pastedowns, 1/1ᵛ frontispiece *Riddle me, riddle me . . .*, 1/2ʳ title, 1/2ᵛ dedication *To all good boys and girls throughout the British Empire*, 1/3ʳ *A wheel-barrow*, incipit: *My pretty Miss, a thing there is*, 2/8ʳ *The wonder, or riddle of riddles*, incipit: *I saw a man*). Pp. 30, [1]. Laid paper. 28 wood engravings. Original gray wrappers, front cover with series title *The Edinburgh Juvenile Library* within wood-engraved cartouche, back cover with wood-engraved left profile *Lady Hearty*, which turned upside down becomes a right profile *Aunt Dorothy*. Reference: Gumuchian 1660.

PML 80866. Gift: Elisabeth Ball.

The covers and frontispiece of this chapbook suggest a Lumsden influence, and "The Edinburgh Juvenile Library" was probably in competition with "Ross's Juvenile Library." The contents of the versified riddles (which are not riddles at all, since they are answered before they are asked) derive from such eighteenth-century compendia as *The Child's New Year's Gift*.

The next guest that came was a rich downy Moth,
Who fed all his life upon superfine cloth.
A pest to the wardrobe he'd long been, 'tis true;
My coat was ate by him soon after 't was new.

See Yonder 's the Dormouse, just crept from his hole;
He 's leading along his blind brother, the Mole.
The wonderful Dragon-fly also was there,
And numbers of insects which fly in the air.

THE BUTTERFLY'S BALL.

THE BUTTERFLY'S BALL.

8   THE BUTTERFLY'S BALL.

The Butterfly's Ball was held in
    July ;
The day, though so long, too soon
    was gone by :
And when it gave way to the
    shades of the night,
The Glowworm illumined them
    all with his light.

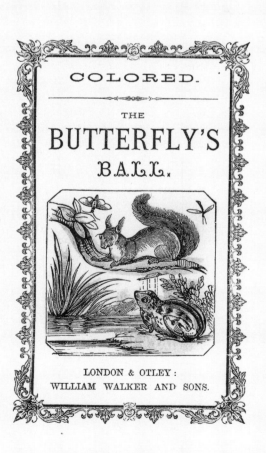

COLORED.

THE

BUTTERFLY'S

BALL.

LONDON & OTLEY :
WILLIAM WALKER AND SONS.

283b. outer forme, *reduced*

OTLEY: W. WALKER

❧ 283a ☙

The Diverting History of Jumping Joan, and her dog and cat. Adorned with fine woodcuts. Otley: Printed by W. Walker at the Wharfdale Stanhope Press, [ca. 1825]. Price one Penny. Quarter-sheet 32° (102 × 61 mm.).

[1⁸] (1·8 mounted as pastedowns, 1ᵛ *Frontispiece*, 2ʳ title, 2ᵛ incipit: *Joan had a dog, and Joan had a cat*). Pp. 15, [1]. Frontispiece and 14 smaller wood engravings (see previous page). Original rust wrappers, title *Jumping Joan. Price One Penny* on front cover, wood engravings within border on both covers.

PML 80176. Gift: Elisabeth Ball.

❧ 283b ☙

Colored. The Butterfly's Ball. London & Otley: William Walker and Sons, [ca. 1840]. Half-sheet 8° (171 × 106 mm.).

[1⁴] (1ʳ title and illustration within border, 1ᵛ incipit: *Come, Lucy, take hold of my hand, lest you fall*). Pp. 8. 8 wood engravings (60 mm. square), only the title-cut hand-colored. Folded and unopened, as issued (see previous page).

PML 81055. Gift: Mrs. Sherman P. Haight.

William Walker began printing in Otley ca. 1810 and established a business that has specialized in cheap wares for a popular market almost down to the present time. The two chapbooks described above show his "early style," when he was, with neatness and a care for design, working a vein from which many of his contemporaries also profited. Later, in Victorian times, Walker's published huge quantities of ephemeral booklets and tracts, and more recently they worked the bottom end of the market, supplying cheap children's papers, bumper books and annuals to such universal outlets as stationery shops, sub post offices, etc. Some idea of the size of their output in the twentieth century can be gained from Sotheby's sale catalogue for 7–8 June 1990, when Walker's modern archive was dispersed in a series of fifty-eight lots. Earlier material and the firm's records were destroyed in a fire.

YORK: R. BURDEKIN

❧ 284 ☙

A Present for Children. York: printed and sold by Richard Burdekin, 16, High-Ousegate, [ca. 1830]. Price One Halfpenny. 48°? (86 × 54 mm.).

[1⁶] (1ʳ title and vignette, 1ᵛ *A Constable*, 6ᵛ *A Cat and Bird* and imprint *R. Burdekin, Printer, York*). Pp. 12. 12 wood engravings and letterpress captions. Stitched, 1ʳ·6ᵛ dyed yellow, as issued, to resemble wrappers.

PML 80383. Gift: Elisabeth Ball.

Richard Burdekin was born in Mansfield, Nottinghamshire, in 1781 and apprenticed to a local bookseller. About 1805 he joined

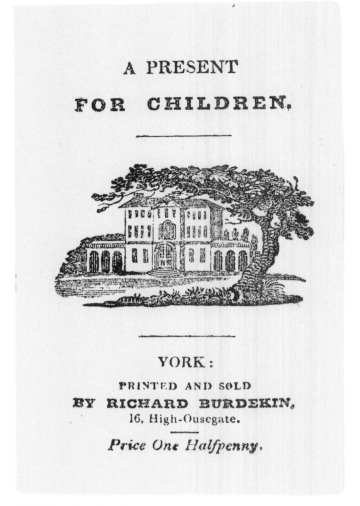

284. fo. 1 recto, *enlarged*

Wilson, Spence & Mawman in York as a bagman, or rider, traveling their printed goods and stationery through large parts of the country (his saddlebags are preserved at the Castle Museum in York). In 1813 he left Wilson's and set up a bookshop with Robert Spence, who retired in 1820, and two years later Burdekin established a printing office which, in one form or another, has continued to the present time. As with so many small printing shops during the 1820s and 1830s, Burdekin turned to small wares to augment his turnover, and the entirely pictorial *Present for Children* (with a seemingly arbitrary series of blocks illustrating animals, a school, and a hairdresser) is a nice example of his line in halfpenny books. Burdekin died in 1860, and the business has been handed down through the family from then onwards.

YORK: J. KENDREW

❧ 285a ☙

The World Turned Upside Down; or, no news and strange news . . . York: Printed by J. Kendrew, [ca. 1820]. Half-sheet 32° (95 × 61 mm.).

[1¹⁶] (1·16 mounted as pastedowns, 1ᵛ *Frontispiece*, 2ʳ title with vignette captioned *Taylor riding a Goose*, 2ᵛ alphabets and

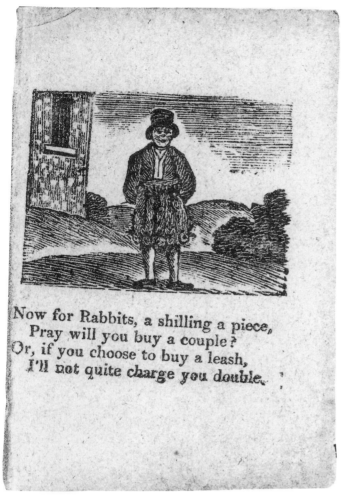

285a. front cover, *enlarged*

285b. front cover, *enlarged*

13 wood engravings (10 illustrating the nursery rhyme, 2 the second text). Original printed yellow wrappers, wood engraving and the first half of a poem from *Rhymes for the Nursery* (1806) by Ann and Jane Taylor *Learning to go alone* (incipit: *Come, my darling, come away*) on front cover, wood engraving and riddle rhyme *A pretty Thing* (incipit: *Who am I that shines so bright*) on back cover. Reference: Davis 34 (variant binding).

PML 83219. Gift: Elisabeth Ball.

❧ 285c ❧

The Life and Death of Jenny Wren . . . York: Printed by J. Kendrew, Colliergate, [ca. 1825]. Quarter-sheet 32° (96 × 63 mm.).

[1⁸] (1ʳ title, 1ᵛ incipit: *As little Jenny Wren / Was sitting by her shed*, 8ᵛ imprint *J. Kendrew, Printer, York*). Pp. 16. 16 wood engravings (25 × 37 mm. and slightly smaller) including title-cut. Stitched, 1ʳ·8ᵛ dyed yellow, as issued, to resemble wrappers. References: Davis 39; Morgan 72.

PML 83897. Gift: Elisabeth Ball

Roger Davis, formerly of the Brotherton Library in the University of Leeds, is the author of a study, *Kendrew of York*, with a checklist of his chapbooks for children (Leeds: The Elmete Press, 1988). Thanks to his investigations, we now have a less sparse knowledge of a prolific chapbook publisher who had always been an obscure figure. Part of the reason for this obscurity is that James Kendrew,

numbers, 3ʳ incipit: *To see a butcher kill a hog is no news*, 16ʳ illustration captioned *Monkey Riding a Bear* and ad *At J. Kendrew's, Colliergate, York: Little Folks may be supplied with great variety of Books of all Sorts*). Pp. 30, [2]. 29 wood engravings (45 × 32 mm. and slightly smaller) including frontispiece and title-cut. Original printed brown wrappers, wood engraving and rhyme (incipit: *Now for Rabbits, a shilling a piece*) on front cover, wood-engraved full-length portrait of *Sir Richard Whittington* on back cover. References: Davis 56 (variant binding); Morgan 68; Hockliffe 876.

PML 83935. Gift: Elisabeth Ball.

❧ 285b ❧

The House that Jack built; to which is added, some account of Jack Jingle, showing by what means he acquired his learning and in consequence thereof got rich, and built himself House. Adorned with cuts. York: Printed by J. Kendrew, Colliergate, [ca. 1821]. 36°? (83 × 63 mm.).

[1¹²] (1·12 mounted as pastedowns, 1ᵛ *Frontispiece*, 2ʳ title, 2ᵛ alphabets and numbers, 8ʳ *The History of Jack Jingle*). Pp. 23, [1]. Wove paper (Birmingham Ref. Lib. copy watermarked 1821).

who was born in the early 1770s, served no apprenticeship and conducted his business in York without being a freeman of the city. Roger Davis suggests that he worked originally as a bookbinder and only began printing ca. 1803. From then on he specialized in popular goods: song sheets, "last dying speeches," almanacs, and children's chapbooks and battledores, and he continued to work as a printer up to his death in 1841. His family showed none of the energy of the Burdekins, however. After his death the printing plant was sold, and the business shrank to what seems to have been a fairly mundane level of bookselling, finally fading away in 1890.

Kendrew's chapbooks were published in three main series, listed by Roger Davis as the 32-page penny books, with sugar-paper covers (twenty-one titles), the 24-page penny books, similarly covered (six titles) and the 16-page halfpenny books with color-brushed covers (twenty-two titles), an example of each of which is shown here. There is a strong possibility that Kendrew was too optimistic in his edition size for many titles. A substantial remainder stock was apparently left after his death, and copies of Kendrew chapbooks (sometimes overprinted with the name of his grandson, J. H. Carr) are commonly found on the antiquarian market in good condition.

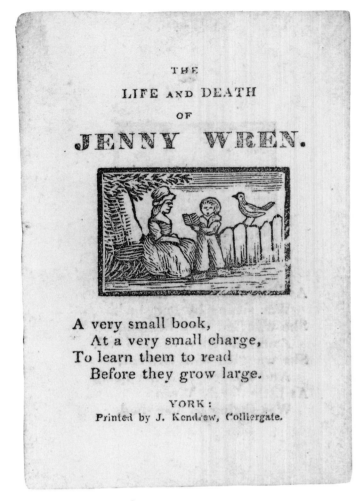

285c. fo. 1 recto, *enlarged*

XIV
TRACTS AND TRANSITION

PICTURE books and chapbooks, games and paper toys represent the sunnier aspect of English children's literature at the start of the nineteenth century. As we have noted once or twice, however, they were only part of a much larger output, which included a high proportion of dull stuff: moral tales, catechistic lesson books, and books of (variably accurate) knowledge. The most significant contributor to this literature was not an individual publisher but a group of reformers, who were concerned to evangelize and bring a new seriousness to the Church of England of their time. They believed that population growth, political unrest, the spread of industry, and a loosening of consensus on national religious topics were leading to a decline in moral values, and they aligned themselves with the founders of the Sunday school movement and other promoters of "the education of the poor" in an endeavor to spread a consciousness of revealed religion to all classes.

One of the leaders in this movement was Hannah More, who, after her years as one of the famed "blue-stockings" of London society, had returned to her native west country to set up parish schools. She and her sisters were also active in an ambitious attempt to beat the chapbook sellers at their own game and, through a network of subsidized centers, to distribute a series of tracts (designed in chapbook style) that would carry the evangelical message to the chapbook public. Hannah More herself, as "Z," wrote a monthly threesome—a tract, a ballad, and an improving tale. With the setting up of the "Cheap Repository" organization (see entry 286), a means was found to subsidize the production and distribution of her work.

Such was the success of this enterprise (for which John Marshall was for a time one of the printers) that in 1799 a regular publishing company was founded: the Religious Tract Society. It grew to be one of the largest producers of children's books in the nineteenth century, including among its wares the century's best-selling story "Hesba Stretton's" *Jessica's First Prayer* (1867) and a best-selling "respectable" magazine, *The Boy's Own Paper*, which ran from 1879 until after the Second World War (and was the place where our entry 26 was first published). In this role the Religious Tract Society (RTS) not only confronted commercial publishers with subsidized competition, but, like another religious organization, the Society for Promoting Christian Knowledge (SPCK), it developed a system of national distribution, which constitutes one of the most successful early attempts at catering to a countrywide mass readership. In 1999 the Children's Books History Society held a conference at the University of East Anglia, Norwich by way of celebrating the two hundredth anniversary of the RTS. A small exhibition tracing the varied contributions of the Society to different areas of publishing was accompanied by a catalogue by Brian Alderson and Pat Garrett: *The Religious Tract Society as a Publisher of Children's Books* (Hoddesdon: The Children's Books History Society, 1999).

The Religious Tract Society is perhaps the most prominent example of the way in which, during the first forty years of the nineteenth century, a "godly" seriousness returned to English children's books. This becomes especially obvious during the late 1820s and the 1830s when the "picture-book enlightenment" was waning, and when zealous religious writers like Mrs. Sherwood and her sister, Mrs. Cameron, dominated the scene. The period has a slight air of stagnation about it, with no new publishers injecting life in what had now become the established norms of the children's book industry and with writers working within the boundaries of accepted ideas. Indeed, in mid-century one even finds a company like Dean & Son (see previous chapter) publishing a series of "Farthing Books" of moral and religious lessons alongside its well known secular entertainments.

This generally serious atmosphere was also conducive to the wide dissemination of those books and magazines that owed their conception to the prolific American entrepreneur Samuel Griswold Goodrich. Inspired by the example of Hannah More he had, as "Peter Parley," set himself up as a sort of one-man educational institute, pouring forth instructional works of unexceptionable sobriety. (Like many educators before and after, he abhorred fairy tales: "monstrosities," reconciling young readers to vice and crime and "Not True" to boot.) His work was pirated in England, and, as we note, much else was published under this homely sobriquet that he did not write. The Darton firm on Holborn Hill was one of the leading purveyors of Parley books and is indeed, through its historic position and its employment of writers like Mrs. Sherwood and Mary Howitt, one of the most prominent companies at the worthy end of the market.

The desultory and rather amorphous character of this period is only lightly touched upon in the following examples. We have chosen to dwell mainly on the growth and diversification of tract publishing, but have also selected a number of more general books to indicate the earnest, dowdy character of secular publishing. Only with Catherine Sinclair's *Holiday House* (1839) does a premonition come of the excitements in store.

◄§ 286 §►

Plan for Establishing by Subscription a Repository of Cheap Publications, on Religious & Moral Subjects; *which will be sold at a half-penny, or a penny, and few to exceed two-pence, each.* [London: J. Marshall (?) for the Cheap Repository, 1795]. Half-sheet 4° (225 × 185 mm.).

[1²] (1ʳ drop-title). Pp. 4. Laid paper, watermarked JH. Unbound, as issued.

The Osborne Collection of Early Children's Books, Toronto Public Library.

The prospectus sets an aim for the proposed publications of brevity, cheapness, and neatness. It recognizes that this will probably entail financial loss: "but it has been thought material to offer [the tracts] at this very reduced rate, chiefly with a view of rendering their sale so advantageous to the Hawkers (to whom also an additional allowance is made) as to supplant the pernicious Publications now in circulation."

This *Plan* seems not to have been known to G. H. Spinney, who published a full account of the Cheap Repository, with details of John Marshall's uneasy relationship with the project, in *The Library* 4th ser., 20 (1939), pp. 295–340.

⤙ 287 ⤚

[HANNAH MORE (1745–1833)]. *Cheap Repository. The History of Idle Jack Brown. Containing the merry story of the mountebank, with some account of the bay mare Smiler. Being the third part of the Two Shoemakers*. London: Sold by J. Marshall, (Printer to the Cheap Repository for Moral and Religious Tracts) No. 17, Queen-Street, Cheapside, and No. 4, Aldermary Church Yard; and R. White, Piccadilly . . . By S. Hazard, Printer to the Cheap Repository, at Bath, and by all Booksellers, Newsmen, and Hawkers in Town and Country.—Great Allowance will be made to Shopkeepers and Hawkers, [1st March 1796]. Price 1d.½ each, or 6s.9d. per 100.—50 for 3s.9d.—2s.3d. for 25. [Entered at Stationers Hall.]. Large 12° (205 × 130 mm.).

[1¹²] signed A–C⁴ (12ʳ⁻ᵛ CR ads). Pp. 21, [3]. Printed from stereotype plates. Woodcut title-vignette. Stitched, uncut, as published. Reference: Spinney 53.

The Osborne Collection of Early Children's Books, Toronto Public Library.

Entered at Stationers Hall on 29 February 1796, *Idle Jack Brown* is one of Hannah More's tract stories. It forms part of a sequence, slightly analogous to Hogarth's print series of the "Idle and Industrious Apprentice," as may be gathered from the titles of its fellows: *The Two Shoemakers*, *The Apprentice Turned Master*, and *Jack Brown in Prison*. These were published at intervals, but, lacking the zest of Hogarth, they can hardly be regarded as a cliff-hanging serial.

⤙ 288 ⤚

[LEGH RICHMOND (1772–1827)]. *The Dairyman's Daughter; an authentic and interesting narrative, in five parts. Communicated by a clergyman of the Church of England*. London: Published by the Religious Tract Society. Printed by Tilling and Hughes, Grosvenor-row, Chelsea; and sold by F. Collins, no. 60, Paternoster-Row; and J. Nisbet, no. 15, Castle-Street, Oxford-Street, [ca. 1820]. Price 21s. 4d. per 100. 18° (138 × 90 mm.).

A¹⁸ B⁸ (6+1). Pp. 54. Wood engraving of a burial on title. Original printed blue-gray wrappers. Reference: Osborne II, 928.

The Osborne Collection of Early Children's Books, Toronto Public Library.

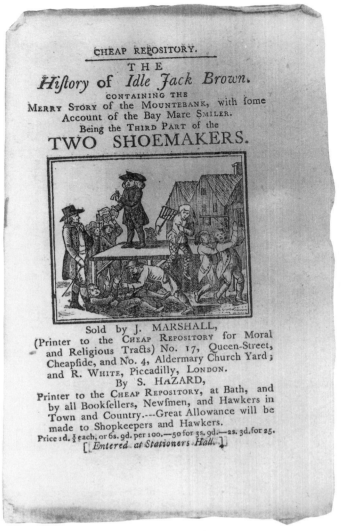

287. *reduced*

Legh Richmond was a clergyman who, during incumbency at Brading on the Isle of Wight, wrote three stories based upon events occurring among the local poor. *The Dairyman's Daughter*, written in 1805, is the most famous of these, but they were later gathered together as *The Annals of the Poor*, in which form they became the first of the Religious Tract Society's best-sellers. (*DNB* gives a figure of two million copies sold before Richmond's early death in 1827.) This expanded version of the original story is a typical tract of the Religious Tract Society's early period, during which Richmond himself was briefly joint secretary of the society. The Alderson & Garrett catalogue describes and illustrates an early version "abridged for the American public" and published by the American Tract Society ca. 1830.

⤙ 289 ⤚

A Voice to the Young. [London:] Religious Tract Society, 56, Paternoster-row, [ca. 1835]. 32° (102 × 66 mm.).

[1²] (1ʳ drop-title, illustration, incipit: *I am going a long way back for my text*, 2ᵛ imprint (as above) and tract number (*170.*)). Pp. 4. Blue-dyed wove paper. Half-page wood engraving. Unbound, as issued.

289. fo. 1 recto, *enlarged*

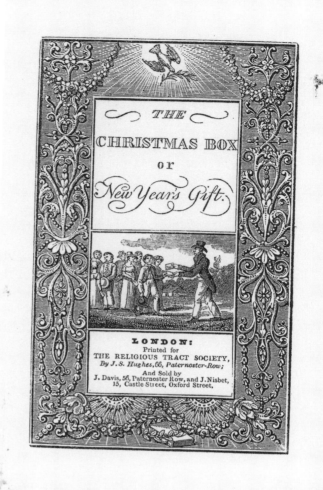

290. A2 recto, *reduced*

PML 85769. Gift: Elisabeth Ball.

Numerous early productions of the Cheap Repository and the Religious Tract Society were intended to be read by adults rather than children. Within a few years, however, the Religious Tract Society perceived that its mission might most easily be directed at a young readership whom it could reach through the growing number of church schools and Sunday schools. As a result, for much of the nineteenth century vast quantities of edifying booklets and leaflets issued from the society at prices from a farthing upward, many to be given away as Sunday-school rewards. An 1875 RTS catalogue lists some 68 series of books, and other publications such as "Hymns on broadsheets" and "Texts on rollers," numbering thousands of items; among children's tracts there are 468 penny, halfpenny, and farthing booklets, organized into packets for sale at one shilling each. *A Voice to the Young* is an example from one of the cheapest series. The Morgan Library possesses two further copies, one on undyed paper (PML 85770) and one on yellow-dyed paper (PML 85768); it also has dozens of other RTS titles, printed on variously colored papers.

ᵅ§ 290 §ᵅ

The Christmas Box or New Year's Gift. London: Printed for The Religious Tract Society, By J. S. Hughes, 66, Paternoster Row, and J. Nisbet, 15, Castle Street, Oxford Street, [1822 or 1823]. 12° (164 × 97 mm.).

A–C¹² D⁶ (A1ʳ half-title, A2ʳ title, D6ᵛ imprint *J.S. Hughes, Printer, 66, Paternoster Row, London*). Pp. 80, [4]. 43 wood engravings including title-border. Original green-roan-backed printed boards, title, wood engraving and *Price One Shilling* on front cover, ads on back cover. Reference: Osborne I, 56.

PML 82654. Gift: Elisabeth Ball.

The dimensions of this little compendium closely correspond with those of the tracts first put out by the Cheap Repository; the organization of its contents—a series of Christmas carols with separate title pages—suggests that each song might be reprinted to sell individually like the old chapbook "garlands of new songs." By this date, however, the careless chapbook cuts have been replaced by wood engravings that show the influence of the Bewick school. (A fairly precise date for the book can be arrived at from the trade addresses on the cover.)

291. frontispiece vignette, *enlarged*

❧ 291 ❧

The Passionate Boy. Published under the direction of the Committee of General Literature and Education, appointed by the Society for Promoting Christian Knowledge. London: Printed for the Society for Promoting Christian Knowledge; sold at the Depository, Great Queen Street, Lincoln's Inn Fields, and 4, Royal Exchange; and by all booksellers, 1849. 32° (101 × 66 mm.).

[1⁸] (1ʳ blank, 1ᵛ wood-engraved frontispiece signed *Whimper*, 2ʳ title, 2ᵛ imprint *London: R. Clay, Printer, Bread Street Hill*, 8ᵛ imprint). Pp. 16. The wood engraving is by Josiah Wood Whymper (1813–1903). Original printed gray wrappers, title on front cover, ads *32mo Tracts (with Cuts)* on back cover.

Provenance: Gumuchian & Cⁱᵉ (1930 cat., no. 1794). PML 83423. Gift: Elisabeth Ball.

The Religious Tract Society was a nondenominational organization but with an appeal to the evangelizing wing of the established church and to the nonconformist sects. Conventional Anglicanism was served by the rival, long-standing Society for Promoting Christian Knowledge, which had been founded in 1698 and was much involved in setting up schools and Sunday schools.

As a publisher the SPCK was a sober institution, and its tracts and schoolbooks at this time must have been among the dullest things ever foisted upon children. The Morgan Library possesses a quantity of tracts such as this *Passionate Boy*, and from the advertisements on the back covers of some of them (showing items numbered as high as 572) it appears that the society had "borrowed" several of Hannah More's Cheap Repository stories, including *The Shepherd of Salisbury Plain* and *Tawny Rachel*.

❧ 292 ❧

Once Angry and My Child. Otley: William Walker & Sons, [ca. 1850]. 32° (118 × 72 mm.).

[4⁸] (1ʳ drop-title *Once Angry*, 4ʳ *My Child*, 7ʳ–8ᵛ four religious poems). Pp. 16; pages 1–12 also paginated 49–60. Wood-engraved initial and tailpiece. Original printed pink wrappers, title (as transcribed above), border and vignette on front cover, ads on back cover for *Reward Books . . . Temperance Dialogues & Recitations*

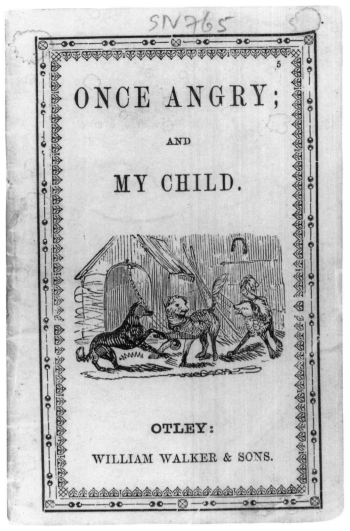

292. front cover, *enlarged*

. . . Gems of Sacred Melody, In Penny Sheets of Excellent Music. Catalogues sent to any Address on receipt of a Penny Stamp.

Provenance: Gumuchian & Cⁱᵉ (1930 cat., no. 1646). PML 80200. Gift: Elisabeth Ball.

This and the following three entries give a token representation to the widespread production and acceptance of tractlike publications once the large, charitable societies had shown the way. William Walker, whom we have primarily noted as a chapbook publisher (chapter XIII), is seen here to be utilizing spare capacity in his Wharfedale Steam-Printing Works for the production of the many cheap reward series advertised on the back of *Once Angry*, which were clearly destined for the flourishing Sunday school market.

The tract's curious system of double pagination indicates that it was worked together with three others of the same dimension on a single sheet. This yielded a continuously paginated volume collating [1–4⁸], of which *Once Angry* formed the final quire. The four individually paginated tracts were presumably marketed collectively as well as separately. The unexpected mention of New York in *Once Angry*, coupled to a slightly unconventional diction ("I didn't mean to speak cross"), allows for the possibility that Walker used the text of an American tract society publication.

293. frontispiece, *enlarged*

❧ 293 ☙

The White Satin Shoes; and Vanity. London: J. and C. Mozley, Paternoster Row; and Joseph Masters, New Bond Street, 1857. 32°? (118 × 81 mm.).

[1¹⁶] (1ʳ title, 2ʳ *The White Satin Shoes*, 11ᵛ *Vanity*, 16ᵛ imprint *John and Charles Mozley, Printers, Derby*); wood-engraved frontispiece by T. Bolton. Pp. 32. 5-line wood-engraved initial G. Original brown-printed glazed green wrappers, title and series number 7 on front cover, wood engraving on back cover.

PML 83941. Gift: Elisabeth Ball.

The Mozleys, whom we first encountered at Gainsborough in the eighteenth century (chapter VIII), are here found at their London office set up in Paternoster Row in 1851, although printing was still undertaken at Derby. By this time the family was much taken up with church affairs; John and Charles Mozley's brother James (1813–78) was to become regius professor of divinity at Oxford, while another brother, Thomas (1806–93), was closely involved with the Tractarians and married John Henry Newman's sister, Harriet, who wrote several books for children. In conjunction with James Burns (see entries 316, 332, and 360c), the Mozleys

published her *Fairy Bower* (1841), a notably accomplished story for its time along with a two-volume sequel, *The Lost Brooch* (also 1841).

As a tract *The White Satin Shoes* is more concerned with behavioral than religious issues and has been selected from a collection of similar Mozley productions held by the Morgan Library.

❧ 294 ☙

Buttercups and Daisies. London: Groombridge & Sons, Paternoster Row, [ca. 1855]. 24°? (114 × 84 mm.).

[1¹²] (1ᵛ frontispiece, 2ʳ title, border and vignette *It was haymaking time*, 2ᵛ text). Pp. 24. 6 wood engravings including 3 signed in the block by Edward Whymper (1840–1911). Frontispiece and illustration on 4ʳ colored in a child's hand. Original printed green wrappers, title, *Price One Penny* and elaborate, wood-engraved decorative border by Whymper incorporating the series title *Buds & Blossoms* on front cover, ad for the full set (i.e. 6 "packets" of 6 titles each) on back cover.

PML 83757. Gift: Elisabeth Ball.

With Groombridge's "Buds & Blossoms" series, the tract moves into a no-man's-land between religious proselytizing and

294. fo. 2 recto

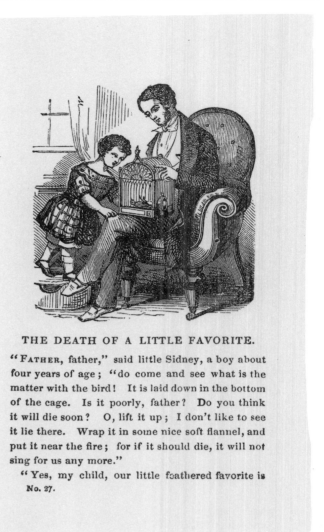

THE DEATH OF A LITTLE FAVORITE.

"FATHER, father," said little Sidney, a boy about four years of age; "do come and see what is the matter with the bird! It is laid down in the bottom of the cage. Is it poorly, father? Do you think it will die soon? O, lift it up; I don't like to see it lie there. Wrap it in some nice soft flannel, and put it near the fire; for if it should die, it will not sing for us any more."

"Yes, my child, our little feathered favorite is No. 27.

295. fo. 1ʳ, *enlarged*

chapbook storytelling. The series was sold in sixpenny packets with six books in each and formed part of a cheap publishing program that was apparently aimed at the market for "acceptable Presents, Birthday and Christmas Gifts." *Buttercups and Daisies* itself borders on the genre of "street Arab" stories, which was to have its heyday in the second half of the nineteenth century, and its moral lesson of probity in poverty is introduced to supply narrative point rather than to display authorial conviction.

Groombridges were a firm with a diverse list, and "Buds and Blossoms" presumably supplied quick turnover to help finance more ambitious popular and scientific publishing, including the distribution of the elaborate color-printed series produced by Benjamin Fawcett of Driffield. The employment of Whymper's cuts in *Buttercups and Daisies* is no more than routine, however. Edward Whymper was the son of the Josiah Whymper noticed at entry 291, and as a member of the wood-engraving firm found himself involved in plenty of jobbing work for tract and popular publishers. (Later in the century he was to win fame as a mountaineer and explorer.)

❧ 295 ❧

Death of a Little Favorite; The Fall of a Tree; and other stories. London: Sunday School Union, 56, Old Bailey, [ca 1860]. Child's Cabinet, No. 27. 24°? (132 × 78 mm.).

[1⁶] (1ʳ drop-title *The Death of a Little Favorite*, 3ʳ *A Blind Man and his Little Daughter*, 3ᵛ *March*, 4ᵛ *The Fall of the Great Tree*,

5ʳ *To my Little Child*, 5ᵛ *The Two New Year's Days*. Pp. 12. Half-page wood engraving to the first story and a small circular one to *March*. Original printed green wrappers, title (as transcribed above) and circular wood-engraved vignette on front cover, ads on back cover.

PML 83431. Gift: Elisabeth Ball.

Like Groombridge in his "Buds and Blossoms" series, the Sunday School Union advertised packets of children's books for giving away (alongside the "Coloured Picture Reward Tickets—twenty different sorts, 4d. per packet"). "The Child's Cabinet: suited to the Younger Children in our Sunday Schools" was one of these series issued in packets, at sixpence for twelve booklets and one shilling for twenty-four. Each item was somewhat like a small magazine, with a miscellany of semi-religious anecdotes, exhortations, and sets of sentimental verses. (The title story of *Death of a Little Favorite* begins with a dying pet bird and ends with Janeway-like exhortations: "O, who shall see to-morrow? Graves are opening for to-morrow... Love Christ to-day!") An occasional concession to liveliness amidst all this earnestness was now and then made in the wood engravings.

FRONTISPIECE.

Evangelist reasons with Christian.

296. *reduced*

◄§ 296 §►

Explanation of the Pilgrim's Progress, &c. &c. abridged and adapted to the capacities of children, in dialogue, between a child and his mother. By a lady. London: printed and sold by J. Barfield, 91, Wardour-street, and by the booksellers in town and country, 1818. 16° (124 × 96 mm.).

A–B⁸ (A1ʳ title, A1ᵛ blank, A2ʳ *Introduction*, B8ᵛ imprint *Printed by J. Barfield, Wardour-street, Soho*); 7 etchings, printed from one or two copperplates, including frontispiece *Evangelist reasons with Christian*. Pp. 32. Wove paper stock for letterpress (watermarked 1816), different from that for etching. Black morocco gilt.

Provenance: Charles Todd Owen (binding). PML 83537. Gift: Elisabeth Ball.

We have already encountered *The Pilgrim's Progress* adapted as subject matter for little picture books (entry 195); further calls were made on it as a means of interpreting Christian doctrine: "*Child.* Does the Celestial Gate mean Heaven? *Mother.* Yes: but Christian has a long way to go; the Hill Difficulty is very steep . . . &c. &c." For some reason Giant Despair and Doubting Castle are omitted in Barfield's tract but are promised for a sequel "containing an account of the Pilgrimage of Christiana," provided that the author is favored with encouragement. Not enough encouragement can have been forthcoming as no copy of a sequel is recorded.

◄§ 297 §►

MARY MARTHA SHERWOOD, née BUTT (1775–1851). *The History of the Fairchild Family; or, the child's manual: being a collection of stories calculated to shew the importance and effects of a religious education.* London: printed for J. Hatchard, 190, Piccadilly; and sold by F. Houlston and Son, Wellington, 1818. 12° (172 × 101 mm.).

A⁴ (–1, 2ʳ title, 3ʳ *Contents*, 4ᵛ blank); B–N¹² O⁸ (O7ᵛ imprint *Ellerton and Henderson, Printers, Johnson's Court, Fleet Street, London*, –O8, quires A and O forming part of the same sheet); etched frontispiece *"Don't tease me Henry" said Lucy "don't you see I am reading." Page 47.* Pp. [6], 302. Wove paper, watermarked 1817. Original half calf, signed inside front cover J. Hatchard & Son. References: Cutt *Mrs. Sherwood* G1; Morgan 258.

Provenance: *Jane Cox the gift of her dear Mamma November 2ⁿᵈ 1818* (inscr.). PML 83364. Purchase: Ball Fund.

The publications of the tract societies constituted only one part of a movement towards religious and moral awakening in the early nineteenth century. As early as 1802, in the *Guardian of Education*, Mrs. Trimmer had praised the "most seasonable and edifying lesson to girls of the lower order" in the story of *Susan Gray*, a short novel published by Hazard, the Cheap Repository's man in Bath, which set out the social purpose of the tracts on a somewhat larger scale. Mrs. Trimmer was not quite accurate, however, in saying that the anonymous author had "employed his pen to a most important purpose," for *Susan Gray* was one of the first published stories by Mary Martha Butt, who as Mrs. Sherwood was to become a dominant figure in the evangelizing of English children's literature.

The History of the Fairchild Family is probably the most famous example of her evangelical style (long made notorious through Harvey Darton's quotation of the passage where the children are taken to see a corpse on a gibbet). The book contains a sequence of prose vignettes of the Fairchilds at home, each of which is devised to feature a religious doctrine but each of which also carries somewhere a sense of Mrs. Sherwood's appreciation of the comforts of a loving family life. Interspersed between these vignettes are prayers, arising out of the story subjects, and hymns, reprinted from unacknowledged sources such as Isaac Watts and William Cowper.

Along with this copy of the first edition of *The Fairchild Family*, the Morgan Library also owns a first edition of Mrs. Sherwood's other early blockbuster, *The History of Little Henry and his Bearer* (1814; Gottlieb 125, PML 85525). Based upon her experience as an army wife in India, this book of missionary fiction became extremely influential, combining, in the words of Nancy Cutt (*Ministering Angels*, pp. 27–8), the devices of the sentimental novel and the children's tract tale.

◄§ 298 §►

MARY MARTHA SHERWOOD, née BUTT (1775–1851). *A Drive in the Coach through the Streets of London. A story founded on fact. Fourth edition.* Wellington, Salop: printed by and for F. Houlston and Son. And sold by

FRONTISPIECE.

Julia and her Mamma in the Bookseller's Shop.

See Page 34.

298.

Scatcherd and Letterman, Ave-Maria Lane, London, 1819. [Entered at Stationers' Hall.]. 18° (142 × 85 mm.).

A–C⁶ (A1ᵛ *Frontispiece. Julia and her Mamma in the Bookseller's Shop. See Page 34*, A2ʳ title, C6ᵛ blank). Pp. 35, [1]. Wove paper, watermarked RVB 1817. 6 full-page wood engravings including frontispiece, wood-engraved title vignette. Original printed gray stiff wrappers, title and *Price Sixpence* on front cover, ads on back cover. Reference: Cutt *Mrs Sherwood* C43 (other eds.).

Provenance: Lysaght (sign.); Gumuchian & Cᵢᵉ (1930 cat., no. 5326). PML 83587. Gift: Elisabeth Ball.

As well as writing longer stories, Mrs. Sherwood was a prolific author of moral tracts and brief tales which, in a more secular vein, came close to being original chapbooks. *A Drive in the Coach* is an intriguing mixture of these two styles and reads almost as though Maria Edgeworth's Rosamond has been taken over by the good-godly movement: "There are not so many jokes in this life, my child, as young people are apt to think," says mamma ominously as her giddy daughter Julia is about to be confronted with a coffinmaker's shop.

A Drive in the Coach was probably first published in 1818 by the Shropshire firm of Houlston's, which had already scored a success

with *Little Henry and his Bearer* in 1814 and went on to issue nearly a hundred of Mrs. Sherwood's little books. The firm had begun as booksellers in 1779, started a printing business in 1805, and did a considerable trade in a variety of chapbooks and other pamphlets. They opened a warehouse in London in 1825 and moved their headquarters there in 1829, but, although the name continued to appear in book trade annals until 1910, Houlston's never quite made the same mark as when they published the early works of Mrs. Sherwood.

◆§ 299 §◆

MARY MARTHA SHERWOOD, née BUTT (1775–1851). *The Gipsy Babes. A tale of the last century.* Wellington, Salop: printed by and for Houlston and Son. And sold at their Warehouse, 65, Paternoster-Row, London, 1826. [Entered at Stationers' Hall]. 18° (137 × 77 mm.).

A–F⁶ (–A1, A2ʳ title, A2ᵛ blank, F2ᵛ imprint *Houlstons, Printers*, F3ʳ–5ᵛ Houlston ads, –F6); hand-colored etched frontispiece (see overleaf) dated *Janʸ 1ˢᵗ 1827*. Pp. 64, [6]. Unwatermarked, wove paper. Blue morocco gilt, by Kelly & Sons (bound in first, with the same publisher's *The Holiday Queen* [by Mrs. Cameron], seventh edition, 1823). References: Cutt *Mrs. Sherwood* C26; Morgan 254.

Provenance: Sara Gracie Iselin (armorial bookplate). PML 84865. Purchase: Ball Fund.

As Nancy Cutt has noted, Mrs. Sherwood's stories evolved beyond the evangelical fervor that governed such writings as *The Fairchild Family*. This process is clearly to be seen in *The Gipsy Babes*, which not only contains no religious proselytizing but also exhibits a variety of characteristics that show how closely Mrs. Sherwood's skill as a storyteller (however sentimental) was rooted in tradition. The story is given a fireside setting—"stir the fire," says grandfather, "and let every one sit still, and you shall hear such a tale as will surprise you;" a conscious parallel is drawn with "The Babes in the Wood;" respect is paid to the detail of events and the forms of dialect speech. Even when the Bible is quoted, it is by way of setting a scene rather than impressing a lesson.

The Morgan Library also owns a sixth edition of *The Gipsy Babes*, bound in paper wrappers, with the imprint: London: printed for Houlston and Son, 65 Paternoster Row; and at Wellington, Salop. 1835 (PML 82454).

◆§ 300 §◆

JAMES JANEWAY (1636?–1674). *A Token for Children; being an enlarged edition of Mr. Janeway's work: containing Thirty-six Memoirs of Young Persons. Collected and revised by Mrs. Cameron, author of "Margaret Whyte," and "The Two Lambs."* London: printed for R. B. Seeley and W. Burnside: and sold by L. B. Seeley and Sons, Fleet Street, 1828. 2 volumes. 12° (138 × 84 mm.).

Vol. I: π² (1ʳ half-title, 1ᵛ imprint *L. B. Seeley and Sons, Weston Green, Thames Ditton*, 2ʳ title, 2ᵛ blank); a–b⁶ c⁴ (a1ʳ *Advertisement*, a2ʳ editor's preface, b2ʳ author's preface, b6ʳ author's dedication to *any who are concerned in the education of children*, c2ʳ *Contents*, c4ʳ divisional title, c4ᵛ blank); B–Z⁶ 2A⁴ (parts 1–3, 2A3ᵛ imprint, 2A4 blank). Pp. [4], xxx, [2], 270, [2]. Vol. II: *a–b*² (a1ʳ half-title, a1ᵛ imprint, a2ʳ title, a2ᵛ blank, b1ʳ *Contents*, b2ʳ divisional title, b2ᵛ blank); B–Y⁶ Z⁴ (part 4, Z3ᵛ imprint, Z4 ads). Pp. [4], ii, [2], 258, [2]. Original roan-backed printed boards, title on front covers, ads on back covers. Reference: Osborne I, 152.

PML 82380–1. Gift: Elisabeth Ball.

Lucy Lyttleton Cameron (1781–1858) was a sister of Mrs. Sherwood and worked closely with her in seeking to "render religion pleasant" to children. From her preface to these volumes, she appears to have been as optimistic as James Janeway himself (see entries 27–28) that such rendering might best be achieved by giving children true accounts of other children's deaths. Acknowledging the classic status of the original *Token*, she makes few alterations to Janeway's funerary text; her additions of subsequently published, similar memoirs are, she says, more heavily abridged, but the essential Janeway spirit remains. (Elizabeth Lucinda reproves the [deistic] author of *L'Ami des Enfants* for not paying due regard to the sacred name of the Almighty. In consequence of this and other pieties, she makes a good end and "a more lovely corpse was never viewed than hers, as she lay prepared for burial.") Among other conjunctions in the book, we should note "The History of Jane S." by Legh Richmond, who wrote *The Dairyman's Daughter* (entry 288), and the complete quoting of Ann Taylor's "My Mother" in "The Life and Death of Jane Teare."

∞§ 301a ¿∞

[CATHERINE SINCLAIR (1800–64)]. *Charlie Seymour; or the good aunt and the bad aunt. A Sunday story* . . . Edinburgh: Waugh and Innes. J. Hatchard and Son; J. Nisbet; and Whittaker & Co. London, 1832. 12° (144 × 85 mm.).

*A*⁴ (1ʳ title, 1ᵛ imprint *Printed by A. Balfour & Co. Niddry Street*, 2ʳ note by John Sinclair, the author's father, 2ᵛ blank, 3ʳ *Preface*); B–P⁶ Q⁴ (Q4ᵛ imprint); hand-colored etched frontispiece by J. & J. Johnstone after the author's design (see overleaf). Pp. viii, 176. Contemporary dark green quarter roan. References: Osborne II, 941; M. Nancy Cutt, "Another side to Catherine Sinclair," *Signal* 42 (1983), pp. 172–84.

Provenance: William Whyte & Co. of Edinburgh (bookseller's label); *John Alexʳ Watt from Lady Carnegie 3ᵈ April 1832* (inscr.). PML 84694. Purchase: Ball Fund.

∞§ 301b ¿∞

CATHERINE SINCLAIR (1800–64). *Holiday House: a series of tales. Dedicated to Lady Diana Boyle* . . . Edinburgh: William Whyte and Co. Booksellers to the Queen Dowager; Longman, Orme, and Co., London; W. Curry, Jun. and Co., Dublin, 1839. 8° (152 × 93 mm.).

*A*⁶ (1 half-title lacking, 2ʳ title, 2ᵛ imprint *Balfour & Jack, Printers,*

Niddry Street, 3ʳ *Preface*); B–Z 2A–2B⁸ 2C² (L4·5 and O2–7 lacking, quires A and 2C belong to the same sheet). Pp. xii, 387, [1]. Contemporary blue hard-grain morocco gilt, hard grain marbled endpapers, gilt edges. References: J. Morris, "The children's books of Catherine Sinclair," *Scottish Book Collector* 2.3 (Feb./March 1990), pp. 4–10; Alderson *Moon* 1.

Provenance: *Mrs Ramsay with kindest remembrances from Catherine Sinclair Jan 7 1839* (author's presentation inscr.). PML 84634. Purchase: Ball Fund.

As with Mrs. Sherwood, but in much smaller compass, these two stories by the same author show something of the shift from a predominantly serious to a more humane storytelling stance that took place during the 1830s.

Charlie Seymour begins with an intriguing preface by Catherine Sinclair in which she gently takes issue with the quantity of Sunday reading for children that was "almost invariably terminated by an early death." Her aim is to show the value of cheerfulness and to make children aware of the happiness that comes from "a judicious system of moral and religious discipline." This she does by placing her hero between two loving aunts and getting him to choose which one he would wish to live with. One is indulgent and always ready for japes and the other is cool and affectionate in a somewhat Edgeworthian fashion; the contrived plot ensures that the young reader shall realize why this Aunt Mary is an altogether more acceptable mentor than her flighty sister, Aunt Jane.

The book does little to prepare one for the surprises of *Holiday House* (published, incidentally, by the bookseller whose label appears in the Morgan copy of *Charlie Seymour*). Darton called this "the best original children's book written up to that time, and one of the jolliest and most hilarious of any period;" although that 1932 judgment may now need to be slightly modified, its essence remains: Catherine Sinclair now allowed free rein to "cheerfulness" and nursery anarchy to a degree never before found in a children's novel. (Oddly though, in view of her preface to *Charlie Seymour*, the more serious second half of the story does include "an early death," which she apparently replaced with a happy ending in an edition towards the end of her life [Alderson *Moon* 7] although this did not survive in later editions.) This first edition is unillustrated, but Catherine Sinclair had made her own illustrations for the story and these were subsequently used by the publisher, who had them printed in color lithography.

∞§ 302 ¿∞

MARY HOWITT, née BOTHAM (1799–1888). *Tales in Verse: for the young*. London: William Darton and Son, Holborn Hill, [1836]. 12° (153 × 96 mm.).

*A*⁴ (1ʳ title, 2ʳ dedication *To the children of her beloved sister Anna*, 3ʳ *Preface*, 4ʳ *Contents*); B–S⁶ T⁴ (B1ʳ *Olden Times*, incipit: *The fields with corn are rich and deep*); 10 engravings, printed from steel plates (?) on thicker paper than the letterpress, including conjugate frontispiece and pictorial title. Original tissues tipped in to face the plates. Pp. iv, [*recte* viii], 212. Original or contemporary blind-blocked red hard-grain roan, gilt edges. References: Osborne I, 68; Darton *Check-list* 756(1).

FRONTISPIECE.

THE GIPSY BABES.

Published by Houlston & Son. Wellington, Salop: and 65, Paternoster Row, London, Jan.ʸ 1ˢᵗ 1827.

Page 185.

Above: **299.**   *Below*: **301a.** frontispiece, *enlarged*   *Above*: **302.** plate facing R3ᵛ, *reduced*

C.S. delᵗ· — J. & J. Johnstone Sc.

Charlie considering which of his two aunts he likes best.

Provenance: *T. Connolly, 6 Chancery Place, Dublin* (nineteenth-century bookseller's label); *English Crooks* (inscr.); Gumuchian & Cie (1930 cat., no. 3103). PML 85131. Gift: Elisabeth Ball.

Mary Howitt was a busy contributor to the children's-book publishing industry during its slow growth through the 1820s and 1830s. Unlike Mrs. Sherwood and Catherine Sinclair, however, she was not impelled to write by any strongly didactic motive, and her very varied output smacks more of professional journalism than tractitis.

Tales in Verse is a collection that typifies her ability as a poet: ballads and descriptive stanzas carried through with a natural facility, but none sufficiently memorable to endure. (She did, however, survive in "The Spider and the Fly," which first appeared in 1834 in her versified *Sketches of Natural History*. The Morgan Library possesses the sixth edition of this book, enlarged by the poet herself in 1845 when she recovered its copyright [PML 82764].)

❧ 303 ❧

[GEORGE MOGRIDGE (1787–1854) or THOMAS TEGG (1776–1845)]. *Tales about Plants, By Peter Parley, author of Tales about Animals, Tales about Europe, Asia, etc. With numerous engravings.* London: printed for Thomas Tegg, Cheapside; Tegg and Co. Dublin; Griffin and Co. Glasgow; and J. Tegg, Sydney, Australia, 1839. 16° (134 × 102 mm.).

303. D1^v, *detail*

A^6 (1^r half-title, 1^v blank, 2^r title and vignette *Negroes beating down cloves*, 2^v imprint *Chiswick: printed by C. Whittingham*, 3^r Preface, 5^r Contents); B–Z AA–II^8 KK^2 (quires A and KK belonging to the same half-sheet, KK2^v imprint *Chiswick Press: printed by C. Whittingham*). Pp. xii, 500. 109 wood engravings. Original blind and gilt-blocked green straight-grain cloth. Reference: Osborne I, 210.

Provenance: *George Young, bookseller, 9, Suffolk-st. Dublin* (trade label); *Frances Mary Anne Smith—from her affectionate father Xmas day 1839* (inscr.). Brian Alderson, Richmond.

One example of a work attributed to "Peter Parley" hardly does justice to the dominance of Parleyism over children's book publishing during the 1830s and early 1840s. The "old storyteller" himself was a New Englander from Connecticut, born Samuel Griswold Goodrich (1793–1860), who published a vast number of educational and didactic books for children and edited or gave his name to magazines for them. Some of these books and, more importantly, his alliterative pseudonym, traveled to England, and a further vast number of Parley books were published there, often bearing little relationship to American originals or to anything that Goodrich himself had had a hand in. (The complicated facts are summarized in F. J. Harvey Darton's *Children's Books in England*, pp. 221–8, while Lawrence Darton's *Check-list* devotes much space to genuine Goodrich titles and works by his imitators.)

Tales About Plants is by one of these English Parleys, picturing the "old man" with his youthful listeners as he inundates them with descriptions of plant life, interspersed with anecdotes and pious ejaculations ("Thus wonderfully and beautifully," he says of the chickweed, "has the Great Creator provided for the protection of this trifling weed!"). In his *Recollections of a Lifetime* Goodrich identifies *Plants* as one of the counterfeits and castigates British authors and booksellers for their "utter disregard of truth, honor and decency." In the light of this denunciation, we need to record that Goodrich's own *Peter Parley's Tales of Animals* (second edition, Boston: 1832, "with many corrections and improvements") contains wholesale, unacknowledged copies of numerous Bewick wood engravings and may possibly have been "improved" after consulting the first British edition of the work, published, like *Plants*, by Thomas Tegg (see PML 82373 and 80666).

"THE Publisher begs to call attention to the great improvement in this series of children's books, being divested of all the pernicious ribaldry, which, for many years, has disgraced much of the infantine reading. The days of giants and goblins are long since past, and it is high time that what is first read and recited to children, should be really of an instructive, as well as of an amusing description." Echoing as they do the sentiments and even the phrases of the "Improvers" from every generation, those words sum up the *dirigiste* philosophy of the "Age of Parleyism." (We have already quoted them in part from an advertisement on the cover of *Kindness and Love*, published by Edward Lacey [entry 108], and among the works commended there is Lacey's *Peter Parley's Primer* [PML 81387].)

For all that the years between 1820 and 1845 seem to be dour ones, however, they could also be seen as a gestation period. The "pernicious ribaldry" of *The Old Woman of Stepney* (entry 54) or the giants and goblins of other cheapjack series (e.g. entry 150) may not have made them *personae gratae* among those who welcomed Lacey's effusions, but even within the stable framework of the "Approved Literature" there were signs of restiveness. New ideas about the potential of children's literature were growing. A more specialized publishing industry, aided by a new print technology, was not going to be content with limited formulae. From the 1840s onward a combination of new talents would create a body of children's literature of which the productions of today are still recognizably a part.

The seeds of change were most fruitfully planted by the Brothers Grimm, whose *Kinder- und Hausmärchen* began to appear in English translation in 1823 (entry 304). With a single book the imaginative potential of folktales was widened far beyond the eighteenth-century norms of Perrault and Mother Bunch. The richness and peculiarity of the folk imagination was seen to be something in the possession of all nations and, as Edgar Taylor says in his preface, the collection frees children from the treadmill of nursery didacticism. The exploration and imitation of folktales were to become the decisive factors behind the changes that would nurture *The Rose and the Ring*, and this chapter sets out some of the ways in which such exploration manifested itself, whether in Ruskin's "Legend from Stiria," or "Felix Summerly's" anti-Peter-Parleyism, or less directly the nonsenses of Edward Lear.

From another point of view, *German Popular Stories* relates to a phenomenon that still awaits more detailed examination: the influence of Germany itself. Apart from the Grimms, this was not really a literary influence, for Germany did not have a strong enough tradition of children's literature to impress the English market. Rather, it was a broader "cultural" influence. On the one hand, things German had an exotic and sometimes rumbustious comic flavor, which appealed to a nation too long preoccupied (where foreign preoccupation could be discerned) with things French. On the other hand, there was a clearly definable influence

from German Romantic art and its concomitant interest in a reconstituted medievalism. One of the turning points, not far in time from Taylor's translation of Grimm, was the publication in England in 1820 of Friedrich August Moritz Retzsch's outline drawings for Goethe's *Faust*, and the resultant fashion among illustrators for both the "outline style" and a sanitized rusticity lasts through the next three decades.

Evidence for this Germanic influence is widespread, and in the following section we have not gone out of our way to demonstrate it but have rather found ourselves falling over it in several directions. Indeed, one of the problems in compiling this chapter was to organize and annotate the material so as to bring out the interlacing of several strands of development in individual books or from one book to another. As a result, our sequence of examples is thematic rather than chronological. We have endeavored to delineate a confluence of ideas and an increasing activity in the field of children's books on the part of men of consequence—factors that were to create a climate in which such books as *The Rose and the Ring* could flourish.

✤ 304 ✤

JAKOB LUDWIG KARL GRIMM (1785–1863) & WILHELM KARL GRIMM (1786–1859). *German Popular Stories, translated* [by Edgar Taylor and David Jardine, vol. II. translated by Edgar Taylor only] *from the Kinder und Haus Marchen, collected by M. M. Grimm, from oral tradition.* London: Published by C. Baldwyn, Newgate Street, 1823. [Vol. II. James Robins & C° London. And Joseph Robins Junr & C° Dublin. MDCCCXXVI.]. 2 volumes. 12° (175 × 99 mm.).

Vol. I: a^6 (1^r half-title, 1^v quotation from *Pref. to Hist. of "Tom Thumbe the Little." – 1621*, 2^r *Preface*); B–L^12 (B1^r *Hans in Luck*, L1^r end of *Rumpel-stilts-kin*, L1^v *Directions to the binder*, L2^r *Notes*, L12^v imprint *Printed by Richard Taylor, Shoe-Lane, London*); 12 etched plates by George Cruikshank, printed in sepia, including pictorial title (first state without the umlaut in Märchen). Pp. xii, 240. Vol. II: *A²* (= M6·7, 1^r half-title, 1^v quotation from *Pref. to "Valentine and Orson . . . . with new pictures lively expressing the history." – 1677*, 2^r *Advertisement*); B–M^12 (B1^r *The Goose-girl*, M2^v end of *The Juniper Tree*, M3^r *Notes*, –M6·7, M11^r translator's note on *"Fairy Legends and Traditions of the South of Ireland,"* M11^v imprint *London: printed by Richard Taylor* and printer's device, M12^r ads for publications by Clementi and Co. and by Longman, Hurst, Rees, Orme, Browne, and Green, M12^v blank); 10 etched plates by George Cruikshank, printed in black, including pictorial title. Pp. iv, 256, [4]. Modern brown morocco gilt, edges gilt, by Riviere & Son; lacking the original paperboard bindings, but the Robins ads originally inserted with

important place in children's reading, these translators (perhaps only Edgar Taylor) may be seen as making the first moves in a campaign that was to lead to the final freeing of constraints upon the writers and publishers of books for children. The epigraphs from *Tom Thumbe* and *Valentine and Orson* are significant, harking back as they do to the chapbook tradition, and the German popular stories that they introduce are the chapbook tradition writ large. These two volumes of Grimm brought into the mainstream of English culture a new exoticism, which nonetheless could be sensed as part of a common storytelling heritage. From the antics of the Bremen Town musicians to the deep magic of "The Goose Girl," we are perceiving old possessions in a new light.

Edgar Taylor, the main translator of the stories, served the Grimms well with his workmanlike versions and his intelligent notes. For all its imaginative novelty, however, the book would not have had the success that it did without George Cruikshank's etchings, which not only came to be seen by some writers, such as Ruskin and Thackeray, as his *chef d'oeuvre*, but which also gave a new critical status to the place of the illustrator in popular literature.

◦§ 305 §◦

Madame LEINSTEIN (fl. 1820's). *Unlucky John and his Lump of Silver. A juvenile comic tale. Translated from the German, into easy verse, by Madame Leinstein. Embellished with fifteen neat coloured engravings.* London: printed and sold by Dean & Munday, Threadneedle-street, [not before 1824 (watermark-date)]. Price Six-pence. 16° (140 × 86 mm.).

[1¹⁶] (1ʳ blank, 1ᵛ *Frontispiece*, 2ʳ title, 2ᵛ–3ʳ blank, 3ᵛ incipit: *Honest John was a simple plodding swain*, 16ʳ *Moral*, 16ᵛ blank). Pp. 31, [1]. Printed on one side of the sheet only. 15 wood engravings (frontispiece full-page, remainder half-page—see overleaf), hand-colored at the publisher's. Original printed blue wrappers, title and wood engraving (repeated from 7ᵛ) on front cover, ads for *Children's Toy Books, uniformly printed* on back cover.

PML 83042. Gift: Elisabeth Ball.

Unlucky John is none other than the Grimms' "Hans im Glück," or, as Edgar Taylor put it, "Hans in Luck," the first story in *German Popular Stories*. Madame Leinstein's mistake in the title, which deflects attention from the point of the tale (Hans *enjoys* not possessing things), also bespeaks a casual attitude to the tale's contents: her versification omits the last incident and supplies a trite moral. Nevertheless, *Unlucky John* is notable for being a very early example of a Grimm story turned into a picture book. It appears to have been quite successful; the Morgan Library has a copy of another edition, dated 1825 (PML 85858=Gumuchian 3712), while at the same time Dean (and Newman) published a companion booklet: *Wishing; or the Fisherman and his Wife*.

◦§ 306 §◦

[GEORGE NICOL (fl. 1837–51)]. *The Story of the Three Bears.* London: Porter and Wright, 60, Pall-Mall, 1837. Oblong 8° (95 × 127 mm.).

304. vol. I, plate facing B1ʳ

them have been preserved. References: Cohn 369; Gottlieb 197; Ray *English* 112 (etched title vol. 1 in 2nd state); for a detailed survey, with concordance, of nineteenth-century translations, see Martin Sutton, *The Sin-Complex* (Kassel, 1996; Schriften der Brüder Grimm-Gesellschaft 28).

PML 75702–3. Bequest: Tessie Jones.

Popular tales, say the translators of this monumental work, "have been too much neglected. They are nearly discarded from the libraries of childhood. Philosophy is made the companion of the nursery." The indictment presumably relates to the generally serious moral and didactic works that were published in the early nineteenth century as the "official" children's literature, subsisting with due formality alongside the altogether unphilosophic picture books which we have dealt with in chapters XI and XII. Nevertheless, by urging that "works of fancy and fiction" have an

306. D7 recto, *detail*

305. fo. 15 verso

A⁴ (1ʳ half-title, 1ᵛ *Entered at Stationers Hall. Printed by W. Nicol, 51, Pall Mall*, 2ʳ title, 2ᵛ blank, 3ʳ–4ᵛ *Dedication* [to Robert Southey] dated July, 1837 and signed G.N.); *B⁸* C–D⁸ *E²*? (B1ʳ blank, B1ᵛ illustration, B2ʳ incipit: *Three Bears, once on a time, did dwell*, E2ᵛ printer's imprint). Pp. [2], vi, 29, [1]. Wood-engraved title-vignette by Rob. Hart after C.J. and 11 full-page wood engravings (incorporated in the signature collation but not in the pagination). Contemporary maroon half roan. References: *Realms of Childhood* 125; for the text, reprinted from the 1841 edition, see Ober.

PML 85110. Purchase: Julia P. Wightman.

Further evidence for the way in which adults began to play about with children's traditional tales can be seen in a series of versifications made by George Nicol. This *Three Bears* was the first and was published very soon after the first appearance of the story in print in the fourth volume of Robert Southey's occasional journal *The Doctor* (1837)—so soon, in fact, that George Nicol did not know the authorship and dedicates his version to the "unknown Author of 'The Doctor.'"

Nicol obviously enjoyed the work (and did a better job on Southey here than Mme Leinstein did on Grimm), and later on produced two more oblong octavos, not only following the design

of *The Three Bears* but also using the bear family as a frame device for telling more stories: *The Vizier and the Woodman* (1840), and, with a nice puff for "Stories of the brothers Grimm," the first picture-book version of "The Wolf and the Seven Kids" in *An Hour at Bearwood* (1839), which was later bound up with the above work as *The Three Bears and their Stories* (1841).

◄§ 307 §►

[JAKOB LUDWIG KARL GRIMM (1785–1863) & WILHELM KARL GRIMM (1786–1859).] *The Charmed Roe; or, the little brother and little sister. A fairy story. Illustrated by Otto Speckter, with twelve plates. Drawn on stone by Louis Haghe and Thomas Picken. Uniform with Otto Speckter's "Puss in Boots"*. London: John Murray, Albermarle Street, 1847. 8° (170 × 145 mm.).

A⁴ (1ʳ half-title in red and black, 1ᵛ blank, 2ʳ title in red and black, 2ᵛ imprint *London: Bradbury and Evans, Printers, Whitefriars*, 3ʳ *List of Illustrations*, 3ᵛ blank, 4ʳ Drop-title *The Charmed Roe* [red] . . . *First Picture*, decorated initial in red, text in black); B–E⁴ (B1ʳ *Second Picture*, B2ʳ *Third Picture* etc., with B3ᵛ, B4ᵛ, D1ᵛ blank and C4ᵛ blank except for a typographic ornament, E1ᵛ imprint *Bradbury and Evans* etc., E2–4 ads). Pp. 34, 6. Wood-engraved half-title decoration, small vignette on C4ʳ and floral initials; XII numbered tinted lithographs including frontispiece, signed by either L. Haghe or T. Picken, printed by Day & Son, Lithʳˢ to the Queen. Original pale blue boards, title and wood-engraved vignette within a rustic border printed in pink on front cover by Vizetelly Brothers and Co. . . . Fleet Street, London, publishers' decorated monogram, within a rustic border, printed in pink on back cover, red cloth spine, decorated endpapers, Reference: Ehmcke 28.

Provenance: Brian Alderson, Richmond.

With the publication of *The Charmed Roe* (the Grimms' "Brüderchen und Schwesterchen"), John Murray effected a new conjunction in the conversion of *German Popular Stories* into picture books. Murray had, a year before, published a successor

307. plate III, *reduced*

308. frontispiece, *reduced*

volume to Edgar Taylor's Grimm: *The Fairy Ring*, translated much less successfully by Taylor's cousin John Edward and supplied with decorations by Richard Doyle. Here, though, Murray commissioned a set of pictures from the German illustrator Otto Speckter, a translation of whose similarly illustrated *Märchen von dem gestiefelten Kater* (Puss in Boots) Murray had published in 1844. Speckter's original drawings were reproduced in a Christmas volume of the Verlag des Deutschen Volkstums (Hamburg, 1920), which allows one to see how completely his English lithographers worked over his powerful images to give them a smoothness acceptable to their Victorian patrons; they also substituted a decorated frontispiece for Speckter's eleventh drawing, which showed the queen suckling her child while caressing the charmed roe (see Brian Alderson, "An Unusual Children's Book: Siblings," Children's Books History Society *Newsletter* 57 [April 1997], p. 38).

Speckter had won an early reputation as an illustrator with his lithographs for W. Hey's *Fünfzig Fabeln* (Hamburg, 1833). His *Puss in Boots* illustrations had been published in Germany in 1843, and these were followed by some impressive Andersen illustrations (1845), four of which appeared in the English edition of *The Shoes of Fortune* (1847). In *The Charmed Roe* he brings to an English publication the cleaned-up, rustic Gothic that was typical of German children's book illustration at this time.

❧ 308 ❧

[JOHN RUSKIN (1819–1900)]. *The King of the Golden River; or, the Black Brothers: a legend of Stiria. Illustrated by Richard Doyle.* London: Smith, Elder, & Co., 65, Cornhill, 1851 [1850]. 8° (177 × 132 mm.).

π^2 (1^v frontispiece, 2^r pictorial title); $A^2(2+1)$ (1^r letterpress title, 1^v imprint *London: Henry Vizetelly*, printer and engraver, *Gough Square, Fleet Street*, 2^r *Advertisement*, 2^v blank, $2+1^r$ *Contents*, $2+1^v$ *List of illustrations. Designed and drawn on wood by Richard Doyle*); B–D^8 $E^4(4+1)$ ($E4+1$ ads including for *Wuthering Heights, Jane Eyre, The Stones of Venice* and *Military Memoirs of Col. James Skinner, C. B.*; quires A and E originally made up a sheet). Pp. [10], 56, [2]. 22 wood engravings (including frontispiece and title) by C. T. Thompson, G. and E. Dalziel, H. Orrin Smith and others, after Doyle. Original buff glazed boards, title, two illustrations (neither repeated from any in the book) and border on upper cover, central ornament and same border on lower cover, lacking spine, gilt edges, green decorated endpapers, cased by Westleys & Co. of London (ticket). References: Wise & Smart 12; Engen p. 196.

PML 133364. Bequest: Gordon N. Ray.

First edition, published at six shillings. Ruskin is one of the key figures in the "Victorian transformation" of children's literature. As will be shown in the next entry, he responded with great readiness to the imaginative possibilities of the books of his childhood, and his early pleasure in folk-tale remained with him throughout his life, making him a formidable advocate of a children's literature that respected its audience. *The King of the Golden River* is a pivotal book. He wrote it with great speed in 1841, "solely for the amusement" of twelve-year-old Effie Gray (who married Ruskin in 1848 and Sir John Millais in 1855). As a "legend of Stiria," it incorporates a Germanic quality that shows Ruskin's debt to the Grimms; at the same time it stands (in 1841) as a remarkable example of an early English *Kunstmärchen*, or artificially conceived fairy tale, while the appearance of Richard Doyle as (a somewhat uneven) illustrator links the book both to the growing tradition of English fairytale illustration and to the *Punch* school of draftsmen.

With or without Doyle's illustrations the work has remained in print as a children's book down to the present time, making it one of the longest-lived of English classics. With regard to the illustration, we should note that only the first two editions of *The King of the Golden River* showed the South West Wind Esquire with his hunting-horn nose. For reasons never fully explained, he was given a conventional, if rather prominent, dwarfish nose from the third edition onwards.

Above: **309.** fo. 9 recto, *reduced*   *Below:* **309.** fo. 19 recto, *reduced*

⊰ 309 ⊱

JOHN RUSKIN (1819–1900). *The Puppet Show or Amusing Characters for Children. With coloured plates. By John Ruskin.* Holograph manuscript. [London, Herne Hill:] 1829. 8° (172 × 108 mm.).

[1³⁰] (1ʳ title, 1ᵛ *Introduction*, 2ʳ⁻ᵛ *George of England*, incipit: *I am the bravest knight of all*, 3ʳ *The Brownie*, incipit: *I am a little dwarf dancing away the day*, 30ʳ *Curdken*, incipit: *My name is Curdken I now am hallooing*, 3–30 all versos blank). Foliated by Ruskin: [1], 1–29; paginated by him: [1], 1–31. One stock of laid paper, with armorial watermark; the quarter-sheet bifolia arranged to a peculiar system, too regular not to be planned: the eight outermost bifolia have their felt sides on the inside and show the extreme tail of the watermark, the seven innermost bifolia have their felt sides on the outside and show the major portion of the watermark. Written in brown ink in a childish but steady upright hand, imitating typography. 57 watercolor drawings by Ruskin, 19 of which have captions, such as: *Water Kelpie* (5ʳ), *Cupid Granadier* (7ʳ), *honour is a mere scutcheon therefore I'll none of it* showing Falstaff (12ʳ), *Don Quixotes Giant* (15ʳ), *Baron Munchausen* (17ʳ), *Ulysses in a Rage* (28ʳ). Bound after the manuscript was completed (foliation at head and drawings at foot of the pages cropped or shaved in places by the binder's knife): contemporary green half roan, gilt fillets, blind tooling in compartments of spine. Reference: Viljoen p.6, no.3.

Provenance: F. J. Sharp of Barrow-in-Furness, Lancashire (1880–1957). MA 3451. Bequest: Professor Helen Gill Viljoen.

Composed by Ruskin at the age of ten, this manuscript is, apart from being a remarkable specimen of childhood artistry, a witness of childhood book lore. What the boy Ruskin has done is to capture images from his own (unphilosophical) nursery library and then to invent verses about them, which do not necessarily reflect the original subjects of the drawings. For instance, Cruikshank's "Hans in Luck," the first etching in the first volume of *German Popular Stories*, appears as the lower illustration for a stanza headed by a monkey:

JACKO

I am a monkey dancing about
Grinning and making a terrible rout
For I but lately broke my chain
And I'll lead them a dance e'er I'm taken again.

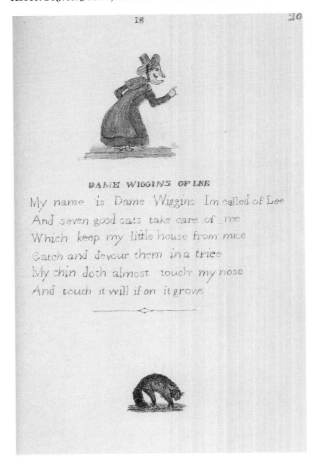

Copies of Cruikshank's Grimm etchings preponderate (there appear to be fifteen in all) and they help us to understand Ruskin's later enthusiasm for these illustrations, which he once called superior to Rembrandt. Similarly, a drawing copied from Dean's *Dame Wiggins of Lee* (see entry 310) reminds us that Ruskin was later to persuade Kate Greenaway to do illustrations for a new edition of the ballad, which Ruskin himself saw through the press. Other sketches may well be traceable to editions of, say, *The Seven Champions of Christendom* or *Don Quixote* which young John Ruskin could have browsed in—but what impresses above everything is the mixture of verve and concentration that the young boy has brought to his "Puppet Show."

ᴥ 310 ᴥ

[RICHARD SCRAFTON SHARPE (ca. 1775–1852) and "Mrs. Pearson," attributed to]. *Dame Wiggins of Lee, and her seven wonderful cats. A humorous tale. By a lady of ninety. Embellished with fifteen neatly coloured engravings* [attributed to R. Stennet, fl. 1820–30]. London: Dean and Munday, Threadneedle-street, [ca. 1842]. Price One Shilling. 8° (150 × 115 mm.).

[1–3⁸ 4⁴] (1/1 and 4/4 mounted as pastedowns, 1ᵛ frontispiece, 2ʳ title, 2ᵛ–3ʳ blank, 3ᵛ incipit: *Dame Wiggins of Lee / was a worthy old soul*. Pp. 54, [2]. Printed on one side of the sheets only. Wove paper, unwatermarked. Large and leaded roman type. 14 wood engravings including full-page frontispiece and small title-vignette (the remainder 74 × 84 mm. each), in publisher's coloring (see overleaf). Original printed mauve wrappers, title (*with seventeen . . . engravings*) and wood engraving (not relating to the text) on front cover, ads on lower cover. References: James p. 77 (editions of 1823 and 1885); Osborne II, 631–2 (editions of 1823 and ca. 1850); Hockliffe 848.

Provenance: *Miss C Dyke* (inscr.). PML 82932. Gift: Elisabeth Ball.

Ruskin's youthful attraction to Dame Wiggins of Lee is evident in *The Puppet Show* (entry 309), where he copies the Dame in her straw hat in the act of admonishing her cats for ice-skating. This is the illustration for the fourth stanza of the rhyme as it appeared in the first edition, which A. K. Newman and Dean & Munday had published in 1823 and which must have been one of Ruskin's childhood books. Many years later, in 1885, he was instrumental in the publication of a new edition of the text, for which he persuaded Kate Greenaway to produce some rather unsatisfactory additional pictures in the style of the original.

The Morgan Library owns two early editions of *Dame Wiggins*, one with a Dean & Munday cover and one with a Newman cover, both with Dean & Munday title pages (PML 85859 and 83023). Both can be dated to ca. 1828 and are in the narrow dimensions typical of Regency picture books, whereas the present edition shows that standard size changing towards the more expansive one of Victorian times. Although all of the original wood engravings are used (apart from Ruskin's favorite, which has disappeared), they are now set into a squarish octavo format, with one picture for each page opening, larger type, and individual titles to the pictures. This reworking, too, remained in print for a number of years (PML 85187 is a "new edition" of it from Thos.

Dean & Co. ca. 1846, in a pretty publisher's cloth binding, but with parsimonious coloring); eventually, ca. 1856, the blocks were again used in Dean's yet more expansive "Miss Merryheart's Series" (250 × 165 mm.), a typical early Victorian picture book with two illustrations per page and the bright hand-coloring done with a hasty brush.

ᴥ 311 ᴥ

RICHARD DOYLE (1824–83). Fifty-one autograph illustrated letters, signed Dick, to his father John Doyle. [London:] Sunday Morning [24] April 1842–Sunday Morning 17 December 1843. (239 × 189 mm. and smaller).

Mostly three pages each and address-page, written in cursive script, each illustrated with several drawings, mostly pen-and-ink, some watercolor. See examples overleaf. Laid and wove paper, various watermarks. Mounted on stubs to form an album and bound with twenty-five autograph letters signed by Henry Edward Doyle (1826–92) and three by Charles Altamont Doyle (1832–93), Richard's two brothers, all to the same recipient. Tan morocco gilt, by Best & Co.

Provenance: Sir Arthur Conan Doyle (Richard's nephew, 1859–1930; armorial bookplate). MA 3315. Purchase: Fellows Fund, with the special assistance of Mr. and Mrs. Walter H. Page.

Like Ruskin, Richard Doyle was also something of an infant prodigy, and like Ruskin his childhood and youth during the 1820s and 1830s were shot through with delight in stories taken from folk and fairy lore. This made him a natural choice to illustrate those books that helped to reassert the imagination in children's literature, the Grimm stories in *The Fairy Ring* (mentioned at entry 307) and Ruskin's own *King of the Golden River* (entry 308); while his straightforward everyday wit, which brought him to the magazine *Punch* at the age of nineteen, also made him a natural choice to illustrate such fiction as Thackeray's *The Newcomes* (1853–55).

These letters were written for his father, the political caricaturist John Doyle (1797–1868) and were something of a weekly task; but they give evidence on almost every page of the new spirit in writing and illustration that was abroad at this time. We reproduce here the start of two letters, which show Doyle writing about his own work as painter and draftsman and exhibit his prodigious talent for comic design. (Lear would have been proud to have done those birds balanced around the rustic frame of our first example; and note, in our second, Punch and Toby fetching wood blocks and lithographic chalk, together with the almost hieroglyphical progression of the artist from stone to canvas to drawing-on-the-block.)

Such examples could be matched by a host of other moments relevant to our purposes, ranging from Doyle's comments on "Rivington an Co's" [*sic*] German Repository of prints in Regent Street (2 April 1843), to the persistent re-appearance of Punch-like figures (e.g. 27 September 1842) and the unbroken succession of fairy and fantasy sketches (e.g. the three tumultuous pages for 19 November 1843). Such drawings remind us not just that Doyle was eventually to create the last word in all fairy illustrations, *In Fairy Land* (1870), but also that in these early years he had created homemade illustrated fairy books such as his *Jack the Giant Killer* of 1842 and his *Beauty and the Beast* (ca. 1842), the

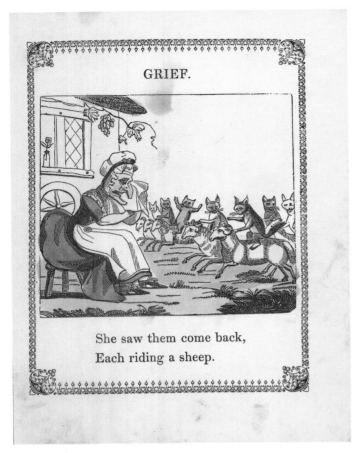

310. 2/8 recto, *reduced*

latter manuscript being in the Morgan Library (MA 2756; Gottlieb 110).

312

The Home Treasury. The Veritable History of Whittington and his Cat. London: Chapman and Hall, 186, Strand, and Joseph Cundall, 12, Old Bond Street, 1847. 8° (165 × 120 mm.).

A–B⁴ (A1ʳ title, A1ᵛ blank, B4ᵛ imprint *C. Whittingham, Printer, Chiswick*); 3 wood-engraved plates including frontispiece, by George and Edward Dalziel after John Absolon, printed in colors from multiple blocks. Pp. [16]. Plates on different paper from the text. Original pale green wrappers, a complex design of Renaissance ornament printed in a shade of brown to imitate gilt, series title *The Home Treasury Ballads Tales Fables Histories*, title *Whittington*, imprint *Chapman and Hall* on both covers, *Price one shilling* on front cover. References: McLean *Cundall* p. 49; Waddleton 1847.51.

PML 86032. Gift: Felix de Marez Oyens, 1991.

Edgar Taylor (see entry 304) was not the only editor to voice doubts about too much rationalism in the nursery. In a serial publication issued between October 1837 and August 1838, *The Child's Fairy Library* (PML 82138–9), we find an orotund preface that repeats Taylor's sentiments: "Happy is mankind, yet in the days of 'Infant Schools,' and of the numberless 'Science made easy's,' that *Imagination* will not yield her exalted empire to the rule of those that have none . . .;" while a year or two later there arrived an even more uncompromising defense of fairy tale,

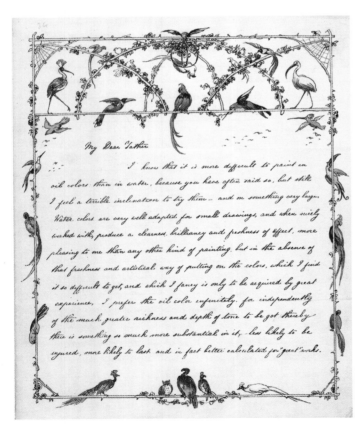

311. letter 48, 29 Oct. 1843, *reduced*

311. letter 34, undated [late May–early June 1843], *reduced*

aimed directly at the philosopher who was presumably the target of the earlier tirade: "The character of most Children's Books published during the last quarter of a century, is fairly typified in the name of Peter Parley...after a narrow fashion [addressing themselves] almost entirely to the cultivation of the understanding of children." By way of redress the author proposed "a series of Works . . . the character of which may be briefly described as anti-Peter Parleyism"—works that would bring back to the nursery "the many tales sung or said from time immemorial."

The controversialist quoted here is Henry Cole, writing in 1843 to introduce his venture of "Felix Summerly's Home Treasury of Books, Pictures, Toys etc.," which he, together with his publisher Joseph Cundall (1818–95), planned as a full frontal attack on the moribund literature of the time. In such elegantly designed little books as this *Dick Whittington* or *Sir Bevis* from a companion series (entry 360b), he set about revolutionizing both the editorial principles and the production methods behind children's books. With a coherent policy in mind, he refurbished the old Regency picture-book tradition, which by now had sunk into decrepitude, and primed the engine of the opulent Victorian years that were to come.

This edition of *Dick Whittington* follows the traditional text of the story and displays two of the special features of "The Home Treasury": an elaborate cover decoration based upon a "design for goldsmith's work by Hans Holbein," as illustrated in Henry Shaw's *Encyclopaedia of Ornament* (1842), and illustrations printed in color. These are among the earliest color-printed pictures in children's books. They were printed from wood blocks, probably by the firm of Gregory, Collins and Reynolds, who were among the first to develop the techniques of George Baxter (see McLean *Victorian Book Design* pp. 40, 191; for the decorated binding, see Margaret M. Smith, "Joseph Cundall and the Binding Design for the *Illustrated Biographies of the Great Artists*," *The Library*, 7th ser., 5 [2004], pp. 39–63).

❧ 313 ❧

Sir HENRY COLE (1808–82) & JOHN CALCOTT HORSLEY (1817–1903). Christmas Card. London: [Printed by Jobbins, Warwick Court, Holborn] Published at Summerly's Home Treasury Office [Joseph Cundall], 12 Old Bond Street, [1843]. (80 × 127 mm.).

Lithograph by Horsley after an idea of Cole, showing in the largest and central scene a merry party and the wish *A Merry Christmas and a Happy New Year to you*, and in the two side panels acts of charity; hand-colored for the publisher by the professional "colourer" Mason. References: Buday pp. 6–10; McLean *Cundall* p. 12.

Provenance: To *James Simpson Esq* From *Wll^m Cole* (inscr.). PML 84814. Purchase: Julia P. Wightman.

Gammer Gurton's Story Books.

A TRUE TALE OF ROBIN HOOD.

BOTH gentlemen and yeomen bold,
Or whatsoe'er you are,
To have a stately story told,
Attention now prepare:

It is a tale of Robin Hood,
Which I to you will tell;
Which being rightly understood,
I know will please you well.

This Robin (so much talked on)
Was once a man of fame,
And styled Earl of Huntingdon,
Lord Robin Hood by name.

In courtship and magnificence
His carriage won him praise;
And greater favour with his prince
Than any in our days.

2   JOSEPH CUNDALL, 12, OLD BOND STREET.

314. plate [5] and 2/1ʳ, *reduced*

313. *reduced*

Henry Cole was a man of protean energy (among his achieve-ments must be numbered the masterminding of the Great Exhibition of 1851 and much positive action in the founding of the Victoria & Albert Museum). He also seems to have been keen that cheerfulness should keep breaking in, and there is a welcome coincidence in date of his founding the "Home Treasury" with his invention of the Christmas card. From a recently reported copy of a salesman's sample of the card it appears that colored copies sold at 6d. each or 13 for 6s. (i.e., buy twelve get one free) with plain copies at 2d. or 13 for 2s. (Bloomsbury Auctions catalogue 507, 25 Nov. 2004, lot 570). Cundall claimed in a letter that "possibly not more than a thousand" cards were sold.

⋙ 314 ⋘

The Old Story Books of England. Illustrated with twelve pictures by eminent artists. Collected and re-edited by [in rebus:] *Ambrose Merton* [i.e. William John Thoms (1803–85)]. [London:] Printed for Joseph Cundall, Old Bond St. in the City of Westminster, [1845]. 8° (163 × 118 mm.).

π² (1ʳ title, rebus-vignette and four-piece border, 1ᵛ blank, 2ʳ editor's dedication, 2ᵛ *Contents* omitting the final book); 1⁸ (Sir Guy of Warwick); 4⁸ (Sir Bevis of Hampton); 10⁸ (Tom Hickathrift); 7⁸ (Friar Bacon); 2⁸ (Robin Hood—see previous page); 6⁸ (The King and the Cobbler); 13⁸ (Patient Grissel); 8⁸ (The Princess Rosetta); 11⁸ (Robin Goodfellow); 9⁸ (The Beggar's Daughter, 9/8ᵛ Chiswick Press device and imprint *Printed by C. Whittingham. 1845*); 5⁸ (The Babes in the Wood; The Lady Isabella's Tragedy); 12⁸ (Fair Rosamond, 12/8ᵛ same device and imprint); 3⁸ (Gammer Gurton's Garland); 13 wood-engraved plates (that for "The King and the Cobbler" inserted as frontis-piece) after Frederick Tayler (1, 4, 10 and 2), John Franklin (7, 13, 11 and 5), John Absolon (6, 8, 9 and 12), and by W. G. & G. E. Mason (3), all except the last printed in colors by Gregory, Collins & Reynolds from multiple blocks, the plate for "Gammer Gurton's Garland" hand-colored at the publisher's. Ff. [2, 104]. Pre-liminaries and plates on different wove paper from the text. Wood-engraved title-border and flower-and-animal borders in the outer margin of each text page (repeated from nine blocks) stencil-colored; wood-engraved initials, tailpieces, rebuses, and

printer's device hand-colored at the publisher's. Original or contemporary blind-tooled maroon morocco over thick boards, gilt edges, marbled endpapers, by James Hayday (d. 1872). References: Waddleton 1845.63; cf. McLean *Cundall* p. 52.

Provenance: Eliza Jane Absolon (sign.), daughter of the artist (?). The Osborne Collection of Early Children's Books, Toronto Public Library. Gift: Felix de Marez Oyens, 1991.

Following the launch of "The Home Treasury" under the editor-ship of "Felix Summerly," Cundall took on a further picture-book series: "Gammer Gurton's Story Books," named after the peasant figure of fun who first comes to light in the sixteenth-century comedy *Gammer Gurton's Needle*. Such a reference is in keeping with the aim of the series, which was to revive those "Histories, which, in bygone days, delighted the Childhood of England's master-spirits." "Ambrose Merton," the editor, was the antiquary W.J. Thoms (to whom we owe the term "folk-lore"). The thirteen stories in the series are here bound up as a compendium, which enhances the pseudo-medievalism of the antique paper, the illu-minated initials, and the decorative borders. There is a striking contrast between the color-printed illustrations and the hand-applied watercolor of the decorative initials and the stenciled borders.

At the height of his career, the bookbinder James Hayday employed between thirty and forty workmen, including ten finishers (see H. M. Nixon, *Five Centuries of English Bookbinding* [Scolar Press, 1978] p. 202). He produced elaborate pastiches and exhibited at Sir Henry Cole's Great Exhibition of 1851. His most important patron was Sir Joseph Walter King Eyton, for whom he executed a sumptuous velvet binding on a vellum copy of the Cole-Cundall edition of Dürer's *Passion* (1844; McLean *Cundall* p. 14).

⋙ 315 ⋘

The Charm. A book for boys and girls. [First Series]. London: Printed by G. Barclay, Castle St. Leicester Sq. for Addey and Co., 21 Old Bond Street. Edinburgh: J. Menzies. Dublin: J. M'Glashan, 1853. 8° (192 × 130 mm.).

[1⁴] (frontispiece, title, preface, lists of contents and illus-trations); [2–39⁴ 40⁸ 41–47⁴] (text and 105 wood engravings); 48⁴ (ads). Pp. [384], 8. Original buff cloth, blocked in blind and gilt.

Provenance: *Marian Alice Anstruther Feb 8ᵗʰ 1853* (inscr.). The Osborne Collection of Early Children's Books, Toronto Public Library.

The second half of the nineteenth century was to be the great age of children's periodicals. The range would stretch from the abhorred penny dreadfuls, such as E. J. Brett's *The Boys of England* (1866–99, under that title), to Charlotte Yonge's genteel High-Church *Monthly Packet* (1851–98). Trade arrangements were also made to ensure English sales for the American *St. Nicholas* (1873–1943), which has claims to being the greatest children's periodical ever.

Hospitable as they were to serialized stories and plentiful illustration, the magazines gave a consistent buoyancy to the children's-book trade, and even overambitious or undercapital-ized ventures like *Good Words for the Young* (1868–72) or *Young*

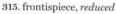

THE LUCKY TUB.

315. frontispiece, *reduced*

316. F2 verso, *reduced*

Folks (1876–96, under varying titles) fostered such masterpieces as "At the Back of the North Wind," with Arthur Hughes's illustrations, and "Treasure Island." *The Charm*, however, was a little too early to catch the floodtide of periodical publishing, and since it was almost certainly undercapitalized, its ambitions were restricted. Undoubtedly Joseph Cundall was at the back of it, working with his shadowy partner Addey, and the magazine reflects in both its contents and its illustrations Cundall's continuing awareness of trends in German publishing. But the staid presentation lacked the editorial energy that later periodicals were to prove a *sine qua non* for success.

Two more series of *The Charm* were edited by Cundall, copies of which are also in the Osborne Collection but with a different provenance and bound in blue cloth.

✣ 316 ✣

Nursery Rhymes, Tales and Jingles. London: James Burns, [September 1844]. 4° (194 × 148 mm.).

a^4 b^2(2+1) (a1^r half-title, a1^v imprint *London: printed by Robson, Levey, and Franklyn, Great New Street, Fetter Lane*, a2^r title, a3^r publisher's dedication to the *Prince of Wales, the Princess Royal and the Princess Alice*, A4^{r-v} *Advertisement*, b1^r *Contents*); B–O^4. Pp. [14], 102, [2]. Wood-engraved half-title, pictorial title gilt-

printed, border on every page, and 78 wood-engraved illustrations including repeats, numerous vignettes. Contemporary cloth. References: Opie *Three Centuries*, 237 note; Alderson *Burns* pp. 117 & 119.

Provenance: *With Nancy's love to her very dear young friend Alice Baine. 23rd January 1851* (inscr.). The Osborne Collection of Early Children's Books, Toronto Public Library.

While much attention has been paid to the Cole-Cundall partnership reviving children's literature in the 1840s, the activities of James Burns have tended to be overlooked. As a publisher Burns was initially involved with the tractarians (he published Harriet Mozley's *The Fairy Bower* in 1841; see note to entry 293), but alongside his more earnest publications he also developed a list drawn from traditional sources, edited and designed in a manner that owed nothing to his immediate competitors. This nursery rhyme book is perhaps his most successful children's book, and an expanded second edition appeared in 1846. Although published soon after James Orchard Halliwell's seminal *Nursery Rhymes of England* (1842), it seems to be an entirely independent compilation—"a very tasteful German-looking book" as a reviewer in *The Examiner* described it—and certainly carries more style than Felix Summerly's rather stubby *Traditional Nursery Songs* of 1843.

Burns's other "popular" books show an equivalent individuality and a similar interest in German decorative and illustrative styles.

YALMER'S VOYAGE WITH OLÉ LUCKOIE.

317. frontispiece, *reduced*

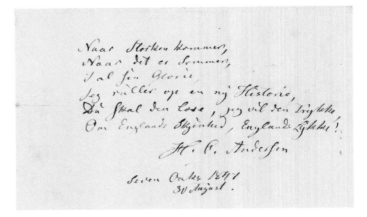

318a. *reduced*

There were series volumes of nursery tales and legends and traditional stories (including newly translated stories from Grimm); there was a peculiar and not very distinguished selection of Andersen, *Tales for the Young* (1847); and there was an attractive series of single tales (see entry 360c). Burns was also involved with the Rugeley publishers of Paget's *Hope of the Katzekopfs* (entry 332), and there is every sign that he would have developed into a pioneering publisher of children's books were it not that he followed Newman into Roman Catholicism and turned his energies to developing England's foremost Catholic publishing company, Burns & Lambert, eventually to become Burns, Oates & Washbourne.

metalcuts including frontispiece. Pp. [4], 127, [1]. Wood-engraved head- and tailpieces and initials. Original blue cloth, blocked in gilt and blind. References: NBL *Andersen*, 34; Alderson *Andersen*, 1; Osborne I, 17.

The Osborne Collection of Early Children's Books, Toronto Public Library.

As has occurred with many ambitious publishing ventures, Cundall's progress was soon hampered by undercapitalization, and his essentially editorial talents had often to be applied to books published by other companies. He seems to have had a good working relationship with Chapman & Hall (who took over the Home Treasury Series in 1846), and his publishing style is clearly evident in *Wonderful Stories for Children*, the first translation of Andersen into English.

Eleven years had elapsed since the first "Eventyr" were published in Denmark, and when Andersen eventually reached England, his stories were translated from inaccurate German editions as well as Danish ones. Mary Howitt at least went to the Danish, but her English renderings in no way matched the spirited originals, and what is more, she silently excerpted "A Night in the Kitchen" from its true position as part of "The Flying Trunk."

Within a year of the appearance of *Wonderful Stories*, at least four more selections from Andersen were issued by English publishers, two of them by Cundall himself. These were *A Danish Story Book* (PML 26350) and *The Nightingale and Other Tales*, both in deeply unsatisfactory translations from the German by Charles Boner. *The Shoes of Fortune* with Speckter's illustrations (noted at entry 307) was published by Chapman & Hall in December 1846.

⧉ 317 ⧉

HANS CHRISTIAN ANDERSEN (1805–75). *Wonderful Stories for Children. By Hans Christian Anderson, author of "The Improvisatore," &c. Translated from the Danish by Mary Howitt*. London: Chapman and Hall, 186 Strand, 1846. 8° (165 × 120 mm.).

π² (1ʳ title, 1ᵛ imprint *Vizetelly Brothers and Co. Printers and engravers, Peterborough Court, 135 Fleet Street*, 2ʳ *Contents*); A–H⁸ (H8ᵛ same imprint); four litho-tinted and hand-colored

⧉ 318a ⧉

HANS CHRISTIAN ANDERSEN (1805–75). Autograph Poem, in Danish, 1 page, 6 lines, signed *H.C. Andersen* and dated from *Seven Oaks 1847 30 August*. (108 × 180 mm.).

MA 2876. Purchase: Fellows Fund, with the special assistance of Douglas C. Ewing.

318b

HANS CHRISTIAN ANDERSEN (1805–75). Two Autograph Letters, in English, signed in full, to the publisher Richard Bentley: 3 pages, dated from *Glorup 31 August 1848*, (205 × 131 mm.); 2½ pages, dated from *Copenhagen 20 October 1852*, (272 × 210 mm.).

MA 2876(4) and 2876(17). Purchase: Fellows Fund, with the special assistance of Douglas C. Ewing.

318c

Pen-and-ink Drawing of Hans Christian Andersen taking tea, perhaps at "Seven Oaks" in 1847. (210 × 185 mm.).

MA 2876. Purchase: Fellows Fund, with the special assistance of Douglas C. Ewing.

In 1847 Andersen paid his first visit to England, where he was much fêted. Among those who tended his fragile susceptibilities was Richard Bentley, who published translations of the fairy tales, novels, and travel sketches by the great man. The Morgan Library has an extensive run of letters from Andersen to Bentley, written over three decades; we are showing one in which he notes the first appearance of an edition illustrated by his chosen Danish artist, Vilhelm Pedersen (published in Leipzig by Carl B. Lorck), and one in which he discusses the English publication of *A Poet's Day Dreams* (Bentley, 1853). Other mementos of this visit are the caricature sketch, possibly done by "Alfred Crowquill" at Bentley's house, Sevenoaks, and a manuscript poem.

> Naar Storken kommer,
> Naar det er Sommer,
> I al sin Glorie
> Jeg ruller op en ny Historie,
> Du skal den laese, jeg vil den trykke,
> Om Englands Skjonhed, Englands Lykke!

> When the storks come,
> And summer comes,
> In all its glory,
> My mind turns to a new story,
> I set it down, and the printing-press
> Tells England's joy and comeliness!

319

EDWARD LEAR (1812–88). *A Book of Nonsense. Third edition. With many new pictures and verses . . .* London: Routledge, Warne, and Routledge, [1861]. Oblong 8° (135 × 213 mm.).

A² (1ʳ title with woodcut and the limerick *There was an Old Derry down Derry...*, 1ᵛ woodcut device of the Dalziel Brothers' Camden Press, 2 *Dedication* lacking); B–P⁸ (B1ʳ incipit: *There was an Old Man with a beard*, P8ʳ printer's imprint *Dalziel Brothers, Camden Press, London*). Ff. 111, [1]. Wove paper, unwatermarked. Printed on one side of the sheets only. 113 wood-engraved illustrations

There was an Old Person of Ischia, whose conduct grew friskier and friskier;
He danced hornpipes and jigs, and ate thousands of figs,
That lively Old Person of Ischia.
14

319. C6 recto, *reduced*

by the Dalziels after Lear, and letterpress limericks. Original cloth-backed printed boards, title-page repeated on both covers. References: Field pp. 132–6; Korn pp. 7–8; Noakes 76.

PML 84569. Purchase: Frederick R. Koch.

So far in this chapter the momentum of a "children's book revolution" has been largely exemplified through the determined promulgation of fairy tales as an essential ingredient in children's culture. In 1846, however, the year of the arrival in England of Andersen's tales, a native contribution appeared which transformed the concept of what an author might or might not do when writing for children. This revolutionary work was Edward Lear's *Book of Nonsense* (2 vols., lithographed throughout; see J. G. Schiller, *Nonsensus* [1988] for a census of extant copies). In historical terms it was not unprecedented, for Lear based his "limericks" on a model that he had found in John Marshall's *Anecdotes and Adventures of Fifteen Gentlemen* (see entry 175). The novelty lay first in the easy flow of the nonsense, which contrasted with the more rough-and-ready versification of the model, and second in the blending of Lear's nonsensical verses to his even more nonsensical illustrations.

From the evidence of both the first and the second editions, Lear's printer/publisher Thomas McLean had problems with the lithography of the book, and in the 1850s his business fell on hard times. Consequently Lear sold the copyright on *A Book of Nonsense* to a regular trade publisher, Routledge, who brought out this third, expanded edition using conventional wood engravings for the illustrations. Lear was apparently pleased with the financial outcome. In November 1862 he wrote to Lady Waldegrave: "I went into the city today to put the £125 I got for the 'Book of Nonsense' into the funds. It is doubtless a very unusual thing for an artist to put by money, for the whole way from Temple Bar to the Bank was *crowded* with carriages and people,—so immense a sensation did this occurrence make."

320. letter 10, *reduced*

⌁ 320 ⌁

EDWARD LEAR (1812–88). *A Nonsense Alphabet*. Holograph manuscript. [England: ca. 1860]. Half-sheets (312 × 197 mm.).

26 pen-and-ink drawings and nonsense alphabet verses, mounted on both sides of 13 cards. A single stock of watermarked, laid paper over board. Incipit: *A* / [drawing] / *A was some Ants* / *Who seldom stood still,* / *And they made a nice house* / *In the side of a hill.* /*a!* / *Nice little ants*!; ending: *Z* / [drawing]. *Z was some Zinc* / *So pretty and bright,* / *Which sparkled & shone* / *In the sun's merry light,* / *Z!* / *Beautiful Zinc!* Reference: *Fellows Report* (1975–77), p. 200.

MA 2946. Gift: Leslie Ten Eyck Michaels and Patricia Michaels Mason, in memory of Arthur Michaels.

For twenty-five years *A Book of Nonsense* stood as the only public evidence of Lear's comic genius; the wonders of his "nonsense songs" and all their attendant fooling did not get into print until a sequence of three books came out in the 1870s. Nevertheless, in private, Lear was (for several complex reasons) a compulsive

"bosh-producing luminary," and his voluminous correspondence abounds in his own highly individual wit. Furthermore, he was generous with his talents and made many copies of nonsense poems or of other "nonsenses" like this alphabet, which he would give to friends and to the children of friends. Where the alphabets are concerned, he often followed the stanzaic model which we see here and often copied the same subjects, "ants" and "zinc" being typical. The unusual items in this set are B for Butterfly, E for Eagle, F for Fan, G for Grasshopper, O for Omnibus and T for Trumpet.

⌁ 321 ⌁

HEINRICH HOFFMANN (1809–94). *The English Struwwelpeter or pretty stories and funny pictures for little children. After the sixth edition of the celebrated German work*. Leipsic: Friedrich Volckmar, 1848. 4° (247 × 195 mm.).

[1²⁴]. Ff. 24. Sheets printed on one side only. Unwatermarked, wove paper. Roman type. Wood-engraved illustrations on each leaf, hand-colored at the publisher's. Original printed light-pink paper boards, type-ornament border, title and imprint (as transcribed above) on front cover, wood engraving of children being read to on back cover. References: Herzog & Siefert p. 105, no. 14; Schatzki 129; Gottlieb 131 (early edition, rebound); *Realms of Childhood* 135.

Provenance: Walter Schatzki (1941 cat., no. 129). Spencer Collection, The New York Public Library, Astor, Lenox and Tilden Foundations.

Very different from the *Book of Nonsense*, but equally revolutionary, was Heinrich Hoffmann's *Struwwelpeter*, which was first published at Frankfurt am Main in 1845, with lithographic illustrations (PML 84753). Here too was nonsense (although literal-minded folk do not perceive how Hoffmann is sending up the traditional features of the cautionary tale); in addition, though, the book has a graphic originality which is all the more remarkable for being the work of an amateur. Symbolic imagery, strip-cartoons, the simultaneous presentation of a sequence of actions, caricature, and decoration are all features which coincide in *Struwwelpeter* to make it one of the most dramatic examples of picture-book art for children. Immediately after its appearance, the book became immensely popular in Germany; the English edition follows the sixth German edition and was produced in Leipzig for distribution through London agents. Its rather flimsy getup (which was intentional on the part of Hoffmann) ensured fairly rapid disintegration, and copies of all early editions of the book in whatever language are of extreme rarity.

A contemporary trade bibliography, Christian Gottlob Kayser's *Vollständiges Bücher-Lexicon* (1834–1912), described the sixth German edition as being illustrated with wood engravings. While acknowledging that Kayser is usually accurate in his descriptions, bibliographers have doubted this entry and assumed on the basis of the book's appearance that it continued to be printed by lithography. But after making a detailed examination of the edition (which was the "parent" to the first English printing), the German authority on illustrative processes Hans Ries has argued convincingly that the illustrations are wood engravings, hand-colored and printed simultaneously with the letterpress text

321. fo. 12 recto, *reduced*

322. plate facing C3ʳ, *reduced*

❧ 322 ❧

CLARA DE CHATELAIN, née DE PONTIGNY (1807–76). *Right and Wrong. By Madame de Chatelain. Illustrated with eight coloured drawings.* London: William Tegg, 85, Queen Street, Cheapside, [ca. 1855]. 4° (240 × 185 mm.).

B⁴ C–E⁴ (B1ʳ title, B1ᵛ imprint *London: printed by W. Clowes and Sons, Stamford Street and Charing Cross*, E4ᵛ same imprint); 8 wood-engraved plates (including frontispiece), in publisher's coloring. Pp. 32. Original printed buff boards, hand-colored wood engraving (repeat of that facing E1ʳ) on front cover, ads on back cover for five picture books in "4to Fancy Boards."

Provenance: *Stassin et Xavier Libraires 22, rue de La Banque* (contemporary label of Parisian booksellers, who specialized in foreign and children's books); Gumuchian & Cⁱᵉ (1930 cat., no. 1687). PML 82525. Gift: Elisabeth Ball.

The arrival of *Struwwelpeter* in England in 1848 marks the start of a rapid expansion in the publishing of what may be termed "new-style" picture books. We have little direct evidence to attribute the change to Hoffmann's book, but it is significant that from 1848 onwards there is a marked increase in the number of books published in quarto; also, publishers and their illustrators began to use subjects directly related to "bad children," and they often adopted the design of variously mixing illustration and text found in Hoffmann's work.

There was a continuing influence from publishing events in Germany, where *Struwwelpeter* had also had a galvanic effect.

Mme de Chatelain, who seems to have worked as an editorial dogsbody, was early on responsible for helping Joseph Cundall (via the firm of Addey & Co.) to publish translations of a couple of German *Struwwelpeter* imitations: *A Laughter Book for Little Folk* (1851) and Dr. Julius Bähr's *Naughty Boys and Girls*, illustrated by Theodor Hosemann (1852). The publisher of *Right and Wrong*, William Tegg, was the English agent for the German publishers of *Struwwelpeter*. There is a strong possibility that Tegg commissioned Mme de Chatelain to write a story to fit the colored plates. Judging by the pictorial content (dress, architecture, ornaments), these plates are almost certainly of German origin. The story itself, centered as it is upon the workings of juvenile conscience, shows no concession to modern trends. This imitation not listed in Rühle.

❧ 323 ❧

[WILLIAM NEWMAN (fl. 1855–1865)]. *The Comical Pictures and Sad Fates of Richard, Lucy, & John.* London: Dean & Son, Printers & Publishers 11 Ludgate Hill, [ca. 1860]. One Shilling mounted on cloth, Coloured. Dean's Sixpeny Colᵈ Picture English Struwelpeters. 4°? (233 × 175mm.).

6 disjunct leaves, printed on rectos only and stabbed to form a codex: 1 *The Little Slattern, a lesson for girls*, incipit: *Lazy was Lucy, so careless, so gay*, 2 *The Dirty Boy*, incipit: *Really, of all the odd, odd things*, 4 *The Cruel Boy*, incipit: *Alas! that I should*

I know not: p'raps for ever
A scarecrow he'll remain,
For boys who think it clever
'To laugh at others' pain.

323. fo. 6 recto, *reduced*

mention, 6 mounted as back pastedown. Nine wood engravings by William McConnell (1833–67), in publisher's coloring. Original yellow wrappers, wood-engraved floral title (as transcribed above) on upper cover, letterpress ads and three wood engravings on back cover and inside front cover. Reference: Rühle 281j.

Provenance: Gumuchian & Cie (1930 cat., no. 5011). PML 82529. Gift: Elisabeth Ball.

Perhaps the most obvious proof of the impact of *Struwwelpeter* lies in the actual use of his name (albeit with only one "w") for a series of picture books, published by Dean & Son and matched by a very similar rival series published by George Routledge. These two publishers were what might be termed "market leaders" in the new-style picture books, and from the mid-fifties onward they put out huge numbers of large-format books, at first hand-colored and then color-printed. (Dean's *Dame Wiggins of Lee* of ca. 1856, noted at entry 310, advertises on its back cover nine different series of "coloured six-penny books," totaling 122 titles in all).

A most noteworthy characteristic of such "Struwelpeters" as *Richard, Lucy and John* is their total failure to live up to their model. The tongue-in-cheek comedy of Hoffmann's original is abandoned in favor of conventional moralizing (often in lamentable verse), and the high distinction of his designs is turned into raw caricature. Rühle plausibly identifies the author of this example as William Newman.

324

[Daniel Defoe (1661?–1731)]. *Deans New Scenic Books N° 2. Robinson Crusoe.* [London: Dean and Son, 1869]. Large 8° (245 × 170 mm.).

[1⁸] (1ʳ drop-title *The Voyages and Adventures of Robinson Crusoe*); eight pull-up chromo-lithographic scenes (about 200 × 140 mm.), hinged to the top of the leaves just above the text, each constructed of three paper cut-outs (foreground, middle distance, background, placed equidistantly in front of one another to provide depth) which are connected with a purple ribbon for pulling up the picture. Ff. 8. Unwatermarked, wove paper. Letterpress printing on both sides of the sheet, but imposed to show text on rectos only. The reverse of the largest (background) section of each of the eight pull-up mechanisms dyed mauve. Original black-cloth-backed boards, chromo-lithographic pictorial title (as transcribed above) on front cover, ad on back cover *Handsomely-bound Books, for Youth. Well adapted for birth day presents, and prize books for schools. By Dean and Son Ludgate Hill, London, E.C.*, yellow front endpapers with ads for *Amusing Picture Story Books*, back endpapers *Juvenile and Instructive Works*. References: Haining pp. 30–1 (Little Red Riding Hood); Montanaro pp. 263–4.

Provenance: *Gerald White / West Knoll / Bournemouth* (inscr.). The Metropolitan Museum of Art, Department of Prints. Gift: Lincoln Kirstein.

Thomas Dean & Son were not content to exploit the picture-book market with their multiplying series. They were also probably the first English publishers to develop a large-scale enterprise in the production of "movable" books (i.e. picture books that are adapted in various ways to bring them into a closer relationship with toys, chiefly by furnishing them with movable parts). The arrival of such books in the late 1850s is further evidence of Victorian playfulness getting under way.

Although this example is not among the earliest of Dean's very varied range of movables, the pop-up device is still in primitive form, requiring manual operation rather than relying, as some could, on the leverage of the book's hinge. The triple scene, with its components graded by size, may owe something to the popularity of peep shows (see entries 169–170). As was so often to occur with future publishers of movables, little attention was paid to the text. The gimmick was all.

325

Darton's Instructive Books. Moveable Trades. Showing the mechanical movements in each trade to instruct and amuse children. London: Darton & C° Holborn Hill, [not after 1860]. Small 2° or 4° (268 × 183 mm.).

Eight disjunct leaves of letterpress; eight hand-colored lithographic plates (with levers for operating the movable parts), and eight blank leaves for backing the plates in order to obscure the mechanisms. Three different paper stocks for letterpress, lithography, and blanks. Stabbed, and glued into original printed pink paper boards, red roan spine, the arms of the City of London, title (as transcribed above) on both covers. References: Darton *Check-list* H93F; Montanaro p. 185.

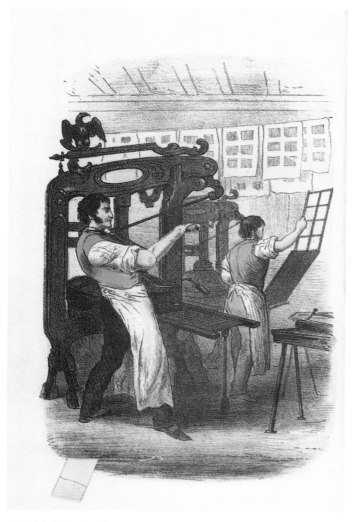

325. plate [1], *reduced*

326. fo. 1 recto, *reduced*

Provenance: *Miles Stavely 1860 from his dear Mamma* (inscr.). PML 84996. Purchase: Fellows Fund.

Dean's chief rival in the early years of movable books was Darton & Co., who were always insistent in their advertisements that "Mr. Griffin, the original inventor of moveable books for children, arranges and fixes the whole of Darton & Co.'s instructive moveable children's books." If this is so, then Mr. Griffin was probably the fixer for *Moveable Trades*, which has a quality in its presentation beyond the cheaper, popular lines in which Dean & Son specialized. The lever mechanisms are, admittedly, simple. They have none of the complex articulated movements that were invented and so ingeniously exploited by the German artist Lothar Meggendorfer later in the century. But the lithographic pictures have a nice sense of detail and are finely colored, and there is a pleasant conversational air to the text. (Bibliographers will take especial interest in the first two trades: "The Printer" and "The Bookbinder." Of the latter it is pertinently said: "How many hands and how much time must be employed over one pretty story book, before Harry or Polly [echoes of Newbery] can have it to read!")

   The Morgan Library has a Dean movable of ca. 1857 which, despite its cheaper production, does have slightly more complex articulations: *The Moveable Mother Hubbard* (PML 85325).

❧ 326 ❧

A Little Play for Little People. Punch's Merry Pranks. Leipsic: Friedrich Volckmar. London: William Tegg & Co. 85 Queen-Street, Cheapside. A. & S. Joseph, Myers & Co. 144 Leadenhall-Street, [ca. 1855]. 4° (263 × 202 mm.).

[1–3⁴ 4⁴(4+1)] (1/1ʳ title, 1/1ᵛ blank, 1/2ʳ *Persons represented*, 1/2ᵛ *Act I . . . Bruno*, incipit: *Dear me! What shall I do? I'm sure I've stood,* 4/4ᵛ *Epilogue*, ending *So give me your applause, that magic spell! / And may I teach the public quite as well!*, 4/4+1ʳ *List of articles to be obtained wholesale of A. & S. Joseph, Meyers, & Co.,* [cancel slip: *A. & S. Joseph, Myers, & Co.,*] *144, Leadenhall Street, London, and retail at the principal booksellers and toy repositories in the United Kingdom,* including *Punch's Merry Pranks* and *The English Struwwelpeter* each advertised at 2s.6d. Pp. 30, [2], [2]. Roman type. 15 large wood engravings, the title-cut by Graeff after Hasselhor, 6 signed B. P., all hand-colored at the German publisher's. Original pictorial orange boards, title-cut repeated on front cover but left uncolored, wood engraving on back cover (not elsewhere in the book). References: Gumuchian 4654; Schatzki 134.

Provenance: Gumuchian & Cⁱᵉ (1930 cat., no. 4654). PML 83421. Gift: Elisabeth Ball.

The Tegg company, who gave us *Right and Wrong*, cannot have had much time for moral uplift. As London agent for Friedrich

Volckmar, they here take on a German play of Punch in which the hero retains all his aggressive and amoral self-confidence, even though the script bears no relation to the traditionally violent English *Punch and Judy*. Whoever prepared the translation was skilled in the music-hall doggerel of the times, and the book has a verve which aligns it with the "pantomime" effects that Thackeray sought to achieve in *The Rose and the Ring*.

The arrival of *Punch and Judy* as a genre within children's literature, and as a theme within the catalogue, deserves some closer consideration.

Mr. Punch · A DIGRESSION

(see entries 327–331)

The figure and the name of Punch can be seen as giving summary expression to the purpose of this catalogue. He hovers in the background of eighteenth-century children's literature among the harlequinades or the fairground characters in *The Fairing* (entry 69):

> From hence we went to see the Puppet Show, and that impudent Rogue *Punch*, who came in *Caw, waw, waw*, strutting and prancing, and turned his Backside to all the fine Ladies.

He is obviously a subversive presence. Not only does he make vulgar remarks and do reverse flashing, but his story is more anarchic than even the roughest of fairy tales. How could anyone dedicated to the improvement of youth permit them to encounter a character who behaves throughout with violence and duplicity and yet, in the end, even subdues the Devil sent to take him down to Hell?

Thus, although Punch maintains a place on the fringes of children's literature in the early nineteenth century, doubtless by virtue of the selling power of his name, his eventual movement to somewhere near center stage closely coincides with the loosening of constraints on the children's book market, and he becomes an omnipresent figure on the road to Paflagonia. The crucial document is a book published for adults: *Punch and Judy*, an essay by John Payne Collier "accompanied by the dialogue of the puppet-show." This was printed in London for S. Prowett in 1828 with illustrations designed and engraved by George Cruikshank (PML 17089), and it had the effect of bringing together in one place the historic Punch from the *commedia dell'arte*, the street-wise hero of the puppet-masters, and a classic set of printed images. Here was a source book of respectable, scholarly pretensions that could validate whatever might be plundered from it by entertainers with no pretensions at all.

Our examples in this section illustrate how Punch made his large-scale incursion into children's books following John Payne Collier's *Punch and Judy*. What should also be apparent is the maze of interconnecting references and influences: that Cruikshank, who illustrated one focal work, the English Grimm, is now illustrating another; that young John Ruskin should fix upon *The Puppet Show* in 1829 (entry 309) as the title for his early creative effort at bookmaking (even though it contained no reference to Punch); that *Punch* should be the

name chosen for a magazine that more than anything was to promulgate a new spirit of comedy in English journalism, ranging from the affable to the biting, and employ in the course of its early years the talents of Richard Doyle, William Makepeace Thackeray, and numerous other artists and authors who were involved with children's books. One of them, Charles Bennett, also worked for an obscure rival called *The Puppet Show* (PML 84837) and was a collaborator in a version of *Punch and Judy* that one authority has claimed to be truly authentic (see entry 333). Mr. Punch, for all his deplorable behavior, takes his place alongside the folk heroes of the nation.

⁕ 327 ⁕

The Tragical Comedy of Punch and Judy. London: D. Martin, Fountain Court, Strand, [not after 1838]. 8° (177 × 105 mm.).

[1–3⁸] (1/1ʳ half-title, 1/1ᵛ blank, 1/2ʳ title, vignette and rhyme, incipit: "*I love thee, Punch, with all thy faults and failings*, 1/2ᵛ imprint *London: printed by J. Green and Co., Bartlett's Buildings*, 1/3ʳ Preface, 1/5ʳ text, incipit: *Let graver folks, to wiser brains*, 3/8ᵛ ending *And thus conclude my song*). Pp. 48. 15 wood engravings (12 half-page, 3 small vignettes), in original or contemporary hand-coloring. Original pictorial yellow wrappers, wood engraving *Punch's Pleasantries* and *Price one shilling* on front cover, wood-engraved ad for *R. Cruikshank's Comic Alphabet* on back cover. Blind-tooled maroon morocco, by Morrell.

Provenance: *With Grannicam's Love to her darling Blanche Shelley Decʳ 15ᵗʰ 1838* (inscr.); Charles Todd Owen (binding). PML 83050. Gift: Elisabeth Ball.

> Oh! how the girls and boys rejoice
> The puppet Punch to greet,
> For well they know his comic voice
> Resounding through the street.

Thus the anonymous author of this *Tragical Comedy* places on record the popular appeal of Punch "Spite of the strait-laced folks and all their railings."

Whoever wrote the one hundred fifty-eight jog-trot quatrains of this version almost certainly had John Payne Collier's edition at his side. He follows the traditional sequence of events as laid out by Collier (beginning with the one-by-one killing of Scaramouch, the baby, and Punch's wife), predictably omitting only such scenes as those with Pretty Polly and with the Devil. The illustrator adopts what, after Cruikshank, became the standard practice of showing the events of the story taking place on a puppet-booth stage. In this instance, a changing variety of heads at the bottom of the illustration bring the audience into the picture as well.

⁕ 328 ⁕

Punch's Puppet Show. Or the humours, of Punch & Judy. London: Orlando Hodgson, 111, Fleet Street, [ca. 1840]. 8° (178 × 107 mm.).

PUNCH AND JUDY.

Then left the room, while Punch, to rub
His wounded nose begun,
And called in Mr. Scaramouch,
To see what he had done.

But Scaramouch, who loved his dog
Much better than his neighbour,
Brought in a stick, and Mr. Punch
Did grievously belabour;

16

327. 1/8 verso, *reduced*

PUNCH, HIS CHILD, AND TOBY.

" Oh ! Routee Toutee, Toutee, here's a noise !
You'll surely frighten all the Girls and Boys.
Who was it bid you fall, and hurt your pate ?
Why do you sob and cry at such a rate ?
Hush ! Judy, hush ! don't keep up such a riot,
Here's the dog Toby bids you pray be quiet,
So then you wont ;" enraged Punch threw her down;
The floor hard was, and fairly crack'd her crown.

328. fo. 3 verso, *reduced*

[1⁸] (1·8 mounted as pastedowns, 1ᵛ relief-cut pictorial title, letterpress quatrain, incipit: *Haste! neighbours, Haste! see the puppet show comes*, and imprint, 2ʳ text, incipit: *"Oh! Routee Toutee, Routee Toutee, Toutee*, 8ʳ ending *The hangman swings in air instead of me."*). Ff. [8]. Printed on one side of the sheet only. 8 half-page wood-engraved illustrations, all with eight-line rhyme (except the title-cut), all in publisher's coloring. Original printed pink wrappers, title *Hodgson's Edition. Punch and Judy . . . Sixpence* and ads *A list of large pictured coloured children's books . . . Many Others in Progress* on front cover. Brown morocco gilt.

Provenance: Charles Todd Owen (binding). PML 85009. Gift: Elisabeth Ball.

By contrast with the previous expansive rendering, Hodgson has here reduced the story to a bare minimum. After dispatching the baby and Dog Toby, Punch is arrested, condemned, and then plays his trick on the Hangman (not named as Jack Ketch as he should be). The illustrations, with their black background and heavy figure-drawing, are suitably ominous, and this is the only text to

give a good transcription of the Punch "whizzer": "Routee Toutee, Routee Toutee."

Hodgson is one of the publishers discussed in chapter XII.

⋘ 329 ⋙

Punch and Judy. Derby: Thomas Richardson, [ca. 1840]. Price sixpence. 8° (163 × 105 mm.).

[1⁸] (1ʳ blank, 1ᵛ incipit: *Punch and Judy one day, full of mirth, full of joy*, 8ʳ ending *And Punch was at last safely lodg'd in the Tower*, 8ᵛ blank). Ff. [8]. Printed on one side of the sheet only. Each leaf with hand-colored wood engraving (105 × 95 mm.) and six-line rhyme. Original gray wrappers, wood-engraved pictorial title on front cover. Blind-tooled green morocco, by Morrell.

Provenance: Charles Todd Owen (binding). PML 85007. Gift: Elisabeth Ball.

Truncated though it be, Hodgson's *Punch's Puppet Show* at least sticks by the essentials of the plot. These were obviously too tough

Above: **329**. front cover, *reduced*

for Richardson, who brings the stage events nearer to vaudeville, seeks excuses for Punch's misbehavior (he lets the baby tumble because his nose itches), and closes the brief sequence by having Punch "safely lodg'd in the Tower." No Jack Ketch, and certainly no Devil.

❧ 330 ❧

[A. CORDIER (fl. 1860–70)]. *Histoire de Polichinel. History of Punch. Amusing Alphabet.* London: Darton & Hodge, 58, Holborn Hill, [ca. 1864]. Panorama (107 × 3360 mm., folded: 107 × 140 mm.).

24 chromo-lithographic plates (T and W excluded from the alphabet), printed on one side of the panoramic strip, letterpress captions in English and French (plate A: *First Appearance of Punch; he comes out of an ostrich's egg. / Apparition de Polichinel, il sort d'un oeuf d'autriche*), plate Z with imprint *Paris. Typ. Henri Plon, rue Garancière, 8.* Original wrappers, letterpress and chromo-lithographic pictorial title on front cover, lacking back cover. Red half morocco, by Henderson & Bisset. Reference: Darton *Check-list* H280.

Provenance: *To dearest* [name erased] *from her loving cousin Janie* (inscr.). PML 82022. Gift: Lincoln Kirstein.

This cunningly produced panorama contrives at one and the same time to give Punch's alphabetic progress a narrative form, to find words for each panel that have equivalent first letters in English and French, and finally to preserve Punch's roistering and volatile character. (Parts almost read like a prompt towards *Pinocchio*.) Darton & Hodge, a sober partnership, are unusual sponsors for this French import, which is part of a dozen similar works

Punch receives a **MESSAGE** and learns that his friend Harlequin has made his fortune.

Polichinel reçoit une **MISSIVE** dans laquelle son ami Arlequin lui annonce qu'il a trouvé une fortune.

330.

published or advertised by them between 1863 and 1865. Although printed in France, the book further supports our awareness of Darton's interest in the uses of lithography.

❧ 331 ❧

Punch and Judy. Otley: William Walker and Sons, [ca. 1840]. 16° (125 × 91/100 mm.).

[1⁴] (1ʳ title, 1ᵛ incipit: *Two comical figures commence this odd book*, 4ᵛ ending *Punch caper'd and danc'd, and in ecstasy sung*). Pp. 8. Probably printed together with three other works from a stereotype plate. Each page with half-page illustration (the first and last in original hand-coloring) and eight-line rhyme (except title). Folded, but unsewn.

PML 80210. Gift: Elisabeth Ball.

As befits a street trader's edition of *Punch*, this mass-production job keeps as close to the popular version of the story as eight pages and a versified text allow. Walker's illustrator was incontestably using Cruikshank as a guide, since almost all of his cuts are reversed and simplified copies of the equivalent illustrations done for Payne Collier.

Walker has been discussed above as a chapbook publisher (chapter XIII) and as a tract publisher (chapter XIV). He followed the sound economic practice of uniform production methods, and this *Punch and Judy* is part of a long series of similarly produced eight-page trifles.

331. fo. 4 verso

XVI
THE ROSE AND THE RING

THE origins of Michael Angelo Titmarsh's fireside pantomime have been explained to some extent by the author himself in his "Prelude" to the story. An aptly named "Miss Bunch" persuades him to draw a set of twelfth-night characters for a children's party, and when the party is over he and Miss Bunch concoct a story around them, "which was recited to the little folks at night" and grew to be the story of *The Rose and the Ring*.

That is only part of the truth. There was one child who could not go to the party: Edith Story, the daughter of Thackeray's American friend William Wetmore Story. She had been ill with malarial fever, and as a consolation Michael Angelo Titmarsh would go to her bedside and read to her day by day from his developing manuscript. Then, as she recorded later, "after he had done reading we talked of the people in the story—they were real people to me and to him;" the elaboration of these real people found a place in the manuscript, which Mr. Titmarsh illustrated with his own perfectly attuned watercolors.

More than a twelfth-night joke went into the tale, however, and the purpose of our preceding chapter has been to show that this book is at once the culmination of a movement that sanctioned "idle fancy" as a vital ingredient in children's books, and also the threshold of a period when English children's literature was to come of age. Before *The Rose and the Ring* there is a plenitude of hints and portents: Grimm, say, and caricature, and various Punches and *The King of the Golden River*. Many of these had been welcomed or written about by Thackeray the journalist: he rejoiced in the arrival of Felix Summerly's "Home Treasury;" he joined with Ruskin in praise of Cruikshank; and he admired Richard Doyle to the point of asking him to illustrate *The Newcomes*. Indeed, *The Rose and the Ring* itself dispatches works like Richmal Mangnall's *Historical and Miscellaneous Questions* and assumes that the traditional tales of the fairies are common currency among the fireside audience. It draws into itself a century of erratic progress (there are even Newbery connections in the very name "Michael Angelo Titmarsh") and gives a shape and an authorial voice to fantasy that has finally escaped all the historic constraints. After *The Rose and the Ring* the way is made clear for an imaginative caravan that can as easily accommodate *The Water Babies* as *The Wizard of Oz*.

In the following entries we seek to touch upon some books and prints that will help to place *The Rose and the Ring* in its time and in its author's working life.

→§ 332 ⅋←

[FRANCIS EDWARD PAGET (1806–82)]. *The Hope of the Katzekopfs: a fairy tale. By William Churne of Staffordshire.* Rugeley: John Thomas Walters. London: James Burns, 1844. 12° (137 × 85 mm.).

a⁸ (1ʳ half-title *The Juvenile Englishman's Library.* I); χ² A–F⁶.⁸ G–I⁶ 2χ² K–M⁶ 3χ² N–P⁶ Q⁴. Pp. xv, [1], 211, [1]. Wood-engraved title-border and ten illustrations. Original or contemporary red half roan gilt. Reference: Alderson *Burns* pp. 112–13.

Provenance: Emma Grove, Wandsworth 1845 (inscr.). The Osborne Collection of Early Children's Books, Toronto Public Library.

Chronologically this little moral fairy tale belongs among the events of the 1840s in chapter XV. Through its title it harks back (as does Ruskin's "Legend of Stiria") to the German influence of the Brothers Grimm.* The London publisher was James Burns,

* On this score, we should record the Morgan copy of a *jeu d'esprit* for adults by Robert Southey, which also has Germanic overtones and pictures by Cruikshank: *The Cat's Tail; being the history of Childe Merlin* by the Baroness de Katzleben (Edinburgh: William Blackwood, 1831; PML 83627).

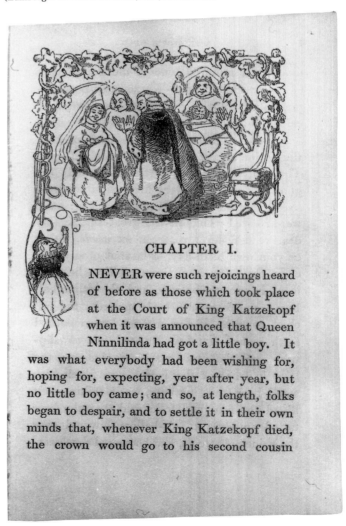

CHAPTER I.

NEVER were such rejoicings heard of before as those which took place at the Court of King Katzekopf when it was announced that Queen Ninnilinda had got a little boy. It was what everybody had been wishing for, hoping for, expecting, year after year, but no little boy came; and so, at length, folks began to despair, and to settle it in their own minds that, whenever King Katzekopf died, the crown would go to his second cousin

332. χ2 recto

who may well have instigated the work and whom we have noted as a rival to Joseph Cundall (entry 316). The book begins with an attack on the contemporary rationalists. Will children, who have been "glutted with Peter Parley, and Penny Magazines, and such-like stores of (so-called) useful knowledge" still "condescend to read a Fable and its moral, or to interest themselves with the grotesque nonsense, the palpable, fantastic absurdities, the utter impossibilities of a Tale of Enchantment?"

The question is addressed as though by a reader to the putative author of the story, "William Churne of Staffordshire," who was celebrated as a man still in touch with the old lore in Bishop Corbet's poem that starts with that pregnant phrase "Farewell, rewards and fairies." And when the story begins we think, briefly, that "William Churne" is going to make the decisive break into fantastic nonsense. The absurdities of the Court of the Katzekopfs seem almost a premonition of later events at the Court of Paflagonia; but unfortunately the Reverend Francis Paget could not sustain his levity and, as he seems to have realized, the fable sinks under the weight of its moral burden. Nevertheless, as one of the first genuine attempts in England at a comic *Kunstmärchen*, Paget's story gives us a measure by which to judge the achievement of Thackeray.

❧ 333 ❧

ROBERT BARNABAS BROUGH (1828–60). *Ulf the Minstrel or the Princess Diamonduckz and the Hazel Fairy. A dragon story for Christmas.* London: Houlston and Wright, [1859]. 8° (158 × 100 mm.).

A^4 (1^v frontispiece, 2^r title, 3^r *Contents*, 4^r *List of engravings*); B–G^8 H^4 (H4^r imprint *H Tuck Printer 16 & 17, New Street Cloth Fair West Smithfield*). Pp. viii, 103, [1]. 21 wood engravings by J. Watkins and N. Walmsley (nine full-page). Original blind- and gilt-stamped red bead-grain cloth, gilt edges, by Leighton Son and Hodge (ticket). References: Osborne II, 972; Gumuchian 935.

Provenance: PML 82140. Gift: Lincoln Kirstein.

The fifteen years that separate *Ulf the Minstrel* from *The Hope of the Katzekopfs* saw enough changes of attitude to explain the differences between these two courtly fantasies; the earlier freighted by its urge to teach moral lessons, the other a light fanciful comedy with no other purpose than to entertain. Nonetheless, Brough's swashbuckling mode of address, his handling of the plot with its foolish king, intriguing courtiers, and put-upon princess, as well as the book's caricature illustrations, are all unlikely inventions without *The Rose and the Ring* as precursor.

Brough himself was a prolific author of burlesques and comic journalism. He was responsible for *The Wonderful Story of Punch and Judy* (as by "Papernose Woodensconce"), which first brought Charles Bennett to the fore as an illustrator and which George Speaight, in his *History of the English Puppet Theatre* (1955), considers to be a more authentic version of the text than John Payne Collier's. But Brough was not a writer with any clear sense of direction and (what with liquor and Bohemian living) he did not have the capacity to build on his natural gifts. For extensive notes on the Brough family and their involvement in publishing see Peter Newbolt, *William Tinsley (1831–1902), "Speculative Publisher": A Commentary* (Aldershot: Ashgate, 2001).

"How dare you say that?" asked the Fairy, sharply.

"I didn't mean it: I didn't know what I was saying."

"The wife of Ulf the Minstrel must always mean what she says, and know what she is saying."

"Oh! how very dreadful! But bring him back to me, and I will try to do, and be, whatever you wish."

333. F4^r, *reduced*

❧ 334 ❧

Lady Spangle [and 7 other stage caricatures]. London: Printed for & Sold by Bowles & Carver.—N° 69 in St Pauls Church Yard, Published as the Act directs, [copperplate ca. 1787–95, impression not before 1801 (watermark-date)]. Oblong broadside (pott-size half-sheet, 182 × 273 mm.).

Etching (173 × 247 mm.): Bowles & Carver picture-sheet 133 (for a description of the series, see entry 159), no title, but the characters captioned *Lady Spangle, Alderman Gobble Guzzle, Miss Gossip Tattle, General Gallypot, Mess. Van Sour Crout's, Signior Stir-stump Shamble-shanks, Sir Soup Saucepan's Entertainment, Young Spend-cash & Old Stingy.* Reference: Bowles & Carver, pp. vii, 85.

Provenance: Walter Schatzki; C. F. van Veen (Sotheby's Amsterdam, 28th Nov. 1984, lot 27). PML 84760.108. Purchase: Mrs. Robert Horne Charles and Mrs. Donald M. Oenslager.

In the prelims to *The Rose and the Ring* references to the customs of pantomime merge with those to "Twelfth-Night Characters." Both were associated by the nineteenth-century reader with winter festivities: pantomimes were set-piece comic dramas that left room within the structure of their traditional stories for contemporary jokes; the characters were designated on paper

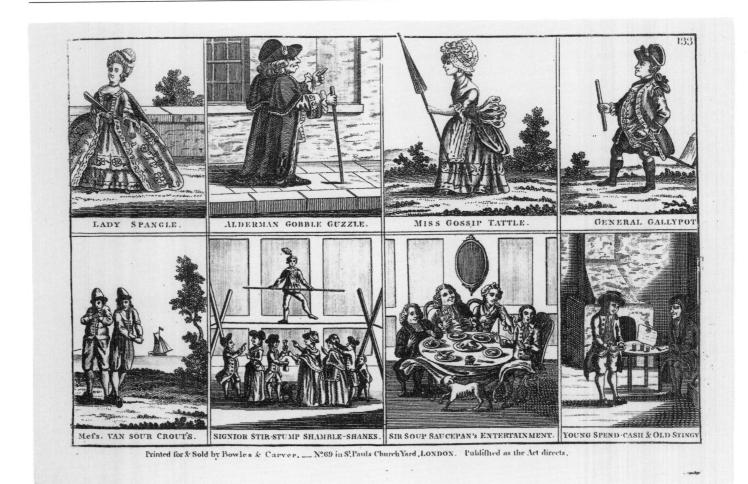

334. Lady Spangle, *reduced*

slips or cards and picked out of a hat by partygoers at twelfth-night parties, the idea being that you had to behave in the role of the character (Captain O'Blunder, say, or Dolly Cowslip) for the duration of the evening.

The date of the emergence of these twelfth-night characters is not easily ascertained (see the discussion in Bridget Ann Henisch's *Cakes and Characters* [London: Prospect Books, 1984]). Many of the publishers we have already discussed (Wallis, Fairburn, Langley, etc.) traded in them, and the present Bowles & Carver print looks very like a prototype of what was to follow. The names and figures do not exactly correspond to a traditional king, queen, courtier, commons run-down of characters, but the caricature element is very similar.

◆§ 335 §◆

New Characters for Twelfth-Night. London: Published by John Wallis, n°, Ludgate Street, Dec. 17ᵗʰ 1798. Full sheet, divided into cards (87 × 51 mm. each).

23 hand-colored etchings of twelfth-night characters, presumably printed from a single copperplate on a sheet, then cut up to form a series of cards. Original pictorial laid-paper wrapper, etched title (as above) showing John Bull presenting to "Egalité" a twelfth-night cake with a victorious British warship on top and marked "Nelson For Ever."

The Metropolitan Museum of Art, Department of Prints, 69.503.9. Gift: Lincoln Kirstein.

With characters like Justice Guttle and Mynheer Sourcrout, these cards clearly belong to the same tradition as the caricatures on Bowles's sheet (entry 334). Here, though, we have twelfth night in full fig, with a master of ceremonies and a king and queen.

> Pray ladies keep distance,
> No Liberties take;
> I'm a Princess To night
> And the Queen of Plumb-cake.

Furthermore, the cards have been cut up by the publisher and packed ready to be dispensed. The series adds to our respect for John Wallis as entrepreneur and innovator (see chapters X and XI). The etching and coloring are prettily done, but the verses are no better than one would expect for the occasion; the master of ceremonies repeats a universal sentiment:

> To Good humour and mirth,
> Doth my Office invite,
> To be merry and wise,
> Is the Law of this night.

Above: **336.** *enlarged*

Above: **336.** *reduced*   *Below*: **336.** *enlarged*

❦ **336** ❧

Fairburn's Characters. [London:] Published by J. Fairburn Upper Holloway & sold by Fairburn Minories, [ca. 1845]. Picture broadside (full sheet, 430 × 345 mm.).

Hand-colored engraving by Robert Cruikshank (1786–1856), showing 24 twelfth-night characters (1 *Nathan Nabob* . . . 24 *Tabitha Take Me*. Reference: Schiller *Five Centuries* 67.

Provenance: This impression is accompanied by Robert Cruikshank's signed original watercolor drawings (about 80 × 50 mm. each) for 16 characters, either designed for the Fairburn print or perhaps more likely, in view of their erratic numbering, for an intermediate stage: *General Gingerbread* 77, *Lady Lustre Gem* 67, *Caledonias Pride* 122, *Whangi Fongo* 29, *Angelic Agnes* 76, *Tragical Toby* 74, *The Star of Prodigys* 124, [Blue Bell of Scotland, cropped] 128, *Grace Gardiner* 140, *Sammy Smart Sack* 134, *Polly Parrot* 71, *Peter Pelican* 82, *Sir Simon Sweepturf* 73, *Tabitha Take Me* 75, *Peter Prospect* 135, *Sabina Sea breeze* 133. Justin G. Schiller Ltd., New York.

With the King of the Night and the Queen of Delight saluting cakes emblazoned with Victorian insignia, John Fairburn brings the twelfth-night figures into Thackeray's time—since Thackeray was an admirer and quondam friend of the designer, Robert

Cruikshank's brother George, there may well be a connection. Much of the caricaturist's panache has gone out of these Fairburn characters compared with their Bowles & Carver and John Wallis forebears (*they* would not have had much time for Amy All Right or Sabina Sea Breeze). The old versified legends have now given way to the kind of riddles that still persist in Christmas crackers and fortune cookies: Q: Why is an Auctioneer like a Man with an ugly countenance? A: Because he's always for bidding.

❧ 337 ☙

[WILLIAM MAKEPEACE THACKERAY (1811–63)]. *Harlequin and Humpty Dumpty: or, Robbin de Bobbin and the First Lord Mayor of Lun'on, a grand historical pantomime. By E. Fitzball, author of "Za-Ze-Zi-Zo-Zu." First performed at the Theatre Royal, Drury Lane, December 26th, 1850.* London: Printed and Published by S. G. Fairbrother, 31, Bow Street, Covent Garden; and may be had in the Theatre, [1850 or 1851]. 12° (166 × 96 mm.).

[1–4⁸.⁴ 5⁸] (1ʳ blank, 1ᵛ frontispiece *Robbin de Bobbin*, 2ʳ title, 2ᵛ–3ʳ blank, 3ᵛ illustration *Humpty Dumpty*, 4ʳ *Characters in the opening*, 4ᵛ–5ʳ blank, 5ᵛ illustration *Old Woman*, 6ʳ *Scene I . . . Old Woman (Air—Meet me by Moonlight)*, incipit: *Stars are fading, dewdrops falling*, 5/8ʳ imprint, 5/8ᵛ blank). Pp. 23, [1]. A single stock of unwatermarked wove paper. 20 full-page wood engravings (part of the collation but omitted from the pagination) after designs by the author, showing full-length portraits of the play's characters. Original printed yellow wrappers, title, *Lessee and Manager, Mr. James Anderson* and *price sixpence* on front cover. References: Lambert 969; Van Duzer 83.

PML 75751. Bequest: Tessie Jones.

As "Christmas Pantomime" *Harlequin and Humpty Dumpty* supplies evidence of Thackeray's liking for the genre (also to be seen in other obscure publications such as his illustrations for John Barrow's *King Glumpus; an interlude. In one act*, privately issued in 1837 and including characters like Lady Popkins and Lord Lollypop). The pantomime text allows for various adult jokes and stage business which a contemporary audience would probably have found uproarious, but it also touches upon our present concerns in several ways: the naming of characters, the inclusion of several nursery rhymes for comic purposes, the resolution of the pantomime into an eighteenth-century style harlequinade, and, of course, the twenty splendid pictures of the leading players.

Although the booklet is barely known (there is no mention of *Harlequin* in Gordon Ray's biography of Thackeray), it is nonetheless to be found in two other states, one with the title reset and without imprint (PML 21714) and one stating "With illustrations by W. West" on the cover-title (Lambert-Van Duzer copy). The pseudonym presumably alludes to William West (1783–1854), who was one of the earliest publishers of theatrical sheets and toy theaters and who gains a mention in *Vanity Fair* where Thackeray is writing about George Osborne's friendship with young Todd (chapter 56): "they both had a taste for painting theatrical characters . . . for going to the play . . . and performed indeed many of the plays to the Todd family and their youthful friends, with West's famous characters, on their pasteboard theatre."

ROBBIN DE BOBBIN.

337. frontispiece, *reduced*

❧ 338a ☙

Mʳ French as Harlequin. London: J. Redington, 208, Hoxton Old Town & Sold by J. Webb, 75 Brick Lane Sᵗ Lukes, [ca. 1850]. Foolscap quarter-sheet (215 × 175 mm.).

Engraved toy-theater portrait, unnumbered, hand-colored as issued. Wove paper, no watermark.

The Thomas Fisher Rare Books Library, University of Toronto.

❧ 338b ☙

Mʳ G. V. Brooke as Othello. London: J. Redington, 208, Hoxton Old Town & Sold by J. Webb, 75 Brick Lane Sᵗ Lukes, [ca. 1850]. Foolscap quarter-sheet (215 × 175 mm.).

Engraved toy-theater portrait, numbered 47, hand-colored as issued. Wove paper, no watermark.

The Thomas Fisher Rare Books Library, University of Toronto.

She was brought out in her night-gown with all her beautiful long brown hair falling down her back, and looking so pretty that even the beefeaters and keepers of the wild animals wept plentifully at seeing her. And she walked with her poor little bare feet (only luckily the arena was covered with sawdust) and sat and leaned up against a great stone in the centre of the amphitheatre, round which the Court and the people were seated in boxes with bars before them for fear of the great fierce red-maned black-throated long-tailed roaring bellowing rushing Lions.

And now the gates were opened & with a Wurrawurrawaraw! two great lean hungry roaring lions rushed out of their den where they had been kept for three weeks on nothing but a little toast-and-water, and dashed straight up to the stone where poor Rosalba was waiting! Commend her to your patron Saints all you kind people for she is in a dreadful state.

There was a hum and a buzz all through the Circus and the fierce King Padella even felt a little compassion. But Count Hogginarmo seated by his Majesty roared out Hooray now for it Soo-soo-soo! — that nobleman being so uncommonly angry still at Rosalba's refusal of him.

But o strange event! o remarkable circumstance! o extraordinary coincidence! wch I am sure none of you could by any possibility have divined! when the lions came up to Rosalba — instead of devouring her with their great teeth it was with kisses they gobbled her up! they licked her pretty feet, they nuzzled their noses in her lap — they moaned they seemed to say dear dear Sister don't you recollect

339. fo. 77, reduced

"West's famous characters," mentioned in the note to the previous entry, were only an early manifestation in the craze for toy theaters (see also chapter X). One of the refinements of the fashion was for toy-theater manufacturers to design and print what passed for portraits of contemporary actors dressed for their most famous roles. At a slightly later date these figures were subject to "tinseling," which was, in effect, dressing them up by sticking small pieces of fabric or metal foil to the paper models. The secret formula for making the foil of punched tinsel ornaments adhere to paper is said to have died with J. Webb (see Speaight p. 131).

Here we show two colored examples (the Fisher Library also owns plain copies of both), ready to be tinseled. "Harlequin" nicely echoes the title of the previous entry, and there is no reason to doubt that the poses which Thackeray gave to his cast list were a takeoff on the theatrical portrait fashion. The actor Gustavus Vaughan Brooke (1818–66) had his greatest triumphs as Othello in 1848 at the Olympic, London, and in 1851 at the Broadway Theater, New York.

◄§ 339 §►

WILLIAM MAKEPEACE THACKERAY (1811–63). The Rose and the Ring. Holograph manuscript. [Rome and Naples: January–March 1854]. (139 × 219 mm. and slightly smaller).

90 disjunct oblong leaves, versos blank, with 39 overlays (for drawings), fo. 67 with spaces for two drawings never supplied. A variety of papers, text written in "fairy script" (so named by Edith Story and not denied by the "great giant") in brown and black inks, mostly single column, occasionally double column, with few deletions and corrections, 81 pen-and-ink drawings (the one on fo. 64 in faint pencil) including many with watercolor and wash. Mounted in a gilt red crushed morocco oblong album (243 × 309 mm.), signed by Holloway of London and commissioned no later than January 1866 by Sir Theodore Martin for the two Thackeray daughters, Anny and Minny (Martin's accompanying A.L.S. mounted in the album). Reference: *The Rose and the Ring; reproduced in facsimile from the Author's original illustrated manuscript in The Pierpont Morgan Library*, introduction by Gordon N. Ray (New York, 1947); on the genesis and progression of the story and the manuscript, see Marchesa Peruzzi de Medici, née Edith Story, "Thackeray, My Childhood Friend" in: *The Cornhill Magazine*, no. 182, new series (August 1911), pp. 178–81.

Provenance: Anne Isabella Thackeray, Lady Ritchie (two-page autograph note signed, dated 1896, recording her recollection of the book's history: "The book was finished & published in England the following Christmas. The Ms. did not go to the printers, but it was copied out by us [i.e. her and her sister] at my Father's wish. He altered it for the press and the Ms varies from the printed

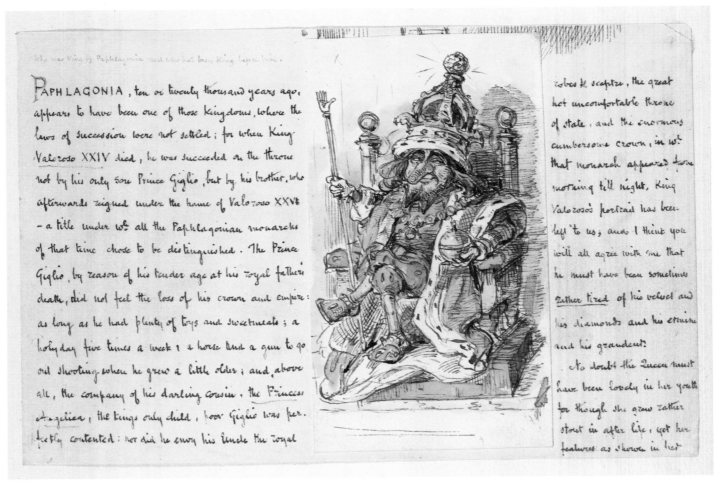

339. fo. 4, reduced

version. The drawings are very much more delicate than the wood blocks"); sold by her to Pearson & Co. of London; Major William H. Lambert of Philadelphia (1914 Anderson Galleries auction-sale catalogue, lot 1016, $23,000 to); George D. Smith, New York bookseller, sold Christmas 1915 to; J. P. Morgan, Jr. MA 926.

There are good practical reasons why Anny and Minny made a new draft of this manuscript when Thackeray was preparing *The Rose and the Ring* for publication. For one thing, it is not very suitable as printer's copy; for another, it was subject to heavy revision in making the final version; and for another, it had to be brought to a conclusion, since two and a half chapters of the story were still unwritten.

Aside from practicality, however, there must have been no question in anyone's mind that this was a very personal document, not to be put to such sordid uses as trade. The story had had its origins as a fireside tale for "the little folks;" it was retold at the bedside of Edith Story; it was composed by Thackeray, as we see it now, as a labor of delight to be shared within the family circle. These comfortable, happy, and above all loving circumstances give the book a sense of coming from the heart. (How could Anny ever have sold it?)

The sustained pleasure which Thackeray took in his work is evident not just in the twelfth-night characters (stuck down in appropriate places in the manuscript) but also in the "fairy script," the casual decorations, and the ironic or comical asides:

Here the children all gather
about Miss Bunch
and say O do, dear kind Miss Bunch,
do tell us all you know about
The Fairies.

The warmth and spontaneity that are so prominent on every leaf set the manuscript of *The Rose and the Ring* (finished or not) among the great documents of children's literature; the author, his story, and his audience are almost palpably present among the disjunct folios.

⌘ 340a ⌘

[WILLIAM MAKEPEACE THACKERAY (1811–63)]. *The Rose and the Ring; or, the history of Prince Giglio and Prince Bulbo. A fire-side pantomime for great and small children. By Mr. M. A. Titmarsh, author of "The Kickleburys on the Rhine," "Mrs. Perkins's Ball," &c. &. Second edition.* London: Smith, Elder, and Co., 65, Cornhill, 1855. 8° (165 × 125 mm.).

A^2 (1ʳ title, 1ᵛ imprint *London: Bradbury and Evans, Printers, Whitefriars,* 2ʳ *Prelude*); B–I⁸ (18ᵛ same imprint); 8 wood-engraved plates after designs by the author, including frontispiece

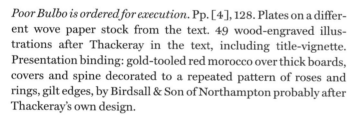

340a. reduced

340b. reduced

Poor Bulbo is ordered for execution. Pp. [4], 128. Plates on a different wove paper stock from the text. 49 wood-engraved illustrations after Thackeray in the text, including title-vignette. Presentation binding: gold-tooled red morocco over thick boards, covers and spine decorated to a repeated pattern of roses and rings, gilt edges, by Birdsall & Son of Northampton probably after Thackeray's own design.

Provenance: *With the author's most respectful compliments* (lithographed) *to Miss Edith Story* (inscribed by Thackeray), a hand-colored touche-lithograph of a deeply bowing character presenting the book, signed in the stone with Thackeray's monogram and dated *Christmas 1854*; James F. Drake, New York bookseller, sold on 10 April 1928 for $1,250 to; Henry S. Morgan, gift to his father; J. P. Morgan, Jr. PML 37762.

✥ 340b ✥

RICHARD DOYLE (1824–83). Thackeray reading *The Rose and the Ring* to little Edith Story in Rome. Wood engraving by Joseph Swain (1820–1909) after Doyle. [London: 1865]. (65 × 80 mm.). Proof impression on India paper (the sheet 285 × 225 mm.).

Provenance: Edith Story (sent to her by Frederick Locker-Lampson, with a two-page A.L.S. dated 11 August 1865 [MA 1189]); same later provenance as 340a.

To anyone absorbed with the original manuscript, the eventual printed version of *The Rose and the Ring* may seem something of an anticlimax. Bradbury and Evans's workaday typography hardly matches the "fairy script." The author drawing on wood blocks and the engraver cutting them cannot capture the free flow of the original drawings; a certain harmony has gone, even if the story is now finished and the book has its own playfulness in the comedy of the rhyming running heads.

Nevertheless, an echo remains in this presentation copy, with its hand-lithographed livery-man handing over the book to Miss Edith Story: a Christmas present on the eve of publication. How, though, it came to be a second edition when Thackeray had said that he would give her the first copy off the press is not explained, and that perhaps accounts for a slightly plangent note in her recollections of "the great Giant," which she published in *The Cornhill Magazine* in 1911.

This figure of "the great Giant" is beautifully evoked in Richard Doyle's wood engraving, even though, like so many artists who drew their illustrations on the block, he complained that the professional engraver had not done justice to his work. The immanent sentimentality of the wan figure on the bed is counterbalanced and occluded by the tousled author peering at his manuscript.

INTRODUCTION TO
CHAPTERS XVII–XX

I N order to show the evolution of children's book publishing a broadly chronological treatment has been inevitable. Houses rise and fall, technologies develop, fashions come and go, attitudes towards childhood change. But in the course of arranging our material we have been conscious that the children's book industry may also be considered under different aspects; although these have been hinted at or have gained passing mention, we were not always able to interrupt our survey to discuss them with any coherence.

This final and somewhat divergent part of the catalogue is designed to show how publishers, booksellers, and the buyers or readers of children's books behaved within the confines of this specialized market. The next four chapters are therefore devoted to specific topics that allow one to distinguish the production, sale, and reception of children's books from those of adult literature. A plan to include a chapter on illustration methods was abandoned, not because the subject is unimportant, but because the various techniques were applied to books of all kinds, even if children's books have occasionally been notable as a proving ground for innovations—witness Kirkall's revival of metalcuts in Croxall's Aesop (entry 57) and its influence on Bewick (entry 132). (Our scattered comments on illustration and printing methods are thus only brought together in the index.)

We have searched the holdings of The Pierpont Morgan Library to exemplify individual points we wanted to make but have in the process been led to other features by the promptings of the collection. Reading through and looking at Mr. Owen's books and Miss Ball's books, which truly represent an amazing range of rarities from two centuries of English children's literature, it is difficult not to note characteristics that must reflect trade practices or market response.

Ever since Caxton posted his advertisement for copies of the Sarum *Ordinal* "good chepe" in 1477 (STC 4890), English printers, publishers and booksellers have shown themselves to be aware of the relationship between the medium of print and the strategies of selling. By 1740 intensive advertising was common in the book trade. But the makers of children's books perceived from the first that new possibilities were present for the marketing of their products, and during the first seventy or eighty years a variety of procedures were adopted which in some way or other related to children as readers or even purchasers of books. The ten examples of marketing methods that follow have all been chosen to show a different ploy (summed up in the headline to each entry). Most of the exhibits are by no means isolated instances, and the Morgan Library could often have supplied us with numerous different titles to illustrate the same point.

SUBSCRIPTION: N. Merridew

◄§ 341 §►

Gabrielle & Augustina; or, virtue its own reward. A moral tale for young people. Translated from the French by Miss S. Fletcher. Coventry: printed and sold by N. Merridew, Cross-Cheaping; and by Longman, Hurst, Rees, and Orme, London, 1811. 8° (155 × 91 mm.).

π^2(2+1) (1^r title, 1^v blank, 2^r dedication *To Her Royal Highness The Princess of Wales*, 2^v blank, 2+1=K4 *Preface*); a^4 χ^2 (*List of Subscribers*); B–I^8 K^4 (B1^r drop-title *The Cavern*, –K4). Pp. xvii, [1], 134. Wove paper. Contemporary tree calf gilt.

Provenance: *L. Fosbrooke 1820* (inscr.); *F. S. Fosbrooke the Gift of her Brother Leonard* (inscr.); *To Ada Mary Potter on her eleventh birthday from her affectionate Mamma. Mar 29. 1855* (inscr.) PML 85361. Purchase: Mrs. Stanley G. Mortimer, III.

Publishing by subscription and listing the subscribers was a common feature of the eighteenth-century book trade, and those trailblazing publishers of children's books Thomas Boreman and John Newbery had introduced in their works lists of children as subscribers (see entry 61). No comparison can be drawn between those playful entrepreneurs and Nathaniel Merridew, who is here engaged in either charity publishing or vanity publishing, probably the former since he lists himself as subscribing to fifty copies and since the book is worthily dull and hardly likely to prop up anyone's self-esteem.

Merridew as publisher has been noted in chapter VIII, and from the locations given for his subscribers he was selling Miss Fletcher's work into the area around Coventry (Birmingham, Kenilworth, Solihull, etc.), but there were a number of sub-

scriptions from Bath and from places as distant as Cirencester and Scotland. L. Fosbrooke, the earliest recorded buyer of this copy, does not figure as a subscriber.

ADVERTISING: H. Roberts

◄§ 342 §►

The History of Miss Sally Strawberry: or, good sense and virtue rewarded. In a pleasing account of her life, intended as a pattern for all little Misses to be good, that they may share the same fortune . . . London: Printed for H. Roberts, at No. 14, Hand-Court, Holborn, 1779. [Price Three-Pence]. 24° (96 × 75 mm.).

A^2 (= D4·5, 1^r title, 1^v blank, 2^r *Contents*); B–C^8 D^8 (3^v blank, –4·5, 6^r ads *New books . . . Each adorned with curious Copper-Plate Cuts, Sold Wholesale and Retail, By the Proprietor H. Roberts . . . And most Booksellers and Toy-shops in Great Britain*, 7^v ads *New turn-ups for the Improvement of Children. Price 6d. Plain, 1s. Coloured*, 8^r ads *Small turn-ups Price 3d. Plain, 6d. Coloured* including *As you like it* and *The Press Gang*, 8^v blank); four etchings (including frontispiece *Miss Sally in her Nurses Arms. Publish'd as the Act directs—Jany the 1st 1776*), apparently printed from one copper-plate and divided for insertion. Pp. [4], 37, [1, 6]. Different paper stocks for letterpress and intaglio. Original marbled wrappers. Brown morocco gilt. Reference: ESTC N033122.

Provenance: *Margaret Toller 1782* (pencil inscr.); Mary Brodrick 1807 (pencil inscr.); Charles Todd Owen (binding). PML 81423. Gift: Elisabeth Ball.

From the days of Boreman onwards children's book publishers followed the common practice of their peers elsewhere and included advertisements at the end of their books, sometimes only filling up blank pages, sometimes adding quires. (John Newbery, followed by John Marshall, saw this as a challenge and sought to include jokes like "given gratis .. only paying one penny for the binding.") These advertisements are a great help today in establishing the range of publications from a particular house, but relying on them for publication dates is often dangerous. For a publisher like Roberts, whose obscurity is commented upon in chapter VI, a list such as that in *Sally Strawberry* is revealing, showing a range of books well beyond those that are known to have survived and confirming Roberts's involvement in making and/or selling both large and small harlequinades.

343. *reduced*

CREATIVE ADVERTISING: E. Wallis

❧ 343 ❧

Explanation to the Royal Game of British Sovereigns; exhibiting the most remarkable events in each reign, from Egbert, the first King, to that of His Present Majesty. Third Edition. London: printed for E. Wallis, 42 Skinner Street, Snow Hill, [not before 1820, not after 1823]. Half-sheet 12° (166 × 102 mm.), imposed for work-and-turn.

A–B⁶ ²B⁶ (A1ʳ title, A1ᵛ imprint *Printed by T. Davis, 102, Minories,* A2ʳ *Explanation. (Should the Game be considered too long, the Players may read only the words printed in Italics.),* ²B6ʳ same printer's imprint, ²B6ᵛ blank); etched plate (470 × 610 mm.), printed on a full sheet, hand-colored, cut up into 12 sections and mounted on cloth (as issued) for protection and folding. Instruction booklet: pp. 35, [1]. Roman and italic type. Original gray wrappers. Game-board: 53 historical scenes spiraling towards a central oval of calligraphic text: *The Royal Game of British Sovereigns . . . Rules of the Game . . .*, large illustrations in

the four corners. Original pasteboard slipcase, hand-colored etched label (147 × 106 mm.), showing the signing of the Magna Charta and incorporating the title. Reference: Whitehouse pp. 25–6 & plate B.

PML 85720. Gift: Reginald Allen.

As we see here and below, publishers also resorted to various less obvious ways of incorporating advertisements into their publications. In this instance Edward Wallis is being particularly ingenious, for on page 35 of his instruction book he notes against the final move of the game, to square no. (53): "Whoever arrives here first is declared winner, and is recommended to proceed immediately to the Publisher's, to purchase another Game, equally instructive and amusing."

344a. frontispiece

344b. front cover, *reduced*

❧ 344a ❧

PICTORIAL ADVERTISING:
B. Tabart, J. Harris

[ISAAC JENNER, formerly JEHNER (b. 1750)]. *Fortune's Football. Most humbly dedicated, by permission, to the young family of the Right Honble Lady Ann Hudson.* London: printed for the author; and sold by Tabart and Co. Juvenile Library, no. 157, New Bond Street, 1806. 12° (134 × 80 mm.).

A–K⁶ (A1ʳ title, A1ᵛ imprint *S. Gosnell, Printer, Little Queen Street,* A2ʳ *The Dedication,* A3ʳ *To the Readers,* B1ᵛ blank, K6ᵛ same printer's imprint); 2 etchings, presumably by the author: frontispiece of a young customer (the artist at nine years old) outside a bookshop, a self-portrait in the stipple manner of the artist in his deformity (tipped in at H3·4). Pp. 120. Wove paper, different for intaglio and letterpress. Gilt-blocked and dab-colored floral boards (*remboîtage*). References: Moon *Tabart* 75; Darton p. 107.

Provenance: Andrew White Tuer (binding); Charles Todd Owen (pencil note). PML 80107. Gift: Elisabeth Ball.

❧ 344b ❧

The Pence Table Playfully Paraphrased by Peter Pennyless. [London:] J. Harris, Corner of St. Paul's Church-Yard, [1818 (date of plate and paper)]. 16° (126 × 105 mm.).

[1–4⁴] (1/1ʳ blank, 1/1ᵛ incipit: *Twelve Pence is just 1ˢʰ / This I gave to buy a Whip,* imprint *Published by J. Harris, corner of Sᵗ Paul's, June 1. 1818,* 3/1ᵛ same imprint, 4/4ʳ *And beg'd hereafter he'd not teaze me. / Nor borrow thus to make me poor,* 4/4ᵛ blank). Ff. [16]. Stipple-engraved throughout: printed from two copperplates on one side of two half-sheets (from the same wove paper stock). 16 nearly full-page illustrations, in publisher's coloring, each with two-line rhyme. Original printed gray stiff wrappers, letterpress title (as transcribed above) and wood engraving of Harris's shop and St. Paul's on front cover, letterpress ad for *Marmaduke Multiply's Merry Method* on back cover, MS price 1/6 on front cover (the usual cost for colored copies of Harris picture books of this size, and presumably thus marked at the publisher's). Reference: Moon *Harris* 613(1).

PML 85074. Gift: Elisabeth Ball.

Booksellers' pride in their premises as well as their wares led many of them to a fairly frequent portrayal of both the interior and exterior of their shops. The treatment was doubtless much idealized, but the presence of these pictures does give some insight into the appearance of bookshops in the age before photography. In

Fortune's Football the engraving illustrates the author in his ninth year "looking over the treasures of an old book-stall"—which may not be exactly an advertisement for Tabart's shop, although the premises portrayed bear a greater resemblance to a respectable juvenile library than to a Farringdon Road barrow.

The illustration of Harris's shop on the cover of *The Pence Table* is a standard view which he used, along with other similar cuts, on numerous occasions. The carriage at the door and the gentry on the pavement outside suggest a highly presentable emporium. If you climbed inside the picture and followed the cathedral railings round to the left behind Harris's shop, you would soon come to the shop in St. Paul's Churchyard where John Newbery had established his business. Neither of these pictures of bookshops is to be found in Sigfred Taubert's iconography of the book trade, *Bibliopola* (Hamburg, 1966).

SUBLIMINAL ADVERTISING:
E. Newbery, J. Harris

➷ 345 ⬥⬥

[RICHARD JOHNSON (1734–93)]. *The Blossoms of Morality; intended for the amusement and instruction of young ladies and gentlemen. By the editor of The Looking-Glass for the Mind. With forty-seven cuts, designed and engraved by I. Bewick. The sixth edition.* London: printed for J. Harris; Scatcherd and Letterman; B. and R. Crosby and Co.; Darton and Harvey; Lackington, Allen and Co.; and J. Walker, 1814. 12° (175 × 105 mm.).

A–T⁶ (A1ʳ title, title-vignette by Bewick, A1ᵛ imprint *Printed by James Swan, 76, Fleet Street, London*, A2ʳ Preface, A3ᵛ Contents, A4ʳ *Ernestus and Fragilis*, T6ʳ imprint *Printed by James Swan, 76, Fleet Street, London*, T6ᵛ blank). Pp. 227, [1]. Wove paper. 23 wood engravings (about 60 × 45 mm. each) by John Bewick and others with 22 wood-engraved tailpieces (mostly pictorial). Modern cloth. References: Moon *Harris* 56(3); Gumuchian 561; Tattersfield JB7; Darton *Check-list* G116(3); Hockliffe 148 (fifth edition, 1810).

Provenance: Gwendoline Wright (pencil sign.). PML 81763. Gift: Elisabeth Ball.

As we have had occasion to notice several times already, booksellers were fond of including advertisements for their titles within the body of their stories. John Newbery was the Great Example, keeping a ready flow of advice going about books which children would find in the shop of their "old friend" in St. Paul's Churchyard, and here we find his nephew's widow instigating the same procedure for her shop round the corner. (*The Blossoms of Morality* was first published solely by Elizabeth Newbery, and her successor, John Harris, continued the phrasing even though shares in the book had been sold to other publishers.)

> My dear papa, said young Theophilus to his father, I cannot help pitying those poor little boys, whose parents are not in a condition to purchase them such a nice gilded library, as that with which you have supplied me from my good friend's at the corner of St. Paul's Church-yard.

The Book of Nature.

My dear papa, said young Theophilus to his father, I cannot help pitying those poor little boys, whose parents are not in a condition to purchase them such a nice gilded library, as that with which you have supplied me from my good friend's at the corner of St. Paul's Churchyard. Surely such unhappy boys must be very ignorant all their lives, for what can they learn without books?

I agree with you, replied his father, that you are happy in having so large a collection of books, and I am no less happy in seeing you make so good a use of them.—There is, however, my dear child, another book, called *The Book of*

345. C2 verso, *reduced*

The Blossoms of Morality was first published unillustrated, apart from a frontispiece, in 1789. Wood engravings for a second edition were commissioned from John Bewick, who died before completing the work, and the outstanding blocks were cut in the workshop of his brother Thomas in Newcastle upon Tyne. Elizabeth Newbery published this and the third edition (1796 and 1801), but when John Harris took over he sold shares in the book to the publishers named in the above imprint, plus Vernor & Hood.

DISTRIBUTING THE COMPETITION:
Harvey and Darton, Dean and Munday

⋄§ 346 §⋄

The Nursery Alphabet for Good Children. London: Printed for Harvey & Darton, Gracechurch Str[t], 1824. 8° (178 × 110 mm.).

[1[8]] (1[r] pictorial title, 1[v] blank, 2[r] incipit: *A stands for Ass*). Pp. 15, [1]. Wove paper (watermark-date 1823). Outer forme printed intaglio, inner forme letterpress. Title-illustration, 26 alphabet illustrations, and 2 emblems (*Learning* and *Ignorance*), all etched and in publisher's coloring. Original pink wrappers, letterpress title *The Nursery Alphabet of Beasts and Birds*, imprint, and *Price One Shilling, coloured* on front cover, Harvey and Darton ads on back cover, ads for books of rival publishers, notably Dean, inside both covers (see overleaf). Brown morocco gilt. Reference: Darton *Check-list* G714.

Provenance: Charles Todd Owen (binding). PML 80903. Gift: Elisabeth Ball.

There seems to be a serious discrepancy here between the publisher's name on the outside of the cover and the advertisements on the inside. The book is "printed for Harvey & Darton," but almost all the traceable titles advertised are books that were published by Dean & Munday or their associate A.K. Newman. Were Harvey & Darton of Gracechurch Street keen to sell stock from their competitor in Threadneedle Street, or was this edition of the book printed for Dean to sell, but with the "official" Darton imprint? A third possibility is that Dean & Munday were the printers of Harvey & Darton's edition of *The Nursery Alphabet* and therefore allowed to advertise discreetly.

347. frontispiece

DISCOUNTING: William Darton

⋄§ 347 §⋄

The Adventures of a Donkey. By Arabella Argus, author of "The Juvenile Spectator." London: printed by and for William Darton, jun. 58, Holborn Hill, 1815. 18° (133 × 85 mm.).

A[2] (1[r] half-title, 1[v] blank, 2[r] title, 2[v] blank); B–U[6] X[4] Y[6] (B1[r] *Prefatory Address*, B2[r] *Chap. I*, quires A and X making up one third of a sheet, X2[v] blank, X3[r] *A list of improved books, &c. for children*, Y3[r] *Penmanship*, i.e. ads for writing-sheets, Y4[r] ads for *Cards*, Y4[v] *Games*, Y5[r] *Dissected maps*, Y6[r] *Dissected puzzles*, Y6[v] *School Books Of most kinds are also kept, and Schools supplied on the usual Terms.* *** *A Quantity of Damaged Books to be Sold Cheap*); etched frontispiece *Poor little foal of an oppressed race.* . . . Pp. [4], 231, [1, 16]. Wove paper (different stock for frontispiece). Original red half roan gilt and gray paper boards, endpapers watermarked 1814. Reference: Darton H32(1).

Provenance: *Elizabeth Ann Pembrook 18 April 1819* (calligraphic inscr.); H. Pembrook (child's sign. in pencil); Gumuchian & C[ie] (1930 cat., no. 365). PML 81508. Gift: Elisabeth Ball.

The presumably pseudonymous but still unidentified "Arabella

Argus" wrote one of Darton's steadiest sellers in *The Adventures of a Donkey*, which remained in print for about fifty years. In this first edition the publisher takes the opportunity to include sixteen pages of advertisements for a wide range of his stock and includes the highly unusual final note on "damaged books." Had there been a fire or a flood, or was he doing some secondhand dealing with the purchase of a much-thumbed private library?

"TAKE YOUR CHOICE": J. Marshall

⋄§ 348 §⋄

SARAH TRIMMER, née KIRBY (1741–1810). *A Series of Prints of Roman History, designed as ornaments for those apartments in which children receive the first rudiments of their education.* London: Printed and Sold by J. Marshall and Co. No. 17, Queen-Street, Cheapside: and No. 4, Aldermary Church-Yard, in Bow-Lane, [1789]. Price, pasted on Boards for hanging up in Nurseries, 3s.—in Sheets 1.4d—sewed in Marble Paper for the Pocket 1s.8d.—neatly Bound in Red Leather 2s.4d. 16° (105 × 90 mm.).

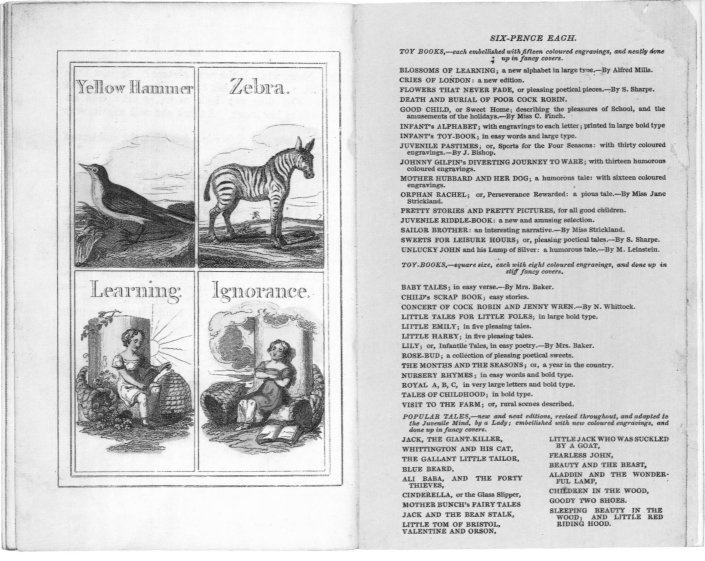

346. fo. 8ᵛ–inside back cover, *reduced*

π1 (recto: letterpress title, verso: ad *The Description of this Set of Prints of Roman History, contained in a Set of Easy Lessons, is sold for 1s. sewed in Marble Paper* [PML 85666],—*or 1s.8d. neatly bound in Red Leather*); [1–32²] (1/1ʳ blank, 1/1ᵛ illustration of Aeneas landing at Latium, imprint dated February 12, 1789, 32/2ʳ illustration of medals of Leo the Boy, Zeno Isaurieus, Basilisc, Anastasius, 32/2ᵛ blank). Ff. [1], LXIV. Unwatermarked, laid paper. Etched and engraved throughout (except title-leaf): 64 illustrations, printed from eight copperplates on one side of half-sheets. Original marbled wrappers (probably lacking a label). References: Osborne I, 175; cf. ESTC T110988; Hockliffe 1152; Bennett p. 52.

Provenance: M. Middleton (contemporary sign., also present in the accompanying text-volume, PML 85666, demonstrating that these two volumes have formed a set since their first sale). PML 85667. Purchase: Ball Fund.

In the general note on prints in chapter X we remark their production for educational purposes as well as for entertainment or decoration. Mrs. Trimmer's "Series of Prints" are an early example of this genre, and it is hard to believe that they found their way into "Nurseries" rather than schoolrooms. John Marshall made further use of the plates, however, by converting them into books to be sold alongside the appropriate *Description*, and as can be seen from the prices quoted above, a variety of choices was offered to the customer, the prices on the title-page differing from those cited on the verso. Among the subjects dealt with by Mrs. Trimmer were *Ancient History*, *English History*, *Scripture History*, and *The New Testament* (treated with all due gravity, of course). Few examples of the prints by themselves, either "pasted on boards" or "in sheets," seem to have survived, but the editions in book form (being fairly boring) are not uncommon.

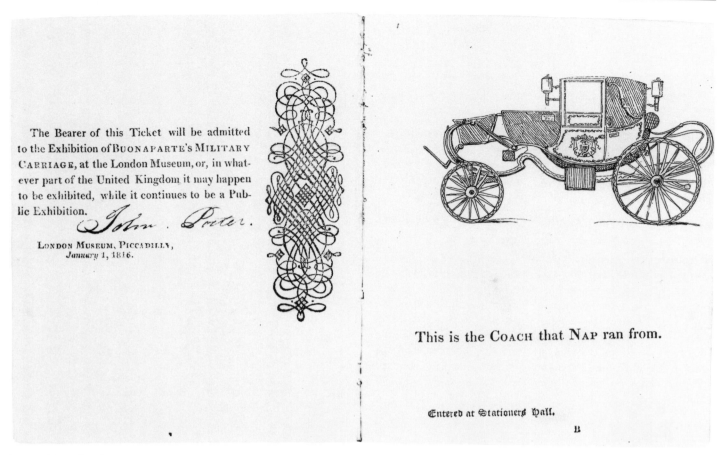

The Bearer of this Ticket will be admitted to the Exhibition of BUONAPARTE'S MILITARY CARRIAGE, at the London Museum, or, in whatever part of the United Kingdom it may happen to be exhibited, while it continues to be a Public Exhibition. *John Porter.*

LONDON MUSEUM, PICCADILLY, *January 1, 1816.*

This is the COACH that NAP ran from.

Entered at Stationers Hall.

B

349. π1ᵛ–B1ʳ, *reduced*

CROSS-SELLING: N. Hailes

∞§ 349 §∞

[*The Coach that Nap Ran From.* London: Nathaniel Hailes' Juvenile Library at the London Museum, 173 Piccadilly, 1816]. 16° (122 × 97 mm.).

π²<B¹² (π1ʳ blank, π1ᵛ *The Bearer of this Ticket will be admitted to the Exhibition of Buonaparte's Military Carriage, at the London Museum, or, in whatever part of the United Kingdom it may happen to be exhibited, while it continues to be a Public Exhibition. London Museum, Piccadilly, January 1, 1816.* [MS. signature:] *John Porter,* metalcut of arabesque ornament in inner margin, B1ʳ illustration, incipit: *This is the Coach that Nap ran from.* [at foot, in gothic type:] *Entered at Stationers Hall,* B1ᵛ–2ʳ blank, B2ᵛ illustration, *This is the Box prepar'd by his Wife, / That lay in the Coach that Nap ran from,* B12ᵛ view of the "Egyptian Hall," London Museum, *The wonderful Coach, from which Nappy flew, / At Bullock's Museum, is open to view; / ... / And if you wish you, may have a step through, / The Carriage so famous, from fam'd Waterloo!,* π2ʳ ad for the third editon of *Sir Hornbook; or, Childe Launcelot's Expedition,* π2ᵛ blank). Ff. [1], 12, [1]. Unwatermarked, wove paper. 12 hand-colored etched illustrations (the one on B9ʳ signed W.H.B.), printed from three copperplates on one side of the quarter-sheets, each with letterpress cumulative rhyme. Longitudinal imprints of the plates disappearing into the gutter: *London Published as the Act directs*

1ˢᵗ January 1816 by W. Bullock Museum Piccadilly. Lacking the original binding (stiff wrappers, presumably with title and imprint on front cover). Orange morocco gilt. Reference: Opie *ODNR* p. 232.

Provenance: Charles Todd Owen (binding). PML 85182. Gift: Elisabeth Ball.

Nathaniel Hailes had begun bookselling with John Sharpe ca. 1810, but in 1814 the partnership was dissolved, and Hailes continued on his own at their premises in "The London Museum." (Marjorie Moon gives a good account of this establishment in her afterword to the reprint of *The Juvenile Review* [Toronto, 1982], where it is explained how William Bullock had it built in 1812 as "The Egyptian Hall" to house his exhibition of curiosities.) Among Bullock's exhibits was Napoleon's traveling carriage, and this little book not only celebrates its wonders in the manner of "The House that Jack Built," but also supplies the purchaser with a ticket for a free inspection of the vehicle.

Harvey Darton (pp. 203–4) records an earlier piece of cross-marketing by Sharpe and Hailes together in their edition of *Sir Hornbook* (1814): "Purchasers [in the bookshop] to the Amount of Ten Shillings are allowed an Admission Ticket to the Museum, and Purchasers to the Amount of Twenty Shillings, a Ticket BOTH to the Pantherion and to the Museum." (The Pantherion was an early example of "living experience" techniques whereby the customers were able to walk through an imitation jungle full of stuffed animals.)

LENDING: P. Humphry

350

[Circulating Library Label]. Chichester: Humphry's, August 1768. Broadside (90 × 53 mm.).

Letterpress, numbered in manuscript *154*. Laid paper. Roman type, 20 lines. Mounted inside front cover of *The Travels of Tom Thumb over England and Wales . . . Written by himself* (London: R. Amey and M. Cooper, 1746. 12°), for another copy of which see entry 63.

The Osborne Collection of Early Children's Books, Toronto Public Library.

P. Humphry (or Humphrey) was in business at least by 1766 and is listed by Pendred as a bookseller and stationer at Chichester in 1785. That he combined a circulating library with his other interests need cause no surprise, since the second half of the eighteenth century saw a rapid growth in both subscription libraries and lending libraries run by the trade. We know little about provision for children in circulating libraries, and the presence of Tom Thumb's *Travels* at Chichester need not argue an extensive stock since the book probably had some appeal to an adult clientele.

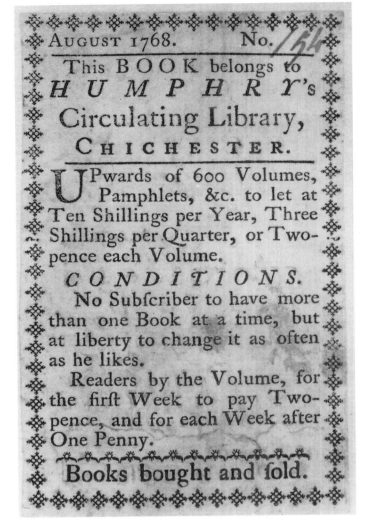

350. enlarged

XVIII

BINDINGS

WITH the invention of children's books as a widely market-able commodity came the recognition that attractive and colorful appearance encourages sales. In addition, the physical insignificance of the product and the nature of the intended market argued for distribution of stock ready-bound rather than in sheets. As a consequence, from before the middle of the eighteenth century children's books have occupied a peculiarly distinctive, if neglected, place in the history of bookbinding. It is not always easy to distinguish between edition-binding done or commissioned by the publisher and book trade binding of individual or groups of copies of an edition, which may have survived only in scattered examples. However, there can be no doubt that children's books were much more commonly published in bound form than printed books for almost any other major market in the eighteenth century, while in the nineteenth century some new ideas for decorative or pictorial binding styles were tried out on juveniles without serious financial risk.

In this chapter we show examples of a dozen different styles of publisher's binding that were found on children's books between 1727 and 1845. Within these categories variations exist which are not shown here (e.g. the Kirkall-Bewick pictorial bindings seen at entries 118 and 144a), and in many instances the kind of binding represented was subject to multiple variations in color or design from one book or one edition to another; the Morgan Library possesses many examples of such variants.

Ending our survey with the decorative paper bindings of the 1830s and 1840s, we have deliberately excluded consideration of the arrival of publisher's cloth in the early 1820s and of nineteenth-century pictorial paper covers. Both of these styles were to develop into a rich and multifarious branch of this applied art during the Victorian period, whose heyday lies outside the confines of this catalogue.

PUBLISHER'S PANELED CALF

⊰ 351 ⊱

Biblia or a Practical Summary of yᵉ Old & New Testaments. Lond. Printed for R. Wilkin. in Sᵗ Pauls-Church Yard, 1727. 128° (38 × 25 mm.).

π² (=S4·5; *The Preface*); A–R⁸ S⁸ (–4·5; 6ʳ *Particular Cuts explain'd*); etched frontispiece, two titles (first as transcribed above, the second preceding K6: *Biblia Vol. II. Book V. Treating of The Evangelical Dispensation by the Ever Blessed Jesus Christ. Lond. Printed for R. Wilkin. 1727*), and 15 other etchings, presumably all printed from a single copperplate on one side of a part-sheet and divided for insertion. Pp. [4], 278, [6]. Laid, watermarked paper; a different stock for the plates. Roman type.

Eight lines and headline to the page. References: Spielmann 15 B; Roscoe *Thumb Bibles* 22; Adomeit B16; ESTC T067305.

Binding: Original blind-paneled calf over pasteboard (see overleaf), spine with four raised bands, edges plain, marbled endpapers.

PML 65843. Purchase: Ball Fund.

Calf and sheepskin have been materials traditional to the market for cheap bookbinding since the Middle Ages (which has not precluded calf, at least, from being used for elaborate and expensive bindings as well). For this "Thumb Bible"—the first edition of the Wilkin summary—the publisher chose to issue the main run in standard calf if only to ensure that his minute book would reach customers with all its text-leaves and illustrations present in the right order. To those wanting a superior cover for their abridgment of scripture, he marketed part of the edition in gold-tooled morocco.

PUBLISHER'S INLAID MOROCCO

⊰ 352 ⊱

The Bible in Miniature [sic] *or a Concise History of the Old & New Testaments.* Lond. Printed for E. Newbery Corner of Sᵗ Pauls Church Yard, 1780 [not before 1809 (watermark-date in C1·8)]. 128° (40 × 27 mm.).

A–Q⁸ (A1ʳ *The Preface*, A3ʳ *Book I*, K3ʳ *Book V. Treating of The Nativity of Christ*, Q8ᵛ imprint *Crowder & Hemsted, Printers, Warwick-Square*); 16 etchings including two titles (first as transcribed above, the second inserted between K2–3: *A Concise History of the New Testament. Lond. Printed for E. Newbery. Corner of Sᵗ Pauls Church Yard. 1780*), presumably all printed from a single copperplate on one side of a part-sheet and divided for insertion. Pp. 256. Wove, watermarked paper; a different stock for the plates. Roman type. Eight lines to the page. References: Roscoe J28(2); Spielmann 17; Roscoe *Thumb Bibles* 32.2; Bennett p. 128; Adomeit B27; cf. ESTC T127074.

Binding: Original gold-tooled red morocco over pasteboard, Holy Monogram on oval black morocco inlays in the center of the sides, flat spine decorated in compartments, edges gilt, blue-and-white headbands, marbled endpapers. Provenance: H. Bradley Martin (Sotheby's New York, 31 Jan. 1990, lot 2306). PML 85996. Purchase: Gordon N. Ray Fund.

The fashion for fancy bindings on miniature Bibles continued well beyond Wilkin's time, and here we find Elizabeth Newbery (or, more likely, John Harris) producing her "concise history" in morocco (goatskin), the material reserved for deluxe bindings

Above: 351. *enlarged*   *Below*: 352. *enlarged*

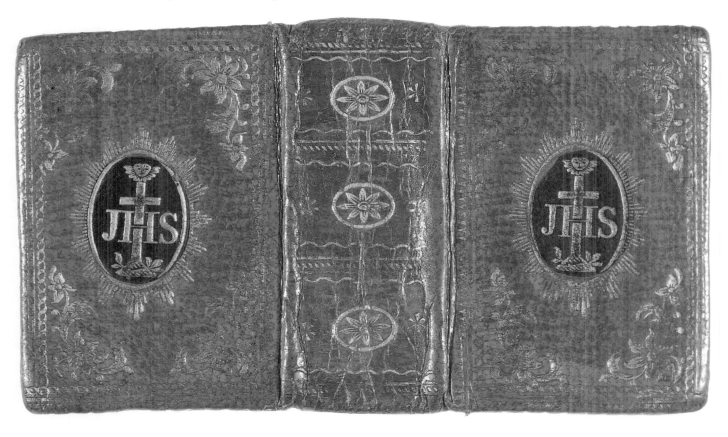

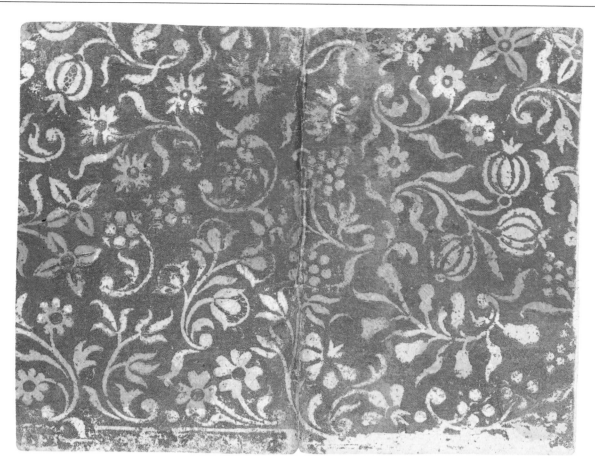

Above: **353.** *enlarged*   *Below:* **355.** *enlarged*

since late medieval times. This superior binding was available in red, olive, or black morocco with inlays of a contrasting color at 2s.; there was also an issue in calf at half the price.

Elizabeth Newbery's abridgment is essentially that of Wilkin's edition, transmitted through W. Harris of 70 St. Paul's Church Yard and J. Harris of Leadenhall Street (not EN's J. Harris), whose text of 1778 is followed here. Her miniature Bible is invariably discussed as a single edition, known in various states or issues, but Mrs. Newbery in fact commissioned a number of different editions from several printers over a period of at least two decades. By 1809 her shop was entirely in the control of John Harris, but changes in the engraved title page of *The Bible in Miniuture* were probably no longer felt to be worth making.

"DUTCH" GILT AND FLOWERED PAPER

⊷§ 353 ?⊷

The New and Entertaining History of Polly Cherry and her Golden Apple. To which is added, the adventures of Prince George. Carefully corrected by Miss Virtue. London: Printed and Sold [by John Marshall] at No. 17, Queen-Street, Cheapside, and No. 4, Aldermary Church-Yard, in Bow-Lane, [not before 1787]. [Price One Penny Bound and Gilt.]. Half-sheet 32° (103 × 64 mm.).

A[16] (1·16 mounted as pastedowns, 1[v] frontispiece *Polly Cherry's Rules for Daily Practice*, verse, incipit: *Soon as the Morn salutes your Eyes*, 2[r] title, 2[v] ad for Marshall's *Juvenile Magazine*, 16[r] J. Marshall and Co. ads). Pp. 30, [2]. Laid paper, no watermark. 12 wood engravings including frontispiece (about 36 × 57 mm. each). Reference: ESTC N041813.

Binding: Original wrappers, cut from an Augsburg or Nuremberg gilt-blocked and dab-colored sheet, the colors including gold, purple, orange, yellow, and green; fragment of a name signed in the block still visible. (See previous page.) PML 82301. Gift: Elisabeth Ball.

From the second quarter to the end of the eighteenth century "Dutch flowered paper" was apparently the most widely used covering for children's books, either glued to the sewn bookblock as here, the pastedowns serving as modest reinforcement, or stretched over more durable pasteboard. In either case, it is notable as perhaps the first widespread, continuously used form of edition-binding and was adopted by the English juvenile book trade for works other than those intended for the schoolroom.

"Dutch paper" is actually a misnomer. It is used to indicate a variety of decorated papers, which were manufactured mostly in southern Germany and probably imported via Dutch merchants, although later in the century there was some local production in England. Albert Haemmerle and Olga Hirsch (*Buntpapier* [1961]) describe the various techniques and reproduce numerous pictorial and ornamental designs, but the most common pattern employed for children's books was boldly floral. The embossing of a sheet was done in copper-gilt (now often vanished) from a wood or metal block or engraved cylinder; color was applied afterwards by means of dabbing or stenciling. A single sheet yielded wrappers for several small-format books. The condition of the binding paper on *Polly Cherry* has remained particularly fresh.

SCHOOL CANVAS

⊷§ 354 ?⊷

[SARAH FIELDING (1710–68)]. *The Governess; or, the little female academy. Calculated for the entertainment and instruction of young ladies in their education. By the author of David Simple. The fifth edition. Revised and Corrected . . .* London: Printed for A. Millar; and Sold by T. Cadell, in the Strand, 1768. [Price Bound Eighteen Pence.]. 12° (160 × 95 mm.).

A[4](4+1 signed B) (1[r] title, 2[r] author's dedication *To the Honourable Mrs. Poyntz*, 3[r] *Preface*); B–F[12] G[12](12+1 signed H) (quire A and leaf G12+1 presumably forming a half-sheet). Pp. x, 146. Laid paper. References: Grey 10 [facsimile]; ESTC T000474.

Binding: Original rough canvas over pasteboard, of a type commonly found on eighteenth-century English schoolbooks. Provenance: Davis (faint pencil-sign.); Gumuchian & C[ie] (1930 cat., no. 2525). PML 85568. Gift: Elisabeth Ball.

Given the always unstable relationship between schoolchildren and their textbooks, there should be no surprise that the trade-binding of schoolbooks has a long history. The books were certain to come in for heavy wear, while at the same time it was in the interests of school proprietors to make them last as long as possible (unless the parents were paying, in which case other interests prevailed). The usual binding material found on textbooks is sheep or some other cheap leather (see *Nolens Volens*, entry 2). In the mid-eighteenth century, however, canvas came to be adopted as an alternative (see *The London Vocabulary*, entry 3). Sarah Fielding's *Governess* was not conceived as a schoolbook but was originally published for "recreational" reading. This later and cheaper edition probably marks the customary descent of a "trade book" to classroom use. The work is famed as the first long story or novel to be written for children in English; the Morgan copy of the first edition is discussed at entry 370 in this catalogue.

RED-PRINTED PICTORIAL WRAPPERS

⊷§ 355 ?⊷

Nurse Truelove's New-Year's Gift: or, the book of books for children. Adorned with cuts. And designed for a present to every little boy who would become a great man, and ride upon a fine horse; and to every little girl, who would become a great woman, and ride in a Lord Mayor's gilt coach. But let us turn over the leaf, and see more of the matter. N.B. You may have this little book of T. Carnan, (Successor to Mr. J. Newbery) at No. 65, in St. Paul's Church-yard, only paying two-pence for the binding; but not unless you are good. Nurse Truelove. [London, ca. 1785]. 32° (96 × 60/64 mm.), turned chain-lines.

[1[32]] signed A[8]<B[8]<C[8]<D[8] (1·32 mounted as pastedowns, 1[v] frontispiece *An honest Man is an Honour to his Country*, 2[r] title, 2[v] blank, 3[r] *The History of Miss Polly Friendly*, 28[r] ads, 32[r]

356. front cover

356. F1 recto

illustration *A virtuous Woman is a Crown to her Husband*). Pp. 54, [10]. Laid paper. 35 cuts including frontispiece (about 30 × 36 mm. each). Reference: Roscoe J270(6)=J270(7).

Binding: Original pictorial buff wrappers, typographical borders and four wood- or metalcuts of children's games printed in red on the sides: bowling and skittles on front cover, dolls and peg top on back cover. (See p. 269.) PML 82436. Gift: Elisabeth Ball.

While the Newberys liked to compose advertising copy for their children's books—"prettily bound and gilt" (i.e. in decorated paper)—they also genuinely experimented with other forms of binding: most notably the pictorial bindings for which Bewick supplied the designs and some rather less august pictorial bindings for which existing metalcuts, or woodcuts, were used or possibly prepared *ad hoc*.

This beautifully preserved copy of Newbery's *New Year's Gift* shows one of these cheaper pictorial bindings in fine state, even though the printer has had trouble getting the red ink to "take" on the rough surface of the cover. The book itself is one of Newbery's spatchcock miscellanies of moral tales, moral adjurations, a catechism, and the story of "Mrs. Williams and her plumb cake," to which twice he draws attention in the text of *Little Goody Two-Shoes*. Amidst all this inconsequential stuff, however, there also appears the first illustrated version of "The House that Jack Built."

The binding suggests something of the book's nature without making direct reference to its contents.

PICTORIAL BOARDS RELATING TO THE TEXT

◦§ 356 ℰ◦

A New Hieroglyphical Bible, for the amusement & instruction of children; being a selection of the most useful lessons, and most interesting narratives: (scripturally arranged) from Genesis to the Revelations. Embellished with familiar figures, & striking emblems; elegantly engraved. To the whole is added a sketch of the life of Our Blessed Saviour, the holy apostles &c. Recommended by the Revd Rowland Hill M.A. London: Printed & Published by G. Thompson N° 43 Long Lane. West Smithfield. (Enter'd at Stationers Hall.), 1794 [but not before 1802]. 18° (134 × 84 mm.).

π^2 (engraved frontispiece and title); A–M^6 (A1^r letter from Hill to Thompson, A1^v preface, A2^v verse by Theodore Beza *On the Incomparable Treasure of the Holy Scriptures*, K6^r *Life of... Jesus Christ*, M4^r–5^r various prayers and hymns, M5^v–6^r *Questions*

357.

and answers out of the Holy Scriptures). Pp. [4], 144. Wove paper with 1802 watermark-date. 485 wood-engraved illustrations (including repeats) of various sizes, identical type-ornament border around every page of the hieroglyphic Bible. References: Bennett p. 93; ESTC T123482; Clouston pp. 53–62.

Binding: Original pictorial buff boards, wood engraving of the Fall *The wages of sin is death* on front cover, Crucifixion *The gift of God is eternal life through Jesus Christ our Lord* on back cover. Provenance: *Edwd Gauntlett Jany 1810* (inscr.); Anne Lyon Haight (bookplate). PML 81079. Gift: Mrs. Sherman P. Haight.

By putting emblematic cuts on the cover—from the Fall to the Redemption—Thompson manages to harmonize his pictorial boards with the hieroglyphic content of his pages. (Bassam employed a somewhat similar contrast of images for his *Hieroglyphic Bible*, see entry 155.) Mrs. Trimmer did not approve of the venture, writing of Thompson's edition that it was "a Book which, however well intended, can answer no one good purpose, but which exposes the Sacred Volume to the ridicule and contempt of infidels." (*Guardian of Education* I [1802], pp. 381–91 for the whole review.) Such strictures did not put off trade, and a copy of the original edition was pirated a few years later by the American bookseller W. Norman for publication in Boston (PML 80885).

CARNAN'S "VELLUM MANNER"

⤙ 357 ⤚

[JOHN NEWBERY (1713–67), editor] *The Newtonian System of Philosophy Adapted to the Capacities of Young Gentlemen and Ladies. And familiarized and made entertaining by objects with which they are intimately acquainted: being the substance of six lectures read to the Lilliputian Society, by Tom Telescope, A.M. And collected and methodized for the benefit of the youth of these kingdoms, by their old friend Mr. Newbery, in St. Paul's Church Yard. Who has also added a variety of copper plate cuts to illustrate and confirm the doctrines advanced . . . The seventh edition.* London: Printed for T. Carnan, (Successor to Mr. J. Newbery) in St. Paul's Church Yard, 1787. [Price One Shilling and Six-Pence.]. 18° (116 × 76 mm.).

A–M^6 (A1^r title, A1^v blank, A2^r dedication, A2^v *Contents*, A3^r *Introduction*, A5^r *Lecture I*, L5^r *Advertisement*, L6^r–M6^v ads); nine etchings (including *Frontispiece*, caption *Lecture on Matter & Motion*), possibly printed from a single copperplate on a half-sheet and divided for insertion. Pp. [4], 140. Laid paper, unwatermarked. Five relief-cut illustrations. References: ESTC N005412; Roscoe J348(7).

Binding: Original green quarter vellum and marbled boards, spine-label lost.

PML 85632. Gift: Elisabeth Ball.

Binding "in the vellum manner" is here shown on a copy of *The Newtonian System*, the first edition of which has been discussed in chapter I (entry 9). This style of binding, in which paper-covered boards, either in a single color or marbled, are supported by a green (or blue) vellum backstrip, came into being towards the end of the 1760s. S. Roscoe in his *John Newbery and his Successors* (1973) gives conclusive arguments for this dating and suggests that the method, which was brought about by a scarcity of leather, may well have been the brainchild of Thomas Carnan. He quotes an advertisement dated 1768, which explains the advantages: "Books bound in the Vellum manner . . . open easier at the Back, and are not so liable to warp in being read [as books in leather]. If . . . the covers should be stained or rubbed, they may be new covered for a Penny."

COVER-TITLE LABELS

ᨺ 358a ᨺ

[WILLIAM COWPER (1731–1800)]. *The Humorous History of John Gilpin and the Historical Ballad of the Children in the Wood*. Glasgow: Published by J. Lumsden & Son, [not before 1811]. 18° (124 × 81 mm.).

A[18] (1[r] incipit: *John Gilpin was a citizen*, 8[r] *Three Black Crows*, incipit: *Two honest tradesmen, meeting in the Strand*, 9[v] *Anecdotes of the Mastiff Dog*, 10[v] *The Sagacity of the Elephant*, 12[r] *The Children in the Wood. A Ballad*, incipit: *Now ponder well, ye parents dear*, 16[v] *Conclusion*, 17[v] *Dishonesty punished*, 18[v] *Wise sayings for the use of children*); eight etchings, including frontispiece *Stop! Stop! John Gilpin, here's the House, they all at once did cry* and conjugate title with vignette printed from one plate and inserted before A1, and six illustrations printed from another copperplate on one side of a part-sheet, divided into three bifolia designated A (inserted around A2·17), B (around A5·14) and C (around A8·11). Pp. 52 (plates included in pagination). Wove paper watermarked 1811. Wood-engraved oval tailpiece (A18[r]). Reference: Roscoe & Brimmell 89a. Not in Russell.

Binding: Original pink stiff wrappers, engraved title-label—see overleaf (63 × 53 mm.) mounted on front cover: *Lumsden & Son's / New Edition / of Johnny Gilpin / & Children in the / Wood*, printed within an oval frame in black ink (the Moon copy described in Roscoe & Brimmell has the label printed in blue). Provenance: Charles Todd Owen (red morocco binding, top edges gilt, by Morrell). PML 85023. Gift: Elisabeth Ball.

ᨺ 358b ᨺ

Marshall's New Riddle-Book for 1819. Embellished with Coloured Engravings. London: printed and sold by John Marshall, 140, Fleet Street, From Aldermary Church-Yard, [1818]. Price sixpence. 32° (96 × 78 mm.).

[1[8]] (1[r] title, 1[v] incipit *I saw a Bird pent in a cage*, 8[v] imprint *Printed and Sold by John Marshall, 140, Fleet Street, from Aldermary Church-yard. London; Of whom may be had a Variety on the same Plan*); engraving of 20 illustrations (hand-colored as issued), printed from a copperplate on a part-sheet, divided into three bifolia (inserted in the middle of the quire and around 2·7 and 4·5). Pp. 30 (*recte* 28; plates included in pagination). Wove paper watermarked 1818.

Binding: Original orange stiff wrappers, hand-colored engraved title-label cut out in the shape of a sunburst and mounted on front cover: *Riddle / Book*. See overleaf. Provenance: Charles Todd Owen (gilt orange morocco binding). PML 85367. Gift: Elisabeth Ball.

ᨺ 358c ᨺ

Juvenile Stories. Embellished with Coloured Engravings. London: printed and sold by John Marshall, 140, Fleet Street, From Aldermary Church-Yard, 1821. Price Sixpence. 16°? (108 × 87 mm.).

[1[8]] (1[r] title, 1[v] *The Cross Man*, 8[v] imprint *Printed and Sold by J. Marshall, 140, Fleet Street, from Aldermary Church-Yard, London. Of whom may be had a Variety on the same Plan*); eight full-page wood engravings including frontispiece (all hand-colored as issued) on four bifolia, inserted around 1·8, 2·7, 3·6 and 4·5. Pp. 30, [2] (plates included in pagination). Laid paper for text, wove paper (1817 watermark-date) for illustrations.

Binding: Original orange-speckled stiff wrappers, hand-colored engraved shaped floral title-label mounted on front cover: *Juvenile / Stories*. Provenance: C. Gresley 1824 (inscr.); Charles Todd Owen (gilt orange morocco binding). PML 85032. Gift: Elisabeth Ball.

Children's books bound entirely in monochrome paper (and not vellum-backed) date from the last years of the eighteenth century, when pink-glazed stiff wrappers with a decorative label were often used. Lumsden (see chapter XI) was especially adept in such bindings, employing a range of attractively colored papers, with handsomely designed labels. This edition of *John Gilpin* also contains several miscellaneous pieces, including the dispiritingly unfunny ballad of "The Three Black Crows." The label serves the simple purpose of indicating the two main poems in the book.

Marshall had been a pioneer of paper bindings (entry 87 describes a copy of his two-volume edition of *Cobwebs to Catch Flies* in pink-glazed paper). With the revival of his activities after 1810, his interest in such bindings was also renewed, and he produced some delightfully individual covers in variously colored papers with variously shaped cut-out labels, engraved and hand-colored. The intention was to reflect the pleasures that resided (perhaps) in the books. As a riddle book the present volume is something of a disappointment, with no consistent relationship existing between riddles and pictures. There is a strong possibility that the text was cobbled up around plates that had been used for a different purpose much earlier in the century.

With *Juvenile Stories* Marshall introduces a speckled variation

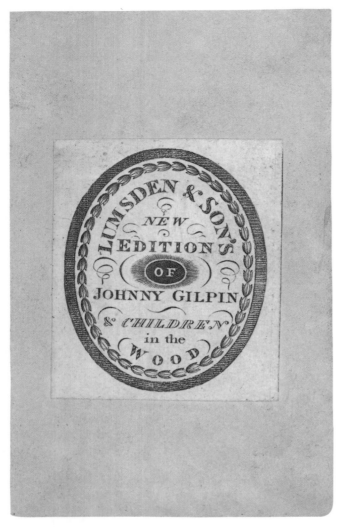

Above: 358a.   *Below*: 358c.

358b. *enlarged*

on the binding for his *New Riddle-Book*. The jolly cover and the brightly hand-colored illustrations within pink-wash frames make an extravagant setting for these dimly moral stories. Several books with similarly fanciful labels appear in our brief survey on Marshall in chapter XI.

PICTORIAL LABEL

❧ 359 ❧

Hodgson's Tom Thumb. [London: Hodgson & Co. or Orlando Hodgson, ca. 1825]. 8° (160 × 96 mm.).

[1⁸] (1·8 mounted as pastedowns, 1ᵛ drop-title, heading *Tom punished for thieving*, incipit: *For stealing cherry stones pray mind!*). Ff. [8]. Etched throughout: printed from a single copper-plate on one side of a sheet. 8 half-page hand-colored illustrations, each with one-line caption and four-line rhyme. Wove paper, apparently unwatermarked.

Binding: Original blue wrappers, hand-colored wood-engraved pictorial label (95 × 71 mm.) with mitred corners, showing three youths and a dog in a park, mounted on front cover. Provenance: Charles Todd Owen (gilt maroon morocco binding). PML 85116. Gift: Elisabeth Ball.

Glazed paper bindings with hand-colored engraved or relief-cut labels became very common during the first three decades of the nineteenth century, and the leading publishers and their epigones, whom we noticed in chapters XI and XII, adopted a

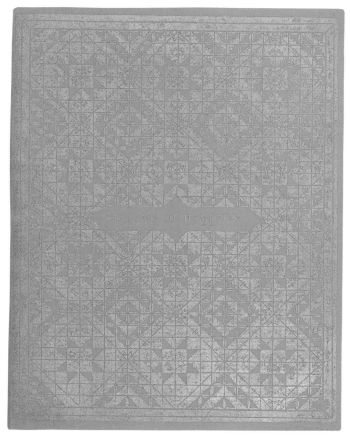

Above: **360b.** *reduced*

Above: **359.** *reduced*   *Below:* **360a.** *reduced*

Below: **360c.** *reduced*

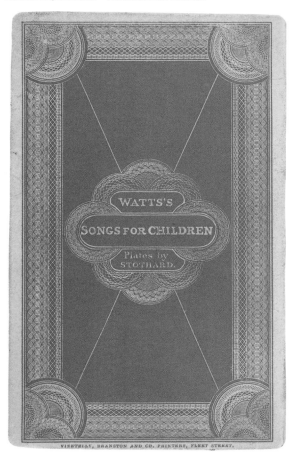

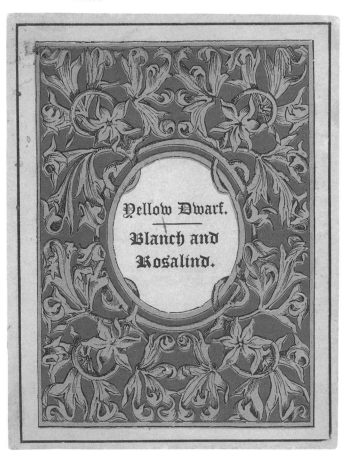

variety of designs. Hodgson, for instance, favored a "series" style, fitting large pictorial cover-labels to the varied colored paper wrappers of his picture books.

This heavily abridged version of *Tom Thumb* retains some of the incidents found in the earliest known edition (entry 41) but does not set them into narrative form. Each leaf of the book simply pictures one isolated incident and describes it in four lines of lamentable verse; for another impression of the copperplate, given another cover in the same style, see entry 226.

DESIGNED COVERS

❧ 360a ❧

Rev. ISAAC WATTS (1674–1748). *Songs, divine and moral, for the use of children.* London: Charles Tilt, 86, Fleet Street, 1832. 8° (162 × 99 mm.).

A^2 (1^r half-title, 1^v blank, 2^r title and vignette, 2^v imprint *Chiswick: printed by C. Whittingham*); B–C^4 D^8 E–F^2 G–I^8 K^2 ($B1^r$ *Preface*, $B4^r$ divisional title *Divine Songs . . .*, $C1^r$ *A general song of praise to God*, incipit: *How glorious is our heavenly King*, $I3^r$ divisional title *Moral Songs*, $I4^r$ *The Sluggard*, incipit: *'Tis the voice of the sluggard; I hear him complain*, $K2^v$ same printer's imprint). Pp. 96. Wove paper. Six half-page wood engravings after Thomas Stothard (1755–1834), including title-vignette, hand-colored in a child's hand. Reference: Pafford B108 (noting a copy given by John Constable to his daughter Emily "from her dear Papa" who had colored the pictures for her).

Binding: Original buff paper boards, a complex center- and corner-piece design of filigree and arabesque ornament, printed white-on-brown on both covers and incorporating title *Watts's / Songs for Children / Plates by / Stothard*, back cover signed *Vizetelly, Branston and Co. Printers, Fleet Street.* (See previous page.) Provenance: *Ellen King Rome 1861* (inscr.); Anne Lyon Haight (bookplate). PML 81090. Gift: Mrs. Sherman P. Haight.

❧ 360b ❧

[WILLIAM JOHN THOMS (1803–85), editor]. *Gammer Gurton's Story Books. The Gallant History of Bevis of Southampton.* [London:] Joseph Cundall, 12, Old Bond Street, [ca. 1845]. 8° (160 × 121 mm.).

4^8 (1^r drop-title, *Chapter I* and imprint); wood-engraved frontispiece after Frederick Tayler (1802–89). Pp. [16]. Laid paper, frontispiece on wove. Wood-engraved outer-margin flower and animal border on every page, printed from four blocks, wood-engraved five-line floral initial I and small tailpiece, all uncolored. Reference: McLean *Cundall* p. 50.

Binding: Original orange and gilt stiff wrappers (Cundall's "gold-paper cover"—see previous page), all-over geometric design on both sides, title *Sir Bevis of Hampton* gilt-printed in center of front cover, ads for *Felix Summerly's Home Treasury* inside front cover, for *Gammer Gurton Story-Books* inside back cover (*Sir Bevis* being no. 4 in the series). PML 84157. Purchase: Ball Fund.

❧ 360c ❧

The Yellow Dwarf [and *Blanch and Rosalind*]. London: James Burns, Portman Street, [ca. 1845]. 8° (165 × 120 mm.).

Wood-engraved frontispiece; 1^8 (Dwarf; 1^v imprint *London: Printed by Robson, Levey, and Franklyn, Great New Street, Fetter Lane*); 2^8 (Blanch; –7, –8 blank). Pp. 16, 11, [1]. Wove paper. Wood-engraved borders and vignettes. References: Osborne II, 617; Alderson *Burns* p. 114.

Binding: Original paper boards, wood-engraved floral design (see previous page) printed in green and black on a brown ground incorporating title *Yellow Dwarf. / Blanch and / Rosalind* on both sides, front cover signed *Gregory, Collins, & Reynolds. 3 Charter House Sq.* Provenance: L.G.E. Bell (book-label). The Osborne Collection of Early Children's Books. Toronto Public Library.

Isaac Watts's *Divine Songs* was to be one of the best-selling titles in Victorian times, lending itself to an amazing variety of illustrated presentations from cheap tracts for Sunday schools to elaborately produced drawing-room editions. This edition, printed and illustrated with refinement and clothed in Vizetelly's chocolate-tracery paper covers, is suggestive of things to come.

We have already noted the importance that Henry Cole attached to all aspects of the production of his "Home Treasury" series (entry 312). With this edition of *Bevis*, which is one of "Gammer Gurton's" offerings, the standard gilt design of the cover is varied, with the pattern now (accidentally) echoing the tessellated game which "Felix Summerly" included among his recreations for children.

The publisher James Burns has been briefly discussed above (chapter XV), where we suggested that he was not so much an imitator of Joseph Cundall as an entrepreneur working on similar lines. This is apparent in his series of popular tales, of which *The Yellow Dwarf* is a part, where both typesetting and illustration have an "open" quality to them. Nevertheless, for his covers Burns went to the same color printers as Cundall, and Gregory, Collins & Reynolds produced a floriated design which, with its black-letter titling, is not dissimilar to the "Home Treasury" series. The design is printed from woodblocks, and the printers varied the color combinations for different titles in the series (see McLean *Bookbindings in Paper* p. 44). Like Cundall, Burns also had the twenty volumes of the series bound up into a composite *Book of Nursery Tales: a keepsake for the young* (3 vols., 1845).

XIX
SPECIAL MARKETS

A NEGLECTED qualification of children's books as a genre is that they cater for a readership whose capacity and expectations are variably unformed. This means, in effect, that the readers subdivide themselves according to a sense of their own status. "Those are books for babies," says the mature seven year old of his or her outgrown picture books; "that's just a book for girls," says the scornful youth of *Little Women*.

These differences within an apparently homogeneous market have not been lost on publishers and, almost from the beginning, specialists in children's books began to edit, however casually, certain titles or groups of titles with the intention of appealing more directly to a narrower group of buyers than "children" in general. In this chapter we provide some indicative examples drawn from the Morgan Library's holdings—aware that many equivalent examples appear earlier in the catalogue where they were selected to show publishing styles rather than marketing approaches.

BOOKS FOR CHILDREN LEARNING TO READ

৶ 361 ৫

[Hornbook. Aberdeen: Edward Raban, 1622]. Broadside, one-eighth of a pott sheet (about 140 × 90 mm.).

Incipit: *Aabc* . . . , followed by a second alphabet and the Lord's Prayer. Five founts of gothic type, 19 lines. Printed on the felt side of a half-sheet (285 × 185 mm.; French paper stock, pot watermark with crescent surmount and initials I F c, cf. Briquet 12691–12817), together with three other settings of the same text (two of 22 lines each, adding a brief syllabary), one of which has 21 lines including imprint *Printed in Aberdene by E. Raban*. The typographical area of each of the four settings measures 112 × 62 mm. The half sheet—here intact—was intended to be cut up and to yield four similar but different *Abecedaria* for mounting on wood, leather or silver, under translucent horn. References: STC (2nd ed.) 21.9 (recording two more copies of the undivided half-sheet, British Library and National Library of Scotland); Tuer 50; Edmond pp. 81–2 (an actual-size reproduction of the Bibliotheca Lindesiana copy); Gottlieb 53; ESTC S118881.

Provenance: J. Pearson and Co. 1912, sold to: Pierpont Morgan. PML 19467.

Hornbooks were portable reading-primers. An alphabet, some numerals, and the Lord's Prayer were printed on one side of a sheet of paper; this was attached to a small wooden paddle and the surface was covered with a sheet of transparent horn. The child would thus carry around his abc to learn outside the school-room—or perhaps to use for games of bat-and-ball. Children with hornbooks occur in sixteenth-century pictures, and the appearance of the term in general circumstances, such as Thomas Dekker's satire *The Guls Horne-Booke* (1609), suggest that the implement was in common daily use. Examples of hornbooks from early times must be viewed with a critical eye, for much faking has occurred. Few happier instances of the prevalence of hornbooks exist, however, than this letterpress sheet which shows the substance of the hornbook at the point of manufacture.

৶ 362 ৫

The Imperial Battledoor. [London: ca. 1800]. Pr 4ᵈ Plain pr 6ᵈ Colour'd. Quarter-sheet 8° (153 × 86 mm.).

[1²] (1ᵛ longitudinal title inside flap, *Lesson I*, incipit: *Ape Bog Cot* (see overleaf), *Lesson II*, incipit: *Pan Qui Rat*, the Lord's Prayer and Arabic numerals inside front cover, 2ʳ six illustrations in publisher's coloring inside back cover). Laid paper. Etched throughout: perhaps printed from a large copperplate together with other battledores, then divided for folding. Mounted on original stencil-colored (in diamond pattern) and gilt-painted floral flexible boards. References: cf. Welsh p. 172; Roscoe J20; Johnson 15.

PML 81747. Purchase: Julia P. Wightman.

Battledores are thought to have evolved as a simpler and cheaper type of hornbook. Welsh (1885) records that Benjamin Collins of Salisbury had entered battledores in his account books by 1746 and had annotated the entry "My own invention." The reference is probably to *The Royal Battledore*, which he published in partnership with John Newbery and James Hodges (Roscoe J21), and the inventive part involves his combining the alphabet and the Lord's Prayer with a pictorial alphabet grid and then printing them on to a piece of card to fold once and to be loosely secured by a vertical folded flap.

Battledores were probably so named from their connection with hornbooks, which, as we have said, are widely recognized as serving the cause of both learning and a primitive form of schoolroom tennis. Few early examples have survived, and the version shown here appears to have been designed at the point when the workaday typographic battledores of Collins and Newbery were giving way to less thoroughly didactic fare. The text matter has been reduced, the pictures have been inserted for their decorative quality, and the engraving and hand-coloring give the little book a prettiness that is more of the nursery than the schoolroom. (James p. 33 illustrates a *Child's Own Battledoor* somewhat similar to this one, with the imprint of Darton & Harvey conjecturally dated 1798. Victoria and Albert Museum.)

362.

❧ 363a ❧

The London New Battledore. Penryn: Whitehorn, [ca. 1840]. 8°? (138 × 86 mm.).

[1²] (1ᵛ 3 wood-engraved illustrations inside flap, *Capital Letters* inside front cover, 2ʳ *Small Letters* inside back cover). Wove paper. Mounted on original pictorial pink wrappers, letterpress title, imprint and wood engraving of an owl (after Bewick?) on flap, three wood engravings on covers (including a scene from "Ali Baba").

PML 83604 [copies also in green (PML 83318) and in yellow wrappers (PML 83603), with only the three illustrations inside the flap different]. Gift: Elisabeth Ball.

❧ 363b ❧

My School Book. Braintree: Shearcroft, Printer, [ca. 1840]. 8°? (137 × 91 mm.).

[1–2²] (1/1ᵛ Arabic numerals and imprint inside flap, capital letters inside front cover, 1/2ʳ small letters, 1/2ᵛ–2/1ʳ blank and pasted together, 2/1ᵛ syllables and phrases, 2/2ʳ phrases inside back cover). Wove paper. Mounted on original pictorial yellow wrappers, longitudinal title on flap, two wood engravings of robbers on covers.

PML 83320 [PML 83319 is a battledore from the same publisher with quite different contents]. Gift: Elisabeth Ball.

❧ 363c ❧

The "Prince Arthur" Battledore. Eastwood: G.R. Barber, [not before June 1857]. Price One Penny. 8°? (138 × 91 mm.).

[1²] (1ᵛ *Evening Prayer* inside flap, upper and lower-case alphabets inside front cover, 2ʳ *Irregular Alphabets, &c.* inside back cover). Wove paper. Mounted on original pictorial blue flexible boards, title and bird-vignette on flap, four oval wood engravings within type-ornament border on covers (*Fort Gwalior, Destruc-*

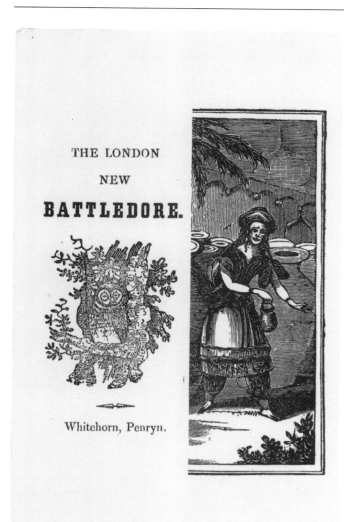

tion of the Chinese fleet June 1857, A Chinese junk of war, Fort at Cawnpore).

PML 83602 [also a copy in green wrappers (PML 83601)]. Gift: Elisabeth Ball.

Prince Arthur (1850–1942) was Queen Victoria's third son and, during the 1850s, several children's books were published with his name optimistically incorporated into their titles.

The popularity of battledores as simple reading matter and the ease with which they could be manufactured made them an obvious source of profit for small printers. With the rapid increase in the stationery and jobbing-printing trades in the nineteenth century, battledore production became a very localized industry, even more widespread than the chapbook printing discussed in chapter XIII above.

We have chosen here three individually-produced battledores, one of which has an additional central leaf, from small provincial towns, manufactured during the early Victorian period, and we have annotated them with Morgan variants which give some idea of the way local printers varied their stock. These three copies come from a very large collection of English provincial battledores in the Library, among which examples may be found from Alnwick (Davison), Birmingham (Rosewarne), Castle Cary (Moore), Gainsborough (Bowden: printed on linen) and Kettering (Toller).

❧ 364 ❧

Aunt Ann's Lesson-Book, for very young children. In words of one and two syllables. By a friend to little children. London:

Left: **363a.**   *Below*: **363c.** *reduced*

printed for Harvey and Darton, Gracechurch-street, 1822. Price 1s.6d. coloured. 12° (178 × 105 mm.).

A¹² B⁶ (A1ʳ title, A1ᵛ blank, B6ʳ imprint *Printed by Harvey, Darton, and Co, Gracechurch-Street, London*); 12 wood engravings in publisher's hand-coloring (see overleaf) on one side of three bifolia (inserted around A1·12, A5·8 and B3·4). Pp. 35. Wove paper, different stocks for text and plates. Original red flexible boards, letterpress title on front cover, ads on back cover. Brown morocco gilt. Reference: Darton *Check-list* G52.

Provenance: *Sarah Ann Storrs from her Grandmama 6 No. 1827* (inscr.); lent to L. A. May (pencil-inscr.); Charles Todd Owen (binding). PML 81510. Gift: Elisabeth Ball.

One gets the impression that Aunt Ann, the "friend to little children," had been reading Mrs. Barbauld and Miss Edgeworth in preparation for these friendly labors. The tone of the earlier writers is faintly to be heard in her thirty-four "lessons," but these little tales are randomly didactic and the publisher has made no effort to place them in a helpful relationship to their illustrations. (Frugal readers will be pleased with the unillustrated lines about "Kind Papa"—an honest grocer who spends fifty pounds on his son Frank's schooling rather than on buying a horse "for it is better that you should learn to read, then that I should ride about." If the schooling included books like this at 1s.6d. a time, one can see that the fifty pounds would be needed.)

365. pl. [14] facing C4ʳ, *reduced*

❧ 365 ❧

[RICHARD ROE (fl. 1808–11)]. *The Assembled Alphabet; or, acceptance of A's invitation; concluding with a glee for three voices. Being a sequel to the "Invited Alphabet." by R. R.* London: published by B. Tabart and Co. Juvenile and School Library, New Bond-Street, 1809. 12° (132 × 120 mm.).

B-D⁶ (B1ʳ title, B1ᵛ imprint *E. Hemsted, Printer, New Street, Fetter Lane, London*, B2ʳ *Preface*, B4ʳ incipit: *No sooner had advising A*, D6ʳ *Notes*, D6ᵛ same imprint); 26 etched plates by Charles Knight after designs by the author, illustrating the alphabet; engraved plate of musical notation *Glee for three voices* printed on one side of a bifolium. Pp. 36. Wove paper watermarked 1808. Stabbed as issued, but lacking wrappers. References: Osborne II, 687; Moon *Tabart* 138(1); James p. 53; Alderson *Moon* 98; Hockliffe 695.

PML 84728. Purchase: Mrs. Louise Melhado.

"R. R." has already put in an appearance in this catalogue with his attractive and original *Good Boy's Soliloquy* (entry 194). That book was preceded by his equally attractive and original *Invited Alphabet* (1809), which incorporated deaf-and-dumb hand-signs into its pictures (PML 85492; Gottlieb 57), and its sequel, described here. A further sequel, *Infantile Erudition* (1810; PML 80760) carried the wittily playful didacticism into the murkier waters of elementary mathematics. Taken together, the four books establish "R. R.," whom we assume to be a certain Richard Roe, as one of the most notable picture-book artists of his period.

The Assembled Alphabet is full of ideas. Quite apart from the end-matter, the harmonized "glee" and the solemn "Notes," the treatment of the letters plays with their character in both the verses and the pictures. Without giving unnecessary explanations, " R. R" leaves the reader to discover how each letter may

dictate varied responses, either through the repetition of words, (six designated words in "L") or through the silent incorporation of objects in the pictures (a volcano in "V") or through the drawing of images which may resemble the shape of the letter (a cottage gable in "A," a diagonally-barred gate in "N"). Truly, as his preface says, learning ceases to be "vexatious drudgery" and "swollen eyes and tear-glazed cheeks will no longer disfigure the otherwise smiling countenance of infancy."

BOOKS FOR BOYS

❧ 366 ❧

[ELIZA FENWICK (1765?–1840)]. *Presents for Good Boys, in words of one and two syllables.* London: Printed for Tabart & C° at the Juvenile & School Library, 157, New Bond Street, March 1ˢᵗ 1805. and sold by all Booksellers & Toy Shops in the Empire. Price One Shilling. 18° (135 × 89 mm.).

A¹⁸ (1ʳ title, 1ᵛ blank, 2ʳ drop-title *Present for Good Boys; or the toy shop*, 18ᵛ imprint *Squire, Printer, Furnival's-Inn-Court, Holborn*). Pp. 36. Wove paper. Etched pictorial title and 11 illustrations (see overleaf) printed from a single large copperplate, apparently before the outer forme went through the letterpress (text and illustration barely clashing on A5ʳ, otherwise only the uninked area of the plate overlapping); illustration on 10ᵛ with publisher's imprint; all illustrations hand-colored, presumably as issued. Plain buff wrappers, presumably original. References: Osborne II, 925; Moon *Tabart* 41(1).

PML 81739. Gift: Elisabeth Ball.

Aunt Ann (entry 364) made sure to divide her lessons equally between the sexes: "A Good Boy" followed by "A Good Girl," "Kind Mamma" by "Kind Papa." Even among young readers, however, the trade was prepared to discriminate, and a number of books came out in which stories for boys in one volume were matched by stories for girls in another. Thus Tabart published Eliza Fenwick's *Presents for Good Girls* alongside the volume described here (both items being indicted by Mrs. Trimmer for their high price: "The expensiveness of children's books is a growing evil!"). Whatever Mrs. Trimmer's views, the fond mama in the present volume doesn't mind, for on page nineteen she takes the children "to Mr. Ta-bart's shop in New Bond Street" and chooses some books for them "which pleas-ed them ver-y much."

BOOKS FOR GIRLS

◄§ 367 §►

The Ladies' School, or the approach of the holydays, by a young lady. Embellished with engravings. [London:] Designed, Engraved, Published and Sold by D. Orme, 308, Oxford-street, opposite Vere-street. Watts and Co. Printers, Southmolton-Street, 1810 [1811]. Quarter-sheet 16° (123 × 101 mm.).

[1⁴] (1ʳ title, 1ᵛ blank, 2ʳ incipit: *In the morning we rise at the sound of a bell*); eight etchings (including frontispiece *The School*), printed from a single copperplate on one side of a half-sheet and divided for insertion, hand-colored as issued; plate-imprint *Published April 29ᵗʰ 1811, by John Wallis, 13 Warwick Square London, [of wh]om may be had as a Companion, The Boy's School or Holydays at Home*, under the illustrations for *Dancing* and *Drawing*. Pp. 8. Wove paper. Stabbed original printed yellow wrappers, title and *Price 1s. Plain, 1s.6d. Coloured* on front cover, *Published & Sold by Daniel Orme, No. 308, Oxford-Street, opposite Vere-Street; Where may be had a variety of Children's Books* on back cover. Reference: Osborne I, 68 (1814 Wallis ed. with the same copperplate).

Provenance: Anne Ellis (early sign.); Gumuchian & Cⁱᵉ (1930 cat., no. 4346). PML 82178. Gift: Elisabeth Ball.

Here again both sexes are served independently, since a boys' companion to *The Ladies' School* is being advertised. We have not seen this alternative so are unable to say what equivalence is found for such lines as:

> And think not, ye Boys, who of mischief are full,
> That we Girls are stupid, inactive and dull;
> Tho' we're not in our pastime and pleasures so rough,
> We enjoy well the game which is call'd Blind-man's-buff.

The publishing history of this insignificant work is curious. The issue described, dated 1810, is published by Daniel Orme, who was best known as an engraver and miniature painter. The plates are engraved with the imprint of John Wallis, dated 1811, and the Morgan Library has a second copy (PML 82179) which is dated 1811 throughout and is published by John Wallis—who there advertises the move from Ludgate Street to Warwick Square.

368.

◄§ 368 §►

[ELLENOR, Lady FENN, née FRERE (1743–1813)]. *The Female Guardian. Designed to correct some of the foibles incident to girls, and supply them with innocent amusement for their hours of leisure. By a Lady* . . . London: Printed and Sold by John Marshall and Co. No. 4, Aldermary Church-Yard, in Bow-Lane, 1784. 18° (148 × 91 mm.).

A⁶ (1ʳ title, 1ᵛ author's note, 2ʳ *Dedication* to the author's aunt, 5ʳ *Contents*, 6ʳ divisional title, 6ᵛ quotation); B-M⁶ (M5ʳ-6ᵛ *Mrs. Teachwell's Library for her Young Ladies*); engraved frontispiece *Female Guardian, Nº XXVII Page 100* by Thomas Cook after Daniel Dodd. Pp. x, [2], 128, [4]. Laid paper. Contemporary sprinkled sheep. References: ESTC TO63518; NCBEL II, 1025; Osborne I, 253.

Provenance: Fanny Elizabeth Hoghton (sign.); Glegg / Withington (pencil inscr.); Samuel F. Pickering (pencil sign.) PML 84922. Purchase.

"Mrs. Teachwell" was boldly adopted as an *alter ego* by Ellenor Fenn, without acknowledging that school-marm's possible

THE PICTURE.

THE LAMBS.

364. frontispiece, *reduced*

16

The next day, when their play hours came, Charles took Ed-ward with him in-to the gar-den, and load-ed the lit-tle fel-low's new cart with stones that he had pick-ed off the bed he was go-ing to dig up with his new spade. Ed-ward drew the cart when it was fill-ed, to the end of the walk, and threw out the stones; and then went back to his bro-ther Charles for more loads. He next took a-way some weeds in the same man-ner; so that Ed-

366. A8 verso

relationship to "Mrs. Teachum" in Sarah Fielding's *Governess*. She also retained that lady's sober policy in matters of education, and she continued to address herself primarily to young ladies rather than young gentlemen (the Blind-man's-buff of *The Ladies' School* looks to have been far too boisterous for the innocent amusement of girls at "The Grove").

This copy of *The Female Guardian* formerly belonged to Samuel Pickering, who mentions it briefly in his *John Locke and Children's Books*. He draws attention to Mrs. Teachwell's "Library for her Young Ladies," listed at the end of the book, which contains a span of titles from Mrs. Barbauld's *Lessons* to Dr. Johnson's *Rambler*. Elsewhere Mrs. Teachwell writes that the library "is selected with the utmost caution, as a point on which depends the health and purity" of her pupils' minds.

CHEAP BOOKS

❧ 369 ❧

The Juvenile Learner; or, the child's early guide. Glasgow: James Lumsden and Son, [ca. 1825]. Price One Halfpenny. 32° (99 × 60 mm.).

[1⁸] (1ʳ title within border, 1ᵛ *Frontispiece*, 2ʳ alphabets, 4ᵛ *Words of two syllables*, 5ʳ *Puss*, 5ᵛ *The charitable girl*, 7ʳ *The ass, the ape and the mole*, 7ᵛ *The Ten Commandments, in Short Rhyme*, 8ᵛ ads within border *Lumsden & Son's Superior Edition of half-penny books, Containing 16 pages each* as listed in Roscoe & Brimmell 8). Pp. 15. Wove paper. 8 wood-engraved illustrations. Fos. 1ʳ·8ᵛ dyed yellow to imitate wrappers. Reference: Roscoe & Brimmell 11 (recorded only from the ad in *Familiar Objects Described* n.d.).

Provenance: Margaret Crawford (inscr. *A Present to Miss M Crawford from RC*). PML 80940. Gift: Elisabeth Ball.

A penny was the standard price for popular books—preserved in such designations as "penny histories" or "penny merriments." Many fewer chapbooks, etc. were published at a halfpenny, which would make for serious inroads on publishers' profit margins, and

A QUAVER (15) is equal to, and must occupy the same time in playing as, two Semiquavers or four Demi-Semiquavers

A SEMIQUAVER (16) is equal to, and repuires the same time occupied in playing as, two Demi-Semiquavers.

A DEMI-SEMIQUAVER (17) is equal to half a Semiquaver.

Practise the preceding Lessons, till you are well acquainted with them, before you proceed farther.

369. fo. 8 verso, *enlarged*   *Below:* 371. etching opposite A7ʳ, *reduced*

372. fo. 7 recto, *reduced*

this edition of *The Juvenile Learner* is almost the only halfpenny book noted in the catalogue (disregarding halfpenny and farthing tracts, which were subsidized).

The Morgan Library possesses a number of Scottish chapbooks priced at a halfpenny—four of them perceptibly inferior to their penny brethren. Two are additonal titles in Lumsden's "Superior Edition" and, like *The Juvenile Learner*, they are inscribed to Miss M. Crawford but by her sister Jane; both are known to Roscoe and Brimmell only through advertisements: *The Babes in the Wood* and *The History of Peter Martin* (PML 80939 and 80935).

EXPENSIVE BOOKS

⋙ 370 ⋘

[SARAH FIELDING (1710–68)]. *The Governess; or, little female academy. Being the history of Mrs. Teachum, and her nine girls. With their nine days amusement. Calculated for the entertainment and instruction of young ladies in their education. By the author of David Simple.* [Quotation from *Midsummer Night's Dream*]. London: Printed for the Author; and Sold by A. Millar, in the Strand, [2nd January] 1749. 12° (162 × 93 mm.).

A⁶(6+1) (1ʳ title, 1ᵛ blank, 2ʳ dedication *To the Honourable Mrs. Poyntz*, 4ʳ *Preface*; B–L¹² M⁴(4+1) (M3ᵛ ads for *Books Printed for A. Millar*, quires M and A originally formed a single sheet and their formes were worked together). Pp. xiv, 245, [5]. Relief-cut head- and tailpieces and initial-frames. Original blind-paneled divinity calf. References: Grey 1; ESTC T134317; Schiller *Five Centuries* 35.

PML 67220. Purchase: Ball Fund.

At the other end of the price scale from halfpenny chapbooks were those story books that were designed for the genteel market. Sarah Fielding's *Governess* was one such, being advertised on 28 December 1748 in the *General Advertiser* to sell at 2s. 6d. (price bound). We do not know whether this price was arrived at by comparison with adult books (Sarah Fielding's two-volume *David Simple* was 6s., for instance), or was part of the agreement with the author, but 2s. 6d. does not seem to have been sustainable and Millar published a second edition on his own account later in the year with the number of pages reduced by over a hundred and the price reduced to 1s. 6d. bound (see also entry 354).

VARIABLY PRICED BOOKS

⋙ 371 ⋘

[DOROTHY KILNER? (1755–1836)]. *Jingles; or, original rhymes for children. By M. Pelham.* London: printed for Tabart and Co. at the Juvenile and School Library, New Bond-Street, and to be had of all booksellers. By W. Marchant, 3, Greville-Street, Holborn, [not before October] 1808. [Price Ninepence without prints, One Shilling and Sixpence with prints, or Half-a Crown with the prints coloured.]. 16° (127 × 102 mm.).

[1³²] signed A¹⁶ <B¹⁶ (1ʳ title, 1ᵛ *[Entered at Stationers' Hall.]*, 2ʳ *Advertisement*, 2ᵛ ad for *Songs for the Nursery, &c. Now first collected, and printed on a large Type. Price Sixpence without plates, One Shilling and Sixpence with, and Half-a-Crown with the plates coloured*, 3ʳ *Billy and Polly*, incipit: *Billy, Billy, come and play*, 31ʳ ads, 32ᵛ imprint W. Marchant, Printer, 3, Greville-street, Holborn); 12 etchings in publisher's hand-coloring (see previous page), printed from two copperplates (dated Augᵗ 1806) on both sides of a part-sheet (watermarked 1805) pp. 60, [4]. Wove paper (different stocks for text and plates). Original letter-press yellow wrappers, apparently a remainder of the binding for the first edition, title, *Price 9d. without Plates, 1s. with Plates, and 1s. 6d. with the Plates Coloured*, and ads on front cover, ad for Tabart's *Popular Nursery Tales* (see entry 382 [ch. XX]) on back cover. Black morocco gilt. References: Moon *Tabart* 88(2); Alderson *Moon* 95 (1806 edition).

Provenance: *M.L.J. MacArthur from grandmama 1853* (inscr.); Charles Todd Owen (binding). PML 82785. Gift: Elisabeth Ball.

Jingles follows in the wake of the Taylors' *Original Poems* (entry 102) and shows the author (assumed without conclusive evidence to be Dorothy Kilner) trying her hand at moral verses. Unlike the Darton books, however, which had a frontispiece for each volume, whether the customers liked it or not, *Jingles* is available in three styles: unillustrated, illustrated plain or illustrated with hand-coloring. Making up and marketing a book with differential pricing may have been difficult and this copy shows the publisher changing his mind. The cover is for the first edition of 1806 and, as we note, gives prices, respectively, of 9d., 1s., and 1s.6d. for the three issues. Here though, against what is thought customary for reprints, the price for all three issues has been raised. The reason for this may well be to align *Jingles* with *Songs for the Nursery*, which Tabart published in the same format round about the same time. (Marjorie Moon records a first edition, unillustrated, for 1805, and a later one, as advertised in *Jingles* above, for 1808 but with the plates dated 1806.)

Tabart's pricing here, taken with Mrs. Trimmer's strictures on his charge for *Presents for Good Boys* (entry 366), prompts the observation that more study is needed of marketing methods at this period. Tabart, for instance, was able to advertise his stock as ranging "from one penny to five guineas in price" (see description of entry 163), and some books from other publishers must have almost priced themselves out of the market (e.g. Lamb's *Beauty and the Beast* [PML 16547, Gottlieb 109], the colored copies of which sold for 5s. 6d., and the anonymous *Elegant Girl* [1817], an unusually large hand-colored book which S. Inman sold for sixteen shillings).

MUSIC FOR CHILDREN

⋙ 372 ⋘

Music Made Easy for Children. Embellished with numerous engravings. London: published by D. Carvalho, 74, Chiswell Street, Finsbury Square, [ca. 1830–32]. Price One Shilling Coloured. Post 8° (177 × 104 mm.).

[1¹⁴] (1·14 mounted as pastedowns, 1ᵛ presentation-form *Carvalho's Edition. The Gift of Friendship from—to—*and two wood-engraved vignettes, 2ʳ blank, 2ᵛ drop-title, 3ʳ imprint, 13ʳ *Steps to Dancing*, 13ᵛ blank, 14ʳ ads for *Superior Juvenile Publications, printed by D. Carvalho, And to be had of every respectable Bookseller in the Kingdom. Price One Shilling each. Post Octavo, uniformly printed in a superior manner, on the best superfine Paper, Hot-pressed, with Twelve Illustrative Engravings neatly Coloured . . . with the Engravings plain, at 6d. each—18mo. Neatly Half-bound, price One Shilling each*). Ff. [14]. Unwatermarked, wove paper. Printed on one side of the sheet. 12 pictorial wood engravings incorporating musical notation—see previous page (62 × 79 mm. each), in publisher's coloring. Original yellow stiff wrappers, title (as given above) and wood engraving (children on a swing) on front cover.

Provenance: from *Aunt Dolly . . .* to *Helen Neville* (gift-leaf completed in pencil, other inscriptions in Helen's childish hand dated from Beardwood, Blackburn Novᵇᵉʳ 30th 1843). PML 81828. Gift: Elisabeth Ball.

Ledger spaces Treble.

G B D F A C E

Ledger lines Bass.

C E G

GOOD BOYS DANCING FOR AUNT CAROLINE'S ENTERTAINMENT.

COWS EAT GRASS.

373. illustrations [6–7], *reduced*

From the days at least of Anna Magdalena Bach, there has been music composed and published for children to exercise their talents on (and by 1797 there were settings of nursery rhymes to be played and sung: see James Hook's *A Christmas Box*, PML 83634). Publishers of children's books—as opposed to children's music—also joined in. Tabart published a musical setting of "There was a Little Man and he wooed a Little Maid" in his 1807 picture-book version of "their" *Memoirs* (Moon *Tabart* 109) together with "glees" in *The Assembled Alphabet* and *Infantile Erudition* (see entry 365). William Godwin, published "Beauty's Song" as a fold-out sheet in his *Beauty and the Beast* (PML 16547). Others converted the business of learning to read music into picture-book form, the best known example being perhaps Charlotte Finch's *The Gamut and Time-Table in Verse*, published by Dean & Munday ca. 1825 (PML 81476). Carvalho's *Music Made Easy* was probably inspired by that book and amounts to a set of pictorial definitions. The illustrations are of some interest from a technical standpoint since Carvalho's wood-engraver has contrived to cut numerals and musical notation normally undertaken by copper-engravers. They are also attractive as examples of "child ownership" for Helen Neville appears to have been giving names to the children in the pictures.

❧ 373 ❧

C. WILLIAMS (fl. ca. 1845). *Musical Notes Learned in a Day, or the child's pictorial friend, by Miss C. Williams, Larkbeare House, Exeter.* Ent^d Sta. Hall. Exeter: Sold by Messrs Fitze and Hannaford, Exeter, and may be had of all Booksellers through Messrs Grant & Griffiths, Publishers, St Paul's Church Yard, London. C. Risdon, Lith, Exeter, [not before 24th May 1845]. (137 mm. square).

One leaf, recto-verso *Preface* dated from Larkbeare House May 24th 1845, verso *Directions*; two double-demy quarter sheets joined to form a continuous folding strip (137 × 1463 mm.). Lithographed throughout: 12 illustrations, each accompanied by musical notation and a mnemonic phrase, incipit: *Lines in the stave Trebb. E G B D F Empty Grandmama's Basket Dear Fanny*, ending: *Spaces below stave Bass. F D B G Frightful Dog, Be Gone.* Wove paper, watermarked J. Whatman 1845. Original roan-backed flexible boards, lithographic title (as given above) on front cover.

Provenance: Miss Buckingham (adult inscr.). PML 84991. Purchase: Fellows Fund.

Anyone who had to learn "Every Good Boy Deserves Favor" will know that the mnemonic method of teaching note sequences has very limited success—nor does "Empty Grandmama's Basket Dear Fanny" contribute a radical improvement. Nevertheless, one must admire Miss Williams's ingenuity in inventing phrases (how *did* she come by a "A Chinese employed Gathering"?) and her work when opened out as a frieze would have looked charming on the walls of the nursery music room. The volume is not noticed in the General Catalogue in Michael Twyman's *Early Lithographed Books*.

374. etching opposite B1ʳ, *reduced*

BOOKS FOR LEARNERS OF FRENCH

◄§ 374 §►

CHARLES PERRAULT (1628–1703) and/or PIERRE PERRAULT DARMANCOUR (1678–1700). *Tales of Passed Times by Mother Goose. With morals written in French by M. Perrault, and Englished by R.S. Gent. To which is added a new one, viz. The Discreet Princess. The six edition. Corrected, and adorned with fine cuts.* London: Printed [in Holland] for J. Melvil, Bookseller in Exeter change in the strand, 1764. *Contes du Tems Passé de Ma Mere L'Oye. Avec des morales. Par M. Perrault. Augmentée d'une nouvelle, viz. L'Adroite Princesse. Sixieme edition. avec des joli estampes.* A Londres: Imprimeé pour J. Melvil, Librairie, 1764. 8° (157 × 98 mm.).

A–O⁸ P² (A1ʳ blank, A1ᵛ English title, A2ʳ French title, A2ᵛ blank, A3ʳ *Table*, A3ᵛ *Tale I*, A4ʳ *Conte I*, K4ʳ French title to Mme L'Héritier's *Finette*, K5ʳ English title, K6ʳ French dedication *A Madame la Comtesse de Murat*, K7ᵛ English dedication *To the Right Honorable The Lady Mary Montagu*, P2ᵛ blank); 9 etchings, printed from two copperplates on one side of a sheet, divided

for insertion into smaller leaves than the size of the bookblock. Pp. 227. Imposed for French text on rectos, English on versos. Contemporary half vellum. Reference: ESTC N044521.

Provenance: Terwout (twentieth-century sign. and note in Dutch). PML 84456. Purchase: Julia P. Wightman.

Perrault's *Contes* were seen by some eighteenth-century publishers as material for teaching French rather than as the start of a folk-tale industry for children. Several of the early Samber editions were therefore bilingual. This "Six Edition, Corrected" forms a mysterious point in the sequence and may be a piracy. The bookseller, J. Melvil, is apparently otherwise unknown as a publisher, whereas the typefounts and ornaments point to Dutch printing (mistakes occur both in the English and French titles). The plates were copied after those by S. Fokke for Jean Neaulme's edition (The Hague, 1745). Melvil's edition is also known with a similar series of plates, but reversed and signed by H. Immink (Oppenheimer copy: Sotheby's London, 2nd June 1982, lot 148). The same iconography was followed by Alexander Anderson for his etchings in the bilingual New York Perrault of 1795, which were also used by the London publisher, T. Boosey, in 1796.

◄§ 375 §►

Methode Amusante pour Enseigner L' A B C avec planches colorieés. Londres: Imprimé par Darton et Harvey, Se vend chez ceux, et chez T. Boosey, et A. Dulau & C°, 1801. 12° (135 × 83 mm.).

A–F⁶ (A1ʳ alphabet, B5ᵛ *Explication des gravures*, E5⁴ *Chiffres Arabes et Romains*, F3ʳ verse *L'Enfant et la Poupée*, F3ᵛ verse *Fanfan et Colas*, F4ᵛ verse *Cloe et Fanfan*, F6ʳ verse *Le Joueur de Gobelets*, incipit: *Escroquillard, fameux escamoteur*, F6ᵛ imprint *De l'Imprimerie de S. Couchman, Throgmorton-Street, à Londres*); 31 illustrations in publisher's hand-coloring on 8 inserted leaves (including frontispiece and pictorial title), probably printed from a single copperplate. Pp. 72. Wove paper (letterpress) and laid paper (intaglio). Blind-tooled green roan, by Morrell. Reference: Darton *Check-list* G631(1).

Provenance: Charles Todd Owen (binding). PML 81520. Gift: Elisabeth Ball.

The cataclysmic events in France at the end of the eighteenth century had the effect of stimulating an English trade in French books—by and for emigrés, and perhaps promulgating a belief that the French language should be more widely understood by children. We have already noted a number of books that were published for some such reasons, and the Darton firms seem to have been particularly interested in developing French connections. This *Méthode Amusante* is entirely in French and may be illustrated with French plates. The text is idiomatic and suggests a French author, but the publisher's contribution in title and imprints is by no means so assured.

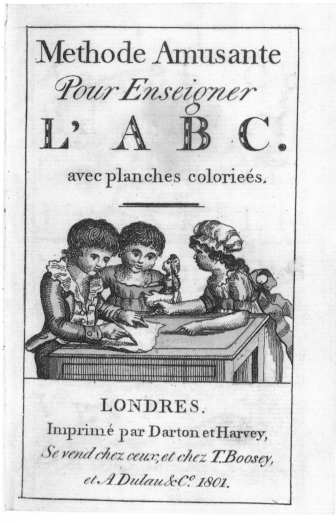

375.

377. frontispiece, *reduced*

❧ 376 ❧

MARY ELLIOTT, née BELSON (ca. 1792–1860s?).
Les Frères Orphelins. Traduit de l'Anglais, de Marie Elliott,
par A.F.E. Lépée, professeur de langue française, à Londres.
Enrichi de gravures en taille douce.* Londres: chez William
Darton, 58, Holborn Hill, [ca. 1830]. 18° (141 × 89 mm.).

A¹⁸ (1ʳ title, 1ᵛ blank, 18ᵛ imprint); hand-colored etched plate,
divided into two bifolia, one inserted as a folding frontispiece
(*"One day, when the good old man slept in his elbow chair…"*), the
other showing two illustrations and inserted around A7·12 (*"One
day they met a pedlar…"* and *"Good morrow, lads,' said he…"*).
Pp. 36. Unwatermarked, wove paper. Original buff stiff wrappers,
letterpress title on front cover, ads for French translation of
other works by Mary Elliott, Mrs. Barbauld, etc. References:
Moon *Elliott* 426; Darton *Check-list* H441.

Provenance: George Hubbard (bookplate). PML 83388. Gift:
Elisabeth Ball.

William Darton II also tried to exploit a demand for French books
by producing French translations of books already in his list in
English. Mary Belson Elliott was the prime focus for this operation and Marjorie Moon lists 62 of her books in French editions
published by Darton. Apparently he could not be bothered to re-
engrave the captions to the plates which remain in English and
carry Darton's proud advertisement of his shop as "the Repertory
of Genius."

BOOKS FOR LEARNERS OF ITALIAN

❧ 377 ❧

[MARY PILKINGTON née HOPKINS (1766–1839)].
*Tales of the Hermitage; in English and Italian. Translated
by V. Peretti. Rules are given in the introduction for properly
placing the accent on the Italian words. Second edition.*
London: Printed by R. Juigné, No. 17, Margaret-Street,
Cavendish-Square. for B. Dulau and Co. Soho-Square, 1809.
12° (173 × 102 mm.).

a² (1ʳ half-title, 1ᵛ blank, 2ʳ title, 2ᵛ blank), b⁶ (1ʳ *Introduction*); B-L⁶ M⁴ (B1ʳ divisional title, B1ᵛ *Tale the First*, B2ʳ *Novella Prima*, M3ᵛ *Jugemens portés par plusieurs Journeaux litteraires et autres, sur la Grammaire et sur les Thêmes de V. Peretti*, M4ᵛ *B. Dulau and Co. having just bought the Copyright of all the much esteemed Publications of Mr. Peretti . . . are going to print them all uniform, with considerable additions by the Author. London, 1809*, quires a and M worked together on a half-sheet); etched frontispiece *My good man, said Mʳˢ Cavendish* . . . Pp. [4], xii, 128. Wove paper. Contemporary tree sheep, one inserted quire of six leaves at the end: *Books for Schools, published by W. Simpkin and R. Marshall, Stationers' Hall Court, Ludgate-Street, London.*

Provenance: *Monsieur Haines, Professeur de Langue Francaise et Allemande, 44* [changed by hand to 33] *Kingsland Place, Southampton* (letterpress label dated in Ms. 1833). PML 81726. Gift: Elisabeth Ball.

Apart from a well-disseminated edition of Mrs. Barbauld's *Inne Gioveniti*, published by Nathaniel Hailes in 1819, translations of early children's books into Italian were rare. Dulau, however, seems to have had some scheme for widely promoting the works of V. Peretti and this translation of Mrs. Pilkington is planned to stand alongside an array of Italian grammars and guides to pronunciation. The first edition of this bilingual English-Italian version of *Contes de l'Hermitage* had been published at Paris in 1805.

XX

MARKS OF POSSESSION

WE have already noted in chapter VII the peculiar interest that attaches to books that carry with them evidence, however slender, of the children who once owned them. Many books elsewhere in the catalogue also carry these mementos, and in this final chapter we attempt to summarize some of the forms taken by such marks of possession. We hope that, in a work so heavily devoted to the making, publishing, and selling of children's books, there is an aptness in leaving the last word to the buyers, the givers, and the readers.

PARENTAL CENSORSHIP

⤚ 378 ⤛

A Museum for Young Gentlemen and Ladies: or, a private tutor for little masters and misses ... I. Directions for reading ... III. An account of the solar system ... V. An account of the arts and sciences ... VIII. Tables of weights and measures ... The seven wonders of the world. XI. Prospect and description of the burning mountains ... With letters, tales and fables, for amusement and instruction; illustrated with cuts. The third edition. London: for J. Newbery, in St. Paul's Church-Yard; and B. Collins, in Salisbury, 1760. [Price 1s.]. 12° (125 × 83 mm.).

A–Q⁶ (A1ᵛ ad for the 1760 edition by R. Baldwin and B. Collins of the *The Polite Academy*) R⁶ (–R1, upper half of R2 also cut away and lower half pasted onto Q6ᵛ, thus canceling the ballad of *The Country Squire*) S⁶ (S6 mounted as pastedown). Pp. vi, 209. 28 cuts of various sizes including a full-page view of Vesuvius. Original dab-colored floral boards. Reference: Roscoe J253 (4).

PML 83084. Gift: Elisabeth Ball.

This title was one of the books owned by Frances Laetitia Earle (entry 113). As we note there, we were surprised to find first that Mr. Newbery had seen fit to include a vulgar ditty in his *Museum* and second that no one had protected Frances Laetitia from its scatological contents. The owner of this copy of the book was more fortunate. By a neat piece of surgery the whole ballad has been excised and the cut remnants of the leaves so joined that the deletion is hardly noticeable. In later editions (e.g. Roscoe J253[19]) the publishers themselves cleaned up the volume, which thus enabled Mrs. Trimmer to give it a tempered welcome in the *Guardian of Education* Vol. II, p. 185.

FINE JUVENILE CALLIGRAPHY

⤚ 379 ⤛

The Renowned History of Primrose Prettyface, who by her sweetness of temper and love of learning, was raised from being the daughter of a poor cottager, to great riches, and the dignity of Lady of the Manor ... Adorned with cuts according to custom. London: Printed in the Year when all little Boys and Girls should be good, and sold by John Marshall and Co. No. 4, Aldermary Church-Yard, in Bow Lane [not after 1786]. [Price Six Pence, Bound, Gilt, and Lettered.] N. B. The lettering of the Book is withinside. 12° (116 × 75 mm.).

A⁶ (–1, 2ʳ blank, 2ᵛ frontispiece *Primrose Prettyface spinning at her father's door, her scholars sitting round her,* 3ʳ title, 3ᵛ blank, 4ʳ

(103)

" *World was at End:* In ſhort, 'twas the moſt
" lamentable Scene that Eyes could behold."
   The King in his Letter on the melancholy
Occaſion, to the King of Spain, concludes thus :
" I am without a Houſe, in a Tent, without
" Servants, without Subjects, without Money,
" and without Bread."

An Italian Man and Woman in their proper
Habits.

An Hiſtorical Deſcription of ITALY.

ITALY in the Scriptures is called Chittim,
and Meſech. Pliny (an ancient Latin Writer)
gives it this Character : ' Italy is the Nurſe-
' Mother of all Nations, elected by the Gods to
' make the Heavens more glorious, and unite
           K   ' the

378. K1, *enlarged*

379. reduced

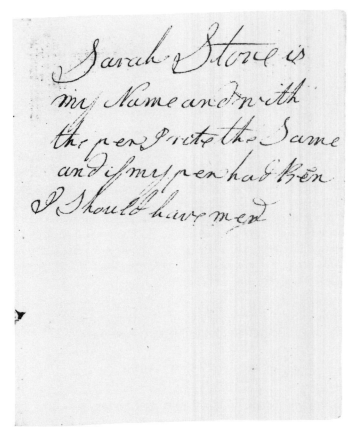

380. enlarged

text); B–G⁶ H⁶(6+1) (H6ʳ–H6+1ʳ ads, H6+1ᵛ blank, H6+1=A1).
Pp. [3]–97. 32 wood engravings (frontispiece full-page, remainder nearly half-page). Original dab-colored floral boards,
lacking title-label. References: Osborne II, 927; Gumuchian
4626; Hockliffe 131 (1818 edition).

Provenance: *Ann Lovejoy. / Her Book Jan: 30: 1786* (child's
calligraphic inscription in red ink on front pastedown); Anne
Lyon Haight. PML 81082. Gift: Mrs. Sherman P. Haight.

This copy of Marshall's *Goody Two-Shoes* imitation may well be a
first edition, admirably celebrated for us by Ann Lovejoy's ownership inscription. Later editions of the book (e.g. PML 85638) were
furnished with copper-engraved frontispieces and title pages. The
publisher's unusual instruction about "the lettering of this Book"
presumably refers to a title-label that was ready-printed for the
owner to place on the spine or the front cover.

OWNERSHIP RHYMES

⊷ 380 ⊷

*The Visions of Heron; the hermit of the Silver Rock: or, a
journey to the Moon. Containing variety of pleasing stories,
moral and entertaining. Particularily, an account of the
celebrated Man in the Moon.* London: Printed for H. Roberts,
No. 56, nearly opposite Great Turnstile, Holborn, 1777. [Price
6d.]. 16° (93 × 73 mm.).

A–E⁸ (A1ʳ title, A1ᵛ blank, A2ʳ text); 7 (of 8?) engraved illustrations, apparently printed from one copperplate on a half sheet,
divided for insertion. Pp. 80. Two paperstocks, one shared by
quires A–C and the plates, quires D–E on paper with turned
chain-lines. Modern marbled boards. Reference: not listed in
Marjorie Hope Nicholson's *Voyages to the Moon* (New York, 1948).

Provenance: *Sarah Stone is / my Name and with / the pen I rite the
same / and if my pen had Ken / I should have men* (contemporary
child's inscription on blank recto of plate [1]); *Stal not this Book /
for fear of Shame / for hear doth Stand / the oners Name / Hannah
/ Norman / May 25 1789* (inscription on blank recto of plate [2]
by a child, who repeated her name on blank recto of plate [3] and

380. enlarged

wrote the following inspired rhymes of ownership: *When this you / se rember me / and kep me in / your minde let / all the world se / what the will / think of me as / your your* (on C1ᵛ blank); *Hannah Norman / is my name and / and with my / pin I rite the / seme and if / my pin had / mended I shald / hve roted beter* (blank verso of plate [3]). PML 85549. Purchase: Julia P. Wightman.

Few books in the catalogue carry such a rich cargo of children's comments as this one—speaking for themselves, as cited above, beyond any need of further annotation.

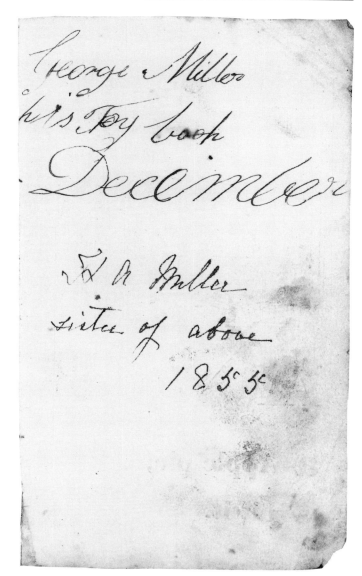

381. *reduced*

A "TOYS POOK"

ᵹ 381 ᵹ

The Life and History of A, Apple-Pie, who was cut to pieces and eaten by twenty-six young ladies and gentlemen, with whom all little people ought to be acquainted. Embellished with sixteen coloured engravings. London: published by Dean & Munday, Threadneedle-street, [ca. 1830]. Price One Shilling. 8° (178 × 101 mm.).

[1¹⁶] (1ʳ blank, 1ᵛ *Frontispiece. Apple-Pie Hall*, 2ʳ title, 2ᵛ–3ʳ blank, 3ᵛ incipit *A B a Apple pie*, 16ʳ *Then & came* . . .). Pp. 31. Wove paper. Printed on one side of two sheets. 16 wood engravings including full-page frontispiece and small title-vignette, the remainder half-page illustrations, all hand-colored at the publisher's. Original printed pink wrappers, title and wood-engraved vignette on front cover, ad for *Nursery Tales and Toy Books* on back cover, type-ornament border on buff covers. Reference: Hockliffe 681.

Provenance: *George Miller his / Toys pook / December 26, 1846* on 2ᵛ, *George Miller / his Toy book / December* on 3ʳ (childish inscriptions); *H A Miller / sister of above / 1855* (adult inscription on 3ʳ); Gumuchian & Cⁱᵉ (1930 cat., no. 1 bis). PML 85085. Gift: Elisabeth Ball.

George Miller's attempted use of the term "toy book" is sanctioned here by the publisher's advertisement, as described. Nevertheless it is nice to see the word as current among buyers as well as sellers since its origins and use have never been fully clarified (*OED* notices it only for "Aunt Louisa's Toy-Books" of 1865). The compound phrase seems to have come into general currency with the publishing innovations of the early nineteenth century (see entry 14), when it stood for what we now call "picture books," and it was in fairly common use in the book trade in both England and the United States from that time onwards.

CHARLES HURT JUN.'S SET OF TABART'S NURSERY TALES

ᵹ 382 ᵹ

At Tabart's Juvenile and School Library, No. 157, New Bond-Street, Are just published, new and beautiful editions of the following popular Nursery Tales:

Cinderella	The Seven Champions
Blue Beard	Robin Hood
Puss in Boots	Valentine and Orson
Fortunio	The Forty Thieves
Sleeping Beauty	Nourjahad
Whittington and his Cat	Aladdin
Griselda	Richard Coeur de Lion
Riquet with the Tuft	Jack and the Bean Stalk
Children in the Wood	Sinbad. Part I.
Jack the Giant Killer	Do. Part II.
Hop o' my Thumb	Fortune and Fatal
Beauty and the Beast	Cendrillon
Fortunatus	La Barbe Bleue
Andolocia	Gulliver's Travels. Part I.
The White Cat	Do. Part II.
Tom Thumb	Do. Part III.
Goody Two Shoes	Do. Part IV.

In all thirty-four sorts. The whole of the above may be had separately, at Sixpence each, with three coloured engravings

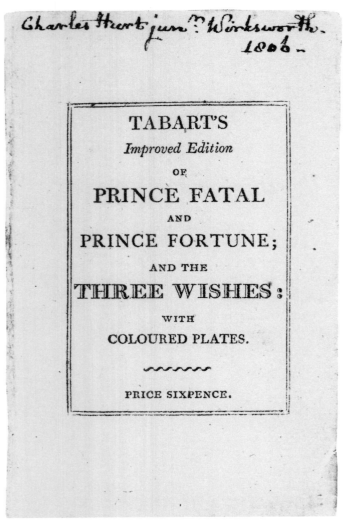

382. enlarged

. . . [back cover ad of *Jack and the Bean Stalk*]. London: 1804–7 [series]. 27 volumes. 18° (largest: 137 × 87 mm., smallest: 119 × 74 mm.).

A[18] (1[r] *The History of Jack and the Bean-Stalk. Printed from the original manuscript, never before published. London: printed for B. Tabart, at the Juvenile and School Library, no. 157, New Bond-Street, 1807*, 1[v] imprint *C. Squire, Printer, Furnival's Inn-Court*, 17[v]–18[v] ads and printer's imprint); 3 etched illustrations after William Marshall Craig (ca. 1765–ca. 1834) and/or Henry Corbould (1787–1844): frontispiece *Jack climbing the Bean stalk*, bifolium <A5·14 *The Giant & Jack in the Oven* and *Jack escaping from the Giant* (printed from a copperplate with illustrations for other volumes in the series), hand-colored at the publisher's. Pp. 34, [2]. Laid paper for letterpress printing, wove paper (watermark date 1806) for intaglio printing. Original yellow wrappers, letterpress title, *Price sixpence* and ad on front cover, ad on back cover as transcribed above and . . . *In justice to themselves, Tabart and Co., shall state, that their editions of the above Stories, consist either of new translations, or of modernized and improved versions, in chaste and correct language, embellished with beautiful engravings, from original designs, made on purpose, by Messrs. Craig and Corbould* . . . Twenty-six other volumes in the series, as listed above, but lacking *Sinbad* II, the French

Cendrillon and *Barbe Bleue*, Gulliver I–IV; most but not all are similarly constructed and illustrated and start their cover-titles with *Tabart's Improved Edition of* . . . . The colors of the wrappers vary. Reference: Moon, *Tabart* 170; Hockliffe 19.

Provenance: Charles Hurt jun[r]. of Wirksworth, Derbyshire, 28th March 1805–9th February 1809 (all volumes inscribed on front cover in his youthful but accomplished hand, except *Richard Coeur de Lion* and *Sinbad* I, which may have joined the set later; wording and dates of inscriptions vary). PML 83144–70. Gift: Elisabeth Ball.

In 1804 Benjamin Tabart made a double-pronged attack on the fairytale market. On one side he set about publishing his "Collection of Popular Stories" in three volumes (with a fourth added in 1809), and on the other he began issuing the booklets in this "Improved Edition of Nursery Tales." Uncertainty still permeates our knowledge of the editing of these two series, which differ in the details of both titles included and the wording of the stories. Nevertheless, from the evidence of advertisements and from notes in William Godwin's unpublished journals, there is no doubt that both he and his second wife were much involved with helping Tabart prepare his texts.

The point is important, because both of these collections make a notable advance, not merely in the bringing together of tales from a variety of sources into two linked series but also in establishing new norms. Where Tabart led, others would follow, and, as Iona and Peter Opie point out in their *Classic Fairy Tales* (1974), he is the first publisher to call Perrault's "Little Thumb" "Hop o' my Thumb," and his *Jack and the Bean-Stalk*, described here, is the first attempt at a complete prose version of the well-known tale to appear.

As a contemporary collector Charles Hurt Jun[r] showed both taste and foresight in building up his set of the "Improved Edition" as issued. The presentation of the tales in this series is more happily done than the "Collection," and our only regret in illustrating this remarkable survival is that it lacks the four volumes of *Gulliver's Travels*, upon which Tabart lavished much care.

A TRIBUTE OF REGARD and A GIFT OF FRIENDSHIP

⋘ 383a ⋙

Food for the Young, adapted to the mental capacities of children of tender years. By a mother. London: William Darton, 58, Holborn-Hill, 1823. 12° (140 × 88 mm.).

A–P[6] (A1[r] title, A2[v] *Printed by G. Smallfield, Hackney*, A3[r] *Preface*, A3[v] *Contents*, P6[v] printer's imprint); 3 etchings including *Frontispiece . . . Lucy crept onward, and then knelt down to the nest*. Pp. 176. Illustrations on different wove paper from text. Inserted at the end an engraved advertisement: *William Darton, Wholesale Bookseller . . . Maps, Charts & Plans of every description. Extensive collections of Books for the Use of Children & Young People and Works of Merit as soon as published . . . either in Plain or Elegant Bindings.* Contemporary maroon quarter roan and marbled boards (but now rebound), engraved label *Sold by John Stacy, Bookseller, Norwich.* Reference: Darton H598 (2 or possibly 3).

Fatal & Fortune.

The Farmer finding Fatal at prayers.

London. Publish'd by Tabart & Cº. Sep.1804.

382. enlarged

Provenance: Originally purchased as a present, with the steel-etched pictorial gift-leaf supplied by Darton and bearing the calligraphic, Quaker-style phrasing: *A Tribute of | Regard, | Presented by | Thy Affectionate | Friend.* (See overleaf.) PML 80663. Gift: Elisabeth Ball.

✌ 383b ✌

The Comical Adventures of Old Mother Muggins and her Dog, Trap... London: Printed and Published by D. Carvalho, 74, Chiswell Street, Finsbury Square, [ca. 1830]. Post 8° (175 × 103 mm.).

[1¹²] (1ʳ title and illustration *Here learn like Trap | To read and spell, | And all your friends | Will use you well,* 1ᵛ–2ʳ blank, 2ᵛ incipit: *Mother Muggins kept a School*). Ff. [12]. Wove paper. Printed on one side of the sheets. 12 wood engravings in publisher's coloring (64 × 78 mm. each). Original printed mauve wrappers, title and vignette on front cover, ads on back cover, advertisement leaf mounted inside back cover *Superior Juvenile Publications printed and published by D. Carvalho, 74, Chiswell Street, Finsbury Square. Price One Shilling each, Post Octavo, Hot pressed, with Twelve Illustrative Engravings neatly Coloured.* Modern brown morocco.

Provenance: Marketed, but apparently not sold, to be given as a present, with Carvalho's wood-engraved gift-leaf mounted inside front cover: *Carvalho's Edition. A Gift of Friendship from—to—* see overleaf; Charles Todd Owen (binding). PML 82994. Gift: Elisabeth Ball.

The coming of steel engraving in the early 1820s coincided with and stimulated the publication of a variety of gift books and annuals as part of the "fancy" market. Darton was not very closely involved in this, but his idea for a steel-engraved gift-label fits in with the pattern of these events. Carvalho, at least, was impressed by it, and his own version shows the elegant Darton flourishes toned down for the popular market. For an example of a Carvalho "gift-label" that has been completed, see entry 372.

SCHOOL REWARDS

✌ 384a ✌

The Juvenile "Sketch Book"; or pictures of youth, in a series of tales. London: H.R. Thomas. Juvenile Repository. 7, Hanover St. Hanover Square. H. Holloway, 8, Wolsingham Place, Lambeth, May, 1825. 12° (157 × 96 mm.).

*A*² (=R3·4) B–Q⁶ R⁶ (–3·4) (A1ʳ Preface, A2ʳ divisional title, R6ʳ imprint *Printed J. Brettell, Rupert Street, Haymarket, London,* R6ᵛ blank); etched frontispiece and pictorial title by R. Fenner (the first after J. Clover), printed from a steelplate. Pp. v, 187. Wove paper. Contemporary tan straight-grain roan, title gilt-tooled on front cover, by a Royston binder (with his label: [name unidentified] *Perfumer, Stationer, Bookseller, Printer and Book Binder, Royston*). Reference: Osborne II, 901.

Provenance: *Ladies' | Seminary | Foulmire | Second Class | Prize | for general attention. | Miss E. Chaplin. | Decʳ 1825* (calligraphic

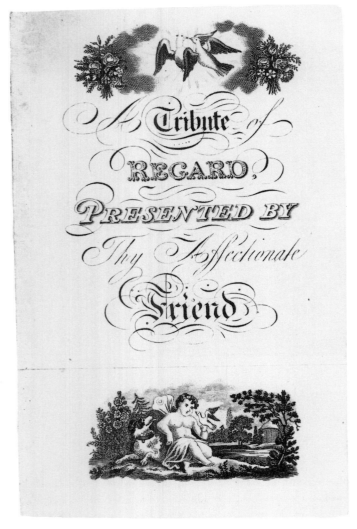

383a.

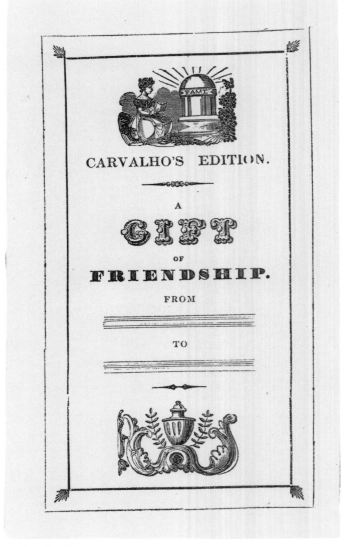

383b. *reduced*

inscription [date partly erased] on school-prize paper label mounted inside front cover), the recipient's signature and the same date on A2^r; Gumuchian & Cie (1930 cat., no. 3479). PML 83280. Gift: Elisabeth Ball.

ᕲ 384b ᕲ

JANE TAYLOR (1783–1824). *Essays in Rhyme on Morals and Manners . . . Fifth edition.* London: printed for Taylor and Hessey, 93 Fleet-Street, and 13, Waterloo-place, Pall-Mall, 1825. 8° (163 × 99 mm.).

A^2 (1^r title, 1^v imprint *London: printed by Thomas Davison, Whitefriars,* 2^r *Contents,* 2^v blank); B–M^8 (M8^v same imprint). Pp. [4], 175. Wove paper. Contemporary red straight-grain morocco, stamps and roll-tools in gilt and blind, gilt edges. Reference: Stewart A 19e.

Provenance: *Presented to / Miss Sarah Ann Newman / for / attention to her lessons / & uniform good conduct / at / The Misses Giles' / Boarding School / Stoke Newington / Christmas 1827* (red morocco school-prize label lettered in gilt and mounted inside front cover—see overleaf). PML 84999. Purchase: Fellows Fund.

In the first appendix to Harvey Darton's *Children's Books in England* reference is made to the "profoundly influential" role which the custom of "reward books" had on children's reading. With the growth of public education and Sunday schools during the nineteenth century, there was a massive growth in the editing, publishing, and distribution of children's books as prizes.

These two examples illustrate the fashion at its superior beginnings. The Ladies' Seminary at Foulmire (now, a trifle more respectably, Foulmere, about seven miles from the Royston bookseller) produced a label where the calligraphy neatly matched the specially designed engraving for Miss Chaplin's "second class prize," while the Misses Giles of Stoke Newington produced what is surely one of the most spectacular prize-labels ever. Furthermore, there is an unusual degree of congruence in this instance between the book's binding and label and its fine printing by Thomas Davison, one of the best printers of the time.

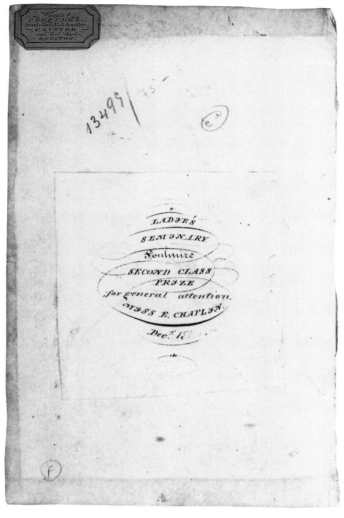

384a. *reduced*

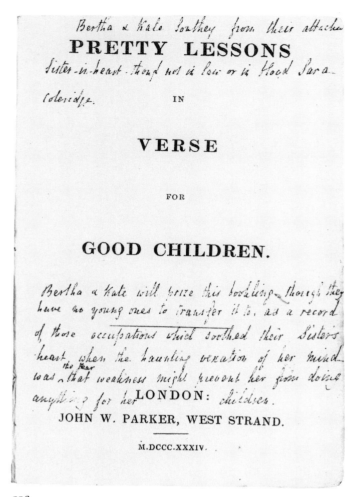

386.

A GODFATHER'S GIFT

✧ 385 ✧

The History of the Apple Pie. [London:] Publish'd by G. Martin 6 Great St Thomas Apostle, [not after 1828]. 12° (101 × 95 mm.).

[1^{12}] (1^r pictorial title, 1^v–2^r blank, 2^v incipit: *A a Apple Pie*). Wove paper, no watermark. Ff. 12. Etched throughout: printed from a single copperplate on one side of the sheet. Title and 22 illustrations hand-colored at the publisher's. Original gray wrappers, hand-colored etched pictorial title-label mounted on front cover (*Price 6^d Coloured | A Apple Pye | Publish'd by G. Martin 6. Great St Thomas Apostle London*, letterpress ads on back cover).

Provenance: *Martha Guest | Book | Birdwell, 1828 | The Gift of her Godfather | Thomas Guest* (adult's inscription inside front cover—see overleaf). PML 85597. Gift: Elisabeth Ball.

We have commented several times on George Martin's insouciant habits as a publisher, which gave his cheap little productions a character all their own. There is therefore a certain satisfaction in seeing so feeble a copycat edition of the Apple Pie rhyme as this treasured by both Thomas Guest and his goddaughter.

WORDS FROM A SISTER-IN-HEART

✧ 386 ✧

[SARA COLERIDGE, née COLERIDGE (1802–52)]. *Pretty Lessons in Verse for Good Children.* London: John W. Parker, 1834. 16° (135 × 90 mm.).

B–E^{16} (B1^v wood-engraved frontispiece, B2^r title, B2^v blank, B3^r *Benoni. Dedication*, incipit: *My Herbert, yet thou hast not learnt to prize*, B3^v blank, B4^r *The Months*, incipit: *January brings the snow*, E16^v imprint *London: printed by J. Moyes, Castle Street, Leicester Square*). Pp. 128. Wove paper. Contemporary pink hexagon-grain cloth, yellow endpapers, engraved label *Shaw, Stationer & Bookseller, Hampstead*. Reference: E.L. Griggs *Coleridge fille* (Oxford University Press, 1940) pp. 83–6, 251; Opie (1977) no. 771.

Provenance: *Bertha & Kate Southey from their attached | Sister-in-heart—though not in law or in blood Sara | Coleridge. | Bertha & Kate will prize this bookling, though they | have no young ones to transfer it to, as a record | of those occupations which soothed their Sister's | heart, when the haunting vexation of her mind | was the Fear that weakness might prevent her from doing | anything for her children* (inscribed by the author on the title page to her cousins, Robert Southey's two youngest daughters);

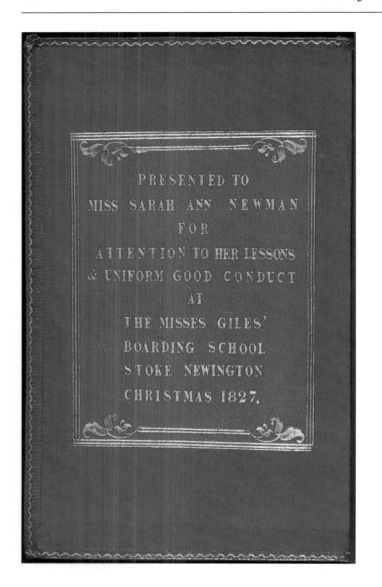

E. Coleridge / from Edith Hawkins / 1894 (presumably inscribed to Samuel Taylor Coleridge's granddaughter, Edith, who was two when her mother published these poems addressed to her older brother, Herbert [born 1830]). PML 85413. Purchase: Julia P. Wightman.

Sara Coleridge's *Pretty Lessons in Verse* became one of the most popular children's books of the 1830s and left us with at least one poem of near-classic status: "January Brings the Snow." This first edition carries an intimate inscription from the author to her cousins, who were, by 1834, no longer child readers but who would recall a childhood shared with Sara at Keswick. Three years later was published her long fantasy novel for children *Phantasmion*, put out in only a small edition by William Pickering and hence little-known as a precursor of the English *Kunstmärchen*.

SISTER TO SISTER

⊷§ 387 §⊶

FRANCES MARY COOPER (born ca. 1834). *The Cat's Festival. Written and illustrated by Frances Mary Cooper, a little girl twelve years old, for the amusement of her younger sister.* London: Longman, Brown, Green, and Longmans. Norwich: J. Tippel, 1846. 8° (180 × 109 mm.).

[1⁸] (1ʳ title, 1ᵛ imprint *J. Tippell, Norwich*, 2ʳ illustration *King Spitfire and Queen Lilly* and verse, incipit: *The King and Queen of Cats began*, 8ᵛ same imprint). Pp. 16. Wove paper. 7 half-page hand-colored wood engravings. Original printed yellow stiff wrappers, title and *Price One Shilling* on front cover.

Left: 384b. reduced   Below: 385.

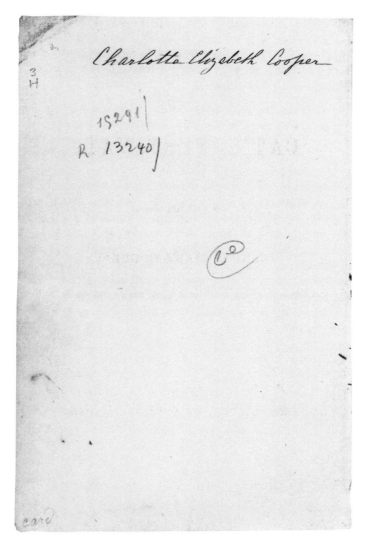

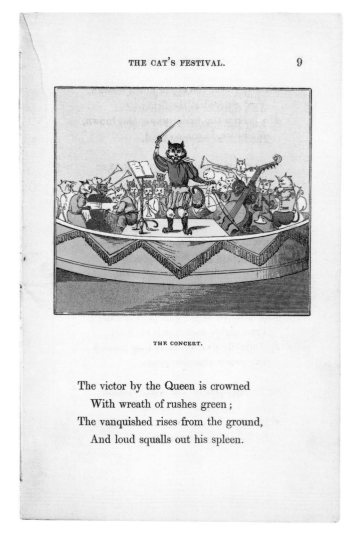

THE CAT'S FESTIVAL. 9

THE CONCERT.

The victor by the Queen is crowned
 With wreath of rushes green ;
The vanquished rises from the ground,
 And loud squalls out his spleen.

Above left: **387**. *reduced*
Above right: **387**. fo. 5, recto, *reduced*
Below left: **388**. plate [2] facing A7ᵛ

PRINCESS FRUTILLA

Provenance: *Charlotte Elizabeth Cooper* (inscription in an adult hand inside front cover), presumably Frances Mary's younger sister, for whose amusement the poem was written and illustrated; Gumuchian & Cⁱᵉ (1930 cat., no. 1853 bis). PML 85072. Gift: Elisabeth Ball.

Every so often publishers take on books written by children in the hopes that they will naturally appeal to other children. (Usually though, if success comes—as with *The Young Visiters*—it is success with an adult audience). In this instance, however, we see not only twelve-year-old Frances Mary Cooper achieving publication but also the copy of her book that was treasured by the sister for whom it was written.

LIGHTING OUT FOR THE TERRITORY

❧ 388 ❧

[MARIE-CATHÉRINE LA MOTHE, Countess D'AULNOY (ca. 1650–1705)]. *Mother Bunch's Fairy Tales. Published for the amusement of all those little masters and misses who, by duty to their parents, and obedience to their superiors, aim at becoming Great Lords and Ladies. Embellished with engravings.* Glasgow: published by J. Lumsden and Son, [ca. 1810]. Price Sixpence. 24° (100 × 85 mm.).

A–C¹² (A1ʳ blank, A1ᵛ wood-engraved *Frontispiece. Yellow Dwarf, p. 19*, A2ʳ title, A2ᵛ blank, C12ᵛ blank); 6 etchings (see previous page), printed in green from a single copperplate on one side of a part-sheet. Pp. 71. Laid paper for letterpress, wove paper for the plates. Mauve stiff wrappers. References: Roscoe & Brimmell 102; Osborne 5, 37; Gumuchian 4205.

Provenance: *A. L. Bartlett—Chicago Ill. / Bought of Sabin / 1872* (inscr. on title); *M. L. Bartlett / Cheyenne. / aug 10, 79 Wyo. Trtry* (inscr. on title); S. Roscoe (inscribed *Bt of L. Bondy 1955 . . . Rebacked by F. L. Wood / The cuts have nothing to do with either Bewick*). PML 84937. Purchase: Julia P. Wightman.

By way of conclusion we have chosen a book that helps to sum up the complex fate that surrounds so many texts conceived with the simplest of motives: to bring enjoyment (and, more rarely, wisdom) to children. The text itself had its origins in France in the seventeenth century, and this edition is a nineteenth-century Scottish reprint of an English version that was first issued by the famous eighteenth-century house of Newbery. Somehow, though, this copy escaped its child-readership. It found its way into the stock of Joseph Sabin, the great Americanist and New York bookseller, and from him it made passage to the shelves of some eager collector or folklorist or child-lover out in the Northwest Territories. From there it returned to the library of the great scholar-collector Sydney Roscoe of Harrow, England, only to journey yet again across the Atlantic to join the treasures of The Pierpont Morgan Library.

Be merry and Wise.

REFERENCES

CITATION FORM	ENTRY
Adomeit	Ruth Elizabeth Adomeit. *Three Centuries of Thumb Bibles: A Checklist.* New York: Garland Publishing Co., 1980.
Alderson *Andersen*	Brian Alderson. *Hans Christian Andersen and His Eventyr in England: Some Notes and Observations by Brian Alderson.* [Wormley, Eng.]: International Board on Books for Young People, British Section, 1982.
Alderson *Burns*	Brian Alderson. "Some Notes on James Burns as a Publisher of Children's Books," *Bulletin of the John Rylands University Library of Manchester* 76 (Autumn 1994): 103–25.
Alderson *Gobwin*	Brian Alderson. "'Mister Gobwin' and His 'Interesting Little Books Adorned with Beautiful Copper Plates,'" *Princeton University Library Chronicle* 59 (1997–8): 159–89.
Alderson *Ludford Box*	Brian Alderson. *The Ludford Box and "A Christmass-Box:" Their Contribution to Our Knowledge of Eighteenth Century Children's Literature.* Los Angeles: Department of Special Collections, University Research Library, University of California, 1989.
Alderson *Miniature Libraries*	Brian Alderson. "Miniature Libraries for the Young," *The Private Library*, 3rd series 6 (Spring 1983): 3–38.
Alderson *Moon*	Brian Alderson. *Childhood Re-Collected: Early Children's Books from the Library of Marjorie Moon.* [Royston]: Provincial Book Fairs Association, 1994.
Alderson *Picture Book*	Brian Alderson. *Sing a Song for Sixpence: The English Picture Book Tradition and Randolph Caldecott.* [Cambridge]: Cambridge University Press in association with the British Library, [1986].
Alderson *Uncle Tom*	Brian Alderson. *Old Uncle Tom Cobbleigh and All: Some Ruminations on Texts and What are called Para-texts.* Toronto: Toronto Public Library, 2002.
Alderson & Garrett	Brian Alderson and Pat Garrett. *The Religious Tract Society as a Publisher of Children's Books; Catalogue of an Exhibition . . . to Celebrate the 200th Anniversary of the Foundation of the RTS.* Hoddesdon: The Children's Books History Society, 1999.
Alston	R. C. Alston. *A Bibliography of the English Language from the Invention of Printing to the Year 1800.* A corrected reprint of volumes I–X, reproduced from the author's annotated copy with corrections and additions to 1973, including cumulative indices. Ilkley [Eng.]: Janus Press, 1974.
Bennett	Stuart Bennett. *Trade Bookbinding in the British Isles, 1660–1800.* New Castle: Oak Knoll Press; London: The British Library, 2004.
Bentley *Blake Books*	G. E. Bentley. *Blake Books: Annotated Catalogues of William Blake's Writings in Illuminated Printing, in Conventional Typography and in Manuscripts.* Oxford: Clarendon Press, 1977.
Bentley *Thorne*	G. E. Bentley. *The Blake Collection of Mrs. Landon K. Thorne.* New York: Pierpont Morgan Library, 1971.
Berry & Poole	W. Turner Berry and H. Edmund Poole. *Annals of Printing: A Chronological Encyclopaedia from the Earliest Times to 1950.* London: Blandford Press, 1966.
Bowles & Carver	Bowles & Carver. *Old English Cuts and Illustrations for Artists and Craftspeople.* Formerly *Catchpenny Prints: 163 Popular Engravings from the Eighteenth Century.* New York: Dover Publications, Inc., [1970].
Briquet	Charles-Moïse Briquet. *Les filigranes: dictionnaire historique des marques du papier dès leur apparition vers 1282 jusqu'en 1600.* A facsimile of the 1907 edition . . . edited by Allan Stevenson. Amsterdam: Paper Publications Society, 1968.
Brown	Philip A. H. Brown. *London Publishers and Printers, c. 1800–1870.* [London]: British Library, [1982].
Buday	George Buday. *The History of the Christmas Card.* London: Rockliff Publishing Corporation, [1954].
Cahoon	Herbert Cahoon, ed. *Children's Literature: Books and Manuscripts; an Exhibition, November 19, 1954, through February 28, 1955.* New York: Pierpont Morgan Library, 1954.
Carpenter	Kevin Carpenter. *Desert Isles & Pirate Islands: the Island Theme in Nineteenth-Century English Juvenile Fiction, a Survey and Bibliography.* Frankfurt am Main: Peter Lang, 1984.
Clouston	William Alexander Clouston. *Hieroglyphic Bibles: Their Origin and History; A Hitherto Unwritten Chapter of Bibliography.* Glasgow: D. Bryce and Son, 1894.

CITATION FORM	ENTRY
Cohn	Albert M. Cohn. *George Cruikshank: A Catalogue Raisonné, of the Work Executed during the Years 1806–1877.* London: The Bookman's Journal, 1924.
CP	*See* Bowles & Carver.
Crane	Walter Crane. *An Artist's Reminiscences.* London: Methuen & Co., 1907. Reprint. Detroit: Singing Tree Press, 1968.
Cutt *Ministering Angels*	Margaret Nancy Cutt. *Ministering Angels: A Study of Nineteenth-Century Evangelical Writing for Children.* [Wormley, Eng.]: Five Owls Press, 1979.
Cutt *Mrs. Sherwood*	Margaret Nancy Cutt. *Mrs. Sherwood and Her Books for Children.* London: Oxford University Press, 1974.
Dahl	Erhard Dahl. *Die Kürzungen des Robinson Crusoe in England zwischen 1719 und 1819 vor dem Hintergrund des zeitgenössischen Druckgewerbes, Verlagswesens und Lesepublikums.* Frankfurt am Main: P. Lang, 1977.
Darton	F. J. Harvey Darton. *Children's Books in England.* Third edition, revised by Brian Alderson. Cambridge: Cambridge University Press, [1982]. Third (corrected) edition revised by Brian Alderson. London: The British Library; New Castle, DE: Oak Knoll Press, 1999.
Darton *Check-list*	Lawrence Darton. *The Dartons; An Annotated Check-list of Children's Books Issued by Two Publishing Houses 1787–1876.* London: The British Library; New Castle, DE: Oak Knoll Press, 2004.
Davis	Roger Davis. *Kendrew of York and His Chapbooks for Children: With a Checklist.* [Collingham, Eng.]: The Elmete Press, 1988.
De Freitas	Leo John De Freitas. *The Banbury Chapbooks.* Banbury: Banbury Historical Society & Robert Boyd Publications, 2004.
DNB	*Dictionary of National Biography.* London: Smith, Elder, & Co., 1885–1901.
Edmond	*Bibliotheca Lindesiana: Catalogue of English Broadsides, 1505–1897.* Compiled by J. P. Edmond. [Aberdeen]: Privately printed [Aberdeen University Press], 1898.
Ehmcke	Fritz Hellmut Ehmcke. *Otto Speckter . . . mit einer Bibliographie von Karl Hobrecker.* Berlin: Furche-Verlag, 1920.
Engen	Rodney Engen. *Richard Doyle.* Stroud, Glos.: Catalpa Press Ltd., 1983.
Esdaile	Arundell Esdaile. *A List of English Tales and Prose Romances Printed Before 1740. Part I: 1475–1642. Part II: 1643–1739.* London: Bibliographical Society, 1912.
ESTC	*English Short-Title Catalogue* (RLIN).
Fellows Report	Pierpont Morgan Library. *Report to the Fellows.* New York: The Library, 1950–1989. Reports acquisitions through 1986.
Field	William B. Osgood Field. *Edward Lear on My Shelves.* [S.L.]: Privately printed, 1933. [Munich: Bremer Press.]
Foxon	David F. Foxon. *English Verse 1701–1750: A Catalogue of Separately Printed Poems with Notes on Contemporary Collected Editions.* London, Cambridge: Cambridge University Press, 1975.
Gagnebin	Jean-Jacques Rousseau. *Oeuvres complètes. Edition publiée sous la direction de Bernard Gagnebin et Marcel Raymond.* [Paris: Gallimard, 1959–]. Vol. 4, *Emile.*
Gottlieb	[Gerald Gottlieb]. *Early Children's Books and Their Illustration.* New York: Pierpont Morgan Library; Boston: David R. Godine, 1975.
Grey	*The Governess; or, Little Female Academy. A Facsimile Reproduction of the First Edition of 1749;* with an introduction and bibliography by Jill E. Grey. London: Oxford University Press, 1968.
Gumuchian	*Les Livres de l'enfance du XVe au XIXe siècle.* Paris: Gumuchian et Cie., 1930. Reprint, London: The Holland Press [1967].
Haemmerle & Hirsch	Albert Haemmerle and Olga Hirsch. *Buntpapier: Herkommen, Geschichte, Techniken, Beziehungen zur Kunst.* Munich: Callwey, 1977.
Haining	Peter Haining. *Movable Books: An Illustrated History . . . from the Collection of David and Briar Philips.* London: New English Library, 1979.
Hall & Muir	Trevor H. Hall and Percy H. Muir. *Some Printers & Publishers of Conjuring Books and Other Ephemera, 1800–1850.* [Leeds]: The Elmete Press, 1976.
Hannas	Linda Hannas. *The English Jigsaw Puzzle, 1760–1890: With a Descriptive Check-List of Puzzles in the Museums of Great Britain and the Author's Collection.* London: Wayland Publishers, [1972].
Hearne	Betsy Hearne. *Beauty and the Beast: Visions and Revisions of an Old Tale.* Chicago: The University of Chicago Press, [1989].

CITATION FORM	ENTRY
Heartman	Charles F. Heartman. *American Primers, Indian Primers, Royal Primers, and Thirty-Seven other Types of non-New-England Primers Issued prior to 1830; A Bibliographical Checklist Embellished with Twenty-Six Cuts.* Highland Park, N.J.: Printed for H. B. Weiss, 1935.
Heawood	Edward Heawood. *Watermarks, Mainly of the 17th and 18th Centuries.* Hilversum, Holland: Paper Publications Society, 1950.
Herzog & Siefert	*Struwwelpeter-Hoffmann: Texte, Bilder, Dokumentation, Katalog.* Hrsg. von G. H. Herzog und Helmut Siefert. Frankfurt am Main: Verlag Heinrich-Hoffmann-Museum, 1978.
Hobbs	Anne Stevenson Hobbs. *Fables.* London: Victoria & Albert Museum, 1986.
Hockliffe	The Hockliffe Project, comp. M. O. Grenby, includes online catalog and digitized full-text images of the Hockliffe Collection of Early Children's Books at De Monfort University. http://malkyn.hum.dmu.ac.uk:8000/AnaServer?hockliffe+0+start.anv (accessed, 15 May 2004). The online catalog is based on Doreen H. Boggis. *Catalogue of the Hockliffe Collection of Early Children's Books.* Bedford: Bedford College of Education, 1969.
Hodnett	Edward Hodnett. *English Woodcuts, 1480–1535.* Reprinted, with additions and corrections. Oxford: Printed at the University Press, 1973.
Howe	Ellic Howe. *A List of London Bookbinders, 1648–1815.* London: The Bibliographical Society, 1950.
Hugo	Thomas Hugo. *The Bewick Collector: A Descriptive Catalogue of the Works of Thomas and John Bewick.* London: Lovell Reeve and Co., 1866. *Supplement.* London: L. Reeve and Co., 1868.
Hunt	C. J. Hunt. *The Book Trade in Northumberland and Durham to 1860: A Biographical Dictionary.* Newcastle upon Tyne: Thorne's Students' Bookshops Ltd for the History of the Book Trade in the North, 1975.
James	Philip James. *Children's Books of Yesterday.* Edited by C. Geoffrey Holme. London: The Studio, 1933.
Jarník	Hertvk Jarník, ed. *Orbis pictus* k vydani upravil H. Jarník.—V Brne: Ústrední spolek jednot ucitelských na Morave, 1929. Latin and German; notes in Czech.
Johnson	Elizabeth L. Johnson. *For Your Amusement and Instruction, the Elisabeth Ball Collection of Historic Children's Materials.* Bloomington: The Lilly Library, Indiana University, 1987.
Juvenile Review	*The Juvenile Review; Or Moral and Critical Observations on Children's Books.* London: Printed for N. Hailes, Juvenile Library, London Museum, Piccadilly, 1817. Reproduction of the Osborne copy. Toronto: The Friends of the Osborne and Lillian H. Smith Collections, Toronto Public Library, 1982.
Keynes *Blake*	Sir Geoffrey Keynes. *A Bibliography of William Blake.* New York: The Grolier Club, 1921.
Keynes *Paradise*	William Blake. *The Gates of Paradise. For Children. For the Sexes. Introductory Volume by Geoffrey Keynes with Blake's Preliminary Sketches.* [Boissia, Clairvaux]: Published by the Trianon Press for the William Blake Trust, 1968.
Kinnell	Margaret Kinnell. "Childhood and Children's Literature: the Case of M. J. Godwin and Co., 1805–26," *Publishing History* 24 (1988): 77–99.
Korn	Frederick B. Korn. *Edward Lear's "A Book of Nonsense": A Description of Holdings in the John M. Shaw Collection, Florida State University.* With an introduction by John M. Shaw. Tallahassee: Friends of the Florida State University Library, 1981.
Lambert	*Library of the late Major William H. Lambert of Philadelphia.* Part I. *Lincolniana*; Part II. *Thackerayana*; Part III. *Civil War*; Part IV. *Lincolniana.* (Sale 1–16 January 1914 at the Anderson Galleries). New York, Metropolitan Art Association, [1914].
Lisney	Arthur A. Lisney. *A Bibliography of British Lepidoptera, 1608–1799.* London: The Chiswick Press, 1960.
Lucas	*The Works of Charles and Mary Lamb.* Edited by E. V. Lucas. Vol. 3: *Books for Children.* London: Methuen & Co., 1903.
McEachern	Jo-Ann E. McEachern. *Bibliography of the Writings of Jean Jacques Rousseau to 1800.* Oxford: Voltaire Foundation, Taylor Institution, 1989–.
McGrath	Leslie A. McGrath, ed. *This Magical Book: Movable Books for Children, 1771–2001* [exhibition catalogue]. Toronto: Toronto Public Library, 2002.
McKenzie	D. F. McKenzie. *Stationers' Company Apprentices, 1701–1800.* Oxford: The Oxford Bibliographical Society, 1978.
McLean *Book-bindings in paper*	Ruari McLean. *Victorian Publishers' Book-Bindings in Paper.* London: G. Fraser, 1983.
McLean *Cundall*	Ruari McLean. *Joseph Cundall, a Victorian Publisher: Notes on His Life and a Check-List of His Books.* Pinner: Private Libraries Association, 1976.

CITATION FORM	ENTRY
McLean *Victorian Book Design*	Ruari McLean. *Victorian Book Design and Colour Printing.* 2nd rev. and enlarged ed. Berkeley: University of California Press, [1972].
Mahony & Rizzo	Robert Mahony and Betty W. Rizzo. *Christopher Smart: An Annotated Bibliography, 1743–1983.* New York: Garland Publishing, 1984.
Maxted	Ian Maxted. *The London Book Trades, 1775–1800: A Preliminary Checklist of Members.* [Folkestone, Kent]: Dawson, [1977].
Montanaro	Ann R. Montanaro. *Pop-Up and Movable Books: A Bibliography.* Metuchen, N.J., and London: Scarecrow Press, 1993.
Moon *Elliott*	Marjorie Moon. *The Children's Books of Mary (Belson) Elliott, Blending Sound Christian Principles with Cheerful Cultivation: A Bibliography.* [Winchester, Eng.]: St. Paul's Bibliographies, 1987.
Moon *Harris*	Marjorie Moon. *John Harris's Books for Youth, 1801–1843: Being a Checklist of Books for Children and Young People Published for Their Amusement and Instruction.* [Cambridge]: Five Owls Press, 1976; *Supplement,* for the Author and Five Owls Press, 1983. Rev. and enlarged ed., Folkestone: Dawson, 1992.
Moon *Tabart*	Marjorie Moon. *Benjamin Tabart's Juvenile Library: A Bibliography of Books for Children Published, Written, Edited and Sold by Mr. Tabart, 1801–1820.* Winchester [Eng.]: St. Paul's Bibliographies; Detroit: Omnigraphics, 1990.
Morgan	F. C. Morgan. *Children's Books Published before 1830 Exhibited at Malvern Public Library in 1911.* Leominster: for the author, 1976.
Muir	Percy H. Muir. *English Children's Books, 1600–1900.* London: B. T. Batsford, [1954].
Muir *NBL*	*Children's Books of Yesterday.* Compiled by Percy H. Muir; foreword by John Masefield. (Catalogue for an exhibition at the National Book League in May 1946). New ed., rev. and enlarged, Detroit: Singing Tree Press, 1970.
NBL *Andersen*	National Book League (Great Britain). *Hans Christian Andersen, 1805–2nd April 1955: Catalogue of a Jubilee Exhibition Held at the National Book League . . . arranged in Association with the Danish Government in Co-operation with the Royal Library, Copenhagen, and Dr. R. Klein.* Organizer Elias Bredsdorff. London & Copenhagen, 1955.
NCBEL	*New Cambridge Bibliography of English Literature.* Cambridge: Cambridge University Press, 1969.
Noakes	Vivien Noakes. *Edward Lear, 1812–1888.* London: Royal Academy of Arts, in association with Weidenfeld and Nicolson, 1985.
Ober	*The Story of the Three Bears: The Evolution of an International Classic. Photoreproductions of Fifteen Versions of the Tale.* Edited and with an introduction and headnotes by Warren U. Ober. Delmar, N.Y.: Scholars' Facsimiles & Reprints, 1981.
OED	*The Oxford English Dictionary, Being a Corrected Reissue . . . of A New English Dictionary on Historical Principles.* Oxford: Clarendon Press, 1933.
Opie *Fairy Tales*	Iona Opie and Peter Opie. *The Classic Fairy Tales.* London: Oxford University Press, [1974].
Opie *Nursery Companion*	Iona Opie and Peter Opie. *A Nursery Companion.* [Oxford]: Oxford University Press, [1980].
Opie *ODNR*	Iona Opie and Peter Opie. *The Oxford Dictionary of Nursery Rhymes.* Oxford: The Clarendon Press, [1951].
Opie *Three Centuries*	Iona Opie and Peter Opie. *Three Centuries of Nursery Rhymes and Poetry for Children.* 2nd ed., rev. and expanded. Oxford: Oxford University Press; New York: Justin G. Schiller Ltd., [1977].
Osborne	*The Osborne Collection of Early Children's Books.* Prepared by Judith St. John. Vol. 1. *1566–1910.* Toronto: Toronto Public Library, 1958; Reprinted 1975. Vol. 2. *1476–1910.* Toronto: Toronto Public Library, 1975.
Pafford	Isaac Watts. *Divine Songs Attempted in Easy Language for the Use of Children*; with an introduction and bibliography by J. H. P. Pafford. London: Oxford University Press, 1971.
PBSA	*Papers of the Bibliographical Society of America.*
Pendred	John Pendred. *The Earliest Directory of the Book Trade.* Edited by Graham Pollard. London: Bibliographical Society, 1955 .
Pilz	Kurt Pilz. *Die Ausgaben des Orbis Sensualium Pictus. Eine Bibliographie.* Nürnberg: Stadtbibliothek, 1967.
Plomer *1726*	H. R. Plomer, G. H. Bushnell, and E. R. McC.Dix. *A Dictionary of the Printers and Booksellers Who Were at Work in England, Scotland, and Ireland From 1726 to 1775.* [Oxford]: The Bibliographical Society, 1932 (for 1930).
Praz	Mario Praz. *Studies in Seventeenth-Century Imagery.* Roma: Edizioni di Storia e Letteratura, 1964.
Quayle	Eric Quayle. *R. M. Ballantyne: A Bibliography of First Editions.* London: Dawsons, 1968.

CITATION FORM	ENTRY
Rammensee	*Bibliographie der Nürnberger Kinder- und Jugendbücher, 1522–1944. Hrsg. aus Anlass der 300. Wiederkehr des Erscheinens des Orbis sensualium pictus des Johann Amos Comenius.* [Bearb. von Dorothea Rammensee. Mit einem Vorwort von Karlheinz Goldmann versehen.] Bamberg: Meisenbach, [1961]
Ray	Gordon N. Ray. *Thackeray: The Uses of Adversity (1811–1846).* New York: McGraw-Hill Book Company, Inc., [1955]. *Thackeray: The Age of Wisdom (1847–1863).* New York: McGraw-Hill Book Company, Inc., [1958].
Ray *English*	Gordon N. Ray. *The Illustrator and the Book in England from 1790 to 1914.* New York: Pierpont Morgan Library, 1976.
Realms of Childhood	Justin G. Schiller. *Realms of Childhood: A Selection of 200 Important Historical Children's Books, Manuscripts and Related Drawings.* New York: Justin G. Schiller, 1983 (Catalogue 41).
Río y Rico	Gabriel-Martín del Río y Rico. *Catálogo bibliográfico de la sección de Cervantes de la Biblioteca nacional.* Madrid: Tip. de la "Revista de Archivos, Bibliotecas y Museos," 1930.
Roscoe	S. Roscoe. *John Newbery and His Successors, 1740–1814: A Bibliography.* [Wormley, Eng.]: Five Owls Press, [1973].
Roscoe & Brimmell	S. Roscoe and R. A. Brimmell. *James Lumsden & Son of Glasgow: Their Juvenile Books and Chapbooks.* Pinner, Eng.: Private Libraries Association, 1981.
Roscoe *Thumb Bibles*	S. Roscoe. "Early English, Scottish and Irish Thumb Bibles," *The Book Collector* 22 (Summer 1973): 189–207.
Rosenfeld	*Orbis sensualium pictus. Faksimiledruck der Ausgabe Noribergae, M. Endtner, 1658, mit Nachwort von Hellmut Rosenfeld unter Beifügung eines vollständigen Faksimiledrucks des Lucidarium-Probedrucks von 1657.* Osnabrück: O. Zeller, 1964.
Rühle	Reiner Rühle. *"Bose Kinder:" Kommentierte Bibliographie von Struwwelpetriaden und Max-und-Moritziaden mit biographischen Daten zu Verfassern und Illustratoren.* Osnabrück: H. Th. Wenner, 1999.
Russell *Cowper*	Norma Russell. *A Bibliography of William Cowper to 1837.* Oxford: The Oxford Bibliographical Society, 1963.
Sadleir	Michael Sadleir. *XIX Century Fiction.* 2 vols. London: Constable & Co. Ltd.; Los Angeles: California University Press, [1951].
Sadler	*Orbis pictus: A Facsimile of the First English Edition of 1659 . . .* Introduced by John E. Sadler. London: Oxford University Press, 1968.
Schatzki	*Old and Rare Children's Books.* New York: Walter Schatzki, 1941. Republished as *Children's Books, Old and Rare.* Detroit: Gale Research Company, 1974.
Schiller	Justin G. Schiller. *Nonsensus: Cross-Referencing Edward Lear's 116 Limericks with Eight Holograph Manuscripts . . . together with a Census of . . . the Genuine First Edition.* Compiled by Justin G. Schiller with introductory remarks by Vivien Noakes. Stroud, Eng.: Catalpa Press Ltd., 1988.
Schiller *Five Centuries*	Justin G. Schiller. *Five Centuries of Childhood, 1497–1897.* New York: Justin G. Schiller, Ltd., 2002 (Catalogue 50).
Shefrin	Jill Shefrin, comp. *Ingenious Contrivances: Table Games and Puzzles for Children* [exhibition catalogue]. Toronto: Toronto Public Library, 1996.
Shoemaker	Richard H. Shoemaker, comp. *A Checklist of American Imprints for 1820–1829.* New York: Scarecrow Press, 1964–1971. Continues *American Bibliography*, compiled by Ralph R. Shaw and Richard H. Shoemaker, 1958–1966.
Slade	Bertha Coolidge Slade. *Maria Edgeworth, 1767–1849: A Bibliographical Tribute.* London: Constable Publishers, [1937].
Sloane	William Sloane. *Children's Books in England & America in the Seventeenth Century: A History and a Checklist; Together with "The Young Christian's Library," the First Printed Catalogue of Books for Children.* New York: King's Crown Press, Columbia University, 1955.
Speaight	George Speaight. *Juvenile Drama: the History of the English Toy Theatre.* London: Macdonald & Co., 1946.
Spencer	Isobel Spencer. *Walter Crane.* London: Studio Vista, 1975.
Spielmann	Percy Edwin Spielmann. *Catalogue of the Library of Miniature Books Collected by Percy Edwin Spielmann, together with some Descriptive Summaries.* London: Edward Arnold, [1961].
Spinney	Gordon Harold Spinney. "Cheap Repository Tracts: Hazard and Marshall Edition," *The Library* 20 (Dec. 1939): 295–340.
STC (2nd ed.)	*A Short-Title Catalogue of Books Printed in England, Scotland, & Ireland and of English Books Printed Abroad, 1475–1640.* 2nd ed. rev. and enl. begun by W. A. Jackson and F. S. Ferguson, completed by Katharine F. Pantzer. London: Bibliographical Society, 1976–1990.

CITATION FORM	ENTRY
Stewart	Christina Duff Stewart. *The Taylors of Ongar: An Analytical Bio-Bibliography.* 2 vols. New York: Garland Publishing Inc., 1975.
Stone	Wilbur Macey Stone. *The Gigantick Histories of Thomas Boreman.* Portland, Me.: The Southworth Press, 1933.
Stone *Watts*	Wilbur Macey Stone. *The Divine and Moral Songs of Isaac Watts; An Essay thereon and a Tentative List of Editions.* New York: Privately printed for the Triptych, 1918.
Tannenbaum	Samuel Aaron Tannenbaum. *Elizabethan Bibliographies.* IX, Sir Philip Sidney. Port Washington, NY: Kennikat Press, [1941].
Tattersfield JB	Nigel Tattersfield. *John Bewick, Engraver on Wood, 1760–1795; An Appreciation of His Life together with an Annotated Catalogue of His Illustrations and Designs.* London: British Library; New Castle, DE: Oak Knoll Press, 2001.
Thwaite	John Newbery. *A Little Pretty Pocket-Book.* A facsimile [of the British Museum copy], with an introductory essay and bibliography by M. F. Thwaite. London: Oxford University Press, 1966.
Todd	William B. Todd. *A Directory of Printers and Others in Allied Trades; London and Vicinity, 1800–1840.* London: Printing Historical Society, [1972].
Tuer	Andrew White Tuer. *History of the Horn-Book.* London: Leadenhall Press; New York: Charles Scribner's Sons, 1897.
Twyman	Michael Twyman. *Early Lithographed Books: A Study of the Design and Production of Improper Books in the Age of the Hand Press.* Williamsburg, Va.: The Book Press; London: Farrand Press & Private Libraries Association, 1990.
Ullrich	Hermann Ullrich. *Robinson und Robinsonaden: Bibliographie, Geschichte, Kritik: ein Beitrag zur vergleichenden Litteraturgeschichte, im besonderen zur Geschichte des Romans und zur Geschichte der Jugendlitteratur.* Teil I. Bibliographie von Hermann Ullrich. Weimar: E. Felber, 1898.
Van Duzer	Henry Sayre Van Duzer. *A Thackeray Library.* New York: Privately Printed, 1919.
Viljoen	Helen Gill Viljoen. *Ruskin's Backgrounds, Friendships, and Interests as Reflected in the F. J. Sharp Collection.* (Catalogue of an exhibition, January–February, 1965) [Flushing, N.Y.]: Paul Klapper Library [Queens College], 1965.
Waddleton	Norman Waddleton. *Waddleton Chronology of Books with Colour Printed Illustrations or Decorations, 15th to 20th Century.* Fifth edition. York: Quacks Books, 1993.
Welch	d'Alté Welch. *A Bibliography of American Children's Books Printed Prior to 1821.* [Worcester, Mass.]: American Antiquarian Society, 1972. Originally published in the *Proceedings of the American Antiquarian Society,* 1963–1965 and 1967.
Wells	Stanley W. Wells. "Tales from Shakespeare (Shakespeare Lecture read 30 April 1987)," *Proceedings of the British Academy* 73 (1987).
Welsh	Charles Welsh. *A Bookseller of the Last Century. Being some Account of the Life of John Newbery and of the Books He Published, with a Notice of the Later Newberys.* London: Griffith, Farran, Okeden & Welsh, 1885.
Whitehouse	F. R. B. Whitehouse. *Table Games of Georgian and Victorian Days.* London: Peter Garnett, 1951.
Wing (2nd ed.)	Donald Goddard Wing. *Short-Title Catalogue of Books Printed in England, Scotland, Ireland, Wales, and British America, and of English Books Printed in Other Countries, 1641–1700.* New York: Index Committee of the Modern Language Association of America, 1972–1998.
Wise & Smart	*A Complete Bibliography of the Writings in Prose and Verse of John Ruskin . . . With a List of the More Important Ruskiniana.* Compiled by Thomas J. Wise and James P. Smart; edited by Thomas J. Wise. London: Printed for Subscribers, 1889–1893.

INDEX OF NAMES

Names listed here designate authors (and some persons of peripheral interest) unless otherwise identified as artists, illustrators, engravers, etc. All references are to catalogue entry numbers, except where they are indicated as page references. Bold entry numbers indicate main references to the person concerned while the non-bold entry numbers indicate subsidiary mentions.

INDEX OF TITLES

All references are to catalogue entry numbers, except where they are indicated as page references.
Bold entry numbers indicate main references to the title concerned, while the non-bold entry numbers indicate subsidiary mentions.

INDEX OF PRINTERS & PUBLISHERS

Entries are for publishers and booksellers, unless otherwise designated. Normally their further activity as printers, where it occurs, is not noted. The index proceeds from London firms to those in (a) the English provinces, (b) Ireland, Scotland and Wales, and (c) the rest of the world, all given in alphabetic sequences except the last.

All references are to catalogue entry numbers, except where they are given as page references. Bold entry numbers refer to items printed or published by the individuals and firms listed below, while those not in bold indicate entries where additional information about these firms may be found.

COVENTRY
Luckman, M./& Suffield **128, 129**
Merridew, Nathaniel **130, 341**

DARLINGTON, Co. Durham
Robson, E., *private pr and etcher* **261b**

DERBY
Mozley, Henry & Sons/John & Charles, *prs*
   274a–b, 293
Richardson, Thomas **275a–d, 329**

DEVIZES, Wilts
Allbut, –, *pr* **263**

DEVONPORT, Devon
Keys, S. & J. **276a–b**

EASTWOOD, Notts
Barber, G.R. **363c**

ETON, Berks
Pote, J. 59

EXETER, Devon
Fitze & Hannaford **373**
Risdon, C., *lith pr* **373**

GAINSBOROUGH, Lincs
Mozley, John/Henry George **43, 138, 139, 145b,**
   147b, 44; *see also under* Derby

GUILDFORD, Surrey
Russell, J. **254**

HUDDERSFIELD, Yorks
Brook, Joseph/and Lancashire **140, 141**

HULL
Stoddart & Craggs 213b

NEWCASTLE UPON TYNE
Hall & Elliot 146b
Hodgson, Solomon **133**
Lane, Isaac, *pr* **58**
Saint, Thomas, *pr* **132,** 146b, p.98
Slack, Thomas **134**
Also, questionable publication **131**

NORTHAMPTON
Adam, William **259a**
Birdsall & Son, *bookbinders* **340a**
Cooper, W., *pr* **259b**

NORWICH
Stacy, John, *bookseller* **383a**
Tippel, J., *pr* **387**

NOTTINGHAM
Dunn, J., *pr* **28**
"For running stationers" **49**

OTLEY, Yorks
Walker, W., *pr* **265, 283a–b, 292, 331**

READING, Berks
Rusher, J. **109b**

ROCHDALE, Lancs
Ashworth, S., *pr* **109a**

RUGELEY, Cheshire
Walters, John Thomas **332**

SALISBURY, Wilts
Collins, Benjamin **67, 76, 113, 378,** 8, 62, 68; and
   battledores 362

SIDMOUTH, Devon
Wallis, John Junr. **179–80**

STOCKPORT, Lancs
Dodge, S. **255**

TAUNTON, Somerset
Marriott, John William **256**
Bishop, John 256

WELLINGTON, Salop *later London*
Houlston, F. & Son/& Wright **297–9**

WORCESTER
Gamidge, Samuel **137**

YORK
Burdekin, Richard **284**
Kendrew, John **285a–c**
Wilson, T. & R. Spence (also separately)/Wilson,
   Spence & Mawman **13, 126, 127, 146b, 147c**

IRISH, SCOTTISH & WELSH FIRMS

IRELAND
DUBLIN
Connolly, T. 302
Curry, W. Jun. & Co. **301b**
Jones, John 20
M'Glashan, J. **315**
Robins, Joseph, Jr. **304**
Tegg & Co. **303**
Young, George 303

SCOTLAND
ABERDEEN
Raban, Edward, *pr* **361**

DUNFERMLINE
Miller, J. & Son **277**

EDINBURGH
Balfour, A & Co.; Balfour & Jack, *prs* **301a–b**
Black, Adam & Charles **25a**
Caw & Elder **282**
Clark, R. & R. **25a**
Menzies, J. **315**
Paterson, D. **143**
Pr "at the Foot of the Horsewynd" **44**
Ross, G. & J. **280,** p.164
Waugh & Innes **301a**
Whyte, William, & Co. **301b**

GLASGOW
Duncan, Robert, *pr* **47**
Griffin & Co. **303**
Paterson, A. **281**
Lumsden, James/& Son **212–15, 278–9, 358a,**
   369, 388, pp.164, 209–10
Niven, –, *pr* **214**

WALES
PENRYN
Whitehorn, – **363a**

EUROPEAN FIRMS

FRANCE
PARIS
Duchesne, Nicolas-Bonaventure **11**
Plon, Henri, *pr* **330**
Stassin & Xavier, *booksellers* **186b, 229b, 322**
Truchy, J.H. **149b**

GERMANY
AUGSBURG
Enderlin, Jakob, *decorated papers* **34**
Engelbrecht, Martin, *peepshows* p.133

LEIPZIG
Volckmar, Friedrich **321, 326**

NUREMBERG
Endter, Michael **1**

THE NETHERLANDS
THE HAGUE, i.e. AMSTERDAM
Néaulme, Jean **11**

SWITZERLAND
ZÜRICH
Orell, Füssli & Co. **15**

OTHER CONTINENTS

NORTH AMERICA
BALTIMORE, Maryland
Raine, William p.184
Warner & Hanna **231**

BOSTON, Massachusetts
Boyles, John, and primers **68**

HARTFORD, Connecticut
Willard, Asaph **149e**

NEW YORK
King, S. **149d**

AUSTRALIA
SYDNEY
Tegg, J. **303**

INDEX OF SUBJECTS

All references are to catalogue entry numbers, except where they are indicated as page references. Bold entry numbers refer to works which can be classed within the given subject area; non-bold entry numbers and page numbers indicate a more general reference to, or mention of, the subject.

CHRONOLOGICAL INDEX

This short author/title index is arranged according to the date of publication of the works in the catalogue. Places of publication other than London are noted. Where earlier (sometimes much earlier) editions are known, their dates are added after the title in brackets. All references are to catalogue entry numbers.